The ABCs
of Mechanical Drafting

with an Introduction to AutoCAD® 2000

Tony Cook
Gwinnett Technical College

Robin Prater
Gwinnett Technical College

Upper Saddle River, New Jersey
Columbus, Ohio

Library of Congress Cataloging-in-Publication Data

Cook, Tony.
    The ABCs of mechanical drafting with an introduction
to AutoCAD 2000 / Tony Cook, Robin Prater.
        p. cm.
    Includes index.
    ISBN 0-13-086586-9
    1. Mechanical drawing. 2. AutoCAD. I. Prater, Robin. II. Title.

T353.C77 2002
604.2--dc21   2001034374

Editor in Chief: Stephen Helba
Executive Editor: Debbie Yarnell
Media Development Editor: Michelle Churma
Production Editor: Louise N. Sette
Production Supervision: Karen Fortgang, *bookworks*
Design Coordinator: Robin G. Chukes
Cover Designer: Linda Fares
Production Manager: Brian Fox
Marketing Manager: Jimmy Stephens

This book was set in Times Roman by STELLARViSIONs and was printed and
bound by Courier Kendallville, Inc. The cover was printed by Phoenix Color Corp.

Pearson Education Ltd., *London*
Pearson Education Australia Pty. Limited, *Sydney*
Pearson Education Singapore Pte. Ltd.
Pearson Education North Asia Ltd., *Hong Kong*
Pearson Education Canada, Ltd., *Toronto*
Pearson Educación de Mexico, S. A. de C.V.
Pearson Education—Japan, *Tokyo*
Pearson Education Malaysia Pte. Ltd.
Pearson Education, *Upper Saddle River, New Jersey*

10 9 8 7 6 5 4 3 2 1
ISBN: 0-13-086586-9

Preface

Drafting is one of the most powerful tools available for translating ideas from the brain of the creator to the reality of a completed product. Too often, drafting is seen as territory belonging strictly to architects and engineers. The purpose of this book is to demystify the art and science of drafting. The techniques covered will be valuable to a variety of fields but will emphasize mechanical drafting.

This book is aimed at providing the maximum comfort level possible for the beginning student. So if you don't have a background in drafting or computer-aided design, don't worry. This book will give you the tools you need to communicate your ideas. Each new concept is accompanied by step-by-step instructions along with illustrations. The examples were purposely chosen to hold the interest of a variety of students. Our approach differs from many classic drafting textbooks in that the emphasis is on helping the student learn on a very basic level. Our purpose is not to make you an expert but rather to provide you with a good working knowledge of the fundamentals of both manual and computer-aided drafting.

The text is divided into three sections: the basics of manual drafting, an introduction to mechanical drawings, and a beginner's guide to AutoCAD®. Our aim was to provide a versatile text that could be used in a variety of classroom settings. Each section stands on its own. An advanced drafting class could begin with Section II and use Section I for review. An AutoCAD® class might choose to begin at Section III and use Sections I and II for reference material. Many examples are cross-referenced between board drafting and AutoCAD®. For example, the construction of an ellipse will be covered as a manual drafting technique as well as included in the AutoCAD® section of the text.

Special Features of the Text

We have tried to provide as many ways as possible to understand the material. Each chapter contains review questions at the end as well as fundamental exercises to underline the basic principles of that particular chapter. These fundamental exercises are then supplemented with Drawing Assignments aimed at deepening the student's understanding of the material.

You will find similar examples used frequently throughout the different chapters. This allows the student to focus on the concept being introduced instead of being distracted by trying to interpret an unfamiliar set of drawings.

In addition, concepts are cross-referenced between chapters. If a command is mentioned that is covered in detail in another chapter, the chapter and section number is generally provided. Appendixes supplement the information as well as provide information for more in-depth work.

Where appropriate, we have provided tips for more efficient drafting whether manually or with AutoCAD®. Placing the notes and reminders outside the body of the text is an effort at drawing attention to a sentence that might otherwise be overlooked. The tips are also easier to find when flipping through a chapter for a review.

Examples within each chapter are also set apart from the rest of the text. Having the example boxed separately allows the students to quickly find their place as they work between the text and their computer.

Each section covering an AutoCAD® command provides ready access to instant information about ways to enter that particular command. The methods are spelled out at the beginning of each section and highlighted with bullets.

Background of the Authors

Tony Cook (ACI) is the Drafting Program Director at Gwinnett Technical College. He has been a drafting and CAD instructor since 1985. He has a two-year drafting diploma from Valdosta Technical College and a Bachelor of Architectural Engineering Technology degree from Southern Polytechnic State University. His industry experience includes working three years in residential construction along with five years in an architectural/interior design firm that specialized in medical buildings, educational facilities, and public utilities buildings.

Robin Prater is a registered professional engineer with Bachelor of Civil Engineering and Master of Civil Engineering degrees from Georgia Institute of Technology. Her years of experience in industry include projects ranging from offshore platforms to coal preparation plants. Since 1995 she has taught classes in blueprint reading, drafting, AutoCAD®, and other related subjects at Gwinnett Technical College in Lawrenceville, Georgia. She has worked with AutoCAD® and residential design for more than seven years.

Acknowledgments

Having just completed the writing of a textbook, both authors have a new appreciation of the importance of acknowledgments. Without the help of a team behind us, this book would never have been completed.

We would like to thank W. Eric Lawrence (AIA, Dean of Continuing Education) for reviewing sections of the text. In addition, a thank you goes out to Todd Cook (Architect, Georgia Perimeter College) for his generosity in supplying several drawings as text illustrations. Donald Mobley (Gwinnett Technical College) also spent many valuable hours reviewing the text for accuracy. Thank you all for your time and efforts.

On the publishing side, we have Carole Horton to thank for starting us on the road to publishing. Steve Helba, Michelle Churma, and Debbie Yarnell provided us with valuable insights along the way.

Thank you to Gwinnett Technical College and the drafting students who helped us in preparing some of the graphics in this text. In particular, thank you to Julie Deehr, Allen Dedels, Bryan Peters, John Pender, Doug Houck, Shannon Parent, Doug Maddox, Lewis Godwin, Danny Cox, Pam Sherwood, and Jason Austin. Many of our other students provided the inspiration for this text. We tried very hard to imagine we were speaking directly to our students as we were writing. The excitement of seeing you begin to accomplish things you never dreamed you were capable of is one of the best parts of teaching.

And now we come to the two persons who absolutely enabled this book to be written. Thank you to Kathy Cook and Cordell Prater for many hours of support and encouragement.

Thanks to the companies who provided drawings and resources for our book:

Georgia Perimeter College

SMC Corporation of America

Cook and Godwin

Barker Cunningham and Barrington

Tony Cook
Robin Prater

Contents

C h a p t e r 9   **199**

Dimensioning Mechanical Drawings

C h a p t e r 1 0   **243**

Pictorial Drawing and Sketching

Section III   □   AutoCAD for Beginners

C h a p t e r 1 1   **301**

Introduction to Computer Basics

C h a p t e r 1 2   **319**

Introduction to AutoCAD®

C h a p t e r 1 3   **339**

Beginning to Draw

Chapter 14 351

View Modification

Chapter 15 369

Creating Simple Geometric Entities

Chapter 16 385

Drawing Aids

Chapter 17 409

Editing and Altering Entities

Chapter 18   **435**

Moving and Duplicating Objects

Chapter 19   **455**

Layers

Chapter 20   **471**

Dimensioning

Chapter 21   **513**

Using AutoCAD Text Commands

Universal Drafting for Everyone

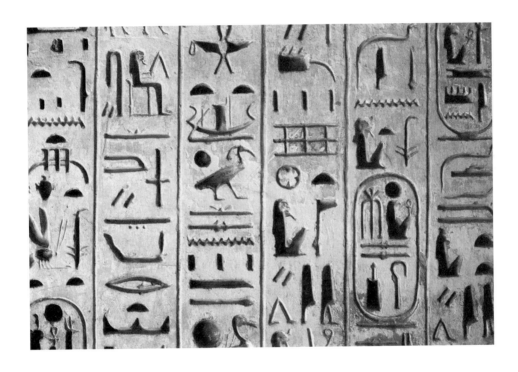

○ ○

CHAPTER 1

Introduction to Drafting Fundamentals

1.1 The History and Origins of Drafting

Imagine having an idea but not being able to communicate it to anyone. Since the dawn of time, humans have been striving to find better and more effective ways to relate their ideas to one another. Examples of the earliest forms of writing such as Egyptian hieroglyphics appear to be composed of a series of pictures (see Figure 1.1). These pictures were eventually streamlined into abstract symbols that we call an *alphabet*. As language and writing developed so did drawing. Bronze compasses made thousands of years ago survive today in museum settings. They look surprisingly like the drafting instruments we use but with pens made of reeds as opposed to graphite leads.

Drafting is not a stagnant discipline. We stand today at an exciting crossroads of change brought on by the introduction of computers. A brief overview of some of the innovations of the past may help you appreciate the ability of drafters to grasp and use new techniques.

Military leaders were quick to realize the advantages of drawing sketches before fortifications and weapons of war were constructed. Stone tablets exist from as far back as 4000 B.C. showing plan views of a fortress constructed by Chaldean engineers [The Louvre, Paris, *Transactions ASCE,* May 1891]. On the civilian side, drawing was used to plan out ideas for dwellings, temples, and burial places. The Egyptian pyramids (see Figure 1.2), burial sites of the pharaohs, were so elaborately and intricately designed that their construction remains a mystery today.

The Greeks developed elaborate systems of architecture, which were later expanded by the Romans. Buildings such as the Parthenon in Athens (see Figure 1.3) were built to precise specifications for the proportions and geometry of the structure. Each column was spaced at an exact distance, and the dimensions of the columns and entablature were determined by precise formulas.

The Roman military engineer Vitruvius (ca. 90–ca. 20 B.C.) left written evidence of the use of technical drawings in his 10-book treatise on architecture, *De Architectura*. The book states, "The architect must be skillful with the pencil and have a knowledge of drawing so that he readily can make the drawings required

FIGURE 1.1 Egyptian hieroglyphics. Courtesy of PhotoDisc, Inc.

FIGURE 1.2 The Egyptian pyramids at Giza. Courtesy of PhotoDisc, Inc.

FIGURE 1.3 The Parthenon on the Acropolis at Athens, Greece. Courtesy of SuperStock, Inc.

FIGURE 1.4 Remains of the Roman Forum with the Colosseum in the background.

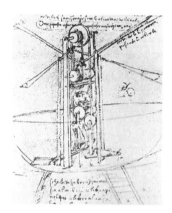

FIGURE 1.5 A flying machine in a drawing by Leonardo da Vinci.

to show the appearance of the work he proposes to construct." Vitruvius also discusses working with drafting instruments as well as developing plan, elevation, and perspective views of a building.

The achievements of the Romans were tremendous. They are credited with developing concrete, which allowed advances in vaulting and domes. Sections of the Roman Forum and Colosseum are still in existence today, as are portions of roads and aqueducts built during the Roman Empire (see Figure 1.4).

Firmly rooted in architecture, the graphic language continued to develop through the ages. As people began to satisfy needs beyond basic food and shelter, they used drafting to prototype products and inventions. Leonardo da Vinci, the ultimate Renaissance man, filled notebook after notebook with sketches for new inventions (see Figure 1.5). In 1651 he published writings on perspective in painting that are considered to be the first ever printed about the theory of projection drawing, a precursor to today's drafting techniques. Fellow Italian architects Leon Battista Alberti and Filippo Brunelleschi also developed ideas on the theory of projections of objects onto imaginary planes—the beginning of three-dimensional drafting.

Mathematics added the next tool to the arsenal of drafting. Frenchman Gaspard Monge is credited with developing theories of descriptive geometry as a response to problems encountered in designing buildings and military fortifications in eighteenth-century France. Descriptive geometry is basically the science of graphic representation. Claude Crozet brought Monge's principles to the United States in 1816, eventually publishing the first English textbook on the subject.

The nineteenth century witnessed several milestones in the profession of drafting. In 1824 Rensselaer Polytechnic Institute was founded "for the purpose of instructing persons in the application of science to the common purpose of life." In 1849 one of the first drafting textbooks, *Geometrical Drawing,* was authored by William Minifie. In 1850 the first drawing instrument manufacturing company to be organized in the United States, Theo. Alteneder & Sons, was founded in Philadelphia. In 1862 The Morrill Act authorizing land grants to support colleges dedicated primarily to teaching agriculture and mechanical arts was passed by the U.S. Congress. In 1890 a second Morrill Act was ratified providing funding for these colleges.

The final innovation of the nineteeth century was the process of blueprinting. Until that time there had been no easy way to reproduce drawings. Invented in 1841 and introduced to the United States in 1876 at the Philadelphia Centennial Exposition, blueprinting changed drafting forever. Until then drawings had been as much art as science. Think of Leonardo da Vinci's sketches, which are prized for their artistic value as much as or more than for their scientific explorations. Drafting involved fine line drawings with shade lines and often watercolor washes. Once blueprinting became established, drawings became streamlined and less ornate in order to provide a better quality reproduction.

As the nineteeth century drew to a close the groundwork had been laid for a shift in the fundamental use of drafting. The emphasis of the twentieth century was on manufacturing, which demanded accurate drawings that could be used to mass produce parts. Previously sketches were typically drawn as a preliminary step to making a particular item. Models were often required to get the dimensions correct before the final product was produced. This process was no longer adequate. The use of projections, the application of descriptive geometry, and the technology of the blueprint process were coupled with the fresh supply of college-trained draftsmen to fill a need sparked by the Industrial Revolution.

Modern technical drafting requires standardization. In the United States the movement toward standardization is being led by the American National Standards Institute (ANSI) in conjunction with the American Society for Engineering Education, the Society of Automotive Engineers, and the American Society of Mechanical Engineers. Together they sponsored the development of the *American Standard Drafting Manual-Y14,* a publication you will become very familiar with if you remain in the drafting profession. The manual has become the authoritative source for uniform drafting practices in the country. American National Standards cover abbreviations, bolts, screws, nuts, dimensioning and surface finish, gears, graphic symbols, keys and pins, piping, rivets, small tools and machine tool elements, threads, tolerances, and washers as well as the Y14 drafting manual and miscellaneous topics. British standards are covered by the British Standards Institution, and Germany is governed by the Deutsches Institut fur Institute. The International Organization for Standardization is headquartered in Geneva, Switzerland, and coordinates efforts toward global standards.

Today is an exciting time because we are riding the crest of yet another innovation in drafting. Computers have already made immense changes in how ideas can be communicated. Drafting is an evolving, ever-changing profession. Who knows what more the future will bring?

1.2   The Function of Drafting in Our World

In today's world drafting provides the universal graphical language that allows engineers and designers to communicate their ideas to the craftspersons and technicians who will ultimately turn these ideas into reality (see Figure 1.6). *Drafting* is graphic communication that is essential to designing, laying out, and developing ideas.

FIGURE 1.6 Drafters at work. Courtesy of IBM Corp.

Graphic representation can be broken down into two basic parts, artistic and technical. Drafting uses elements of both of these disciplines. The design process usually starts with an idea that then takes the form of sketches. Computational sketches may be used in testing the feasibility of this idea. If the idea holds up, technical drawings are then produced so that the structure or product can be manufactured. Exact mechanical drawings can often be useful in finding flaws or refining ideas that were not apparent in the freehand sketch.

Today, almost everything with which you come in contact needed some form of drawing to be built or constructed. The clothes you wear, the furniture you sit on, and the car you drive all needed drawing to become a reality. In this country you cannot even begin constructing a house without first taking a set of drawings to the local building department for approval. Consider the following areas where drafting is utilized:

Construction Related

- Architecture
- Civil Engineering/Site Plans/Mapping/Surveying/Road and Bridge Design
- Electrical Engineering/Power and Lighting Plans
- Fire Protection
- Landscaping
- Interior Design
- Mechanical/Heating and Air Conditioning/Plumbing
- Structural Engineering

A typical architectural or engineering firm employs people with many job descriptions. Architects and engineers work as a team to put together construction drawings and specifications for industrial, commercial, residential, and government projects. An architect or engineer is hired to design and oversee the construction of a project and engineers and designers from disciplines auxiliary to the project are assembled and added to the project team (see Figure 1.7).

Building components such as heating and air conditioning, plumbing, fire protection, electrical, and structural elements are included with the architectural drawings. The architect must hire engineers to prepare a full complement of drawings and specifications in order to complete his or her obligation to the owner. The

FIGURE 1.7   Team meeting at job site.

architect is not normally responsible for services such as interior design or landscape design; however, some firms do have these departments and for an additional charge will provide these services. Otherwise, landscaping and interior design are contracted out separately. Drafting is also utilized in the following industrial and manufacturing sectors:

Industry

- Computer Science
- Geology/Geophysical
- Military Engineering Nuclear Engineering
- Nuclear Engineering
- Oil and Gas
- Patents
- Photogrammetry
- Technical Illustration
- Telecommunications

Manufacturing

- Aeronautical Design
- Apparel Design
- Automated Manufacturing
- Automobile Design
- Electronic Design
- Furniture Design
- Machine Tool Assembly
- Mechanical Engineering
- Plastic Design
- Sheet Metal Assembly

The drawings used by manufacturing groups run through stages similar to those in the building construction fields. The initial design phase aims at refining the design to the point at which basic drawings can be utilized to construct a prototype or model of the desired product (see Figure 1.8). Once a real-life model is put together, it can be evaluated and tested to see if the product will work. At this point the product may be accepted, improvements may be made, or the entire project may be scrapped. If the bugs are worked out, then

FIGURE 1.8 Prototype batter's helmet for baseball and softball with a flip-off mask. (Designed by Mike Hamilton. Drawn by Doug Maddox.)

FIGURE 1.9   Drawing of an integrated circuit.

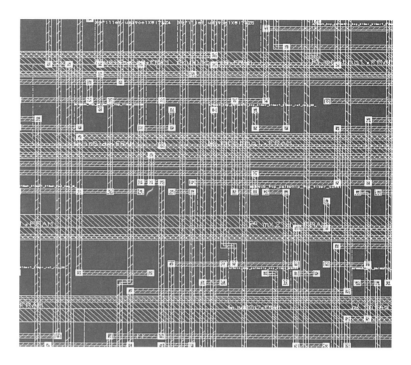

the working or construction drawings can be drafted. This set of plans can then be used to patent or to mass-produce the product.

The electronics industry also uses drafting as a design tool, and most of the drafting is now computerized. Special CAD programs are designed to aid in the layout of integrated circuits and printed circuit boards (see Figure 1.9). In a product such as a cell phone, even the case holding the electronic components is designed using a CAD program.

The list of disciplines that use drafting is extensive and is constantly changing as technology continues to advance. The terms *designing* and *engineering* will always be associated with drafting. The drafter is an integral part of a team that prepares drawings for a builder or manufacturer to use to make a desired end product.

1.3   Board Drafting versus Computer-Aided Design (CAD)

In the last few decades the computer has spawned a major revolution in drafting. Computers were around for several years before they had any impact on drafting; however, the development of CAD software changed things considerably. The early software programs were cumbersome and fairly elementary, but today's CAD packages have brought computers to the forefront of drafting technology (see Figure 1.10).

In the late 1970s, most schools and colleges had only drawing boards in their labs. The only way students got to see CAD back then was by taking a field trip to a manufacturing company with a large engineering department.

By the early 1980s, schools were setting up a few labs with CAD, but it was far from smooth sailing. In its infancy, CAD had quite a few problems. The CAD software locked up the computers daily, and with limited computer memory, drawing was slow. Many industry people did not want to upgrade from drawing boards to computers because of the cost of the software and equipment. A number of bugs were still showing up in the software packages. Toward the end of the 1980s, the computers improved and so did the software, and the cost of the CAD packages became more affordable. AutoCAD emerged as the leading software for drafting. Today, very few companies and schools are without CAD, a powerful and productive tool.

Will Board Drawing Disappear?

A drafter is expected to learn both board and CAD skills. When you encounter the term *drafter,* you need to think of a person skilled in both CAD and board drawing. Board drawing remains a valuable tool for instruction, and elements of board drawing skills are still needed to help build a fundamental understanding of drafting basics (see Figure 1.11).

There are several skills that most industry professionals believe should be taught on a drawing board: freehand sketching, lettering, reading scales, and geometric construction (see Figure 1.12). There is a real art

FIGURE 1.10 A CAD workstation.

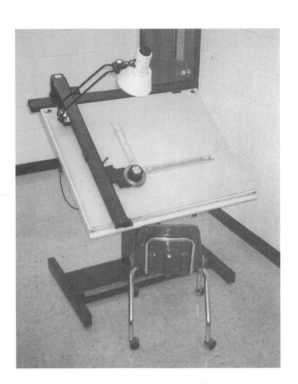

FIGURE 1.11 A drawing board station.

FIGURE 1.12 A drafter doing a freehand sketch in the field.

and skill to board drawing that not everyone can manage, but fortunately the computer can compensate to some degree. Interestingly, it is extremely rare for an individual who is a really good board drafter not to be an exceptional CAD operator.

Board Essentials

Freehand sketching and lettering are the most free-form skills in drafting and two of the most difficult to master. There was a company in Atlanta in the early 1980s that gave a drafting skills test to prospective employees. The only thing on the test was a sheet of lettering. The company reasoned that an individual who had mastered lettering could learn to master anything else involved in drafting.

Today, some people claim that a portable notebook computer loaded with CAD software is replacing lettering and sketching. Freehand sketching is normally done out of the office while visiting a field or job site. Much of the time you are standing up holding a pad of grid paper with a pencil and eraser. Now, it is possible to take the notebook computer to the field, but imagine standing up balancing your computer while trying to punch keys and drag the cursor. The pencil begins to sound more enticing. Plus, sketching commands in most current software packages do not give you the control to sketch easily and effectively.

Most sketches are brought back to the office to be redrawn to scale using the equipment of your choice. It is important that the sketch be easy to understand because someone else back at the office who was not on the field visit may have to do the drawing. That person will be counting on your sketch to be accurate and readable.

This concept applies to lettering as well as sketching. Any notes taken in the field must be clear and concise. Your lettering skills will be counted on to produce information that others can comprehend.

Engineers and designers often use the technique of freehand sketching for their preliminary ideas. Most find it much easier and faster, initially, to sketch on paper. The ideas are then turned over to a drafter to draw the design to scale using a computer or a drawing board. Interior designers find this technique particularly useful. A quick sketch at the job site can ensure that their ideas reflect their clients' desires. This can save time and money later on in the project.

1.4　Scales and Geometric Constructions

Two other skills that are better learned on the drawing board are reading scales and geometric construction. It is possible to learn them using a computer, but the drafter then relies on the computer software to do a lot of thinking and problem solving. This leaves the drafter in the dark as to how the skill is accomplished. When a difficult geometric or scaling problem comes along that the computer will not handle, the drafter is at a loss as to where to start.

Think back to when you were a child learning to add, subtract, multiply, and divide. Did a teacher hand you a calculator and show you how to press the buttons? You might have wished for this to happen, but it did not. You learned, your parents learned, and your grandparents learned by writing numbers down and using the tool called the brain. This type of training helps develop a problem-solving ability that is very helpful. Once the basics are mastered, calculators become time-saving tools for solving difficult problems not crutches to cover poor math skills.

Learning to draft utilizes the same process. Mastering the basics on the board enhances CAD use for more difficult problems. Walk through a business that uses drafting. Look at the computer stations and notice the drafting scales beside them. Every once in a while a drafter needs a scale. Believe it or not, the scale is not for laying on a computer screen. Computer-aided drafting is just a tool—a time saver—and not a replacement for thinking. When the drafter is faced with a problem the computer may not be able to do, then the brain must take over.

1.5　CAD Is the Workhorse

Today, CAD drives the drafting industry and has worked its way into most fields (see Figure 1.13). The advantages of CAD are clear. Even people who hated the thought that a computer would replace the majority of board drawing have come around to accepting CAD as a valuable tool.

Here are some of the advantages of computer-aided drafting:

1. *Revisions*—Remember: almost all drawings get changed. Changes on a computer are done with ease as well as being neater and less time consuming.

FIGURE 1.13 CAD worksta-
tions showing different displays.
Courtesy of Hewlett-Packard Co.

2. *Speed*—Most drawing is much faster on a computer. Time is a big factor when crunch time comes and the drawing must get completed. Once a drawing has been completed using CAD, the finished product can be easily transmitted to most areas of the globe.

3. *Consistency*—Human beings can work as a team. They can even try to copy each other's style of lettering and line work, but when many people work on the same project, it is easy to distinguish different styles when the set of drawings is done. With CAD you can make every drawing look like the same person drew it. Duplication and copying is an exact science with CAD software. Drawings are easy to read and use for construction.

4. *Neatness and layouts*—With a computer-generated drawing, components of a job can easily be moved and oriented into any position. Smearing is a thing of the past. If an original drawing gets torn or ripped, you just print out another copy from a floppy disk or hard drive.

5. *Storage*—Putting drawings on floppy disks, CDs, and tape backups has helped reduce the size of the storage space needed in an office. A box of floppy disks takes up much less room than a large flat file drawer for 24 ″ × 36 ″ sheets.

6. *Precision*—No one can draw on the board more accurately than the computer or change the entire scale of a drawing in a matter of seconds. Think of a computer as a big calculator that you can set up to be as exact as the drawing requires.

1.6　Summary

Although the drawing board is no longer the primary focus of drafting in today's world, it still retains value. The competencies and skills learned at the drafting board provide valuable lessons that complement rather than compete with CAD skills. A good board drafter as well as a good CAD operator need to possess similar skills: speed, accuracy, neatness, making revisions without complaining, and using industry standards. When you encounter the term *drafter*, think of an individual proficient in CAD as well as in board drawing. This book will endeavor to teach you how to do both well.

REVIEW QUESTIONS

1. Why were hieroglyphics developed by early humans?
2. What were some of the earliest civilizations to use drawings to build structures?
3. The Romans were credited with the development of what construction material?
4. What advanced structural forms did the Romans use?
5. Define *drafting* in today's terms.
6. List eight industries or professions that use drafting.
7. What development has made the largest impact on the drafting field?

8. Why did it take so long for most companies to start using CAD?

9. Name four skills in drafting that should be taught on the drawing board.

10. What are some advantages to sketching by hand?

11. List the advantages of CAD over board drawing.

12. What does ANSI stand for?

13. Develop your own definition or description of drafting.

14. List five objects that needed design drawings to be drafted in order to be built or constructed.

15. What does the acronym CAD stand for?

RESEARCH ASSIGNMENTS

1. Research ancient Greek architecture and list five different structures from that time as well as two contributions the Greeks made to architecture.

2. Make a list of five architects of the past and include their more famous buildings or structures.

3. Research ancient Roman architecture and make a list of famous structures still standing today.

4. Research the Renaissance period of architecture in Europe and list some of its architects and the structures they designed.

5. List three modern-day architects or engineers and include photocopies of their work.

6. Research the history of the development of CAD.

CHAPTER 2

○ ○

Learning the Basic Tools and Terminology of Drafting

2.1 Drafting Equipment from A to Z

The first step in learning to draft manually is to assemble your tools. A wide variety of items are available, so you will need to decide how extensive your kit needs to be. The details given in this chapter should help you in your decision. A list of typical equipment needs follows:

- Drafting board and/or table (see Figure 2.1)
- Chair
- Drafting tape
- Drafting pencils, mechanical pencils, or automatic pencils
- Leads, lead sharpener (if using lead holder)
- Erasers, erasing shield, and dusting brush
- Triangles (30°-60°-90°, 45°-45°-90°, adjustable)
- T square, parallel rule, or drafting machine
- Scales (triangular architect's, triangular engineer's)
- Dividers, compass
- Protractor
- Lettering guides and other templates
- Irregular curves (French curves and/or flexible curves)
- Technical pen set and drafting ink
- Dry cleaning pad or drafting powder
- Carrying case or box

FIGURE 2.1 A manual drafting station. Courtesy of Alvin & Co.

Drafting Furniture

Drafting Boards and Tables

Drafting tables are generally referred to by the dimensions of the top of the table (see Figure 2.2). Standard sizes range from 24 ″ × 36″ (610 × 915 mm) to 42″ × 84″ (1067 × 2134 mm). If you are buying a table, you should base your decision on the size drawings with which you plan to work, the space available for the table, and the cost you can afford. It is important that the surface of the table be hard and smooth. Imagine trying to draft precisely on a surface that is wavy or ridged. Materials range from soft- and hardwoods to Masonite or particleboard with a vinyl veneer. Some tops come ready to use, whereas others must first be covered. Vinyl is often used for this purpose. Covering material needs to be smooth and of the proper density for drawing, otherwise you will be able to inscribe the cover as you draw, leaving ridges that will create difficulties for future drawings. The covering material also should be self-healing so that small holes made by instruments such as a compass will close up. The left edge is generally considered the working edge or the edge on which the T square slides, so this edge must be straight. It can be tested with a framing square or a T-square blade that is true.

When you have decided on your basic table, you can look at the bells and whistles. It is very important to be able to adjust the position of the drafting table to fit your comfort level. A one-hand tilt control as well as a one-hand or -foot height control are very desirable features. The capability of positioning the board in the vertical position is also advantageous. In addition, many professional drafting tables come equipped with electrical outlets and drawers in which to store tools or drawings.

If you do not want to invest in a drafting table, a drafting board may be a good alternative (see Figure 2.3). Some drafting boards come with a base that acts as a support and allows the board to be tilted. A drafting board is a good accessory to have even if you have a full-sized drafting table because of the portability of the board. Boards range from as small as 9″ × 12″ for sketching and field work to as large as 48″ × 72″. Choose a board that is slightly larger than the sheet size that you plan to use most often. For example, a 20″ × 24″ board will work well for 17″ × 22″ drawings. The criteria for selecting a drafting board are similar to those for choosing a drafting table: the board must have a smooth surface without warpage, and the ends must be square and true. Traditionally, boards were made of a softwood such as basswood and were either solid or hollow, often with a metal edging. One reason for this choice was to allow the drafter to use thumbtacks to anchor drawings to the board. This practice eventually left evidence in the form of tiny holes that could interrupt the smooth flow of a penciled line. Today, most drafters choose to use drafting tape to attach their drawings to the board. Boards, just like tables, now come in a variety of surfaces such as particleboard with a vinyl veneer, Masonite, or the traditional wood.

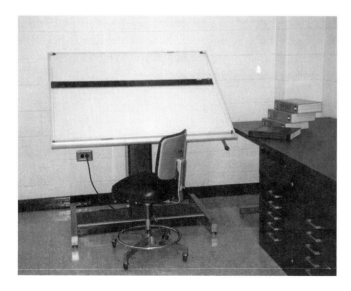

FIGURE 2.2　A professional drafting board.

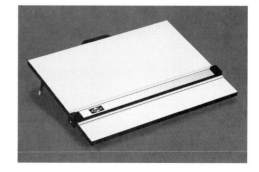

FIGURE 2.3　A drafting board with a parallel ruler. Courtesy of Keuffel & Esser Co.

Drafting Chairs

Investing in a good-quality drafting chair can save you many aches and pains down the road. Take time to find a chair that fits your body style. Some drafters prefer to use a stool rather than a chair. Seats should be padded or contoured and of sturdy construction. Select a fabric that allows air to circulate. Height adjustment is also important.

Lamps

Adequate lighting is critical to successful drafting. Lamps may be attached to the drafting table or placed on a table nearby. Most drafting lamps are adjustable so that they can be positioned according to the needs of the drafter. It is difficult to draw accurately in a shadow. Lamps may be either incandescent or fluorescent. If fluorescent is used, you may want to experiment with lamps of a different spectra.

Drafting Pencils, Leads, and Sharpeners

Drafting Pencils

What is more inspirational than a handful of newly sharpened pencils? It makes you want to jump in and start drawing. Drafting pencils can be distinguished from regular pencils by their lack of an eraser on the end. The grade of the pencil is marked on one end. As with regular pencils, keeping a sharp point requires a continual process of sharpening. After several trips to the sharpener, the pencil becomes awkwardly short. For this reason, many professional drafters do not use drafting pencils but look to alternatives.

Mechanical and Automatic Pencils

The first improvement in drafting pencils was the mechanical pencil or lead holder (see Figure 2.4). A long piece of lead, approximately the same diameter as a drafting pencil lead, is inserted manually into the holder. Grips at the end of the tube keep the lead from slipping out. As the lead wears away, the drafter presses a button on the top of the mechanical pencil to release the grips so more lead can be pulled from the holder. Mechanical pencils overcome the problem of shortening pencils, but they must still be sharpened using special sharpening tools.

The next generation of pencils was the automatic pencil. The lead in these pencils is advanced by increments with the push of a button or tab. Automatic pencils are designed for thin leads that do not need sharpening. They are available in widths of 0.3, 0.5, 0.7, and 0.9 mm. These pencils generally have a small eraser hidden in the end button. Pretend this eraser does not exist. If it wedges down in the pencil, it will plug the hole and lead will not drop down in the base of the barrel when refills are needed.

Drafting Leads

The lead used for drafting is made of graphite with enough kaolin (clay) added to produce the hardness required for each particular grade. Leads come in 18 grades ranging from 9H, which is the hardest, to 7B, which is the softest (see Figure 2.5). If you look at a cross section of the leads you will notice that the harder grades have a smaller diameter than the softer grades. The softer grades need a larger diameter to give them enough strength to be useful. You can generally divide the eighteen grades of lead into three categories. Grades 9H up to 5H are considered "hard" grades; 4H and 6H leads are commonly used for a light linetype referred to as construction lines. Grades 3H, 2H, H, F, HB, and B are considered "medium" in hardness. The grades most commonly used for line work on architectural drawings are H and 2H. The softer grades in this category, such as F and HB, are better suited to technical sketching and other freehand work such as arrow-

FIGURE 2.4 Examples of mechanical and automatic pencils. Courtesy of C.B. White.

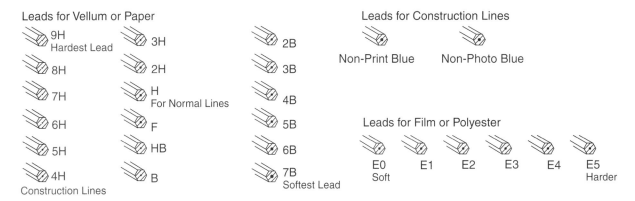

FIGURE 2.5   Lead diameters and examples of their common usage.

heads. The third category ranges from 2B to 7B, the softest grade. These leads are more suited for artwork than technical drafting. They smudge easily and are very difficult to keep sharp.

Special leads are also available through drafting supply stores. Polyester or plastic leads are useful for drawing on the polyester drafting film commonly referred to as Mylar. Normal drafting lead does not adhere as well to this type of drafting media and is easily smudged. The plastic leads are usually labeled with an S or E. The grades available are equivalent to F, 2H, 4H, and 5H. Some companies produce a combination lead for use on both vellum and polyester film.

Colored leads serve a variety of purposes. Red and yellow leads are often used for corrections; however, these colors will appear on prints as black (or blue). If you have information that you wish to place on a drawing but not have it appear on a print, blue lead is a good choice. Blue lead will not reproduce on a diazo (blueprint) machine; it will however reproduce on a photocopy if special photo blue lead is not used. Some drafters prefer to use blue lead for guideline and construction lines.

Sharpeners
Drafting pencils may be sharpened with the same type of pencil sharpeners used for regular pencils. The leads used in lead holders (mechanical pencils) can be sharpened with a pencil pointer made for lead only (see Figure 2.6a). Sanding blocks are another method of sharpening pencils or lead (see Figure 2.6b). With a sanding block the lead can be sharpened to a conical, wedge, or elliptical shape (see Figure 2.7).

Erasers, Erasing Shields, and Dusting Brushes

Erasers
Now that you have selected your drafting pencils, you will most likely find yourself in need of some good erasers. Erasers are commonly found in two basic shapes, rectangular and stick. The stick erasers are good

FIGURE 2.6   (a) A pencil pointer and (b) a sanding block. Courtesy of Alvin & Co.

(a)   (b)

FIGURE 2.7 Conical, wedge, and elliptical leads.

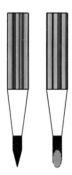
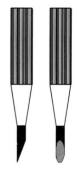

Cone Shape   Wedge Shape   Elliptical Shape

for erasing in tight areas because they are small in diameter. Erasers also come in a variety of compositions that are tailored for different media and drawing instruments, so before you select an eraser, you need to know whether you will be drawing in pencil or pen and on vellum or polyester film. Proper selection can make the eraser your best friend instead of your worst enemy.

White Pencil Eraser.   A white pencil eraser is a good general-purpose eraser for pencil on paper. It contains a small amount of pumice, which is an abrasive material sometimes added to make the eraser more effective.

Pink Pencil Eraser.   Pink pencil erasers have less pumice than the white pencil erasers. They work well at erasing pencil marks off most types of office papers.

Soft Green and Soft Pink Pencil Eraser.   These types of erasers contain no pumice, so they are useful for working with delicate papers. The erasing characteristics of the two colors are the same. The eraser is manufactured in two colors just to satisfy individual preferences.

Gray Ink Eraser.   Gray ink erasers are designed to remove ink from paper. They contain a fair amount of pumice and are firm to the touch. Use care when using this type of eraser; it can easily erase a hole right through your sheet of vellum.

Red Pencil Eraser.   This is the firmest of all pencil erasers and, not surprisingly, contains the largest amount of pumice. As with the gray ink eraser, use care when using this type of eraser.

Kneaded Eraser.   At the other end of the spectrum is the kneaded eraser. This eraser is soft, pliable, and nonabrasive. It is a great stress reliever because it can be kneaded and shaped into any size you need. The kneaded eraser is used mostly for pencil and charcoal. In addition, it is a useful tool for shading. Many drafters also use the kneaded eraser for cleaning up smudges on drawings and work surfaces.

Caution: When erasing on polyester film, take care not to rub off the matte finish. If the matte finish is removed, ink and pencil will no longer adhere to the surface of the medium. Wipe the film with a paper towel after erasing to remove any oil residue on the surface. Otherwise, the ink will run when reapplied to the portion of the film that has been erased.

Vinyl Eraser.   The vinyl eraser contains no abrasive material and is used on polyester drafting film (Mylar) to erase ink or plastic lead.

India Ink Erasing Machine Refill.   The India ink refill eraser is used for removing India ink from vellum or polyester film. A solvent dissolves the binding agents between the ink and the vinyl, allowing the ink to be removed. This substance is specially made for ink and consequently does not work well with pencil.

Electric Erasers.   Electric erasers use a motor to spin a stick eraser around at high speeds to facilitate erasing. You do not need to press down hard with an electric eraser; it does the job for you. Electric erasers are available in models with or without a cord. Some students think using the electric eraser is one of the highlights of manual drafting.

Erasing Shields.   An erasing shield is a thin metal or plastic sheet covered with holes of different shapes and sizes (Figure 2.8). These holes allow you to isolate the particular mark you wish to erase without accidentally erasing nearby lines and symbols. Slightly bend one corner to make the erasing shield easier to pick up when it is lying flat.

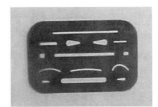

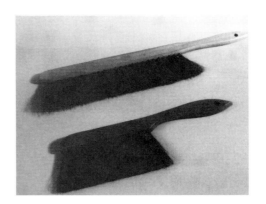

FIGURE 2.8 An erasing shield with tooled openings. Courtesy of C.B. White.

FIGURE 2.9 Wooden dusting brushes. Courtesy of C.B. White.

Dusting Brush.   Using your hand to sweep away eraser dust and graphite particles can leave oily residue from your skin and smudge your drawing. A dusting brush (see Figure 2.9) solves this problem. The fine bristles on the brush clear away unwanted particles without smearing your drawing.

Triangles

Triangles, made of shaped transparent plastic, are used as straightedges to draw lines. They are produced in two standard shapes, which are referred to by the size of the angles at the three corners of the triangle. The first of these triangles, shown in Figure 2.10a, has angles of 30°, 60°, and 90° and is called a 30°-60°-90° triangle. The other standard triangle (see Figure 2.10b) has angles of 45°, 45°, and 90° and is called a 45°-45°-90° triangle. The bigger the number of an angle, the larger the angle. Therefore, the 60°angle is larger than the 30° angle. Also, the three angles of a triangle must always add up to 180° (30° + 60° + 90° = 180°) (45° + 45° + 90° = 180°). The designation of these triangles refers only to the shape of the triangle; both shapes of triangles are available in a variety of sizes depending on the size of your drawing.

Using the two shapes of triangles individually and in combination allows the drafter to draw lines at any 15° increment (see Figure 2.11). Adjustable triangles (see Figure 2.12) are also available. These triangles come with a built-in protractor that allows the drafter to adjust the edge of the triangle to draw a line at any angle.

FIGURE 2.10   A 30°-60°-90° triangle and a 45°-45°-90° triangle. Courtesy of C.B. White.

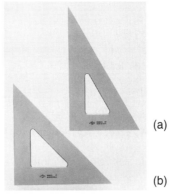

(a)   30°-60°-90°

(b)   45°-45°-90°

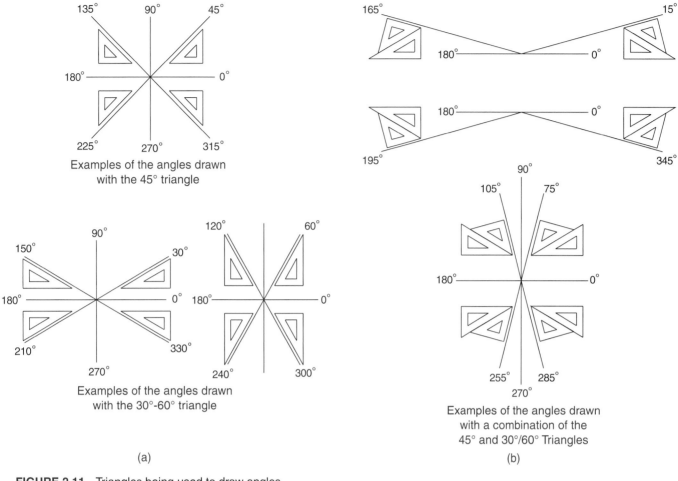

Examples of the angles drawn
with the 45° triangle

Examples of the angles drawn
with the 30°-60° triangle

(a)

Examples of the angles drawn
with a combination of the
45° and 30°/60° Triangles

(b)

FIGURE 2.11 Triangles being used to draw angles.

FIGURE 2.12 An adjustable
drafting triangle. Courtesy of
C.B. White.

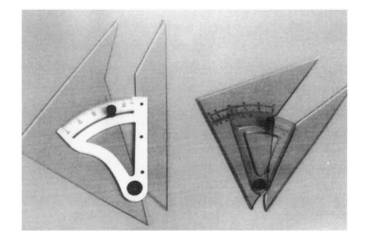

T Squares, Parallel Rules, and Drafting Machines

T squares

In many minds, the T square is the piece of equipment that seems to symbolize drafting. Notice how often the symbol is displayed on the corner of a business card or in a letterhead. The T square (see Figure 2.13) consists of a long strip, called the *blade*, that is fastened tightly at right angles to a shorter piece known as the *head*. The long edges of the blade are the working edges of the T square. They must be perfectly straight and free of any nicks. These edges are usually made out of transparent plastic about ⅜″ wide. This allows the drafter to see what is surrounding the line being drawn.

Treating the T square gently is very important. If the blade becomes nicked or the head loose, the T square will be of very little value. Never use your T square to drive a tack into the board or to cut paper. Check periodically to make sure that the head remains at a 90° angle to the blade. Place the head against a straight edge such as a framing square or a drafting board that has been tested and found true. If the T square wiggles, it needs to be adjusted or replaced. To check the trueness of the blade carefully draw a line along one edge of the blade. Use a hard pencil so the line will be clearly defined. Turn the blade over and draw a line along the same edge. The two lines should coincide (see Figure 2.14). If they do not, the space between the lines will be twice the error of the blade. Again, the T square should be corrected or replaced.

Parallel Rules

Parallel rules or bars (see Figure 2.15) are mounted directly on the drafting board or table using a system of cables running through pulleys attached at the four corners of the board. The parallel bars slide up and down the board on the cable enabling the drafter to draw horizontal parallel lines. Vertical lines and angled lines can be drawn using the parallel bar with triangles (see Figure 2.16). As with a T square, the edges must be kept straight and nick free.

Parallel bars are particularly suited to drawing lines reaching almost the full length of the board. Many architectural drawings fall into this category. A T square may have a tendency to deflect when extremely long lines are drawn. The bar and any triangles must be kept securely in place while drawing. More sophisticated parallel bars are equipped with a locking device to ensure that the bar does not move. Parallel bars can be used even when the board is in the vertical position.

FIGURE 2.13   A drafter's T square.

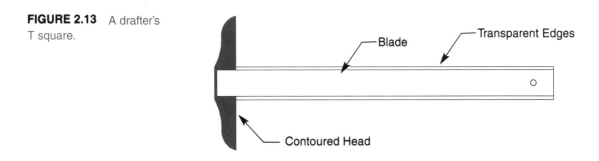

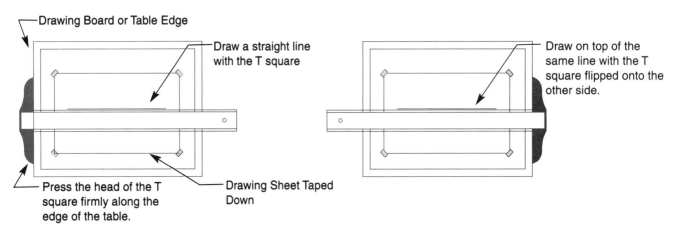

FIGURE 2.14   One method for checking the trueness of a blade.

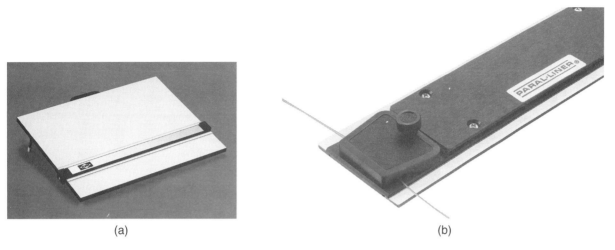

(a)   (b)

FIGURE 2.15   Parallel rules. Courtesy of Alvin & Co.

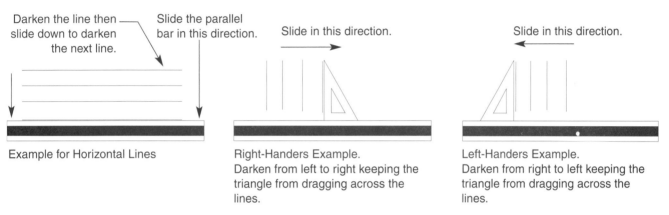

Darken the line then slide down to darken the next line. ⟶ Slide the parallel bar in this direction.

Example for Horizontal Lines

Slide in this direction. ⟶

Right-Handers Example.
Darken from left to right keeping the triangle from dragging across the lines.

⟵ Slide in this direction.

Left-Handers Example.
Darken from right to left keeping the triangle from dragging across the lines.

FIGURE 2.16   Drawing lines with parallel rules.

Drafting Machines

A drafting machine attaches directly to the drawing board and combines the function of triangles and parallel bars. The main body of the machine (see Figure 2.17) consists of a vertical and a horizontal bar clamped to a circular control that allows the angle of the machine to be rotated. While the two bars remain at 90° to each other they can be rotated in order to draw lines at any angle. The center control contains a protractor and vernier plate that allows the rotation of the bars to be measured to within 5′ (minutes). The two bars of the drafting machine serve the combined function of a straightedge and a scale.

The main body of the drafting machine is mounted in either an arm system or a track system. The aptly named arm system (see Figure 2.18) functions just as your arm does using two sections connected by an elbow to position the drafting machine at the desired location on the board. The track system (see Figure 2.19) attaches the main body of the drafting machine to a vertical track that traverses the length of the board on a horizontal track mounted at the top of the board. The body of the drafting machine can be moved up and down along the vertical bar and from side to side using the horizontal bar. A locking device on both bars allows the drafting machine to be fixed at any location on the board.

FIGURE 2.17   Close-up of a drafting machine.

FIGURE 2.18   An arm drafting machine mounted on a drafting table. Courtesy of Keuffel & Esser Co.

FIGURE 2.19   A track drafting machine mounted on a drafting table. Courtesy of Vemco Corporation.

Both the arm and the track drafting machines work well. The arm drafting machine is more compact and slightly less expensive than the track drafting machine; however, the track drafting machine can be used with the board in a vertical position. Because the drafting machine must be able to be situated at any position across the drafting board, both types of machines come in sizes relative to the size of the drafting board. Drafting machines tailored for left-handed drafters are available.

Operating the Drafting Machine Controls

The controls of a drafting machine allow movement horizontally, vertically, and at an angle. Models of drafting machines will vary slightly, so have your instructor demonstrate the controls for your particular machine. In a track drafting machine, horizontal and vertical locks are usually located on the vertical track. The rotation control for both arm and track drafting machines will be on the center control with the protractor and vernier. The protractor and vernier scale allow you to set the angle of the bars with precision. First, try setting the bars to a specified whole degree. Place your hand on the center knob and use your thumb to depress the index thumbpiece. This releases the head and allows the bars to rotate. As you experiment with this control, notice that the head automatically re-locks every 15°. You will have to press the index thumbpiece to continue rotating the machine. Pay attention to the protractor and vernier scales as you rotate the drafting machine (Figure 2.20). Each tick mark or increment of the protractor represents 1° of rotation, with every 10° marked with a number. The zero mark on the vernier plate will line up with the degree of rotation. If the zero mark on the vernier scale lines up exactly with one of the tick marks on the protractor scale, the drafting machine will have been rotated that many whole degrees (see Figure 2.21).

Always be aware whether you are measuring an angle off the position of the vertical or the horizontal bars. The horizontal bar rotates from a base position at 0°, so the readings for the horizontal bar come directly off the protractor and vernier scales. The vertical bar, however, has a base position at ninety degrees. To position the vertical bar you must determine the angle change from 90°. Figure 2.22 shows examples of measuring angles for both the horizontal and vertical bars. The trick is always to determine whether you are working with the horizontal bar, which references to 0°, or the vertical bar, which references to 90°.

After experimenting with rotating your drafting machine to various angles you should be able to see how easy it is to measure whole angles. Now let's learn how to read angles to an accuracy of 59 (minutes). [As a reminder, 1 degree equals 60 minutes ($1° = 60'$), and there are 60 seconds in each minute ($1' = 60''$)]. On the vernier scale, positive angles read upward, and negative angles read downward from zero. Each tick mark on the vernier scale represents $5'$. In the illustration shown in Figure 2.23, the zero on the vernier plate is resting between 9° and 10°, therefore, the drafting machine has been rotated at an angle greater than 9° and less than 10°. Use the vernier scale to narrow this reading down further. Look upward on the vernier scale above the zero mark and find the location where the tick marks on the vernier and the protractor scale line are most closely aligned. In Figure 2.23, this occurs at $25'$ on the vernier scale, so the correct reading for this angle is $9°25'$. A negative angle is read the same way, except the vernier scale is aligned using the lower half of the scale.

FIGURE 2.20 Close-up of a protractor and vernier on a drafting machine.

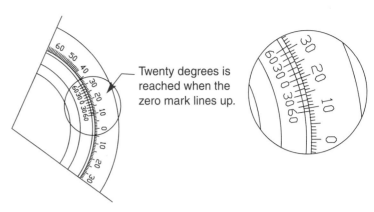

Twenty degrees is reached when the zero mark lines up.

FIGURE 2.21 Protractor and vernier set at 20°.

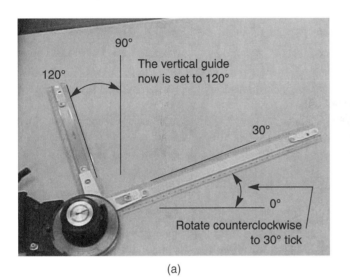

90°

120°

The vertical guide now is set to 120°

30°

0°

Rotate counterclockwise to 30° tick

(a)

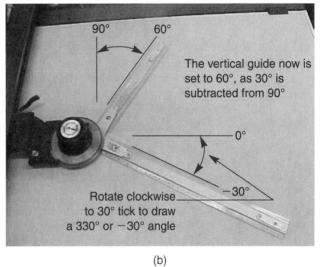

90° 60°

The vertical guide now is set to 60°, as 30° is subtracted from 90°

0°

−30°

Rotate clockwise to 30° tick to draw a 330° or −30° angle

(b)

FIGURE 2.22 A vernier measuring an angle from the horizontal and the vertical.

FIGURE 2.23 A vernier reading of 9°25′.

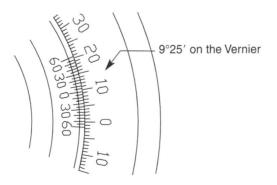

9°25′ on the Vernier

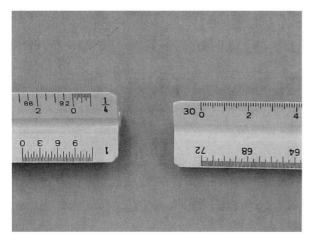

FIGURE 2.24 Architectural and engineering scales.

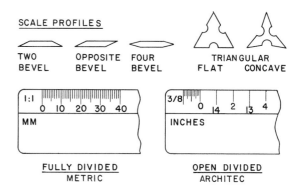

FIGURE 2.25 The four basic shapes of drafting scales.

Scales

Because objects are rarely drawn full size, scales or rulers play an important role in drafting. Typical scale types are mechanical, engineering, and architectural. Units are either metric (millimeters) or English (inches). Figure 2.24 shows typical scales used for engineering and architectural drawings. Scales come in four basic shapes, which are illustrated in Figure 2.25. Some two-bevel scales are equipped with attachments so they can be used as arms on a drafting machine. Triangular scales combine many scales on one instrument, which gives them an advantage over the other styles of scales. Directions for reading architectural and engineering scales are provided in Section 2.3.

Compass and Dividers

Compass

The compass is used for drawing circles and arcs (see Figure 2.26). One leg of the compass has a needle point, and the other contains lead for drawing. This lead must be kept sharp in order for your drawings to remain accurate. A conical or wedge point may be used. The lead is sharpened in the same way as is the lead for a mechanical pencil. An adjusting screw is the most common device for opening and closing the legs of the compass. Some less expensive models swing the compass open and shut with a metal arc. These tend to become loose over time.

FIGURE 2.26 A compass in use. Courtesy of C.B. White.

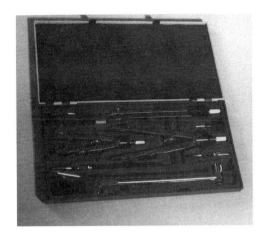

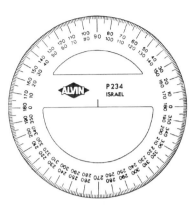

FIGURE 2.27 A compass and divider set. Courtesy of C.B. White.

FIGURE 2.28 A protractor. Courtesy of Alvin & Co.

If you plan to do much drafting, it is well worth the extra investment to purchase a high-grade instrument. Professional compass sets usually come with removable ends, an extender bar, and an adapter for ink pens.

A compass set and dividers are often packaged together in a specially lined and divided case (see Figure 2.27). A compass adapter will allow the drafter to use an automatic pencil or an ink pen with the compass.

Dividers

A divider is similar to a compass, except both ends are needle points. It may have a center wheel for adjustments, or it may simply use pivot adjustment under friction. Whichever method is used, the divider must be easily adjusted with one hand and remain steady in the new position. Dividers are used for transferring dimensions and dividing a distance into some number of equal parts.

Protractor

Drafters not using a drafting machine will want to include a protractor (see Figure 2.28) in their drawing kit. Protractors are circular instruments marked off in 360°. They can accurately be used to measure angles to within a tolerance of 0.5°.

Lettering Guides and Other Templates

Lettering guides and templates make life easier for the drafter. They are sheets of plastic with various shapes and symbols cut out for tracing. Lettering guides are available in many sizes and styles of lettering. Other templates range from circles and ellipses to unique symbols. Specialized templates exist for almost any discipline, whether it be electrical, plumbing, or even computers. The most common architectural templates are at ¼″ = 1′ scale and provide door swings, plumbing fixtures, appliance symbols, roof pitches, circles, cabinets, and electrical symbols (see Figure 2.29). Some mechanical templates consist of nuts, bolts, threads, and welding symbols.

FIGURE 2.29 Examples of templates. Courtesy of C.B. White.

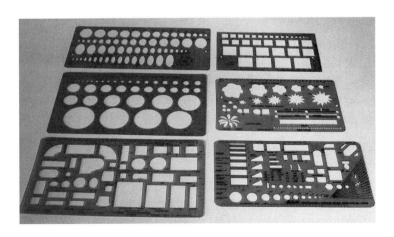

If you plan to use ink with your template, buy one with risers built in to keep the template slightly above the drawing. Otherwise, capillary action may cause the ink to run under the template and create a smear. If your template does not have risers, a few layers of tape under the template may serve the same purpose.

Irregular Curves

The curves required in drafting are not always circles or portions of circles. Irregular or French curves (see Figure 2.30), made out of transparent plastic, provide a solution to the problem of drawing curves that do not have a constant radius (i.e., circles or arcs). French curves come in a variety of shapes, but the one constant is that none of the curves on the template have a constant radius. Shapes such as parabolas, hyperbolas, ellipses, and logarithmic spirals are used to construct the French curves.

Flexible curves are another answer to the problem of drawing irregular shapes (see Figure 2.31). Made out of plastic with a flexible core, they allow the drafter to bend them into the desired shape. The core holds the curve in place so the line can be drawn.

Technical Pen Sets and Drafting Ink

Technical Drafting Pens

Technical drafting pens work on the principle of capillary action. A needle acts as a valve to allow ink to flow out of the main body of the pen through a small tube that monitors the amount of ink. Different sized needles are used to draw lines of different width. For this reason, technical pens are usually purchased in a set (see Figure 2.32).

Price range varies for technical pens and is partly determined by the choice of points for the needle part of the pen. Points should be selected based on how you intend to use them. Stainless steel points are well suited for vellum but wear out quickly when used on polyester film (Mylar). Tungsten carbide points are a good choice for polyester film (Mylar) and can also be used on vellum. The longest lasting points are jewel points, which can be used with excellent results on either polyester film or vellum. Jewel points provide the smoothest flow of ink for polyester film.

Careful cleaning and maintenance are critical to keeping technical pens in good working order. Triangles with a special edge for inking are useful accessories when working with technical pens.

Drafting Ink

Drafting ink has its own set of requirements for usefulness. It must dry quickly, not clog the pen, adhere well to the drafting media, and provide even color for reproducing. Select ink that is recommended for the surface on which you plan to draw. Ink must be kept tightly sealed so that it does not dry out or become thick. Some inks can be thinned with a combination of four parts aqua ammonia to one part distilled water.

FIGURE 2.30 Examples of French curves.

FIGURE 2.31 A flexible curve. Courtesy of C.B. White.

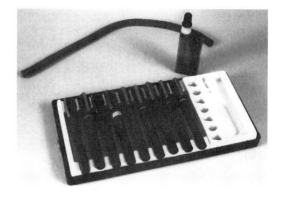

FIGURE 2.32 A set of drafting pens and ink. Courtesy of C.B. White.

2.2 Drafting Media and Title Blocks

Drafting Media

The goal of most drafting projects is to produce a finished drawing that is accurate and professional in addition to being easily reproducible. Choosing the right drafting media is key to reaching this goal. Factors to take into consideration when selecting drafting media include transparency, durability, smoothness, erasability, dimensional stability, and cost.

Transparency becomes an important consideration primarily because of reproduction processes. Rarely does the original of a manual drawing get anywhere near a job site. The original usually stays safely in a file drawer while the various trade professionals use sets of copies. Traditionally, the originals have been copied using a diazo process commonly referred to as *blueprinting*. This process requires that light pass through the material being reproduced. If drawings are to be reproduced using a photocopy process, transparency is not important.

Durability becomes an issue when the drawing will be used and handled over a period of time. The amount of use will determine the amount of durability required. If the drawing becomes wrinkled with constant use, it may become difficult to read. Certain types of media are more resistant to crumpled edges and torn corners than others.

The smoothness of the paper is critical to producing sharp, crisp lines that are easily read. Drafting media should be easy to draw and letter on without disproportionate effort. Imagine trying to draw a straight line across a surface that is even slightly bumpy or wavy. The smoothness of the paper also determines how the media will accept ink and pencil.

Whenever humans are involved in drafting, erasability becomes a consideration. A paper that erases easily allows the drafter to make changes without leaving behind telltale marks. A medium that does not erase easily may tempt the drafter to work so hard at getting rid of unwanted lines that the paper becomes worn through or torn. If a residue is left behind on the medium, it may "ghost" through and appear when the drawing is reproduced.

Some media may expand or contract as the temperature or the humidity changes. This can play havoc with figures drawn carefully to scale. The ability of a medium to maintain its size in spite of the ambient conditions is referred to as *dimensional stability*. Media used for drafting should always have good dimensional stability.

The final criterion for selecting drafting media is, as with most things, cost. Transparency, durability, smoothness, erasability, and dimensional stability come at a price. The drafter must decide how to maximize these factors for a price that is affordable. The two most common drafting media are vellum and polyester film.

Vellum

Vellum is commonly used in drafting because it is one of the least expensive papers with good smoothness and good transparency. It is specifically designed to accept either ink or pencil. The erasability of vellum is good, although some brands are better than others. The two most widely used weights of vellum are 1000H and 2000H (see Figure 2.33).

There are some trade-offs to using vellum. It is not as dimensionally stable as some other materials and so it is affected by humidity and other atmospheric conditions. In addition, vellum must be handled carefully because it is not the most durable of the drafting media. Frequent handling can cause the material to deteriorate. In spite of these slight flaws, lead on vellum is still the most prevalent combination used in manual drafting today.

Polyester Film (Mylar)

Polyester film is a plastic material commonly referred to by the trademark name Mylar. It is more expensive than vellum but possesses excellent characteristics of transparency, durability, smoothness, erasability, and

FIGURE 2.33 A table of paper weights.

Typical Vellums

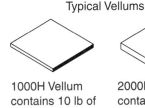

1000H Vellum contains 10 lb of rag or cloth.

2000H Vellum contains 20 lb of rag or cloth.

Typical Film Sizes Range from 3mils to 9mils

Film can be found as thin as .003″ or 3 mils.

Film can be found as thick as .009″ or 9 mils.

dimensional stability. Regular graphite lead will smear when used on polyester film, so it is better to use ink or special polyester leads.

Polyester film is produced with a single- or double-matte surface. The matte surface gives a texture to the film so that it will accept ink or polyester lead. With the single-matte style, one side has a matte surface that can be drawn on, whereas the other side is slick and will not accept drawing. This is the most common type of polyester film. The double matte style is surfaced on both sides and is slightly more expensive than the single matte.

You need to take the following precautions when drawing on polyester film. Avoid getting any moisture on the surface of the film. Moisture interferes with the adhesion of ink or lead to the polyester film, giving the appearance that the area was skipped when lines are drawn. Dirt can also interfere with the adhesion of ink to polyester film. The ink may appear to flow nicely but will flake or wear away with time. So keep your hands clean and dry when working on polyester film. If the surface becomes soiled, clean it with a cleanser formulated for use on polyester film. Make sure the surface is completely dry before you begin drawing.

Erasing on polyester film takes a certain amount of technique. If you are not careful, you can erase not only the ink you applied but also the factory-applied matte surface. If the matte surface is destroyed, the film will not accept ink or lead on that spot on the drawing. Always erase at right angles to the line you are changing, using a light touch without too much pressure. Ink erasers leave an oil residue that needs to be wiped before more ink is reapplied.

Sheet Sizes for Drafting Media

Drafting media come in either rolls or precut sheets. Figure 2.34 shows the most common sizes for precut sheets. The sheet size chosen for various types of jobs will usually be standardized within a particular office.

FIGURE 2.34 ANSI specifications for sheet sizes.

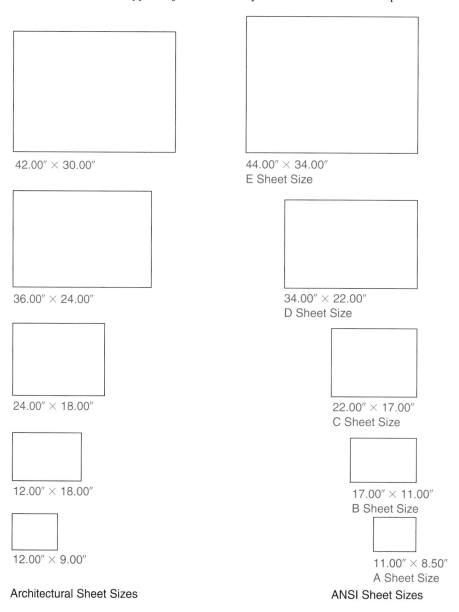

42.00″ × 30.00″

44.00″ × 34.00″
E Sheet Size

36.00″ × 24.00″

34.00″ × 22.00″
D Sheet Size

24.00″ × 18.00″

22.00″ × 17.00″
C Sheet Size

12.00″ × 18.00″

17.00″ × 11.00″
B Sheet Size

12.00″ × 9.00″

11.00″ × 8.50″
A Sheet Size

Architectural Sheet Sizes

ANSI Sheet Sizes

Attaching Drafting Media to the Drafting Board

Although other systems exist, drafting media are most often attached to the board using drafting tape. This tape is specially prepared to hold the paper down without damaging the board or destroying the paper when it is removed. To remove the tape, pull it off slowly in the direction of the edge of the paper, pulling from the outside can cause the paper to tear. Drafting tape is also manufactured in the shape of round dots that are easily removed.

It is best if your drafting board is larger than the sheet size on which you are working. This will allow you to place your paper so that you can use your T square or drafting machine to reach any section of the sheet (see Figure 2.35). If using a T square, place the paper close to the edge of the board with the head of the T square. This will minimize errors resulting from the flex of the T square. Allow enough room at the bottom of the board to support your arm as well as to provide room for the T square or drafting machine.

Title Blocks and Borders

Borders on architectural drawings are usually thick solid lines around the outside of the entire sheet. Typically they are indented ⅜″ to ½″ on the top, bottom, and right sides of the sheet. The left side of the border is indented ¾″ to 1½″ to allow room for binding (see Figure 2.36). Borders are not required, but they provide an excellent frame for the drawing as well as adding a professional looking finish.

The placement of the title block on a drawing will vary with different disciplines. Architectural title blocks are typically found on either the right side or the bottom of the sheet. Both the title block and border can be preprinted on the drafting media for an additional charge. Borders and title blocks are often created in AutoCAD to suit a particular individual's or company's requirements.

The information provided in the title block will vary slightly from company to company. The following items may be included in the title block:

- Name of the project
- Name, address, and phone number of firm
- Name and address of the client
- Drawing name
- Drawing number (Example: Sheet 2 of 10)
- Job or file number
- Scale of the drawing
- Designer or architect
- Drawn by
- Checked by
- Date completed
- Revisions with dates

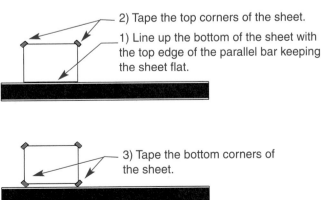

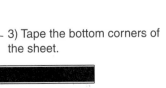

FIGURE 2.35   Paper positioned correctly on a drafting board.

Form 1. Title Block

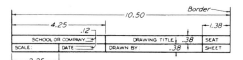

Form 2. Title Block

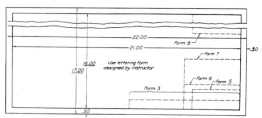

Form 3. Title Block

Sheet Sizes

American National Standard	International Standard
A – 8.50″ × 11.00″	A4 – 210 mm × 297 mm
B – 11.00″ × 17.00″	A3 – 297 mm × 420 mm
C – 17.00″ × 22.00″	A2 – 420 mm × 594 mm
D – 22.00″ × 34.00″	A1 – 594 mm × 841 mm
E – 34.00″ × 44.00″	A0 – 841 mm × 1189 mm
	(25.4 mm = 1.00″)

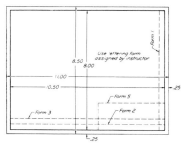

Fig. I Size A Sheet (8.50″ × 11.00″)

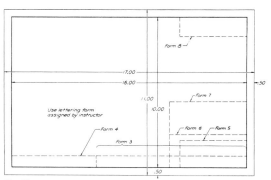

Fig. V Size B Sheet (11.00″ × 17.00″)

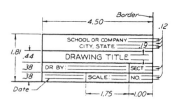

Fig. VI **Size C Sheet (17.00″ × 22.00″)**

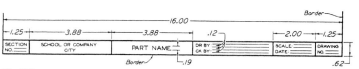

Fig. VII **Form 4. Title Block**

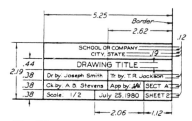

Fig. VIII **Form 5. Title Block**

Fig. IX **Form 6. Title Block**

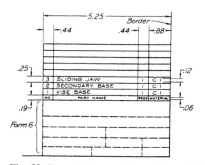

Fig. X **Form 7. Parts List or Material List**

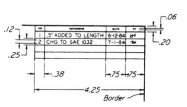

Fig. XI **Form 8. Revision Block**

FIGURE 2.36 ANSI standards for title blocks.

2.3   Reading Scales

Rulers measure the actual size of an object in the "real" world. A scale, on the other hand, allows you to measure the size that the object is drawn to represent. Thus, instead of measuring the actual length of a line on a drawing and then multiplying by a scale factor, you can read the number directly off your scale. The work is done for you. The scale of a drawing should always be noted either in the title block or as a note in the body of the drawing. This section discusses using three types of scales: architectural, engineering, and metric.

Architectural Scales

Architectural scales are available in several different shapes, as discussed in Section 2.1. The triangular scale is the most versatile because it combines eleven scales on one piece of equipment. Learning to use a scale is best done as a hands-on experience.

Take a minute to pick up your scale and look it over. The type of numbers on the ends distinguish the architect's scale from other scales. Architect's scales have a fraction at the end of each scale. One edge contains a full-size scale that measures just like a traditional ruler (see Figure 2.37). It is marked with a 16 at the end because each inch is further subdivided into sixteenths. All the other edges contain two scales. One scale is read from left to right, and the other scale is read from right to left. The scales that share an edge are always multiples of each other. For example, ¼ is twice ⅛. With the exception of the full-size scale, the numbers at the end of the scale represent the number of inches on the scale that represent a foot. Thus, the ⅜ at the end of one scale stands for ⅜ inch = 1 foot. Each foot of the actual object will take up ⅜″ on your drafting paper when it is drawn to this scale.

The incremental markings between the zeros represent feet and half feet, depending on which scale you are using. Turn your scale over until you find the ⅛″ and ¼″ scales (Figure 2.38). Most residential drawings are drawn at a ¼″ = 1′ scale. Commercial architectural drawings are generally drawn using the ⅛″ = 1′ scale. Notice that each edge contains two rows of numbers. On the ⅛″ and ¼″ scales, the top set of numbers go from zero on the left to 92 on the right. The bottom set of numbers start at zero on the right and go to 46 on the left. The numbers on the top correspond to the ⅛″ scale. The zero is closest to the ⅛″ designation, and the numbers get larger as you move to the right. The bottom numbers correspond to the ¼″ scale, since the zero on the bottom right is closest to that designation.

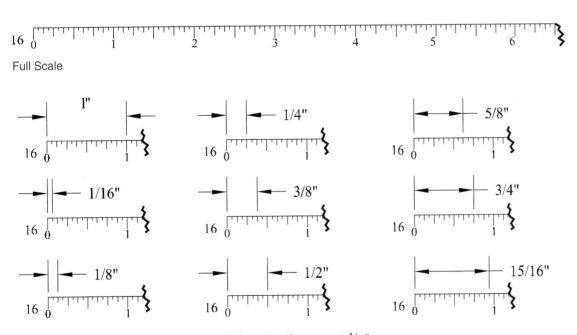

If this scale is used as 1″ =1″, then every tick mark will represent ⅟₁₆″.

FIGURE 2.37   Full scale.

FIGURE 2.38 Architectural scales ⅛″ = 1.0′ and ¼″ = 1.0′.

The left side is the ⅛″ =1′-0″ scale.

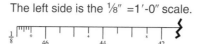

The right side is the ¼″ =1′-0″ scale.

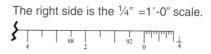

Every tick mark to the left of the zero represents 2″ on this scale.

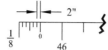

Every tick mark to the right of the zero represents 1″ on this scale.

Every tick mark to the right of the zero represents 1′ on this scale.

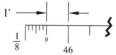

Every long tick mark to the left of the zero represents 1′ on this scale.

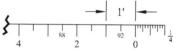

This line measures 2′-8″ at this scale.

This line measures 4′-5″ at this scale.

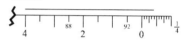

The next step is to determine the significance of each tick mark for each particular scale. Every tick mark between the two zeros serves a double duty. On one scale, every tick mark represents a full foot. On the other scale, every *other* tick mark represents a foot, making the marks in between equal to a half foot, or 6″. Let's look at the ⅛″ = 1′ scale. (see Figure 2.38). Remember, we are using the top numbers for that scale. Notice that the first tick mark is labeled with a zero. The next three tick marks bear no labels on the top and are followed by a tick mark labeled with a four. Thus, each tick mark represents a foot using the ⅛″ = 1′ scale. Now, examine the ¼″ = 1′ scale (see Figure 2.38). Looking at the numbers on the bottom, notice that the far right tick mark is labeled with a zero. Moving to the left, the next three ticks marks are not labeled on the bottom. The next tick mark to the left is labeled with a two. Thus, each tick mark represents a half foot or 6″. The full foot marks fall on the tick marks that are slightly longer. All the scales except the full scale work in this manner. Experiment with using the other scales.

Now let's look at the portion of your scale outside the zeros. Each divided portion to the left and right of the two zeros represents one foot subdivided into inches and portions of inches. The number of subdivisions depends on the room available. The 3″ = 1′ scale has room for many more divisions than the ³⁄₃₂″ = 1′ scale. Take a look at the 3″ = 1′ scale (Figure 2.39). Space is available to actually label 3, 6, and 9″ on the scale. The tick marks get slightly shorter at each subsequent division until the smallest increment, which represents ⅛″. Now look at the ³⁄₃₂″ = 1′ scale (Figure 2.40). The section to the left of zero is divided into only six sections, so each subdivision represents 2″. Take time to check out the other scales and find out how they are divided into inches at the ends.

The best way to measure with a scale is to position the instrument in such a way that it does not have to be picked up to complete the measurement. Moving the scale introduces a chance for error. Figures 2.39 and 2.40 show some examples of measuring with various scales.

Engineer's Scales

Engineer's scales are used for reading and constructing drawings such as plot plans, landscape designs, and topographic maps. The triangular engineer's scale contains six scales labeled 10, 20, 30, 40, 50, and 60. Notice that there are more divisions on the 60 scale than on the 10 scale. This is because the 60 scale is divided into sixty increments per inch, whereas the 10 scale is divided into only ten increments per inch.

The drafter has the option of using each scale in several ways. For example, the 20 scale can represent 1″ = 20′, 1″ = 200′, 1″ = 20 miles, and so forth. The engineer's scale is graduated in decimals rather than feet and inches, so there are ten divisions between numbers on the scale. Figures 2.41a–e show some examples of measuring with the engineer's scale.

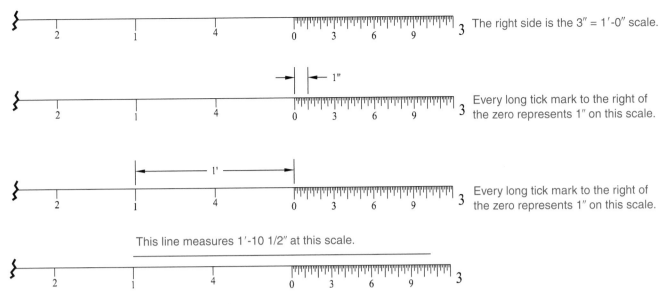

The right side is the 3″ = 1′-0″ scale.

Every long tick mark to the right of the zero represents 1″ on this scale.

Every long tick mark to the right of the zero represents 1″ on this scale.

This line measures 1′-10 1/2″ at this scale.

FIGURE 2.39 Architectural scale 3″ = 1.0′.

FIGURE 2.40 Architectural scales 3/32″ = 1/0′ and 3/16″ = 1.0′.

The left side is the ³⁄₃₂″ =1′-0″ scale.

The right side is the ³⁄₁₆″ =1′-0″ scale.

Every tick mark to the left of the zero represents 2″ on this scale.

Every tick mark to the right of the zero represents 1″ on this scale.

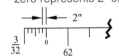

Every tick mark to the right of the zero represents 1′ on this scale.

Every long tick mark to the left of the zero represents 1′ on this scale.

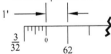

This line measures 2′-8″ at this scale.

This line below measures 4′-5″ at this scale.

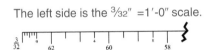

Metric Scales

Metric scales are divided into sections of ten just like engineering scales. The numbers at the end of a metric scale indicate the proportion of the drawing to the actual object being drawn. Figures 2.42a–c show some examples of measuring using a metric scale. Most mechanical drawings use millimeters or centimeters, whereas architectural drawings use meters. Metric scales are used in many countries and are very flexible, just like the engineer's scale. Architectural drawings that use metric are almost nonexistent in the United States.

An example of the engineer's 10 scale. Notice the 10 on the left-hand side, which indicates the number of scale increments per inch.

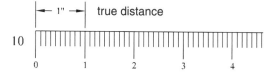

If you use the scale as 1″=10′, then each short tick mark represents 1′, and each long tick mark represents 10′.

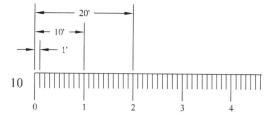

This line measures 43′ at the 1"=10' scale.

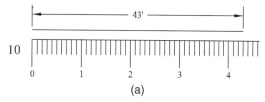

(a)

An example of the engineer's 40 scale. Notice the 40 on the left-hand side, which indicates the number of scale increments per inch.

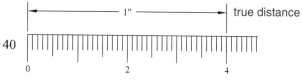

If you use the scale as 1″=40′, then each short tick mark represents 1′, and each long tick mark represents 10′.

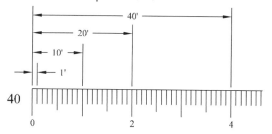

This line measures 37' at the 1"=40' scale.

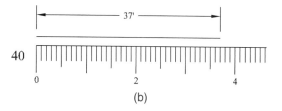

(b)

An example of the engineer's 60 scale. Notice the 60 on the left-hand side, which indicates the number of scale increments per inch.

If you use the scale as 1″=60′, then each short tick mark represents 1′ , and each long tick mark represents 10′.

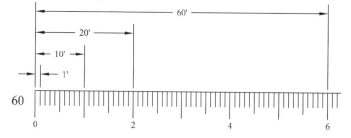

This line measures 57' at the 1"=60' scale.

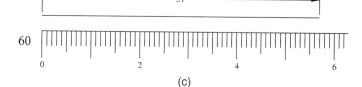

(c)

FIGURE 2.41   Measuring with engineer's scales.

If you use the scale as 1"=1" (full scale), then each short tick mark represents 0.1", and each long tick mark represents 1".

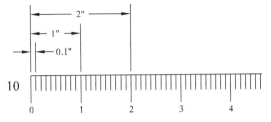

If you use the scale as 1"=100', then each short tick mark represents 10', and each long tick mark represents 100'.

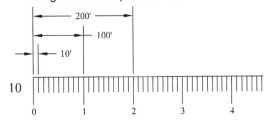

This line measures 3.3" at full scale.

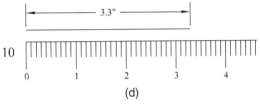

(d)

This line measures 430' using the 1"=100' scale.

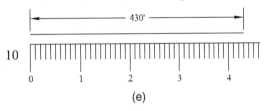

(e)

FIGURE 2.41 *continued*

An example of the metric scale. The .05 and 1:20 on the left-hand side indicate the number of scale increments per one meter.

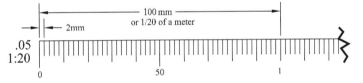

This line measures 78 mm.

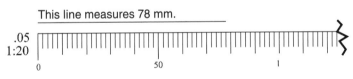

An example of the metric scale. The .01 and 1:100 on the left-hand side indicate the number of scale increments per one meter.

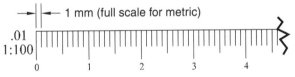

It takes 1000 mm to make 1 meter.

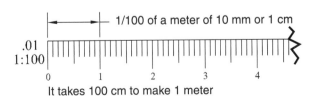

It takes 100 cm to make 1 meter

This line measures 42 mm at full scale.

(a)

An example of the metric scale. The .03 and 1:33 1/3 on the left-hand side indicate the number of scale increments per one meter.

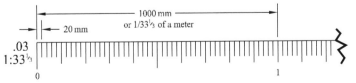

This line measures 1120 mm.

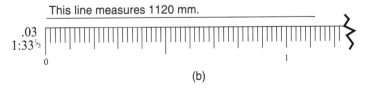

(b)

FIGURE 2.42 Measuring with metric scales. *continued on next page*

An example of the metric scale. The .025 and 1:40 on the left-hand side indicate the number of scale increments per one meter.

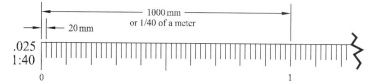

This line measures 740 mm at full scale.

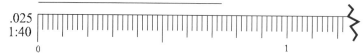

The metric scales are blown up very large for the reader to see.

(c)

FIGURE 2.42   *continued*

Mechanical Scale

Mechanical engineers draw a variety of objects, ranging from tiny parts the size of needles to large parts used in airplanes and ships. The challenge is the same in all drafting fields and that is to scale a drawing so that it will fit on a standard sheet size and be readable. Some of the scales used by mechanical engineers are listed here:

Some Typical Mechanical Scales

$1'' = 1''$ Full scale

$1/2'' = 1''$ Half scale

$1/4'' = 1''$ Quarter scale

$1/8'' = 1''$

$2'' = 1''$ Double scale

$4'' = 1''$ Quadruple scale

As you can see, the mechanical engineer uses the inch as the basis for measurement. Any scale less than an inch, such as ¼″=1″, compresses the scale, or makes the object shrink. Scales larger than 1″ are used to enlarge the size of a small object to make it big enough to be seen and dimensioned. There are also customized half and quarter scales.

Figure 2.43 shows the engineer's 16 scale being used at full scale. Each inch is divided into sixteen increments. Some manufacturers make a full scale on which each tick mark represents 1/32″ for even more exact measurements. Figure 2.43 also gives some examples of fractional components with their decimal equivalents. A mechanical drafter needs to learn the decimal equivalents of the fractions. Appendix D lists these equivalents.

Figure 2.44 shows the engineer's 10 scale being used at full scale. Each inch is divided into 10 equal increments with each mark representing .10″. The longest ticks represent whole inches, and the second longest tick marks represent .5″ or ½″. This scale may be more convenient to use if your measurements are in decimals. To measure more exactly than to .1″, you must estimate between the .10 tick marks. For instance, a .05 measurement would fall halfway between the tick marks, as in the .75 example in Figure 2.44.

The 16 scale can be used to generate a $2'' = 1''$ or double scale equivalent (see Figure 2.45). To use this scale you must read the measurement at full scale and then mentally double the value. Study the examples to become familiar with reading at a $2'' = 1''$ scale.

A typical small scale that mechanical engineers use is the $1/2'' = 1''$. It reduces the real size of an object by half and thus it is referred to as *half scale*. Both the engineer's 16 scale and the 20 scale can be used to produce a half-scale drawing. See Figure 2.46 for half-scale examples using the 16 scale. Reading this full scale as a half scale takes a little time to grasp. Observe how the engineer's 20 scale in Figure 2.47 can be used as a half scale.

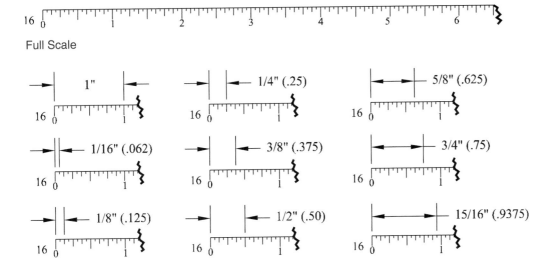

Full Scale

This line measures 3.5625″ or 3⁹⁄₁₆″ at this scale.

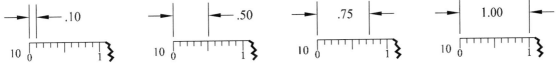

If this scale is used as 1″ = 1″, then every tick mark will represent ¹⁄₁₆″.

FIGURE 2.43 Engineer's 16 scale.

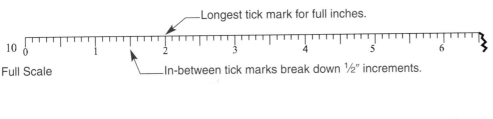

Full Scale

This line measures 2.8″ at full scale.

FIGURE 2.44 Engineer's 10 scale.

FIGURE 2.45 Double scale.   This distance measures 1″ at 2″=1″ scale.

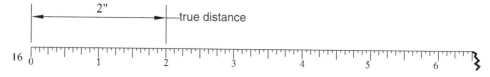

Double Scale Using ¹⁄₁₆″ Scale.

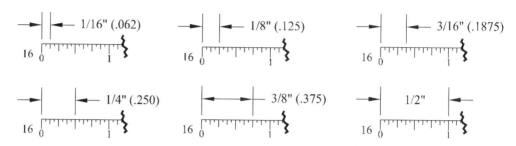

Some Examples at Double Scale

This line scales to 1.5″ at double scale.

FIGURE 2.46 Half scale.   This distance measures 1″ at ½″=1″ scale.

Half Scale (½″=1″) Using ¹⁄₁₆″ Scale.

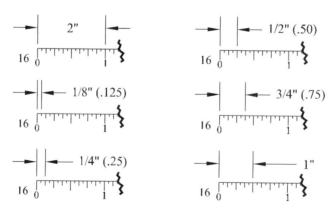

Some Examples at Half Scale

This line scales to 7″ at half scale.

FIGURE 2.47 Engineer's 20 scale used at half scale.

An example of the engineer's 20 scale. Notice the 20 on the left-hand side, which indicated the number of scale increments per inch. This distance measures ½″ at full scale and 1″ at half scale.

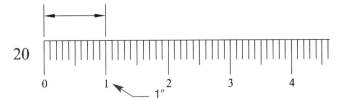

At ½″=1″ scale each of the shortest tick marks represents ¹⁄₁₀″.

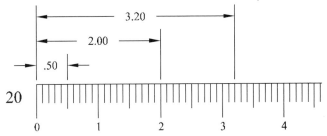

This line scales 2.9″ at half scale.

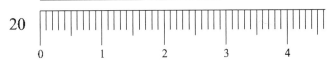

FIGURE 2.48 Quarter scale.

This distance measures 1″ at ¼″=1″ scale.

Quarter Scale (¼″=1″)Using ¹⁄₁₆″ Increments.

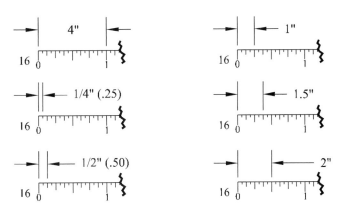

Some Examples at Quarter Scale

This line scales to 16″ at quarter scale.

The 20 scale may be easier to read because you do not need to convert the readings in your head. Just read the numbers and count the individual tick marks as .10 when a measurement falls between the numbers.

At quarter-scale (1/4″ = 1″) an object is drawn at one quarter of its actual size. See Figure 2.48 for examples of how to use a full scale as a quarter scale.

Do not be afraid to experiment with the scales. They are easily adaptable to your needs. Look at your engineer's 40 scale and see if you can visualize how to use it as a 1/4″ = 1″ scale without an example. When you think you know how, give your instructor a demonstration.

2.4   Freehand Drawing

Many people mistakenly think that sketching is an artistic skill requiring a natural skill or ability. For a drafter, freehand sketching can be quite different from what an artist might do. An artist sketches to bring life to a picture, giving great attention to shades and shadows and sometimes even adding colors, whereas a drafter makes sketches that are heavily geared toward explaining and communicating to colleagues. Drafters are normally exposed to sketching in two ways:

1. In the office, sketching is a quick method for a boss or coworker to organize, detail, design, and plan out drawings. This type of sketching occurs in both the design process and in the working drawing stage. The sketches are not necessarily analyzed on how pretty they are (unless they are being shown to a client) but more on how clear and understandable they are to read. This type of sketching is used to share ideas.

2. In the field or on a job site being able to sketch well is a must. This type of sketching is used by an individual to bring back details or ideas to the office. These sketches must be clear enough to be read by the office staff in order for them to develop the sketches into detailed scaled drawing. Remember, it can be very embarrassing not to be able to read or interpret your own sketch.

Basic Tools for Freehand Sketching

- Blueline grid pads of paper or translucent sketch paper
- Soft leads and blue lead
- Color markers/pencils
- Erasers

One of the most important tools a drafter can bring to a job site for sketching is a pad of gridded vellum. The paper comes in a wide range of sizes. Two of the most common sizes used in technical sketching are the 8 × 8 gridded boxes (⅛″ × ⅛″ actual box size) and 10 × 10 gridded boxes (¹⁄₁₀″ × ¹⁄₁₀″ actual box size). The grids are highlighted in 1″ bold blue boxes with the smaller boxes inside them (see Figure 2.49).

The gridded vellum gives the drafter instant vertical and horizontal guidelines or construction lines and, it is hoped, a sense of a controlled sketching environment. When students are first learning to sketch, the guidelines are invaluable, but as they get better and more confident it is common for them to use rolls of white or yellow transparent tissue vellum. A lot of professionals (including instructors) use this medium to sketch out examples quickly.

The drawing techniques for sketching can vary just like in board drawing. Generally, softer leads work better. The drawback is that smearing will increase as the leads get softer. Varying line weights is important when sketching, so pick a lead that is versatile enough to draw thick and thin lines easily. Start off with HB or F to see how they work. Some drafters and designers draw and sketch with H lead all the time, relying on hand pressure to get the thick lines. Blue lead can also be used to lay out or construct sketches just like on normal drawings. The drafter or designer then darkens the sketch with the soft lead. If the designer wants the sketch to take a more artistic form, then color markers or pencils can be used to give the drawing a more realistic feel.

Sketching to Communicate Ideas

The first thing to learn is to treat a sketch just like a drawing. Pull the pencil to draw, keep the pencil vertical and bear down hard to get thick lines and ease off the pressure to get thin lines. While learning to sketch it is acceptable to lay out and plan out the sketch in blue lines, just as when drawing with all your tools. This will give you a much nicer looking sketch.

FIGURE 2.49 Gridded vellum.

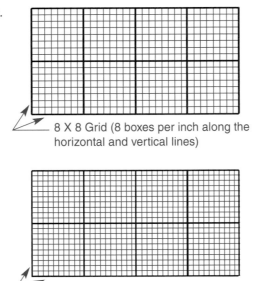

8 X 8 Grid (8 boxes per inch along the horizontal and vertical lines)

10 X 10 Grid (10 boxes per inch along the horizontal and vertical lines)

Sketching without a scale tends to give students a bit of a challenge. The grid paper can be used as a scale in a number of ways.

1. An easy method to use is to count boxes in order to stay proportional. Simply look at the object to be drawn and evaluate the proportions of the length, width, and height of the object. Establish an overall size for the length, width, or height by a box count (see Figure 2.50). Get your overall sizes set and work within the limits to sketch out the smaller items using smaller boxes (see Figure 2.51). Most students can use this method well with a little practice.

2. Using the grid as a real scale is another method. If the gridded vellum is divided into eight boxes per inch, then it can be used for many scales (see Figure 2.52).

3. Another method is to use a visual measuring stick for proportions. Some drafters use their thumb or pencil to measure for scaling a sketch. A person up against a wall can also be used as a scaling guide.

Having to sketch rather than draw can cause an uneasy feeling. Take the tools away from a new drafting student and the challenge begins. A student forgets that sometimes tools and computers cannot be hauled

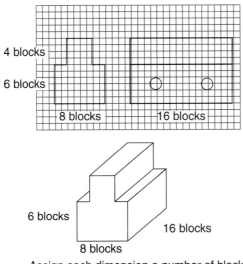

4 blocks

6 blocks

8 blocks   16 blocks

6 blocks

16 blocks

8 blocks

Assign each dimension a number of blocks.

FIGURE 2.50 A simple shape gridded on paper.

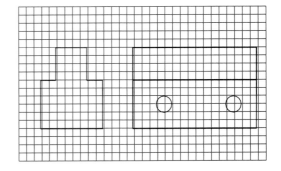

FIGURE 2.51 Add holes using the small squares as a guide.

FIGURE 2.52　Gridded paper.

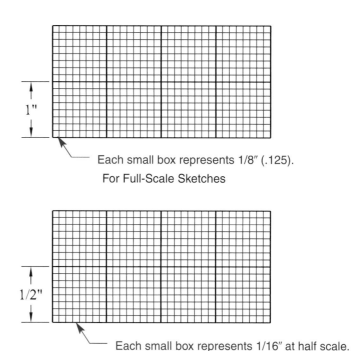

Each small box represents 1/8″ (.125).
For Full-Scale Sketches

Each small box represents 1/16″ at half scale.
For Half-Scale Sketches

everywhere a drafter needs to go, so some basic freehand survival skills are needed. Being a drafter rather than an artist does have some advantages, especially when it comes to sketching. An artist may draw one line with several strokes of a pencil, whereas a drafter needs to draw that line with one long stroke (see Figure 2.53). Approach your sketch just like a drawing. It needs to be clear, and readable line splits and split ends are not acceptable for a drafter.

The grid method of sketching works extremely well for horizontal and vertical lines. The challenge comes when angled lines, arcs, and circles are needed. It is normal for sketched circles and lines to be less than perfect, but there is no excuse for the sketch to look sloppy.

Angled lines should be sketched in one continuous stroke. Locate where the endpoints need to go. A couple of points in between the two ends may be added if needed (see Figure 2.54). Simply draw the angled line pulling through the points. Do not think too much about it. Just do it. It gets easier with practice.

FIGURE 2.53　The difference between an artist's sketch line and a drafter's sketch line.

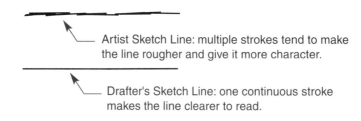

Artist Sketch Line: multiple strokes tend to make the line rougher and give it more character.

Drafter's Sketch Line: one continuous stroke makes the line clearer to read.

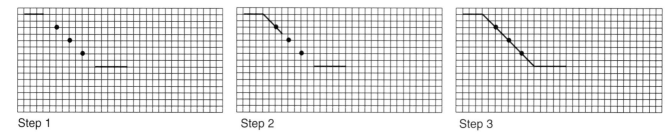

Step 1　　　　　　　　　　　　　Step 2　　　　　　　　　　　　　Step 3

FIGURE 2.54　Sketching an angled line.

FIGURE 2.55 Sketching a circle.

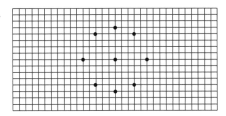

FIGURE 2.56 Completing the circle sketch.

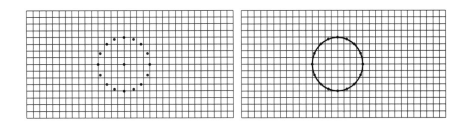

Once you reach a good comfort level on angled lines then it is time to tackle circles and arcs. Circular motions seem to be fairly easy and natural on small shapes, but as they grow in size the circle form becomes harder to hold true. Using grid boxes will help you plot the bigger circles and arcs.

Start out by marking the center, then the four quadrant points (see Figure 2.55). Some good drafters can sketch a great circle using these four points and drawing through the grid proportionally. When you are in the learning stages laying out three points between the quadrants may help a great deal (see Figure 2.56). Using this method allows you to make a much smoother circle when you sketch. As you gain competency you may bypass sketching points and using grid paper. It is a little like taking the training wheels off a bicycle. Start off with small shapes and sizes, and progress to bigger and more difficult shapes.

Beginning students have a tendency to want to use their triangles and circle templates on their sketches to make them look better. Remember that if the instructor wanted the sketches to look better, then students would be allowed to use all their tools. The purpose of sketching is to learn to draw with bare minimum tools. Do not fear sketching. Embrace it for what it is: a fast method for gathering, designing, and sharing ideas. Practice can make a drafter or designer an exceptional sketcher, so be patient. Learning to sketch will take time, patience, and a good eraser.

REVIEW QUESTIONS

1. Make a list of equipment to include in your own personal drafting kit.
2. What features should you look for in a top-quality drafting table?
3. Name three criteria for making a decision about the type and size of drafting table to buy.
4. What is the difference between a 9H drafting lead and a 7B drafting lead? What grades of lead are most commonly used for line work on architectural drawing?
5. Why would a drafter use blue lead for a drawing?
6. Why should you use a drafting brush rather than simply brushing away the eraser dust with your hand?
7. List the six factors that influence the choice of drafting media. Briefly summarize why each of these elements is important.
8. Compare vellum with polyester film.
9. List 10 pieces of information that might be placed on a title block.
10. What is the difference between a ruler and a scale?
11. Explain the advantage of using grid vellum sheets when you sketch.

EXERCISES

Scales exercises should be done on 8″ × 11″ sheets.

EXERCISE 2.1
Reproduce the patterns shown in Figure 2.57 using freehand sketching methods (i.e., use no triangles, drafting machines, etc.).

EXERCISE 2.2
Try your hand at sketching the drawings in Figure 2.58 freehand.

EXERCISE 2.3
Practice reading the angle shown on the vernier and protractor settings in Figure 2.59.

EXERCISE 2.4
Use your scales to complete the following exercise. Use four different mechanical scales to draw a line that measures 2.25″.

EXERCISE 2.5
Read the architect's scale illustrated in Figure 2.60. What are the lengths of the lines being measured?

FIGURE 2.57　Exercise 2.1.

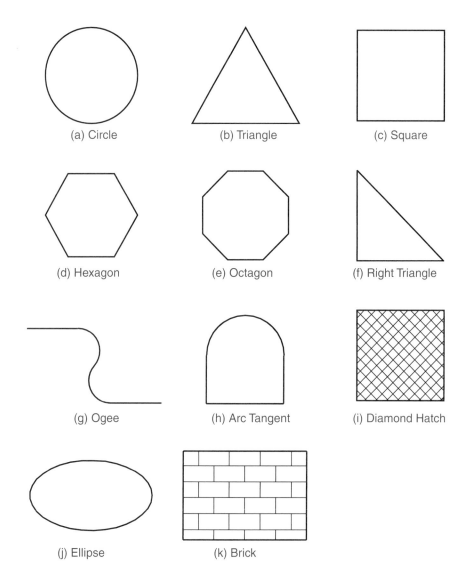

(a) Circle　　　　(b) Triangle　　　　(c) Square

(d) Hexagon　　　(e) Octagon　　　(f) Right Triangle

(g) Ogee　　　(h) Arc Tangent　　　(i) Diamond Hatch

(j) Ellipse　　　(k) Brick

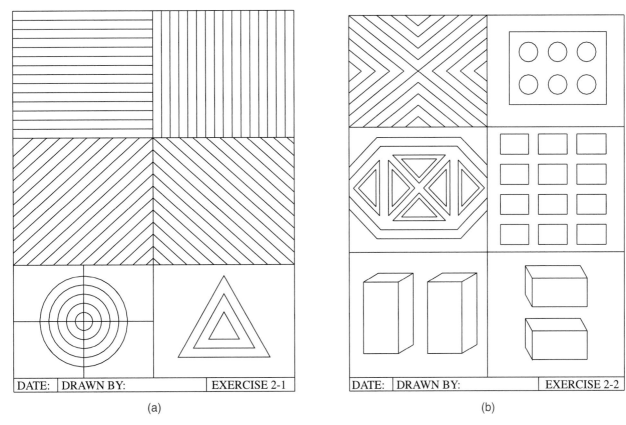

(a)   (b)

FIGURE 2.58 Exercise 2.2.

EXERCISE 2.6

Use your scale to draw a line of the length specified using the given scale.

Problem	Length of Line	Scale
1	7½″	¼″=1″
2	16″	½″=1″
3	10′-5″	¼″=1′−0″
4	1′-9″	¼″=1′−0″
5	4′-6″	⅛″=1′−0″
6	1′-9″	⅛″=1′−0″

EXERCISE 2.7

Use an engineer's scale to measure 36′ on each of the six scales.

For Exercises 2.8 through 2.11, use your scales to draw a line of the assigned distance for the given scale. Use thin vertical lines as the endpoints.

EXERCISE 2.8

Draw the following distances using a ¹⁄₁₆″ = 1′-0″ scale.

- 48′
- 16′-6″
- 12″
- 25′-9″

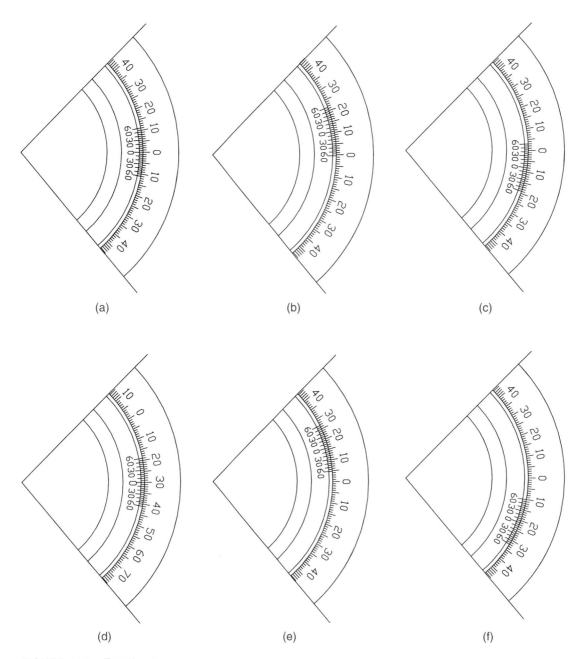

FIGURE 2.59   Exercise 2.3.

FIGURE 2.60   Exercise 2.4.

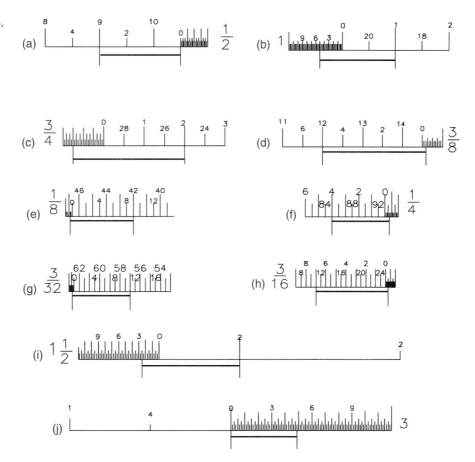

EXERCISE 2.9

Draw the following distances using a 2″ = 1″ scale.

- 4 ″
- ³⁄₄″
- ⁹⁄₁₆″
- 1¹⁄₁₆″

EXERCISE 2.10

Draw the following distances using a ¼″ = 1″ scale.

- 4″
- 12³⁄₈″
- 7¹¹⁄₁₆″
- 15½″

EXERCISE 2.11

Draw the following distances using a ¼ ″=1′-0″ scale.

- 31′-3″
- 5′-9″
- 12″
- 21′-10″

○ ○

CHAPTER 3

Manual Drafting Skills: A Masterly Art

Manual drafting skills come naturally to some and can be acquired by those who practice and do not give up in the early stages. In a few weeks, beginners will start to get the hang of it with a little practice and patience. Some persons may never become great board drafters but may learn enough skill to be competent at it when they occasionally step away from CAD. As discussed earlier, there is much value to board drawing and lettering, so do not take it for granted. It just may sneak up and take a bite out of you in the workplace.

3.1 How to Make Your Lines Look Good

Lead Drawing Techniques

The technique of good line work is not a secret but it does take a little bit of getting used to. First, select a good automatic drawing pencil with a 0.5-mm lead width (see Figure 3.1). The old-fashioned lead holders require a little more skill to master and less upkeep, so try the automatic pencil first. Another factor that seems to help in the beginning is picking a pencil with a wide barrel at the base. The wider the base, the more control you will have. Think of first graders starting to learn to write with large pencils. Large pencils are much easier to control.

The next step is to hold the pencil using a comfortable grip so the hand will not tire out quickly. The grip must allow you to draw with the pencil perpendicular to the paper or vellum. This is not a natural writing position so it will take some getting used to. Some teachers demonstrate a standard method of holding the pencil (see Figure 3.2). You may need to experiment a little in the beginning to find a comfortable grip that fits your hand.

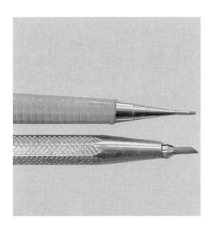

FIGURE 3.1 Two types of drafting pencils. Courtesy of Alvin & Company, Inc.

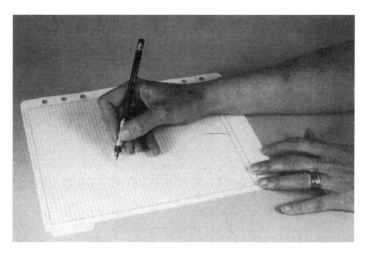

FIGURE 3.2 Correct hand position. Courtesy of C. B. White.

FIGURE 3.3 Pencil lead chart.

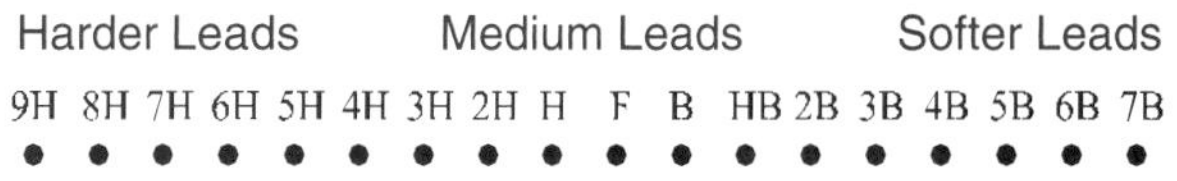

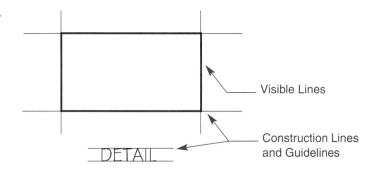

FIGURE 3.4 Drawing with construction lines.

Choosing the Right Lead

Once you have selected a good grip, then the next step is picking the right lead to use (see Figure 3.3). For construction layouts blue nonprint lead is the best to use, but some drafters use 6H lead because that was what they were taught when they first learned years ago. Blue lead is better because it does not print when reproduced in blueline prints using a diazo process.

After the construction lines are drawn on the sheet then it is time to use H or 2H lead for darkening lines (see Figure 3.4). The H is a softer lead, so it is easier to make wide dark lines with it, but the drawback is that it will smear more than the harder 2H lead. The 2H lead is acceptable to use for darkening a drawing; however, it does require a lot more pressure bearing down on the paper with the pencil to get wide dark lines. Most instructors want you to try using the H lead and learn some techniques to avoid smearing your lines.

Helpful Hints for Achieving Good Line Quality

Drawing bold thick lines may require at least two hard passes with the 0.5-mm pencil to darken the lines. Thin lines can be drawn with one hard pass over the construction lines. Remember that both lineweights need to be of the same darkness. The only difference should be the width of the lines.

Perfecting your line work can take some time and practice, but there are some things that can help. The automatic pencils are sold in different widths, namely, 0.9 mm, 0.7 mm, 0.5 mm, and 0.3 mm. The 0.9 mm is the largest, and the 0.3 mm is the smallest. If you do not mind changing pencils as you draw, this can be a shortcut to developing good line work. A combination of a 0.7 mm for the thick lines and a 0.5 mm for the thinner lines will vary the line width using only one pass at a time when darkening.

If smearing is a problem, locate the source of the smearing. It can be only one of two things. Either the bottom of the hand (below the little finger) is dragging, or some of the drafting tools are dragging across the sheet. If the problem is the hand, then avoid sliding it on the paper/vellum as much as possible. It is fine to rest the hand on the paper, but just keep from sliding it.

The triangles and scales are supposed to slide on the paper, so use a drafting powder pad or can and sprinkle the powder on top of the paper (see Figure 3.5). The dry cleaning pad creates a gap between the paper and the tools and reduces the smearing. Another way to cut down on smearing is to brush the graphite off the sheet of paper, but remember to brush in the direction the lines are running (see Figure 3.6). Brush every 5 minutes or so.

Drawing in a pattern can help cut down on smearing by keeping the equipment from dragging back and forth across darkened lines. Horizontal lines should be drawn from left to right and from top to bottom of the page. Left-handed drafters should draw horizontal lines from right to left (see Figure 3.7). You may draw vertical lines from either direction, but just keep from crossing over them with the triangle (see Figure 3.7). Circles, angled lines, and other shapes need to be darkened last along with the border lines and title block to prevent unnecessary smearing. Practicing these techniques can make a major difference in the neatness of a drawing.

FIGURE 3.5 Applying powder to a drawing.

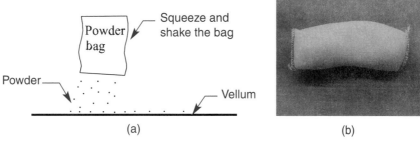

(a)

(b)

FIGURE 3.6 Proper brushing technique.

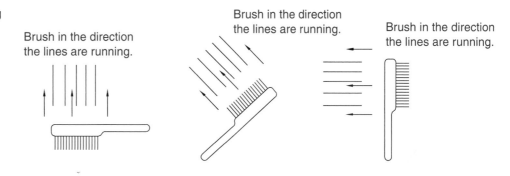

Brush in the direction the lines are running.

Brush in the direction the lines are running.

Brush in the direction the lines are running.

FIGURE 3.7 Drawing lines with a triangle.

Darken the line, then slide down to darken the next line.

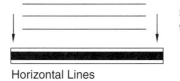

Slide the parallel bar in this direction.

Horizontal Lines

Slide in this direction.

Right-Handers: Darken from left to right, keeping the triangle from dragging across the lines.

Slide in this direction.

Left-Handers: Darken from right to left, keeping the triangle from dragging across the lines.

Vertical Lines

3.2   The Alphabet of Lines

The purpose of drafting is to communicate ideas. Lines, symbols, lettering, and dimensions form the "language" of a drawing. The drafter has a choice of linetypes to convey the necessary information. Over the years, particular types of lines have acquired special meanings. These lines are referred to as the *alphabet of lines* (see Figures 3.8, 3.9, and 3.10).

Construction Lines and Guidelines

Construction lines are used to lay out drawings. If drawn properly, they are so light that they can barely be seen when the drawing is held at arm's length. Typically, construction lines are drawn with a sharp 4H or 6H lead with very little pressure applied by the drafter. These lines are used for preliminary work, so they should not be able to be reproduced. For this reason, some drafters prefer to use blue lead for construction lines because it does not reproduce in a diazo process.

Guidelines and construction lines differ only in purpose. Guidelines are used to provide a boundary or guide for lettering. Much like the writing tablets used in kindergarten, guidelines keep your letters uniform and level. Just like construction lines, guidelines should be drawn very lightly so that they do not reproduce. Neither guidelines nor construction lines should need to be erased.

Visible or Object Lines

Visible or object lines form the principal lines of a drawing. They are relatively thick lines (see Figure 3.9) that form the outlines of the object being drawn. These lines should stand out in comparison with other lines on the drawing. On an architectural plan, object lines are used to draw the outline of the walls. They are thicker than the lines used for dimensions or notes (see Figure 3.10). Occasionally, this rule will be ignored

Alphabet of Lines for Mechanical Drawing

Thicker/Wide Lines
Line width around $\frac{1}{32}''$ or about the same
width as a 0.7-mm drawing pencil lead

Thin lines
Line width around $\frac{1}{64}''$ or a little wider
than a 0.3-mm drawing pencil lead

Visible or Object Line	Thick continuous line	**Long Break Line**	Thin line with jagged Z shape that varies in size depending on space limitations
Cutting-Plane Line	Thick line with $\frac{1}{4}''$ segments and $\frac{1}{8}''$ gaps	**Hidden Line**	Thin line with $\frac{1}{8}''$ segments and $\frac{1}{16}''$ gaps
Viewing-Plane Line	Thick line with $\frac{1}{8}''$ segments and $\frac{1}{16}''$ gaps	**Centerlines**	Thick line broken by $\frac{1}{8}''$ short lines with $\frac{1}{16}''$ gaps in between
Short Freehand Break Line	Thick rough line drawn freehand across short distances	**Section or Hatch Line**	Thin continuous line
Chain Line	Thick line with alternating segments of $\frac{3}{8}''$–$\frac{3}{4}''$ and $\frac{1}{8}''$ with $\frac{1}{8}''$ gaps.	**Dimension Line** / **Extension Line**	2'-0" Used when dimensioning objects Architectural dimensioning style uses slashes instead of arrowheads
		Leader Line	Used when pointing to parts of a drawing
		Phantom Line	Thin line broken every $\frac{3}{4}''$–1.50 by two $\frac{1}{8}''$ lines with $\frac{1}{16}''$ gaps in between

FIGURE 3.8   Alphabet of lines for mechanical drawing.

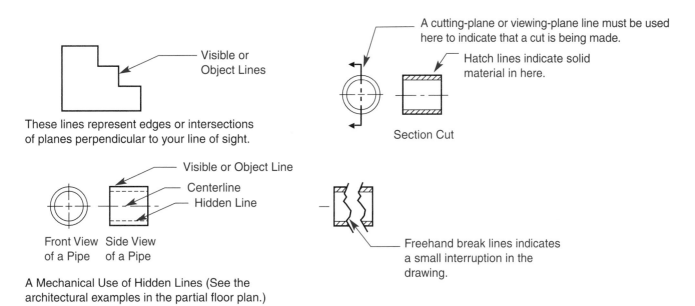

FIGURE 3.9 Examples of mechanical uses of the alphabet of lines.

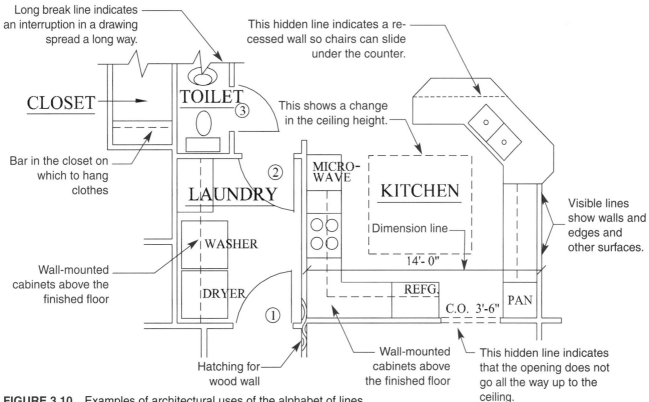

FIGURE 3.10 Examples of architectural uses of the alphabet of lines.

and all the lines will be drawn with the same weight or thickness. In this case, shading can be used to emphasize the importance of the walls (see wood hatching in Figure 3.10). The lead chosen for outline or object lines is in the range of 2H, H, or F.

Dashed or Hidden Lines

Dashed lines are used on a drawing to indicate features that are not visible in the view being shown. For example, in an architectural drawing, a dashed line would be used to show the location of closet rods, undercounter appliances, electrical circuit runs, cased openings, sky lights, overhead cabinets, ceiling fans, roof overhangs, and so on; footings below the ground, existing contours, and other features being blocked from view; cabinet door swings, window swings, and all kinds of bracing and reinforcing for steel. Hidden lines are placed on drawings only when they provide useful insights. (See Figure 3.10 for some hidden line uses in architectural drawing.)

Dashed lines are of medium thickness, intermediate between thick object lines and thin dimension lines. The ideal proportions are ⅛″ to ⅜″ long dashes with ¹⁄₁₆″ to ⅛″ spaces in between. When manually drafting, make your dashes and spaces as close to these sizes and as uniform as possible without measuring each pencil mark.

Dimension and Extension Lines

Dimension and extension lines are used together to clarify the size of the object being shown. The extension lines show the extent of a dimension. In other words, they show that the dimension is being measured from point A to point B. The extension lines should not connect with the object lines of the drawing. A small space should always be left between the extension line and the object being dimensioned.

The dimension lines are drawn along the length being measured at right angles to the set of extension lines (see Figure 3.11). A number indicating the measurement for the dimension is placed near the center of the dimension line, either slightly above the line or inserted in a broken line (see Figure 3.11). Dimensions are given in either feet and inches or in millimeters and meters. One system of units should be used consistently throughout a set of drawings.

Both dimension and extension lines are relatively thin, but this does not mean they are to be drawn lightly. Use an H or 2H lead to make the lines thin but dark. The intersection of the extension and dimension lines can be marked with either an arrowhead, a slash, or a dot (see Figure 3.11). The placement of the dimension and extension lines plays a critical part in the readability of a drawing. They should be spaced as evenly around the drawing as possible. Avoid the appearance of crowding whenever possible.

Leader Lines

The purpose of a leader line is to connect notes to their related feature on a drawing. Leader lines can be drawn either as a freehand curve or as a straight line and shoulder drawn with a straightedge (see Figure 3.12). The end of the line terminates in a dot or an arrowhead pointing to the feature being discussed. In architectural drafting, arrowheads are often an expression of individuality (see Figure 3.13), but once again, it is important to be consistent in your choices. Use the same type of leader line and arrowhead throughout a set of drawings.

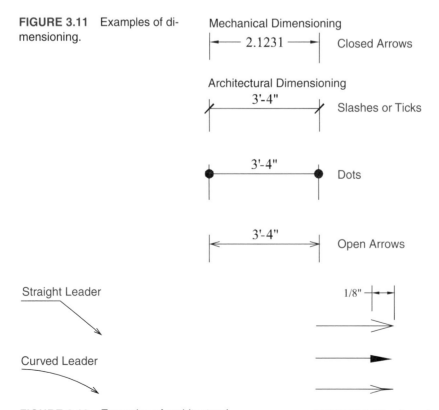

FIGURE 3.11 Examples of dimensioning.

Mechanical Dimensioning
2.1231   Closed Arrows

Architectural Dimensioning
3'-4"   Slashes or Ticks

3'-4"   Dots

3'-4"   Open Arrows

Straight Leader

Curved Leader

1/8″

FIGURE 3.12 Examples of architectural style leader lines with open arrowheads.

FIGURE 3.13 Arrowheads should be around 1/8″ (.125) long and about 1/3 as wide. Arrowheads are drawn freehand.

Centerlines

A centerline is used to mark the center of an object such as a column or a beam. It is also used to indicate the finished floor line on a building. A centerline consists of a long line alternating with a short dash. Figure 3.14 shows some typical proportions for this type of line.

Break Lines

Break lines are used to indicate that a portion of an object has not been shown on the drawing. For example, you may have a long object of uniform cross section that will not fit on the page at the scale being used. The solution would be to show the object with break lines at the center indicating that a section was left out in order to fit the ends on the drawing. Figure 3.15 illustrates a long break line. The short break line is merely a thick wavy freehand line. It is used when the distance required is relatively short. Imagine how difficult it would be to draw a line of this type over several inches without imparting an amateurish feel to the drawing. When a longer break is required, a long break line, consisting of a straight line broken periodically by a freehand jagged line, is used. The long break line is more common on architectural drawings.

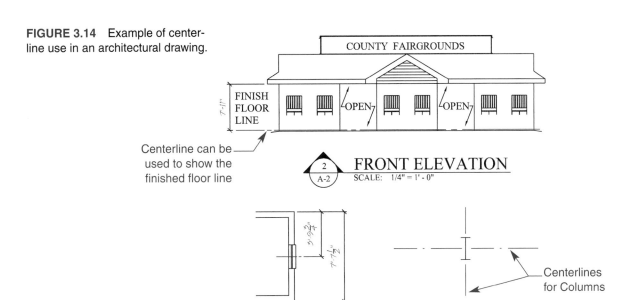

FIGURE 3.14 Example of centerline use in an architectural drawing.

FIGURE 3.15 Example of break line usage.

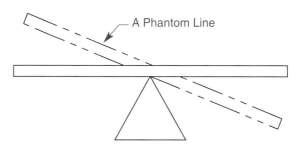

FIGURE 3.16 Example of phantom line usage.

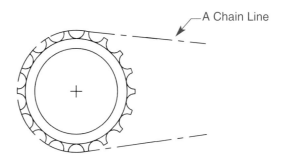

FIGURE 3.17 Example of chain line usage.

Phantom Lines

Phantom lines are used on a drawing to indicate an alternative position for a portion of the drawing. It may be something as simple as showing the rotation of a playground teeter-totter (see Figure 3.16) or the movement of a pivot arm on a piece of machinery.

Chain Lines

Chain lines are placed on a drawing to indicate the location of a section of chain. (Think of the chain that wraps around the gears on a bicycle.) Alternating short and long segments differentiate a chain from other types of lines on a drawing (see Figure 3.17).

Special Lines Used on Architectural Drawings

Some architectural drawings may also contain lines and symbols with special meanings. The key to understanding these variations is found in the drawing legend (see Figure 3.18a). Look at the legend and then find where all the special lines occur in the site plan (see Figure 3.18b). Without the legend you would be at a loss to understand the drawing.

Most architectural plans also have a symbols legend. It is a reference that explains how the drawing details will be organized and laid out on the drawing sheets. The example in Figure 3.18c is a basic one. Depending on the particular architectural firm the symbols legend will vary somewhat, so always look carefully at the legends in all drawings. The American Institute of Architects (AIA) has set standards that an architect can use as guidelines. These guidelines can be found in a book or CD ROM called *Architectural Graphic Standards.*

SITE LEGEND

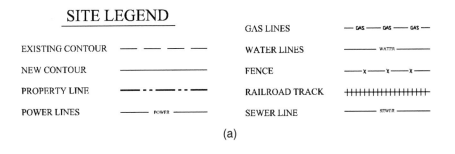

(a)

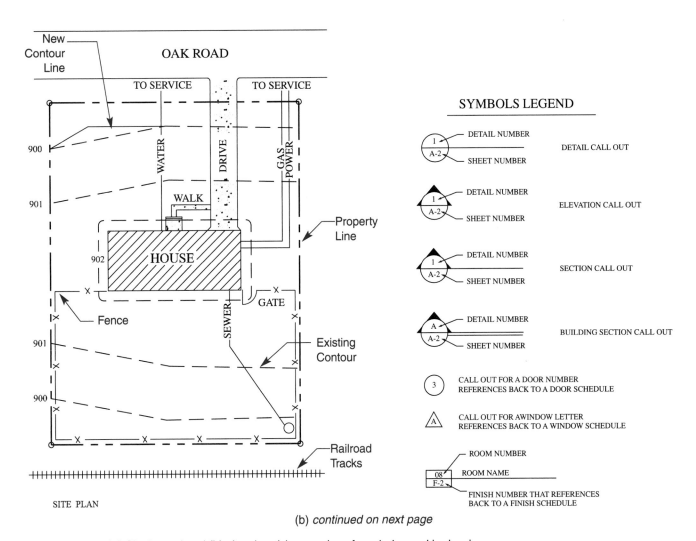

SITE PLAN

(b) *continued on next page*

FIGURE 3.18 (a) Site legend and (b) site plan; (c) examples of symbols used in drawing.

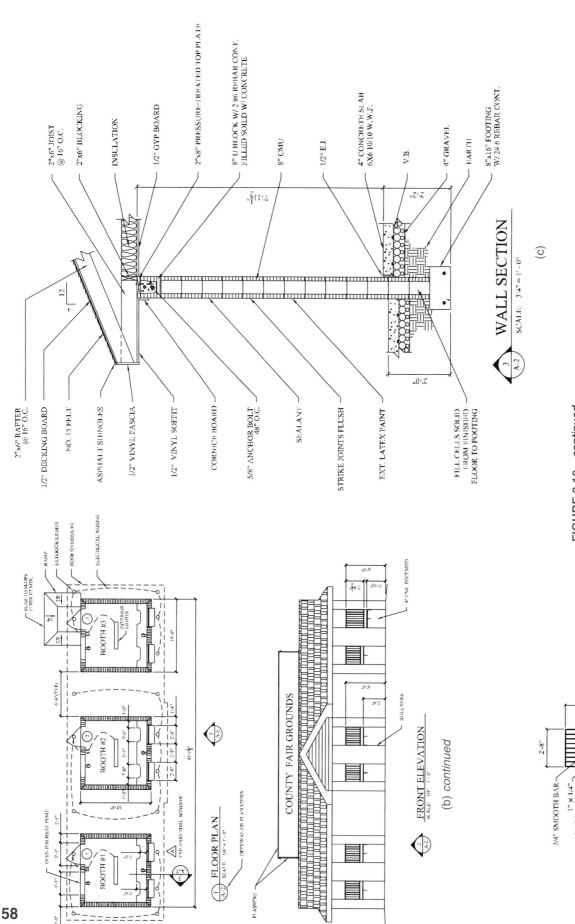

WALL SECTION

2"x6" RAFTER @ 16" O.C.

2"x6" JOIST @ 16" O.C.

2"x6" BLOCKING

INSULATION

1/2" DECKING BOARD

NO. 15 FELT

ASPHALT SHINGLES

1/2" VINYL FASCIA

1/2" VINYL SOFFIT

CORNICE BOARD

5/8" ANCHOR BOLT 48" O.C.

SEALANT

STRIKE JOINTS FLUSH

EXT. LATEX PAINT

1/2" GYP BOARD

2"x8" PRESSURE-TREATED TOP PLATE

8" U BLOCK W/ 2 #4 REBAR CONT. FILLED SOLID W/ CONCRETE

8" CMU

1/2" E.J.

4" CONCRETE SLAB 6X6 10/10 W.W.F.

V.B.

4" GRAVEL

EARTH

8"x16" FOOTING W/ 2 #4 REBAR CONT.

FILL CELLS SOLID FROM FINISHED FLOOR TO FOOTING

SCALE: 3/4" = 1'-0"

3 A-2

(c)

FIGURE 3.18 *continued*

FLOOR PLAN

SCALE: 1/4" = 1'-0"

BOOTH #1

BOOTH #2

BOOTH #3

SLAB TO SLOPE 1" PER FT MIN.

RAMP

EXTERIOR LIGHTS

ROOF OVERHANG

ELECTRICAL WIRING

INTERIOR LIGHTS

OPEN FOR HEAT PUMP

TYP. PASS THRU WINDOW

OPTIONAL OR PLAN VIEWS

FRONT ELEVATION

SCALE: 1/4" = 1'-0"

COUNTY FAIR GROUNDS

4" CMU RECESSED

BULL NOSE

FLASHING

(b) *continued*

WINDOW ELEVATION DETAIL

SCALE: 1/4" = 1'-0"

1/8" ALUMINUM SHELF & BRACES

3/4" SMOOTH BAR

1" x 1/4" SMOOTH BASE

3.3 Tackling Different Styles of Lettering

There are two things that most drafters hate and lettering is both of them. It is one of the most difficult skills to master. Until a level of competency is reached, lettering will always detract from (see Figure 3.19) drawings. The longer a drafter puts off learning to letter decently the more of a burden it becomes.

Variations among Lettering Styles

Lettering styles can vary drastically, with some being quite interesting. Depending on the drafting field there may not be many choices of lettering styles. Mechanical drafting uses ANSI (American National Standards Institute) for guidelines to drawings. The lettering styles for mechanical drawings are restricted, with single-stroke Gothic being recommended, since it is the most legible and readable style of lettering. The letters may

FIGURE 3.19 Example of poor lettering. Being sloppy and inconsistent is unacceptable in all drafting fields.

ABCDF

FIGURE 3.20 Examples of mechanical lettering styles. Courtesy of *Architectural Drawing and Light Construction* by Edward J. Muller.

ABCDEF
GHIJKLM
NOPQRS
TUVWXYZ
01234
56789

Sloped Style at 72° Angle

ABCDEF
GHIJKLM
NOPQRS
TUVWXYZ
01234
56789

Vertical Styles

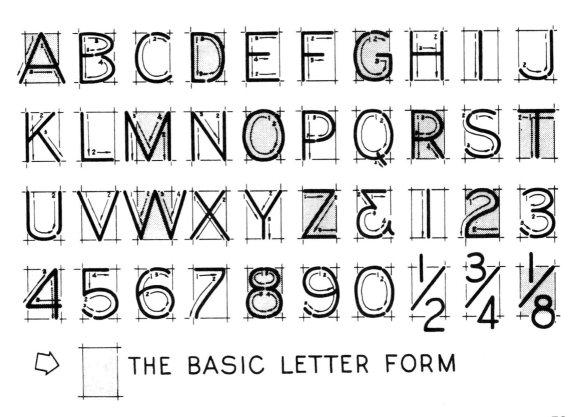

THE BASIC LETTER FORM

be either vertical or sloped (see Figure 3.20). These styles are very basic and easy to read with few accents or characters and are widely accepted in other drawing and engineering fields.

Lettering in Architecture and Related Construction Fields

Architecture has a more freestyle approach to lettering. An artistic flare is put into lettering to give individuals more control over how their lettering should look. There are many architectural styles of lettering. Some are shown in Figures 3.21 and 3.22. If a drafter develops a good style it is even possible to use it on CAD drawings. The image of the letter can be put in a font file and loaded into a software package.

FIGURE 3.21 CAD architectural lettering styles.

ABCDEF
GHIJKLM
NOPQRS
TUVWXYZ
01234
56789
CITYBLUEPRINT
lettering style

ABCDEF
GHIJKLM
NOPQRS
TUVWXYZ
01234
56789
STYLUS BT
lettering style

ABCDEF
GHIJKLM
NOPQRS
TUVWXYZ
01234
56789
COUNTRYBLUEPRINT
lettering style

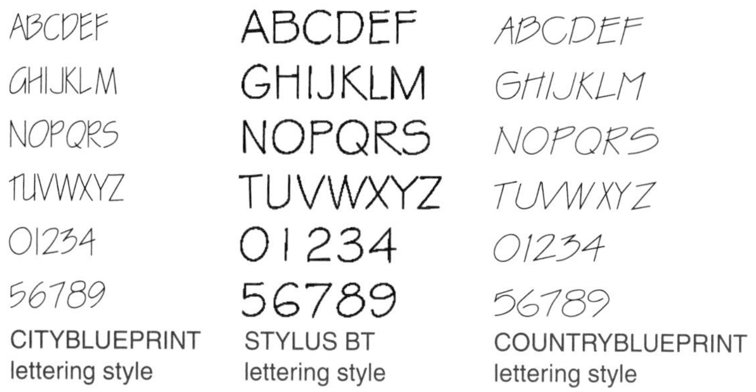

FIGURE 3.22 Architectural lettering styles. Courtesy of *Architectural Drawing and Light Construction* by Edward J. Muller.

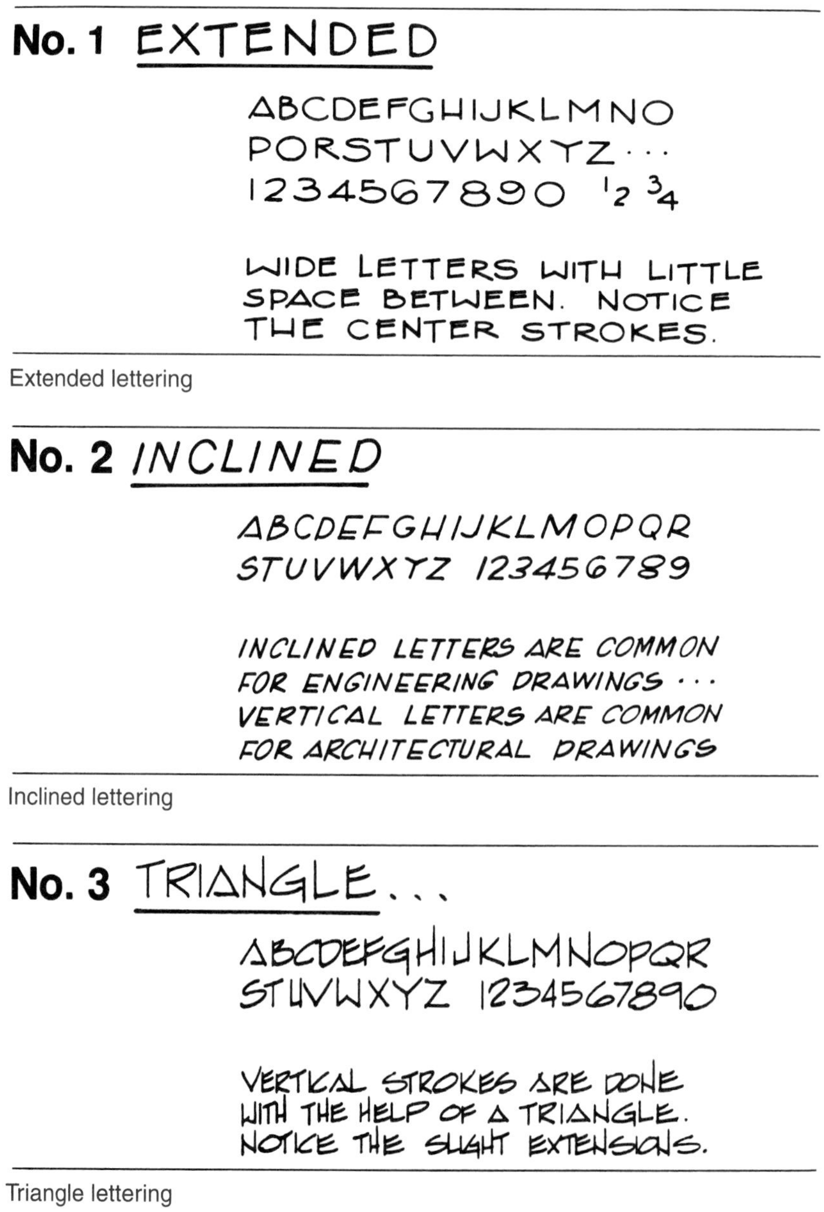

No. 1 EXTENDED

ABCDEFGHIJKLMNO
PORSTUVWXYZ···
1234567890 $\frac{1}{2}$ $\frac{3}{4}$

WIDE LETTERS WITH LITTLE
SPACE BETWEEN. NOTICE
THE CENTER STROKES.

Extended lettering

No. 2 INCLINED

ABCDEFGHIJKLMOPQR
STUVWXYZ 123456789

INCLINED LETTERS ARE COMMON
FOR ENGINEERING DRAWINGS ···
VERTICAL LETTERS ARE COMMON
FOR ARCHITECTURAL DRAWINGS

Inclined lettering

No. 3 TRIANGLE...

ABCDEFGHIJKLMNOPQR
STUVWXYZ 1234567890

VERTICAL STROKES ARE DONE
WITH THE HELP OF A TRIANGLE.
NOTICE THE SLIGHT EXTENSIONS.

Triangle lettering

Keys to Good Lettering

There are three major components to good lettering.

- **Uniformity:** Always use horizontal guidelines to keep the heights the same. In the beginning use vertical guidelines to gauge the widths of your letters. Spaces between words should be about the width of the widest letter, like a W or O.
- **Legibility:** Keep the letters clear and distinct. If the letters are hard to read, then the person reading the drawing must guess at the words.
- **Consistency:** Once you have chosen a style, then you must try and match each individual letter or number each time it is made. Keep the slope consistent on sloped letters, and keep vertical letters as straight up and down as possible. Never allow them to slope back to the left (see Figure 3.23).

An angle of 68° is the maximum slope allowed for lettering (see Figure 3.24). Guides can be used to establish this angle.

The Ames lettering guide is a very useful tool that helps the drafter lay out all the construction lines dealing with lettering (see Figure 3.25). This lettering guide is the most popular tool for lettering drawings because of the speed with which it can be used. Other templates tend to slow you down. Using all uppercase letters is standard for working drawings. However, some designers use lowercase letters for presentation drawings. There are minimum standard heights for lettering (see Figure 3.26) .

Fractions in mechanical drawing are shown stacked with a horizontal line (see Figure 3.27). The overall fraction height is always two times the height of the letter that is being used. Fractions in architectural lettering use an angled slash or solidus (see Figure 3.28). This style allows the height of the fractions to fit within normal lettering guidelines.

Lettering Tip:
When learning to letter, stick to short exercises and concentrate on making good letters. Short assignments tend to bring out the best in a beginner.

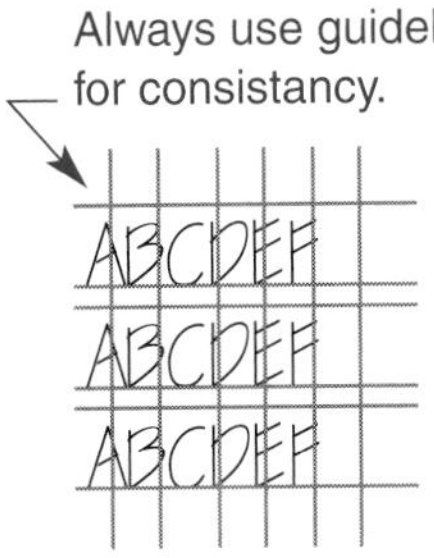

Always use guidelines for consistancy.

Try to make each letter look the same. Always be consistant with the letter shapes and strokes.

FIGURE 3.23 Lettering hints.

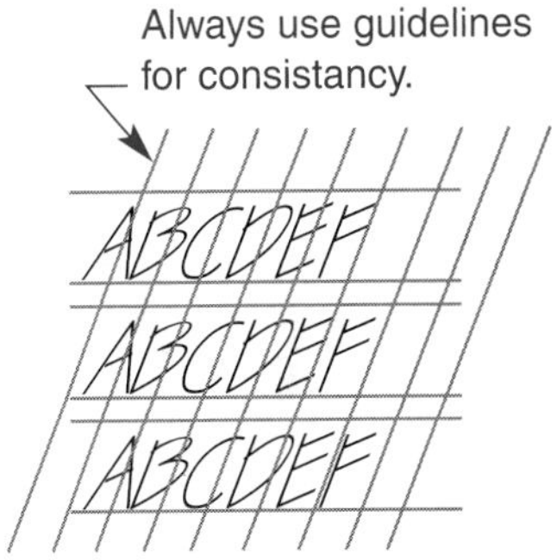

Never slope your letters back to the left. This is unacceptable in any drafting field.

Always use guidelines for consistancy.

Sloped style should be between 90° and 68°.

FIGURE 3.24 Sloped lettering style.

FIGURE 3.25 The Ames lettering guide. Courtesy of Alvin & Co.

VERIFY ALL DIMENSIONS ON THE FLOOR PLAN.

Use ⅛″-tall letters for notes as a minimum.

BILL OF MATERIALS

Use ¼″-tall letters for your titles as a minimum.

FIGURE 3.26 Examples of lettering heights.

$$\frac{1}{4} \quad \frac{1}{2} \quad \frac{7}{8}$$

FIGURE 3.27 Examples of mechanical fractions.

1/4   1/2   7/8   3/16   1/4

(a)   (b)

FIGURE 3.28 Examples of architectural fractions.

Crafting Your Skill

One problem that shows up in beginner's work is weak lines and weak letters. Remember that originals must be printed or reproduced and will require dark lines to generate good prints. Do not be afraid to bear down hard when drawing lines and letters. Carve them out with meaning. Yes, the lead will break on the end of the pencil frequently, but soon the combination of the right amount of pressure and holding the pencil at a 90° angle will develop good, consistent dark lines and letters. If the lead breaks, have a scrap piece of paper beside the drawing and scribble off the sharp edges of the lead. Remember to reset the lead so that the tip is about $\frac{1}{16}''$ long.

Being consistent is a goal for all quality drafters, but even the best drafters have occasional bad days when it comes to lettering and line work, even when they have achieved a good level of consistency. Don't be hard on yourself when you have a bad day.

3.4   Ink Drafting

When it comes to ink drawing throw out all the rules that pertain to pencil drafting. Inking tends to make board drawing much slower and meticulous. New tools with new rules create a whole new set of skills to develop and learn (see Figure 3.29).

Inking Tools, Equipment, and Resources

The medium best suited for inking is polyester film (Mylar). Technical Rapidograph pens in a variety of widths are a must for doing the best inking job. Make sure to get fast-drying latex ink for film. It cuts the drying time down by at least half.

General drafting tools such as a triangle, circle template, and French curve are manufactured for inking. As a rule, look at the base of these tools for risers that raise up the edges where the tip of the ink pen glides along. If the risers are present, the tool has been altered for inking pens (see Figure 3.30).

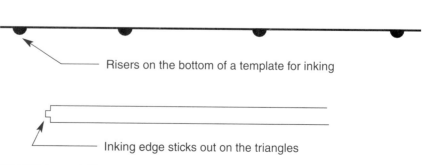

Risers on the bottom of a template for inking

Inking edge sticks out on the triangles

FIGURE 3.29   An ink pen.

FIGURE 3.30   Inking-aided equipment.

If the ink touches anything other than the film it will run everywhere and leave a mess. If you intend to do some ink drawing in the future, buy the tools made for inking, because they work with lead drawings also. A compass adapter can hold an ink pen or pencil, so be sure to include one in your drafting kit along with special ink erasers made for erasing on film.

Drawing Film Basics

Film comes in a variety of thicknesses for durability and transparency for printing—as thin as 3 mils (0.003″) or as thick as 9 mils (0.009″). The surface of the film is matted (treated) to make the ink adhere to the plastic better. Make sure the surface is clean and oil free. A mild thinner or alcohol can be rubbed on the surface to clean it. Lay out construction lines with blue lead as usual, then when it is time to ink just draw right on top of the blue.

The big advantage of inking on film is that the lines go down smoothly without your having to apply much pressure to the pen. This is easier on the hand. Erasing ink on paper or vellum is a challenge because the paper tears when you try to erase. Film can be erased and look great. Knowing that mistakes are fixable, the drafter will ink faster and draw with more confidence. A print made from a polyester original looks great and is much sharper and crisper than a pencil-on-paper drawing. The transparency of the film gives it a superior print quality.

One thing to remember on ink drawings is that it is more critical to keep the surface as clean as possible. Any bit of dirt that the pen picks up will cause the lines to vary in thickness. Use a paper towel to wipe the end of the pen to keep it clean. Ink erasers will also leave an oil residue on the film. After using an ink eraser make sure to wipe the area that has been erased with a damp paper towel to remove the oil from the surface in order to keep the ink from running when reapplied.

Ink Pens

Ink pens come in different widths, which makes it very easy to change pens when you need a thick line (visible) versus a thin one (center) (see Figure 3.31). Read the instructions that come with the pens. The instructions will show the pen widths, will give disassembly directions, and will describe the correct methods for caring for and cleaning the pens. The pens come with either a steel tip or a jewel tip depending on how much money a person wants to spend and how long the pens need to last.

A good tip to remember is to keep the pens full of ink. Air bubbles create internal pressure, which causes pens to drip and skip when they are used (see Figure 3.32).

Ink Lettering Woes

An instrument called the Leroy Lettering Device performs ink lettering. The manual one, which comes only in a right-handed model, takes a little getting used to. The automatic Leroy has a keyboard and is easier to use no matter which hand you prefer using. However, most offices prefer freehand ink lettering on working drawings done by hand.

Learn to letter with pencil and paper first before trying to freehand with ink. Once you have style and have developed some consistency, then it is time to try the ink. Ink pens require little or no pressure at all and

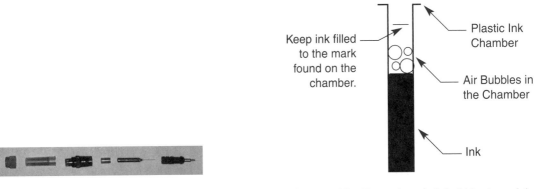

FIGURE 3.31 An exploded view of an ink pen.   **FIGURE 3.32** Formation of air bubbles in an ink pen.

show every tiny shake and jerk that occurs in the hand. The trick to ink lettering is to relax and let the hand make the letters you have practiced over and over. No real pressure is being applied, so let the hand take control and flow freely and quickly. If you have already mastered lead lettering, then the inking will come quickly.

Tips for Left-Handed Drafters

A left-hander will find it rough going no matter if the lettering is in lead or in ink. The problem that cannot be avoided is dragging the hand across the letters as the lettering is done from left to right. The left-handed drafter has to become very creative in dealing with this problem. Some possible solutions follow:

1. Cock the hand above or below the lines of letters.
2. Use a piece of paper to rest the hand on to keep from smearing.
3. Overextend the pen or pencil out from the hand.
4. Rotate the sheet at an angle.
5. Brush the graphite away frequently.

Some individuals prefer ink drafting once they get used to the timing of letting the ink dry and planning out a fast path for the drawing. If a drafter loves to draw, then inking is just another hurdle to jump.

REVIEW QUESTIONS

1. Why should a beginner choose a wide-barrel drawing pencil?
2. Automatic drawing pencil leads come in how many different widths?
3. What leads are used by a drafter to produce dark wide lineweights?
4. Smearing is caused by the drafter's hand or by the equipment. How can a drafter prevent smearing?
5. List and define the different line types in the standard alphabet of lines.
6. List the symbols used on architectural drawings or elevation callouts and section callouts. Name two methods used to draw dark thick lines.
7. How are architectural lettering styles different from those of other drafting professions?
8. List the major points to good lettering.
9. What is the maximum angle of slope used in lettering?
10. Guidelines for lettering are drawn with which tool?
11. When is it acceptable to use lowercase letters on drawings?
12. What is the minimum letter height used for notes and dimensions? For titles?
13. Sketch an example of how architectural and mechanical fractions are lettered.
14. In the alphabet of lines which ones are drawn to be thick/wide?
15. List some reasons why an alphabet of lines is necessary.
16. Sketch out the alphabet of lines and write the name beside each line.
17. Ink can be used on both paper and polyester. What are the advantages of using it on polyester?
18. If you have a sheet of single-matte polyester film, which side do you draw on? Why?
19. Make a list of special drawing equipment used for ink drafting.
20. What are some of the tools that a drafter can use for lettering?
21. Illustrate the three methods that can be used to mark the intersection of dimension and extension lines.
22. Why should you use guidelines when lettering?
23. What is the most legible and readable style of lettering?

EXERCISES

Lettering exercises using all uppercase letters and guidelines.

EXERCISE 3.1

Using a lettering style of your choice, letter the alphabet A–Z and numbers 1–20 three times. Use ¼″ tall guides for letters and ¼″ spacing between your rows.

EXERCISE 3.2

Repeat Exercise 3.1 using a 68° slope to your letters, and ⅛″-high letters and ⅛″ spacing between your rows.

EXERCISE 3.3

Using ¼″-tall letters and ¼″ spacing between your rows, make a list of your 10 favorite movies, numbering them from 1 to 10.

EXERCISE 3.4

Using ⅛″-tall letters and using ⅛″ spacing between your rows, make a list of 12 singers or musical groups/bands, numbering them from 1 to 12.

EXERCISE 3.5

Using ¼″ sloped letters list 20 of your favorite songs.

EXERCISE 3.6

Letter five of your favorite quotes using ¼″-tall lettering.

EXERCISE 3.7

Pick 10 television shows and letter their names using ¼″-tall sloped letters and numbering them from 1 to 10.

EXERCISE 3.8

Using the title block in Figure 3.33 as a guide, design a title block of your own using similar information in it.

FIGURE 3.33 Exercise 3.8.

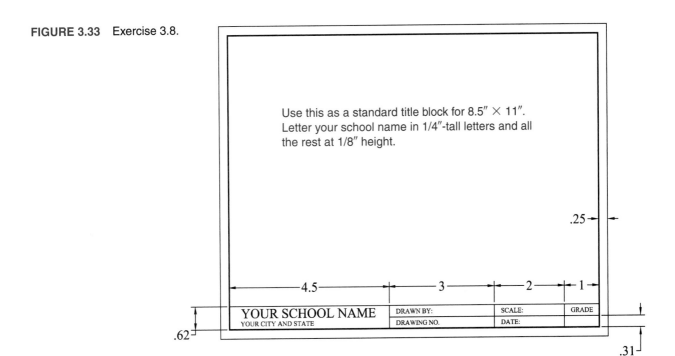

EXERCISE 3.9

Practice your uppercase lettering on an 8.5″ × 11″ sheet of vellum using the lettering layout in Figure 3.34.

EXERCISE 3.10

Practice your uppercase lettering on an 8.5″ × 11″ sheet of vellum using the lettering layout in Figure 3.35.

EXERCISE 3.11

Practice drawing your thick lines on an 8.5″ × 11″ sheet of vellum using the same format as in Figure 3.36.

EXERCISE 3.12.

Practice drawing your thin lines on an 8.5″ × 11″ sheet of vellum using the same format as in Figure 3.37.

FIGURE 3.34 Exercise 3.9.

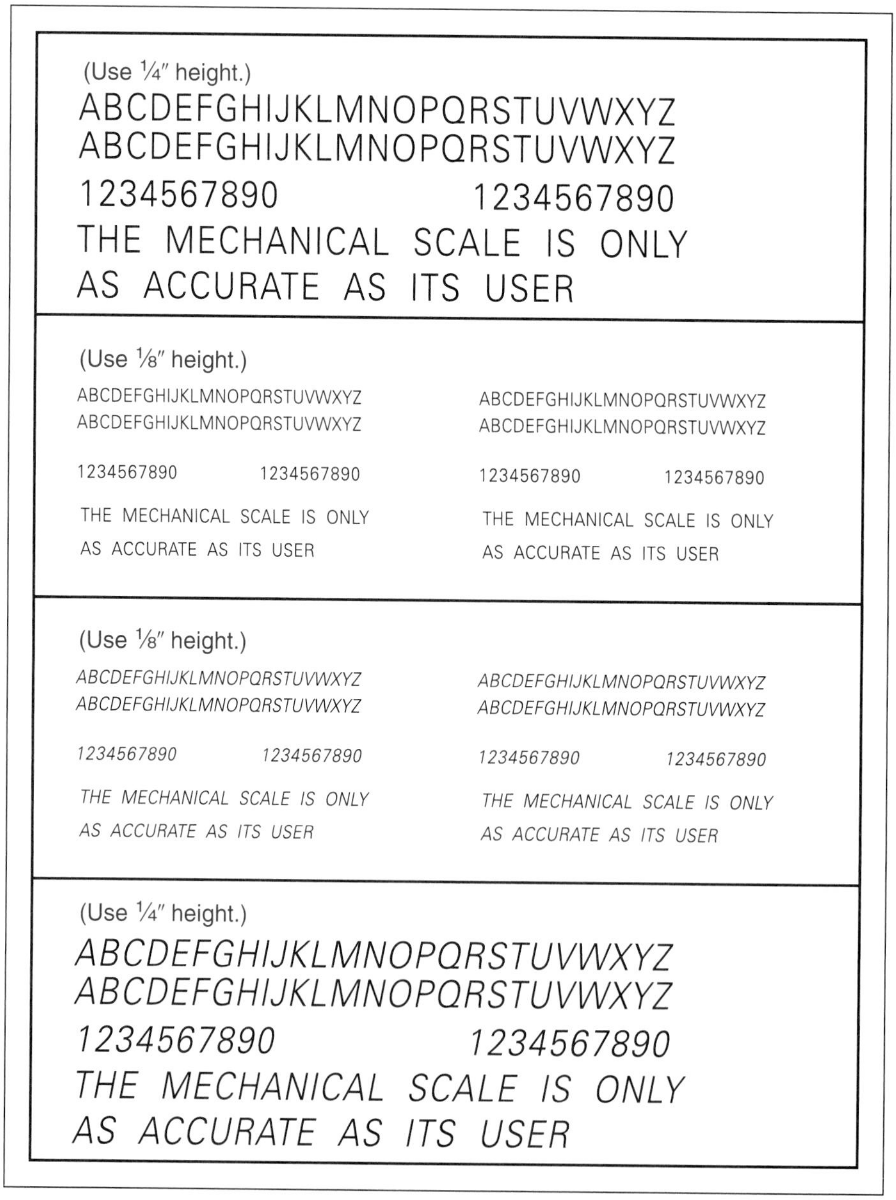

(Use ¼″ height.)
ABCDEFGHIJKLMNOPQRSTUVWXYZ
ABCDEFGHIJKLMNOPQRSTUVWXYZ
1234567890   1234567890
THE MECHANICAL SCALE IS ONLY
AS ACCURATE AS ITS USER

(Use ⅛″ height.)
ABCDEFGHIJKLMNOPQRSTUVWXYZ   ABCDEFGHIJKLMNOPQRSTUVWXYZ
ABCDEFGHIJKLMNOPQRSTUVWXYZ   ABCDEFGHIJKLMNOPQRSTUVWXYZ

1234567890   1234567890   1234567890   1234567890

THE MECHANICAL SCALE IS ONLY   THE MECHANICAL SCALE IS ONLY
AS ACCURATE AS ITS USER   AS ACCURATE AS ITS USER

(Use ⅛″ height.)
ABCDEFGHIJKLMNOPQRSTUVWXYZ   ABCDEFGHIJKLMNOPQRSTUVWXYZ
ABCDEFGHIJKLMNOPQRSTUVWXYZ   ABCDEFGHIJKLMNOPQRSTUVWXYZ

1234567890   1234567890   1234567890   1234567890

THE MECHANICAL SCALE IS ONLY   THE MECHANICAL SCALE IS ONLY
AS ACCURATE AS ITS USER   AS ACCURATE AS ITS USER

(Use ¼″ height.)
ABCDEFGHIJKLMNOPQRSTUVWXYZ
ABCDEFGHIJKLMNOPQRSTUVWXYZ
1234567890   1234567890
THE MECHANICAL SCALE IS ONLY
AS ACCURATE AS ITS USER

FIGURE 3.35 Exercise 3.10.

(Use ¼″ height.)

BDPRS AEFHILT CGOQ IJKMNUVWYZ
38 96 07 S 5ZX   38 96 07 S 5ZX
STAY WITH ONE STYLE SO YOU WILL
BE MORE CONSISTENT.

(Use ⅛″ height.)

BDPRS AEFHILT CGOQ IJKMNUVWYZ   BDPRS AEFHILT CGOQ IJKMNUVWYZ

38   96   07   S5ZX   38   96   07   S5ZX   38   96   07   S5ZX

STAY WITH ONE STYLE SO YOU WILL BE MORE CONSISTENT.

STAY WITH ONE STYLE SO YOU WILL BE MORE CONSISTENT.

(Use ⅛″ height.)

BDPRS AEFHILT CGOQ IJKMNUVWYZ   BDPRS AEFHILT CGOQ IJKMNUVWYZ

38   96   07   S5ZX   38   96   07   S5ZX   38   96   07   S5ZX

STAY WITH ONE STYLE SO YOU WILL BE MORE CONSISTENT.

STAY WITH ONE STYLE SO YOU WILL BE MORE CONSISTENT.

(Use ¼″ height.)

BDPRS AEFHILT CGOQ IJKMNUVWYZ
38 96 07 S 5ZX   38 96 07 S 5ZX
STAY WITH ONE STYLE SO YOU WILL
BE MORE CONSISTENT.

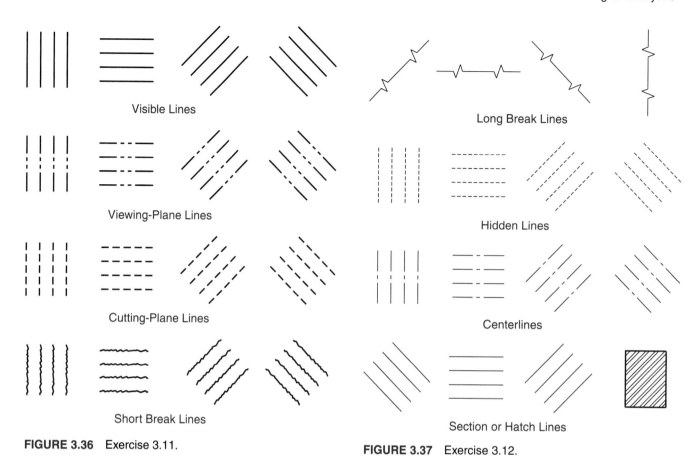

FIGURE 3.36   Exercise 3.11.

FIGURE 3.37   Exercise 3.12.

DRAWING ASSIGNMENTS

1. Construct drawings 3.1–3.5 in Figure 3.38 at full scale to give you some practice using inches and fractional parts of an inch. Use the sample title block shown earlier. Do not dimension your drawings, but center them inside the title block drawing area. Have your instructor demonstrate techniques for centering drawings.

2. Construct architectural drawings 3.6–3.11 in Figures 3.39 using the asigned scales.

3. Do site drawing assignment 3.12 in Figure 3.40.

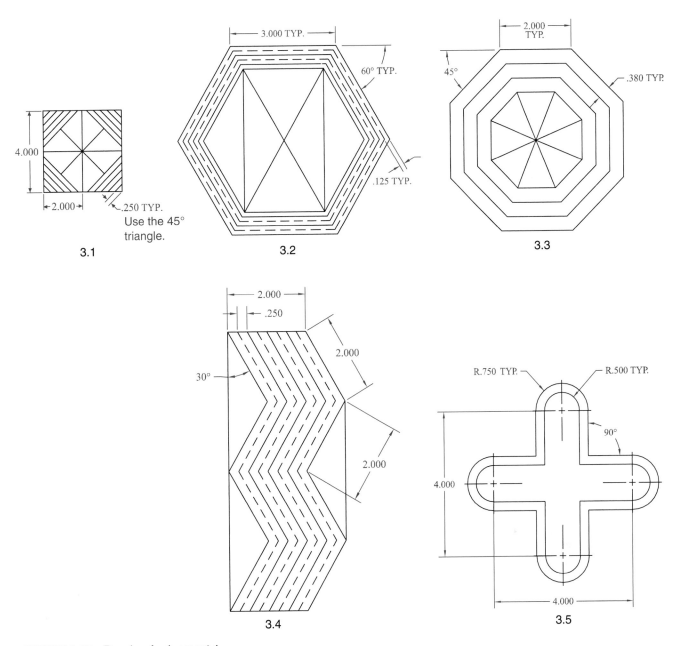

3.1

3.2

3.3

3.4

3.5

FIGURE 3.38 Drawing Assignment 1.

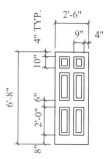

3.6
Scale ½″ = 1′-0″

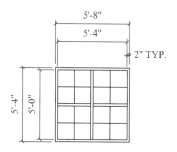

3.7
Divide the window into four equal sections, then divide the glass into four equal sections. Scale ¾″ = 1′-0″

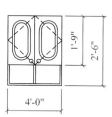

3.8
Choose any dimensions that are not given, and custom-design the rest of the cabinet. Scale ¾″ = 1′-0″

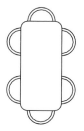

3.9
Draw this table with a basic overall size of 3′ × 6′. Choose the radius of the circles and fillets. Scale 1″ = 1′-0″

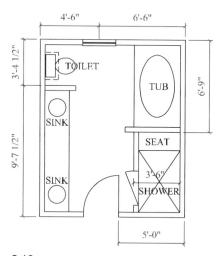
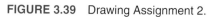

3.10
Some wall dimensions are given. Use a 4″ thickness for your walls. Research the dimensions that are not given to you by looking in the *Architectural Graphic Standards* or a manufacturer's catalog. Scale ¼″ = 1′-0″

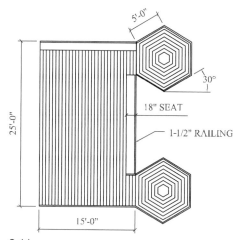

3.11
This deck has 6″ wide deck boards. Scale ¼″ = 1′-0″

FIGURE 3.39   Drawing Assignment 2.

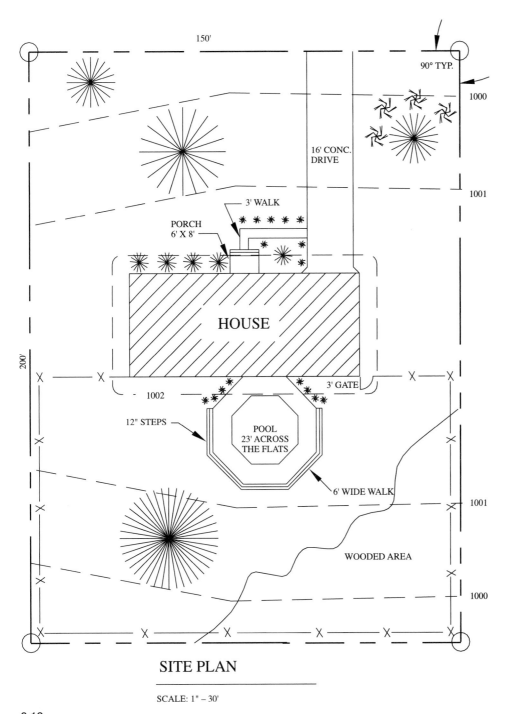

SITE PLAN

SCALE: 1" – 30'

3.12

Redraw this site plan at a Scale 1" = 20'. You can freehand the contours, plants, and trees. The house is 35' × 80' and should be 65' back from the road and 15' from both side property lines as a minimum.

FIGURE 3.40 Drawing Assignment 3.

CHAPTER 4

Drawing Basic Shapes and Patterns

4.1 Mastering Geometric Constructions

Take a moment to look at a technical drawing. Use a floor plan layout, a landscape design, or even the assembly drawings for a tool such as a drill press. Break these drawings down into their most basic elements and you will find geometric shapes. In some ways, learning geometric constructions is similar to learning to form the alphabet before writing words and sentences. Geometric constructions allow you to become familiar with your drafting instruments. The skills that you develop become the stepping stones for more complex projects.

Accuracy is a key factor in successful geometric construction. Keep leads sharp in both your pencil and your compass. A variation on the old carpenter's rule works well here: measure twice, draw once. Construction lines should be drawn as lightly as possible or with nonprint blue lead. Remember the rule about drawing construction lines so lightly that they can hardly be seen if the drawing is held at arm's length. You do not want your technique to show through to your clients, only the results.

The Terminology of Geometric Constructions

Points and Lines

A point represents a position in space or on a drawing. In drafting, this location is shown as the intersection of two lines (see Figure 4.1). A dot or a period should never be used to indicate a point. A dot big enough to be seen easily will also be big enough to be inaccurate. Instead, use a short crossbar on a line or a cross to show the location of a point.

Now that you have mastered points, let's move on to lines. Simply put, a line connects two points. A line may be either straight or curved. Remember, though, that the shortest distance between two points is a straight line. Sometimes a line is drawn and the beginning and end are not defined. (Think of a rainbow.) In this case, the endpoints are not marked. If the endpoints are significant, they are marked with a crossbar (see Figure 4.2).

By definition, parallel lines never intersect, since they remain an equal distance apart along the length of the lines. Parallel lines can be either straight or curved (see Figure 4.2). The symbol used to indicate parallel lines is //. Two lines are called perpendicular if they intersect or form at 90° (see Figure 4.2). The symbol for perpendicular is ⊥. As shown in Figure 4.2, a small box will sometimes be shown at the intersection of two lines that are perpendicular to each other.

Angles

When two lines intersect, they form an angle. The lines are referred to as the *legs* of the angle. The point at which the lines meet is called the *vertex*. Angles come in three basic varieties: right, acute, and obtuse (see Figure 4.3). A right angle is formed when two lines meet at 90°. If the lines meet at less than 90°, the angle is called *acute*. Angles of greater than 90° are called *obtuse*. The symbol for an angle is ∠.

FIGURE 4.1 Point styles.

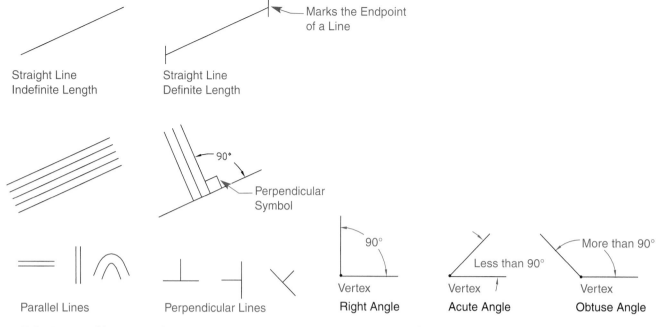

FIGURE 4.2   Line conventions.   **FIGURE 4.3**   Angle terminology.

Polygons

A polygon is defined as any plane figure that is bounded by straight lines. If all the sides and angles are equal, the figure is a regular polygon (see Figure 4.4). Triangles, octagons, and quadrilaterals are types of polygons.

Triangles

Mathematically, a triangle is a two-dimensional or plane figure with three sides and three interior angles. The three interior angles always add up to 180°. If you use straight lines to connect three points that are not in a straight line, you form a triangle. Give it a try.

Like angles, triangles come in different flavors (see Figure 4.5). In a *right triangle*, one of the interior angles is 90°. The longest side is called the *hypotenuse* of the triangle. The two other sides are called the *legs* of the triangle. In a right triangle, the square of the hypotenuse is equal to the sum of the squares of the two legs.

An *equilateral triangle* has three equal sides and three equal angles. An *isosceles triangle* has two sides of equal length and two equal angles. None of the sides or angles are equal on a *scalene triangle*.

Quadrilaterals

A quadrilateral is a plane figure bounded by four straight sides. Depending on whether the sides are equal and/or parallel, the figure can also be defined as a square, a rectangle, a rhombus, a rhomboid, a trapezoid, or a trapezium (see Figure 4.6).

Circles and Arcs

A circle is a closed curve with all points on the circle the same distance away from the center point (see Figure 4.7). The shortest distance from the center of the circle to a point on the circle is called the *radius*. The distance across the circle through the center is called the *diameter*. The diameter is twice the length of the ra-

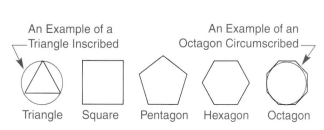

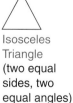
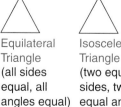
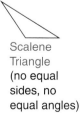

FIGURE 4.4   Regular polygons.   **FIGURE 4.5**   Types of triangles.

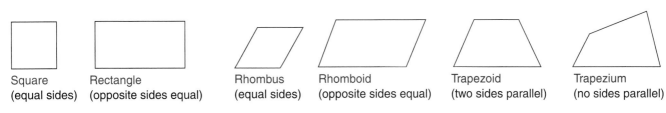

Square
(equal sides)
Rectangle
(opposite sides equal)
Rhombus
(equal sides)
Rhomboid
(opposite sides equal)
Trapezoid
(two sides parallel)
Trapezium
(no sides parallel)

FIGURE 4.6 Types of quadrilaterals.

FIGURE 4.7 Components of a circle.

Diameter
Radius
Circumference

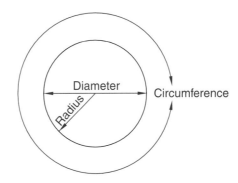

dius. The distance around the circle is referred to as the *circumference*. A circle can be divided into 360 segments called degrees.

An arc is simply a piece or section of a circle.

Tangents

In geometric constructions, a tangent can be thought of as a point of touching (see Figure 4.8a). The tangent point may be the spot at which one line ends and another line begins (see Figure 4.8d). If two circles or arcs touch at only one point, that point is a tangent point (T.P.) (see Figure 4.8c). A straight line touching a circle at only one point is another example of tangency (see Figure 4.8a).

FIGURE 4.8 Examples of tangency.

T.P.
(a)
T.P.
T.P.
(b)
T.P.
(c)
T.P.
T.P.
(d)

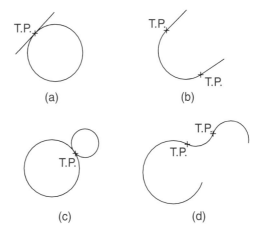

CONSTRUCTION: Parallel Lines

Given: Line AB, distance X (see Figure 4.9a)
Problem: Draw a line parallel to line AB at a distance X.
Solution I—Using a Compass:

Note: This methods works for curved as well as for straight lines.

1. Measure the distance X with your compass. Place the pointed end of the compass on one endpoint and adjust the lead until it lines up with the other endpoint. This setting will determine the radius of the arcs you will draw in the next step.

2. Keeping the compass on the same setting, place the point of the compass anywhere on the line AB. Lightly draw an arc. Repeat this process until you have a series of arcs along the line (see Figure 4.9b).

3. Draw a line tangent to the series of arcs. In other words, draw a line that just touches each of the arcs at a single point.

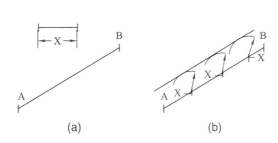

FIGURE 4.9   Parallel line construction using a compass.

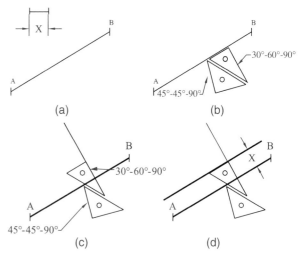

FIGURE 4.10   Parallel line construction using triangles.

Solution II—Using Triangles (see Figure 4.10):

1. Align the shortest leg of your 30°-60°-90° triangle with the line AB (see Figure 4.10b).

2. Place the hypotenuse of the triangle against the hypotenuse of your 45°-45°-90° triangle (or the edge of your T square).

3. Holding the 45°-45°-90° triangle firmly in place, slide the 30°-60°-90° triangle upward so the edge intersects line AB. Keep the edges of the triangles together. Draw a construction line along the edge of the 30°-60°-90° triangle (see Figure 4.10c).

4. Mark the distance X from line AB along the construction line drawn in step 3.

5. Check to make sure the triangles are still aligned with line AB. Slide the 30°-60°-90° triangle up until the short edge is distance X from line AB. Draw your parallel line (see Figure 4.10d).

Given: Line AB, point C (see Figure 4.11a)
Problem: Draw a line parallel to line AB through point C.
Solution:

1. Place the point of your compass on point C and draw an arc that intersects anywhere along line AB. Call this point D (see Figure 4.11b).

2. Leaving your compass at the same setting, put the point on point D (the intersection of line AB and the arc drawn in step 1). Draw an arc that passes through point C and intersects line AB. Call this point E (see Figure 4.11c).

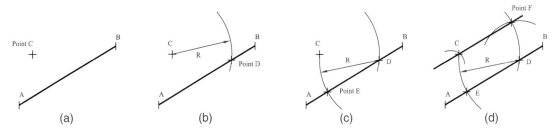

FIGURE 4.11 Parallel line construction.

3. Place the point of your compass on point E (the intersection of the line AB and the arc drawn in step 2). Adjust the compass until the lead passes through point C.

4. Move your compass to point D and draw an arc. This arc will intersect the arc drawn in step 1. Call this intersection point F (see Figure 4.11d).

5. Draw a line through points C and F. This line will be parallel to line AB and will pass through point C. The problem is solved.

CONSTRUCTION: Perpendicular Lines

Given: Line AB, point C (on line AB) (see Figure 4.12a)
Problem: Construct a line perpendicular to line AB at point C.
Solution I:

1. Place the point of your compass on point C. Draw an arc that intersects line AB on either side of point C. Call the two intersections points D and E (see Figure 4.12b).

2. Adjust your compass to a larger setting. Draw an arc with the point of the compass on point D. Repeat on point E. The two arcs should intersect at a point we will call point F (see Figure 4.12c).

3. A line drawn through points F and C will be perpendicular to line AB (see Figure 4.12d).

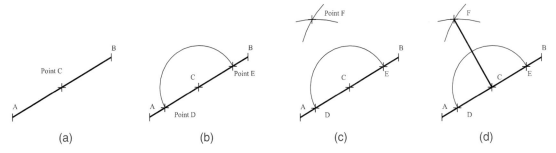

FIGURE 4.12 Perpendicular line construction (Solution I).

Solution II (see Figure 4.13):

1. Use your compass to draw a circle that intersects line AB at point C and one other location (point D) (see Figure 4.13b). The center of this circle must be away from line AB. Mark the center of the circle with a cross.

2. Draw a construction line through point D and the center of the circle. Continue the line until it intersects the opposite side of the circle (point E) (see Figure 4.13c).

3. A line drawn through points E and C will be perpendicular to line AB (see Figure 4.13d).

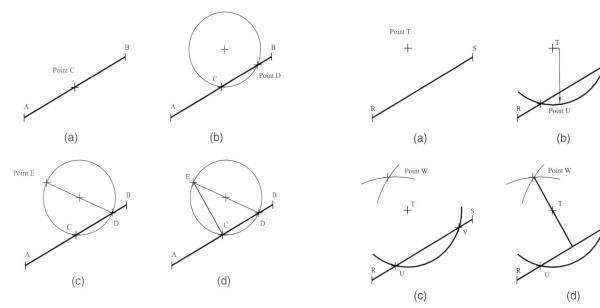

FIGURE 4.13 Perpendicular line construction (Solution II).

FIGURE 4.14 Perpendicular line construction with point not on line.

Given: Line RS, point T (not on line AB) (see Figure 4.14a)
Problem: Construct a line perpendicular to line RS and passing through point T.
Solution:

1. Place your compass point on point T. Swing an arc that intersects line RS in two places. Call these intersections points U and V (see Figure 4.14b).

2. Adjust your compass to draw a larger arc. Draw arcs with points U and V as the centers of the arcs. The two arcs should intersect. Call this intersection Point W (see Figure 4.14c).

3. A line drawn through points W and T will be perpendicular to line RS (see Figure 4.14d) .

CONSTRUCTION: Bisecting a Line

Given: Line AB (see Figure 4.15a)
Problem: Divide line AB into two equal parts.
Solution I—Using a Compass:

1. Place the point of your compass on one endpoint of the given line AB. *Lightly* draw an arc that intersects the line anywhere between the midpoint of the line and the other endpoint (see Figure 4.15b).

2. Now, use your compass to construct another arc of the same radius but with the center of the arc being at the other endpoint of line AB (see Figure 4.15c). (In other words, keep your compass at the same setting that you used for Step 1.) Notice that the two arcs intersect at two points not on line AB. One point is above the line, and the other is below the line. Call those intersections points C and D.

3. Draw a construction line through points C and D (see Figure 4.15d). The point at which this line intersects your original line AB is at the midpoint of line AB. You have divided the line into two equal parts.

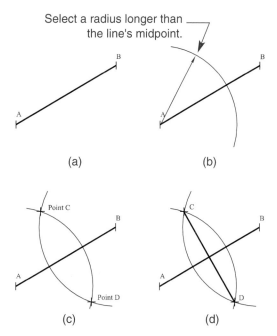

FIGURE 4.15 Bisecting a line. (Solution I)

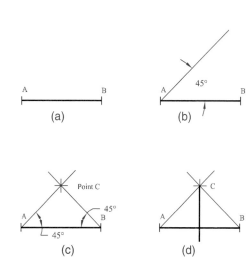

FIGURE 4.16 Bisecting a line using triangles.

Solution II—Using Triangles (see Figure 4.16):

Note: This method may be used with any equal angles; 45° angles were chosen because they are easy to draw using a standard triangle.

1. Align your drafting machine or T square with the given line AB. Use your 45°-45°-90° triangle to draw a construction line at a 45° angle to line AB through point A (see Figure 4.16b).

2. Draw a similar line through point B. The two lines should form a triangle with line AB as the base. Define the point of the triangle as point C (see Figure 4.16c).

3. Use your triangle to draw a line running perpendicular to line AB and through point C. This line will divide line AB into two equal segments (see Figure 4.16d).

CONSTRUCTION: Construction: Dividing a Line into Any Number of Equal Segments

Given: Line AB (see Figure 4.17a)
Problem: Divide line AB into any number of equal segments.
          For this example you will divide the line into seven equal segments.
Solution:

1. Draw a construction line that connects to the given line AB at an acute angle (labeled line AC in this example) (See Figure 4.17b.)

2. Use a scale or ruler to divide the construction line into seven equal spaces (see figure 4.17c). You do not need to use the entire length of the construction line. Find any number (on any scale) that conveniently divides into 7. For example, if 21 fit on the line, you would place tick marks at 3, 6, 9, 12, 15, 18, and 21.

3. Draw a construction line connecting the open endpoint of line AB and the last tick mark on the construction line AC.

FIGURE 4.17 Dividing a line into an equal number of segments.

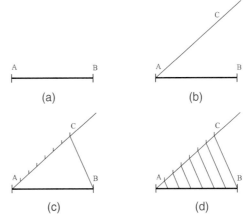

4. Draw lines parallel to this new line and intersecting each of the divisions marked on line AC. The intersections of these parallel lines and line AB will be the seven equal divisions required to solve the problem.

CONSTRUCTION: Dividing a Line into Proportional Parts

Given: Line AB (see Figure 4.18a)

Problem: Divide line AB into proportional parts.

 For this example, divide the line into 2, 3, and 5 proportional parts

Solution:

1. Add the numbers of proportions together, 2 + 3 + 5 = 10.

2. Draw a construction line that connects to the given line AB at an acute angle (labeled line AC in this example) (see Figure 4.18b).

3. Use a scale or ruler to divide the construction line into 10 equal spaces (see Figure 4.18c). You do not need to use the entire length of the construction line. Find any number (on any scale) that conveniently divides into 10. Place tick marks at the proportional locations. This first mark will be at 2. The next mark will be at 5, three spaces past the 2.

4. Draw a construction line connecting the open endpoint of line AB and the last tick mark on the construction line AC (see Figure 4.18d).

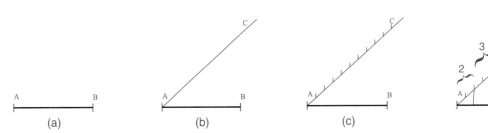

FIGURE 4.18 Dividing a line into proportional parts.

5. Draw lines parallel to this new line and intersecting each of the divisions marked on line AC. The intersections of these parallel lines and line AB will be the proportional divisions required to solve the problem.

CONSTRUCTION: Divide a Space into Equal Parts

Given: Space between two lines (see Figure 4.19a)
Problem: Divide the space into a number of equal parts.
For this example, you will divide the space into five equal parts.
Solution:

1. Place your scale across the two lines at an angle. Find a scale that will allow you to place the zero on one line and a 5 (or multiple of 5) on the other line. Place a tick mark at each of the increments between 0 and 5 (see Figure 4.19b).

2. Take the scale away (see Figure 4.19c). Draw a series of four lines parallel to the initial lines and through each of the divisions marked in step 1 (see Figure 4.19d). This will divide the space into five equal parts.

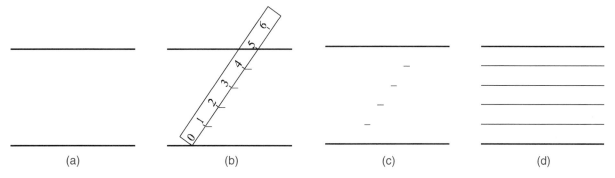

(a)   (b)   (c)   (d)

FIGURE 4.19   Dividing a space into equal parts.

CONSTRUCTION: Adding or Subtracting Lines

Given: Line AB of length X, line CD of length Y (see Figure 4.20a)
Problem: Add line AB to line CD.
Solution:

1. Draw a construction line in the desired position for the finished line. Assign one end of the line to be the endpoint of your new line (AB) + (CD). Mark this point with a cross or crossbar (see Figure 4.20b).

2. Use your compass to measure the length of the given line AB by placing the pointed end of the compass on one end of the line and adjusting the lead end of the compass to rest on the other endpoint of the line.

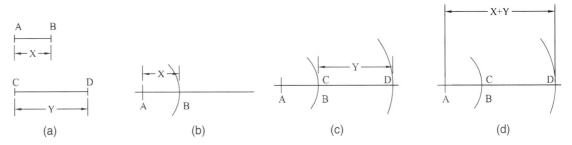

FIGURE 4.20 Adding lines.

3. Without adjusting the compass opening, place the pointed end of the compass on the end-point of the new line. Lightly draw an arc intersecting the previously drawn construction line. You have just transferred the length of line AB to your construction line (see Figure 4.20b).

4. Now, position your compass on the given line CD, just as you did for line AB in step 2.

5. Using this new compass position, place the pointed end of the compass on the intersection of the construction line and the arc drawn in step 3. Draw another arc intersecting the construction line (see Figure 4.20c).

6. Darken the section of your construction line between the point defined in step 1 and the arc drawn in step 5. This is your new line of length (AB) + (CD) (see Figure 4.20d).

Given: Line AB of length X, line CD of length Y (see Figure 4.21a)
Problem: Subtract line AB from line CD.
Solution:

1. Draw a construction line in the desired position for the finished line. Assign one end of the line to be the endpoint of your new line (AB) – (CD). Mark this point with a cross or cross-bar (see Figure 4.21b).

2. Use your compass to measure the length of the given line CD by placing the pointed end of the compass on one end of the line and adjusting the lead end of the compass to rest on the other endpoint of the line.

3. Without adjusting the compass opening, place the pointed end of the compass on the end-point of the new line. Lightly draw an arc intersecting the previously drawn construction line. You have just transferred the length of line CD to your construction line (see Figure 4.21b).

4. Now position your compass on the given line AB, just as you did for line CD in step 2.

FIGURE 4.21 Subtracting lines.

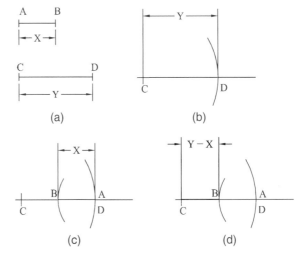

5. Using this new compass position, place the pointed end of the compass on the intersection of the construction line and the arc drawn in step 3. Aiming your compass toward the beginning endpoint of your new line, draw an arc intersecting the construction line (see Figure 4.21c).

6. Darken the section of your construction line between the point defined in step 1 and the arc drawn in step 5 (see Figure 4.21d). This is your new line of length AB − CD.

CONSTRUCTION: Draw an Arc or Circle through Three Points

Given: Point 1, point 2, and point 3 (see Figure 4.22a)
Problem: Construct a circle (or arc) that contains the three given points.
Solution:

Note: Follow the same steps for constructing arcs.

1. Draw two lines to connect the three points. For example, draw a line from point 1 to point 2 then another line from point 1 to point 3 (see Figure 4.22b).

2. Construct the perpendicular bisectors for the two lines (see Figures 4.14 and 4.22c).

3. Notice that the two bisectors intersect. This will be the center of your circle. Call it point 4 (see Figure 4.22d).

4. Place the point of your compass on point 4. Adjust the compass so that the lead touches point 1, 2, or 3. If you have done the previous steps correctly, points 1, 2, and 3 will all be the same distance from point 4, the center of your circle. Use your compass to draw this circle (see Figure 4.22e).

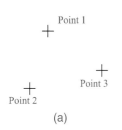 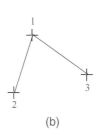 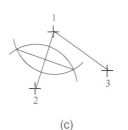 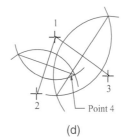 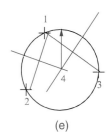

(a)   (b)   (c)   (d)   (e)

FIGURE 4.22 Constructing an arc or circle through three points.

CONSTRUCTION: Bisect an Angle

Given: Angle ∠SUN (see Figure 4.23a)
Problem: Bisect or divide the given angle into two equal angles, that is, divide the angle in half.
Solution:

1. Place your compass point on the vertex of the angle, the point where the two legs of the angle come together. Swing an arc at any location that intersects both legs of the angle. Label these intersections points A and B (see Figure 4.23b).

2. Place your compass on point A and swing an arc. Use any size arc that is convenient. Keep your compass at the same setting and draw an arc with the compass point on point B. Notice that the two arcs intersect at a location we will call point C (see Figure 4.23c).

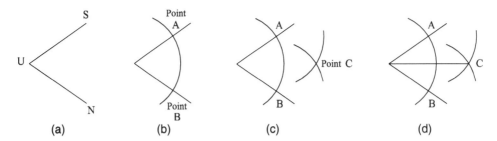

FIGURE 4.23   Bisecting an angle.

3. A straight line drawn through point C to the vertex of the angle will bisect or divide the angle in half (see Figure 4.23d).

CONSTRUCTION: Transfer an Angle

Given: ∠ABC, location A′B′ (see Figure 4.24a)
Problem: Transfer ∠ABC to a new location at A′B′.
Solution:

1. Place your compass point on point B. Strike an arc at any location along ∠ABC. Make sure the arc passes through both legs of the angle (see Figure 4.24b).

2. Duplicate the arc with your compass point on point B′. Designate the intersection of line A′B′ and the arc as point 1 (see Figure 4.24c).

FIGURE 4.24   Transferring an angle.

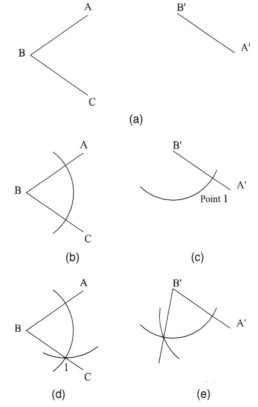

3. Use your compass to measure the chord length between the intersections of the arc in step 1 and the legs of ∠ABC. Place the point of your compass on the intersection on one leg while adjusting the lead of the compass until it goes through the other intersection. Keeping your compass on the same setting, place the sharp end on point 1 and strike an arc (see Figure 4.24d).

4. Draw a line from point B′ to the intersection of the two arcs drawn in steps 2 and 4 to complete the transfer of the angle to its new location (see Figure 4.24e).

CONSTRUCTION: Fillets

Given: Right angle ∠XYZ, radius R (see Figure 4.25a)
Problem: Construct a fillet of radius R tangent to ∠XYZ.
Definition: A fillet is basically a rounded interior corner.
Solution:

Note: This method works only for right-angle fillets.

1. Adjust your compass to the distance given for the radius R. Keep the compass on this setting for the entire construction.

2. Place the point of your compass on the vertex of ∠XYZ. Draw an arc of radius R that passes through each of the legs of the angle. These intersections are labeled points 1 and 2 in Figure 4.25b.

3. Leaving your compass on the same setting, draw an arc whose center is point 1. Draw another arc with a center at point 2. Notice that the two arcs intersect at the point labeled point 3 in Figure 4.25c.

4. Place the point of your compass on point 3 and draw an arc of radius R tangent to the legs of ∠XYZ (see Figure 4.25d).

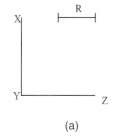
(a)

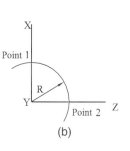
(b)

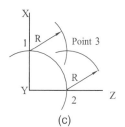
(c)

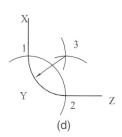
(d)

FIGURE 4.25   Constructing a right-angle fillet.

Given: ∠ABC, radius R (see Figure 4.26a)
Problem: Construct a fillet of radius R tangent to ∠ABC.
Solution:

1. Construct a line parallel to each leg of ∠ABC at a distance R (see Figures 4.9 and 4.26b).

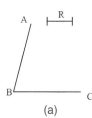
(a)

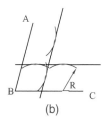
(b)

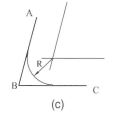
(c)

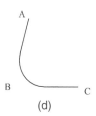
(d)

FIGURE 4.26   Constructing a fillet of any angle.

Note: This method
works for acute, ob-
tuse, and right an-
gles. Give it a try
with several sizes of
angles.

2. The two lines should intersect. Place your compass point on this intersection and draw an arc of radius R tangent to the legs of ∠ABC (see Figure 4.26c).

3. Darken the visible lines (see Figure 4.26d) to complete the drawing.

CONSTRUCTION: Round—Two Circles

Given: Circle 1 of radius X, circle 2 of radius Y, radius R (see Figure 4.27a)
Problem: Construct a round of radius R tangent to circles 1 and 2.
Solution:

1. Placing the point of your compass on the center of circle 1, draw an arc of radius R – X (see Figure 4.27b).

2. With the point of the compass on the center of circle 2, draw an arc of radius R – Y (see Figure 4.27c).

3. Locate the intersection of the two arcs drawn in steps 1 and 2. This point is labeled Z in Figure 4.27c. Use this point as the center of your round. Construct an arc of radius R that is tangent to the two circles (see Figure 4.27d).

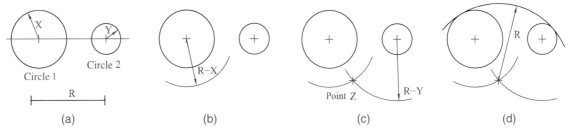

FIGURE 4.27   Constructing a round between two circles.

CONSTRUCTION: Drawing Triangles

Given: Three lines of lengths A, B, and C (see Figure 4.28a)
Problem: Draw a triangle with sides of lengths A, B, and C.
Solution:

1. Lightly draw a construction line to assemble your triangle on. Use your compass to measure the longest of the three lines, line C. Mark off that length on the construction line. This will define side C (see Figure 4.28b).

2. Measure length B with your compass. Place the point of your compass on one end of line C and draw an arc.

3. Measure length A with your compass. Place the point of your compass on the end of line C that you did not use in step 2. Draw an arc (see Figure 4.28c). This arc should intersect the arc drawn in step 2.

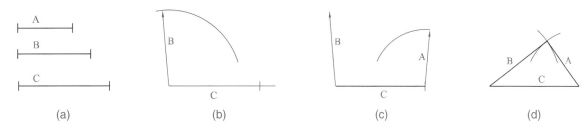

FIGURE 4.28   Constructing a triangle with three given sides.

4. Draw a line from each endpoint of line C to the intersection developed in step 3. These lines define sides A and B of your triangle (see Figure 4.28d).

Given: Length L (see Figure 4.29a)
Problem: Draw an equilateral triangle with sides of length L.
Solution:

1. Draw a construction line to begin building your triangle. Set your compass to measure length L. Mark this distance on your construction line with an arc. This will define the first side of your equilateral triangle. This line is labeled AB in Figure 4.28b.

2. Keeping your compass on the same setting, strike an arc from each end of the line defined in step 1. The two arcs should intersect.

3. Draw lines from each end of line AB to the intersection of the arcs drawn in step 2 (see Figure 4.29c). These lines define the other two sides of the triangle.

FIGURE 4.29   Constructing an equilateral triangle.

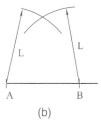

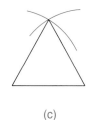

CONSTRUCTION: Drawing Squares

Given: Length J, location of center (see Figure 4.30a)
Problem: Construct a square with sides of length J.
Solution:

1. Lay out the center of the square with perpendicular construction lines.

Note: The radius of a circle is equal to half the diameter.

2. Next lay out a circle with diameter J. First, bisect the line of length J. This will give you the radius for your circle.

3. Place your point on the center laid out in step 1. Draw a circle of radius J/2 (see Figure 4.30b).

4. Use your triangle to draw four construction lines tangent to the circle (see Figure 4.30c). Two of the lines will be horizontal, and two will be vertical.

5. Check the four lines drawn in step 4 to make sure they are of equal length. If so, darken the four lines to define your square (see Figure 4.30d).

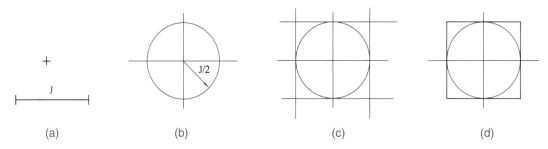

FIGURE 4.30 Constructing a square given the length of the sides.

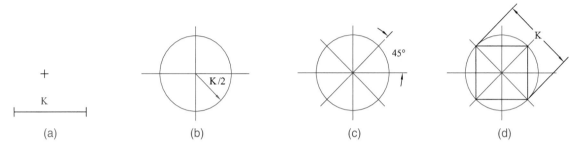

FIGURE 4.31 Constructing a square given the diagonal distance.

Given: Length K, location of center (see Figure 4.31a)
Problem: Construct a square with a diagonal distance between corners of length K.
Solution:

Note: The radius of a circle is equal to half the diameter.

1. Lay out the center of the square with perpendicular construction lines.
2. Next, lay out a circle with diameter K. First, bisect the line of length K. This will give you the radius for your circle.
3. Place your point on the center laid out in step 1. Draw a circle of radius ½K (see Figure 4.31b).
4. Use your 45°- 45°- 90° triangle to draw four construction lines. The lines will go from the center of the circle (the intersection of the circle with the horizontal and vertical lines) to the outside of the circle (see Figure 4.31c).
5. Draw horizontal and vertical lines between the intersections of the 45° lines and the circle (see Figure 4.31d).
6. Check the four lines drawn in step 5 to make sure they are of equal length. If so, darken the four lines to define your square.

CONSTRUCTION: Enlarge or Reduce a Rectangle

Given: Rectangle EFGH (see Figure 4.32a)
Problem: Enlarge or reduce rectangle EFGH proportionately.
Solution:

1. Draw a straight line from corner to corner. Extend the line beyond the triangle (see Figure 4.32b).
2. Use the diagonal to find the correct proportions by which to enlarge or reduce the triangle.

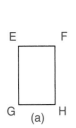
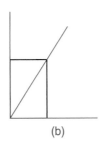

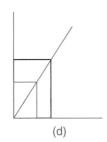

FIGURE 4.32 Enlarging or reducing a rectangle.

Lines projected horizontally and vertically from the diagonal will define a rectangle of the correct size (see Figures 4.32c and d).

CONSTRUCTION: Octagons

Given: Circle of diameter A (see Figure 4.33a)
Problem: Draw an octagon with the distance across the *flats* (the distance between opposite sides) of length A.
Solution:

1. Use construction lines to draw a circle with a diameter of length A (see Figure 4.33a).
2. Draw horizontal lines tangent to the top and bottom of the circle (at 90° and 270° (see Figure 4.33b).
3. Draw vertical lines tangent to both sides of the circle (at 0° and 180°).
4. Use your 45°-45°-90° triangle to draw four lines tangent to the circle at 45° and −45° to horizontal (see Figure 4.33c).
5. The intersection of these eight lines forms an octagon (see Figure 4.33d). Darken in the eight lines to finish the octagon (see Figure 4.33e).

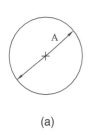
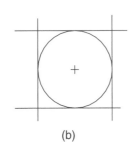
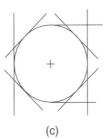
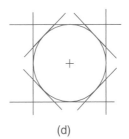
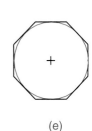

FIGURE 4.33 Constructing an octagon around a circle. Circumscribed example.

Given: Square with sides of length B (see Figure 4.34a)
Problem: Draw an octagon with the distance across the flats of length B.
Solution:

1. Use construction lines to draw diagonal lines between opposite corners on the square. The intersection of these lines will define the center of the square.

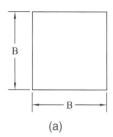 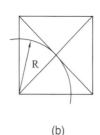 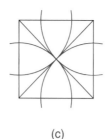 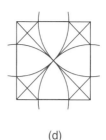 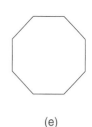

(a)　　　　　　　　　　(b)　　　　　　　　　(c)　　　　　　　　　(d)　　　　　　　　(e)

FIGURE 4.34　Constructing an octagon around a square.

2. Adjust your compass so the point is on one corner of the square and the lead is at the center of the square. Keeping your compass at this setting, draw an arc that intersects the two sides of the corner. Repeat this step at each corner of the square (see Figures 4.34b and c).

3. The arcs drawn in step 2 should intersect the square at eight points. Connect these points to form an octagon (see Figures 4.34d and e).

CONSTRUCTION: Pentagons

Given: Circle of diameter K
Problem: Construct a pentagon inscribed in the given circle (see Figure 4.35).
Solution:

1. Using construction lines, draw intersecting horizontal and vertical lines longer than length K. With the compass point at the intersection of these two lines, draw a circle of diameter K (see Figure 4.35a).

2. Define point 0 as the center of the circle. Define point 1 as the right-side intersection between the circle and the horizontal line. Define point 2 as the left-side intersection of the circle and the horizontal line (see Figure 4.35b).

3. Bisect the distance between points 0 and 1. Define that midpoint as point 3 (see Figure 4.35b).

FIGURE 4.35　Constructing a pentagon inside a circle.

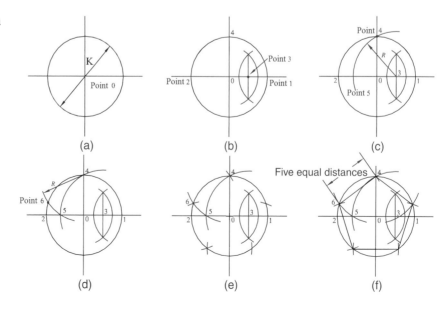

(a)　　　　　　　　　　　(b)　　　　　　　　　　　(c)

(d)　　　　　　　　　　　(e)　　　　　　　　　　　(f)

4. Define point 4 as the top intersection between the circle and the vertical line (see Figure 4.35c).

5. Place your compass point on point 3. Draw an arc passing through point 4 and the horizontal line. Define the intersection of this arc and the horizontal line as point 5 (see Figure 4.35c).

6. Place your compass point on point 4. Draw an arc that passes through point 5 and the edge of the circle (see Figure 4.35d). Define the intersection of this arc with the circle as point 6.

7. The distance between points 4 and 6 defines the length of one side of your pentagon. Adjust your compass to span these two points. Work your way around the circle marking off this distance around the circumference of the circle (see Figure 4.35e). You should end up back at point 4 having marked five intersections around the circle (including points 4 and 6). Connect these five points to form a pentagon (see Figure 4.35f).

CONSTRUCTION: Hexagons (five methods)

Given: Circle of diameter D
Problem: Construct a hexagon of distance D across the corners. (The corners of the hexagon will be on the circle.)
Solution I (see Figure 4.36):

1. Lightly draw a circle of diameter D (see Figure 4.36a). (Remember, you should set the compass to the length of the radius of the circle, not the diameter. You may need to bisect the length D in order to determine the radius.)

2. Keeping your compass on the same D/2 setting, place the point of your compass on the circle. Strike an arc through the circle (see Figure 4.36b).

3. Move the point of your compass to the intersection of the circle and the arc drawn in step 2. Strike another arc through the circle.

4. Continue striking arcs and moving to the intersection until you work your way around the circle. When you get back to the original point, you should have intersected the circle at six points (see Figure 4.36c).

5. Connect these six points to form the sides of the hexagon.

FIGURE 4.36 Constructing a hexagon (Solution I). Inscribed example.

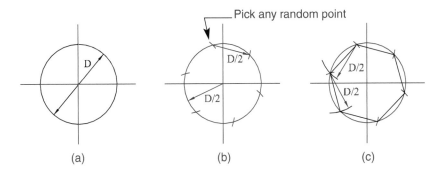

(a)　　　(b)　　　(c)

Solution II (see Figure 4.37):

1. Use construction lines to draw intersecting horizontal and vertical lines. Draw a circle of diameter D whose center is on the intersection of the horizontal and vertical lines at point 1 (see Figure 4.37a). (Remember to use the radius to set your compass. Since the radius is one-half the length of the diameter, you could find the radius length by bisecting the length D.)

2. Define point 2 as the top intersection of the circle and the vertical line. Define point 3 as the bottom intersection of the circle and the vertical line (see Figure 4.37b).

FIGURE 4.37 Constructing a hexagon (Solution II).

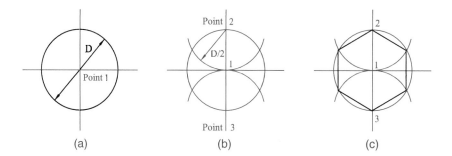

3. Keeping the same compass set on D/2, place the point of your compass on point 2. Strike an arc through the center of the circle and two points on the circle (see Figure 4.37b).

4. Place the compass point on point 3. Strike an arc through the center and the circumference of the circle.

5. The arcs drawn in steps 2 and 3 intersect the circle at four points. These four points plus points 2 and 3 define the corners of the hexagon. Connect these six points to form the hexagon (see Figure 4.37c).

Solution III (see Figure 4.38):

1. Use construction lines to draw intersecting horizontal and vertical lines. Draw a circle of diameter D whose center is on the intersection of the horizontal and vertical lines (see Figure 4.38a). (Remember to use the radius to set your compass. Since the radius is half the length of the diameter, you could find the radius length by bisecting the length D.)

2. Define point 1 as the left intersection of the circle with the horizontal line. Define point 2 as the right intersection of the circle with the horizontal line (see Figure 4.38b).

3. Use your 30°-60°-90° triangle to draw a construction line that begins at point 1 and runs 60° to the horizontal (see Figure 4.38b). Draw another line starting at point 1 and running −60° to the horizontal (see Figure 4.38b). These two lines form two sides of the hexagon. Darken the lines between point 1 and the circle.

4. Draw lines starting at point 2 and running at 60° and −60° to the horizontal. These two lines form two more sides of the hexagon. Darken the lines between point 2 and the circle (see Figure 4.38c).

5. Use horizontal lines to connect the ends of the lines drawn in steps 3 and 4 and form the final two sides of the hexagon (see Figures 4.38d and e).

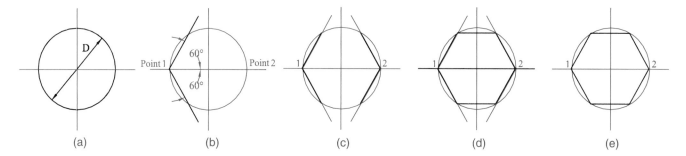

FIGURE 4.38 Constructing a hexagon (Solution III). Inscribed example.

Solution IV (see Figure 4.39):

1. Use construction lines to draw intersecting horizontal and vertical lines. Draw a circle of diameter D whose center is on the intersection of the horizontal and vertical lines (see Figure 4.39a). (Remember to use the radius to set your compass. Since the radius is half the length of the diameter, you could find the radius length by bisecting the length D.)

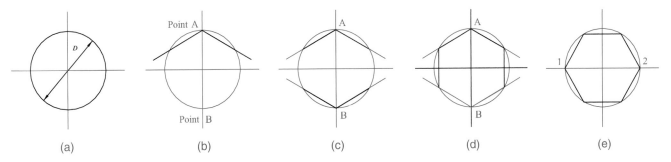

(a)   (b)   (c)   (d)   (e)

FIGURE 4.39 Constructing a hexagon (Solution IV). Inscribed example.

2. Define point A as the intersection of the top of the circle and the vertical line. Define point B as the intersection of the bottom of the circle and the vertical line (see Figure 4.39b).

3. Use your 30°-60°-90° triangle to draw two lines starting at point A and running at −30° to horizontal. One line will go toward the left, the other toward the right (see Figure 4.39b). These lines form two sides of the hexagon. Darken the lines between point A and the circle.

4. Draw two lines starting at point B and running at 30° to the horizontal (see Figure 4.39c). These lines form two sides of the hexagon. Darken the lines between point B and the circle.

5. Complete the hexagon by using two vertical lines to connect the ends of the lines drawn in steps 3 and 4 (see Figures 4.39d and e).

Given: Circle of diameter M
Problem: Construct a hexagon of distance M across the *flats* (the distance between *opposite* sides) (see Figure 4.40).
Solution:

1. Use construction lines to draw intersecting horizontal and vertical lines. Draw a circle of diameter M whose center is on the intersection of the horizontal and vertical lines (see Figure 4.40a). (Remember to use the radius to set your compass. Since the radius is half the length of the diameter, you could find the radius length by bisecting the length M).

2. Lightly draw two vertical lines tangent to the circle on the left and right sides (see Figure 4.40b).

3. Use your 30°-60°-90° triangle to draw four construction lines tangent to the circle at 30° to the horizontal (see Figure 4.40c).

4. The intersections between the four lines from step 3 and the two lines from step 2 form six points (see Figure 4.40d). Connect these six points and darken the lines to form the hexagon (see Figure 4.40e).

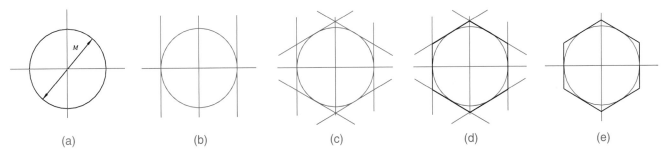

(a)   (b)   (c)   (d)   (e)

FIGURE 4.40 Constructing a hexagon with a given distance across the flats. Circumscribed example.

CONSTRUCTION: Concentric-Circle Ellipse

Given: Lengths A and B (see Figure 4.41a)
Problem: Construct an ellipse with major diameter A and minor diameter B.
Solution:

1. Use construction lines to draw intersecting horizontal and vertical lines. Define the intersection of the two lines as Point 0 (see Figure 4.41b). Draw all the lines in this method as very light construction lines.

2. Draw a circle of radius A/2 whose center is at point 0.

3. Draw a circle of radius B/2 whose center is at point 0.

4. At this point, the circles are divided into four quadrants. Next, use your 30°-60°-90° triangle to divide the circles into 12 equal sections. Draw lines through the center (point 0) at ±30° and ±60° to the horizontal (see Figure 4.41c).

5. Define the top intersection of the smaller circle the vertical line as point 12 (think of a clock face). Define the intersection of the bottom of the circle with the vertical line as point 6. Define the intersection of the right side of the circle with the horizontal line as point 3. Define the intersection of the left side of the circle with the horizontal line as point 9 (see Figure 4.41c).

6. Because the two concentric circles correspond to the lengths given for the major and minor axes of the ellipse, points 3, 6, 9, and 12 will form four points on your ellipse.

7. Now you need to define eight more points on the ellipse. Work with one radial line at a time. Start at the center of the circles. Move out along the line until you reach the smaller of the two circles. Draw a horizontal line outward from the intersection of the small circle with the radial line. Now, continue on the radial line until you reach the intersection of the larger circle with the radial line. Draw a vertical line downward from this point until it intersects the horizontal line just drawn. The intersection of the horizontal and vertical lines from this step forms a point on the ellipse (see Figure 4.41d).

8. Repeat step 7 until you have worked your way around the entire ellipse (see Figure 4.41e). Remember that you do not have to do anything at points 3, 6, 9, or 12. They are already defined.

Note: For extremely large ellipses, you may wish to divide the circles into more than 12 sections.

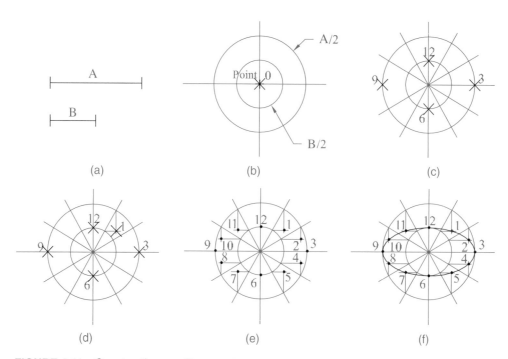

(a)   (b)   (c)

(d)   (e)   (f)

FIGURE 4.41   Constructing an ellipse.

9. Lightly connect the intersections defined in steps 7 and 8 to get a rough outline of your ellipse. Include points 3, 6, 9, and 12 in the ellipse (see Figure 4.41f).

10. Use a flexible curve or a French curve to darken in the ellipse with a smooth, continuous line.

CONSTRUCTION: Reverse or Ogee Curve (S-Curve)

Given: Points A and B
Problem: Draw an S-curve between points A and B (see Figure 4.42).
Solution:

Note: The S-curve in this example is symmetrical. The method for constructing asymmetrical S-curves is beyond the scope of this text.

1. Lightly draw a straight line between points A and B.

2. Divide line AB into four equal sections (see Figure 4.42a). (*Hint:* Bisect the line, then bisect each of the halves.)

3. Draw a line 90° to the horizontal beginning at point A and intersecting the line marking the nearest quarter section of line AB. This point of intersection is labeled point C in Figure 4.42b.

4. Draw another line at −90° to the horizontal beginning at point B and intersecting the line marking the nearest quarter section of line AB. This point of intersection is labeled point D in Figure 4.42b.

5. Using points C and D as centers, draw in the S-curve of radii CA and DB (see Figure 4.42c).

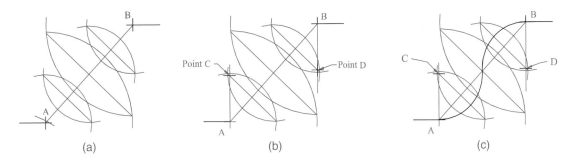

FIGURE 4.42 Constructing a reverse or ogee curve.

CONSTRUCTION: An Arc Tangent to Two Arcs and Enclosing One and Both

Given: Arc 1 with center A and radius B, arc 2 with center X and radius Y, radius RP for the desired arc tangent
Problem: Construct an arc of radius RP that encloses both given arcs (see Figure 4.43).
Solution:

1. Draw an arc that has point A as the center and a radius of (RP−B) (see Figure 4.43b). Look at Figure 4.21 for a review of how to subtract lines.

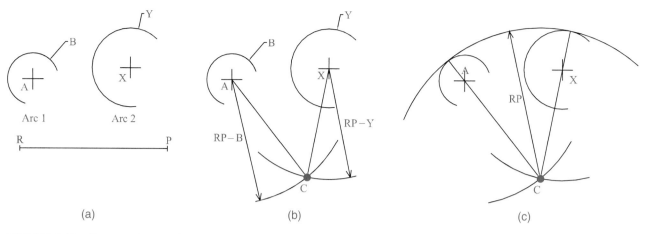

FIGURE 4.43 Constructing an arc tangent to two arcs and enclosing both.

2. Draw another arc using point X as the center with a radius of (RP−Y) (see Figure 4.43b).
3. The two arcs will intersect at a point shown on Figure 4.43b as point C.
4. Using point C as the center, construct an arc with a radius of RP. This arc will be tangent to each of the two given arcs and will enclose both arcs (see Figure 4.43c). The points of tangency will be at the intersection of an extension line CA with arc 1 and an extension of line CX with arc 2.

Given: Arc 1 with center A and radius B, arc 2 with center X and radius Y, radius RP for the desired arc tangent
Problem: Construct an arc of radius RP that encloses one of the given arcs.
Solution:

1. Draw an arc that has point A as the center and a radius of (RP + B) (see Figure 4.44b).
2. Draw another arc using point X as the center with a radius of (RP − Y) (see Figure 4.44b.)
3. The two arcs will intersect at a point shown on Figure 4.44b as point C.
4. Using point C as the center, construct an arc with a radius of RP. This arc will be tangent to each of the two given arcs and will enclose arc 2. The points of tangency will be at the intersection of line CA with arc 1 and an extension of line CX with arc 2 (see Figure 4.44c.)

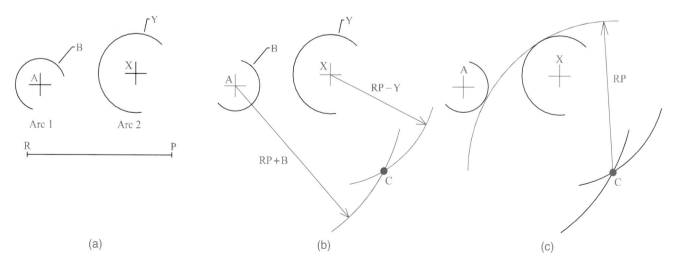

FIGURE 4.44 Constructing an arc tangent to two arcs and enclosing one.

FIGURE 4.45   One-view drawing.

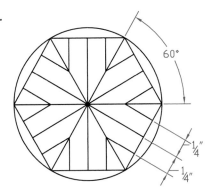

4.2   Getting Started with One-View Drawings

Once you have mastered the fundamentals of geometric construction, you are ready to move on to more complex figures. The key to mastering this skill is to teach your eye to recognize basic patterns within the figure. Find an element that you know how to construct and start from there.

For example, look at Figure 4.45. At first glance it is rather intimidating. But look again. You know how to draw a circle with a given diameter. You have also inscribed hexagons within a circle of given diameter. (The same process as drawing a hexagon when the distance from opposite corners is defined.) Once the circle and hexagon are drawn, recognize that the three lines through the center of the circle simply connect the points of the hexagon. You are left with having to draw three parallel lines within each pie-shaped section. The lines are equally spaced, so one way to approach the problem would be to divide each side of the hexagon into four equal parts. This can be accomplished in several ways. You could use the method illustrated in Figure 4.17. Alternatively, you could bisect each side and then bisect each half. Either way, once each side is proportioned into four equal parts, notice that the center line connects with the center of the circle. Once that line is defined, all you need to do is draw a line on either side that is parallel and starts at the appropriate division point. Repeat this procedure for each piece of the "pie," and before you know it you are done.

The illustration just provided should give you an idea of the basic approach to take in solving one-view drawings. Rarely will you be given a geometric construction that stands alone. Just relax and find the pieces. Remember, you can never solve a jigsaw puzzle unless you pick up the first piece and begin. Each piece works with the previous pieces to form your finished design.

REVIEW QUESTIONS

1. Why should you never use a dot or a period to represent a point in drafting?
2. When should the endpoints of a line be marked? How should they be marked?
3. Define a parallel line. What symbol is used to represent that two lines are parallel?
4. At what angle do two lines intersect if they are perpendicular to each another? What symbol is used to indicate this?
5. What term is used to refer to an angle of less than 90°?
6. Name three types of polygons. What makes them polygons?
7. What is the sum in degrees of the three angles inside a triangle? (*Hint:* Use your drafting triangles as a visual aid.)
8. What is the difference between an isosceles triangle and an equilateral triangle? Define both.
9. Define the terms *radius, diameter,* and *circumference.* You may want to use a sketch.
10. What is a quadrilateral?
11. Can a line and a circle be tangent to each another? How about two circles?

EXERCISES

EXERCISE 4.1

Divide an 11″ × 17″ sheet into six equal spaces.

Part A: In the top three spaces, going from left to right, construct the following geometric techniques.

First construction: Draw a 2.375″ horizontal line and divide it into seven equal spaces.

Second construction: Draw a 1.875″ line and bisect it.

Third construction: Draw an acute angle of 72° and bisect it.

Part B: In the bottom three spaces, going from left to right, construct the following geometric techniques.

Fourth construction: Draw a square with 1.5″ legs. Draw a circle tangent to the four sides.

Fifth construction: Draw a line 2.125″ long and divide it into three proportional parts.

Sixth construction: Draw an ellipse with a major diameter of 1.75″ horizontally and a minor diameter of 0.875″ vertically.

EXERCISE 4.2

Divide an 11″ × 17″ sheet into six equal spaces.

Part A: In the top three spaces, going from left to right, construct the following geometric shapes.

First construction: Inscribe a hexagon inside a circle with a radius of ⅝″.

Second construction: Circumscribe a hexagon about a circle with a radius of ⅞″.

Third construction: Circumscribe an octagon about a circle with a radius of ¾″.

Part B: In the bottom three spaces, going from left to right, construct the following shapes.

Fourth construction: Construct an equilateral triangle with 1″ sides, and bisect the interior angles. Do the lines intersect at one point or two?

Fifth construction: Construct an isosceles triangle with 0.5″ base and 1.5″ sides. Bisect the sides to find the center of the triangle.

Sixth construction: Inscribe a pentagon using a 1.25″-diameter circle as a base. Locate the center by bisecting the angles.

EXERCISE 4.3

Place the geometric constructions shown in Figure 4.46 on an 8½″ × 11″ sheet of vellum. Work the problems as shown.

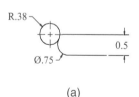

(a)
Draw an arc tangent to the given circle and line using a .75″ diameter.

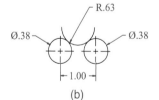

(b)
Draw an arc tangent to the given circles using a .625″ radius.

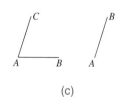

(c)
Transfer the given 72° angle to the horizontal line to the right using a compass and a straightedge.

(d)
Draw a triangle with the three given lines using your compass and a straightedge.

FIGURE 4.46   Exercise 4.3.

ASSIGNMENTS

1. Draw the one-view drawings in Figure 4.47 using the scales listed with the assignment.

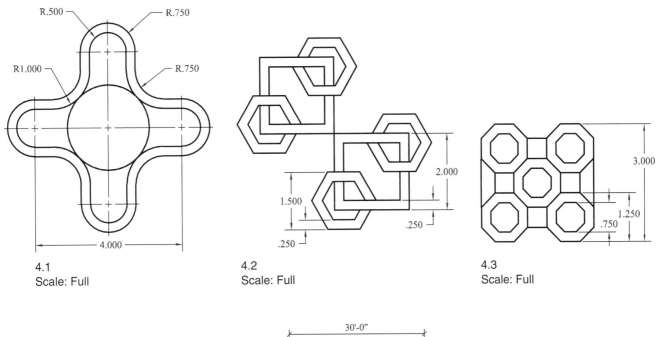

4.1
Scale: Full

4.2
Scale: Full

4.3
Scale: Full

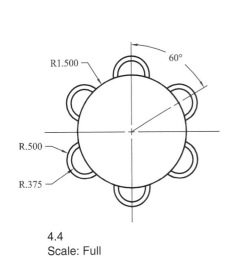

4.4
Scale: Full

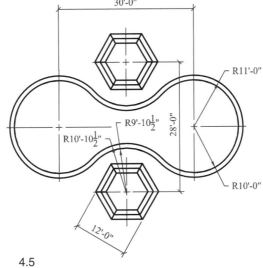

4.5
Scale: ⅛″ = 1′-0″

FIGURE 4.47 Drawing assignment 1.
continued on next page

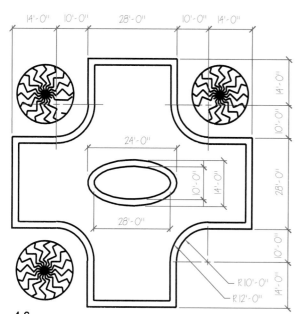

4.6
Scale: ¹⁄₁₆″ = 1′-0″

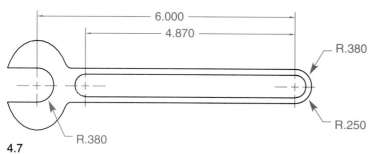

4.7
Ellipse has a major $\varnothing$ of 2″ and a minor $\varnothing$ of 1.5″

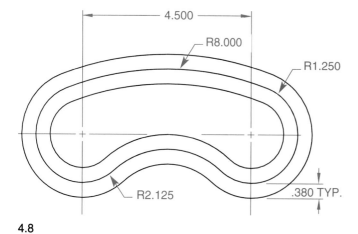

4.8

FIGURE 4.47   *continued*

○ ○

Introduction to Drawing Conventions

The purpose of any drawing is to convey information. The different types of drawings used in drafting can be broken down into two categories: artistic or pictorial (illustrating what the human eye might see) and technical or working drawings that are used in building or manufacturing. Both have their functions in drawing and are used across all fields of drafting.

Pictorial or artistic drawings can be used to give a nontechnical person or client a good idea of what the project will look like when it is completed, just as three-dimensional models make useful sales tools for marketing construction projects (see Figure 5.1).

If you have ever purchased a piece of furniture that had to be assembled, you have probably seen another type of pictorial drawing. A drawing (exploded pictorial) is usually provided to show the purchaser how to put together the various pieces into a fully assembled product. These three-dimensional drawings show width, length, and depth, but because paper is two dimensional, some distortion will occur (see Figure 5.2).

Technical drawings are geared toward building or manufacturing and are very detailed and exact. They show measurements and many different views and sectional cuts in order to show how to produce, manufacture, or build. Parts lists, bills of materials, and all types of schedules can also be used to get the desired end result. People also refer to technical drawings as *working drawings*. They build on one another like a technical manual, explaining and showing every aspect that is required. The major characteristic of these drawings is their true flat two-dimensional views. No depth is shown in the individual views (see Figure 5.3).

FIGURE 5.1 A 3D model of a house. Courtesy of Doug Maddox.

FIGURE 5.2 Exploded isometric of a pressure gun assembly. Courtesy of Innovative Penning Systems.

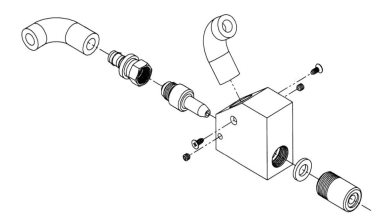

FIGURE 5.3 Example of a house elevation drawing.

The advantage in using technical drawings is that flat views make it easy to dimension. Dimensioning is much clearer to read in flat views, which makes them easier for the builder to read and understand.

The drafting world needs both types of drawing to complement each other. Neither one is more important than the other; they merely serve different functions. The following chart shows the types of drawings that fall under the two different categories while Figure 5.4 provides examples for you to compare.

Technical/Working	Artistic/Pictorial
Orthographics—Elevations	Axonometric
Auxiliary views	Isometric
Sections	Dimetric
Plan views	Trimetric
	Oblique
	Perspectives
	One-point
	Two-point
	Three-point
	True 3-D computer-generated drawing

FIGURE 5.4 Examples of technical and pictorial drawings.

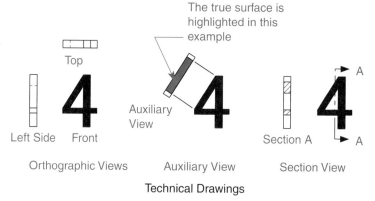

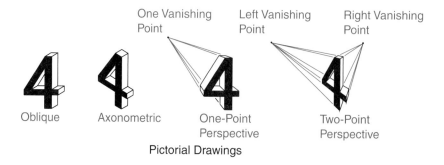

This chapter explains the different types of drawing and some of their characteristics. Later chapters will explain how to actually draw working drawings and pictorials.

5.1 Orthographic Drawings

The orthographic drawing is the backbone of technical drafting. Almost all forms of working drawings originate from the orthographic concept. Most schools spend a lot of time teaching orthographic drawing because once the fundamental concepts are grasped they can easily be applied to other fields of drafting.

The standard orthographic principles are largely mechanically based and are explained using a flat plane view approach. For example, look at the dice in Figure 5.5 in pictorial form. Each side is a flat surface with dimples. There are six total sides with six different dimple patterns to distinguish the sides (see Figures 5.6 and 5.7). Almost everyone is familiar with dice and knows the dimple pattern of the dots.

So far the dice have been shown in pictorial form or as a three-dimensional concept. The orthographic views are drawn looking at one surface at a time. Each surface has a different orthographic view showing only the true flat two-dimensional surface (see Figure 5.8). If the drawing was going to be used in typical orthographic form, then the views would be laid out as in Figure 5.9.

Now let's look at a different example using a stairway and letters (see Figure 5.10). The hidden lines represent corners or edges blocked by solid material in front of the viewing plane.

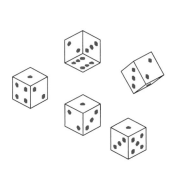

FIGURE 5.5 Pictorial drawings of dice.

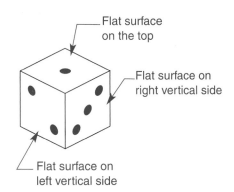

FIGURE 5.6 Die surfaces.

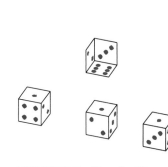

FIGURE 5.7 The six different surfaces of a die.

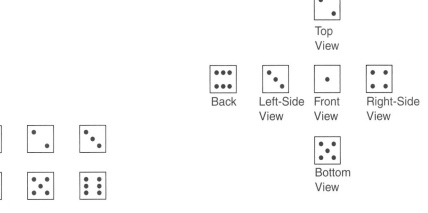

FIGURE 5.8 The six orthographics/elevations of a die.

FIGURE 5.9 An example of how orthographic views would be flipped out using third-angle projection. This alignment is used in mechanical drawing.

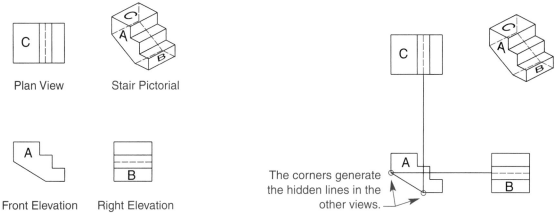

FIGURE 5.10 Isometric and ortho-graphic representations of stairs.

FIGURE 5.11 A view of Figure 5.10 shows how lines project to other views.

The example in Figure 5.11 shows how standard orthographic views are laid out. An architectural version of these views would leave out the hidden lines, and the view alignment would be left up to the drafter for balance and readability.

A good example of how an architect uses the flat orthographic view is in an elevation view. Let's visualize the pictorial example and then look at the same example in elevation or orthographic form.

First, go to a door and open it to about a 45° angle. Stand back about 5 ft and look at the door and the wall (see Figure 5.12) This is a pictorial showing all three dimensions of the door—height, width, and depth. Once you have the picture locked into your brain, shut the door, return to the same spot, and look again (see Figure 5.13). This time when you look, notice that the depth perception has been taken away because the door is shut and your eyes are perpendicular to the door. This is the difference between the orthographic view and its cousin the elevation.

One of the major differences is in hidden line use. In architectural elevations the hidden lines can be used to show how doors or windows open or pivot (see Figure 5.14). They can also show forms below the ground such as footing and basement outlines (see Figure 5.15).

Although the orthographic view and elevations are both two-dimensional flat views they differ in the view alignment. The mechanical orthographic has a very strict set of guidelines for laying out views and showing lines. The architectural elevations have a lot more freedom in layouts with no rigid format to follow. Architects treat elevations almost like artistic drawings, using shading and dressing up the views for aesthetic purposes even though they are technical drawings (see Figure 5.16).

Most drafters enjoy drawing elevations, trying to bring a two-dimensional drawing to life. It may take you a little while to grasp the pictorial and orthographic concepts and relationships. The real fun begins when you are learning to draw a three-dimensional space from flat views and vice versa (see Figure 5.17).

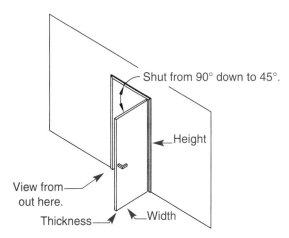

FIGURE 5.12 A pictorial drawing of a door.

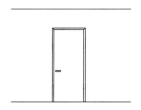

FIGURE 5.13 A door elevation.

FIGURE 5.14 Door and window elevations with hidden lines.

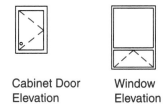

Cabinet Door Elevation

Window Elevation

FIGURE 5.15 Front elevation with hidden lines showing a basement below.

FRONT ELEVATION
Scale: 1/4" = 1'-0"

FIGURE 5.16 Hatched elevation of a church.

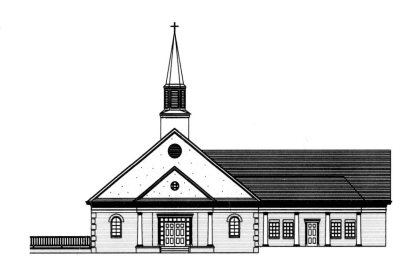

FRONT ELEVATION

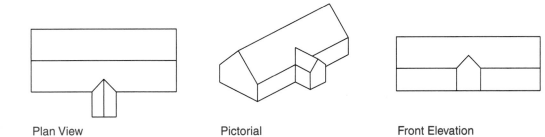

Plan View   Pictorial   Front Elevation   Right Elevation

FIGURE 5.17 Pictorial and elevations of a basic shape of a house.

5.2   Auxiliary Views

Once you have mastered orthographics, you have laid the foundation for the rest of the technical drawings. Next are auxiliary views, which use the same basic principles as the orthographic with a slight twist. Auxiliary views are flat two-dimensional drawings that are projected off angled surfaces (see Figure 5.18). Auxiliary views provide a length and width just like orthographics, but these views are projected off the inclined surface of the orthographic to avoid the distortion a side view would give (see Figure 5.19).

Auxiliary views can be split into two types: primary and secondary. The primary auxiliary is used when a view is needed off a single inclined surface (see Figure 5.20). A secondary auxiliary view is used for multiangled surfaces. It is not used often but does occur from time to time (see Figure 5.21). The secondary auxiliary view is a two-dimensional flat view that is flipped and aligned off the primary auxiliary.

Auxiliary views are heavily rooted in mechanical drawing but occasionally one will pop up in an architectural offshoot. You will most likely see it used in architectural drawing in elevations of bay windows or some other angled walls where true views and true dimensions are needed (see Figure 5.22). If you were trying to follow the mechanical layouts, the same drawing would look like Figure 5.23—flipped and aligned off the plan view. Architectural drafters are free to align the views to meet their needs.

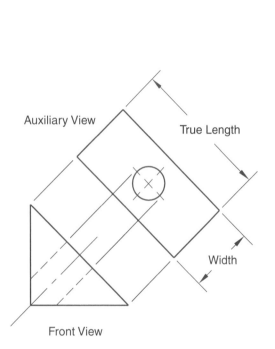

FIGURE 5.18   An auxiliary view.

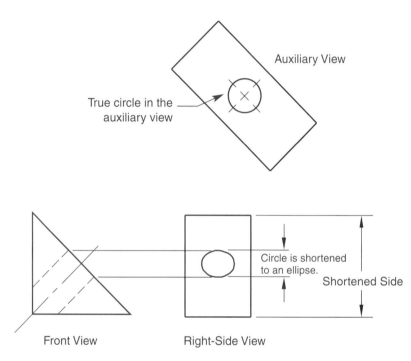

FIGURE 5.19   Detail of an auxiliary view.

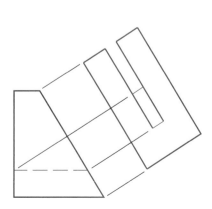

FIGURE 5.20   Example of a primary auxiliary view.

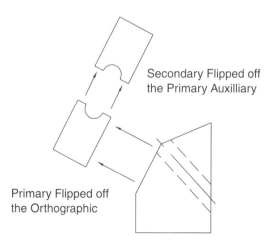

FIGURE 5.21   Example of a primary and a secondary auxiliary view.

FIGURE 5.22 Plan with bay elevation.

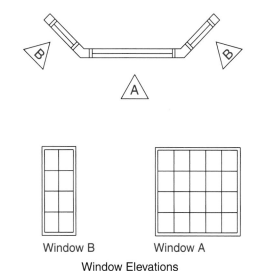

Window B   Window A

Window Elevations

FIGURE 5.23 Plan with bay elevation orthographically aligned.

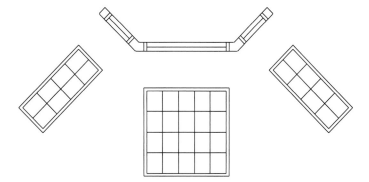

5.3 Section Views

Section views are the final piece in the technical drawing puzzle. The two-dimensional theme is continued in section drawing, but this type of drawing represents a cut through one or more objects. The task of a section drawing is to make it easier to read something that is complicated or blocked from sight.

Section views make unnecessary the hidden lines found in orthographics because you are no longer on the outside looking in, being blocked by solid material; instead you are cutting through to the inside with nothing blocking your vision at the critical viewing position (see Figure 5.24).

Section drawing is very common in most drafting fields. There are many types of sections, and most relate to the placement of the cutting-plane line (see Figure 5.25).

The key to reading sections is to imagine yourself behind the cutting plane looking in the same direction as the arrowhead is pointing (see Figure 5.26). Not all sections need cutting-plane lines such as the broken-out, removed, revolved, and rotated; however, it is very rare for an individual in architecture not to use a section callout or cutting-plane line. The cutting-plane line placement is extremely important. It allows the person reading the drawing to know exactly where the section is taken from.

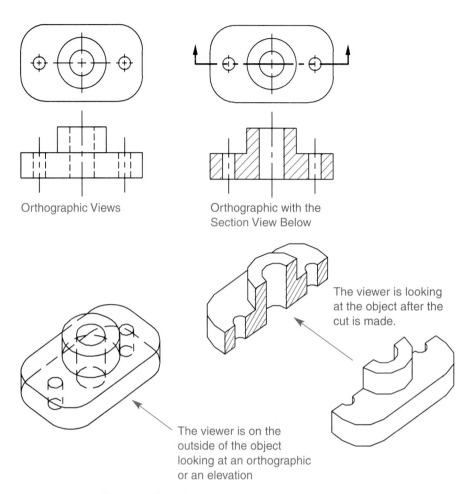

Orthographic Views

Orthographic with the
Section View Below

The viewer is looking
at the object after the
cut is made.

The viewer is on the
outside of the object
looking at an orthographic
or an elevation

FIGURE 5.24   Example of sections.

Architectural drawings use many sections to explain materials and to show how they are assembled or put together. In architecture, most sections are cut vertically through walls or buildings. Plan views are usually sections that are cut horizontally (see Figure 5.27). For example, a floor plan is a section on a horizontal plane cut about 4′ above the finished floor. A wall section is a vertical section or cut that goes all the way through from top to bottom showing the footing in the ground and the roof assembly on the very top of the wall (see Figure 5.28).

Building sections are typically cut all the way across the building, showing walls in section, but they can include interior and exterior elevations of objects not in the direct path of the cutting-plane line (see Figure 5.29). Sections can be very small, representing cuts through door frames or counters or cabinets or any detail that might need explaining to the builder to get it constructed according to the designer's vision (see Figure 5.30).

Here are some tips for understanding sections in architectural drawing.

1. Learn the material's hatching symbols and look on all drawings for a hatching legend just in case someone is using atypical hatch patterns (see Figure 5.31).

2. Visit real-life examples so you can learn how construction materials are attached together. During construction is the best time because when the project is finished too much is covered up.

3. Look at models or even put a model together to learn how a building goes together.

4. Get some practice, and do not hesitate to ask a mentor for advice. There is nothing that can replace years of experience in the profession.

Section drawings are beneficial and irreplaceable when it comes to taking the mystery out of the construction and assembling of buildings.

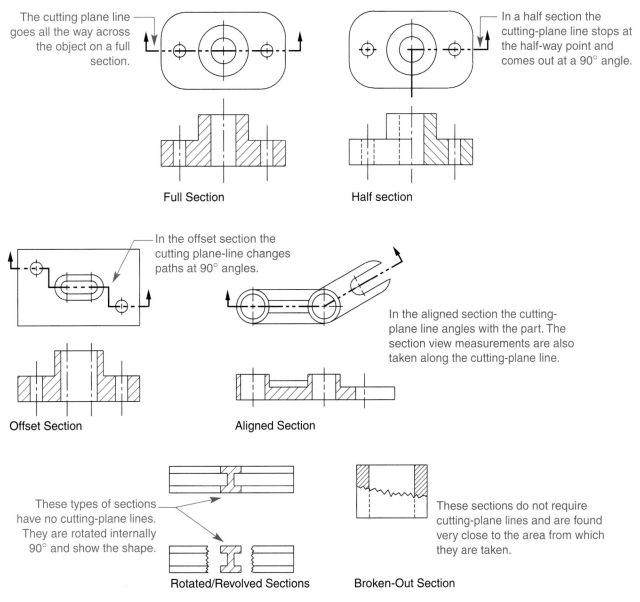

The cutting plane line goes all the way across the object on a full section.

In a half section the cutting-plane line stops at the half-way point and comes out at a 90° angle.

Full Section

Half section

In the offset section the cutting plane-line changes paths at 90° angles.

In the aligned section the cutting-plane line angles with the part. The section view measurements are also taken along the cutting-plane line.

Offset Section

Aligned Section

These types of sections have no cutting-plane lines. They are rotated internally 90° and show the shape.

These sections do not require cutting-plane lines and are found very close to the area from which they are taken.

Rotated/Revolved Sections

Broken-Out Section

FIGURE 5.25 Example of various sections.

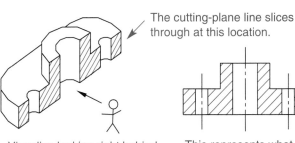

The cutting-plane line slices through at this location.

Visualize looking right behind the cutting-plane line and pick out the edges that are visible.

This represents what is seen in the section. Hidden lines beyond are ignored.

FIGURE 5.26 Isometric section.

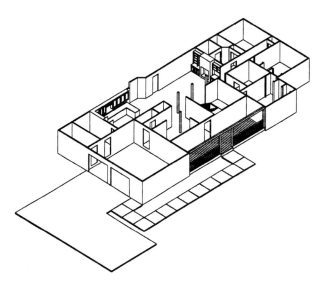

FIGURE 5.27 Isometric house plan with a horizontal cut made just below the ceiling.

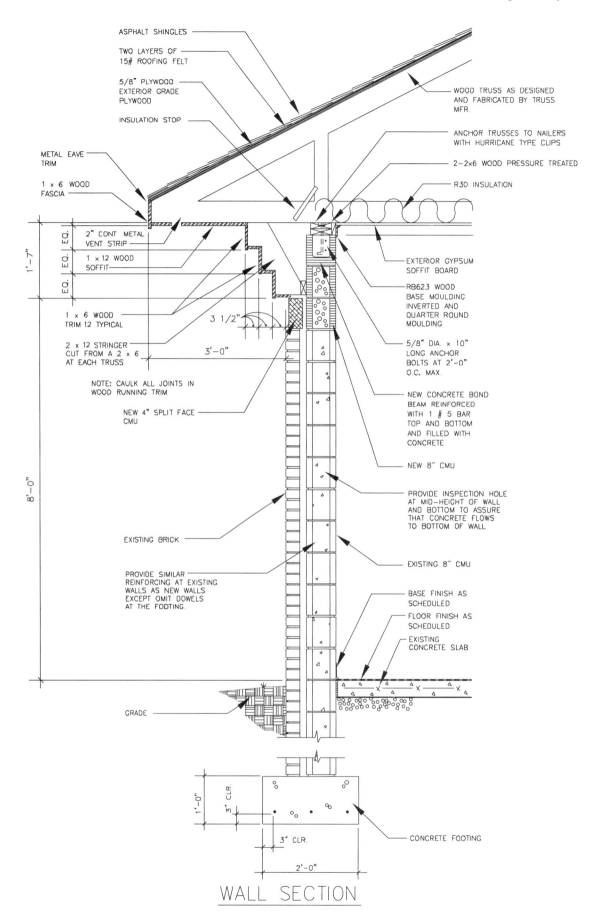

ASPHALT SHINGLES

TWO LAYERS OF
15# ROOFING FELT

5/8" PLYWOOD
EXTERIOR GRADE
PLYWOOD

INSULATION STOP

METAL EAVE
TRIM

1 x 6 WOOD
FASCIA

2" CONT METAL
VENT STRIP

1 x 12 WOOD
SOFFIT

1 x 6 WOOD
TRIM 12 TYPICAL

2 x 12 STRINGER
CUT FROM A 2 x 6
AT EACH TRUSS

NOTE: CAULK ALL JOINTS IN
WOOD RUNNING TRIM

NEW 4" SPLIT FACE
CMU

EXISTING BRICK

PROVIDE SIMILAR
REINFORCING AT EXISTING
WALLS AS NEW WALLS
EXCEPT OMIT DOWELS
AT THE FOOTING.

GRADE

3 1/2"

3'-0"

1'-7"

8'-0"

WOOD TRUSS AS DESIGNED
AND FABRICATED BY TRUSS
MFR.

ANCHOR TRUSSES TO NAILERS
WITH HURRICANE TYPE CLIPS

2-2x6 WOOD PRESSURE TREATED

R30 INSULATION

EXTERIOR GYPSUM
SOFFIT BOARD

RB623 WOOD
BASE MOULDING
INVERTED AND
QUARTER ROUND
MOULDING

5/8" DIA. x 10"
LONG ANCHOR
BOLTS AT 2'-0"
O.C. MAX.

NEW CONCRETE BOND
BEAM REINFORCED
WITH 1 # 5 BAR
TOP AND BOTTOM
AND FILLED WITH
CONCRETE

NEW 8" CMU

PROVIDE INSPECTION HOLE
AT MID-HEIGHT OF WALL
AND BOTTOM TO ASSURE
THAT CONCRETE FLOWS
TO BOTTOM OF WALL

EXISTING 8" CMU

BASE FINISH AS
SCHEDULED

FLOOR FINISH AS
SCHEDULED

EXISTING
CONCRETE SLAB

1'-0"

3" CLR.

3" CLR.

2'-0"

CONCRETE FOOTING

WALL SECTION

FIGURE 5.28

FIGURE 5.29

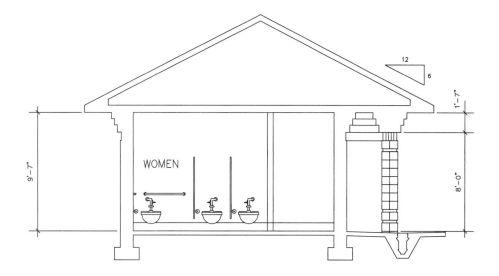

BUILDING SECTION
Scale: 1/4" = 1'−0"

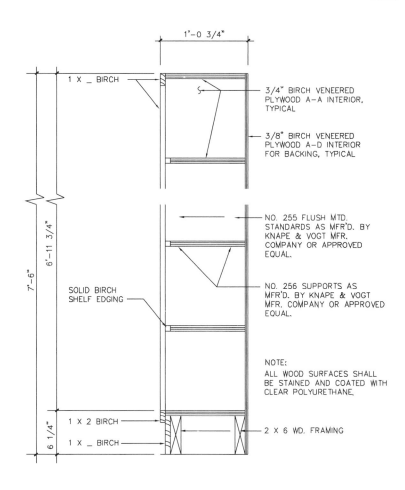

1 X _ BIRCH

3/4" BIRCH VENEERED
PLYWOOD A−A INTERIOR,
TYPICAL

3/8" BIRCH VENEERED
PLYWOOD A−D INTERIOR
FOR BACKING, TYPICAL

NO. 255 FLUSH MTD.
STANDARDS AS MFR'D. BY
KNAPE & VOGT MFR.
COMPANY OR APPROVED
EQUAL.

NO. 256 SUPPORTS AS
MFR'D. BY KNAPE & VOGT
MFR. COMPANY OR APPROVED
EQUAL.

SOLID BIRCH
SHELF EDGING

NOTE:
ALL WOOD SURFACES SHALL
BE STAINED AND COATED WITH
CLEAR POLYURETHANE.

1 X 2 BIRCH

1 X _ BIRCH

2 X 6 WD. FRAMING

SECTION THRU SHELVING
Scale: 1 1/2" = 1'−0"

ADJUSTABLE SHELVING
TYPICAL

PLASTIC LAMINATE
COVERED DOORS

PLASTIC LAMINATE
COVERED WALL CABINET

PLASTIC LAMINATE
COVERED COUNTERTOP
WITH BACKSPLASH

PLASTIC LAMINATE
COVERED BASE CABINET

PLASTIC LAMINATE
COVERED DOORS

BASE AS SCHEDULED

FLOOR FINISH
AS SCHEDULED

ADJUSTABLE SHELVING −
TYPICAL

* NOTE: ALL SURFACES SHALL RECEIVE PLASTIC
LAMINATE FINISH

CABINET SECTION
Scale: 3/4" = 1'−0"

FIGURE 5.30
continued on next page

FIGURE 5.30 *continued*

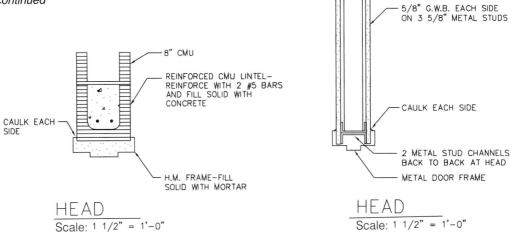

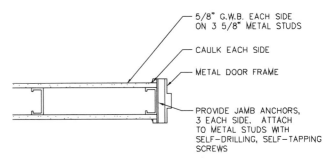

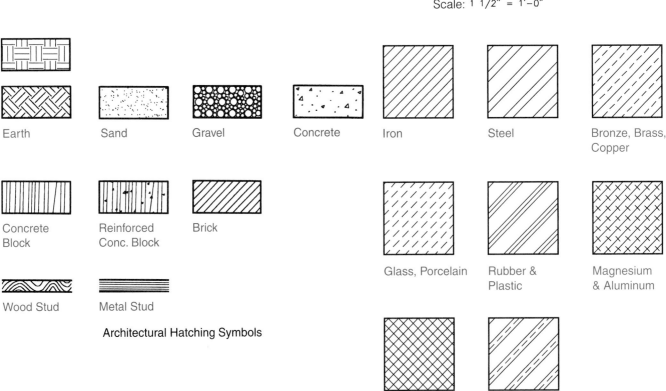

Earth   Sand   Gravel   Concrete   Iron   Steel   Bronze, Brass,
                                                                                         Copper

Concrete   Reinforced   Brick   Glass, Porcelain Rubber &   Magnesium
Block   Conc. Block   Plastic   & Aluminum

Wood Stud   Metal Stud   Zinc, Lead,   Titanium

Architectural Hatching Symbols

Babbitt

FIGURE 5.31 Typical hatching
symbols for section and plan view.

Mechanical Hatching Symbols

5.4 Pictorial Drawings

Pictorial drawings are some of the easiest ones to understand. A person sees a pictorial and can visualize what the project looks like. Most drafters really enjoy pictorial drawings and do not seem to be able to get enough of this type of drawing. However, pictorial drawing normally makes up only a small part of drawing in most architectural offices compared with the multitude of working drawings that must be done on projects.

When learning about pictorials, it is best to start with the easiest and work your way into the more complicated because each type lays down a foundation for the following one.

Oblique Drawings

The oblique drawing style of pictorial is the easiest to use and draw (see Figure 5.32). Some individuals in the field also refer to it as a cabinet drawing. It borrows some features from two-dimensional drawings and uses an angled line for depth. One major drawback to oblique drawings is that although it may be one of the simplest to draw, it is one of the most deceptive to view because of the combined principles. Most drafters counteract the distortion by changing the scale of the depth.

The face that appears to be closest to the viewer represents the two-dimensional part (true measurement) of the oblique, along with any surface that is parallel to the front face (see Figure 5.33). These faces are measured just like an orthographic would be.

Distortion on an oblique occurs along the angled lines. Circles on this surface become ellipses (see Figure 5.34). The combination of true and distorted surfaces makes the oblique unique to the pictorial world.

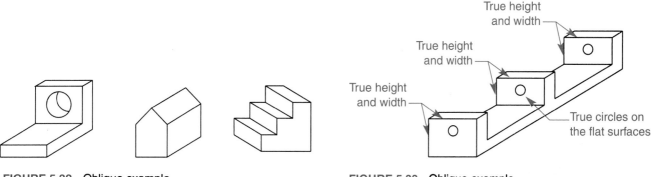

FIGURE 5.32 Oblique example.

FIGURE 5.33 Oblique example.

FIGURE 5.34 Oblique example.

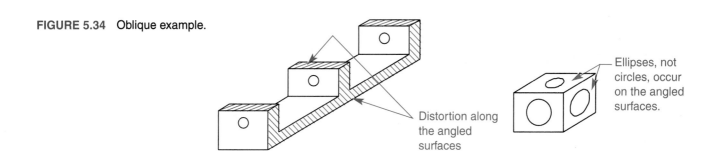

Axonometric Drawings

In axonometric drawing there is no true two-dimensional surface. All the surfaces are on angles in this kind of pictorial. There are three types of axonometric drawings: isometric, dimetric, and trimetric. The angles used determine the type.

1. Isometric drawing is one of the most commonly used pictorials today in manual drawing. The surfaces are created with vertical lines (90°) and 120° equal interior angles (see Figure 5.35). Dimensions and measurements are taken along the interior angles in isometric drawing (see Figure 5.36).

2. Dimetric drawing follows the same principle with some minor changes. The *di* in dimetric means 2, and in this case it means that two of the interior angles are equal instead of all three, as in the isometric. It does not matter which two of the angles are equal (see Figure 5.37).

   Another difference in dimetric drawing is that some techniques allow the drafter to adjust the scales along the depth in order to make the drawing more proportional and less distorted to the viewer. The changing of the angles and of the depth scale is an attempt to make the viewing closer to real life (see Figure 5.38).

3. In trimetric axonometric drawing the three central interior angles are unequal (see Figure 5.39). Just as in dimetric drawing the scale along the angled lines can be adjusted to cut down on distortion to make the pictorial more like real-life viewing. All three scales should be proportionally different.

Axonometric and oblique drawings do not show objects the way the human eye sees them; you must use a perspective to achieve this effect.

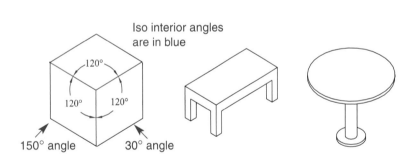

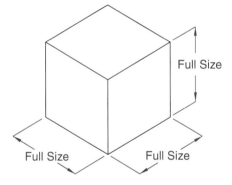

FIGURE 5.35   Iso box with interior angles.

FIGURE 5.36   Measurements can be taken along the interior angles or along parallel angles of an iso box.

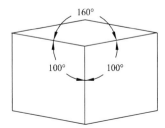

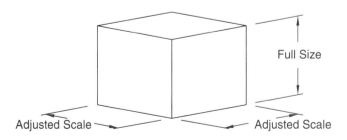

FIGURE 5.37   Dimetric box with interior angles. Any two angles can be equal to form a dimetric.

FIGURE 5.38   Measurements along a dimetric box.

FIGURE 5.39 Trimetric box. All three interior angles must be different to form a trimetric.

150°

100°   110°

Full Size

Adjusted Scale

Adjusted Scale

Perspective Drawings

Perspective drawing is the most complicated pictorial but the benefit is that this type of drawing emulates what the human eye would see. Architectural perspectives are a big selling tool when marketing a design (see Figure 5.40).

A good perspective looks as if an artist did the work instead of a drafter. This sometimes leads people to confuse a drafter with an artist. A perspective drawing is done with tools and is not a freehand sketch, so it is not as hard as it might seem. Euclid, the father of geometry, developed basic principles for perspective drawing more than 2000 years ago. Perspectives can be categorized into three groups: one-point, two-point, and three-point.

One-Point Perspectives

The best way to understand a one-point perspective is to see a real-life example. Find a building that has a long narrow hallway and stand at one end. Look down the hall and notice what is happening (see Figure 5.41). The doors look as if they get smaller the farther down the hallway you look, and the ceiling seems to drop lower. Your eyes cause this illusion, and it can be duplicated on paper by using one point of convergence where all the corners meet. The same phenomenon occurs outdoors. Look down a long straight road or down

FIGURE 5.40 Rendered perspective of a building. Courtesy of *Architectural Drawing and Light Construction* by Edward J. Muller.

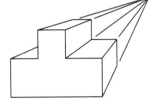 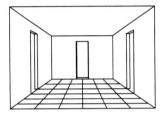

FIGURE 5.41   Examples of one-point perspectives.

FIGURE 5.42   Example of a railroad track that vanishes to one point. Courtesy of Kathy Cook.

a set of railroad tracks (see Figure 5.42). Outdoors, the view does not stop at the back wall but instead vanishes to a point. The trait of vanishing to one point defines this type of perspective.

Two-Point Perspectives

Two-point perspective works best when the object's focus is one corner. This two-point perspective relates more to an isometric, as the two sides head off in different directions. A two-point perspective uses two different vanishing points to generate depths (see Figure 5.43). Notice that as the sides head closer to their individual vanishing points, the vertical lines are drawn shorter, just like in the one-point perspective. The advantage to using two-point perspective is that it can give a more realistic view. For this reason, it is often used by interior designers to illustrate room designs.

Three-Point Perspectives

The three-point perspective incorporates a third vanishing point, which can be used in a variety of ways. A third point can be placed high in the sky to have the object's vertical lines taper in, or a light source, like the sun, can be placed in the drawing and a vanishing point can be projected down to the horizon. Using a light source and a third vanishing point helps plot out shadows on a drawing (see Figure 5.44).

Some drawings have many more vanishing points than three, but understanding how to use two points is a good starting place. Adding shades and shadows tends to bring out the artist in the drafter.

Vanishing Point Left   Vanishing Point Right

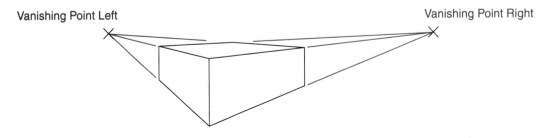

FIGURE 5.43   Two-point perspectives.

FIGURE 5.44 Three-point perspectives.

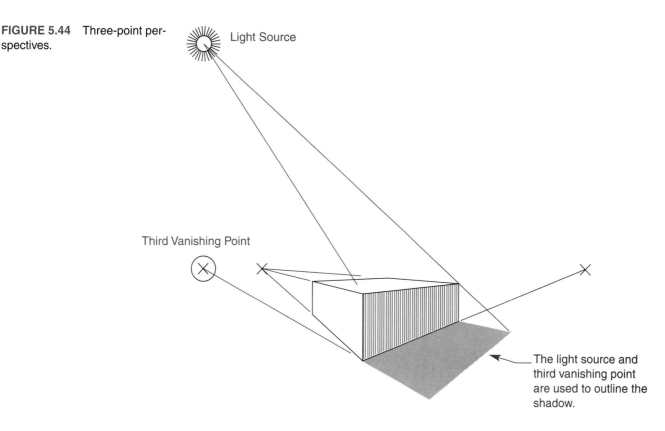

Light Source

Third Vanishing Point

The light source and third vanishing point are used to outline the shadow.

These examples of perspective drawing are very basic. The techniques allow for tremendous detail and complexity. Perspectives really test a drafter's love of drawing; however, the end result can be well worth it.

Computer-Aided 3D Drawings

Before the advent of CAD, pictorials were drawn and constructed on a two-dimensional surface. None of the pictorials were true three-dimensional ones because paper and polyester have no real depth to them. It was only an illusion created by the drafter. Now, with CAD, drawing in 3D is a reality. All the different types of pictorials can be drawn in AutoCAD; however, the fastest way to generate a pictorial is to use true 3D.

Two methods for drawing in true 3D are wireframe and solids. A 3D wireframe is a hollowed-out object (see Figure 5.45). It produces the effect of a glass box. A solid 3D, on the other hand, has solid mass just like an ice cube. The lines behind the solid features can be blocked out very easily (see Figure 5.46).

One problem with 3D drawing is that although the drafter can draw with true lengths, widths, and depths on the computer, when the drawing is printed or plotted it comes out on flat, 2D paper. The best way to view the drawing in 3D is on a computer screen or on a videotape (see Figure 5.47).

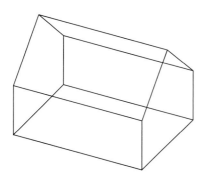

FIGURE 5.45 Example of a 3D wireframe.

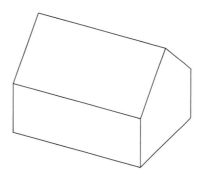

FIGURE 5.46 Example of a 3D solid drawing.

FIGURE 5.47   Rendered 3D
solid. Courtesy of Jason Austin.

FIGURE 5.47   Rendered 3D
solid. Courtesy of Jason Austin.

Presentation Drawings

So far we have discussed construction drawings and working drawings, which are used to make ideas a reality. One drawing area not discussed yet is presentation or marketing drawings. Presentation drawing incorporates all types of drawings in order to sell a design to a client.

Presentation drawings are not detailed like a set of working drawings. Often dimensions are omitted along with other items needed for construction that are not critical when trying to get funding for a project. Typically, a set of architectural presentation drawings includes perspectives, floor plans with basic dimensions, exterior and interior elevations, a very basic site plan, and building sections. See Figure 5.48 for presentation examples.

It is not unusual for a designer or drafter to ink, color, or even render/shade these drawings. These drawings are a designer's selling tool when competing for projects against other design groups. In today's

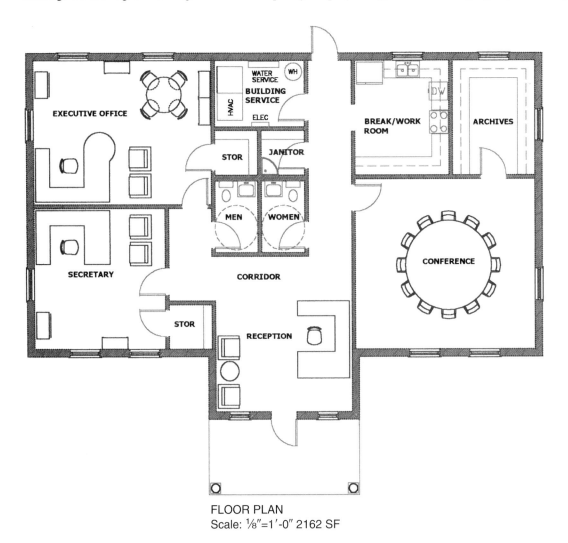

FLOOR PLAN
Scale: ⅛″=1′-0″ 2162 SF

FIGURE 5.48   Presentation drawings.

FIGURE 5.48   *continued*

FRONT ELEVATION
Scale: ⅛″=1′-0″

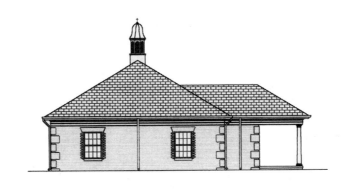

SIDE ELEVATION
Scale: ⅛″=1′-0″

world, with the help of computers and animation software, a designer can walk a client through a virtual building on a computer screen or on a video, producing the most real-life effect possible.

REVIEW QUESTIONS

1. List all the different types of technical drawings.
2. What are the characteristics of a technical drawing?
3. Explain how an auxiliary view is different from an orthographic view.
4. What are some typical sections found in architectural drawings?
5. Sketch an example of an oblique drawing.
6. What are the characteristics of an oblique drawing?
7. Sketch an isometric cube and label the interior angles.
8. Why would a dimetric or trimetric drawing be used instead of an isometric drawing?
9. List all the types of pictorial drawings.
10. What are some disadvantages when drawing dimetrics or trimetrics?
11. Sketch an example of a one-point perspective.
12. What is the purpose of the third vanishing point in perspective drawing?
13. What type of pictorial drawing is a true 3D drawing?
14. When is a pictorial drawing needed? What determines the need for a technical drawing?

EXERCISES

View Identification

EXERCISE 5.1

For the given 3D Figure 5.49, circle the letter of the correct view to match the isometric shown.

EXERCISE 5.2

Sketch out three views for each example in exercise 5.1, using 8 × 8 gridded vellum.

EXERCISE 5.3

Sketch the shapes in Figure 5.50 three times each on 8 × 8 gridded vellum.

1. Find the top view.
Choose a, b, or c.

(a)   (b)   (c)

2. Find the front view.
Choose a, b, or c.

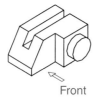

Front

(a)   (b)   (c)

3. Find the front view.
Choose a, b, or c.

 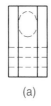 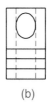 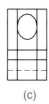

Front

(a)   (b)   (c)

4. Find the front view.
Choose a, b, or c.

Front

(a)   (b)   (c)

FIGURE 5.49   Exercise 5.1.

FIGURE 5.50 Exercise 5.3.
Courtesy of Mirella Lancaster.

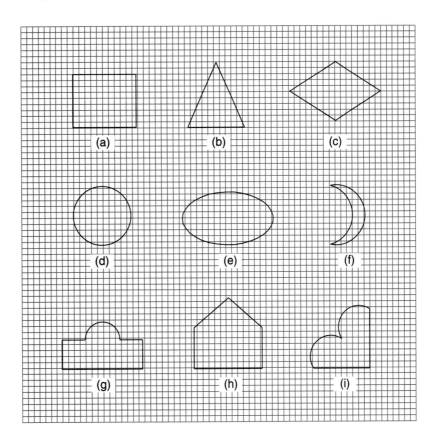

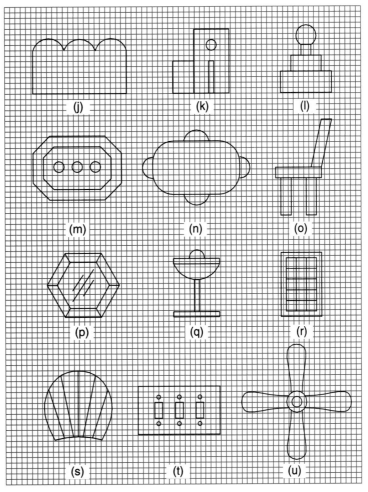

EXERCISE 5.4

Sketch the shapes in Figure 5.51 in isometric form.

EXERCISE 5.5

Sketch figures a, b, d, e, and f from exercise 5.4 in oblique form.

EXERCISE 5.6

Sketch figures c, d, i, j, and k in orthographic form (two views only).

FIGURE 5.51   Exercise 5.4.

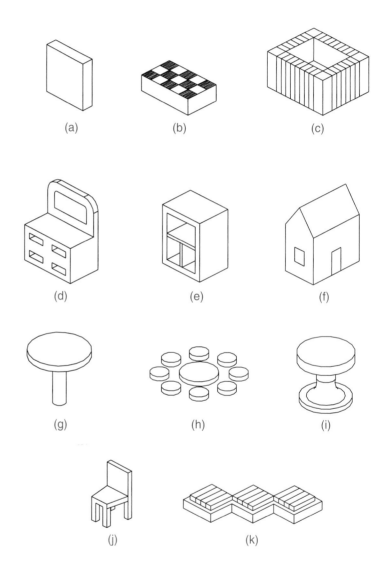

Mechanical Concepts

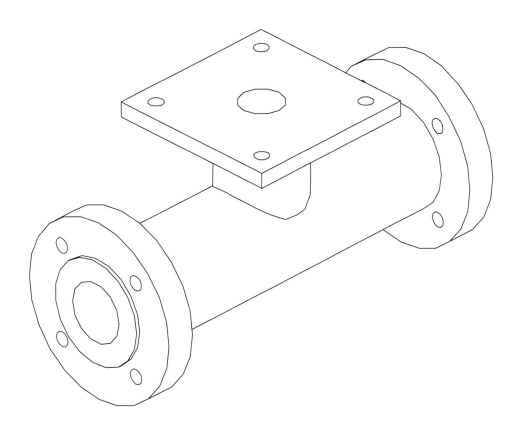

CHAPTER 6

Orthographic Drawing

Orthographic drawing also goes by the names *three-view drawing* and *multiview projection drawing,* among others. We will use the term *orthographic drawing* or *views* in this chapter. The three types of technical drawings used in mechanical or machine drafting are orthographic views, auxiliary views, and sectional views. Orthographic drawing is the most important not only because it is used the most often but because the other technical drawings use the same basic principles.

Basic orthographic concepts were introduced in Chapter 5. Because no skill in technical drawing is more important, this chapter provides a more in-depth look at constructing orthographic views. The majority of all drawings done in the drafting field are technical, so it is necessary to learn and develop a good understanding of orthographics.

People just learning to draw orthographics tend to fall into two categories: those who can look at an object and instantly see the images two-dimensionally in their brain and reproduce them on a drawing versus those who cannot see the two-dimensional image and must work to piece together lines, shapes, and surfaces to construct the drawing. This difference is analogous to that between people who play musical instruments by ear—reproducing the notes they hear in their head—and those who must learn to read musical notes in order to play the music. Do not worry if drawing orthographic views does not come easily right away. It may be a matter of figuring out your particular learning style. The skill will develop over time.

6.1   The Basic Orthographic Layout

As shown previously in Chapter 5, there is a standard layout that must be followed when drawing orthographic views in mechanical or machine drawing. The United States and Canada use a *third-angle projection* alignment, which is shown in Figure 6.1. Third-angle projection is an alignment that rotates each flat projection plane parallel to the viewer's eyes. Many other countries use a *first-angle projection* alignment, which has the exact same views as the third-angle alignment but in different locations, except for the front view, which is still used as the base view from which the other views are projected (see Figure 6.2). The difference is in the rotation or flipping of the object being drawn. In a third angle projection the object is rotated using the corner where the view is located as the pivot line or hinged corner (see Figure 6.3). Although the third-

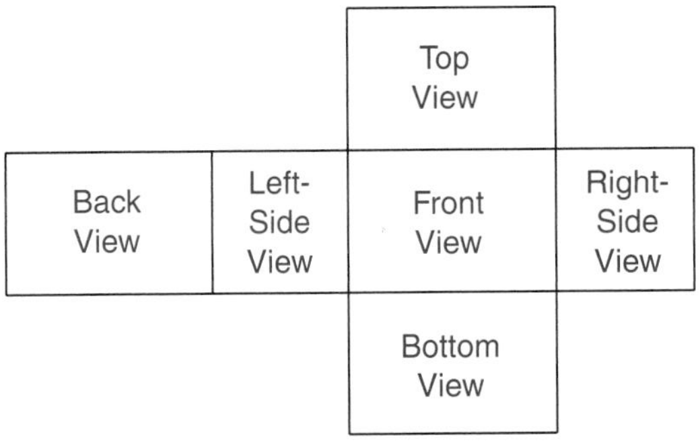

		Top View	
Back View	Left-Side View	Front View	Right-Side View
		Bottom View	

Third-Angle Projection Alignment for Orthographic Views

FIGURE 6.1   Third-angle projection symbol and layout.

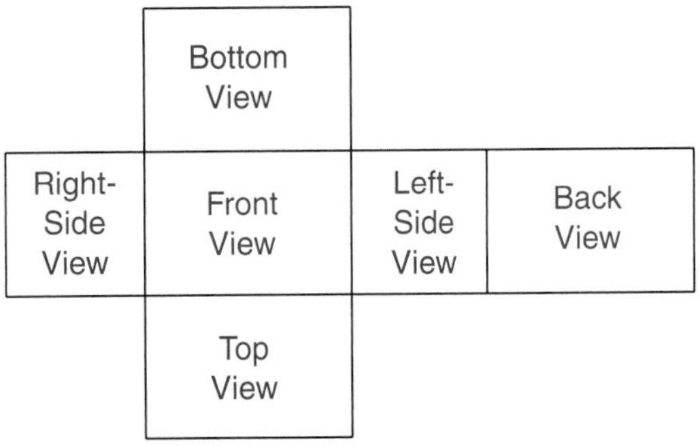

		Bottom View	
Right-Side View	Front View	Left-Side View	Back View
		Top View	

First-Angle Projection for Orthographic Drawing

FIGURE 6.2   First-angle projection symbol and layout.

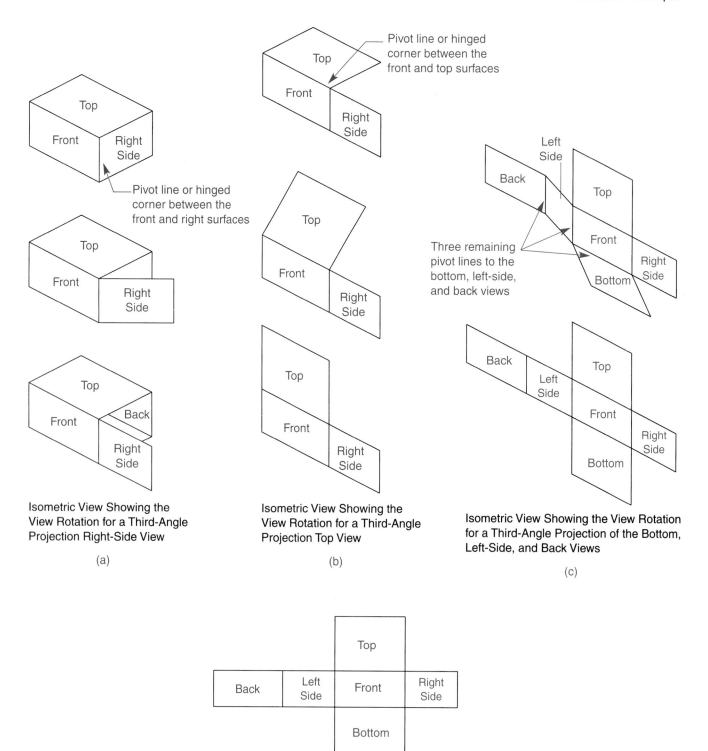

Isometric View Showing the
View Rotation for a Third-Angle
Projection Right-Side View

(a)

Isometric View Showing the
View Rotation for a Third-Angle
Projection Top View

(b)

Isometric View Showing the View Rotation
for a Third-Angle Projection of the Bottom,
Left-Side, and Back Views

(c)

All Six Views in a Flat Orthographic Viewing Plane

(d)

FIGURE 6.3   View rotations for a third-angle projection.

angle projection alignment is the primary format used in the United States, a good drafter must be flexible and be able to adapt to first-angle projection because so many different foreign companies now operate in the United States.

A first-angle projection looks like the opposite of the third-angle format because the first-angle projection views are rotated from the opposite back corner instead of from the front corner, as with third-angle projection (see Figure 6.4). It takes a little time to get used to the rotations. One real challenge is to switch thinking modes when you are working on two different projects and are using third-angle projection on one and first-angle projection on the other. A major mistake would be to combine both systems on the same drawing or project. Universal symbols are used to identify which format is being used on a drawing (see Figure 6.5).

Students typically ask the following questions about the two systems:

1. Why are there two different systems for aligning mechanical drawings?
2. Which method is correct?

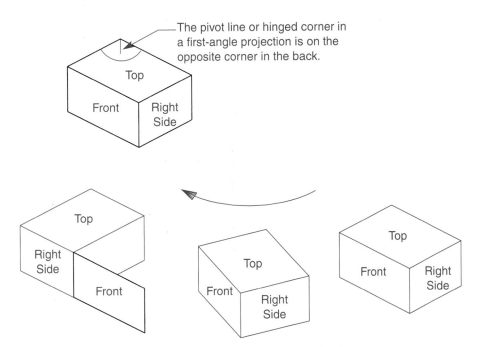

In first-angle projection imagine picking up the object, rotating it 90°, and placing it on the left side of the front view.

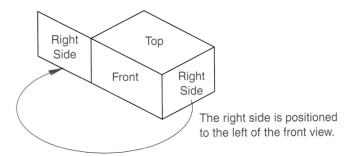

Isometric View Showing the View Rotation for a First-Angle Projection Right-Side View

(a)

FIGURE 6.4 View rotations for a first-angle projection.
continued on next page

FIGURE 6.4   *continued*

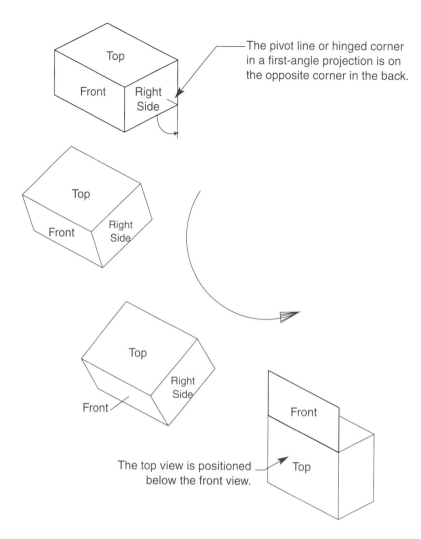

The pivot line or hinged corner in a first-angle projection is on the opposite corner in the back.

The top view is positioned below the front view.

Isometric View Showing the View Rotation for a FIrst-Angle Projection Top View

(b)

FIGURE 6.5   Universal symbols for third-angle and first-angle projections.

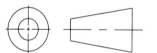   

Third-Angle Projection Symbol

First-Angle Projection Symbol

Let's answer the first question with a question. Why do automobiles in the United States drive on the right-hand side of the road and those in Great Britain and Japan drive on the left? Both ways will get you from point A to point B. The two systems were introduced in different parts of the world and have become a way of life. The difference really is minor to someone who knows the rules. So learn both systems of alignment and be versatile.

As far as determining which method is correct, obviously both are. It just depends on where in the world the parts are to be built. After all, both projection systems should produce the same end product.

6.2   Visualizing the Views

In Figures 5.8 and 5.9 a dice was used to demonstrate how each of its six surfaces can be thought of as an orthographic drawing. An example of a closed door showing only its height and width was used in Figure 5.13

to demonstrate the basic concept of an orthographic drawing. We will build on those concepts to develop your skills even further using a glass-box approach.

The Glass Box

The glass-box technique is a very popular method used to teach students how to draw orthographic views of a three-dimensional object. The best way to start is to picture the object suspended inside a glass box (see Figure 6.6). Real-life examples that may be more familiar to you are a model ship in a glass bottle or a clear paperweight with an object inside it, like a coin. Looking into a corner of the glass box the human eye sees the three-dimensional object in an isometric view (see Figure 6.7a). Now, if the glass box is turned to a flat side or surface parallel to the eyes, the shape flattens out (see Figure 6.7b). This is similar to what you need to visualize when drawing orthographic views. Sometimes if the object is large and you do not have your eyes lined up exactly on the center of the flat surface, the object may still seem three-dimensional, so you must train your eyes to focus on the flat parallel surfaces.

Now, picture the flat glass surface and imagine taking a felt marker and tracing the outline of the object showing only the surfaces parallel to your eyes. This is an orthographic drawing (see Figure 6.8). An ortho-

FIGURE 6.6 An object inside a glass box.

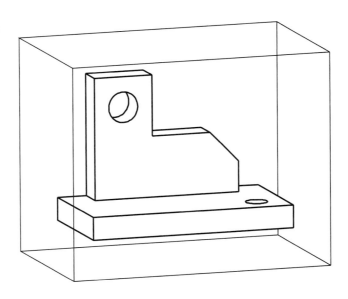

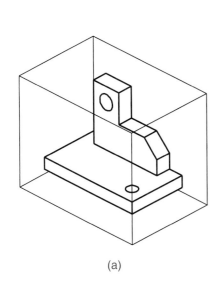

(a)

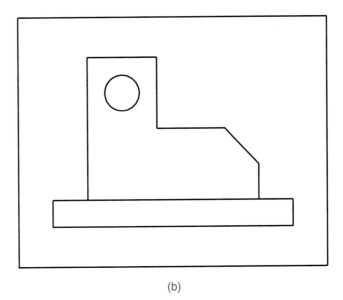

(b)

FIGURE 6.7 (a) Looking into the corner of the glass box.
(b) Looking at a flat surface of the box.

FIGURE 6.8 Outlining the object on the surfaces of the glass box.

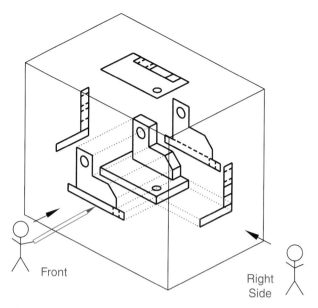

Each view is drawn with no depth perception or three-dimensional effect. The bottom-view and centerlines were omitted for clarity.

FIGURE 6.9 The glass box unfolded in third-angle projection form.

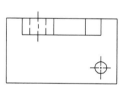

Top View

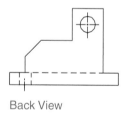

Back View

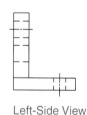

Left-Side View

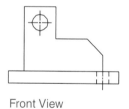

Front View

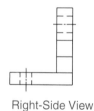

Right-Side View

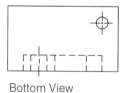

Bottom View

graphic view can thus be traced on each surface of the glass box. It then becomes a matter of unfolding the box to the desired alignment using third-angle projection (see Figure 6.9).

Guidelines for Choosing and Setting Up Views

As shown in Figure 6.9, the orthographic views line up perfectly. Note that once the front view is established, the limits for the other views are set. As Figure 6.10a shows, the outline of the front view is drawn first to set the overall height and width of the part. The outline of the front view can then be extended in the desired directions to lay out the other views (see Figure 6.10b).

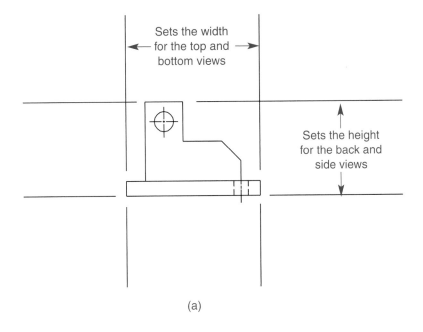

(a)

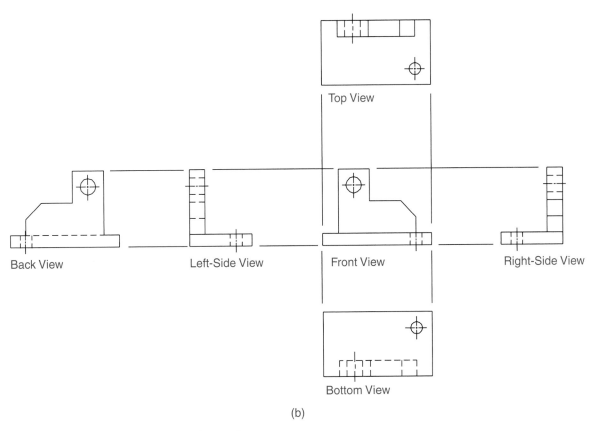

(b)

FIGURE 6.10 Extending the front view perimeter.

FIGURE 6.11   (a) Front view of a gasket. (b) Undistorted geometric shapes.

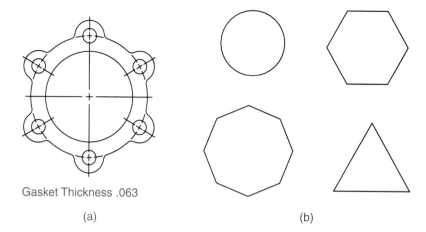

Gasket Thickness .063

(a)   (b)

You as a drafter must decide early on how many views the machinist or builder is going to need to make the part. By now you may have realized that six views are available for use. Six views are normally overkill, repeating information from view to view and taking up too much room. The following are some general rules to help you choose the right number of views:

Rules for Determining the Correct Number of Views

1. Most objects require a minimum of two views. Certain exceptions, such as a thin gasket, can have a front view and a note calling out the thickness (see Figure 6.11a).

2. Use enough views to show the nondistorted geometric shapes found on the object as they appear in true form (see Figure 6.11b).

3. Draw enough views so that all the features can easily be dimensioned later.

Following these rules will help you pick the correct number of orthographic views for each part. Early planning using a rough sketch and shear practice will bring most students up to speed.

You must also determine which surface should be shown as the front view. The best view should be the front view, since it shows the most detail of the object. Look the three-dimensional object over thoroughly to find the best views. Start by choosing the front view, then compare the remaining views to see which one gives the most detail. Use the following guidelines to determine the best views.

Guidelines for Picking the Best Views

1. Look for the view with the fewest hidden lines.

2. Look for the view that shows the best features or geometric shapes.

3. Make the best view the front view based on guidelines 1 and 2.

4. Determine how many views will be needed for the object, and include a spacing of 2″ between each orthographic view. (The 2″ space will allow dimensions to placed later.)

5. If two views are required, choose the second best view using guidelines 1 and 2 (see Figure 6.12a).

6. When three views are needed, choose the best remaining view. Note that the left-side view and the right-side view may show similar features. In this case a top or a bottom view should show a full detailed surface not shown with the front or side views. The combinations in Figure 6.12b and c show some good examples and surfaces as well as some poor ones.

When More Than Three Views Are Required

Sometimes more than three views may be needed to detail the object well enough for a machinist to build it. In almost all these cases the part is fairly complicated. In such instances follow the established guidelines for choosing views, finding all the key features needed for a machinist to build the complete part (see Figure 6.13).

FIGURE 6.12
continued on next page

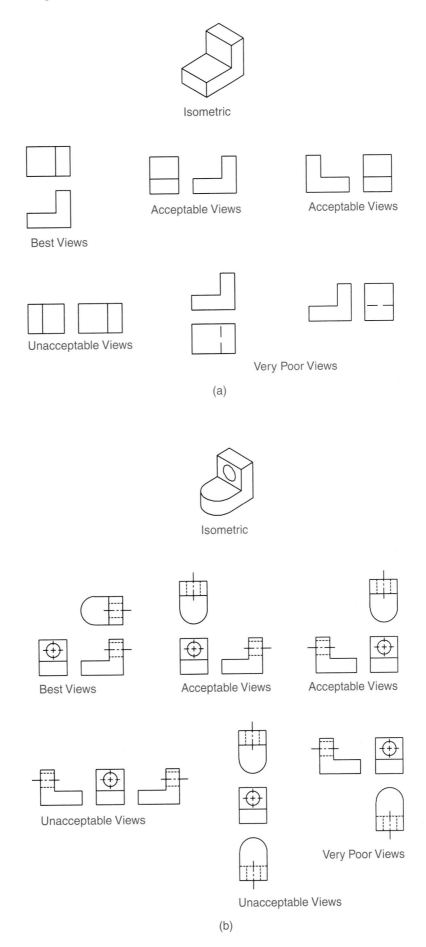

Isometric

Best Views

Acceptable Views

Acceptable Views

Unacceptable Views

Very Poor Views

(a)

Isometric

Best Views

Acceptable Views

Acceptable Views

Unacceptable Views

Very Poor Views

Unacceptable Views

(b)

FIGURE 6.12
continued

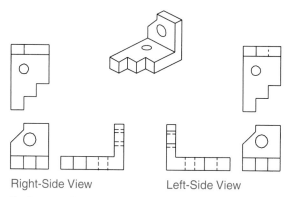

Right-Side View   Left-Side View

Both examples are good orthographic drawings. The left- and the right-side views show the same shape along with the same number of hidden lines, and therefore either is acceptable. Centerlines were omitted in these examples.

(c)

FIGURE 6.13

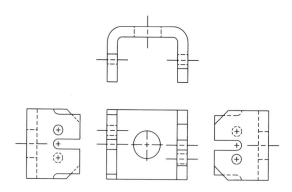

A drawing such as the one in Figure 6.13 can get confusing when views repeat information, such as when a right-side view and a left-side view appear on the same orthographic. A good solution is to use what is called a *partial view*. A partial view allows the drafter to eliminate lines on the lapping views in order to clarify and enhance the readability of the drawing (see Figure 6.14). Notice that partial views may leave out hidden lines and even some visible lines that are found on the view beyond. A drafter may eliminate the lines from the view beyond and let the other side take care of itself when it is rotated out on the other side of the front view (see Figure 6.15).

Remember that the purpose of a partial view is to make an orthographic drawing easier to read. It is not to be used as a shortcut because a drafter does not feel like drawing all the lines in the view. A partial view is not a tool for the lazy.

FIGURE 6.14   Partial views.

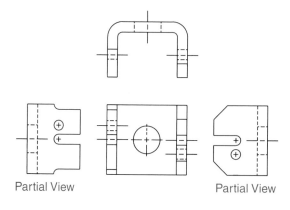

Partial View   Partial View

FIGURE 6.15 Blow-up of side views.

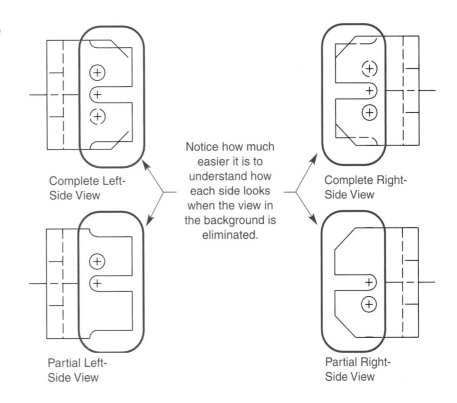

Notice how much easier it is to understand how each side looks when the view in the background is eliminated.

Complete Left-Side View

Complete Right-Side View

Partial Left-Side View

Partial Right-Side View

Minimizing Drafting Time

Before starting a drawing, plan out the views on a sheet of paper, roughly sketching each view using the guidelines previously given in this chapter (see Figure 6.16). Use grid paper if you want to cut down on the roughness of the sketches. This type of planning will cut down on wasted time, energy, and mistakes. Speed is a good trait in a drafter. Most drafters can do a great job on a drawing when given all the time in the world, but some projects are under strict time requirements. If you plan out the drawing ahead of time, surprises along the way should be cut down to a minimum, and you will increase your speed and productivity. No one likes redoing a drawing, but it is a way of life in drafting. Making design changes just feels so much better than correcting mistakes.

Centering the Drawing

Centering the drawing is normally a simple mathematical process. It can be done in the planning and sketching phase and can be quickly learned.

1. Sketch out a title block with borderlines and assign values to the drawing area (see Figure 6.17). These numbers are based on an A size sheet, or 8½″ × 11″.

FIGURE 6.16 Rough sketch of views.

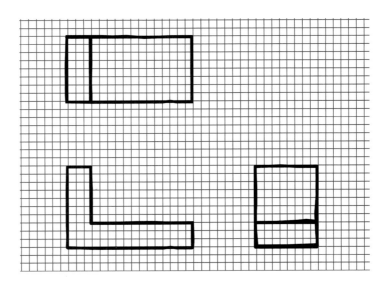

FIGURE 6.17   Drawing area and title block.

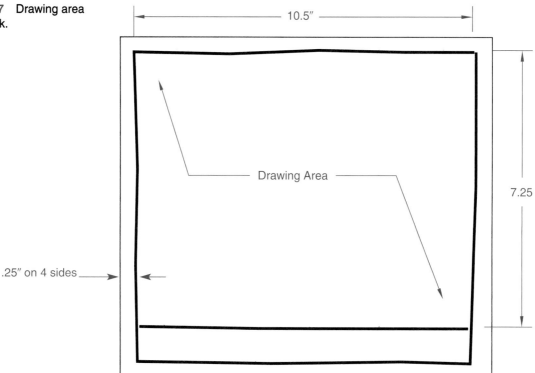

FIGURE 6.18   Views sketched in the drawing area

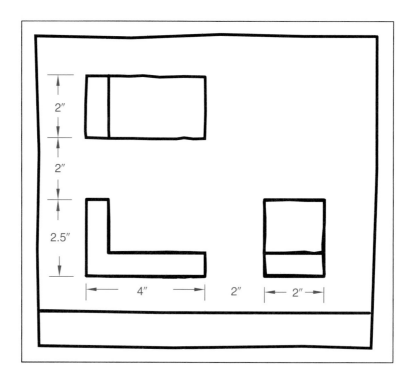

2. Make sure you have the orthographic views you want. Sketch them and include their measurements along with the 2″ spacing callout between all views. The example in Figure 6.18 uses three views.

3. Using the outside lines on the three orthographic views draw a rectangle on their outer perimeter. This rectangle represents the area that will hold the drawing (see Figure 6.19).

4. The next step is to center the area determined in Figure 6.19 inside the drawing sheet border and title block.

FIGURE 6.19 Perimeter of the drawing.

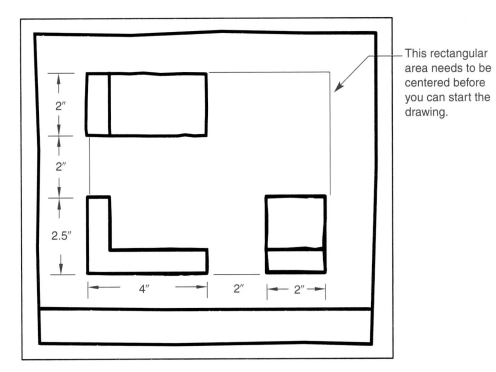

This rectangular area needs to be centered before you can start the drawing.

Example.

- The total height of the drawing area is 7.25″ (see Figure 6.17). The height of the orthographic drawing area is 2″ + 2″ + 2.5″ = 6.5″, which is the width of the top view plus the height of the front view plus the 2″ spacing between them. Once you have calculated this total, subtract it from the total height. In this case, 7.25″−6.5″ = .75″. Divide the .75″ by 2, which gives you a value of .375″. (.75″ / 2 = .375″) This distance will be used to measure down from the top border line and up from the bottom border line (see Figure 6.20).

- Repeat this process for the total width. This example has a total width of 10.5″. The front view is length 4″, the spacing in between views is still 2″, and the width of the right-side view is 2″:

$$4″ + 2″ + 2″ = 8″$$

Subtract the required orthographic width from the total width:

$$10.5″−8″ = 2.5″$$

Now, divide 2.5″ by 2:

$$\frac{2.5″}{2} = 1.25″$$

- The side-to-side centering is determined in the same way. Measure 1.25″ in from both the left-hand border and the right-hand border (see Figure 6.21).

You now have the information to center the complete drawing inside the borders, before even beginning the scaled drawing.

FIGURE 6.20   Centering the drawing top to bottom.

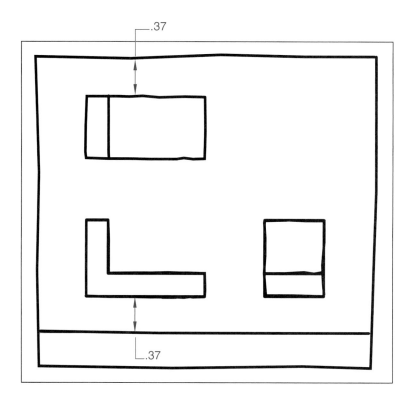

FIGURE 6.21   Centering the drawing side to side.

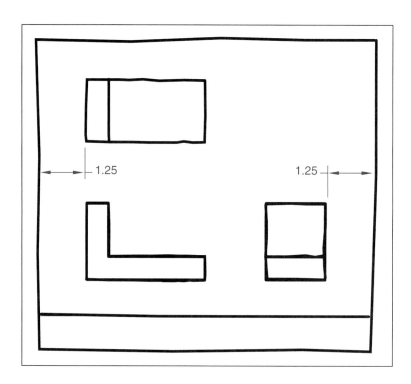

This method works well and needs to be used in the planning stage. Other spacing factors like how close should a view get to the border lines and title block can be addressed ahead of time also. A good rule of thumb is to use the same spacing that you used between orthographic views. In our example we used 2″, but this spacing can vary depending on how many dimensions will be needed. Chapter 9 will discuss spacing for dimensions, but for now 1″ to 2″ is a good range.

6.3 Projecting Shapes in Orthographic Form

Using the glass-box technique is a lot like taking a camera and snapping a picture on all sides of the object. A shape can look totally different when seen from the side or top versus head-on in a front view, when all you can see is going to look flat on paper. Learning how to draw a shape from all possible sides can be an education in itself. As stated earlier in this chapter, some individuals can analyze the orthographic forms from any direction, whereas others must work hard to develop the skill. The following examples will give you a feel for some of the distortion you get on orthographic views.

Circle Distortion

The circle is a good shape to begin with. When you clearly see a circular shape head on in a view, then there is no distortion. The other orthographic views of a circle can fool you, however (see Figure 6.22).

In real life it is quite obvious to the human eye that a hockey puck is not flat on the outside. However, in an orthographic top and side view the puck is drawn in a flat-looking rectangular shape. This shape would need only two views in orthographic form: the front view to see the true circle, and the distorted top or side view to show the depth of the puck. The views work together to show different projected planes.

Figure 6.23 shows an example of half a hockey puck. One end is curved, and the other is perfectly flat. The two different side views do not give any clue as to which surface is curved or flat. How can they when they project the same shape? The front view is the key piece of information, and if the drafter is using third-angle projection, then the left side is flat, and the right side is curved. This example reinforces that it is important to select the best view to be the front view. It is extremely important to find all true circular shapes and show them as circles. How is a machinist going to build a circular shape if you never show it in circular form?

Now look at some combination curves and observe some of their characteristics in Figure 6.24. Notice what it takes for a curve to generate lines in the side and top views. Notice that if the tangent circles and arcs on the outside occur at the top and bottom quadrants, lines will be drawn on the right-side view. If the tan-

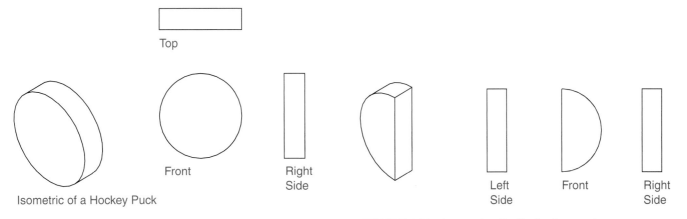

FIGURE 6.22 Isometric of a hockey puck.

FIGURE 6.23 Isometric of half a hockey puck.

FIGURE 6.24 Combination curves.

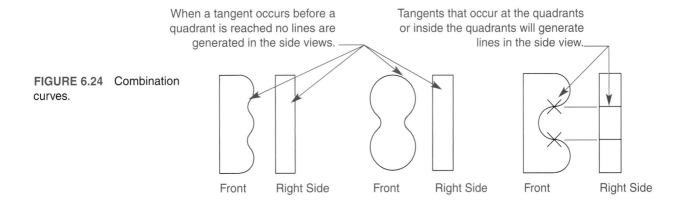

FIGURE 6.25   Angle distortion
in orthographic views.

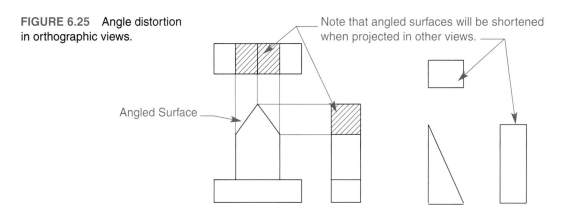

Note that angled surfaces will be shortened
when projected in other views.

Angled Surface

gents occur inside the quadrants, hitting a little more to the left, lines will still be shown. Examine Figure 6.24 very closely to see where the quadrants occur, then look at other views to see when a line is generated. The more of them you see, the easier it becomes to figure out when a line will be generated.

Angled Surface Distortion

Curved surfaces are not the only ones that cause distortion in different views. An angled surface even though it comprises straight lines will be distorted on views where the angle is not shown in profile. Check out the orthographic views in Figure 6.25 for an example of angle distortion. The front view is very descriptive in showing where the angle is formed. The other two views primarily show the depth of the surface. If a view is needed to show the true shape being formed on the angled surface, then an auxiliary view (see Chapter 5 and 7) may be used to get a nondistorted surface view.

Distortion in orthographic views is quite common. The main objective is to have enough views so the true shape is seen at least once in a view or can easily be laid out by a machinist with dimensions from the views that are given. Remember that drafting is a form of graphic communication, and your job as a drafter is to let your drawing speak for you and cover every detail necessary for the building of the part.

Hidden Lines on Orthographic Views

A fundamental concept in the rules for choosing the best views is to avoid hidden lines. Avoiding them means choosing the views with the *fewest* hidden lines. You cannot avoid hidden lines entirely, and they will occur frequently. When you draw orthographic views without hidden lines, look really closely to see if you have missed any. Only very basic objects with very little detail do not have hidden lines somewhere (see Figure 6.26). These are very basic shapes to draw. A lot of fairly easy drawings will generate hidden lines, so the question most beginners need answered is, How do you find hidden lines on an orthographic view? Drafting instructors know that looking is one thing and seeing is another for a student.

FIGURE 6.26   Basic shapes.

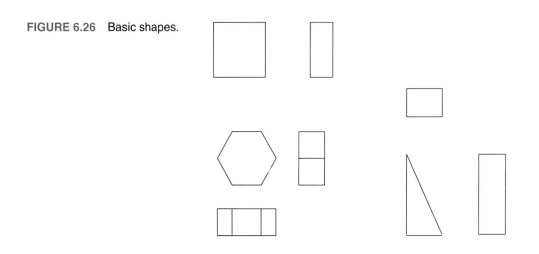

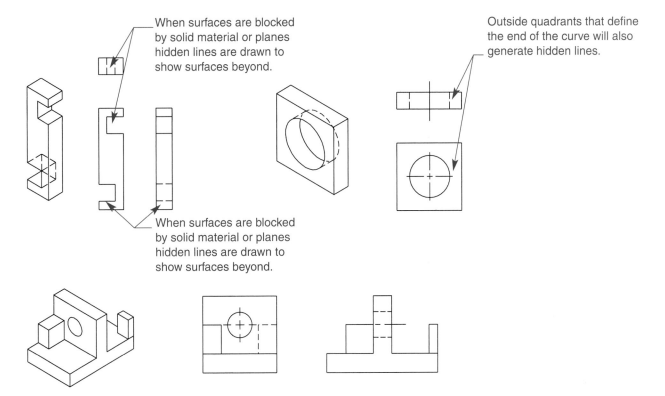

When surfaces are blocked by solid material or planes hidden lines are drawn to show surfaces beyond.

Outside quadrants that define the end of the curve will also generate hidden lines.

When surfaces are blocked by solid material or planes hidden lines are drawn to show surfaces beyond.

FIGURE 6.27 Hidden lines.

Note: Hidden lines also need to be examined in CAD drawings. In AutoCAD the spacing of lengths and gaps can easily be adjusted with a Linetype Scale command; however, the hidden line techniques shown in Figure 6.28 are not always executed in AutoCAD. Be aware of this when drawing with AutoCAD later on in the text.

In an orthographic drawing, a hidden line is developed when a solid object is blocking other lines or surfaces in the flat orthographic viewing plane. Remember the glass box and how objects are drawn flat on the glass plane? Well, if you cannot see around a big flat surface, then hidden lines are used to identify those surfaces that cannot be seen (see Figure 6.27). As you can see, it does not take much for an object to generate hidden lines. A hollowed-out piece or a blocked extruded part will require hidden lines on the orthographic.

Hidden lines need to be drawn according to a set of guidelines. Look at the examples in Figure 6.28 showing hidden line techniques for various conditions. Proper hidden line length and spacing make a draw-

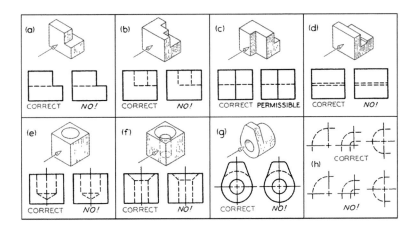

FIGURE 6.28 Hidden line techniques.

ing look more professional. Being consistent on a board drawing takes practice. Use the recommended spacing (⅛″ length with ¹⁄₁₆″ gaps) from Chapter 3's alphabet of lines (Figure 3.8). An exception to this rule occurs when hidden lines are drawn on very thin pieces (.25″ or less). In these cases, the hidden lines can be shorter.

Centerlines

Next in the drawing sequence of an orthographic view is placing the centerlines on the drawing. In mechanical drawing, the centerlines and center marks are used to show symmetry and balance as well as to help locate the exact center for dimensioning and building the part.

Center tick marks need to be drawn when round shapes are seen in a view, as shown in Figure 6.29. The center tick marks should be ⅛″ long with ¹⁄₁₆″ gaps between the tick marks and the centerline, which should extend ⅜″ outside the largest circle. These lines will be used later on when dimensioning to the center of an object.

Centerlines are also drawn along the surface where the circular form is not seen. This helps show the path that the circle is running along and also helps identify the circle even though it may not be visible in a particular view (see Figure 6.30). Notice again that the centerlines extend ⅜″ outside the visible lines. It could cause confusion if they stopped at the visible lines. Extending them out only ⅜″ will keep them from interfering with dimension lines later on.

Overlapping Lines

Lines will overlap on occasion, which causes problems when a drawing is being read. The solution is to prioritize the lines and make the most important lines override the others. Use the following guidelines to rank lines and eliminate less important ones.

FIGURE 6.29   Center tick marks.

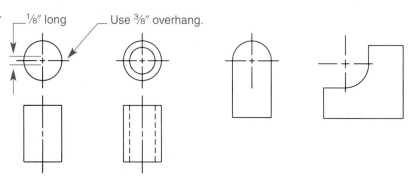

FIGURE 6.30   Drawing center-lines and center tick marks.

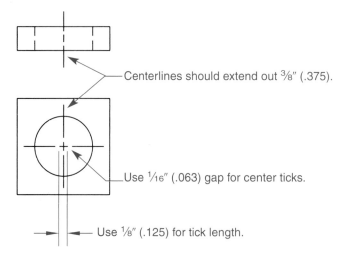

Centerlines should extend out ⅜″ (.375).

Use ¹⁄₁₆″ (.063) gap for center ticks.

Use ⅛″ (.125) for tick length.

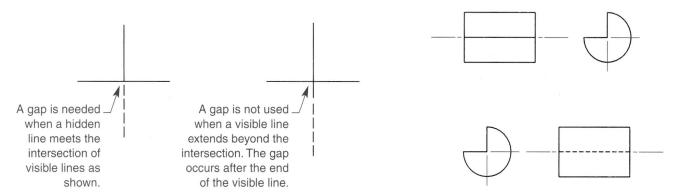

A gap is needed when a hidden line meets the intersection of visible lines as shown.	A gap is not used when a visible line extends beyond the intersection. The gap occurs after the end of the visible line.

FIGURE 6.31 Drawing hidden lines at intersections.

FIGURE 6.32 Drawing centerlines.

Guidelines for Overlapping Lines

1. Visible lines are the most important and should always be shown instead of hidden lines or centerlines when lapping occurs. If visible lines lap other visible lines, then only one standard-width visible line is drawn. Trying to make lines wider when lapping occurs may make a drawing only harder to read and should be avoided.

2. Hidden lines are the second most important and always override centerlines. Make sure to use the hidden-line techniques discussed earlier in the chapter when lines get close. See Figure 6.31 for examples.

3. Centerlines are the least important but the most flexible when it comes to placement. They can be placed off the drawing if needed, unlike visible and hidden lines, which have an exact location (see Figure 6.32).

Fillets and Rounds

Sharp corners on objects are not always desirable on the finished product. Small curves can be placed in those areas of the drawing to generate a smooth transition between the intersection of surfaces such as the ones seen in Figure 6.33. The internal corners are called *fillets* (pronounced 'fi-lets) and the external ones are known as *rounds*. A standard diameter of ¼″ (.250) is the most commonly used. For a curved surface to be considered a fillet or round it can be no larger than ¼″ in diameter. This may not seem very important, but it does make a difference when it comes to projecting lines on orthographic views. Any curve larger than a ¼″ (.250) diameter will not generate lines when drawn on the intersections of surfaces or planes (see Figure 6.34). Just remember to treat a standard-size fillet and round like a normal corner with a sharp intersection

FIGURE 6.33 Fillets, rounds, and runouts.

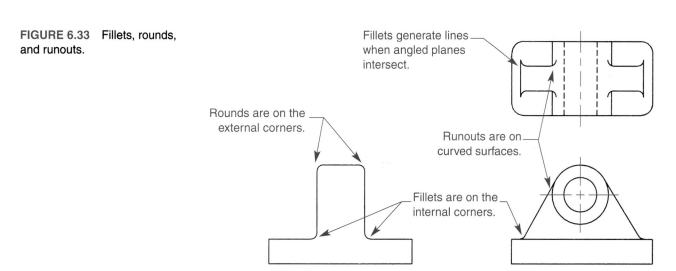

Fillets generate lines when angled planes intersect.

Rounds are on the external corners.

Runouts are on curved surfaces.

Fillets are on the internal corners.

FIGURE 6.34

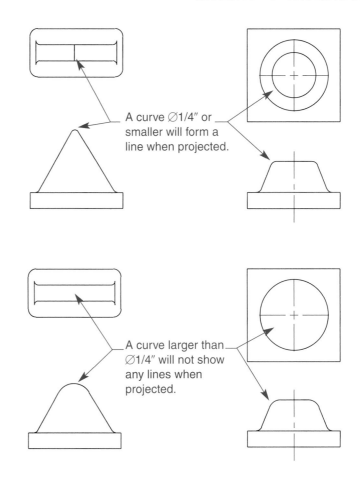

A curve ∅1/4″ or smaller will form a line when projected.

A curve larger than ∅1/4″ will not show any lines when projected.

when projecting it to another view. These ¼″ sizes are used to smooth out rough edges and not to remove lines in the other orthographic views.

Runouts on Curves

When angled surfaces or ribs intersect curved surfaces, a *runout* is used to blend the surfaces together (see Figure 6.33). Once again a ¼″ diameter is used as standard unless specified elsewhere on the drawing. Projecting the runouts correctly on other views will take a little time and practice. A big key to showing the views correctly is determining whether a tangent occurs. Tangents do not ever generate lines, but the runouts are shown in all the views (see Figure 6.35). If a rib intersects instead of creating a tangent, then a line is shown in addition to the runout curves.

FIGURE 6.35 Tangent runouts.

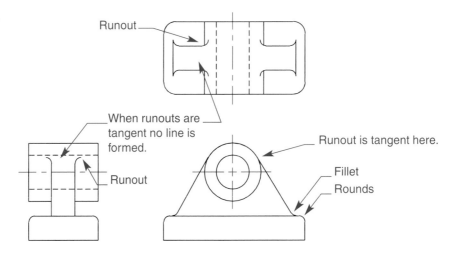

Runout

When runouts are tangent no line is formed.

Runout

Runout is tangent here.

Fillet

Rounds

6.4   Transferring Views and Plotting Points

The six orthographic views repeatedly use the same three dimensions of parts, namely, length, height, and width (see Figure 6.36). Various techniques are used to speed up the transfer of measurements from one view to another.

The Scale Technique

Measure each dimension with a scale every time you draw it. This process can be quite slow sometimes (see Figure 6.37).

The Divider Technique

You can use the dividers in your drafting kit to transfer existing sizes or dimensions to additional views (see Figure 6.38).

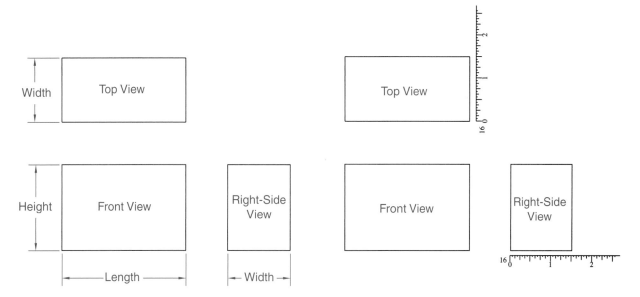

FIGURE 6.36   Standard dimensions.

FIGURE 6.37   Measuring dimensions.

FIGURE 6.38   Transferring dimensions with dividers.

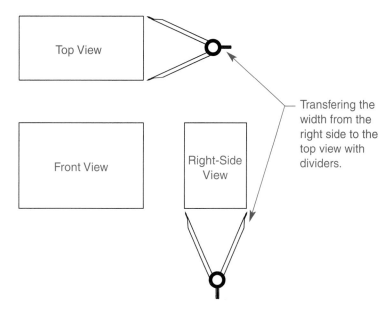

Transferring the width from the right side to the top view with dividers.

The Angled-Line Technique Using 45°

The angled-line method uses angled lines to transfer existing measurements from one view to the next. It works well on views that are at 90° increments to each other. On the top view extend the back horizontal line to the right if drawing a top and right-side view, then extend the far right-hand vertical line on the right-side view up until it intersects the previously drawn horizontal line off the top view (see Figure 6.39a). Now, draw a 45° angled line through this intersection in toward the existing front view (see Figure 6.39b). Once this line is in place you can transfer measurements along the depth direction from the top view to the right side or vice versa (see Figure 6.39c).

Transferring existing measurements to other views will cut down on your drawing time. A good example is the height of a part on the front view. You must measure it correctly with a scale the first time on the front view, but then you can transfer that height with your tools using a horizontal line if you need a right-side, left-side, or back view (see Figure 6.40a). You can use the width of the front, top, and bottom views the same way to draw vertical lines using your tools (see Figure 6.40b).

Use each view as a guide to help develop the others. Lining up the views on one another also helps eliminate mistakes that may be generated by much manual remeasuring. Of course, transferring measurements does not eliminate having to use a scale but only reduces the number of times is has to be used. When you use a scale, double-check your measurement to avoid transferring an incorrect measurement to the other orthographic views.

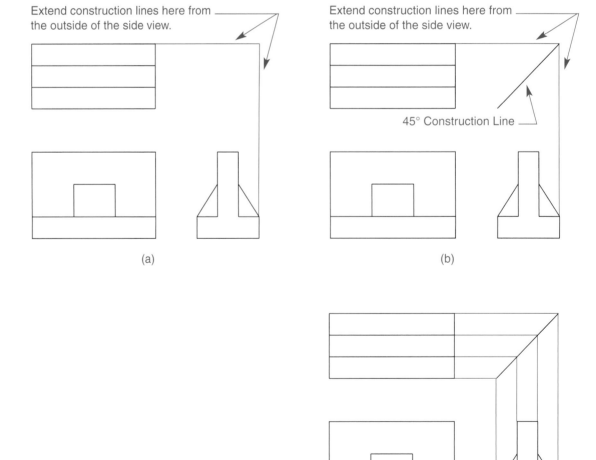

FIGURE 6.39 Using the angled-line technique to transfer dimensions.

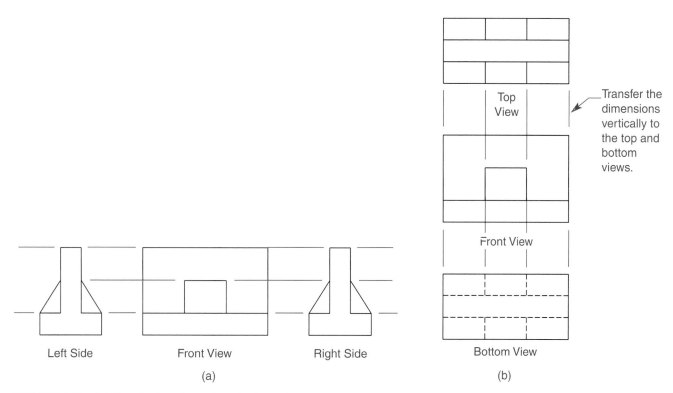

FIGURE 6.40   (a) Transferring dimensions horizontally.
(b) Transferring dimensions vertically.

Plotting Points

You will often need to plot out views in order to get the correct shape in the desired orthographic view. The angle technique can help with plotting on curved and angled surfaces. The following example shows how to plot a curved shape on a top view (see Figure 6.41).

FIGURE 6.41

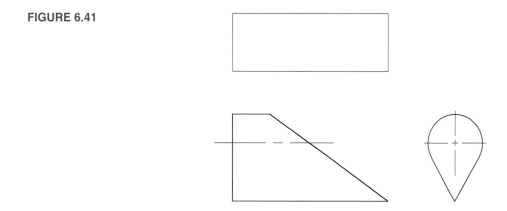

Example: Plotting a Curved Shape

Plot out the curves on the angled surface using the front and right-side views.

1. Go to the view where the circle is true, and divide it into equal parts. This example uses 30° increments along the circle. More increments may be used for a more accurate plot (see Figure 6.42a).

2. Transfer the new points to the front view's angled surface using horizontal lines (see Figure 6.42b).

3. Next, draw vertical lines from the intersections on the angled surface up toward the top view. Numbering the intersections is a way to keep track of your lines (see Figure 6.42c).

4. Now, locate the 45° angled line for transferring points and measurements from the right-side view to the top (see Figure 6.42d).

5. Once you have drawn the 45° measuring line, go to the right-side view and draw vertical lines up from the division points on the curved surface to the 45° line (see Figure 6.42e).

6. Draw horizontal lines from the intersections on the 45° angled line toward the top view, intersecting the ones drawn earlier. Draw the lines one at a time and place a point and number where they intersect with the corresponding lines and numbers projected from the front view (see Figure 6.42f).

7. When you have placed all the points on the top view, darken in the view. Use a French curve if you do not have a template that fits the curve. Take your time and do a good job (see Figure 6.42g).

It takes some time to plot out the shape, but take the time to get it right. Angled surfaces can be plotted out using the same method. Just plot where the corners are, then connect the points with a straight line (see Figure 6.43).

All the techniques used in orthographic drawing will work on the other technical drawings (auxiliary views and sections). Once you understand orthographic drawings, the other technical drawings will seem easy because they use and build on the same principles. Orthographic knowledge will be the key to guiding you through the technical drawing world.

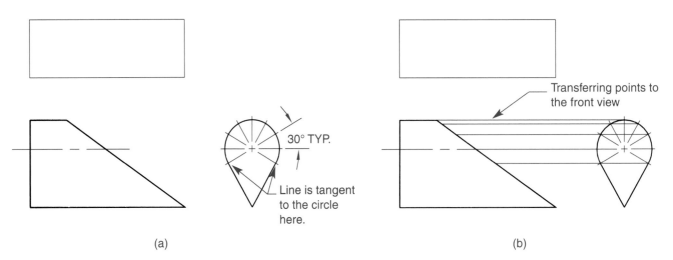

FIGURE 6.42   Plotting a curved shape.

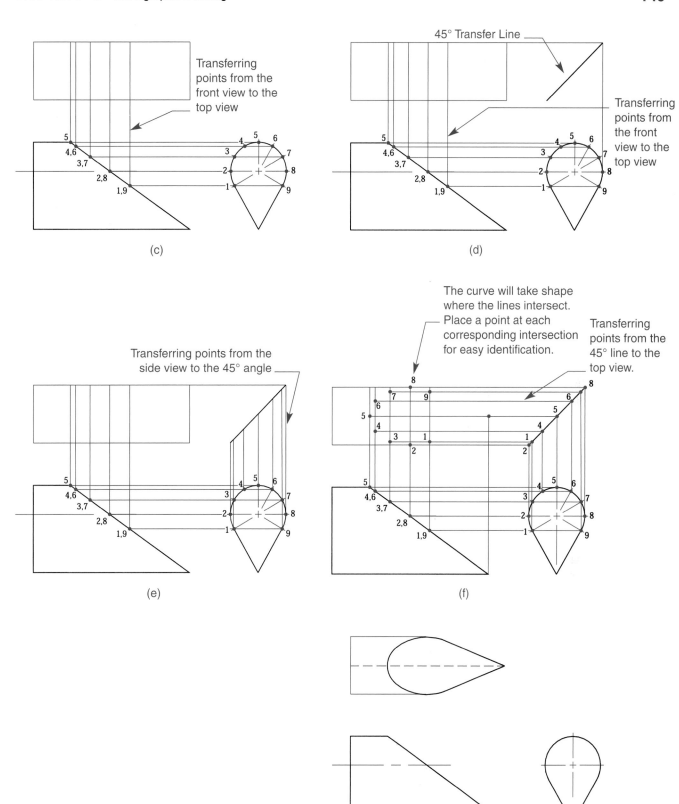

FIGURE 6.42 *continued*

FIGURE 6.43   Plotting angled surfaces.

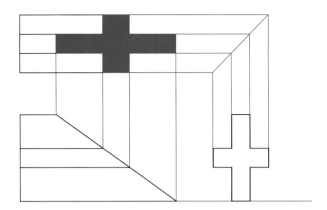

6.5   Tricks of the Trade

The key to orthographics is visualization, whether it comes naturally or is a learned concept for you. Understanding that round objects or angled surfaces can appear as rectangular shapes will give you confidence in your drawing.

In the beginning, students need a three-dimensional shape or drawing (pictorial) to visualize. Holding the object in your hand and lining it up parallel with your eyes verifies in your mind what the view should look like, but this convenience does not always exist in the real world. Sometimes a rough three-dimensional sketch or drawing is handed to the drafter to develop the orthographic views. Occasionally some rough orthographic views are sketched or drawn out and it is up to the drafter to transform them into usable orthographic drawings.

Taking one or two views and developing the others can seem challenging. Some companies will give a drafting test that includes a minimum amount of information when they are interviewing candidates for drafting positions. Mechanical companies like to test the visualization ability of prospective drafting candidates, often by giving a problem in which one or two views are given and the others are to be sketched or drawn.

The best way to prepare for these types of situations is to practice and gain experience. Seeing all the possible ways a drawing can be developed over a period of time is a valuable lesson. Figure 6.44 gives a few examples for you to study. The best way to play this game of hide and seek is to not assume anything because the shapes change depending on your viewpoint. Always ask yourself, What possible shapes can generate a rectangular outline? The answer is, a large number! (see Figure 6.45). Always second-guess the rectangular shape when analyzing a problem because too many other shapes also can form a rectangle. Explore all the

FIGURE 6.44   Typical geometry on drawings.

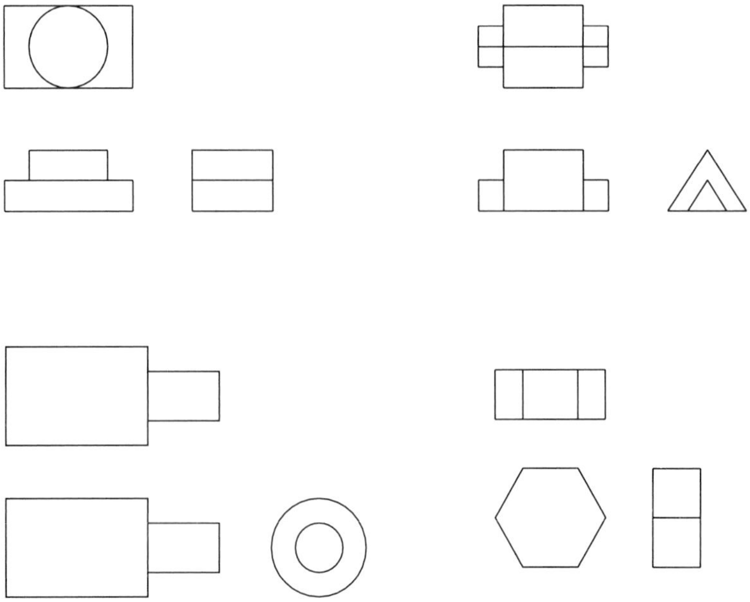

FIGURE 6.45

Rectangular
View

Possible end views for the given rectangle

options to find the different solutions. Work with all the given information to nail down the real shape of an object. If you are given a bare minimum of information on a company's test, show a few possible solutions just to let them know you can see multiple solutions.

Developing a Front View into a Pictorial

A good way to grasp what a part may look like is to turn it into a pictorial view. For a beginner, developing an oblique drawing is an easy technique to learn and use. Start by sketching an orthographic view (see Figure 6.46a). Next, give the orthographic view an oblique form. To do this you must choose a standard oblique angle such as 30°, 45°, or 60°. Thirty degrees works well in most cases, so try it first. Draw your angled lines at each corner in a direction that produces the fewest lines crossing into the part (see Figure 6.46b). Use short equal distances on each angled line. Now, connect the endpoints with lines parallel to the front side (see Figure 6.46c). This is a great method to use for visualizing what an object could look like. Figure 6.46d shows the orthographic views of these simple parts. Although the parts are simple, this method is a great learning tool for working with a bare minimum of information.

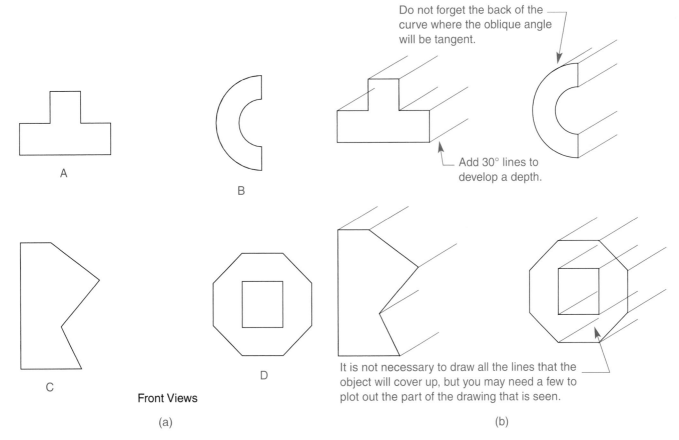

Do not forget the back of the curve where the oblique angle will be tangent.

Add 30° lines to develop a depth.

It is not necessary to draw all the lines that the object will cover up, but you may need a few to plot out the part of the drawing that is seen.

A

B

C

D

Front Views

(a)

(b)

FIGURE 6.46
continued on next page

FIGURE 6.46
continued

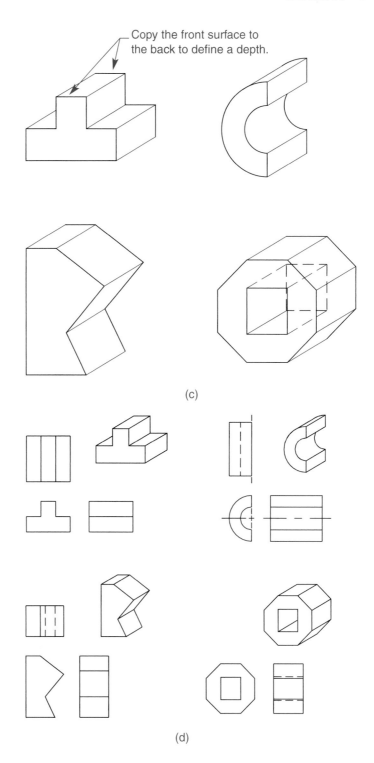

Copy the front surface to the back to define a depth.

(c)

(d)

Here is another technique for exercising the left side of your brain. The examples in Figure 6.47 show three orthographic views per object, but some of the views are missing lines. A good way to find the missing lines is to develop an oblique or isometric drawing with the given orthographic information. It takes time to develop this skill, but it is well worth the endeavor.

Company drafting tests are not designed to trick you but instead are used to find out if a candidate knows the trade. Learn the shapes and embrace the challenges. Drafting is a profession that must be practiced and learned.

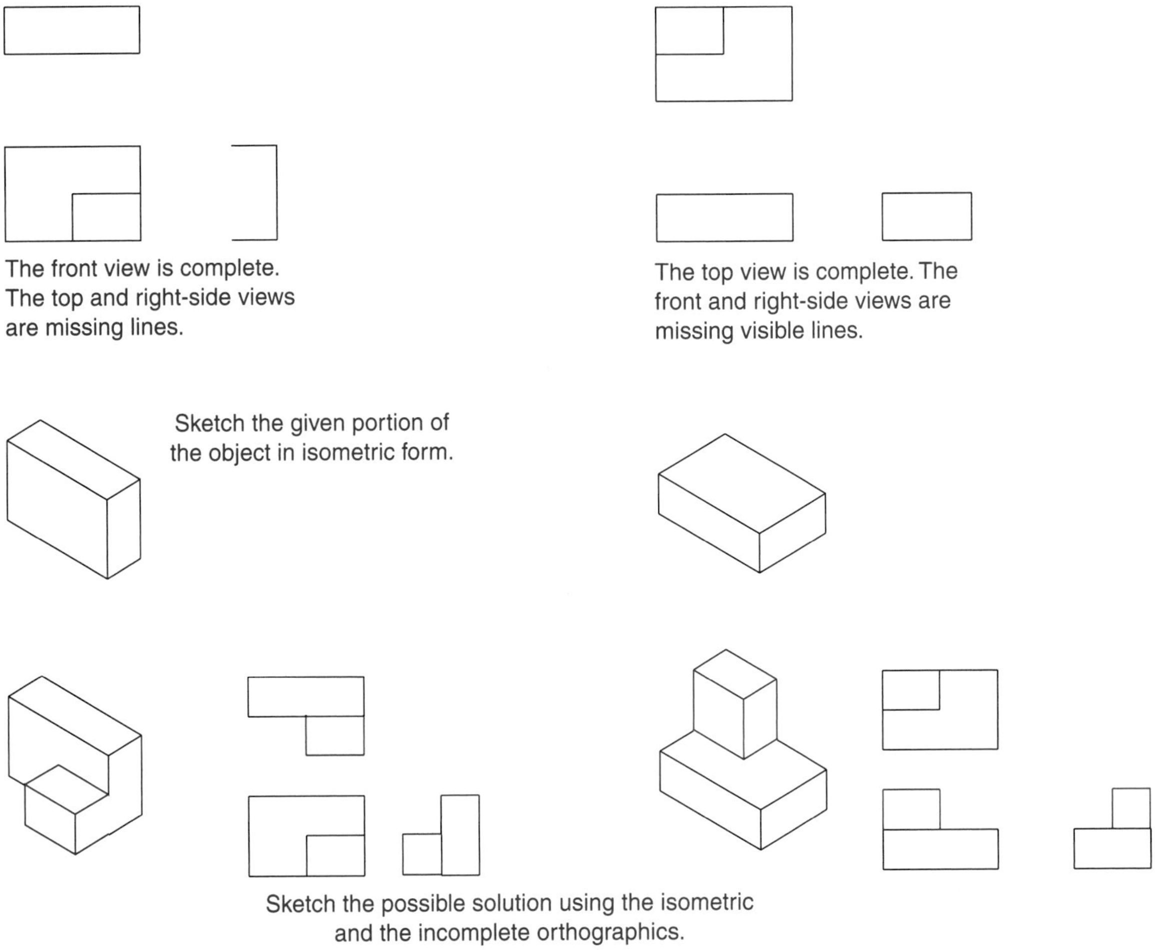

The front view is complete.
The top and right-side views
are missing lines.

The top view is complete. The
front and right-side views are
missing visible lines.

Sketch the given portion of
the object in isometric form.

Sketch the possible solution using the isometric
and the incomplete orthographics.

FIGURE 6.47

REVIEW QUESTIONS

1. How many orthographic views can be projected from an object?
2. What type of object would require only one orthographic view?
3. Explain the difference between third-angle projection and first-angle projection.
4. Sketch the symbol that represents first-angle projection drawing.
5. How are hidden lines formed in orthographic drawings?
6. Explain the difference among fillets, rounds, and runouts.
7. Give some instances when centerlines should be used on orthographic views.
8. Sometimes different linetypes will overlap or stack on each other in orthographic views. Which linetypes have priorities over other linetypes?
9. What factors should be considered when selecting the best orthographic views?
10. Give an example of when a partial view may be helpful.

EXERCISES

EXERCISE 6.1
Sketch the given pictorials in Figure 6.48 in orthographic form. Choose the best three views. Sketch each exercise in third-angle projection form, then repeat the assignment in first-angle projection form.

EXERCISE 6.2

Draw the pictorials in Figure 6.49 in orthographic form. Choose the best three views and alternate between first-angle and third-angle projection formats.

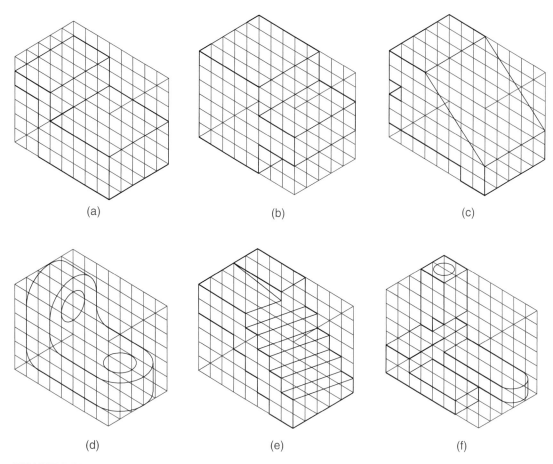

(a)   (b)   (c)

(d)   (e)   (f)

FIGURE 6.48   Exercise 6.1.

FIGURE 6.49   Exercise 6.2

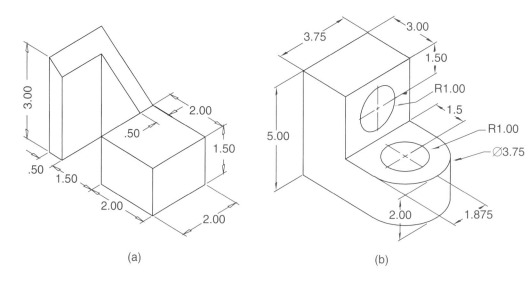

(a)   (b)

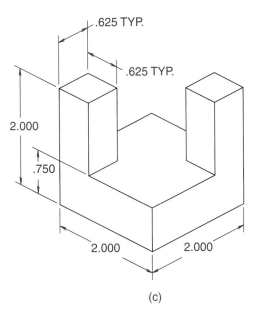

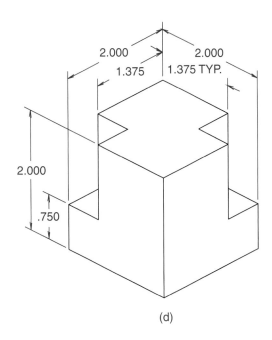

(c)

(d)

FIGURE 6.49 *continued*

DRAWING ASSIGNMENTS

Construct the required orthographic views for the given pictorials in Figure 6.50. Pick a sheet size and scale that will give the drawing a clearance of 2″ from the borders. Use your school's standard title block or the one shown earlier in Chapter 3.

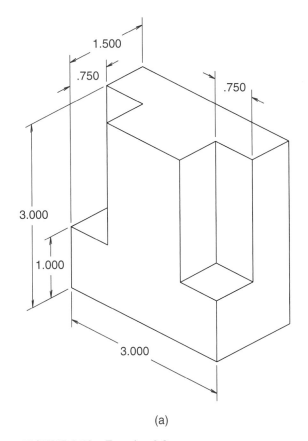

(a)

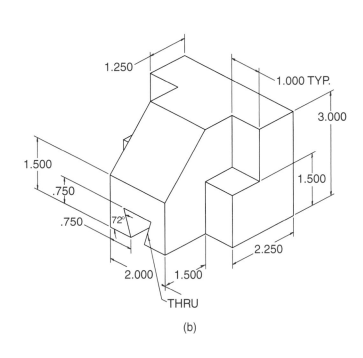

(b)

FIGURE 6.50 ○ Exercise 6.3
continued on next page

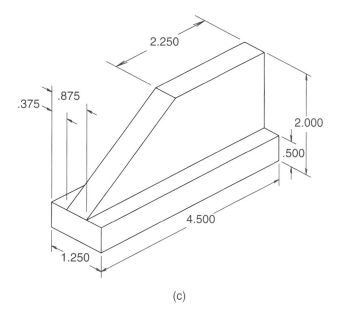

(c)

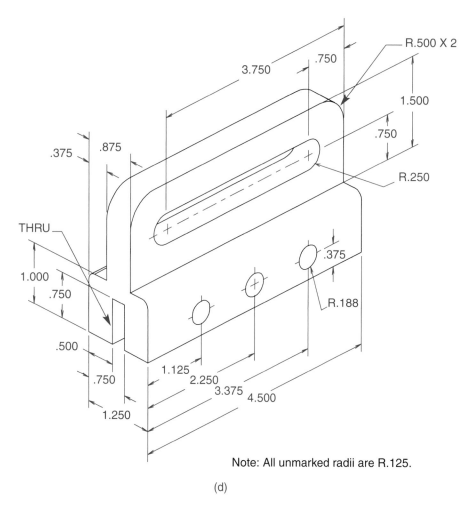

Note: All unmarked radii are R.125.

(d)

FIGURE 6.50
continued

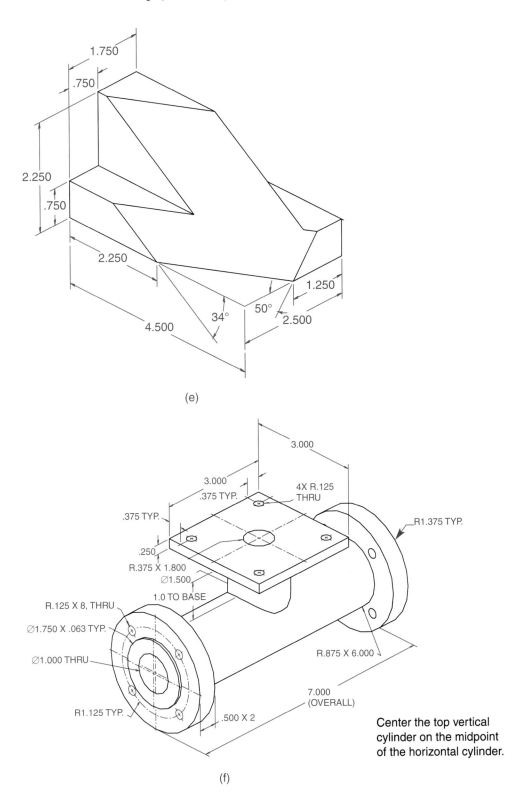

(e)

(f)

Center the top vertical
cylinder on the midpoint
of the horizontal cylinder.

FIGURE 6.50
continued on next page

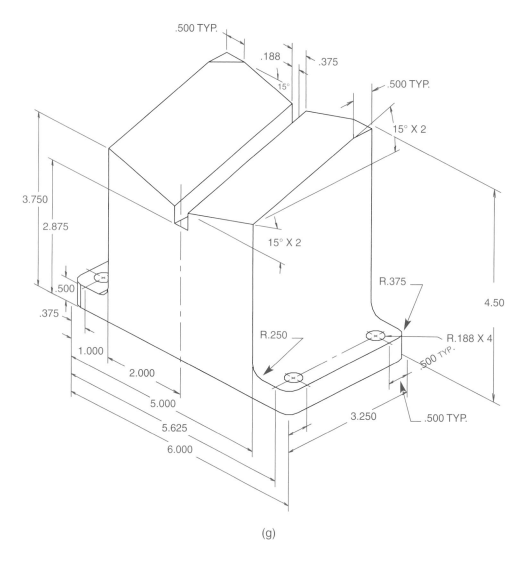

(g)

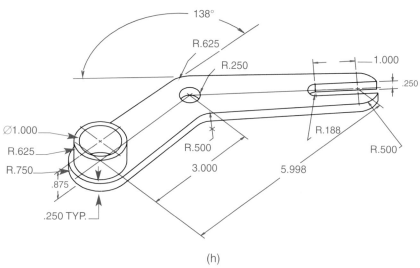

(h)

FIGURE 6.50
continued

Auxiliary Views

Auxiliary views were introduced in Chapter 5 as a part of the overview of technical drawings. Auxiliary views can be used in various ways on drawings not only to show true surfaces but also to revolve the whole object, allowing a look at endless viewpoints. In this chapter we will look at primary and secondary auxiliary views as they are predominantly used in technical drawings.

7.1 Principles of Auxiliary Views

If you understand how to project orthographic views, you have a foundation for learning how to draw auxiliary views. The concept is very similar and easy to transfer to auxiliary drawing.

You may be wondering why, if these two types of drawing are so closely related, auxiliary views are needed. Well, orthographic views work well when surfaces are parallel to the viewing plane and no distortion occurs. Recall that angled surfaces cause distortion, and the true surface is not seen in a normal orthographic view. The solution was to develop a view that shows the true shape of an angled surface.

Think of an auxiliary view as a helper. When orthographic views are not adequate to fully describe a part, then an auxiliary may be used to complete the job. For example, Figure 7.1 shows an object with an angled surface that has a hole drilled in it. The orthographic views do not show all the true shapes needed to describe the part to a machinist. Using an auxiliary view in this case shows the true angled surface as well as the true circle perpendicular through it. You can see how this extra view helps show the hole as a circle in the shaded auxiliary view.

FIGURE 7.1

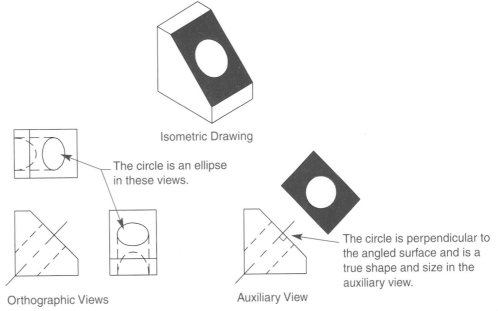

Isometric Drawing

The circle is an ellipse in these views.

Orthographic Views

Auxiliary View

The circle is perpendicular to the angled surface and is a true shape and size in the auxiliary view.

7.2   Projecting Primary Auxiliary Views

A primary auxiliary view is projected off an angled surface on an orthographic view. It can come off any of the orthographic views. The auxiliary surface is flipped or rotated much like in the orthographic layout. Recall the hinged glass box used to explain orthographic projection. A corner is used as a pivoting hinge, and the box is unfolded (see Figure 7.2). In the case of the auxiliary view, imagine that the glass box has an angle shaped like the object. In the auxiliary view the angled corner on the box acts as the pivoting hinge, allowing the surface to be rotated 90° out in perfect alignment with the angled line (see Figure 7.3).

FIGURE 7.2

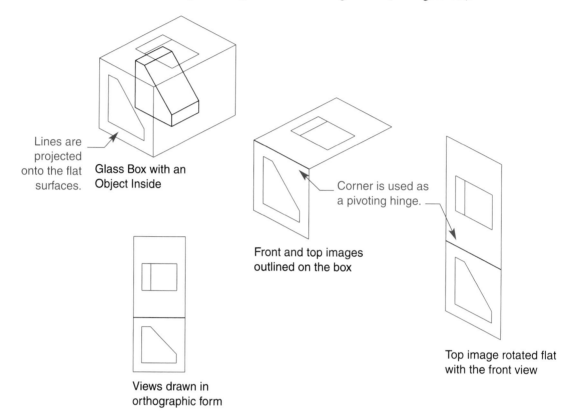

Lines are projected onto the flat surfaces.

Glass Box with an Object Inside

Corner is used as a pivoting hinge.

Front and top images outlined on the box

Top image rotated flat with the front view

Views drawn in orthographic form

FIGURE 7.3

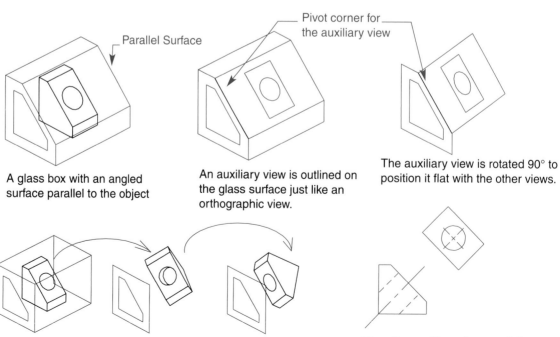

Parallel Surface

Pivot corner for the auxiliary view

A glass box with an angled surface parallel to the object

An auxiliary view is outlined on the glass surface just like an orthographic view.

The auxiliary view is rotated 90° to position it flat with the other views.

The object is rotated until the auxiliary view surface is flat with the front view.

Draw the auxiliary view parallel to the angled line.

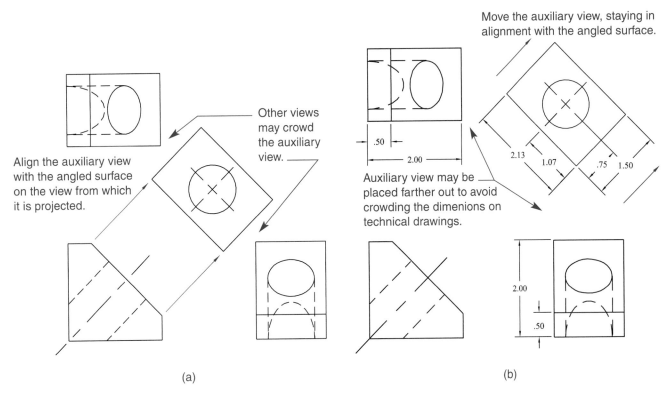

Move the auxiliary view, staying in alignment with the angled surface.

Align the auxiliary view with the angled surface on the view from which it is projected.

Other views may crowd the auxiliary view.

Auxiliary view may be placed farther out to avoid crowding the dimenions on technical drawings.

.50

2.00

2.13

1.07

.75   1.50

2.00

.50

(a)

(b)

FIGURE 7.4

The technique works like the orthographic layout method with a few modifications. The spacing between the auxiliary view and the orthographic from which it is projected will vary from drawing to drawing. Two factors determine how far away the view should be positioned:

1. The surrounding orthographic views may crowd or overlap the auxiliary view, forcing you to shift it farther out. Make sure to keep the auxiliary view aligned correctly with the surface from which it is projected (see Figure 7.4a).
2. Dimensions may start to crowd the views so it may be necessary to push the auxiliary view even farther out to avoid crowding (see Figure 7.4b).

Clarifying Auxiliary Views

1. Generally, hidden lines are not shown on the auxiliary view. If they do not help clarify the view, then leave them off.
2. The auxiliary view is projected to give a true view of the inclined surface. Some professionals eliminate everything else but the angled surface, emphasizing only what is on the true surface (see Figure 7.5).

An auxiliary view may also be used to replace an orthographic view if it is not as descriptive as the auxiliary. Think about why a particular view is needed to construct the object.

- Does it show relevant geometry (true shape and surfaces)?
- Does it help eliminate distortion?
- Can all the unique features be seen and dimensioned easily?

Any view that repeats existing information from other views is not necessary. Remembering this will help you when choosing an auxiliary view over an orthographic (see Figure 7.6).

FIGURE 7.5

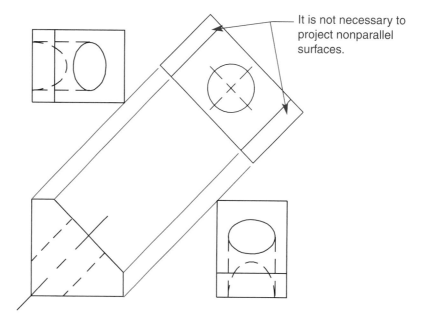

It is not necessary to
project nonparallel
surfaces.

FIGURE 7.6

The top and right-side views repeat information.
An auxiliary view can replace an orthographic.

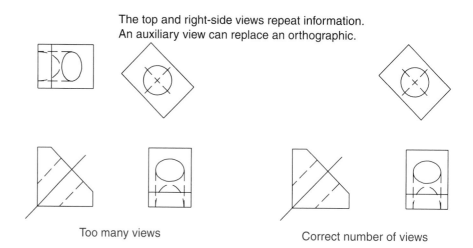

Too many views   Correct number of views

7.3   Plotting Out Auxiliary Views

Laying out auxiliary views can be simplified by using a reference line placed in a convenient location on the orthographic view across from the angled surface (see Figure 7.7). The reference line is used as a guide for locating points on the orthographic view then transfering them first to the angled plane and then out to the area where the auxiliary view will be constructed. The reference line on the auxiliary view is placed parallel to the angled surface. The exact distance of the reference line off the angled surface is up to the drafter. The auxiliary view will be plotted off the line; therefore it needs to be positioned so there is plenty of room between the other views and dimensions that will follow (see Figure 7.8). Common locations for reference lines are centers and outer edges of the view.

Steps in Plotting a Primary Auxiliary View

Step 1   Draw the orthographic views required.

Step 2   Place a reference line (RL) or plane on the true orthographic view opposite the orthographic view with the angle profile (see Figure 7.9a).

Step 3   Divide the orthographic that shows the true shape into equal parts. Label the points for easy identification (see Figure 7.9b).

Step 4   Draw lines perpendicular to the reference line passing through the equally spaced points. Make sure to extend the lines far enough to intersect the angled surface (see Figure 7.9c).

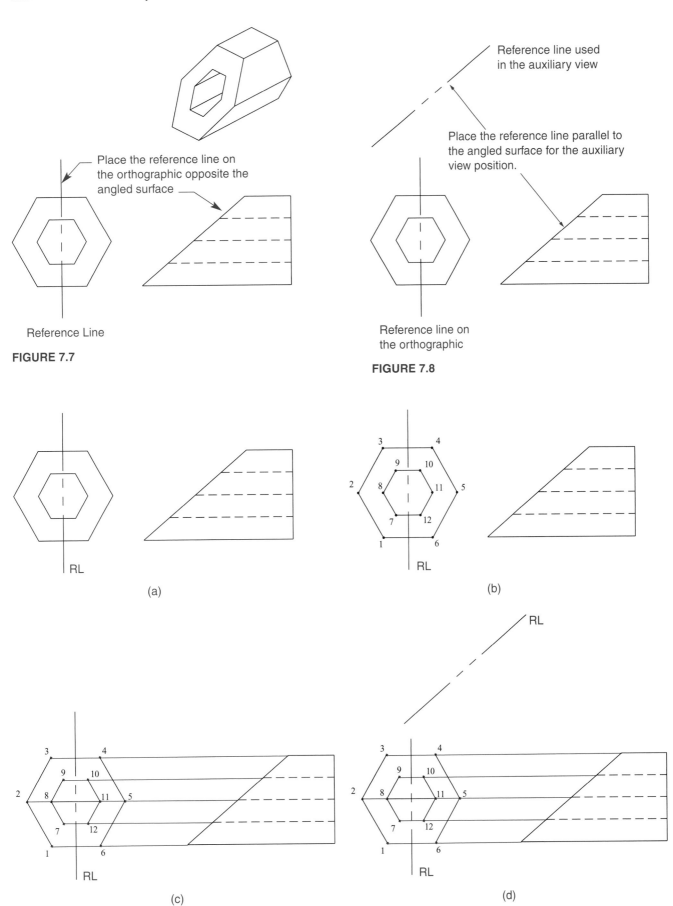

Place the reference line on the orthographic opposite the angled surface

Reference Line

FIGURE 7.7

Reference line used in the auxiliary view

Place the reference line parallel to the angled surface for the auxiliary view position.

Reference line on the orthographic

FIGURE 7.8

(a)

(b)

(c)

(d)

FIGURE 7.9
continued on next page

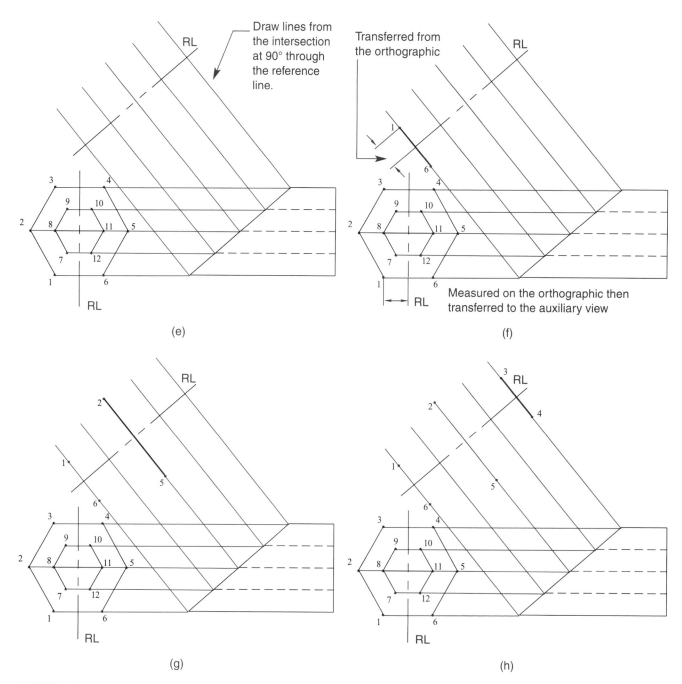

FIGURE 7.9
continued

Note: When plotting curves, the more increments you use, the smoother and truer the curves will be. Straight lines need only two points to be plotted out accurately—the beginning and the end of the line, as shown in Figure 7.9j. See Figures 7.10a through 7.10d for an example of plotting a curved shape.

Step 5   Place the auxiliary view reference line parallel to the angled line and far enough out to avoid interfering with any other views (see Figure 7.9d).

Step 6   Draw lines from the intersection points on the angled surface perpendicular to the reference line that is parallel to the angled surface (see Figure 7.9e).

Step 7   Now, take the measurements along the reference plane on the orthographic view and transfer them to the reference line that runs parallel to the angled surface one at a time (see Figures 7.9f through 7.9i). When all the points have been plotted, connect the points in the same way they are connected in the orthographic view (see Figure 7.9j).

Transferring measurements or distances between views on a drawing can be done quickly using dividers. Always use construction lines to plot out auxiliary views, and darken the visible lines when the view has been completely plotted out. Darken centerlines and reference plane lines last.

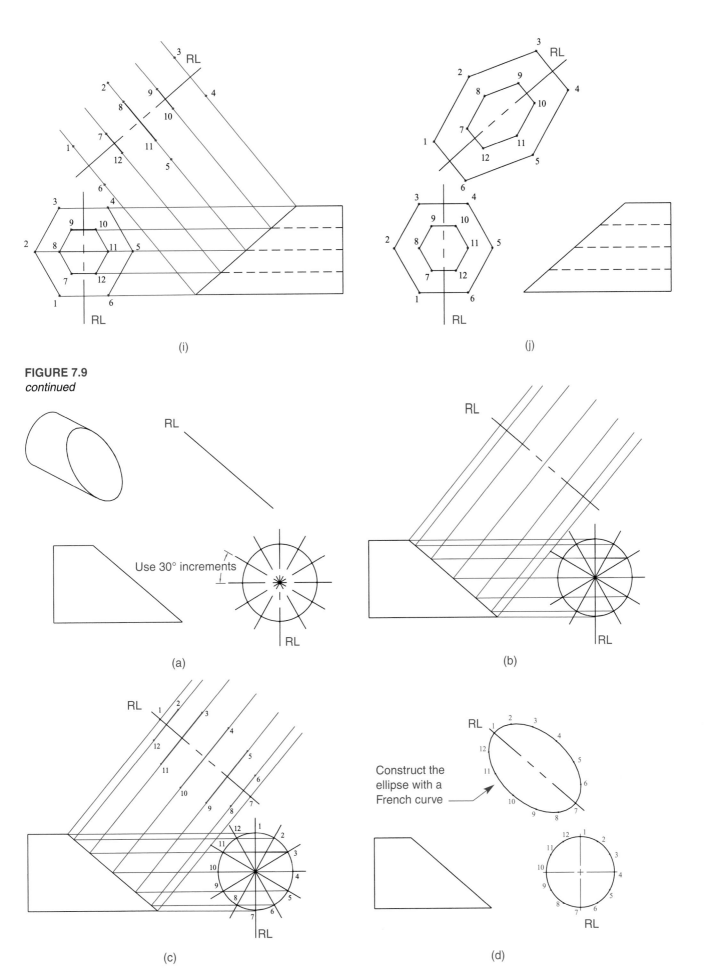

(i)

(j)

FIGURE 7.9
continued

Use 30° increments

(a)

(b)

Construct the
ellipse with a
French curve

(c)

(d)

FIGURE 7.10

7.4   Adding Secondary Auxiliary Views

So far all that has been shown is how to draw a basic primary auxiliary view. Some objects have additional angled surfaces that may need to be shown to see their true surface and shape. A secondary auxiliary view is projected off the primary auxiliary view (see Figure 7.11).

Once again, the techniques shown earlier in Chapter 6 will help simplify the process used to generate secondary auxiliary views. The corner that connects the primary auxiliary view to the secondary is used as a hinge point to pivot and rotate the surface completely flat and aligned with each angled surface.

Laying Out a Secondary Auxiliary View

Step 1   Draw the orthographic views along with the primary auxiliary view as needed (see Figure 7.12).

Step 2   Extend the reference line out beyond where the secondary auxiliary will be projected. Also extend the sides of the primary auxiliary view to set the width for the secondary (see Figure 7.13).

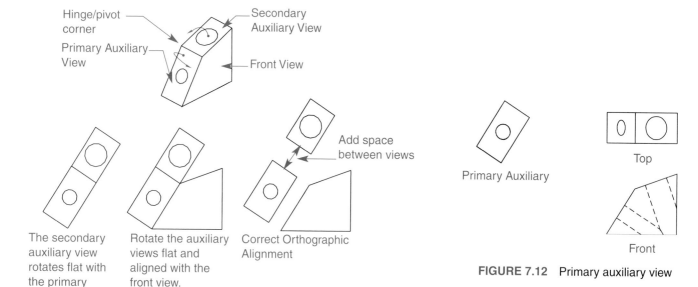

The secondary auxiliary view rotates flat with the primary auxiliary view.

Rotate the auxiliary views flat and aligned with the front view.

Correct Orthographic Alignment

FIGURE 7.11

FIGURE 7.12   Primary auxiliary view

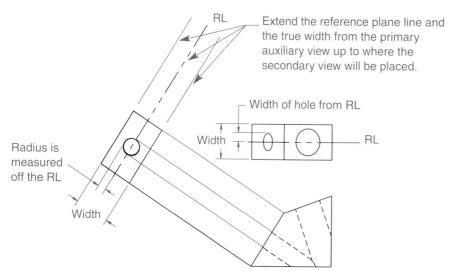

FIGURE 7.13   Guidelines for secondary auxiliary views width

Step 3 Draw a parallel line 1″ away from the top line (pivot corner) of the primary auxiliary view. This will be your spacing between the primary and secondary views (see Figure 7.14).

Step 4 Next, go to the angled surface on the orthographic view that represents the secondary view, and measure all necessary lines and points that will be needed to draw the true length along the secondary view. Take the measurements and transfer them to the secondary auxiliary view, as shown in Figure 7.15.

Step 5 After determining the location of the true lengths go to the reference line of the orthographic and measure the true widths needed (see Figure 7.16).

Step 6 Complete the secondary auxiliary view by drawing in the true shapes using the combined measurement of the true length and true width. The holes are true circles in the auxiliary views (see Figure 7.17).

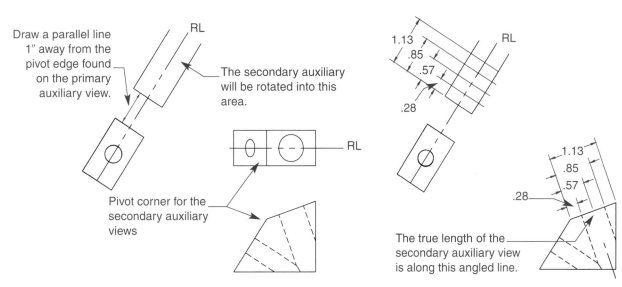

FIGURE 7.14   Location of the starting edge

FIGURE 7.15   Transferring lengths to the secondary auxiliary view

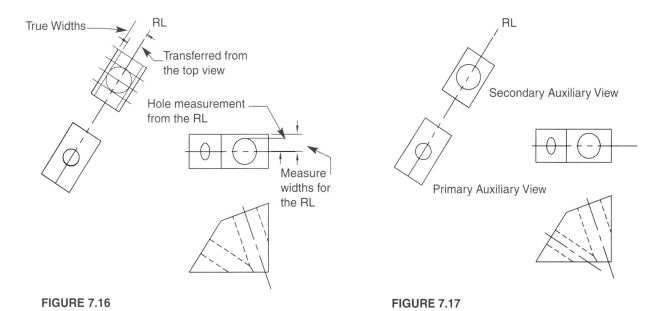

FIGURE 7.16

FIGURE 7.17

FIGURE 7.18

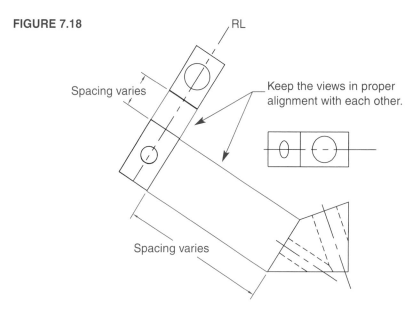

Spacing the secondary auxiliary view is a matter of room availability. The primary auxiliary view is used to align and help lay out the true width of the secondary. The distance between the two views can be flexible. As in the primary auxiliary example, there are different factors such as sheet size, other views (orthographic), and dimensions that will dictate where to place the secondary view. Avoid crowding to keep the views easy to read and understand. Move the auxiliary views as needed for clarity, but always keep the primary auxiliary view aligned with the angled surface (on the orthographic), and the width of the secondary view aligned with the width of the primary auxiliary view (see Figure 7.18).

The auxiliary view examples we have used so far have shown the true shape and size of an angled surface. Remember to use an auxiliary view when the angled surface needs to be described in true form. Just because an angled plane is found on an orthographic view does not always justify using an auxiliary view. The surface may be smooth, flat, and ordinary. Use the following two guidelines to determine if an auxiliary view is warranted:

1. The angled surface has a true shape running perpendicular to the angle that needs to be shown (see Figure 7.19a).
2. An auxiliary view can be used to replace an orthographic if it shows more detail and truer shapes (see Figure 7.19b).

In working drawings, auxiliary views can be altered to suit different needs. A half auxiliary may be used when the view is symmetrical, and crowding is a problem. Partial auxiliary views are also an option when only certain details need to be shown (see Figures 7.20a and 7.20b).

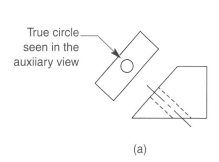

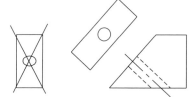

The left-side view shows only distorted geometry and can be replaced with the auxiliary view.

(a)   (b)

FIGURE 7.19

FIGURE 7.20

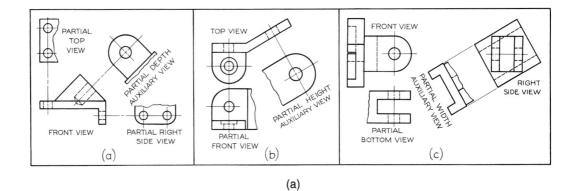

(a)

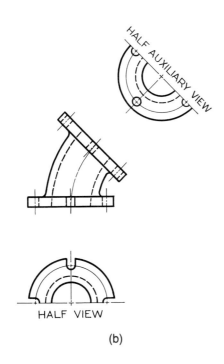

(b)

An auxiliary section may be used to project a sectional view out for hatching (see Figure 7.21). You may use any number of auxiliary views depending on how many angled surfaces are present. Do not be afraid to seek new solutions that may present themselves.

FIGURE 7.21

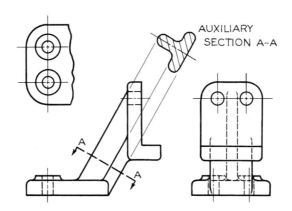

7.5   Introduction to Multipurpose Auxiliary Views

So far we have introduced you to the typical auxiliary views used in technical drawing, which stick to a two-dimensional orthographic approach. Auxiliary views can be projected in many other ways. Some methods include folding lines, descriptive geometry, piecing points, planes, and intersections that can be used to rotate auxiliary views to get true oblique surfaces (see Figure 7.22).

Notice that the four sides in the figure have angled surfaces making the drawing complex. The techniques used are quite detailed. These types of auxiliary views are easily drawn in three dimensions using CAD. The drawing can be turned and manipulated to obtain any view or angle desired. Figure 7.23 shows a simple part turned various ways to illustrate that auxiliary views can be endless. The part does not really need auxiliary views at all; however, a complex part might benefit from multiple views that show many different viewing points. These types of auxiliary views are not really describing angled surfaces but instead are toying with three-dimensional exposure. Using a pictorial drawing may be a good idea in some cases. In CAD, a three-dimensional drawing can be used as a pictorial or an auxiliary view.

The principles discussed in this chapter are geared toward giving the student a background in the typical areas an auxiliary view is used in technical drawing. The concepts involving primary and secondary views will give you the knowledge to develop some basic auxiliary views. The more advanced auxiliary views can be learned later when the student has a good understanding of drawing basics.

FIGURE 7.22

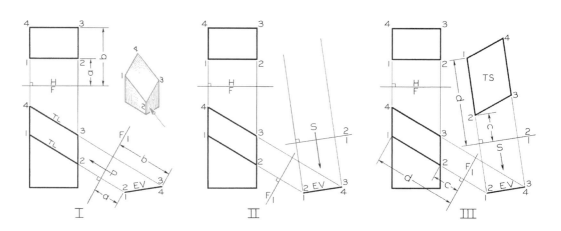

FIGURE 7.23

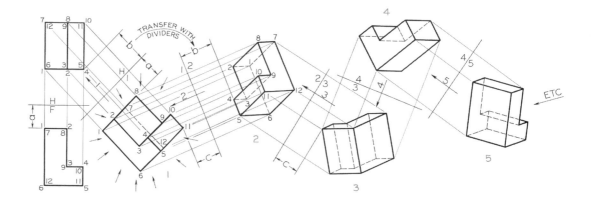

CHAPTER SEVEN REVIEW QUESTIONS

1. For what purpose is the auxiliary view used?
2. How is a reference plane line used to help construct an auxiliary view?
3. Should the reference plane line on the auxiliary view be placed parallel or perpendicular to the angled surface from which it is projected?
4. How are hidden lines used on auxiliary views?
5. When would a secondary auxiliary view be needed?
6. What technique should be used to project circles, curves, and arcs in an auxiliary view?
7. True or False. Auxiliary views are always projected off the front view.
8. What determines the spacing distance for an auxiliary view?

DRAWING ASSIGNMENTS

1. Draw all necessary views (orthographic and auxiliary) to fully describe the object or views given in Figure 7.24.
2. Draw the primary and secondary auxiliary view for each example in Figures 7.25a through 7.25c.

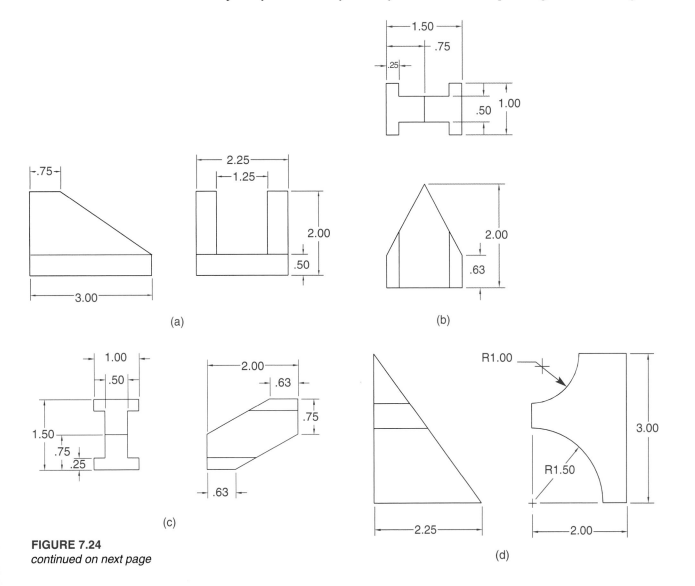

FIGURE 7.24
continued on next page

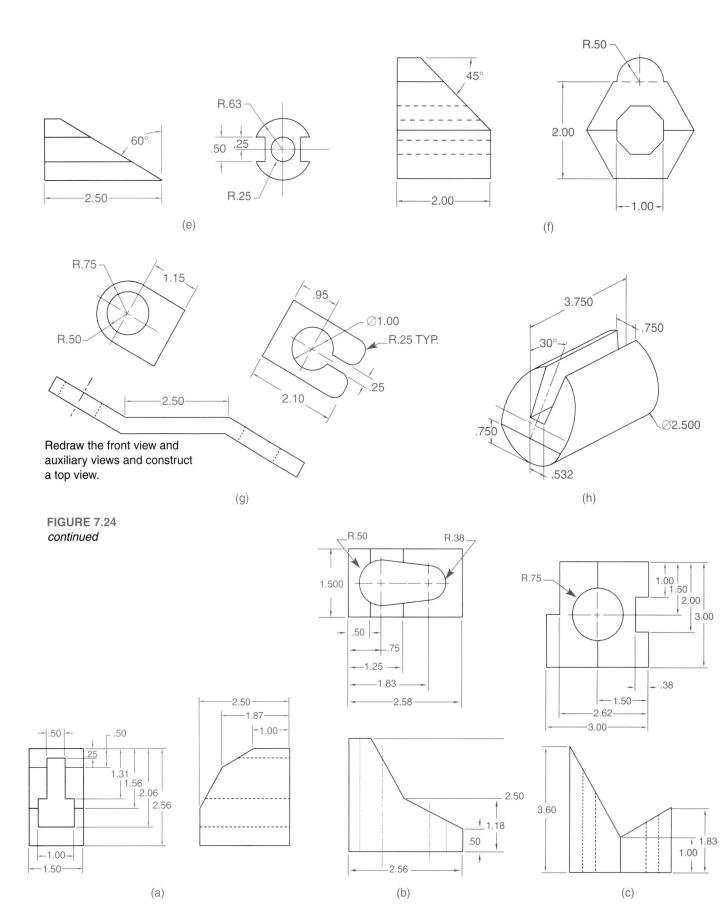

(e)

(f)

Redraw the front view and
auxiliary views and construct
a top view.

(g)

(h)

FIGURE 7.24
continued

R.25 TYP.

(a)

(b)

(c)

FIGURE 7.25

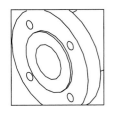

CHAPTER 8

○ ○

Sections

The final piece of the technical drawing puzzle is the sectional view. An overview in Chapter 5 gave some examples of sections and explained the various types. This chapter describes some methods and techniques for drawing sections. Techniques similar to those used with orthographics are used to draw sections. In addition, some unique characteristics are associated with the different types of sections.

8.1 Principles of Section

The purpose of section views in mechanical drawing is to simplify a complex orthographic view by removing the hidden lines, thus showing the inside features with visible lines. Sectional views are therefore used to replace orthographic views that have many hidden lines. A normal three-view orthographic drawing may use the best three views, but if a section would show more detail, then a section may be used in place of an orthographic.

The following different types of sections are used in mechanical drawing:

- Full section
- Half section
- Offset section
- Aligned section
- Revolved/Rotated section
- Broken-out section
- Removed section
- Assembly section

Drawing section views gives the drafter a certain freedom when it comes to creating a more readable view.

First, a cutting-plane/viewing-plane line is placed on an orthographic view. The drafter chooses its location to generate the position of an imaginary cut that passes through the object being drawn. Cutting-plane lines are very versatile and will be demonstrated with the different section types as each one is explained. Hidden lines are normally left out of section views, but the versatility of section drawing allows them to be used to help clarify a section view on occasion. Look for examples in the different sections throughout the chapter.

Visualizing the Cutting Plane

Learning to draw sections starts with visualizing how a cut will look when it passes through a part. The process is similar to viewing an orthographic, the difference being that an internal cut reveals the internal feature while removing the outer shell. Let us start with an easy example like a pipe. In Figure 8.1a, an isometric and two orthographic views of the pipe are shown. Now, imagine taking a saw and cutting the pipe right down the middle perpendicular to the circle. The walls of the pipe are thus exposed and a hollowed-out half circle is left (see Figure 8.1b). To draw the figure as a section view, you would use the following process.

FIGURE 8.1

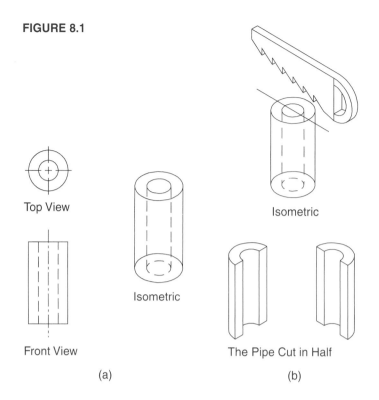

Top View

Isometric

Front View

Isometric

The Pipe Cut in Half

(a)   (b)

Step 1   Draw the best orthographic view that shows true geometry and all visible lines, which in this case is the view showing the circles.

Step 2   Place the cutting plane on this view illustrating where your cut is to be made. (In chapter 3, see Figure 3.8 for types of cutting-plane lines and thicknesses.) Extend the cutting plane line .38″ outside the object on both sides, then draw a 90° line .38″ on each end in the direction you wish to see the part (see Figure 8.2a). Place arrows on the cutting-plane ends showing the direction from which the cut is being viewed. Make the arrows approximately .25″ long and .09″ wide. Remember to remove everything that was on the front side of the cutting plane line from your mind. It is not used when the section view is drawn (see Figure 8.2b).

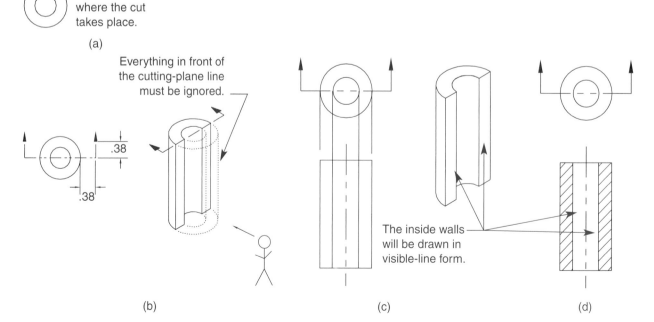

Best view to show where the cut takes place.

(a)

Everything in front of the cutting-plane line must be ignored.

.38

.38

The inside walls will be drawn in visible-line form.

(b)   (c)   (d)

FIGURE 8.2

Step 3 Draw what you see along the cutting plane line and beyond. Project from the top view to locate the lines just as in orthographic drawings (see Figure 8.2c). Recall that circles can project into rectangular shapes in orthographic drawings. They can do so in section views as well.

Step 4 Add section or hatch lines along with centerlines if needed (see Figure 8.2d).

This example is easy to follow when a simple part is used. In a real-world situation a section view is normally used on more complicated parts. Section views tend to take more time to draw, so if an orthographic view is simple or very descriptive, a section may not be necessary. Now, let us walk through each type of section.

8.2 Types of Sections

Full Sections

A full section is very straightforward. A very descriptive orthographic view is typically drawn first, and a cutting plane line is placed on the view. Since it is a full section the cutting-plane line will run all the way across this view for a full, continuous cut through the part. Instead of an orthographic, a section view is projected from it as the cutting-plane line intersects features of the part where the solid material and air chambers exist and converge. The section view is placed behind the direction the arrowheads are pointing and is flipped out just like an orthographic view in third-angle projection but showing features only where the cut is made along with any details seen beyond the cut. In our example of the full section (see Figure 8.3) a more complex part is demonstrated, but the steps are exactly the same as the ones used in the pipe example.

Notice that the area being cut along the cutting-plane line is hatched where solid material was present. Now look at the lines and features that were found and picked up beyond the cutting-plane line. Do not overlook items past the cut. They are seen beyond the cut and must be accounted for on a section view. Pick up all the visible lines and any other linetypes that help describe the features. In the section in Figure 8.3, hidden and centerlines were added to show more of the features beyond.

In most sections it is common to hatch all the solid material that the cutting plane passes through, as shown in Figure 8.4. One exception occurs when the cutting plane passes through a rib running in the long or longitudinal direction. Even though the cut is made through solid rib material, no hatch or section lines are shown. The rib is simply shown as it would appear in orthographic form (see Figure 8.5). This breaks the rule for sectioning, but it is done for clarity as well as to save time.

Full sections can be used to replace any orthographic view in the typical third-angle alignment. See Figure 8.6. The key is in positioning the arrowheads correctly on the cutting-plane line and then placing the section behind the arrowheads.

FIGURE 8.3

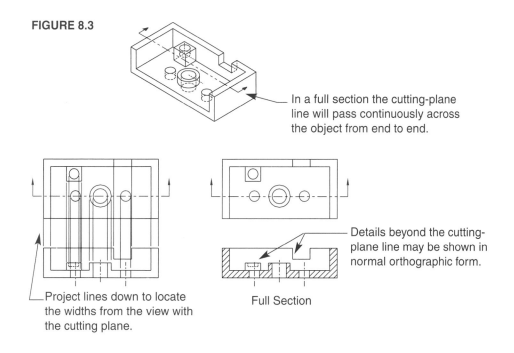

In a full section the cutting-plane line will pass continuously across the object from end to end.

Details beyond the cutting-plane line may be shown in normal orthographic form.

Project lines down to locate the widths from the view with the cutting plane.

Full Section

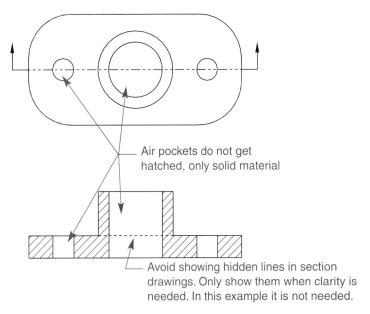

Air pockets do not get hatched, only solid material

Avoid showing hidden lines in section drawings. Only show them when clarity is needed. In this example it is not needed.

FIGURE 8.4

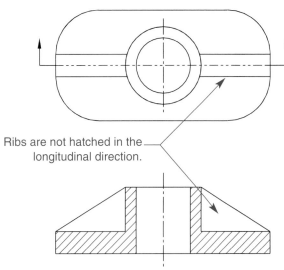

Ribs are not hatched in the longitudinal direction.

FIGURE 8.5

FIGURE 8.6

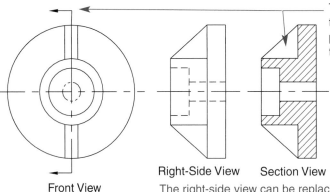

Front View

Right-Side View   Section View

The right-side view can be replaced with a section view to show more visible lines and detail.

The section view is placed behind the direction the arrowheads are pointing. It is rotated in the same third-angle projection format.

Let us now look at some examples of a full section using the same front view with the projections of different sections placed in the correct location to replace the customary orthographic view. Just about any orthographic view can be turned into a section. Pay attention to the arrowheads and flip the section out just as if you were using third-angle projection (see Figure 8.7).

FIGURE 8.7   Sections can be placed in different locations. Make sure to place the view on the side that the arrowheads are not pointing toward, as in these examples.

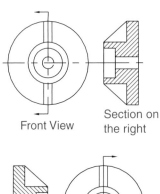

Front View   Section on the right

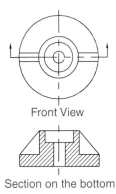

Front View

Section on the bottom

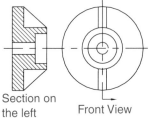

Section on the left   Front View

The following steps summarize the process of drawing a section.

- Draw a good orthographic view first. Usually, it is a front view.
- Draw a thick cutting-plane line on the orthographic showing where the cut is to be made. The cut should pass through key features or areas of the part to show their detail.
- Place arrowheads on a 90° line off the cutting-plane line to show the position or the side from which the section is to be viewed. (Remember, the arrows are pointing in the direction the viewer is looking.)
- Flip the sectional view to the side that the arrowheads are pointing toward. For instance, if the arrowheads are pointing to the left, then the section view will go on the right side of the view being cut. Align the view using the third-angle projection technique.
- Project from the lines on the orthographic view as they intersect the cutting-plane line. Pick up any features beyond the cut that shows detail.
- Add section or hatch lines along with centerlines to complete the view.

In full sections the steps are repeated over and over. It does not matter which views are to be sectioned or if multiple sections are cut on the same orthographic (see Figures 8.8a and 8.8b).

Half Sections

Drawing a half section is easy to learn once drawing the full section has been mastered. The rules and steps are almost identical, and the cutting-plane line is the key to drawing and understanding a half section. An example of a half section is shown in Figure 8.9. Notice the following differences between a full section and a half section:

- The cutting-plane line does not go all the way across the orthographic view. It goes halfway across, then turns 90° and exits the object.
- Only one arrow is used on the half that is to be cut.
- A half-section drawing leaves one side in orthographic form.

A drafter might want to use a half section when an object is symmetrical along the cutting-plane line. A line down the middle of the view is used to separate the section view on one side from an orthographic rep-

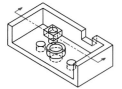

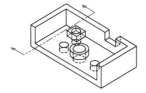

In a full section the cutting plane line passes continuously across the object from end to end.

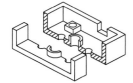

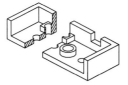

Full section taken from the long direction

Full section taken from the short direction

(a)

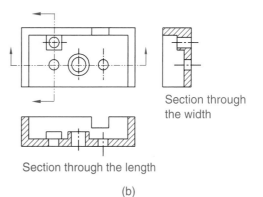

Section through the width

Section through the length

(b)

FIGURE 8.8 Multiple sections on the same drawing

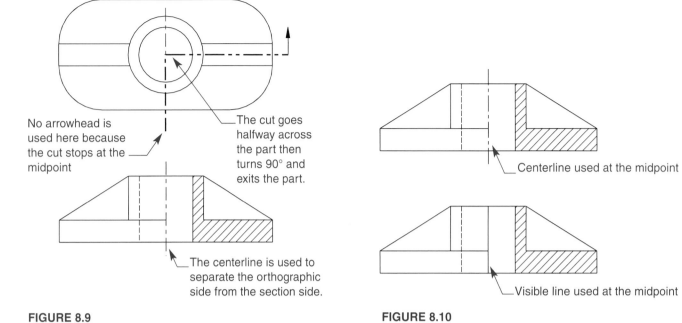

No arrowhead is used here because the cut stops at the midpoint

The cut goes halfway across the part then turns 90° and exits the part.

The centerline is used to separate the orthographic side from the section side.

Centerline used at the midpoint

Visible line used at the midpoint

FIGURE 8.9   **FIGURE 8.10**

resentation on the other. The line used to separate the different drawing types may be a centerline or a visible line, as shown in Figure 8.10. Centerlines tend to cause less confusion.

A half section may not work as well as a full section if there are many details or features along the cut. Later in the text you will learn about dimensioning views. When dimensioning to an object you must dimension to visible lines only. A half section may have too many hidden lines on the orthographic and thus restrict how many dimensions can be placed on a view.

The half section forces you to think and draw in two different modes on the same view. It can cause some confusion at times if you try to do too much at once. The best approach is to draw each side by itself. Draw the section part of the view first, using the techniques for drawing full sections. Let the intersections of the cutting-plane line and the visible lines be your guide for developing the section part of the view. You may take the height measurements from a pictorial drawing to complete the section half. Once the section part is done, switch thinking modes over to an orthographic train of thought. Go back to imagining yourself viewing the object from in front of it (see Figures 8.11a and b).

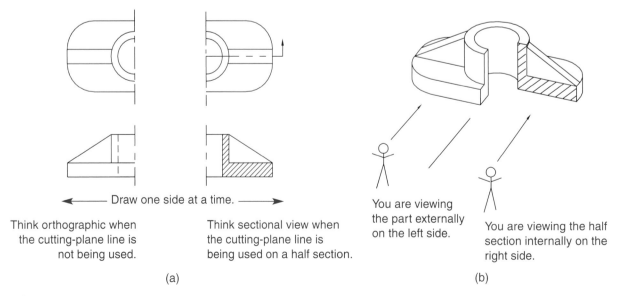

◄——— Draw one side at a time. ———►

Think orthographic when the cutting-plane line is not being used.

Think sectional view when the cutting-plane line is being used on a half section.

You are viewing the part externally on the left side.

You are viewing the half section internally on the right side.

(a)   (b)

FIGURE 8.11

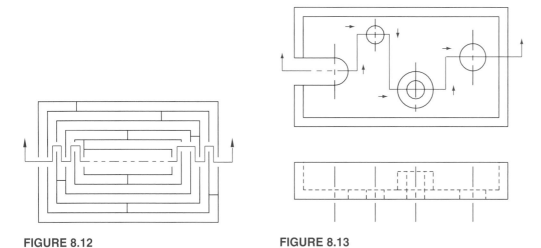

FIGURE 8.12

FIGURE 8.13

Offset Sections

Some parts are not very symmetrical and so present a dilemma when it comes to selecting a straight cutting-plane line that shows a lot of features. An *offset section* provides a solution to a part with juggled or spread-out features. The offset cutting-plane line can change directions at 90° intervals, allowing you to choose a route that reveals the most detail. Think of it as trying to find a path through a maze (see Figure 8.12).

Now, notice the many 90° changes of direction on the cutting line in Figure 8.13. After a feature has been cut through, a 90° change of direction is made toward another feature such as a hole or another form of interruption on the surface of the part. The direction change is best made about halfway to the next feature to be cut. This is not a rule set in stone, but it does help keep the drawing from getting confusing and does keep it more readable. The cutting-plane line should pass all the way through the feature, as shown in Figure 8.14. Changing the cutting-plane direction inside a feature will not help show the full characteristics and should be avoided.

Now let us look closely at drawing the offset section view. We will follow most of the same guidelines used for drawing and projecting a full section. When the cutting-plane line intersects planes along the surface of the part, the lines are projected down to form the widths (see Figure 8.15).

As in the full section, arrows are placed on both ends of the cutting-plane line showing the direction in which the viewer is looking. One rule you must learn is that the change of direction of the cutting-plane line does not generate a line in the sectional view. The reason is simple—it is not a feature of the part but only a tool used to shift through the part. These lines are always ignored (see Figure 8.16).

Offset sections can be found in all fields of drafting. The versatility of this type of section makes it very useful. When using an offset section, do not forget the sectioning basics discussed earlier in this chapter.

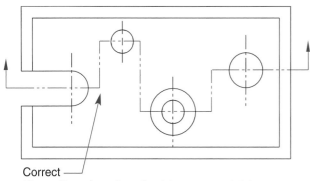

Correct
The cutting-plane line should pass completely
through the feature before changing directions.

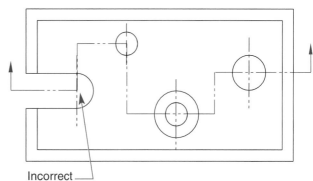

Incorrect
Avoid changing the direction of the cutting-plane line before it passes through completely.

FIGURE 8.14

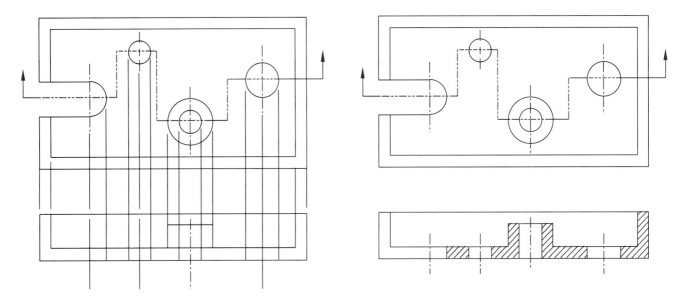

FIGURE 8.15

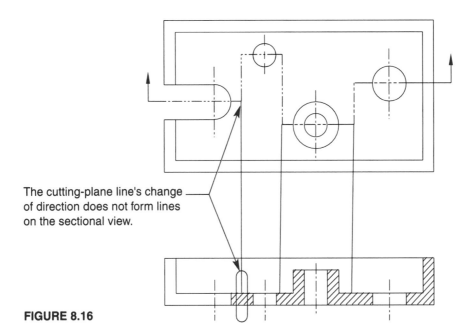

The cutting-plane line's change of direction does not form lines on the sectional view.

FIGURE 8.16

Aligned Sections

Another form of sectioning that also alters the direction of the cutting-plane line is an *aligned section.* This type of section is most often used on symmetrical circular parts (see Figure 8.17). The first half of the cut goes straight across, as for a full section. As shown in Figure 8.18, the cutting plane line angles off the center of the main circle, slicing through an area that has more detail to show. There is no hard-and-fast rule for choosing the angle. It can be set to whatever is needed for the view.

In some cases an aligned section can be used in combination with an offset if needed (see Figure 8.19). When this combination is used the change in direction for the offset is a partial circle based on the center point of the largest circle. The circular arc replaces the 90° line that changes direction. The arc proceeds up to the next feature, stopping where the center of the largest circle would connect with a straight line to the center of the circle that will be sliced through (see the Figure 8.20 blow-up for a closer look). This section combination works well when holes or other features are sporadically placed around a circular part.

The real challenge to drawing an aligned section is not in placing the cutting-plane line on the ortho-graphic view but in properly aligning the sectional view to show where the cutting plane is passing through. To do this you need to imagine rotating the angled cutting-plane line back to a full-section position. The fea-

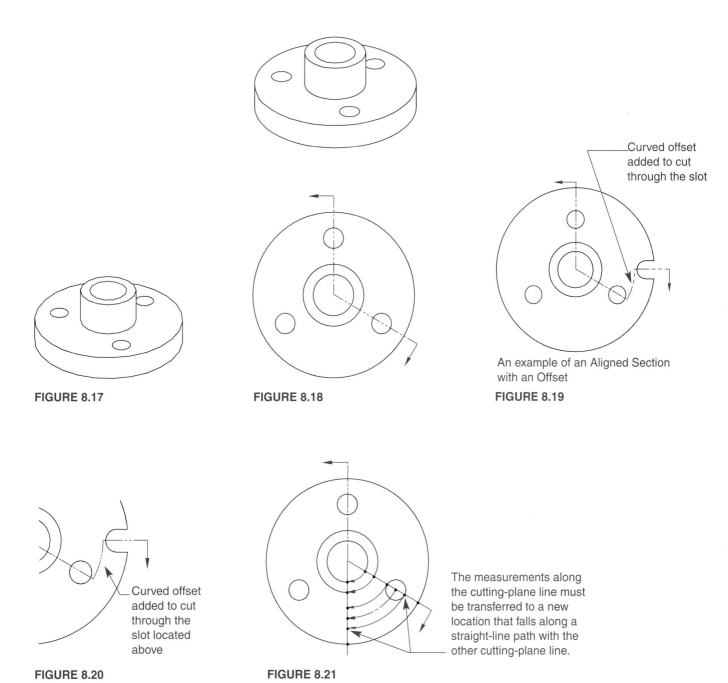

FIGURE 8.17

FIGURE 8.18

Curved offset added to cut through the slot

An example of an Aligned Section with an Offset

FIGURE 8.19

Curved offset added to cut through the slot located above

FIGURE 8.20

The measurements along the cutting-plane line must be transferred to a new location that falls along a straight-line path with the other cutting-plane line.

FIGURE 8.21

tures along the cutting plane line are also rotated to the new position then projected down to draw the section view. See Figure 8.21 to see where the features are relocated. Two techniques can be used to accomplish this task.

Method 1: Using a Compass

Use the center of the large circle as a base point. Place a compass needle point at the base point and open it up along the angled cutting-plane line where the feature lines intersect it. At every intersection point use the lead point in the compass and lightly draw an arc from the intersection point to where the cutting-plane line would normally be located if a full section were being cut. This will align the angled cutting plane back into a straight line, keeping the feature measurements at the right spacing as they are rotated into position. Once the measurements are in the new location, just project them to the sectional view (see Figures 8.22 and 8.24).

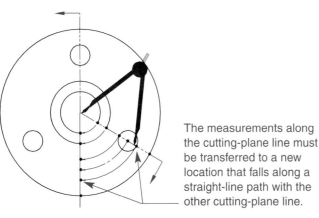

The measurements along the cutting-plane line must be transferred to a new location that falls along a straight-line path with the other cutting-plane line.

FIGURE 8.22

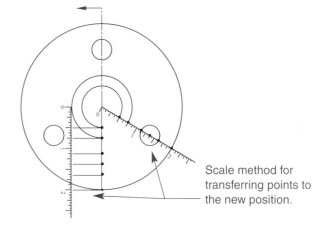

Scale method for transferring points to the new position.

FIGURE 8.23

Method 2: Using a Scale

Use a scale and measure the distances of the features from the center base point along the angle cutting-plane line as the features intersect it. Each time you make a measurement along the angled cutting-plane line, go back to the center base point and measure the same distance straight out as if the cutting plane line did not angle but went continuously across the part just like in a full-section cut. In this example, the measurements are transferred using a scale, but the end result is the same as with the compass method (see Figure 8.23). The section view may be drawn after the points have been repositioned (see Figure 8.24).

As seen in the offset and align sections, the cutting-plane line is critical for defining the section cut. Knowing which alignment to project from and which rules to follow will come with time and practice. Figure 8.25 gives an example of how *not* to project the sectional views on aligned sections. This traditional projection is considered wrong for aligned sections, so avoid it for this type of section drawing.

Ribs on aligned sections may also be placed in a nontraditional position, making the section easier to project and understand. Symmetrical ribs on a round object may be relocated on the orthographic view in order to project them more true to form. The process is just like aligning features that fall on the angled cutting-plane line; however, in this case a rib may not fall on the cutting-plane line. When this happens, you use the full length of the rib and place it on the cutting plane. See Figure 8.26 for some examples. Recall that ribs are not hatched when shown in the longitudinal direction.

Revolved or Rotated Sections

So far all the different types of sections shown have used a cutting-plane line to help project a sectional view. Sometimes only small portions of a drawing need sectioning, so a cutting plane is not used. Basically, a re-

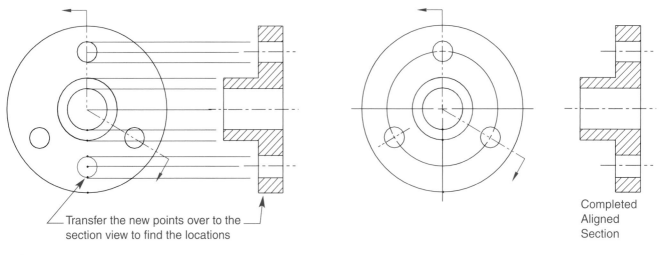

Transfer the new points over to the section view to find the locations

Completed Aligned Section

FIGURE 8.24

FIGURE 8.25

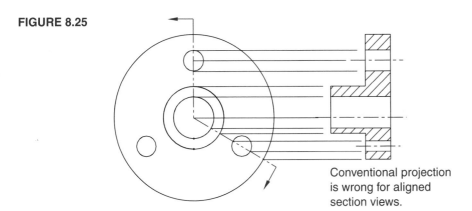

Conventional projection
is wrong for aligned
section views.

Ribs may be repositioned on
aligned sections for a more
readable drawing.

A rib is projected as if it were
along the cutting-plane line.

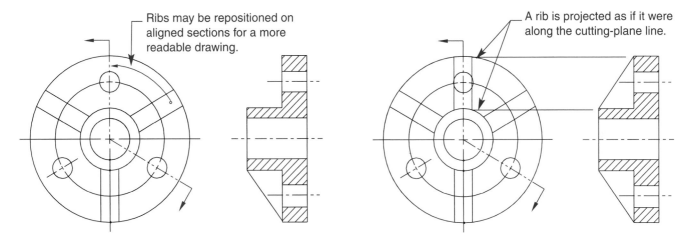

FIGURE 8.26

volved or rotated section is used to generate a small cross-sectional area that runs perpendicular to the viewing plane or to your eyes. This area is not normally shown on a orthographic view; however, the drafter can choose to use a revolved section to turn this area toward the viewing plane 90° in order to see the shape (see Figure 8.27).

Notice in Example A that the part is stopped with a short break line, then the revolved section is drawn, and then the part is continued after another short break. In Example B the same view uses another option showing the section rotated without the use of short break lines. Either method is acceptable; however, if the short break line technique is used, the thickness of the break lines will draw the reader's attention to the section area faster because the thicker lines stand out to the viewer.

One good use of a revolved/rotated section is when dealing with ribs that run in the longitudinal direction on an orthographic. Recall that ribs are not sectioned when running in the long direction along the cutting plane. A revolved/rotated section is a perfect opportunity to use on a rib to show its width with this type

FIGURE 8.27

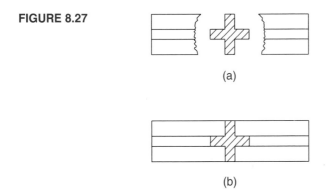

(a)

(b)

FIGURE 8.28

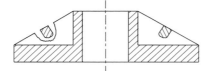

Two different ways of rotating ribs

FIGURE 8.29

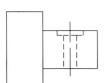

Orthographic view
with a hole and
counterbore

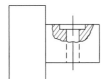

Orthographic view with
a hole and counterbore
shown in a broken-out
section.

(a)

(b)

of section view (see Figure 8.28). This form of sectioning is ideal for clarifying small areas and flipping them into the viewing plane.

Broken Out Section

A broken-out section is used much like a revolved or rotated section. It is most often used to generate sections for small areas without using a cutting-plane line. The major difference is that a broken-out section is not revolved or rotated 90° to the viewing plane or viewer's eyes. A broken-out section simply removes solid material in front of a portion of the view so that interior features or details may be seen in visible-line form. Think of a broken-out section as a rough opening poked in the front of an object similar to the hole in the face of a building caused by a big steel demolishing ball when the building is being knocked down (see Figures 8.29a and b).

Remember that broken-out, revolved, and rotated sections are partial sections and are used in an orthographic view. They enhance an orthographic view by giving the viewer a better look at a key feature.

Removed Section

A removed section breaks away from the traditional method used to flip out sectional views. So far most types of sections we have seen have been lined up with an orthographic view and flipped out and aligned with some third-angle projection concepts. Using a removed section gives the drafter freedom to place the section view in any alignment needed. The following are two good reasons for using this type of section:

1. A drawing sheet may be very crowded and have limited space. A more creative or sensible alignment can be used to keep the drawing as readable as possible.
2. A small area may need to be scaled up to be seen better or to be dimensioned. Trying to combine a larger scale drawing with a smaller scale drawing makes using a standard alignment impossible. See Figure 8.30 for an example of a removed section that blew up the scale.

FIGURE 8.30

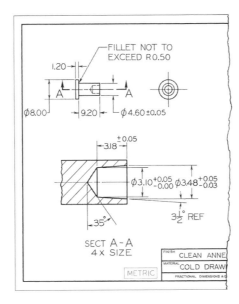

It will be difficult to track down where the sections belong without a set alignment or position; therefore, a section callout or letter will be needed along with a cutting-plane line (see Figure 8.31 for an example). It is preferable to lay out the section with the letters in alphabetical order. Set it up like a book, going from left to right and top to bottom. One thing to remember when placing the view of a removed section on the drawing is to use its correct orientation. Just because the view does not line up with the orthographic from which it is cut does not change its position/orientation as dictated by the cutting plane and the direction in which the arrowheads are pointing (see Figure 8.31).

Assembly Sections

Thus far you have been shown section applications for individual parts. Now it is time to show you sections that are cut through multiple parts when they are assembled together. Normally, individual parts are drawn separately in technical drawings, keeping them as simple as possible. Each part may be detailed in any of the technical drawing forms such as orthographic, section, or auxiliary views (see Figure 8.32). These types of drawings along with the dimensions are given to the machinist who will build the parts. This may be an excellent drawing for building the individual pieces; however, it does not put the parts together to show how they fit and function together when assembled.

An *assembly section* is one of several options that can be used to show how the individual pieces fit together. The following is a list of the different options for assemblies:

Note: A combination of the two assembly forms may be used to generate the desired result. Some features on the assembly may be very easy to understand and can be left in orthographic form, whereas other, more complex portions of the assembly may need to be displayed in sectional form (see Figure 8.33c).

1. *Orthographic Assembly*—The parts are put together showing their location and fit in orthographic form. Because it is an orthographic, hidden lines can become confusing and may not give enough detail when showing the assembly, but it can be used for simple assemblies (see Figure 8.33a).

2. *Section Assembly*—The parts are assembled together showing their normal position; however, the parts are sectioned to remove hidden lines, making the drawing easier to read. A full section down the middle is fairly common, but any type of section can be used depending on the shape of the assembly. In a section assembly some pieces do not get hatch lines, such as shafts and ribs cut in the long direction (see Figure 8.33b).

You make a section assembly easy to read by assigning hatching symbols or section lines to the different types of materials. Single sections on a part use a general or common hatch pattern. See Figure 8.34 for the general hatch symbol. This general hatch pattern may be used for all materials when sectioning an individual part. If more than one section view is on the same drawing sheet with different materials, then you should use the ANSI hatching for the different materials, as shown in Figure 8.34. For a complete list of section symbols check a machinist's handbook.

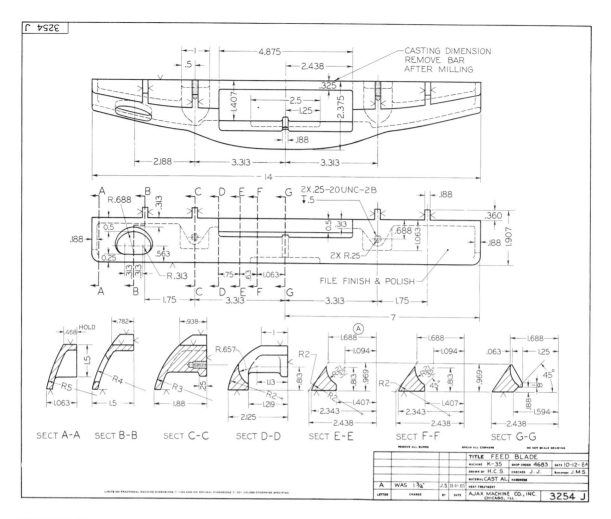

FIGURE 8.31

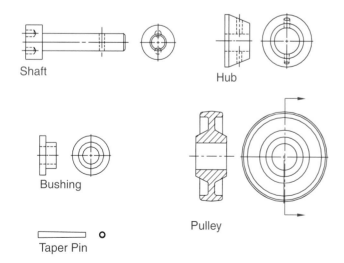

FIGURE 8.32

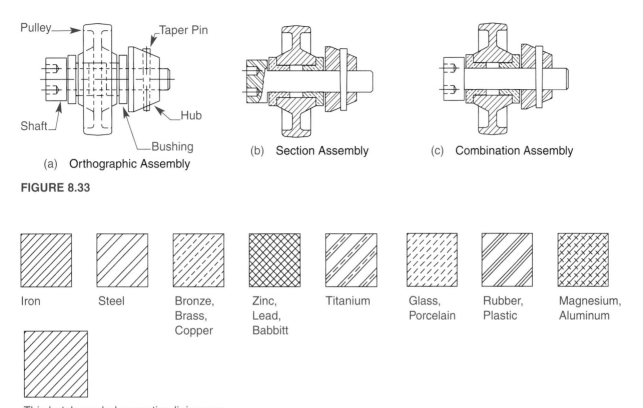

(a) **Orthographic Assembly**

(b) **Section Assembly**

(c) **Combination Assembly**

FIGURE 8.33

Iron

Steel

Bronze, Brass, Copper

Zinc, Lead, Babbitt

Titanium

Glass, Porcelain

Rubber, Plastic

Magnesium, Aluminum

This hatch symbol or section lining can be used as a general symbol for all materials in a single hatch.

FIGURE 8.34   Typical symbols for sectioning mechanical materials

FIGURE 8.35

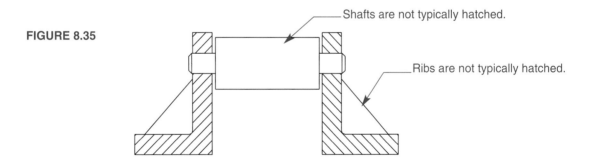

Shafts are not typically hatched.

Ribs are not typically hatched.

It should be obvious that a section assembly drawing must use different material symbols to separate the elements that make up the assembly. Using the general section symbol would make the drawing much more difficult to read and understand and therefore is never done. Use the correct material symbols and follow your normal sectioning rules. Do not hatch ribs running in the longitudinal direction even if the cutting plane line passes through them. Leave them as they would appear in a normal orthographic view. Likewise, drawing section lines for shafts is a waste of time. Hatching these items does not aid the readability and should be avoided (see Figure 8.35).

8.3   Sectioning Rules and Techniques

The readability of a section is the responsibility of the drafter. There are some hard-and-fast rules, but there is also a great deal of flexibility in using different techniques to help enhance the view. The following is a review to help you remember some of the rules.

The same part has section or hatch lines set to the same angle and spacing.

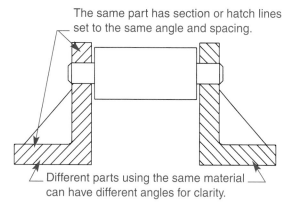

Different parts using the same material can have different angles for clarity.

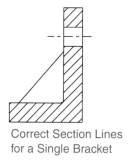

Correct Section Lines for a Single Bracket

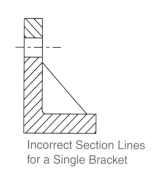

Incorrect Section Lines for a Single Bracket

FIGURE 8.36

1. Section lines on the same part are hatched in the same direction (see Figure 8.36).

2. The visible lines along the cutting-plane line and beyond are seen and drawn. Show all visible lines (see Figure 8.37).

3. Hidden lines are rarely shown in the cutting-plane area on section views. The object of a sectional view is to remove hidden lines and to make the drawing clearer. Hidden lines can be used only to help clarify a nonrepetitive part of the drawing (see Figure 8.38).

4. The arrows on the cutting plane show the direction the viewer is looking. The sectional view is flipped out and flipped similar to third-angle projection format. (A removed section does not follow this alignment.) (See Figure 8.39.)

5. Section lines should be set to a 30°, 45°, or 60° angle referenced off the longest side of the sectioned area. Parallel or perpendicular lines are never used in the section view (see Figure 8.40).

6. A sectional view shows the area the cutting-plane line passes through. Even revolved sections follow this rule, although no cutting-plane line is used at its location (see Figure 8.41).

7. When different sectioned pieces touch in an assembly section, the section or hatch lines may be altered for better readability. The following options may be used.

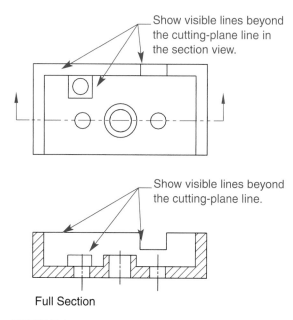

Show visible lines beyond the cutting-plane line in the section view.

Show visible lines beyond the cutting-plane line.

Full Section

FIGURE 8.37

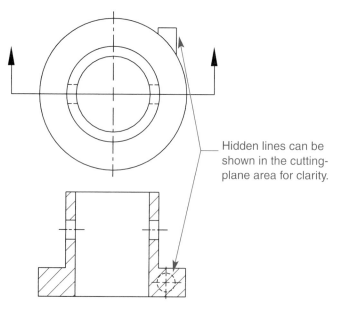

Hidden lines can be shown in the cutting-plane area for clarity.

FIGURE 8.38

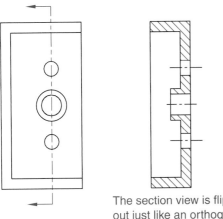

30° Angle

Do not use a
90° angle.

45° Angle

Do not use a
0° angle.

60° Angle
**Common Angles for
Section Lines**

Unacceptable Angles

The section view is flipped
out just like an orthographic
view with the viewer looking
at the cut in the direction of
the arrowheads.

FIGURE 8.39

FIGURE 8.40

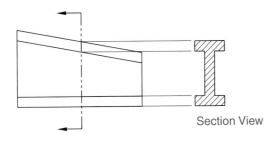

Section View

Staggering the hatch lines helps
show that there are two different
parts in the assembly.

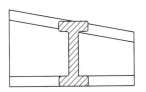

Correct Revolved Section
It projects just like a section
with a cutting-plane line.

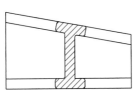

Incorrect Revolved Section
It never runs with the angle.

FIGURE 8.41

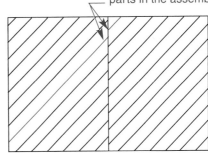

FIGURE 8.42

a. The section lines are staggered or offset to clearly show that two parts are being sectioned (see Figure 8.42).

b. Different parts may use a mirror hatch pattern alternating every other part. Mirrored and staggered section lines may also be combined for clarity. See Figure 8.43 for both examples.

c. The angle of the section lines may be altered from part to part. Combinations of 30°, 45°, and 60° give the best results (see Figure 8.44).

All the examples have shown the same hatch symbol or section lines being used. When different materials are used side by side, these techniques make the parts stand out even more.

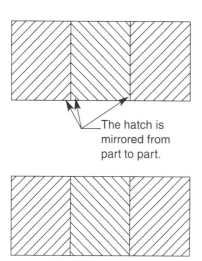

The hatch is mirrored from part to part.

A combination of staggering and mirroring is also very effective in separating parts.

FIGURE 8.43

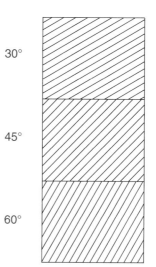

30°

45°

60°

Changing the section-line angles is another way to accent the different parts in an assembly.

FIGURE 8.44

Tips for Good Section Drawing

Let us start by emphasizing lineweights. Recall from the alphabet of lines how lineweights help accent the drawing and make them much more readable. Well, section lines or hatch lines are drawn at .35mm or about half the thickness of a visible line (.7mm), so the two should not be confused. Keeping the section lines spacing consistent is another concern of the drafter. Most experienced drafters can eyeball the spacing of section lines. They have practiced enough section drawings to let their vision control the spacing. The spacing is not set in stone, however. A small area needs small spacing (1/16″ minimum) between section lines (see Figure 8.45a), whereas larger areas may be spaced farther apart (see Figure 8.45b). As a beginner, it is a good idea to lay out the section lines using blue nonprint lead or hard lead like 4H or 6H when doing board drawing. Use a lettering guide to lay out the lines quickly using consistent spacing. Go back and darken the section lines with a .35 mm thick H or 2H pencil to complete the section. Remember to draw the section lines last on a drawing because they smear very easily (see Figure 8.46).

Some of the more common section line problems are shown in Figure 8.47. They include lines that overlap, inconsistent line quality and spacing, and general smearing, which tends to happen when many lines are drawn in a small area. On a board drawing make sure to use the drafting powder on the vellum surface to help prevent your equipment from smearing as you work.

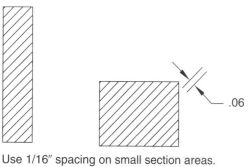

Use 1/16″ spacing on small section areas.

(a)

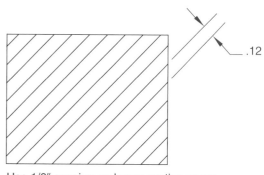

.12

Use 1/8″ spacing on larger section areas.

(b)

FIGURE 8.45

FIGURE 8.46

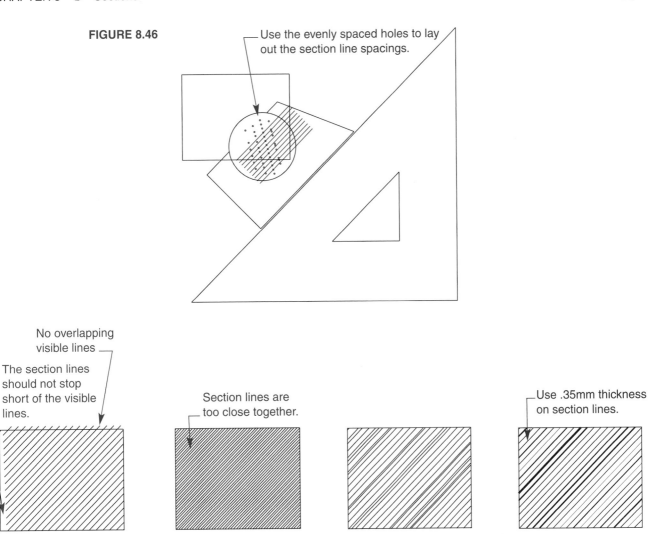

Use the evenly spaced holes to lay out the section line spacings.

No overlapping visible lines

The section lines should not stop short of the visible lines.

Section lines need to terminate on the visible lines.

Section lines are too close together.

Section lines need to have adequate spacing.

Section lines need to have consistent spacing.

Use .35mm thickness on section lines.

Section lines need a consistent line weight.

FIGURE 8.47 Examples of poor sectioning

Sectioning Shafts

All the sectioning described thus far gives the viewer a two-dimensional feel. The shaft section called an S-break (see Figure 8.48) is used on shafts in a 2-D orthographic view. Although the view is flat, the section will give the impression of a 3-D break on the shaft. The following steps are used to draw an S-break on a shaft.

Step 1 Outline a small rectangle on the end of the shaft where you want to place the break. The width of the rectangle should be one-third of the radius and run the full height (diameter) of the shaft (see Figure 8.49a).

FIGURE 8.48

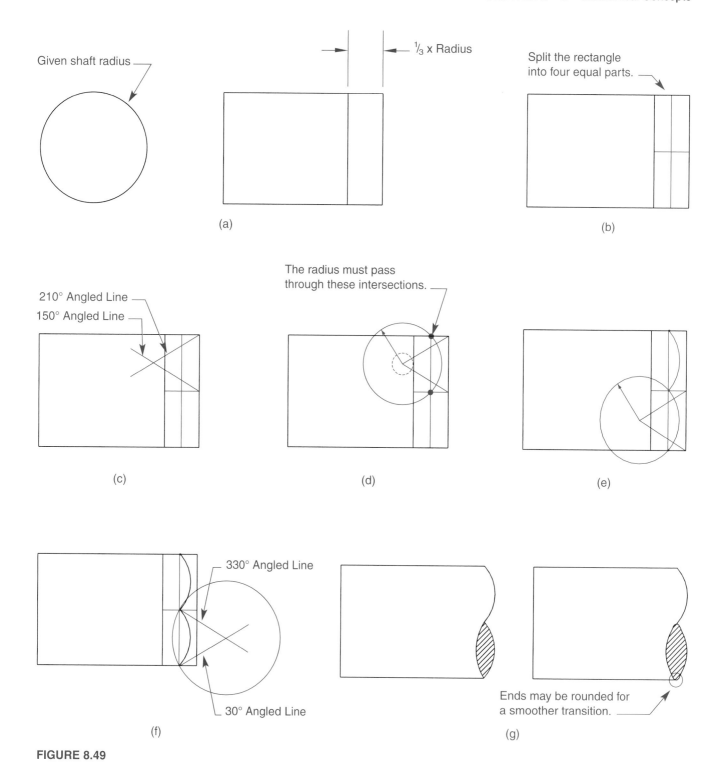

FIGURE 8.49

Step 2 Draw two lines from the midpoints, splitting the small rectangle into four equal pieces (see Figure 8.49b). In the top right-hand corner draw two angles converging into the shaft at 210° and 150° (see Figure 8.49c).

Step 3 Using the intersection of the 210° and 150° lines as the center, draw an arc that intersects the top and bottom corners on the left-hand side of the top right rectangle (see Figure 8.49d).

Step 4 Repeat steps 2 and 3 on the bottom right rectangle portion of the shaft (see Figure 8.49e).

Step 5 Continue on the bottom right rectangle part and reverse the process, going the other way in a mirror image. Draw the 30° and 330° angles converging outside the shaft (see Figure 8.49f).

Step 6 Remove all the construction lines so the end of the shaft is clearly seen. Hatch or add section lines to the area inside the bottom arcs (see Figure 8.49g). The ends may be rounded off with small arcs for a smoother look.

REVIEW QUESTIONS

1. What type of drawing or representation does a section replace?
2. List the different types of sections found in mechanical drawing.
3. When are hidden lines used on a section drawing?
4. Why is a cutting-plane line so important?
5. Which sections do not require cutting plane lines?
6. What purpose do the arrowheads on the cutting-plane line serve?
7. Sketch the typical symbols used when sectioning steel, iron, brass, and aluminum.
8. How are hollowed-out areas handled in section views?
9. Why is drawing a half section more challenging than drawing a full section?
10. Explain how the path of an offset section should be determined.
11. Which type of parts would an aligned section be used for?
12. Explain when ribs should be sectioned.
13. When is a general sectioning symbol *not* used?
14. What are some of the techniques used to clarify parts in an assembly section when they touch?
15. When should a drafter draw a section view?

EXERCISES

1. Draw a shaft 4″ long with a 1″ diameter. Break the shaft using the S-break method.
2. Practice drawing the cutting-plane and viewing-plane lines as shown in the alphabet of lines in Figure 3.8. Draw six of each using the correct lineweight and darkness. Add the arrowheads in the correct location. Use your triangles to draw these larger arrowheads.

DRAWING ASSIGNMENTS

1. Convert each of the drawings in Figure 8.50 into an orthographic view along with the appropriate section view.

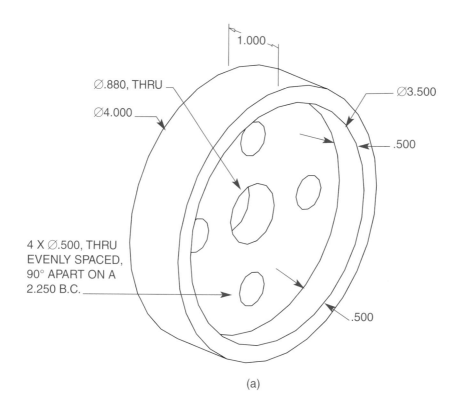

Ø.880, THRU

Ø4.000

1.000

Ø3.500

.500

4 X Ø.500, THRU
EVENLY SPACED,
90° APART ON A
2.250 B.C.

.500

(a)

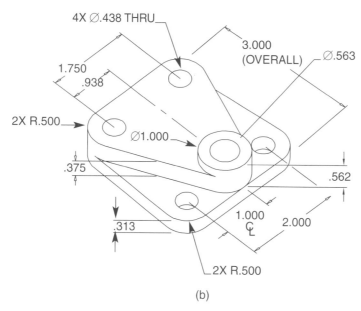

4X Ø.438 THRU

3.000
(OVERALL)

Ø.563

1.750

.938

2X R.500

Ø1.000

.375

.562

.313

1.000
C̶L

2.000

2X R.500

(b)

FIGURE 8.50

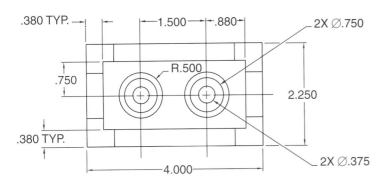

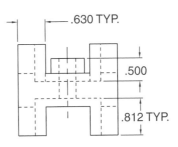

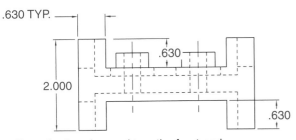

Draw the top view and turn the front and
right-side orthographic views into sections.

(c)

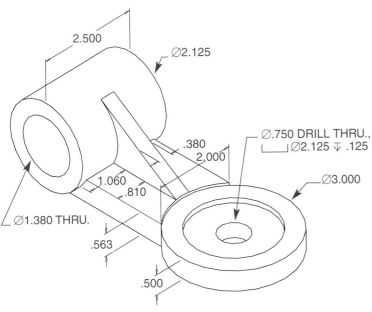

NOTE: Overall length is 6.823.

(d)

FIGURE 8.50
continued on next page

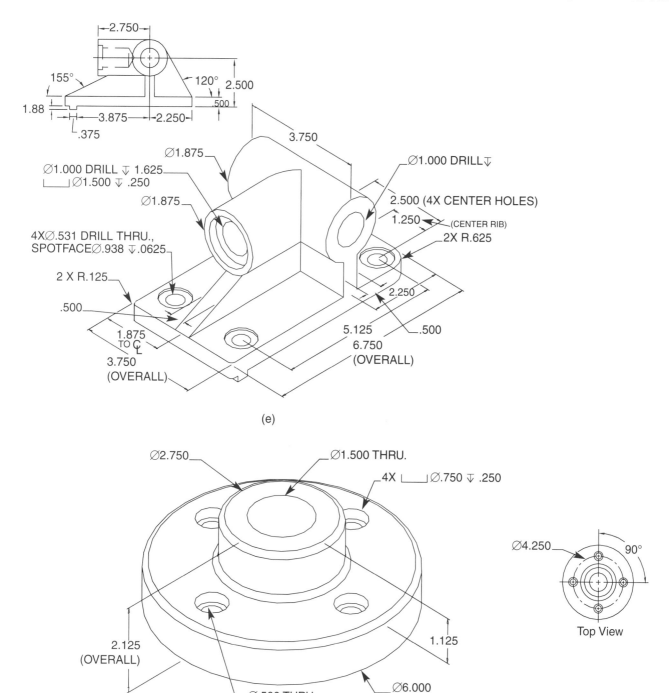

(e)

(f)

NOTE: All fillets are to be .125 radius on the edges.

FIGURE 8.50
continued

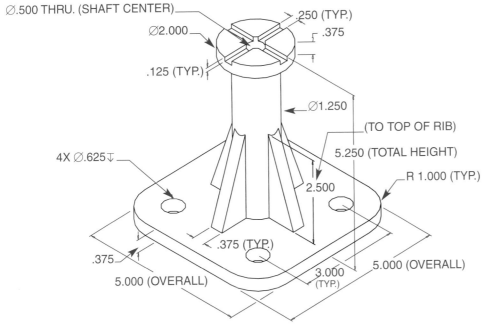

Ø.500 THRU. (SHAFT CENTER)

Ø2.000

.125 (TYP.)

.250 (TYP.)

.375

Ø1.250

4X Ø.625↧

(TO TOP OF RIB)

5.250 (TOTAL HEIGHT)

R 1.000 (TYP.)

2.500

.375 (TYP.)

.375

5.000 (OVERALL)

3.000
(TYP.)

5.000 (OVERALL)

NOTE: Center all ribs on base plate.

(g)

FIGURE 8.50
continued on next page

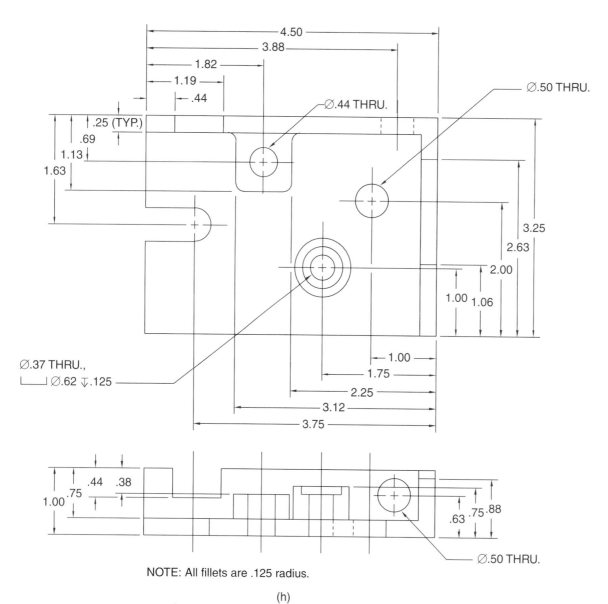

NOTE: All fillets are .125 radius.

(h)

FIGURE 8.50
continued

CHAPTER 9

Dimensioning Mechanical Drawings

All forms of technical drafting involve dimensions and annotations. Machine tool design and engineering graphics are forms of mechanical drawing with their own dimensioning requirements. In fact, these types of graphics appear to have more rules and standards than all the other types of drafting combined. In addition, these standards and guidelines are much more rigid than most. If you stop to think why, the reasons become clearer. Take a look at some of the other drafting fields and see what is being built.

Architecture deals with buildings and large components, as does civil engineering. When dimensions are placed on these drawings the measuring units are feet and inches. Dimensions and sizes of large items can sometimes vary without affecting the function or form of the design. For instance, if a hotel lobby is designed to be 80′ × 100′, but during construction it is actually built to a size of 79′-11″ × 99′-11″, this variation usually is not a problem. An error of 1″ in both directions when the room size is large may not affect the building design, and the architect can often live with this amount of inaccuracy.

In contrast, mechanical drawings deal with mechanical parts that tend to be small in size—many can fit in the palm of your hand—and whose functions are varied. Mechanical parts are used in many ways you hardly think of in your day to day life. For example, a car has so many mechanical parts that perform so many different functions it would take a long while to name all of them. The following are some with which you are probably familiar:

- Braking system
- Steering system
- Locks, latches, and hinges
- Engines, transmissions, axles

Think about these items. You should be familiar with all of them as a whole, but probably not with every component of the unit. Now, compare these items with the hotel lobby. A mistake of 1″ in the manufacture of automotive parts could cause major problems, not to mention malfunctions and accidents, if the parts worked at all.

9.1 Dimensioning Units and Standards

Obviously, most machine tool parts need to be built with great precision and accuracy. For example, in automobile engines a thin film of oil is used to lubricate metal and reduce friction. This thin oil film keeps metal parts from rubbing against one another, and allowing the engine to function properly and helping prevent excessive wear. Thus, part sizes must be exact and uniform.

Dimensioning Units

You might ask, What precision is necessary when dealing with machine tool parts? In the United States decimal inches are predominantly used for dimensioning. A machinist can manufacture a part to a tenth (.1), a hundredth (.01), or a thousandth (.001) of an inch or less. In most other countries the metric system is predominantly used. The common metric dimensioning unit is the millimeter, which is $\frac{1}{1000}$ of a meter (approximately 39″). A machinist can manufacture a part to $\frac{1}{10}$ of a millimeter, or .1 mm. The following is the equivalence between the decimal inch and the millimeter:

$$1″ = 25.4 \text{ millimeters (25.4 mm)}$$
$$.039″ = 1 \text{ millimeter (1 mm)}$$

In the United States, dimensions for mechanical parts such as nuts, bolts, threads, welds, and other fasteners are given in fractions. Thus, it is necessary to learn the following decimal equivalents of fractions:

Fraction		Decimal Equivalent
1/64″	=	.015625
1/32″	=	.03125
1/16″	=	.0625
1/8″	=	.125
3/16″	=	.1875
1/4″	=	.25
5/16″	=	.3125
3/8″	=	.375
7/16″	=	.437
1/2″	=	.500
9/16″	=	.5625
5/8″	=	.625
11/16″	=	.6875
3/4″	=	.750
13/16″	=	.8125
7/8″	=	.875

Dimensioning Standards

Due to technological advances and almost instantaneous communications, today's world has "shrunk" dramatically, forcing many companies to think and compete globally to survive. Thus, many U.S. companies have facilities spread throughout the country and sometimes the world. Producing parts at a plant in one part of the world, then combining the parts with others from different corners of the planet and assembling them into a mechanical device is a logistical nightmare. Having the mechanical device work correctly takes good standards and excellent communication. If a company manufactures all its own parts, it can create its own dimensioning standards for its employees to follow; however, this is often not the case.

Let us look at a company that buys parts throughout the world from other companies. The company standards manual is not applicable in such a case, but there are uniform standards that companies can use to ensure uniformity of parts throughout the world. The following groups publish dimensioning and tolerance standards:

- **ASME**—the American Society of Mechanical Engineers. This group has adopted the ASME Y14.5M—1994 (also ANSI/ASME Y14.5M—1994) standards for drafters, designers, and engineers. These standards are also referred to as the former ANSI Y14.5M dimension standards (ANSI—American National Standards Institute).
- **ISO**—International Standards Organization
- **SI**—International Bureau of Weights and Measures (International System of Units)

The ISO standards are used by professionals in many companies outside the United States. A key difference is that countries other than the United States use the metric system; the United States primarily uses decimal inches.

9.2 Linear Dimensioning

In this text we will use the ASME Y14.5M—1994 standards as a guide to explaining acceptable dimensioning practices. Once you have learned some of the basic concepts of dimensioning in this book, buy yourself a copy of the *ASME Y14.5M—1994* standards book. It is the ultimate reference for resolving arguments and gray areas. Use this chapter as a training tool, but check the standards for your industry.

Dimension Components

We start by studying the components of a typical linear dimension (see Figure 9.1). The key components are labeled in this linear or straight-line dimension example. To begin, let's look at the dimension text and its options.

The Dimension Value

- Decimal-inch dimensions are expressed according to the tolerance desired. A *tolerance* is the total amount by which the dimension is permitted to vary. Tolerances vary depending on the precision needed for a particular part (see Figure 9.2). Always check in or near the drawing's title block to see what general tolerance is being applied to the drawing. Remember that a dimension is normally expressed to the same number of decimal places as its tolerance. In Figure 9.2 as well as on mechanical drawings, the number of Xs to the right of the decimal represent the tolerance found in the general tolerance note. This information tells you how much the dimension can vary.

- If a dimension value is less than 1″, it is written without a zero to the left of the decimal (see Figure 9.3).

FIGURE 9.1

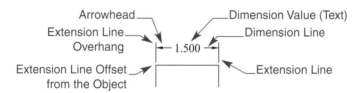

FIGURE 9.2

A general tolerance to apply to this dimension would appear as follows in the title block:

.XX=±.02

Refers to any dimensions on the drawing with two decimal places.

Use this tolerance when a dimension has two decimal places, unless noted otherwise.

(a) Two places

A general tolerance to apply to this dimension would appear as follows in the title block:

.XXX=±.001

Refers to any dimensions on the drawing with three decimal places.

Use this tolerance when a dimension has three decimal places, unless noted otherwise.

(b) Three places

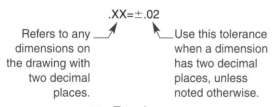

A general tolerance to apply to this dimension would appear as follows in the title block:

.XXXX=±.0005

Refers to any dimensions on the drawings with four decimal places.

Use this tolerance when a dimension has four decimal places, unless noted otherwise.

(c) Four places

FIGURE 9.3

Yes	No	Yes	No
Correct decimal-inch dimension	Incorrect decimal-inch dimension	Correct decimal-inch dimension	Incorrect decimal-inch dimension

FIGURE 9.4

.125 Minimum Height for Text

.750

- The dimension should be a minimum of .125″ (⅛″) high (see Figure 9.4). Some companies use .187″ (³⁄₁₆″) to make the dimension easier to read. The larger size also helps if the drawing is reproduced later in a smaller size. Recall that dimensions and notes should have the same letter height on the drawing. If there is more than one drawing sheet, then the height should also be the same on all the sheets.

- Dimension text and lettering styles are defined in ANSI 14.2M. Single Stroke Gothic Lettering is the universally accepted style for mechanical drawing. The letter style of the dimensions and of the notes must be the same on the drawing.

- Fractions are not used to dimension linear distances. Fractions are used in other capacities such as thread notes and welding callouts (see Figure 9.5).

- A unidirectional system is used to align the units. The number is drawn vertically, aligned from the top of the drawing sheet to the bottom. The dimension lines may be drawn in various directions; however, the number always appears in the same orientation (see Figure 9.6).

- A visible gap of about ¹⁄₁₆″ is used between the number and the dimension line (see Figure 9.7).

- Both the number and the decimal point must be clear, dark, and distinctive. If doing the drawing on a drawing board, use guidelines to letter the numbers. Apply a lot of pressure when lettering to make the letters and decimal point bold and readable, just like a visible line.

- The inch symbol is not used following the numerical value.

Metric or Millimeter Dimensions.   Many but not all of the rules for decimal inches apply also to millimeter dimensions in ASME Y14.5—1994 standards. The main difference is in the appearance of the numerical value. The following rules apply to millimeter dimensions.

- If a dimension is less than 1 mm, place a zero in front of the decimal point or to its left (see Figure 9.8).

- If the dimension value is in whole millimeters, then omit a decimal point or zero (see Figure 9.9).

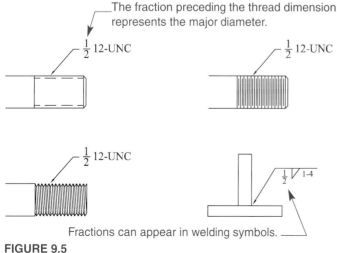

The fraction preceding the thread dimension represents the major diameter.

½ 12-UNC

½ 12-UNC

½ 12-UNC

½ ∨ 1-4

Fractions can appear in welding symbols.

FIGURE 9.5

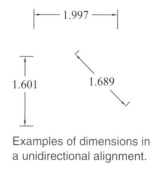

1.997

1.601   1.689

Examples of dimensions in a unidirectional alignment.

FIGURE 9.6

Use a .06 gap here.

2.000

FIGURE 9.7

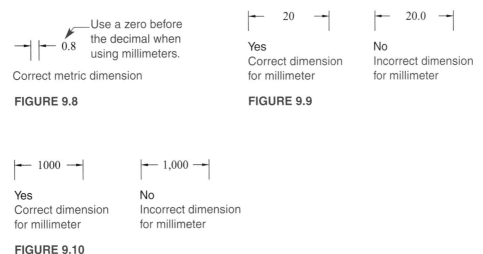

FIGURE 9.8

Correct metric dimension

FIGURE 9.9

Yes
Correct dimension
for millimeter

No
Incorrect dimension
for millimeter

Yes
Correct dimension
for millimeter

No
Incorrect dimension
for millimeter

FIGURE 9.10

- Do not use commas and spaces to separate digits into groups in showing millimeter dimensions (see Figure 9.10).

Applying Tolerances to the Dimensions. Earlier in this chapter it was stated that tolerances control how a dimension is expressed. A dimension expressed to three decimal places (thousandths) should have a tolerance that also controls the variance to three decimal places (see Figure 9.11). At times it may be necessary to control dimensions individually rather than have a general tolerance apply to the whole drawing. The following examples show how tolerances can be applied and drawn with the dimension instead.

- **Limit dimensions** display two values: an upper limit and a lower limit. The tolerance is included in the dimensions and reflects the total variance allowed (see Figure 9.12).
- **Unidirectional tolerancing** allows the dimension to vary in one direction only. The tolerance may be in a positive direction or in a negative one but not both (see Figure 9.13). The tolerance is drawn beside the dimension to its right and overrides a general tolerance.
- **Bilateral tolerancing** allows the dimension to vary in both the negative and positive directions, either by the same (symmetrical bilateral tolerance) or different amounts (deviated bilateral tolerance). A general tolerance does not apply when bilateral tolerancing is used (see Figure 9.14). *Note:* The tolerance should also be a minimum of .125″ (⅛″) tall to ensure its readability on a drawing.
- A **reference dimension** is one given for informational purposes or estimated sizes. A reference dimension appears in parentheses. Other dimensions around the reference dimension will determine its actual size (see Figure 9.15).

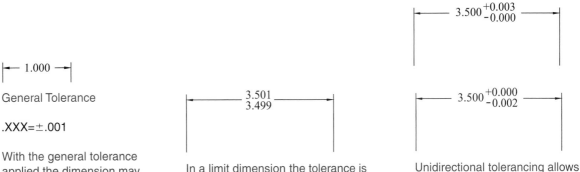

General Tolerance

.XXX=±.001

With the general tolerance applied the dimension may become as large as 1.001 or as small as .999.

FIGURE 9.11

In a limit dimension the tolerance is already applied, and the variance range is shown.

FIGURE 9.12

Unidirectional tolerancing allows the tolerance to be applied in only one direction.

FIGURE 9.13

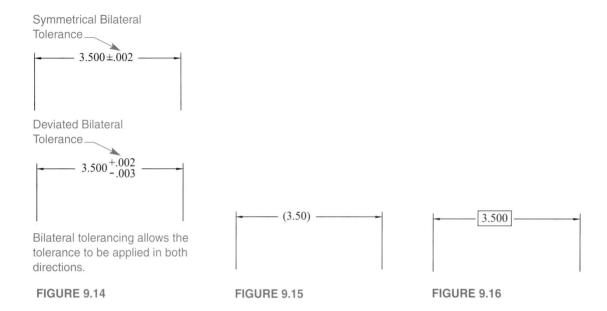

Symmetrical Bilateral Tolerance

Deviated Bilateral Tolerance

Bilateral tolerancing allows the tolerance to be applied in both directions.

FIGURE 9.14   **FIGURE 9.15**   **FIGURE 9.16**

- A **basic dimension** is a theoretically exact size. A basic dimension appears enclosed in a rectangle. The general tolerance displayed in a title block or a general note does not apply to basic dimensions. They are usually controlled by a more advanced geometric tolerance not discussed in this text. A general note stating that all untoleranced dimensions are basic may also be used instead of a rectangle (see Figure 9.16). *Note:* All untoleranced dimensions are basic dimensions.

- A **not-to-scale dimension** indicates that the dimension is inconsistent with the scale of the drawing. A not-to-scale dimension can be indicated by underlining the dimension (see Figure 9.17).

Dimension and Extension Lines

The lineweights for dimension and extension lines should be of the thin, dark variety. A width of .35 mm or 1/64″ is called for in the alphabet of lines. Certain guidelines are followed for using these lines in mechanical drawing:

- A dimension line must be spaced a minimum of .38 (10 mm) or 3/8″ away from the visible line being referenced (see Figure 9.18).

- A gap of .06 or 1/16″ must be used to separate the extension line from the visible line (see Figure 9.18).

- No gap is used when the extension line is used to dimension to the centerline of a circle (see Figure 9.19).

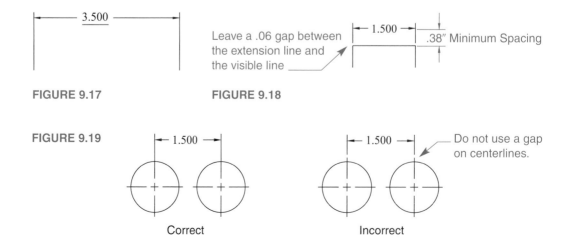

FIGURE 9.17   **FIGURE 9.18**

FIGURE 9.19

Correct   Incorrect

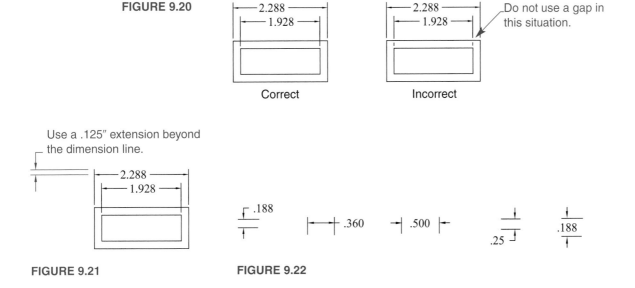

FIGURE 9.20

Correct   Incorrect

FIGURE 9.21

FIGURE 9.22

- When extension lines are used inside a part, no gaps are used when passing through a visible line (see Figure 9.20).
- The extension line must extend .125 (⅛″) beyond the dimension line (see Figure 9.21).

Some versatility is allowed when it comes to arranging the dimensions, dimension lines, and extension lines. (See the different alignments shown in Figure 9.22.) These are all acceptable when there is not much room for the arrows or dimension.

Arrowheads

Mechanical drafting requires arrowheads to be placed on the ends of a dimension line or at the end of a leader line for notes or size callouts. It is acceptable in most mechanical drawings to make the arrowhead size proportional to the dimension text height. Use of the .125″ minimum height of a dimension character will determine the arrowhead size:

- The length of the arrowhead will be the same size as the text height (see Figure 9.23).
- The width of the arrowhead should be one-third of the length measurement (see Figure 9.24).

Arrowheads are drawn freehand for board drawing. A little practice is required to get arrowheads to look uniform, consistent, and proportional. Many students make too wide arrowheads at first. See Figure 9.25 for some strokes to practice making arrowheads for board drawing. The arrowhead needs to be kept narrow, with the strokes gradually coming off the dimension line. Hugging the dimension line will help keep the arrowhead slimmed down. Jumping off the dimension line too quickly often results in an unacceptably wide arrowhead.

In AutoCAD, arrowhead shapes and sizes are set with variables. It becomes a matter of adjusting the settings or variables to get desired results. This subject will be discussed in Chapter 20. Figure 9.26 shows

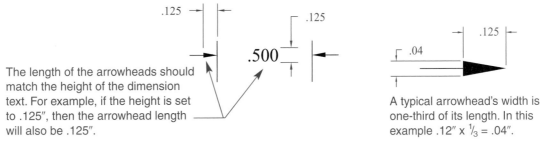

The length of the arrowheads should match the height of the dimension text. For example, if the height is set to .125″, then the arrowhead length will also be .125″.

A typical arrowhead's width is one-third of its length. In this example .12″ x ⅓ = .04″.

FIGURE 9.23   **FIGURE 9.24**

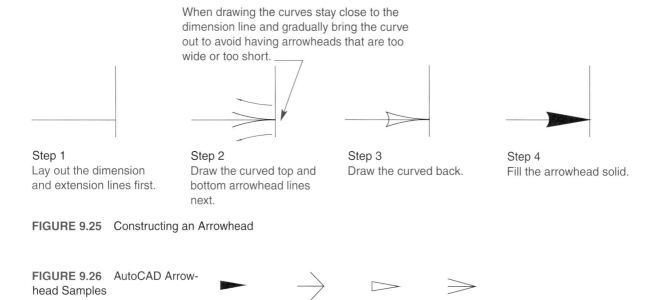

When drawing the curves stay close to the dimension line and gradually bring the curve out to avoid having arrowheads that are too wide or too short.

Step 1
Lay out the dimension and extension lines first.

Step 2
Draw the curved top and bottom arrowhead lines next.

Step 3
Draw the curved back.

Step 4
Fill the arrowhead solid.

FIGURE 9.25   Constructing an Arrowhead

FIGURE 9.26   AutoCAD Arrowhead Samples

Closed Fill   Right Angle   Closed Blank   Open 30°

some arrowhead shapes found in the AutoCAD selections. The AutoCAD software can make every arrowhead perfect on a drawing. This is one reason that some of the arrowhead types in Figure 9.26 are allowed on mechanical drawings. The closed filled is the most widely accepted.

Dimensioning Systems for Drawings

Different dimensioning systems or styles can be used to place or orient dimensions on a drawing. Several factors may determine how a drawing will be dimensioned, namely,

1. How the dimensions are to be toleranced
2. The space needed to place dimensions
3. The size of the drawing

Depending on the circumstances, any of the following systems may be used:

- Chain dimensioning
- Parallel dimensioning
- Baseline or datum dimensioning
- Ordinate dimensioning

We shall examine the positive and negative aspects of each of the different styles.

Chain Dimensioning

Chain dimensioning is also referred to as a **point-to-point system.** A string of dimensions are placed along a straight continuous line. This style is very straightforward to use and understand (see Figure 9.27).

Each feature such as a corner or circle center has an extension line referencing off it. The dimension line is then placed a minimum of ⅜″ (.375) away from the closest visible line. All the extension lines must stop ⅛″ outside the dimension line on the chain. These lines follow the same guidelines explained previously. The dimension values are then placed in the chain or straight-line form (see Figure 9.28).

One problem with chain dimensioning is that it tends to appear crowded when small spaces are dimensioned. There are a few options for adjusting the dimension placement (see Figure 9.29). These options are acceptable to use on chain dimensioning when you are faced with a crowded situation.

It is typical to place an overall dimension above a chain dimension set (see Figure 9.30). Using an overall dimension allows the drafter to exercise another option on chain dimensioning, that is, to leave out one of

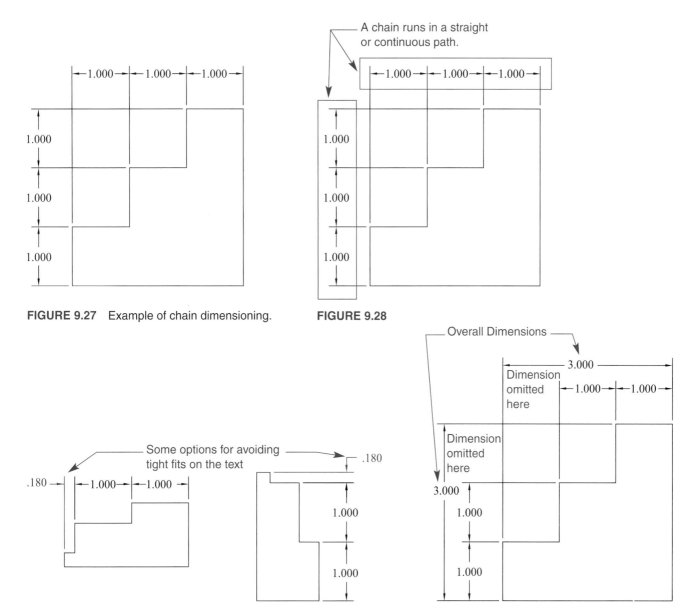

FIGURE 9.27 Example of chain dimensioning.

FIGURE 9.28

FIGURE 9.29

FIGURE 9.30

the dimensions in the chain system. If a dimension is left out of a chain, it can still be calculated when an overall dimension also accompanies the group (see Figure 9.30).

To add an overall dimension to a chain, simply place another dimension line 1/4″ (when using minimum spacing) to 3/8″ (when using maximum spacing) outside the chain. Use the outside extension lines and draw them 1/8″ above the overall dimension line (see Figure 9.31).

A close examination of the chain system will reveal its weaknesses: the chain system references the previous dimension drawn (see Figure 9.32). Referencing from the previous point causes a tolerance accumulation. Simply put, if a tolerance variance is allowed on the first dimension, then the second dimension in the chain is referenced from the first, causing the tolerances to accumulate. The actual size of the first one may be smaller or larger depending on the machinist's accuracy. This accumulation goes on throughout the chain (see Figure 9.33).

The possible dimension values with the tolerances added in tell the story: a chain system can allow the actual production size to change a good bit from the given dimensions on the drawing. This may be acceptable for some parts. If it is not, then you may want to place an individual tolerance with the dimension value for greater control on the produced part (see Figure 9.34).

Tolerancing decisions are normally made by an engineer, whereas the drafter must place them correctly on the finished drawing following the ASME Y14.5M standards.

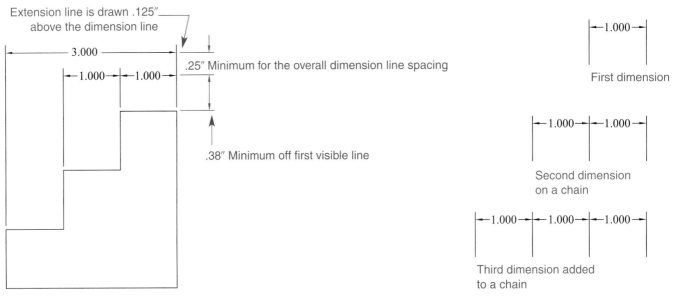

Extension line is drawn .125″ above the dimension line

3.000

1.000 — 1.000

.25″ Minimum for the overall dimension line spacing

.38″ Minimum off first visible line

FIGURE 9.31

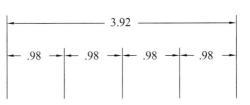

1.000

First dimension

1.000 — 1.000

Second dimension on a chain

1.000 — 1.000 — 1.000

Third dimension added to a chain

FIGURE 9.32

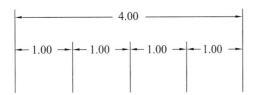

4.00

1.00 — 1.00 — 1.00 — 1.00

(a)   A chain with a general tolerance of .XX=±.02

3.92

.98 — .98 — .98 — .98

(b)   The effect of a (−.02) tolerance on the chain

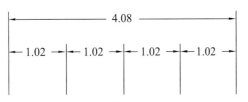

4.08

1.02 — 1.02 — 1.02 — 1.02

(c)   The effect of a (+.02) tolerance on the chain

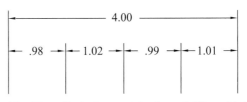

4.00

.98 — 1.02 — .99 — 1.01

(d)   The effect of a combination of different tolerances

FIGURE 9.33

FIGURE 9.34

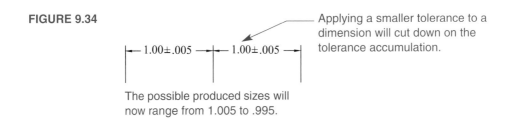

Applying a smaller tolerance to a dimension will cut down on the tolerance accumulation.

1.00±.005 — 1.00±.005

The possible produced sizes will now range from 1.005 to .995.

Parallel Dimensioning

A very different form of dimensioning is the **parallel** system in which each dimension stands alone, not relying on any other dimension for reference (see Figure 9.35). This method may be applied by placing the inner-most dimension line 3/8″ (.38) minimum off the outermost visible line. The other dimensions may then be added starting from the inside and working outward, using the normal 1/4″ spacing (see Figure 9.36).

It is important to stagger dimension numbers in order to keep the drawing easier to read. Even though nonstaggered dimensions look symmetrical, it is too easy to confuse numbers, as they tend to blend together because they are so close to each other (see Figure 9.37).

A shortcoming of this dimensioning system is its lack of continuity between dimensions. Problems can occur when tolerances are once again applied. Figure 9.38 shows the possible results on a produced part. What you see in conditions A–D in Figure 9.38 is probably what you expected; however, splitting the accumulated tolerance on each side becomes a guessing game for a machinist. Since there are no criteria tying the features together, they could be adjusted in a variety of positions. Let us look at condition C for instance (see Figure 9.39). Such a situation can cause some major problems if not handled correctly. One way to avoid this problem is to simply add more dimensions to critical spots when more control is needed between the dimensions (see Figure 9.40).

Datum or Baseline Dimensioning

Datum or **baseline dimensioning,** as it is called in AutoCAD, is a very precise and controlled system that eliminates tolerance accumulation. The best way to use a datum system is to pick the longest outside surface

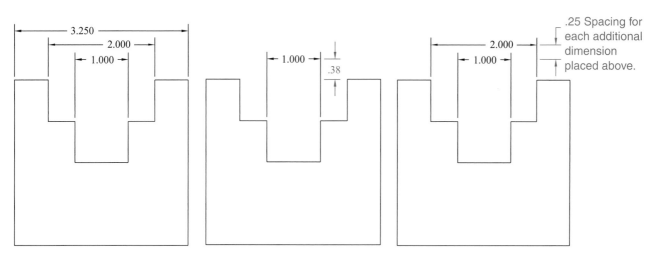

FIGURE 9.35   **FIGURE 9.36**

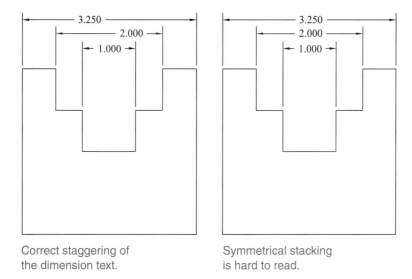

Correct staggering of
the dimension text.

Symmetrical stacking
is hard to read.

FIGURE 9.37

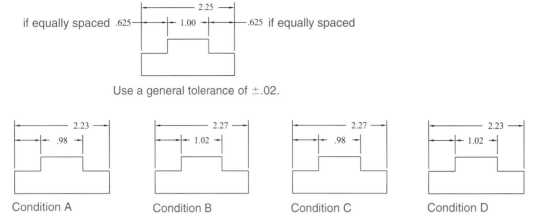

Use a general tolerance of ±.02.

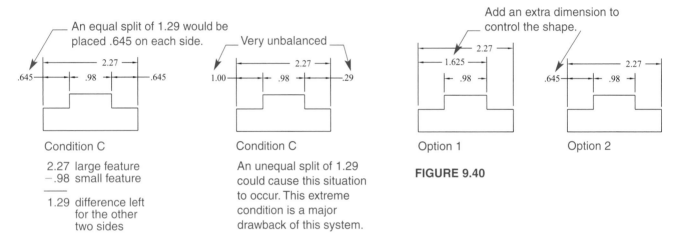

FIGURE 9.38

Condition A   Condition B   Condition C   Condition D

FIGURE 9.39

An equal split of 1.29 would be placed .645 on each side.

Very unbalanced

Condition C

2.27 large feature
−.98 small feature
————
1.29 difference left
      for the other
      two sides

An unequal split of 1.29 could cause this situation to occur. This extreme condition is a major drawback of this system.

Add an extra dimension to control the shape.

Option 1   Option 2

FIGURE 9.40

parallel to the direction you intend to dimension as your reference. This is called the *datum* or *baseline*. All the dimensions shown in this direction will be referenced back to this baseline (see Figure 9.41).

Setting Up a Datum.   Once you determine a good side to use as a baseline, draw a line off the side with a 1/16″ (.06) gap off the corner (see Figure 9.42). Place points on the baseline in blue lead representing the minimum spacing for stacking dimension lines according to ASME Y14.5 standards. After the points are placed, it is time to start laying out the dimensions. Begin by dimensioning the closest feature to the baseline 3/8″ above the visible line (see Figure 9.43). Dimension the next feature placing it on the next point 1/4″ above the first dimension (see Figure 9.44). Continue dimensioning and stacking until all the features in that direction are dimensioned. Repeat the process on the rest of the drawing until all the features have been dimensioned (see Figure 9.45).

Now, let us look at the dimension values and tolerances and see how the baseline system controls or minimizes the tolerance accumulation. As in the chain system, the dimension values vary as determined by the allowable tolerance (see Figure 9.46). However, notice in the baseline examples that none of the dimension numbers and tolerances exhibit the accumulation problem found earlier in the chain examples. Since the dimensions are taken from the baseline independently, they do not build up across the part. The baseline or datum system is the answer to stopping a tolerance accumulation.

The baseline method can also be used instead of the parallel system to eliminate any guesswork when it comes to coordinating where the tolerance variance should be placed. Recall Figure 9.39, where the machinist has to make a choice and try and balance out dimensions not called out. The baseline system resolves this problem because all the features are dimensioned and referenced from the same line.

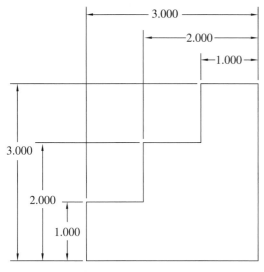

An example of a datum dimensioning system

FIGURE 9.41

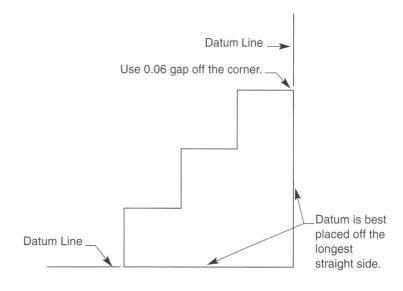

FIGURE 9.42

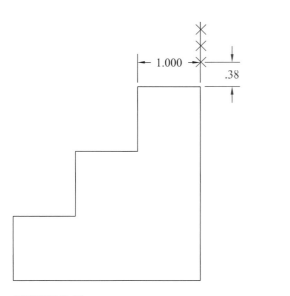

FIGURE 9.43

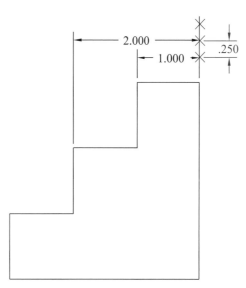

FIGURE 9.44

A major downside to a baseline system is the amount of space it takes up. The drawing area can fill up quickly with a baseline system, but proper planning will help prevent crowding a drawing. Two things that can help give you enough space are getting a big enough drawing sheet to hold the drawing and the dimensions as well as using enough space between your views. A normal spacing of 2″ between orthographic views may not always work with a baseline dimensioning system. Always examine how many dimensions will be needed and the space required to hold the dimensions comfortably. Some typical planning will be covered in Section 9.3.

Ordinate Dimensioning

The **ordinate dimension system** is a good way to avoid crowding a drawing with dimensions. Rather than using dimension lines and arrowheads, this system uses one extension line with a dimension that is referenced from an established origin on the view. The origin is placed in a lower-left corner or the center of a hole closest to the left-hand corner. One good option for identifying the origin is to use arrowheads as directional indicators for the X and Y values, although this is not an ASME Y14.5M requirement (see Figure 9.47).

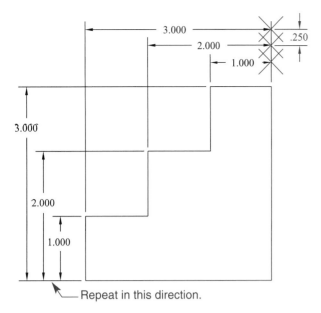

Repeat in this direction.

FIGURE 9.45

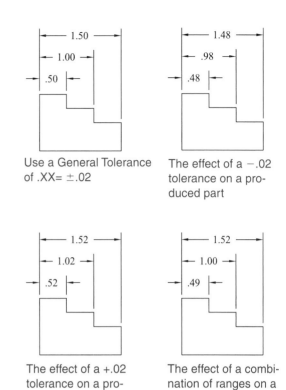

Use a General Tolerance of .XX= ±.02

The effect of a −.02 tolerance on a produced part

The effect of a +.02 tolerance on a produced part

The effect of a combination of ranges on a produced part

FIGURE 9.46

FIGURE 9.47

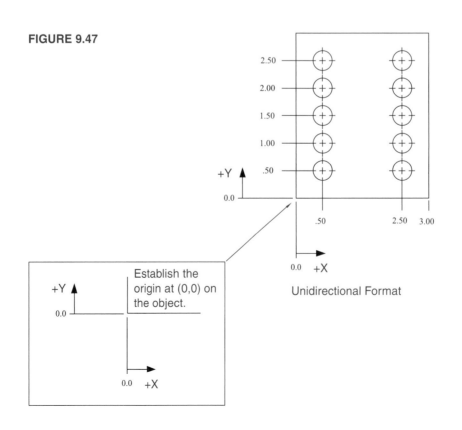

Establish the origin at (0,0) on the object.

Unidirectional Format

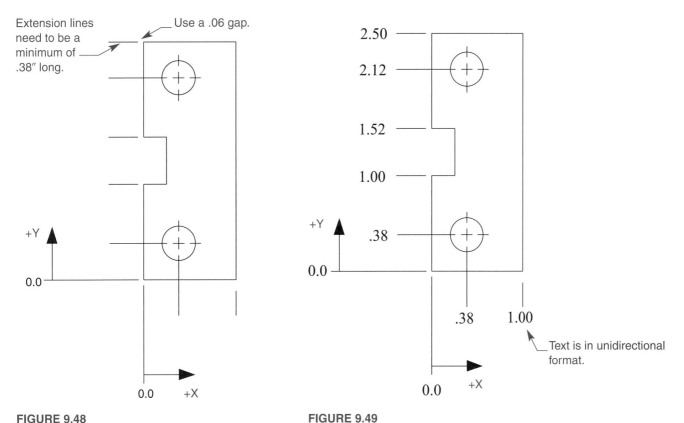

FIGURE 9.48

FIGURE 9.49

Once an origin (0,0) is established, you can start placing extension lines 1/16″ (.06) off each feature, one set running in the X direction, then another in the Y direction (see Figure 9.48). Each distance is measured from the origin in the X or Y direction and placed at the end of the extension line.

A standard unidirectional system is used in Figure 9.49. If a part has many features close together, an aligned system may be used (see Figure 9.50). Note that the dimension is placed on top of the extension line with a 1/16″ spacing off the line if the text height is drawn to the minimum 1/8″.

FIGURE 9.50

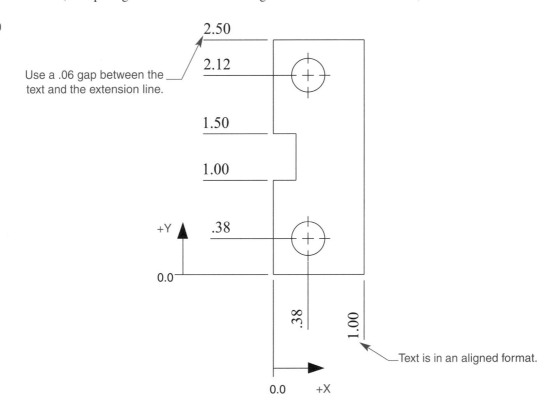

FIGURE 9.51

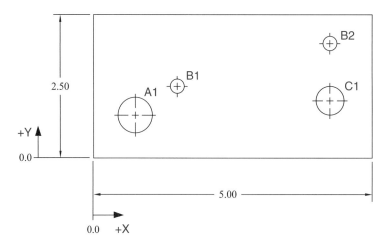

Holes with the same diameter may use the same letter but are assigned different numbers.

Symbol	Hole Location +X	+Y	Hole Size
A1	.75	.75	⌀.50
B1	1.5	1.25	⌀.25
B2	4.25	2.00	⌀.25
C1	4.25	1.00	⌀.31

Tabulated Dimensions

A **tabulated system** is an even more basic use of the ordinate system. In this system each feature is given a symbol that is an alphanumeric code. The drafter establishes an origin (0,0) as previously shown in the ordinate system. This time instead of using an extension with a dimension, the drafter draws a table or chart and places the dimensions in the appropriate columns. X and Y columns are used for dimensions to locate the features of the drawing (see Figure 9.51).

The advantage of the ordinate and tabulated dimensions are that time and space are saved, and tolerances to not accumulate on the dimensions. Having an origin is analogous to using a baseline when it comes to a tolerance variance, because every dimension has the same reference.

The negative aspect of the ordinate and tabulated systems can easily be understood. A drawing with tabulated dimensioning forces a person interpreting the work to look at the line drawing and then to look at the table containing the dimensions. Having to coordinate the two pieces of information can create problems. An ordinate system has a slightly different problem in that the reader has no arrowheads to point to where the dimensions are referencing. The viewer must always remember to look at the dimension location, which can be confusing.

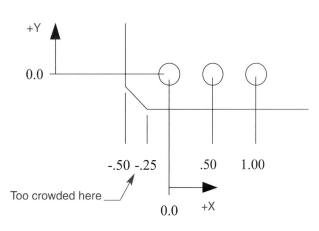

FIGURE 9.52

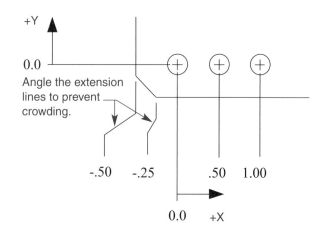

FIGURE 9.53

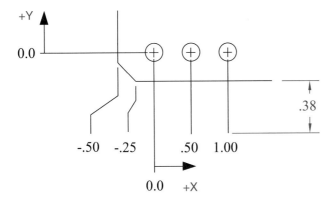

FIGURE 9.54

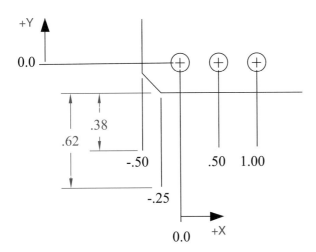

FIGURE 9.55

Even ordinate and tabulated dimensions can have crowding problems with the dimension text (see Figure 9.52). Using an angled extension line is a solution (see Figure 9.53). The angles used on the extension line may be varied as needed, but staying between 30° and 60° is the most acceptable. Remember to use a consistent spacing between the dimension text and the outside visible lines (see Figure 9.54).

It may not always be possible, though, to use this spacing for really crowded drawings. One solution is to place some of the dimensions on a 3/8″ spacing and others on 5/8″. This is the same spacing used for the baseline system with the minimum text height of 1/8″. If you need more space, continue stacking the text another 1/4″ farther out.

You may use a combination of the ordinate and tabulation systems. This method allows you to create a table for the hole sizes while still using the ordinate system to locate the X and Y points (see Figure 9.56).

FIGURE 9.56

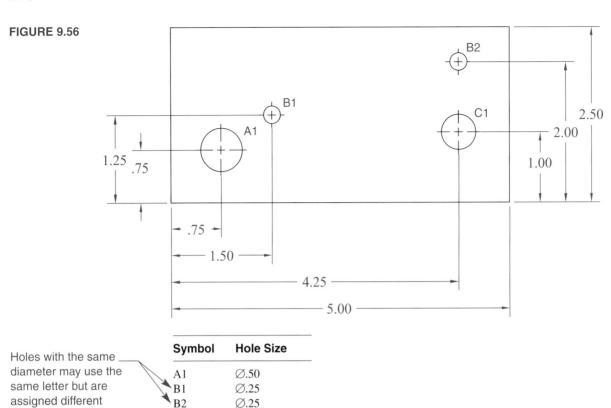

Symbol	Hole Size
A1	$\varnothing.50$
B1	$\varnothing.25$
B2	$\varnothing.25$
C1	$\varnothing.31$

Holes with the same diameter may use the same letter but are assigned different numbers.

9.3　Dimensioning Shapes and Sizes

Linear or straight-line dimensioning methods were shown in Section 9.2. This section covers the other miscellaneous types of dimensioning that must be used on the different shapes that occur in technical drawing. Symbols play a large part in dimensioning different geometric shapes, so let us examine the standard dimensioning symbols in Figure 9.57.

These symbols can occur in different locations throughout a drawing. Learning the symbols will be your first step in understanding their meaning and in turn will allow you to place them on your drawing. Look for them as you go through the different drawings and examples.

Dimensioning Angles

In mechanical drawings angular units are expressed in degrees and decimal parts of a degree (see Figure 9.58a), in degrees and minutes (see Figure 9.58b), or in degrees, minutes, and seconds (see Figure 9.58c).

Dimension angles require the same basic dimensioning components (angle value, dimension line, extension lines, and arrowheads). Because of the nature of an angle, the dimension lines are curved or circular. Figure 9.59 shows some acceptable ways to dimension angles. Remember to use the 1/16″ extension line gaps off visible lines and 1/8″ extension line overhangs past the dimension lines. These are very direct methods of dimensioning an angle.

If the slope of the angle is known, then it may be used instead of the angle. A leader line is used with a note containing slope information (see Figure 9.60). To call out the slope use the slope symbol first followed by the numerical value. Point to the angled surface with an arrowhead, then use a 3/8″ long angled leader line (30°–60°) connected to a 1/4″ long horizontal line (see Figure 9.61).

Leader lines play an important part in calling out sizes. They are very versatile and can make a call-out very easy in a tight location (see Figure 9.62).

Symbols	Purpose	Abbreviations	Example
∅	**Diameter** A measurement indicating the length of a line segment passing through the center point of a circle or circular arc and extending from one side to another.	**DIA.**	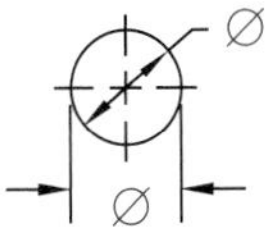 ∅ ∅
R	**Radius** A measurement indicating the length of a line segment passing from the center point of a circle or circular arc to one side.	**R**	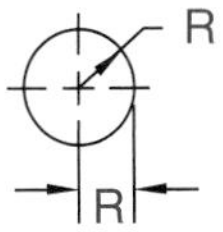 R R
S∅	**Diameter of a sphere** A measurement indicating the length of a line segment passing through the center point of a sphere or partial spherical shape and extending from one side to another.	**S∅**	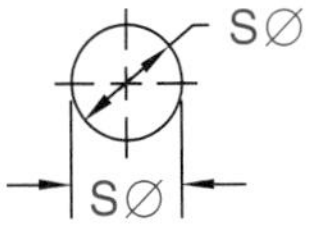 S∅ S∅
SR	**Radius of a sphere** A measurement indicating the length of a line segment passing from the center point of a sphere or partial spherical shape to one side.	**SR**	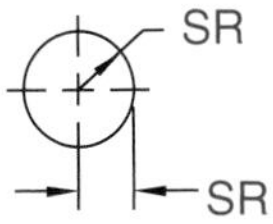 SR SR
⌒	**Arc length** A measure of the circular distance along an arc.	**None**	 .50
⌴	**Counterbore or Spotface** A flat bottom hole cut with a boring bit. Used to recess a hole into an object so a bolt or fastener will not stick outside the part when the assembly is completed.	**CBORE, SFACE**	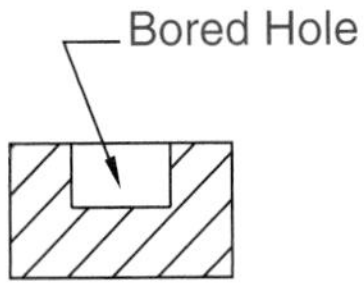 Bored Hole
∨	**Countersink** A hole with angled or tapering sides. It is used to recess tapered screw heads.	**CSK**	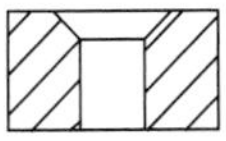
↧	**Depth** Indicates how deep a feature is in a part.	**DP**	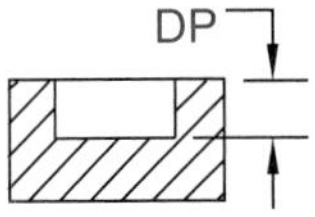 DP
□	**Square** Indicates the shape of the object or that it is equal in length and width.	**SQ**	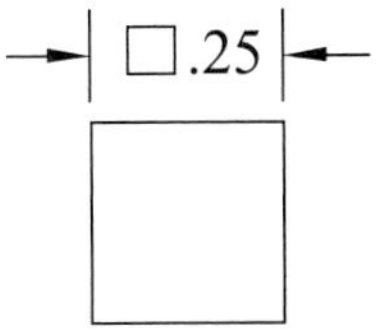 □.25
	**Slope** The slope symbol is used to call out the ratio of the rise over run for flat surfaces. 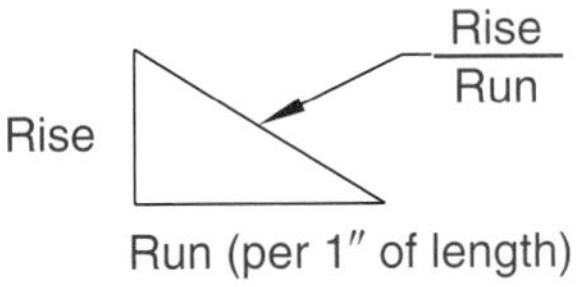 Rise / Run · Rise · Run (per 1″ of length)	**None**	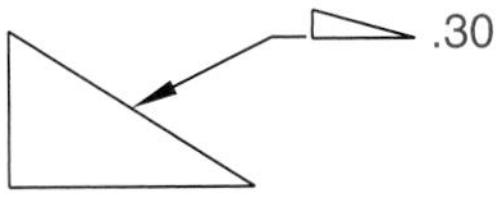 .30
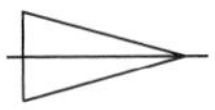	**Conical Taper** This symbol is used for shapes with a cone taper. 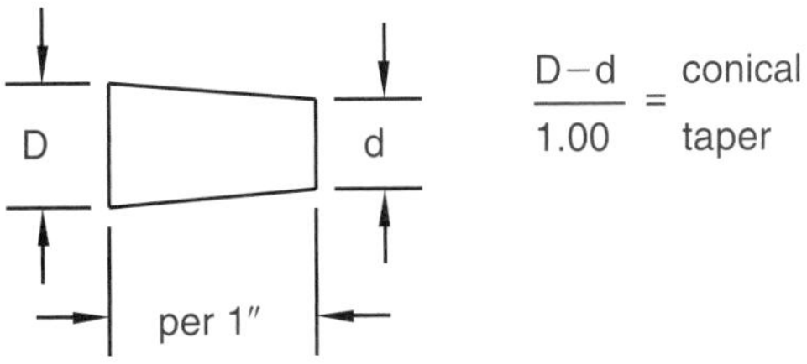 D · d · per 1″ · D−d / 1.00 = conical taper	**None**	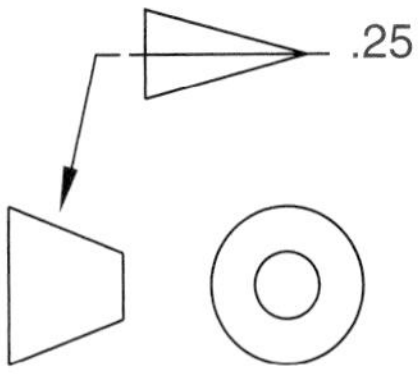 .25

FIGURE 9.57
continued on next page

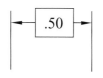

Basic Dimension
A basic dimension indicates a theoretical exact size. A general tolerance will not apply to this dimension.

Reference Dimension
A dimension used for information purposes only.

X

This symbol can be used in two different ways on a drawing. It can represent a multiplication symbol indicating how many of the same size or feature are repeated on a drawing.

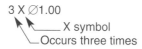

3 X ⌀1.00
⌐——— X symbol
⌐—Occurs three times

The symbol can also be used to represent decimal places in a drawing. It is commonly found near or in the title block to indication general tolerances.

.XX ◀——— Indicates any dimension taken
——to two decimal places

.XXX ◀——— Indicates any dimension taken
——to three decimal places

FIGURE 9.57
continued

FIGURE 9.58

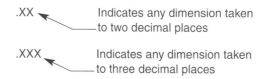

39.5°   39°30′   39°40′21″
                Degrees and Minutes   Degrees, Minutes, and Seconds

(a)   (b)   (c)

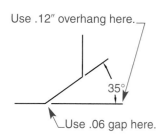

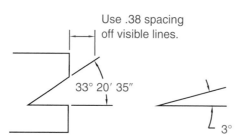

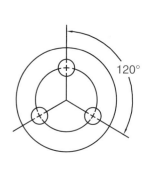

FIGURE 9.59

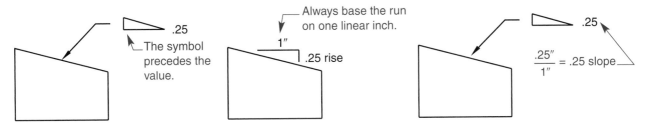

FIGURE 9.60

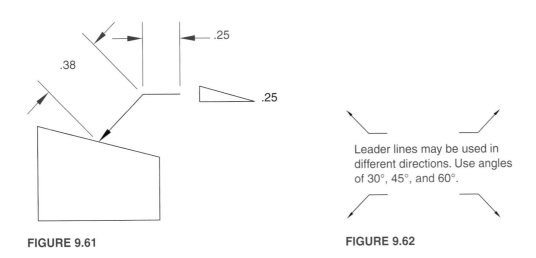

FIGURE 9.61　　　　　　　　　　　　　　**FIGURE 9.62**

Dimensioning Circles

To dimension a circle, a radius or diameter symbol must be used. The symbol must precede the dimension. A leader line is used when dimensioning the circle profile (see Figure 9.63). The leader line can be placed in any quadrant, and it must extend from the center of the circle and be drawn using an angle of either 30°, 45°, or 60° (see Figure 9.64). To dimension a circle's diameter from a position where the circle appears as a line use the style shown in Figure 9.65. Shafts should be dimensioned in this fashion.

FIGURE 9.63

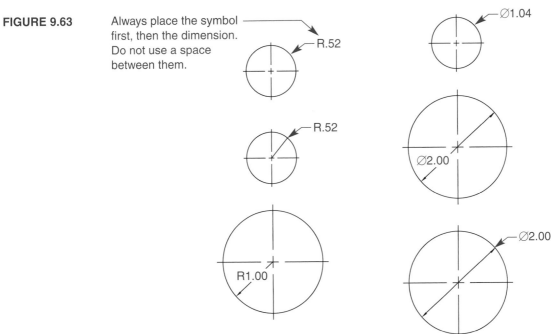

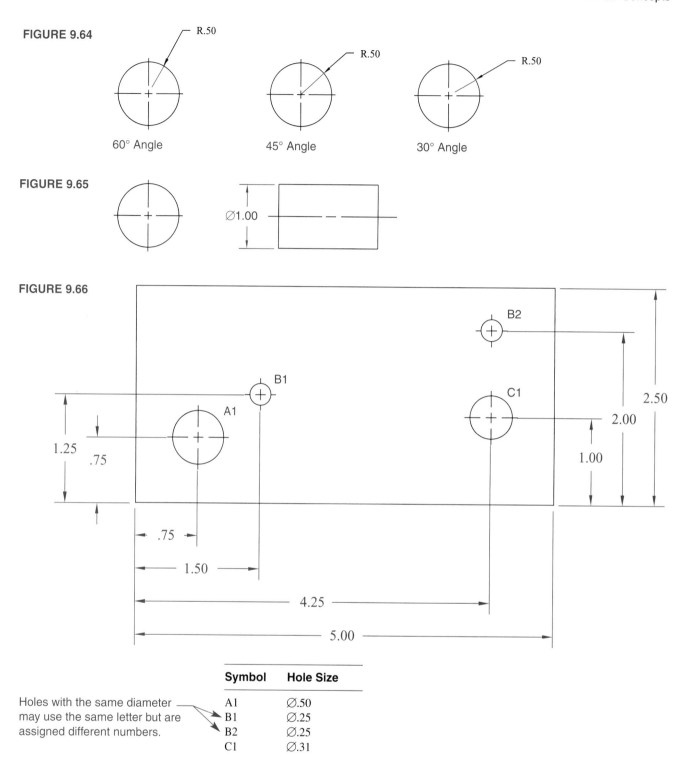

FIGURE 9.64

60° Angle   45° Angle   30° Angle

FIGURE 9.65

Ø1.00

FIGURE 9.66

Symbol	Hole Size
A1	Ø.50
B1	Ø.25
B2	Ø.25
C1	Ø.31

Holes with the same diameter may use the same letter but are assigned different numbers.

Another option for dimensioning the size of a circle or hole it to use the tabulated system shown earlier. In this system the holes are assigned an alphanumeric code. Another column is created in the table so sizes can be assigned to the individual holes, which eliminates the use of leader lines. A table may be created just for the hole sizes while the other features may be dimensioned using another system such as a datum (see Figure 9.66).

Ordinate and tabulated combinations may be used to reduce crowding to a minimum. Figure 9.67 shows an example listing the hole or circle sizes in a table while using an ordinate system for the feature locations.

FIGURE 9.67

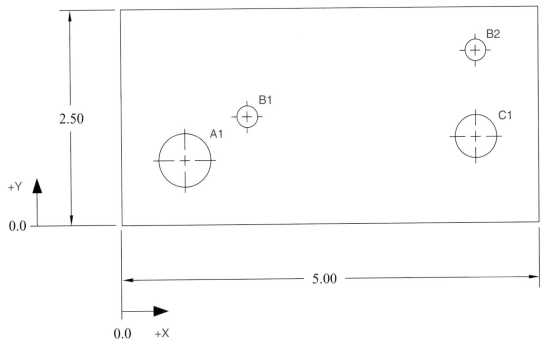

Symbol	Hole Location		Hole Size
	+X	**+Y**	
A1	.75	.75	∅.31
B1	1.5	1.25	∅.25
B2	4.25	2.00	∅.25
C1	4.25	1.00	∅.50

FIGURE 9.68

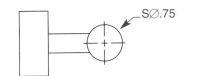
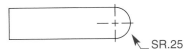

Dimensioning Spheres

A spherical shape may be dimensioned similarly to a circle. The symbols for a spherical shape (S∅ for a spherical diameter and SR for a spherical radius) must be used to denote the geometry (see Figure 9.68). *Note:* One factor to consider when deciding whether to use a radius versus a diameter call out on a circle is the tolerance effect. Examine Figures 9.69 and 9.70 with a tolerance of ±.02. These figures demonstrate how much of a difference a radius versus a diameter dimension makes. It is obvious that when the tolerance is applied to the diameter dimension, the circle size has a more restricted amount of change. Choosing a radius essentially doubles the tolerance effect on the circle's overall size.

Dimensioning a Conical Shape

A cone or tapering cylinder shape may be dimensioned with a note and leader line. The conical taper symbol must be used in the note. It calls out the taper per 1″ unit of length. Figure 9.71 shows an example of how to dimension. An explanation is highlighted in color to show exactly what the dimension is controlling.

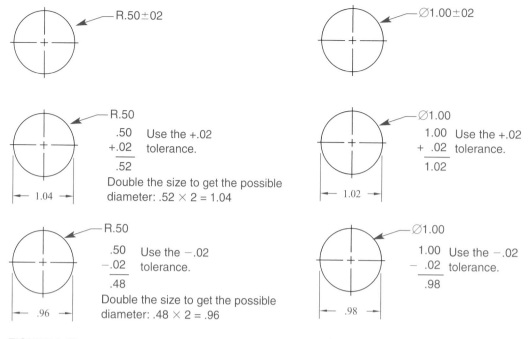

FIGURE 9.69

FIGURE 9.70

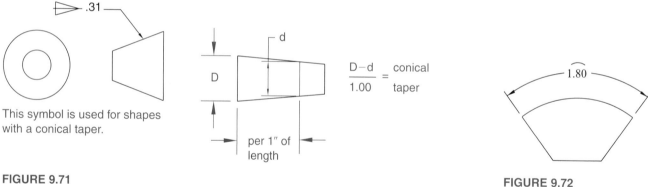

FIGURE 9.71

FIGURE 9.72

Dimensioning an Arc's Length

The length of an arc is expressed or dimensioned similarly to an angle. Extension lines are used along with a curved dimension line. The dimension of the arc is placed between the dimension line, and the arc length symbol is placed above the number (see Figure 9.72).

Dimensioning an Arc's Radius

An arc or partial circle with a uniform radius may be dimensioned using only the radius. The placement of the dimension depends on the arc's size and room for the dimension (see Figure 9.73 for different layout options). Leader lines must always be oriented to pass through the arc's center, and the radius symbol must precede the dimension value. These values are the same ones used for dimensioning circles. A crosshair or center tick mark is used on large circles with a radius greater than 1/8″ (.125). Small circles such as fillets, rounds, and runouts do not require ticks and may have a note calling out their typical radius instead of having a dimension and leader placed on the individual arcs.

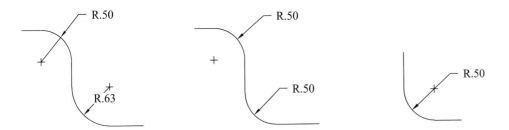

FIGURE 9.73

Divide the curve into equal parts and dimension the points. The more points you use, the more accurate the curve will be when it is built.

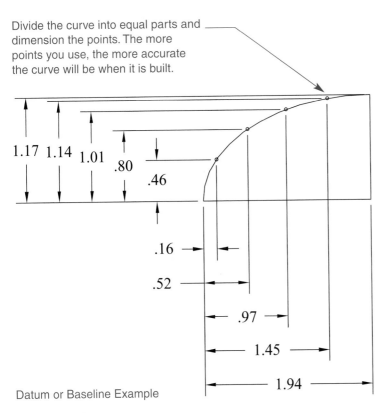

Datum or Baseline Example

FIGURE 9.74

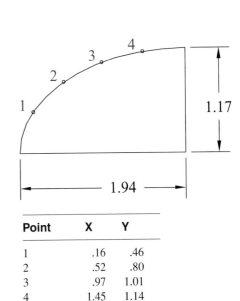

Tabulated System

Point	X	Y
1	.16	.46
2	.52	.80
3	.97	1.01
4	1.45	1.14

Dimensioning Irregular Curves

An irregular curve has no uniform center used to construct its shape. Without a consistent radius, a set of dimensions indicating points that fall on the curve must be identified. The best methods to use are the datum/baseline system or a tabulated system. They both set up a reference point or surface and supply the X and Y coordinates for each point (see Figure 9.74 for a demonstration of how to dimension a curve).

Dimensioning Counterbores

To dimension a counterbore you must dimension to visible lines. A leader line with the counterbore symbol, diameter symbol, and depth symbol is one option for dimensioning the orthographic views. Notice in Figure 9.75 that the counterbore is hidden when viewed from the side. The leader line and note should therefore be placed on the visible lines in the other view. If you want to view the counterbore in visible-line form on the side view, a section is a solution. Using a section here showing the counterbore will allow you to dimension it there (see Figure 9.76). Remember to use the standard symbols and place them in the correct order (see Figure 9.77). The symbols precede the values.

FIGURE 9.75

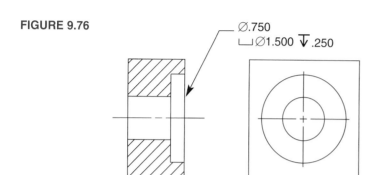

The first drilled hole is called out.

∅.750

⌴∅1.500 ▽.250

The depth symbol precedes the value.

Next is the counterbore symbol with its diameter called out.

The counterbore in the side view

FIGURE 9.76

∅.750

⌴∅1.500 ▽.250

FIGURE 9.77

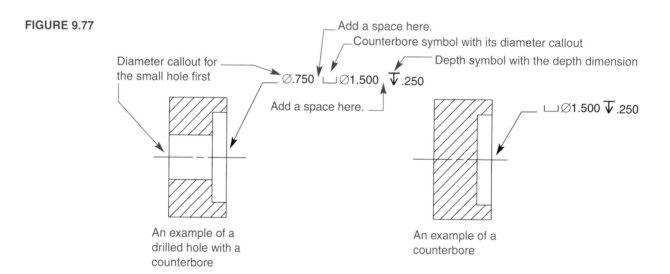

Add a space here.

Counterbore symbol with its diameter callout

Depth symbol with the depth dimension

Diameter callout for the small hole first

∅.750   ⌴∅1.500 ▽.250

⌴∅1.500 ▽.250

Add a space here.

An example of a drilled hole with a counterbore

An example of a counterbore

Dimensioning a Countersink

A countersink is drilled to form a conical taper around a previously drilled hole to allow a screw with a cone-shaped head to be recessed inside the part. As with the counterbore, a leader with the countersink information is needed. Even though the shape is different from the counterbore, the situation is similar as far as dimensioning. Once again the orthographic views may contain hidden lines, forcing you to make some choices. The front view may be dimensioned because all the lines are visible (see Figure 9.78). If a section view is drawn for the side view, then it may be dimensioned in visible-line form. Figure 9.79 breaks down the dimension note for the countersink.

A drilled hole that stops short in a part may be dimensioned using one of the following methods (see Figure 9.80). Method A points to the visible circle in an orthographic view using a leader line with a note showing the diameter of the drill bit and the depth symbol followed by the dimension for the depth. Method B may be used when a section view is shown. The depth of the hole is drawn in visible-line form and therefore may be dimensioned. The diameter may be dimensioned as indicated on the outside surface. The depth may be dimensioned from the outside of the part to the flat portion of the hole. The 30° angled drilled tip is not included in the dimension but must be drawn as shown in Figure 9.81.

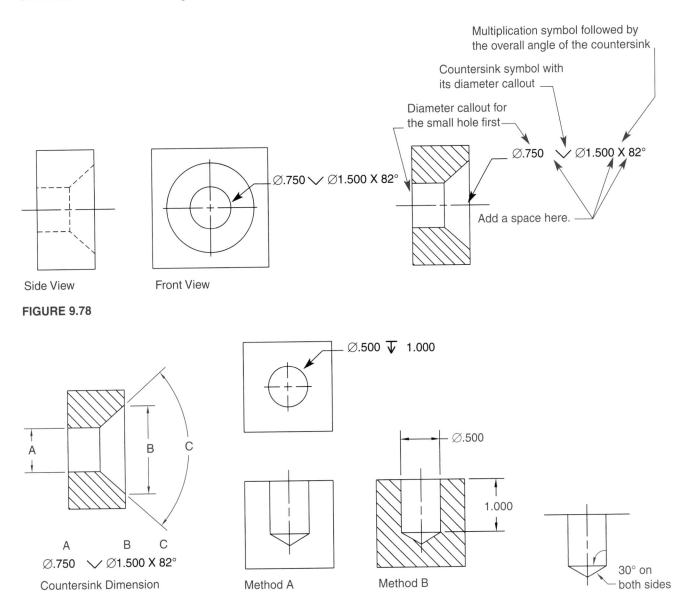

FIGURE 9.78

FIGURE 9.79

Countersink Dimension

FIGURE 9.80

Method A

Method B

FIGURE 9.81

Dimensioning a Slot

A slot is basically a rectangle with two circular ends. It can be dimensioned in several different ways. Two good methods are described next.

Method 1: If the overall size of the slot is a concern, then this method is recommended. Dimension to the overall shapes as shown in Figure 9.82.

Method 2: If the location of the center marks needs to have the least amount of variance when the tolerances are applied to the dimensions, then method 2 will work better. Dimension from tick mark to tick mark while using a radius callout or diameter (see Figure 9.83).

Curved slots can require a slightly different approach (see the example in Figure 9.84). A slot like this will definitely need to nail down the center locations, so a combination of an angle and radius dimensions will be required. Dimensions to the center tick marks are essential to successfully completing the drawing. Polar dimensioning using the angles works well.

The next two examples discuss dimensioning holes around the center of a large circle.

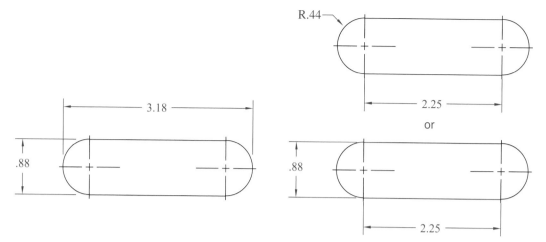

FIGURE 9.82   **FIGURE 9.83**

FIGURE 9.84

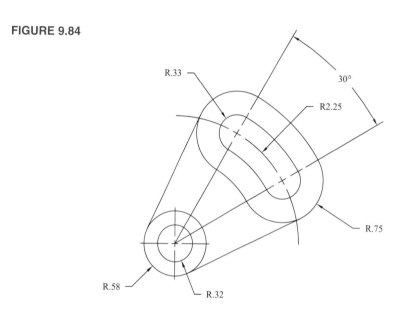

Dimensioning a Symmetrical Hole

If holes are placed in a circular symmetrical pattern, that is, equally spaced off a center and from one another, they are in what AutoCAD calls a *polar array*. A circular pattern like this should be dimensioned using a polar system (angles) (see Figure 9.85). If the holes are equally spaced at a 45° angle, then only one angle needs dimensioning, and all the others are assumed to be the same angle unless noted otherwise or called out with separate dimensions. The distance from the center is also the same for all the holes in a polar array. A circle needs to be drawn in centerline form through the centers of all the holes, as shown in Figure 9.85.

This circle is called a *bolt circle* because each bolt hole's center is located on the circle. The diameter of the bolt circle should be dimensioned. The holes can be called out with the bolt circle dimension or placed on a hole (see Figure 9.86).

An option to the polar system is a rectangular system in which the centerlines of the large circle are used for rectangular (chains or datums) dimensioning. The vertical line is used to dimension in the X direction, and the horizontal centerline controls the dimension in the Y direction (see Figure 9.87). As you can see, this method eliminates the need for angles because of the X and Y coordinate control. Both methods are acceptable in the ASME Y14.5M standard. The choice may depend on how the engineer wants the tolerance to affect the design of the part.

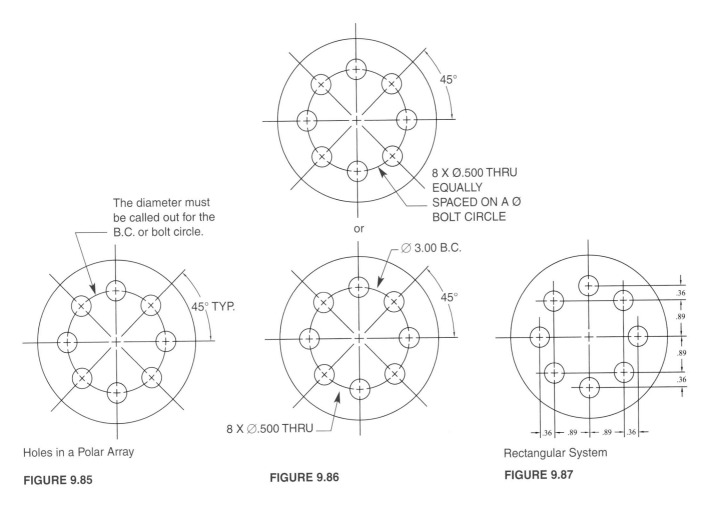

The diameter must be called out for the B.C. or bolt circle.

Holes in a Polar Array

FIGURE 9.85

8 X ∅.500 THRU

FIGURE 9.86

Rectangular System

FIGURE 9.87

9.4 Placing Dimensions on a Drawing

Dimensioning is an art that is evolving into a science. In Sections 9.2 and 9.3 we showed you different systems, methods, and rules that are acceptable in mechanical drawing. Once you have seen and read about the various systems of dimensioning, the next step is to put your knowledge into practice. Understand that it may take some time to sort out all the various options that you will be faced with. Part of the process will be learning to accept that a drawing can be correct even though it can be dimensioned several different ways depending on the intended function of the part.

Dimensioning and designing go hand in hand. With time a drafter can grow into a designer by learning the profession. Understanding how a part works sets the stage for dimensioning it. Just practicing the process on different types of parts is a good beginning. Your instructor can give you some insight and pointers on the different parts and geometric shapes. The first step to good dimensioning is to plan before you draw.

Planning Out Dimensions

Think back to the chapter on orthographic drawing. Recall that a good practice was to start a drawing by identifying the best views and sketching them out in third-angle projection form first to eliminate errors and to save time before actually drawing a line. Once you have sketched out the views, it is time to plan out the dimensions that go with it. Guidelines for choosing good views are similar to those you can use to start planning the dimensions. You choose orthographic views based on the following criteria:

- A view that shows the geometric shapes in true form
- A view with the fewest hidden lines

FIGURE 9.88

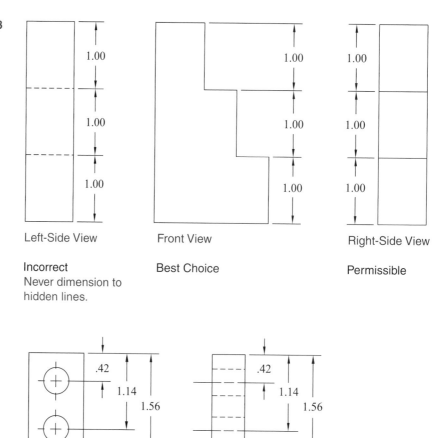

Left-Side View

Incorrect
Never dimension to
hidden lines.

Front View

Best Choice

Right-Side View

Permissible

Correct

Incorrect

In the same way, it is better to dimension views when the details and geometry are clearly seen and never to dimension to hidden lines. Figure 9.88 gives a few examples of these techniques. The ones labeled "correct" should stick in your mind. The views that best describe the object should get the majority of the dimensions, because they show the best shapes and have the fewest hidden lines. Keep these goals in mind before you start placing dimensions on the rough sketches.

Dimensioning Order

When you are staring at a drawing asking yourself which dimensions to start with, it is useful to remember that dimensions generally fall into three categories:

- Location
- Mating
- Size Description

Location dimensions are basically used to locate features as they reference off edges such as corners and centers (see Figure 9.89). **Mating dimensions** are used in areas where parts interact, as in mounting into or sliding through one another. Dimensions common to both parts as they fit together are considered mating (see Figure 9.90). **Size descriptions** are used to call out various shapes like the ones shown in Section 9.3. Often, leader lines with symbols and notes are used for the size description dimensions (see Figure 9.91). The leaders can be set to many different angles and directions depending on the space around the drawing.

Planning the Location and Mating Dimensions

In the preliminary stages you must plan out the dimensions to keep them spaced properly and readable on the finished drawing. The ASME Y14.5M rules apply, and it is up to you to choose the layout and the particular systems such as datum/baseline, chain, parallel, or ordinate. The following steps will help you plan:

FIGURE 9.89

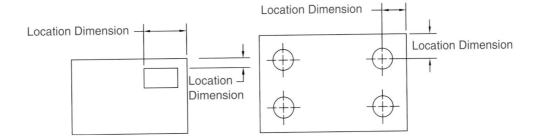

FIGURE 9.90

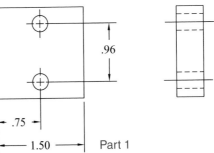

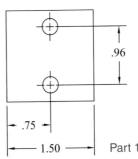

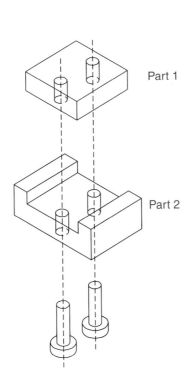

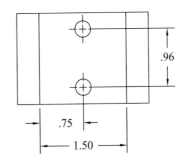

Isometric of the mating parts
showing how they go together.

All the dimensions shown are
mating dimensions.

FIGURE 9.91

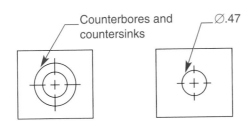

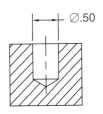

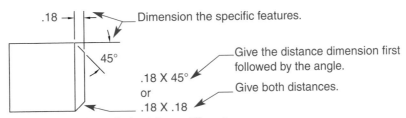

Chamfers may be called out three different ways.

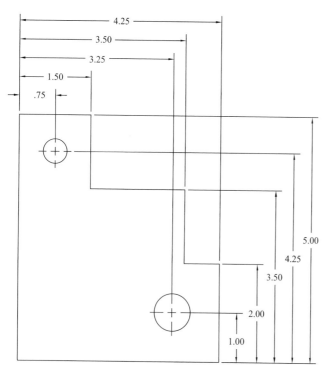

FIGURE 9.92

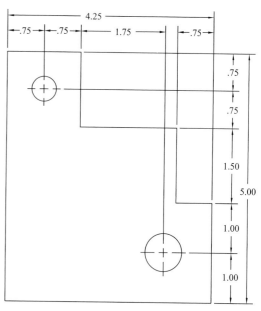

FIGURE 9.93

1. Lay out the location and mating dimensions first. They do not have the flexibility that the size descriptions do. Figures 9.92 and 9.93 show a datum and a chain system. This is a good example showing where the location dimensions should be placed. If the dimensions were on the opposite sides, they would have extension lines passing through too much of the drawing, making it more difficult to read. Also, remember to dimension where the geometry is clearly seen.

- Keep dimensions outside the view, staying out of the interior.
- Avoid using extension lines that pass a long way through the drawing (see Figure 9.94).

FIGURE 9.94

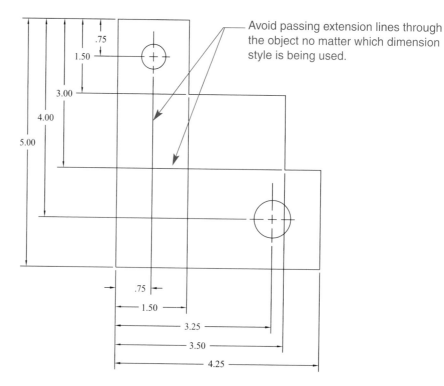

Avoid passing extension lines through the object no matter which dimension style is being used.

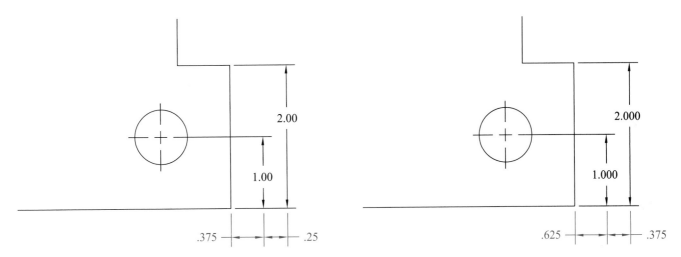

FIGURE 9.95   **FIGURE 9.96**

Note:
■ If you have three or more views, you must use equal spacing between all views. Determine the largest space needed and use it for all view spacing (see Figure 9.98).
■ You may space an auxiliary view differently than the other views for better readability. Feel free to place it as far away as needed. Dimension only the nondistorted features on the auxiliary view.

2. Spacing is a major key to good dimensioning. The minimum spacing works well for dimensions that are carried out to two decimal places (1.50). Use a .375″ (10 mm) spacing off the first visible line to place the first dimension line, then use .25″ (6 mm) spacing for each additional dimension line as they extend farther out (see Figure 9.95). If the dimensions are carried out to three or four decimal places, then use an initial spacing of .625″ (20 mm) with a .375″ (10 mm) offset for any additional dimensions that are added (see Figure 9.96).

3. In the orthographic chapter we recommended a 2″ spacing between the views. This spacing can be linked to the number of dimensions needed between the views. Add up the number of dimensions you will need, calculate the spacing needed between the dimension lines, and add some clearance between the other view and its dimensions. Dimension spacing should be consistent throughout the drawing (see Figures 9.97 and 9.98).

4. You must place the longer dimensions outside the shorter ones no matter which dimension system you use to keep the number of times extension lines cross to a minimum.

5. Do not extend the centerlines across into the next view. A trained machinist can read a technical drawing and knows that centers line up from view to view (see Figure 9.99).

FIGURE 9.97

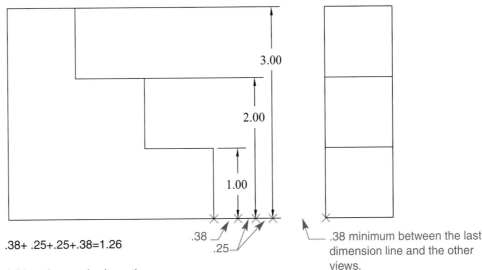

.38+ .25+.25+.38=1.26

.38 minimum between the last dimension line and the other views.

Add up the required spacing for dimensions in order to get the spacing between views.

FIGURE 9.98

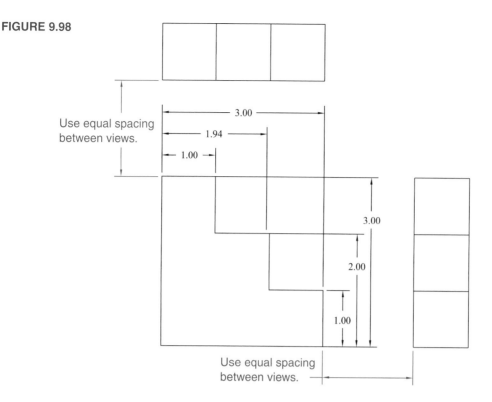

Use equal spacing between views.

3.00
1.94
1.00
3.00
2.00
1.00

Use equal spacing between views.

FIGURE 9.99

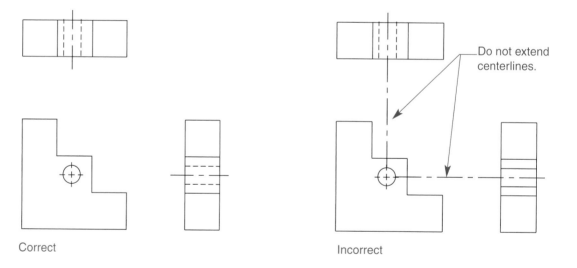

Do not extend centerlines.

Correct

Incorrect

6. Make sure every location and mating feature is accounted for in the drawing. Do not repeat dimensions from view to view, because redundancy crowds the drawing unnecessarily. Dimensioning once where a feature is best described is sufficient. In a chain dimension system, it is permitted to leave out a dimension when an overall dimension is also used (see Figure 9.100).

Planning the Size Descriptions

After you have added the location and mating dimensions to the preliminary sketch, it is time to concentrate on the size descriptions. Look at all the views and start planning out dimensions where the visible-line features are seen and where the notes and leaders will be placed. Keep in mind that flexibility is the key; leader lines can be positioned in many different places and still be correct (see Figure 9.101). Even with this flexibility, though, some guidelines need to be followed:

FIGURE 9.100

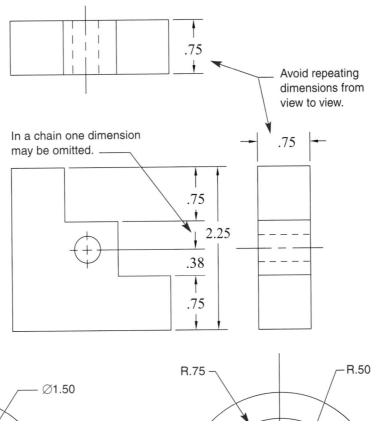

Avoid repeating dimensions from view to view.

In a chain one dimension may be omitted.

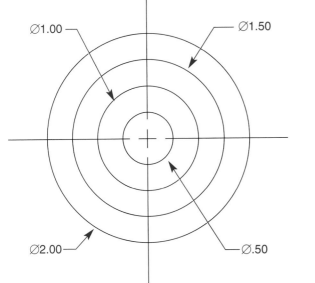
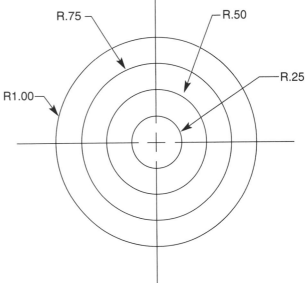

Use any quadrant needed when dimensioning with leader lines. Use variations of 30°, 45°, and 60° angles.

FIGURE 9.101

1. Leader lines may cross other lines; however, keep crossings to a minimum and avoid passing through intersections (see Figure 9.102).
2. Use either straight lines or sloped ones using variations of 30°, 45°, or 60° angles for leaders with a .25 horizontal line on the end (see Figure 9.103).
3. When the leader is pointing to a circle, line it up as if it were going to pass through its exact center (see Figure 9.104).
4. Place the horizontal shoulder that comes off the leader line at the beginning of the note or at its end. The shoulder must also start at the center of the height of the text (see Figure 9.105).
5. Avoid putting dimensions inside the view; however, in crowded situations or with very large views, size descriptions may be placed inside the view (see Figure 9.106).

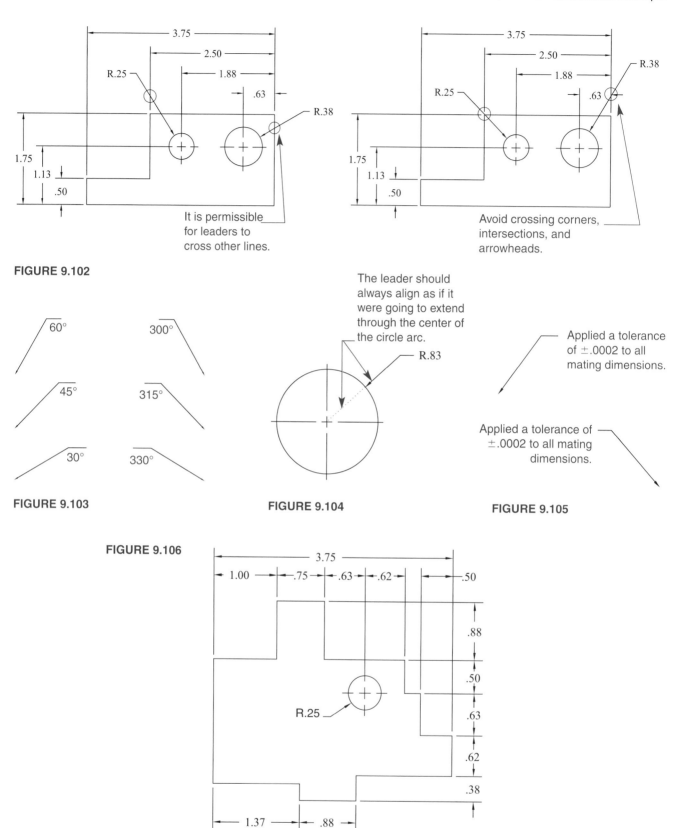

FIGURE 9.102

It is permissible for leaders to cross other lines.

Avoid crossing corners, intersections, and arrowheads.

FIGURE 9.103

The leader should always align as if it were going to extend through the center of the circle arc.

FIGURE 9.104

Applied a tolerance of ±.0002 to all mating dimensions.

Applied a tolerance of ±.0002 to all mating dimensions.

FIGURE 9.105

FIGURE 9.106

Keep these guidelines in mind during the preliminary sketch to help develop a good dimensioning plan. Do not be afraid to make changes if you dislike your first attempt. Very rarely does anyone do it right the first time. After all, the purpose of these early sketches is to plan things out and to eliminate problems before starting the scaled drawing. When the dimensioning plan has been completed on your initial sketch, it is time to start the scaled drawing.

Laying Out the Scaled Drawing

Start by drawing the views, using construction lines. After you have laid out the views, using construction lines, carefully add the dimension components to the views, using the same order you previously used on the sketch. Do not put in the text component of the dimension yet; only lay out the guidelines for the height of the dimensions and notes. After you are done, look the drawing over for any unforeseen problems that may have occurred in the scaling process. Have your instructor or boss look at anything you are not sure of before beginning the hard-line process.

When you are confident that the drawing is ready to be darkened, repeat the sequence. Start with the views first, working from the top of the sheet to the bottom, darken the horizontal lines, then darken the vertical lines going side to side. Darken the circles and angles next. Once the views are complete, go on to the dimensions. Use the same technique, drawing from the top of the sheet to the bottom, catching all the horizontal extension and dimension lines. Darken the vertical lines next, then the angled lines and leaders. The last components to be darkened are the arrowheads and text. Save your best for last. It is easy to spoil a drawing with poor arrowheads and text when dimensioning. Remember that dimensioning is an art that has evolved into more of a science in machine tool design.

REVIEW QUESTIONS

1. What kind of units are used to dimension mechanical drawings?
2. Why do mechanical dimensions have to be more exact/precise than those in other drafting fields?
3. Name the group that governs mechanical dimensioning practices in the United States.
4. What standard controls text and lettering styles?
5. Explain the term *unidirectional* as it applies to dimensions and tolerances.
6. When is it acceptable to use fractions on mechanical drawings?
7. Sketch examples of the following:
   (a) Bidirectional tolerance
   (b) Limit dimension
   (c) Reference dimension
8. Sketch an example of a datum dimensioning system, and label the minimum sizes and spacing that apply to it.
9. Name three features of well-drawn arrowheads.
10. Sketch examples of parallel, chain, and ordinate dimensioning.
11. What factors dictate the type of dimension style to be used?
12. Where on an ordinate dimensioning system should the origin be placed?
13. Sketch a small drawing that combines ordinate and tabulated dimensioning.
14. List 10 symbols used to dimension shapes and sizes. Explain what each one represents. Use a small sketch for each one.
15. Compare dimensioning a circle as a radius versus as a diameter when a tolerance is applied.
16. Sketch an example showing how an irregular curve should be dimensioned.
17. What is meant by the term *bolt circle*?
18. Sketch examples using two different methods for dimensioning to the centers of holes symmetrically placed in a circular pattern.
19. Explain how a location dimension is different from a mating dimension.
20. If you were given a three-dimensional sketch and told to draw it orthographically, including the dimensions, what steps would you follow to complete the task?

EXERCISES

EXERCISE 9.1
Draw the parts in Figure 9.107 on three different sheets of velum. Dimension each one using the following methods:
  (a) Datum
  (b) Chain
  (c) Ordinate

EXERCISE 9.2
Draw and dimension the parts in Figure 9.108. Use a method that combines a table format for the holes and arcs.

FIGURE 9.107

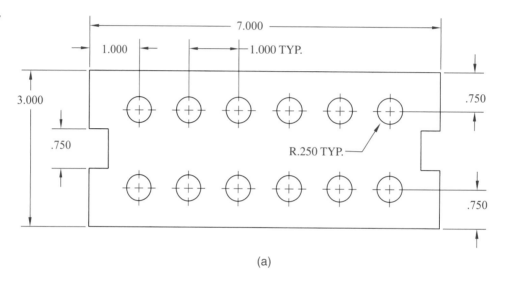

(a)

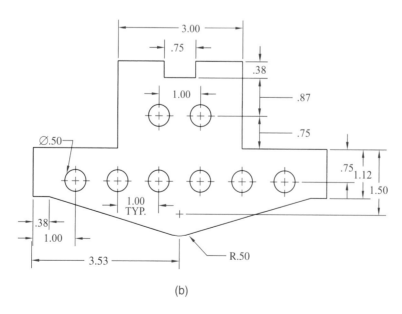

(b)

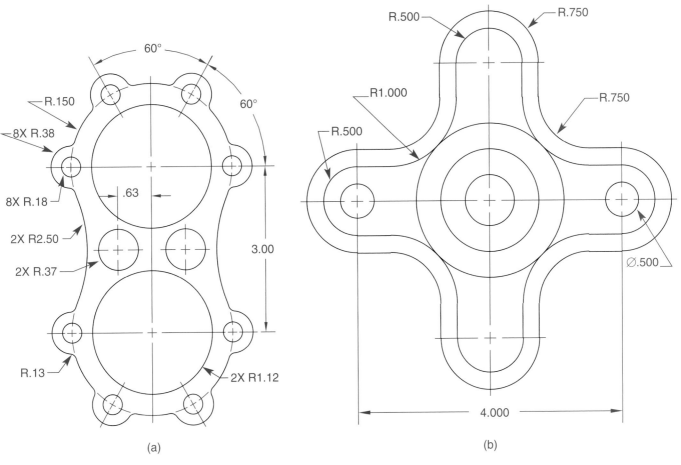

(a)

(b)

FIGURE 9.108

ASSIGNMENTS

1. Draw and dimension the parts in Figure 9.109 shown in orthographic form.
2. Draw and dimension the parts shown in Figure 9.110. Use orthographic views, auxiliary views, and sections as needed.

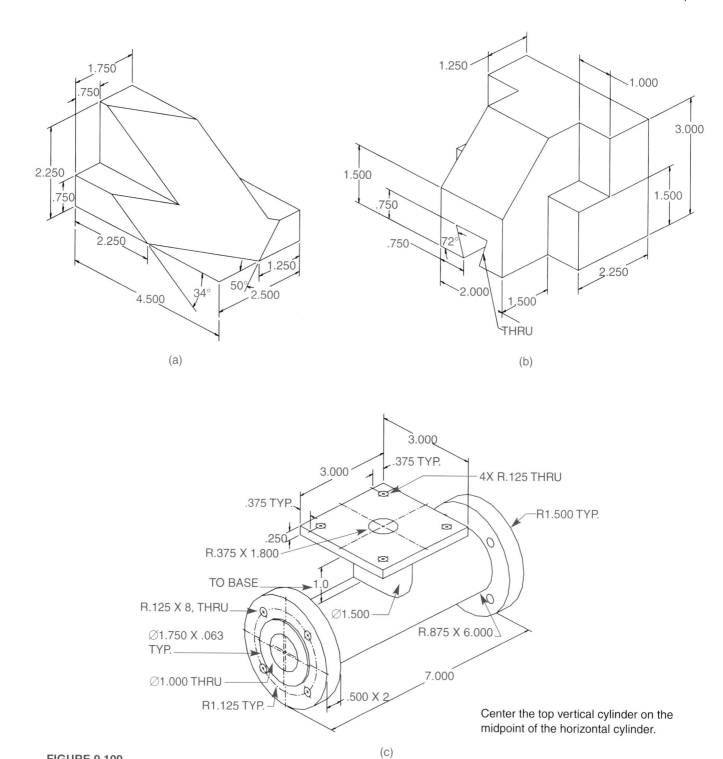

(a)

(b)

Center the top vertical cylinder on the
midpoint of the horizontal cylinder.

(c)

FIGURE 9.109

FIGURE 9.110
continued on next page

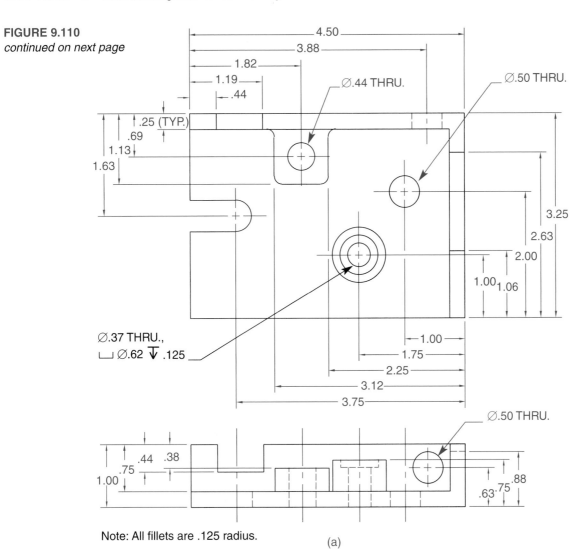

Note: All fillets are .125 radius.

(a)

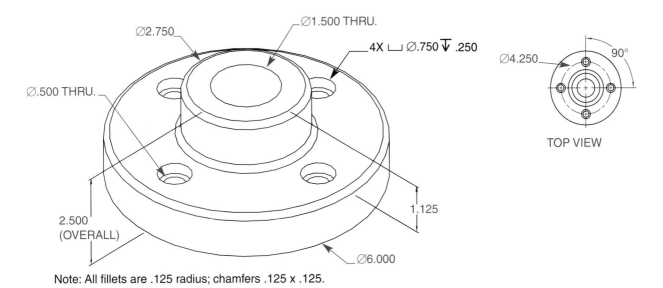

Note: All fillets are .125 radius; chamfers .125 x .125.

(b)

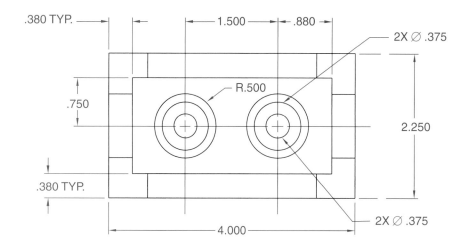

.380 TYP.

1.500

.880

2X ⌀ .375

R.500

.750

2.250

.380 TYP.

2X ⌀ .375

4.000

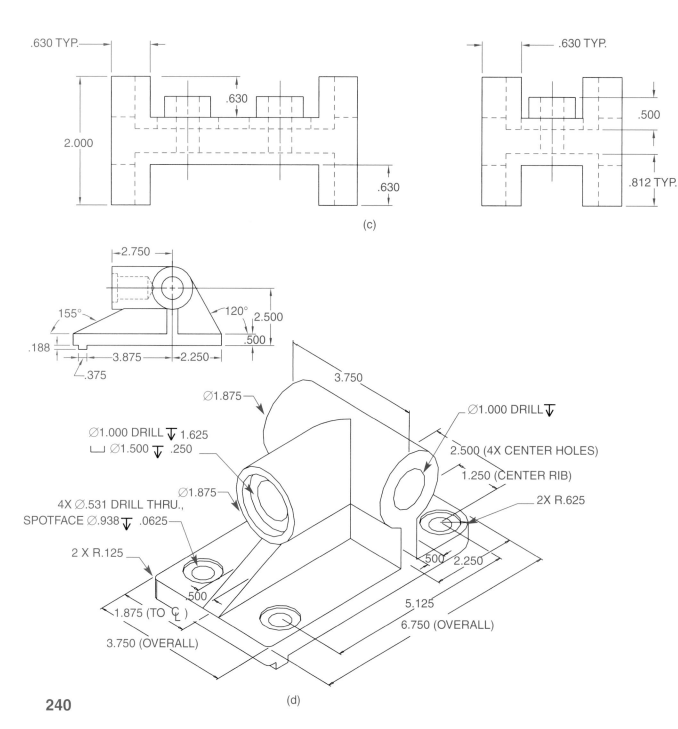

.630 TYP.

.630

2.000

.630

.630 TYP.

.500

.812 TYP.

(c)

2.750

155°

120°

2.500

.500

.188

3.875

2.250

.375

3.750

⌀1.875

⌀1.000 DRILL ⌴

⌀1.000 DRILL ⌴ 1.625
⌴ ⌀1.500 ⌴ .250

2.500 (4X CENTER HOLES)

1.250 (CENTER RIB)

⌀1.875

2X R.625

4X ⌀.531 DRILL THRU.,
SPOTFACE ⌀.938 ⌴ .0625

2 X R.125

.500

.500

2.250

5.125

1.875 (TO ℄)

6.750 (OVERALL)

3.750 (OVERALL)

240

(d)

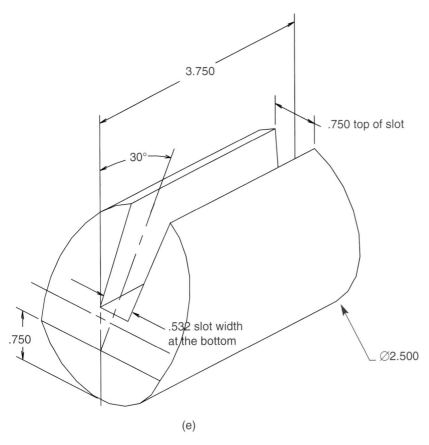

(e)

FIGURE 9.110
continued

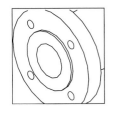

CHAPTER 10

Pictorial Drawing and Sketching

Learning how to draw and sketch pictorials is one of the most fun parts of drafting. It can be quite rewarding visually to draw something that looks three dimensional (3-D). Time and practice are required to be proficient at pictorial drawings. If you struggle somewhat in the beginning and your instructor comes over and makes it look easy, take a deep breath and remember that your instructor has done these drawings a few hundred times. The power of practice and knowing the concepts of the drawing will empower you one day.

10.1 Axonometric Drawing

The three types of axonometric drawings were explained in Chapter 5. An isometric drawing has three equal isometric axes. A dimetric drawing has two equal axes, and a trimetric drawing has three different angles (see Figure 10.1).

Isometric drawing is one of the most popular pictorials used in drafting. It becomes fairly natural to most people after a short time. Recall the isometric example from Chapter 5.

Steps for Drawing Isometrics

Step 1. When drawing an isometric object, you need a scaled orthographic drawing from which to take measurements (see Figure 10.2).

Step 2. Draw the vertical line located where the three isoaxes intersect (see Figure 10.3 and the isometric example in Figure 10.1). This is needed to view your object looking at the top or bottom.

Step 3. Using a 30°-60°-90° triangle go the bottom of the vertical line and draw your length along the right side at a 30° angle (see Figure 10.4). Then go back to the bottom of the vertical line and draw the width along the left side at a 150° angle (see Figure 10.5).

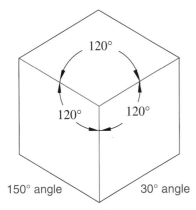

Isometric Example

Iso interior angles are true to scale and highlighted in blue.

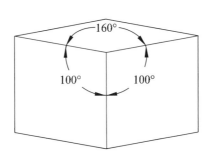

Dimetric Example

Any two angles can be equal to form a dimetric. Scale along axes can be adjusted.

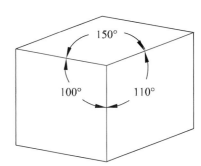

Trimetric Example

All three interior angles must be different to form a trimetric. Scale along axes can be adjusted.

FIGURE 10.1 Isometric, dimetric, and trimetric examples.

FIGURE 10.2   Orthographic
drawing of a building.

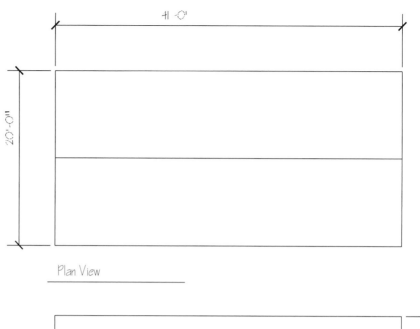

Plan View

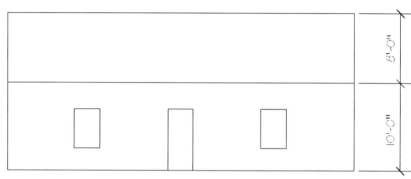

Front Elevation

FIGURE 10.3

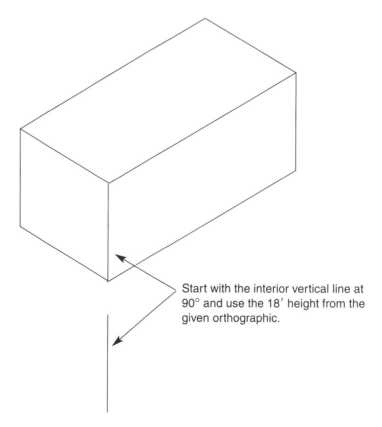

Start with the interior vertical line at
90° and use the 18′ height from the
given orthographic.

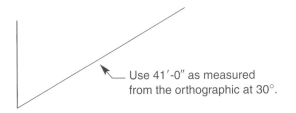

FIGURE 10.4 Isometric construction.

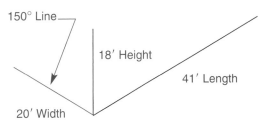

FIGURE 10.5 Isometric construction.

Step 4. Go to the end of the 30° angled line and draw an 18′-tall vertical line on the far right end (see Figure 10.6). Then go to the end of the 150° width line and draw another 18′-vertical line on the far left end (see Figure 10.7).

Step 5. Go to your interior vertical line and connect from its endpoint a 30° line along the right-hand side going to the end of the vertical line on the right-hand side (see Figure 10.8). Now, go back to the interior vertical line and do the same thing going to the left (see Figure 10.9). At this point you see the walls or sides being established.

Step 6. Starting at the top of the right-hand vertical line draw a line using a 150° angle back to the left (see Figure 10.10). Now, go to the top of the left-hand vertical line and draw a line at 30° going back to the right, finishing off the top vertical surface (see Figure 10.11). When drawing or sketching isometrics always lay out the overall box to be constructed and draw within it.

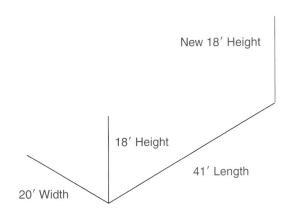

FIGURE 10.6 Isometric construction.

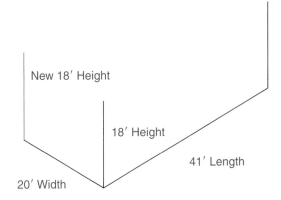

FIGURE 10.7 Isometric construction.

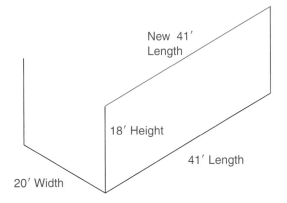

FIGURE 10.8 Isometric construction.

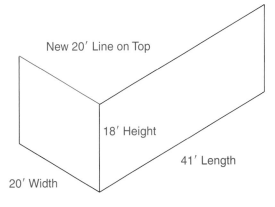

FIGURE 10.9 Isometric construction.

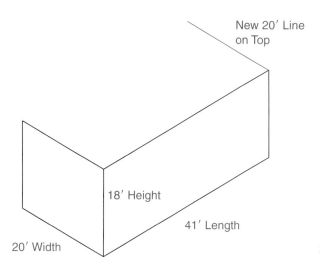

FIGURE 10.10   Isometric construction.

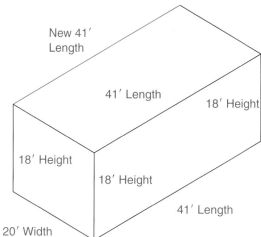

FIGURE 10.11   Completed iso box. The iso box is constructed with the overall length, width, and height. All angles are formed with angles of 30°, 90°, and 150°.

Note: Remember that with orthographic drawing, all vertical and horizontal lines are drawn to scale. On isometric drawing all vertical lines and lines parallel to the 30° and 150° axes are drawn to scale.

Step 7.   Once the overall box is finished, it is time to start measuring within the box using the iso box lines (see Figure 10.12). Start from the bottom and work your way up going from side to side. Then go to the vertical lines and measure across the 150° line and get the width dimensions (see Figure 10.13). *The key is always to measure along the iso lines for your width and lengths (see Figure 10.14). Always measure heights along the vertical lines (see Figure 10.15).*

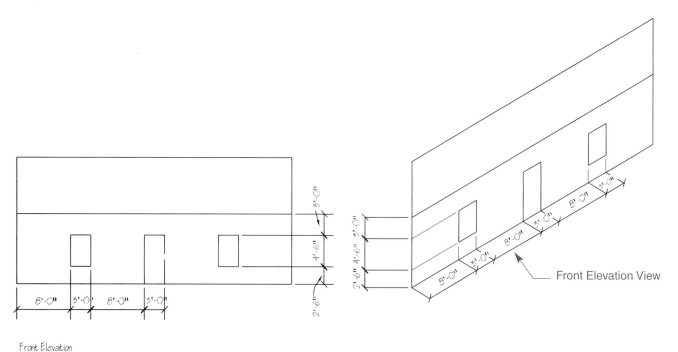

FIGURE 10.12   Iso house I. Laying out the front elevation on the iso drawing. Note that all measurements are taken along the iso axes when transferred from the orthographic.

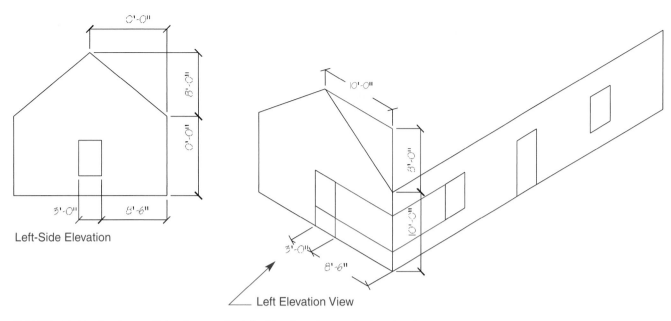

Left-Side Elevation

Left Elevation View

FIGURE 10.13 Iso house II. Laying out the left-side elevation on the iso drawing.

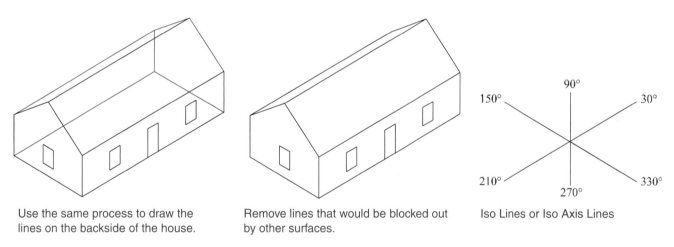

Use the same process to draw the lines on the backside of the house.

Remove lines that would be blocked out by other surfaces.

Iso Lines or Iso Axis Lines

FIGURE 10.14 Finished iso house.

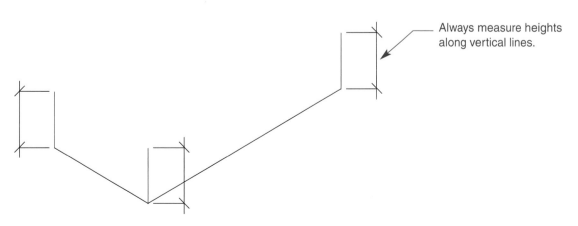

Always measure heights along vertical lines.

FIGURE 10.15 Iso vertical line.

Nonisometric Lines

In an isometric some lines will not fall on or be parallel with the isometric lines. When this happens you must plot out the nonisometric line, finding its endpoints based off the isometric lines (see Figure 10.16). In the previous example the roof had to be done this way.

Figure 10.16 shows how nonisometric lines are drawn. It is a matter of plotting out the endpoints and connecting the points with lines (see Figure 10.17).

Now, let's look at an example of a hip roof that also requires an additional point to plot (see Figure 10.18). Using the same technique as shown on the earlier example, plot the left side (see Figure 10.19).

In general, pictorial drawings do not show any centerlines or hidden or construction lines in the final drawings. Sometimes it is necessary to draw them in during the construction of visible lines.

One thing that tends to give students a problem in pictorials is changing directions around corners. The next drawing will use corner 2 as the starting point to start the construction of the isometric.

An Example of Plotting out Corners on an Isometric Drawing (see Figure 10.20)

Step 1. Draw a vertical line for corner 2 first using the height measured from the front or side view (see Figure 10.21). This will be our starting reference line.

Step 2. Draw a 30° and 150° line off the bottom endpoint of corner 2 (see Figure 10.22).

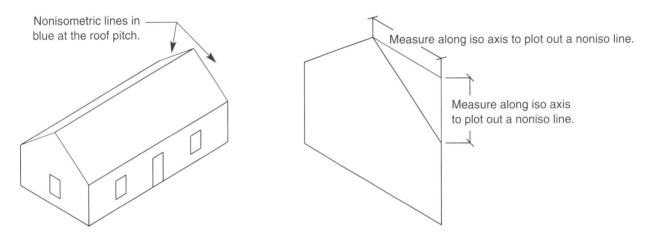

Nonisometric lines in blue at the roof pitch.

Measure along iso axis to plot out a noniso line.

Measure along iso axis to plot out a noniso line.

FIGURE 10.16   Example of an iso roof.

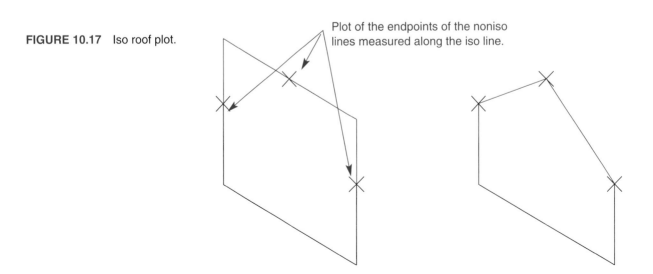

FIGURE 10.17   Iso roof plot.

Plot of the endpoints of the noniso lines measured along the iso line.

Get this distance to plot it on the isometric view.
Hip example has two new points that need to be plotted out.
Plan View of Roof
Side Elevation
Front Elevation
Hip roof noniso lines need to be plotted out.

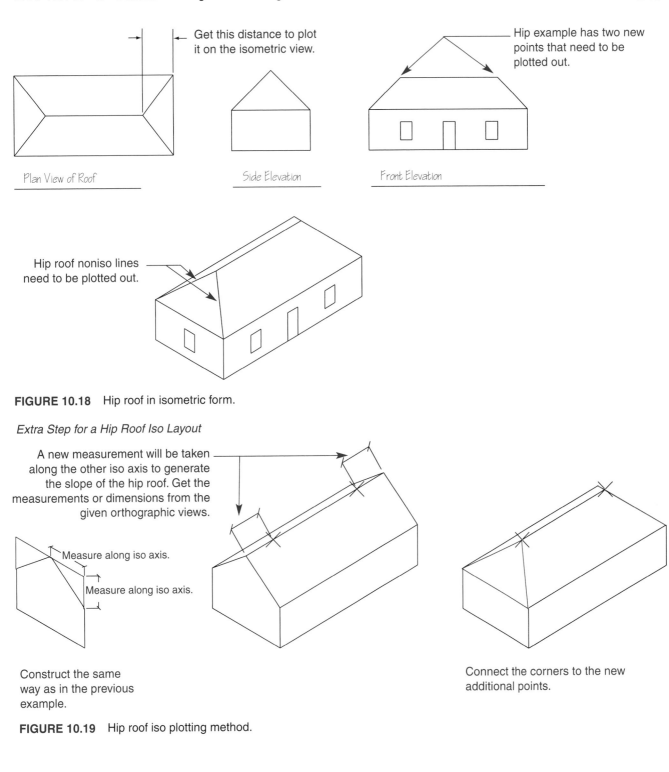

FIGURE 10.18 Hip roof in isometric form.

Extra Step for a Hip Roof Iso Layout

A new measurement will be taken along the other iso axis to generate the slope of the hip roof. Get the measurements or dimensions from the given orthographic views.
Measure along iso axis.
Measure along iso axis.
Construct the same way as in the previous example.
Connect the corners to the new additional points.

FIGURE 10.19 Hip roof iso plotting method.

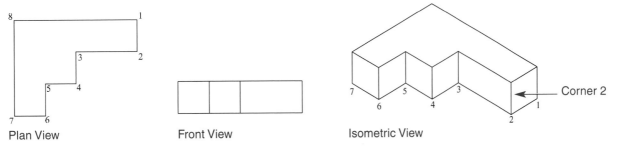

8
1
3
2
5
4
7
6
Plan View
Front View
7
6
5
4
3
1
2
Corner 2
Isometric View

FIGURE 10.20 Iso corner ortho.

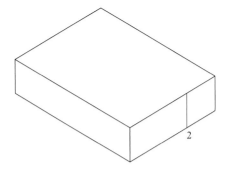

FIGURE 10.21 Take the overall dimensions and construct an iso box.

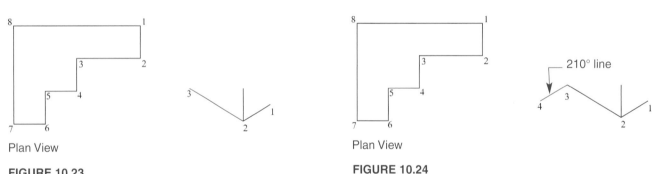

Plan View

FIGURE 10.22

Step 3. Measure where corner 1 will be drawn along the 30° line going toward the right side, then take a 150° line from the bottom of corner 2 and draw it back to the left, stopping at the measured distance from the top view (see Figure 10.23).

Step 4. Now, draw a line going 210° from corner 3 heading to the left. Stop at the distance measured from the orthographic for corner 4 taken from the plan view (see Figure 10.24). Continue on to corner 5 by drawing a 150° line from corner 4. The base is being laid out first, which is the best way to learn (see Figure 10.25). Going to corner 6 is just a matter of starting from corner 5 and drawing a 210° angled line back down toward the left (see Figure 10.26). Find-

Plan View

FIGURE 10.23

Plan View

FIGURE 10.24

FIGURE 10.25

Plan View

FIGURE 10.26

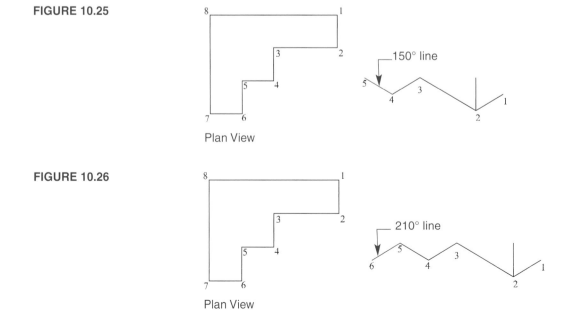

Plan View

FIGURE 10.27

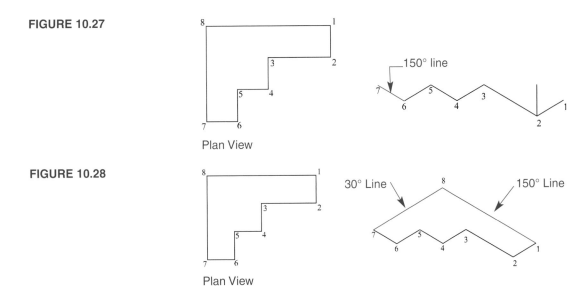

Plan View

FIGURE 10.28

Plan View

ing where corner 7 will be is just a matter of drawing a 150° line upward toward the left using the distance measured off the plan view (see Figure 10.27). The final corner, 8, can be found by drawing a 30° line from corner 7 and a 150° line from corner 1 and intersecting the two lines to complete the base (see Figure 10.28).

Step 5. With the base completed, go to each corner and draw the vertical lines at 90°. Use the height from the front orthographic view for the correct distance (see Figure 10.29).

Step 6. The top position is left to complete. It is easy to go to each top corner and simply connect the top ends with lines parallel to the base (see Figure 10.30). After the top lines are drawn, go back and erase the baselines on the back side (see Figure 10.31).

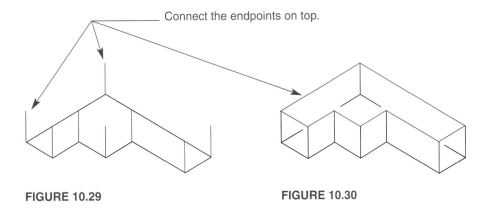

Connect the endpoints on top.

FIGURE 10.29

FIGURE 10.30

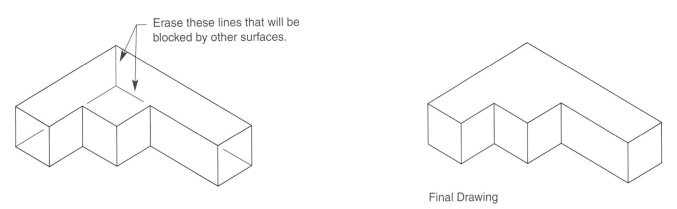

Erase these lines that will be blocked by other surfaces.

Final Drawing

FIGURE 10.31 Completed iso example.

Distortion does occur in isometrics. Do not be fooled just because your dimensions along the axis are true to scale. The iso lines sloped at 120° each create a 3-D look but also cause distortion. Circles are distorted into ellipses and require special techniques to be drawn. This topic will be covered later for all pictorials. The same principles can be applied to each one.

Dimetric Drawing

In dimetric drawing, the central angles are set up so that two of them are equal (as explained in Chapter 5). Any two can be equal, but the three added together must sum to 360° (see Figure 10.32).

The philosophy behind using a dimetric instead of an isometric is that changing the angle measurements allows the drafter to emphasize a certain side with the unequal angle and can reduce some of the distortion on that surface. Full or the true scale may be used and applied to the desired surface. The other surfaces with the sharper angles are drawn at reduced scales. Different drafters use a variety of scales such as ½, ⅝, or even ¾. It is not an exact science; sometimes trial and error is the only way to find the scale that looks the best (see Figure 10.33). Except for setting up the new angles and scales, you repeat all the steps and principles used in isometric drawing for dimetric drawing.

Trimetric Drawing

The final axonometric, known as a trimetric, uses three unequal central angles and allows the drafter to choose the scales along the angled lines (see Figure 10.34). Thus, trimetric puts a lot of control in the drafter's hands to find a good view. As with the dimetric, the versatility found in the trimetric is designed to reduce distortion and give a more realistic view. Once the angles and scales are set, the drawing principles of a trimetric copy that of the isometric and dimetric.

Considering the distortion created with an isometric view, you may wonder why the isometric is very popular and why the other two axonometrics are seldom used. The answer lies in the drafter's tools and equipment. The isometric has all the tool benefits over the other two. The 30°-60°-90° triangle draws all the iso lines for quick iso drawing (see Figure 10.35). Even the drafting arms and machines are set up to lock

FIGURE 10.32   Dimetric example.

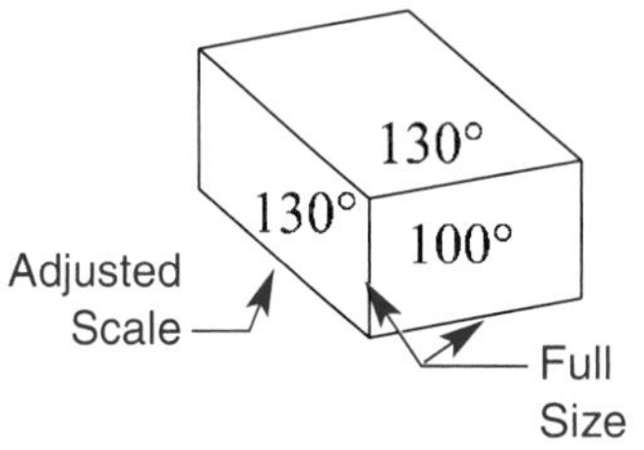

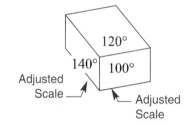

FIGURE 10.33   Dimetric example
adjusted scale.

FIGURE 10.34   Trimetric example.

FIGURE 10.35   Isometric triangle example.

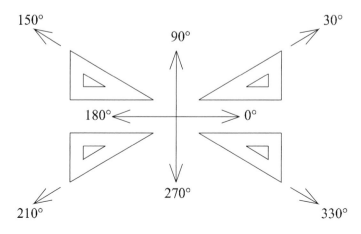

every 15°, which works well with iso drawing. The AutoCAD program also favors isometric lines. An Auto-CAD operator can turn on an isogrid, which sets up an automatic iso environment for easy drawing.

Another advantage of isometrics is the isometric templates used for drawing elliptical circles in iso form. The templates are the fastest way to draw iso ellipses on the drawing board, and they come in a wide range of sizes. AutoCAD can draw iso circles or ellipses quickly and easily if the isogrid is turned on. It can even change from a horizontal ellipse to left vertical to right vertical with the touch of a key on the keyboard (see Figure 10.36).

Axonometrics can be drawn in a variety of forms. They can be exploded or assembled (see Figure 10.37). Sections can be cut through them (see Figure 10.38). The viewing positions can be shifted to many

FIGURE 10.36   Isometric cube with ellipses.

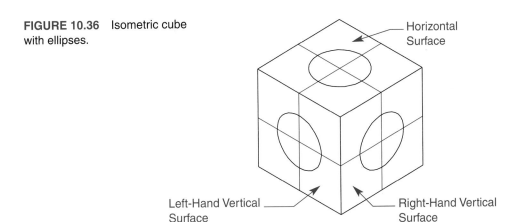

FIGURE 10.37   Isometric exploded and assembled.

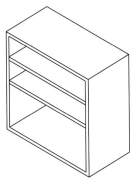

Assembled Isometric of a Bookshelf

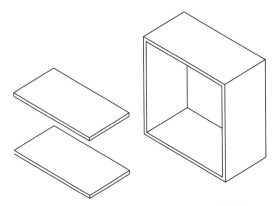

Partial Exploded Isometric of a Bookshelf with the Shelves Out

FIGURE 10.38   Isometric section at a footing.

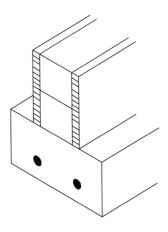

Looking Down on
the Top Surface

Looking Up at the
Bottom Surface

Looking at the Right
Surface

Looking at the Left
Surface

FIGURE 10.39   Isometric views of a cube.

orientations (see Figure 10.39). Given the different options of viewing, most people still tend to visualize better looking down on objects.

10.2 Oblique Drawing

As discussed in Chapter 5, oblique drawing combines a true flat 2-D surface with an angled distorted surface (see Figure 10.40). Just as with the axonometric, there is flexibility in adjusting the scales on the distorted or stretched surface. As seen in Figure 10.41, there are three types of obliques:

1. *Cavalier style* uses true scale for the depth.
2. *Cabinet style* uses half the true scale for the depth.
3. *General style* allows the drafter to adjust the depth scale as needed to reduce distortion.

Drawing an oblique begins with deciding which surface will be drawn true and which one will be distorted. The obvious answer to this question is to take the most complex side and put it on the true surface or shape and to place the simpler side on the angled surface. This approach works fairly well except with some rare exceptions when the appearance of the depth is too distorted (see Figure 10.42). Then a good drafter or designer tries to adjust the depth scale to make the drawing more realistic. Other options the drafter has are to change the angle of the sloped side. The angles used for oblique drawing as a rule are between 30° and 60°. The three commonly used angles are 30°, 45°, and 60°. Once again the drafting equipment is geared toward making these angles easily with the 30°-60°-90° triangle, 45°-45°-90° triangle, and the ability of the drafting

FIGURE 10.40   Oblique example.

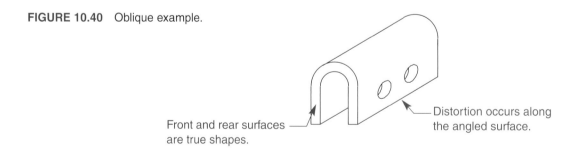

Front and rear surfaces
are true shapes.

Distortion occurs along
the angled surface.

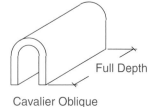

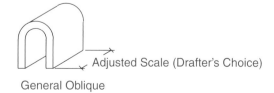

Full Depth

Half Depth

Adjusted Scale (Drafter's Choice)

Cavalier Oblique

Cabinet Oblique

General Oblique

FIGURE 10.41   The three types of obliques.

FIGURE 10.42 House oblique.

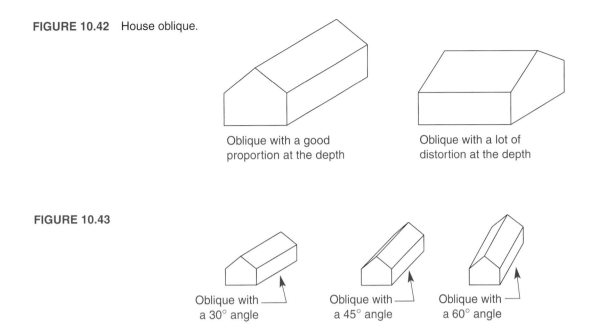

Oblique with a good
proportion at the depth

Oblique with a lot of
distortion at the depth

FIGURE 10.43

Oblique with
a 30° angle

Oblique with
a 45° angle

Oblique with
a 60° angle

arms/machines to lock every 15°. In AutoCAD, using a 30° angle will give the drafter a little bit of an edge. An iso setting will allow an AutoCAD operator to draw 30° lines quickly with this iso mode turned on (see Figure 10.43).

The following are some steps and strategies to use when learning to draw an oblique.

Step 1. Get two scaled orthographic views or elevations and select the view to be drawn on the flat surface and the one to be placed on the angled surface. Construct an oblique box using the overall dimensions from your orthographic views. Most drafters start off trying a 30° angle for the sloped surface along with using the cavalier style oblique in order to use the same scale for all surfaces (see Figure 10.44). If the drawing is not looking quite right, you may want to construct a box using a cabinet or general style.

FIGURE 10.44 House ortho-
graphic with oblique setup.

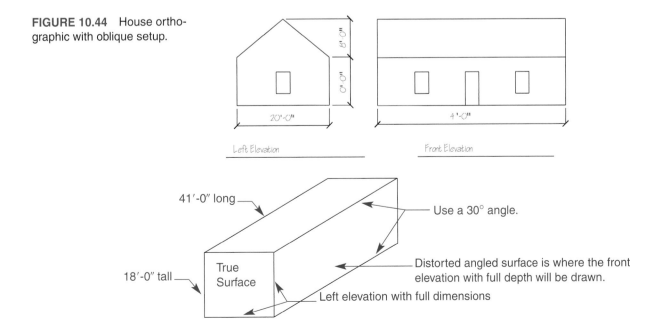

Left Elevation

Front Elevation

41'-0" long

Use a 30° angle.

Distorted angled surface is where the front
elevation with full depth will be drawn.

18'-0" tall

True
Surface

Left elevation with full dimensions

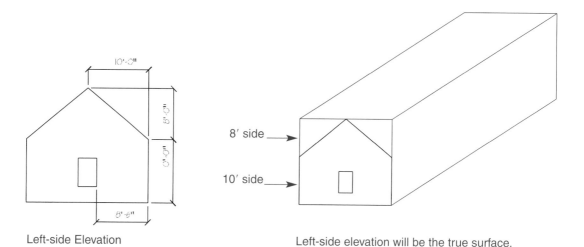

Left-side Elevation

FIGURE 10.45   Oblique showing true surface.

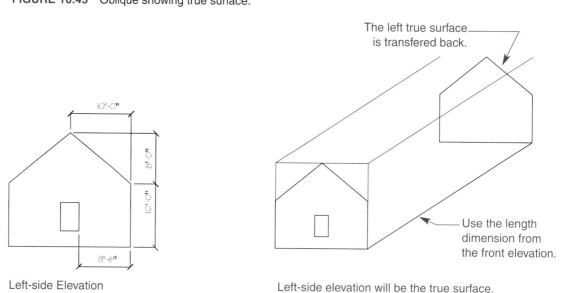

Left-side Elevation

FIGURE 10.46   Oblique transferring back surface.

Step 2.   Once the overall box is laid out with construction guidelines start drawing the true view inside the box (see Figure 10.45). If there are other true surfaces parallel to the front, drop back along the angled base line for the depth setback, then draw the true surface at its new position (see Figure 10.46).

Step 3.   Now that the 2D surfaces are laid out, go to the angled surface and connect endpoints between the true surfaces (see Figure 10.47). Erase lines as you need to. As you develop the drawing you will want the drawing to appear solid, so eliminate lines that make the view look hollowed out (see Figure 10.48).

Step 4.   Take your orthographic view and measure the lengths needed for plotting out the lines on the angled surface (see Figure 10.49). Then measure on the vertical edge to get the height set correctly. Use lines parallel to the angle on the bottom and draw them angling across the sloped surface (see Figure 10.50).

This technique is the same one used in axonometrics found earlier in the chapter. To get the best looking drawing possible, do not darken the visible lines until everything is laid out and correct. This will help keep you from smearing and having to erase mistakes that were darkened prematurely. Some drafters will erase their construction lines on a pictorial to make the drawing look as much like a real picture as possible.

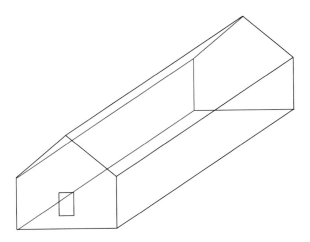

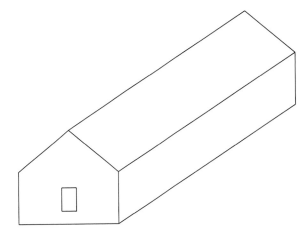

FIGURE 10.47 Oblique transferring distorted surface.

FIGURE 10.48 Oblique with wire-frame line removed.

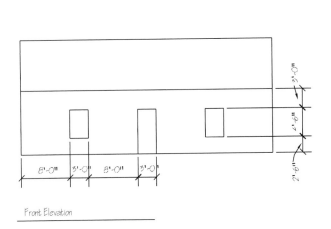

Front Elevation

FIGURE 10.49 Oblique laying out windows.

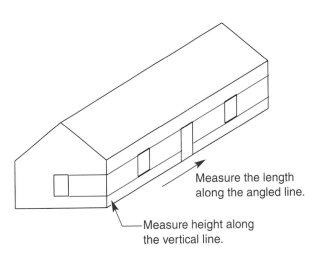

Measure the length along the angled line.

Measure height along the vertical line.

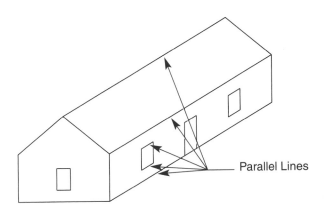

Parallel Lines

FIGURE 10.50 Oblique showing parallel lines.

FIGURE 10.51 Oblique showing hip roof layout.

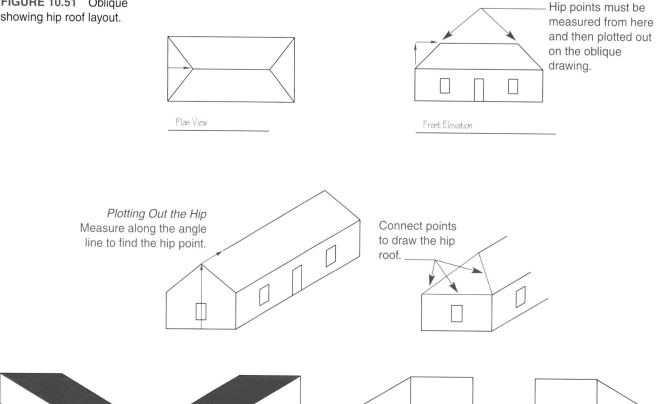

Hip points must be measured from here and then plotted out on the oblique drawing.

Plan View

Front Elevation

Plotting Out the Hip
Measure along the angle line to find the hip point.

Connect points to draw the hip roof.

Looking down at the top with the angle going up to the left

Looking down at the top with the angle going up to the right

Looking up at the bottom with the angle going down to the left

Looking up at the bottom with the angle going down to the right

FIGURE 10.52 Oblique views of box.

Lines that are not parallel to the oblique box must be measured and plotted out just like the noniso lines in an isometric drawing. Measure the height needed on the true view and then the depth along the slope surface (see Figure 10.51). The possible viewing layouts for an oblique drawing are shown in Figure 10.52.

Circles in Pictorial Drawing

The only true circles in pictorial form exist on the 2-D surface of an oblique or in a 3-D computer-generated drawing. Due to the angles generated in pictorial drawing, circles are transformed into ellipses (see Figure 10.53). Isometric ellipses are drawn in two forms: isometric drawing and isometric projection. In true isometric drawing the ellipse diameter is measured along the isometric axis (see Figure 10.54). This is the easiest and most common one used in drafting because measuring with the iso axis keeps the scale uniform throughout the drawing. Isometric projection is not used as often. This technique allows you to measure the diameter along the horizontal line (see Figure 10.55). This alters the drawing scale along the iso axis by approximately 20%.

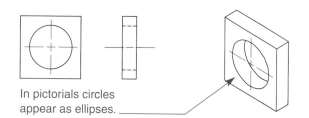

In pictorials circles appear as ellipses.

FIGURE 10.53 Circle in orthographic and isometric forms.

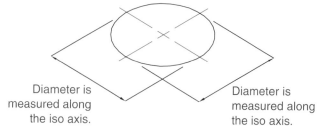

Diameter is measured along the iso axis.

Diameter is measured along the iso axis.

FIGURE 10.54 Ellipse in Isometric Drawing form.

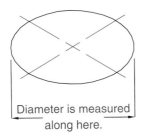

Diameter is measured along here.

FIGURE 10.55 Example of isometric projection. Notice that the ellipse is reduced by 20% when the projection method is used.

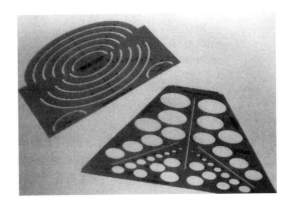

FIGURE 10.56 Isometric templates.

Ellipses can be drawn either way by using one of the following four methods.

Method 1

Templates. Templates for isometric drawing or projection can be used for drawing ellipses (see Figure 10.56). Using templates is the preferred method because of the speed and accuracy. Just make sure you are using the correct template for drawing versus projection. Look at the template and see if it reads "dimensions refer to isometric axes." If it does, it is an isometric drawing template.

Method 2

Four-Center Method. The four-center method requires a compass.

Step 1. Use a 30°-60°-90° triangle to construct the isometric box. All four sides are as long as the ellipse's diameter. Place tick marks at the midpoints (see Figure 10.57).

Step 2. Draw some construction lines from the midpoints to the vertex of the wide angles (see Figure 10.58).

Step 3. The intersection of these lines will give you two of the four centers required. Use these intersections as centers to draw the first two arcs using the compass. Stop when you hit the midpoints (see Figure 10.59).

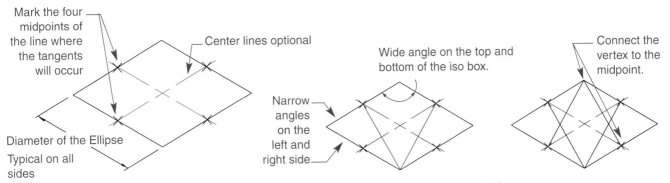

Mark the four midpoints of the line where the tangents will occur

Center lines optional

Diameter of the Ellipse Typical on all sides

FIGURE 10.57 Isometric projection.

Wide angle on the top and bottom of the iso box.

Narrow angles on the left and right side

Connect the vertex to the midpoint.

FIGURE 10.58 Isometric projection.

FIGURE 10.59 Isometric projection.

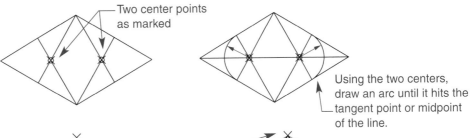

Two center points as marked

Using the two centers, draw an arc until it hits the tangent point or midpoint of the line.

FIGURE 10.60 Isometric projection.

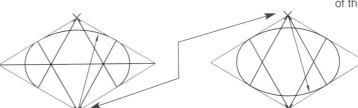

Use the corners of the 120° angles as the centers to complete the ellipse. Draw the arc from tangent to tangent.

Step 4.   Draw the final two arcs from the big angles. Insert the compass needle at the intersection of the big angle and open the compass until it tangents the two arcs on the other side. The method is not that accurate; the ellipse is shorter (see Figure 10.60).

Method 3

   Plotting from the Orthographic Using X and Y Coordinates. Plotting out the ellipse will require a scaled drawing in orthographic form, a French curve, and drafting triangles.

Step 1.   First, take the orthographic and divide the circle into 15° segments. (The more you divide it, the more accurate the plot will be.) Also label the horizontal axis X and the vertical axis Y (see Figure 10.61).

Step 2.   Lay out the X and Y iso axes on the iso box. Measure the radius distance on all four axis lines (see Figure 10.62a). Get the measurements from the orthographic drawing and plot them along the iso X and Y axes. Follow the arrows.

FIGURE 10.61

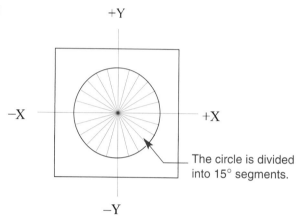

The circle is divided into 15° segments.

FIGURE 10.62   Isometric ellipse plotting.   *continued on next page*

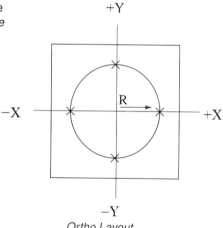

Ortho Layout

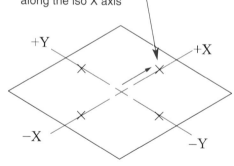

Point being transferred along the iso X axis

Iso Layout

(a)

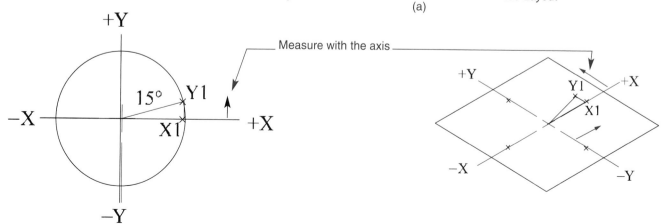

Measure with the axis

(b)

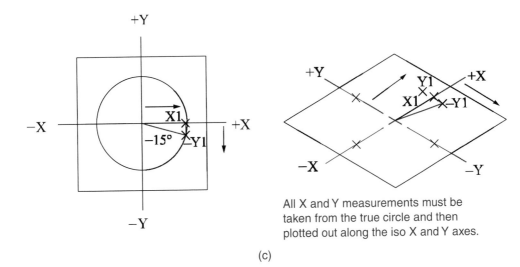

All X and Y measurements must be taken from the true circle and then plotted out along the iso X and Y axes.

(c)

FIGURE 10.62 *continued*

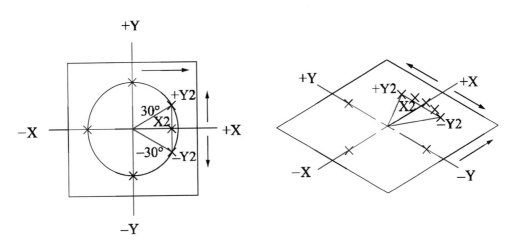

FIGURE 10.63 Circle and isometric plotting points.

Step 3. Go to the orthographic and draw a line from the intersection point where the 15° angled line meets the circle down to the X axis. Once you have the X1 and Y1 measurements, go to the iso box and plot the 15° intersection measurement along the iso X and Y axes (see Figure 10.62b).

To save time go ahead and measure the Y1 in the negative direction (see Figure 10.62c).

Step 4. Repeat Step 3 for the each of the 15° segments that you divided the orthographic circle into (see Figure 10.63).

You need to plot out every increment to give you enough points to use a French curve to connect the ellipse (see Figure 10.64). A smooth ellipse requires a good set of plotted points that allow you to run your French curve through as many points as possible in order to get a continuous smooth arc.

FIGURE 10.64 Plotted points form an ellipse pattern.

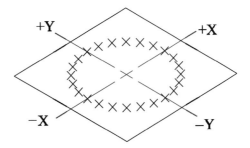

FIGURE 10.65 Isometric grid method part 1.

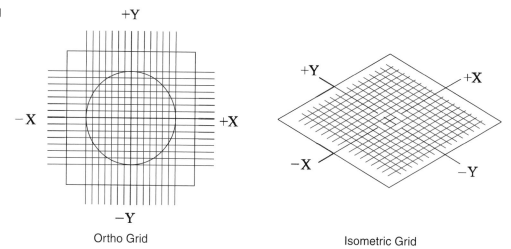

Ortho Grid   Isometric Grid

FIGURE 10.66 Isometric grid method part 2. Locating the quadrants on the X and Y axes.

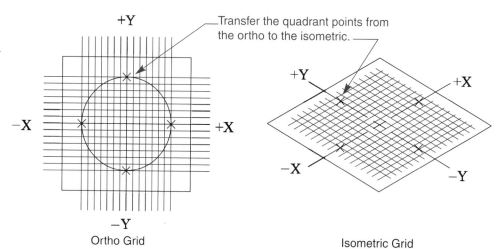

Ortho Grid   Isometric Grid

Method 4

Grid Method for Plotting Ellipses. The grid method is very similar to the X and Y coordinate plotting method. It requires an orthographic drawing from which to measure. A grid is laid out on the orthographic drawing and then the same grid is drawn in isometric form on the pictorial (see Figure 10.65). Basically, you transfer the points where the circle intersects the grid boxes on the orthographic drawing, then reproduce the same grid in isometric form locating the intersection points on the boxes by measuring or visually approximating the distances.

Step 1. Draw the circle in orthographic form. Choose the size the little grid boxes should be. The smaller the circle, the smaller the grid boxes should be. (Just as in the previous method, the more points you use to construct the ellipse, the more accurate the ellipse will be.) (See Figure 10.66.) Lay out the isometric axes, X and Y, and divide the boxes using the same distances found and the orthographic.

Step 2. Start out on the end of the X axis and mark a point on the grid box where the circle intersects it, then move to the isometric drawing and count out the same number of boxes used on the orthographic and place a mark at the corresponding grid box (see Figure 10.66).

Step 3. Move up or down to the next row of boxes and measure from the orthographic the next intersection points. Go to the isometric drawing and measure where the intersection points would occur on the isometric grid (see Figure 10.67). Once this row is complete, continue on to the next rows, repeating this sequence for every row until all the intersecting points have been plotted out (see Figure 10.68). Complete the ellipse by connecting all the plotted points (see Figure 10.69).

The grid method can be used to plot out any shape. It is not normally used on regular ellipses because templates are much faster to use on predictable shapes. Irregular shapes on flat surfaces and irregular shapes

FIGURE 10.67 Isometric grid method part 3. Placing points where the circle intersects the grid.

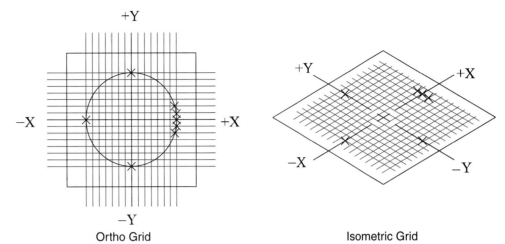

Ortho Grid

Isometric Grid

FIGURE 10.68 Isometric grid method part 4. Points completed.

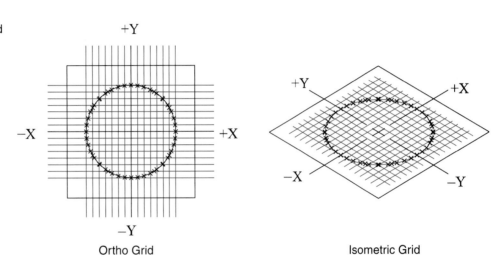

Ortho Grid

Isometric Grid

FIGURE 10.69 Completed ellipse. Connect the points to form the ellipse.

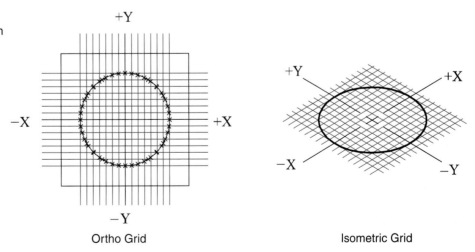

Ortho Grid

Isometric Grid

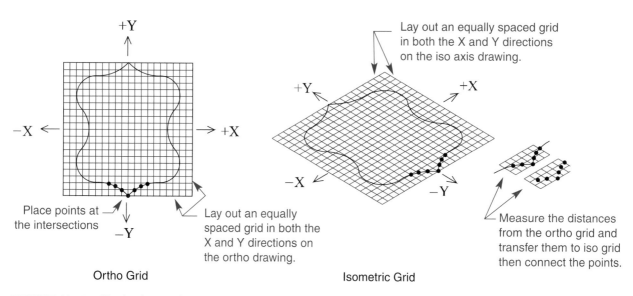

FIGURE 10.70   Plotting isometric curves from an orthographic.

on irregular surfaces can be drawn fairly easy using the grid method or even the X and Y plotting technique (see Figure 10.70). Using grids is not limited to isometric drawing but can be used in all the pictorials, especially the ones that do not have time-saving templates.

10.3 Perspective Drawing Basics

Structured perspective drawing began two thousand years ago and was initially based on some of Euclid's geometric principles. The evolution of perspective drawing has spawned different techniques. If you watch several skilled designers draw a perspective of an object it is quite possible that each one will use a different method. This book demonstrates the technique called the *plan method*. It is a technique that is fairly easy to understand after a few tries.

The plan method can be used for one-point, two-point, and three-point perspectives. Each one of these perspectives will be demonstrated using a basic setup to help build a foundation for understanding this particular form of drafting.

Perspective Drawing Setup and Definitions

Phase I: Setting Up a Plan View with the Picture Plane

Step 1.   First, on a small sheet of paper at the scale of your choice, draw a plan view (top view) of the object to be drawn in perspective form. Next, on a large sheet of paper draw a horizontal line near the top representing what we will label as the picture-plane line (see Figure 10.71).

Step 2.   Pick a point on the picture-plane line and draw a line at a 30° angle. Lay a front corner from your plan view on the corner where the 30° line touches the picture-plane line. Put the

FIGURE 10.71   Start of perspective drawing.

Plan View

Front View

FIGURE 10.72 Alignment for two- and three-point perspectives.

FIGURE 10.73 Alignment for one-point perspectives.

FIGURE 10.74 (a) Example of a two- and a three-point perspective. (b) Example of a one-point perspective.

Note The actual distance from the picture-plane line to the ground line has no scale to it and is not important to the perspectives. It is important that you have a long triangle or drafting machine that can draw vertically from the picture plane to the ground line.

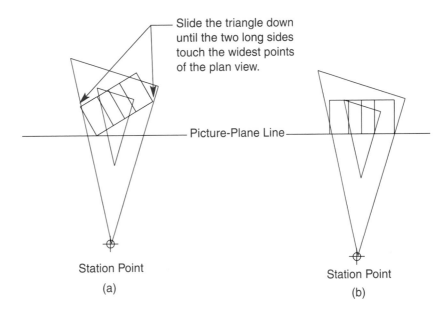

Slide the triangle down until the two long sides touch the widest points of the plan view.

Picture-Plane Line

Station Point
(a)

Station Point
(b)

longest side of the plan view (or the side you want to emphasize) along the 30° line and tape it down (see Figure 10.72). If a one-point perspective was desired, then the plan view side would be placed on top of the picture-plane line (see Figure 10.73).

Step 3. Choose a station point (the distance the viewer is imagined to be standing away from the object) (see Figure 10.74). To cut down on distortion, most instructors will have beginning students use a 30°-60°-90° triangle to set the station point location.

Timeout for Definitions and Analysis

Definitions:
  A. The plan view is the top view of your object.
  B. The picture plane is similar to a viewing window or the film in a camera. It defines the surface where it will be seen by the viewer. The objects tend to taper to a smaller size (see Figure 10.75).

Analysis: The plan view can be located in a variety of positions on the picture plane (see Figure 10.76). For a beginner, it is much easier to put the front corner for a two-point or for a three-point perspective on the picture plane. For one-point perspective, it is easier to put the front of the object on the picture-plane line. Your instructor can change this setup when you are ready for advanced work.

Phase II: Setting Up Ground and Horizon Lines
  Step 1. Drop down below the picture-plane line toward the bottom of the large sheet. Draw a horizontal line across the sheet that is parallel to the picture-plane line. This will be your ground line (see Figure 10.77).

  Step 2. You have the following three choices or options when drawing the next line, which will represent the horizon line. This horizon line will be parallel to the ground line, and the distance for the ground line will be a scaled measurement.

FIGURE 10.75 Example of a picture plane.

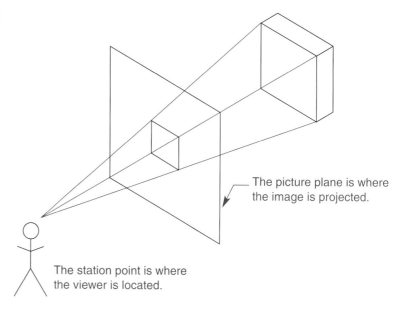

The picture plane is where the image is projected.

The station point is where the viewer is located.

Picture-Plane Line

Back corner touching

Plan view floating off the picture-plane line

Picture-Plane Line

FIGURE 10.76 Object and picture-plane locations.

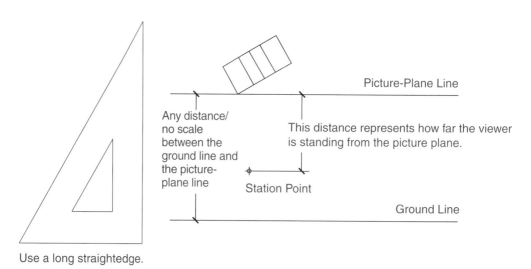

Picture-Plane Line

Any distance/ no scale between the ground line and the picture-plane line

This distance represents how far the viewer is standing from the picture plane.

Station Point

Ground Line

Use a long straightedge.

FIGURE 10.77 Perspective with picture-plane line and ground line.

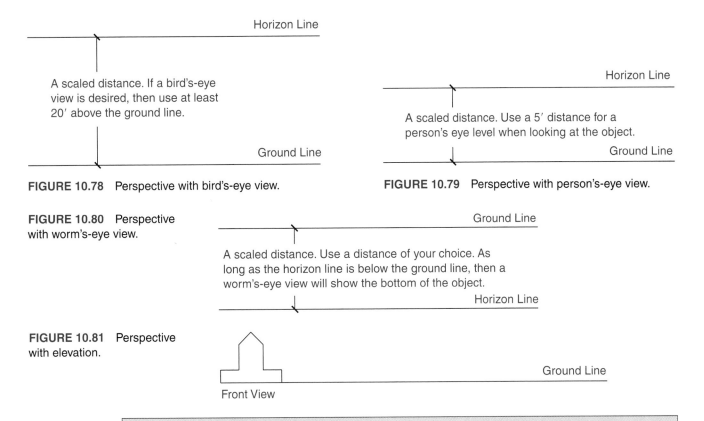

FIGURE 10.78 Perspective with bird's-eye view.

FIGURE 10.79 Perspective with person's-eye view.

FIGURE 10.80 Perspective with worm's-eye view.

FIGURE 10.81 Perspective with elevation.

Horizon Line Location Tips

1. *A bird's-eye view* is obtained by placing the horizon line high above the ground line. Measure the height desired, 30′ or higher works well (see Figure 10.78).
2. *A person's-eye view* is obtained by placing the horizon line around 5′ to 6′ above the ground line. This height is supposed to give a view that an average person would see standing on the ground (see Figure 10.79).
3. *A worm's-eye view* is obtained by placing the horizon line well below the ground line. The purpose of a worm's-eye view is to see the bottom of the object. The farther down the horizon line is placed the more of the base will be seen by the viewer (see Figure 10.80).

Step 3. Draw a front or side elevation (at the same scale as the plan view) of the object on a small sheet and tape it down on top of the ground line, aligning the bottom with the ground line (see Figure 10.81).

At this point the setups will look similar to Figure 10.82.

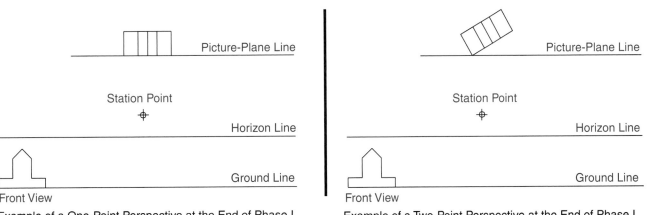

Example of a One-Point Perspective at the End of Phase I

Example of a Two-Point Perspective at the End of Phase I

FIGURE 10.82 Perspective, phase II.

Phase III: Getting the Vanishing Points and the True-Height Line

Step 1.   The true height is determined when the plan view touches the picture-plane line. Draw a line straight down from this point and stop when it intersects the ground line (see Figure 10.83).

Step 2.   (Go to step 3 if you are setting up a two-point layout.) When placing the vanishing point in a one-point perspective, draw a line through the station point and stop when it intersects the horizon line (see Figure 10.84). This is where your vanishing point is located, and it is always on the horizon line. This is the basic layout for a one-point perspective. Step 3 will show you the complete two-point layout.

Step 3.   In a two-point perspective the vanishing points require a little more work. Transfer the 90° angle on the plan view down to the station point, and extend the lines to the picture-plane line, shown in Figure 10.85 as points A and B.

Step 4.   Draw vertical lines straight down from points A and B until they touch the horizon line. These new points represent the left and right vanishing points on a two- and three-point perspective (see Figure 10.86). Adding a third vanishing point will be shown when the three-point method is demonstrated later.

Figure 10.86 shows the completed setup needed to start drawing a two-point perspective. Use this format for your perspective drawing. One-point perspectives (see Figure 10.84 for the completed setup) work well for a lot of interior drawing or when you desire to converge the elements of the drawing to a single vanishing point. (This tends to give an oblique effect.) The two- and three-point perspectives work well for a more realistic effect.

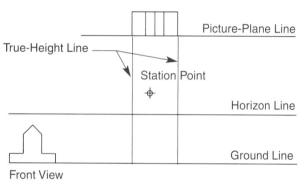

Example of a One-Point Perspective
Showing the True-Height Line

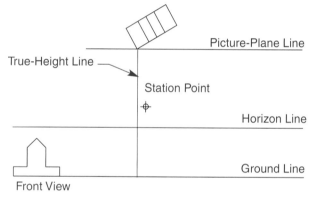

Example of a Two-Point Perspective
Showing the True-Height Line

FIGURE 10.83   Perspectives with true-height line.

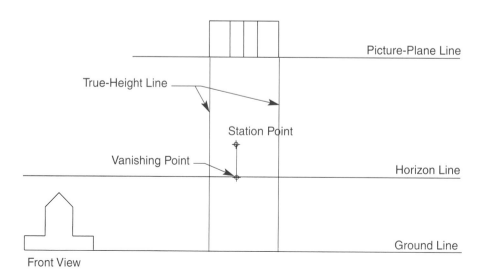

FIGURE 10.84   Perspectives finding one vanishing point.

FIGURE 10.85 Perspectives finding two vanishing points.

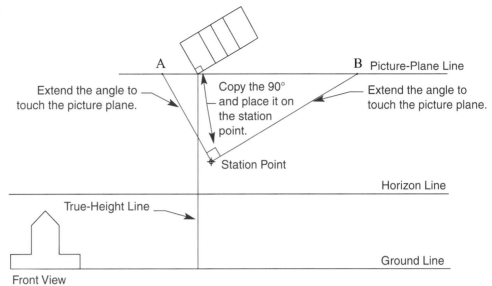

FIGURE 10.86 Completed two-point perspective layout.

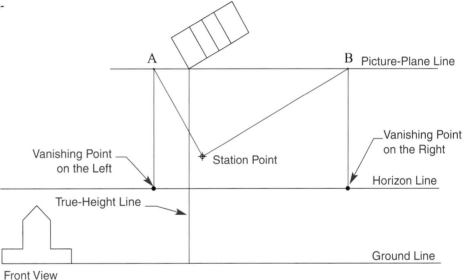

The following examples will use these abbreviations:

GL—ground line

PP—picture-plane line

HL—horizon line

VP—vanishing point

SP—station point

TH—true-height line

One-Point Perspective Example (see Figure 10.87)

Step 1. Draw a plan view and elevation on separate 8½″ × by 11″ sheets. Get a big sheet (17″ × 22″) and lay out the picture-plane line, ground line, and horizon line (see Figure 10.88). Use a scale of ⅛″ = 1′-0″ as a minimum choice. Tape the plan view sheet down on a picture-plane line. Next, tape the elevation down on the ground line (see Figure 10.89).

FIGURE 10.87 Isometric of floor plan.

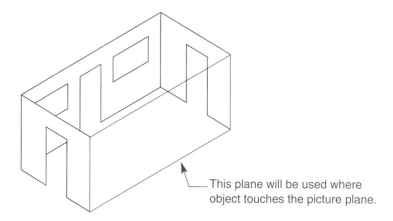

This plane will be used where object touches the picture plane.

FIGURE 10.88

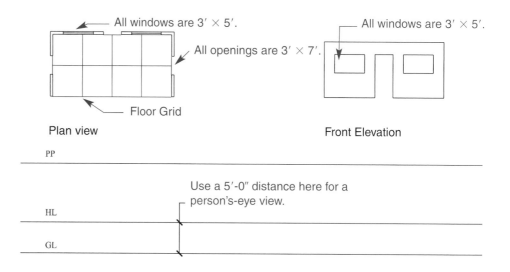

All windows are 3′ × 5′.

All openings are 3′ × 7′.

All windows are 3′ × 5′.

Floor Grid

Plan view

Front Elevation

PP

Use a 5′-0″ distance here for a person's-eye view.

HL

GL

FIGURE 10.89 One-point-perspective setup.

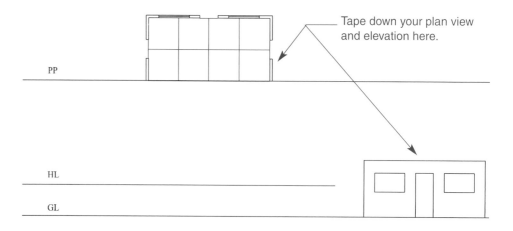

Tape down your plan view and elevation here.

PP

HL

GL

FIGURE 10.90 One-point perspective finding the station point.

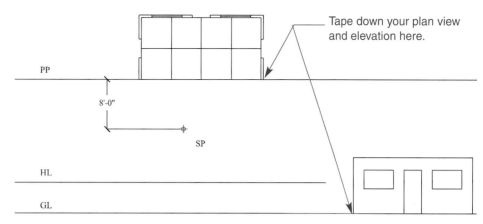

Step 2. Locate the station point. This example will put the viewer 8′ away from the picture-plane line and slightly to the left of the building's center (see Figure 10.90).

Step 3. Next, locate the true-height lines by passing a line through the front corners that touch the picture plane straight down until it intersects the ground line. Note that heights can be measured only off the true-height line (see Figure 10.91).

Step 4. Find the vanishing point by drawing a vertical line through the station point and intersecting the horizon line (see Figure 10.92).

Step 5. The setup is complete, and it is now time to start drawing the perspective. It works well to start at the bottom and work your way up, laying out the walls first. Go to where the ground line and the true-height line intersect. These are your two outside corners (see points 1 and 2 on Figure 10.93).

FIGURE 10.91 One-point perspective finding true heights.

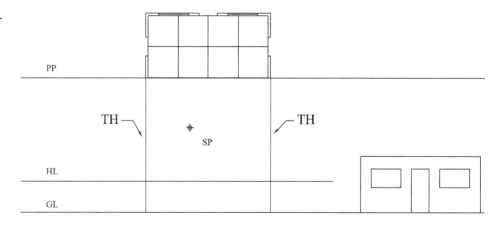

FIGURE 10.92 One-point perspective finding vanishing point.

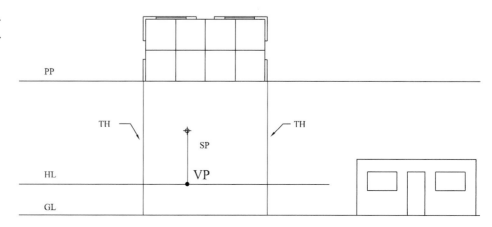

FIGURE 10.93 One-point perspective finding base of wall.

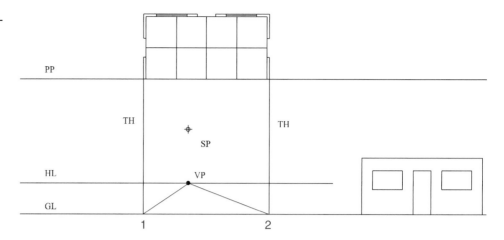

FIGURE 10.94 One-point perspective finding ceiling line.

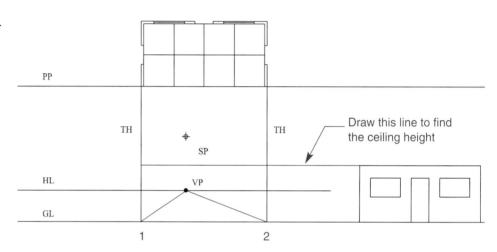

Step 6. From the ground line draw lines from points 1 and 2 back to the vanishing point. Now go to the elevation and project a horizontal line from the top of the wall over to the true-height lines (see Figure 10.94).

Step 7. Starting at the top points on the true-height, draw lines back to the vanishing point (see Figure 10.95).

Step 8. To find the back wall go to the plan view's back corners labeled 3 and 4 on Figure 10.96, and draw a line from the station point to these corners crossing the picture-plane line. From these intersections, labeled A and B, draw vertical lines straight down, crossing the tapering lines (see Figure 10.96).

FIGURE 10.95 Taking walls to the vanishing point.

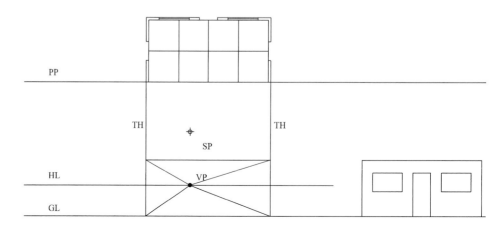

FIGURE 10.96 Locating back corners.

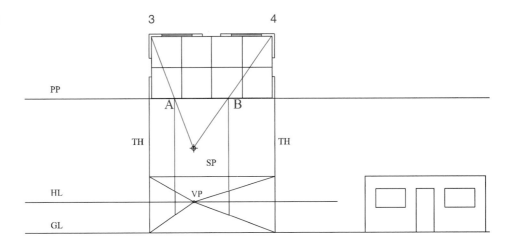

FIGURE 10.97 Locating back wall.

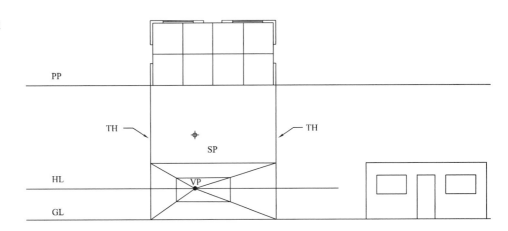

Step 9. These two lines represent the back corners on the one-point perspective. To finish up the back floor and ceiling lines connect the bottom points as well as the top points with a straight line (see Figure 10.97). Now, erase the inside lines that should disappear behind the back wall (see Figure 10.98).

Step 10. To draw the big tile floor follow the same pattern. Go to the plan view and draw the vertical lines straight down from the picture-plane line to the ground line (see Figure 10.99).

Step 11. The vertical lines mark where the grid will start on the ground line. Simply draw from these intersections back to the vanishing point (see Figure 10.100). (Remember to erase the lines that disappear behind the back wall.)

Step 12. To get the horizontal grid line go to the plan view, locate the intersection with the left wall, and draw a line from this point back to the station point. Where it crosses the picture-plane line draw a vertical line down to the bottom left wall in the perspective drawing (see Figure 10.101). Connect the bottom points with a straight line to complete the floor grid.

Step 13. Next, you are going to lay out the heights for the doors and windows on the true-height lines. Draw horizontal lines from the elevation that shows the height of the doors and windows (see Figure 10.102).

FIGURE 10.98 Darkening back wall.

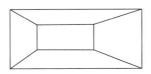

The overall room size is now outlined.

FIGURE 10.99 Floor grid part I. Transferring grid from the picture plane to the ground line.

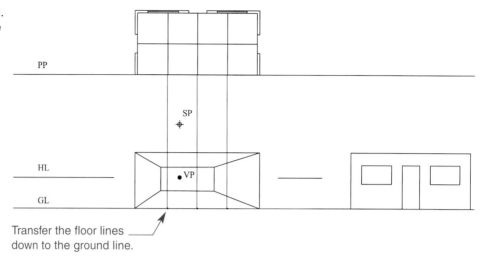

Transfer the floor lines down to the ground line.

FIGURE 10.100 Floor grid part II. Drawing the grid from the ground line to the vanishing point.

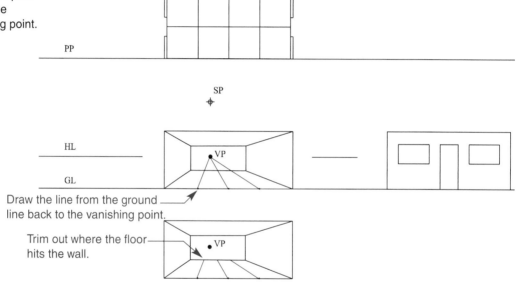

Draw the line from the ground line back to the vanishing point.

Trim out where the floor hits the wall.

FIGURE 10.101 Drawing the horizontal grid line.

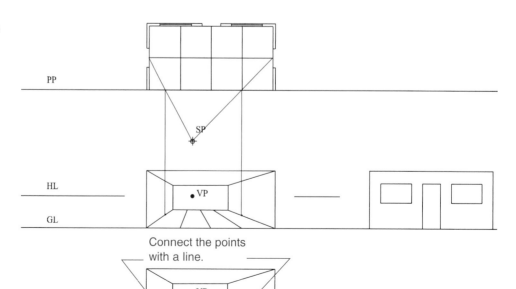

Connect the points with a line.

FIGURE 10.102 Getting door and window height #1 (height on the side wall).

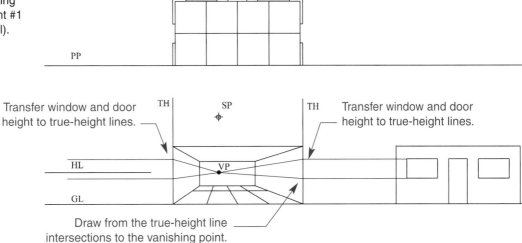

Transfer window and door height to true-height lines.

Transfer window and door height to true-height lines.

Draw from the true-height line intersections to the vanishing point.

FIGURE 10.103 Getting door and window height #2 (height on the back wall).

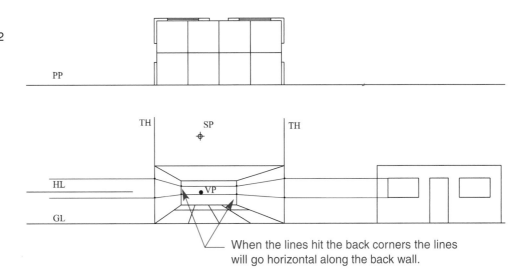

When the lines hit the back corners the lines will go horizontal along the back wall.

Once the heights are established on the true-height line, draw lines from those intersections to the vanishing point (see Figure 10.103).

Step 14. By now you may have realized that the plan view is needed to find the vertical lines that belong with the perspective shown in Figure 10.105. Using the plan view, go to each corner on the doors and windows and draw a line from there to the station point, passing the lines through the picture plane (see Figure 10.104).

Step 15. The intersection points along the picture-plane line can be projected down with a vertical line to form the openings on the door and windows (see Figure 10.105).

Erasing lines when they are no longer needed can make it easier to see the perspective. Perspectives are not complicated once you have mastered the system because so much is repetition that can be picked up quickly.

Two-Point Perspective Example
Use the plan view and elevation given in Figure 10.106 to construct a two-point perspective. If you use the two-point setup method shown earlier in this chapter, a basic setup should look like Figure 10.107.

Step 1. Lay out the bottom of the object first. Find the outside corners in the plan view and draw a line from the corners to the station point, passing the lines through the picture-plane line

FIGURE 10.104 Locating corners of door and window #1 (drawing from the corners through the station point).

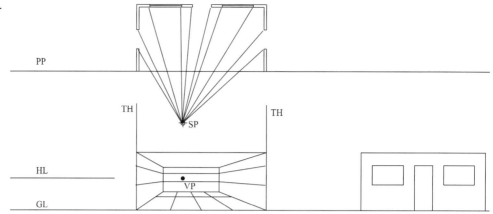

FIGURE 10.105 Locating corners of door and window #2 (transferring the corners from the picture plane to the floor line).

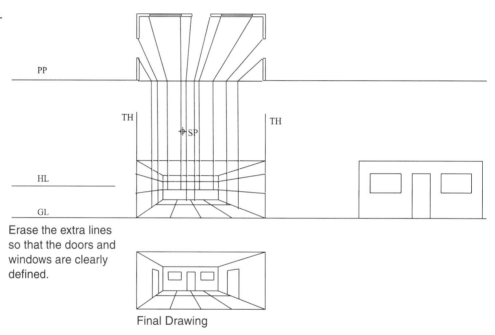

Erase the extra lines so that the doors and windows are clearly defined.

Final Drawing

FIGURE 10.106 Plan and elevation for two-point perspective.

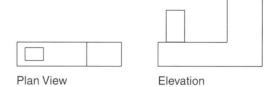

Plan View   Elevation

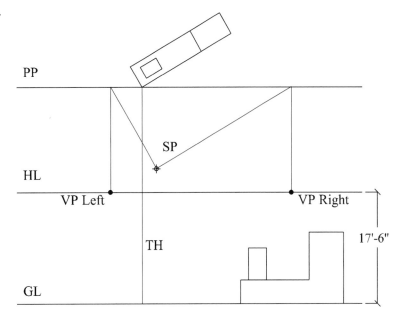

FIGURE 10.107 Two-point perspective layout.

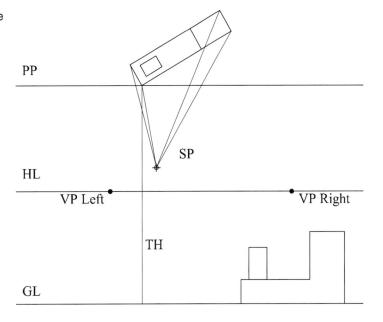

FIGURE 10.108 Drawing a line from the station point to the corners.

(see Figure 10.108). Project these intersection points on the picture-plane down with vertical lines to the ground line (see Figure 10.109).

Step 2. The corner that touches the picture-plane line in the top view is also where the corner touches the ground line in the perspective part of the drawing. Use this intersection on the ground line to start boxing out the base by drawing lines back to the vanishing points (see Figure 10.110).

Step 3. Go to the plan view and locate the box shape with the little rectangle inside it. Draw lines from the corners back to the station point, passing through the picture plane. Use these intersections to draw vertical lines down to locate the corners in the perspective (see Figure 10.111).

Step 4. On the elevation drawing, transfer the height of the box across to the true-height line. Take the point where it intersects the true-height line, and vanish it to the left vanishing point and then to the right vanishing point (see Figure 10.112).

FIGURE 10.109 Transferring vertical lines.

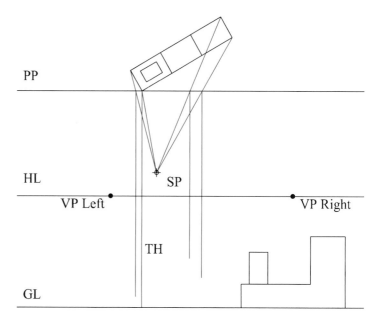

FIGURE 10.110 Finding the base.

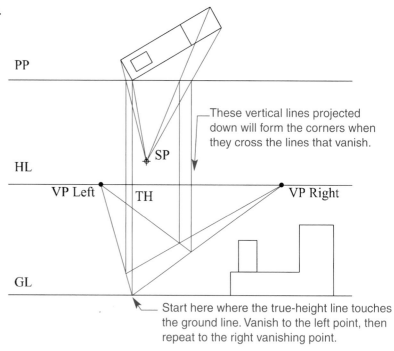

These vertical lines projected down will form the corners when they cross the lines that vanish.

Start here where the true-height line touches the ground line. Vanish to the left point, then repeat to the right vanishing point.

FIGURE 10.111 Darkening the base.

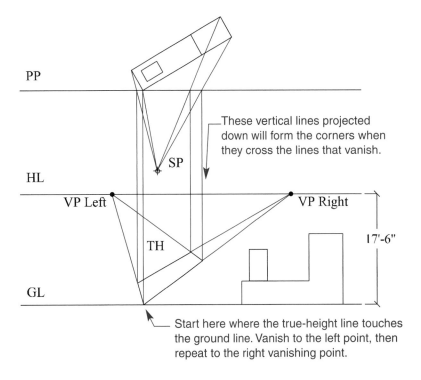

PP

These vertical lines projected down will form the corners when they cross the lines that vanish.

SP

HL

VP Left · VP Right

17'-6"

TH

GL

Start here where the true-height line touches the ground line. Vanish to the left point, then repeat to the right vanishing point.

FIGURE 10.112 Drawing level 2 height.

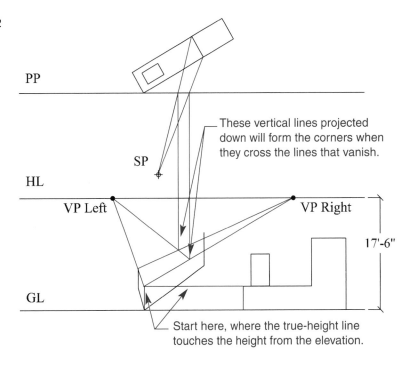

PP

These vertical lines projected down will form the corners when they cross the lines that vanish.

SP

HL

VP Left · VP Right

17'-6"

GL

Start here, where the true-height line touches the height from the elevation.

FIGURE 10.113 Showing changing direction at corner (vanishing to the left).

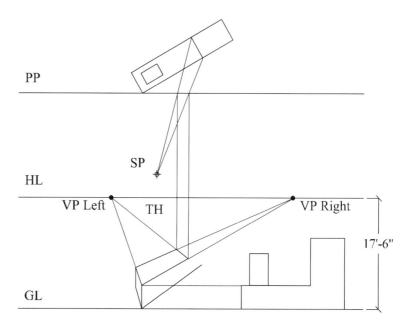

When the vertical lines are intersected, you must vanish back to the other vanishing point to make the change of direction (see Figure 10.113). (This is very similar to changing directions in isometric drawing but instead of going from a 30° line to a 150° line where a corner stops, you go from the left vanishing point to the right vanishing point.)

Step 5. Repeat steps 3 and 4 for the highest box on the object (see Figure 10.114).

Step 6. The final part of drawing is the minitower coming out of the middle part of the object. The best way to find the correct location is to use a grid on the plan view (see Figure 10.115). This grid needs to be redrawn on the perspective part of the drawing, but it must be transferred down just like every other point. This requires repeating the steps of going to the plan view and drawing lines from the corners back to the station point and crossing the picture-plane line (see Figure 10.116). Once you have done this, use vertical lines to transfer down the locations of the corners. When you have brought the four points down, vanish them back to the correct vanishing points to form the grid (see Figure 10.117).

Note: The most common error made is transferring the height from the true-height line along the lines that follow the vanishing points. Sometimes you must do a little work to find the right height at the right location. A good example appears in the final part of our drawing.

FIGURE 10.114 Showing top level.

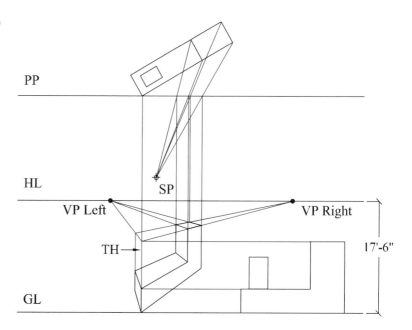

FIGURE 10.115 Grid minitower plan view (extend lines to intersect the outside edge).

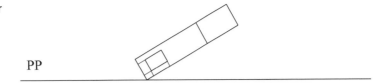

FIGURE 10.116 Transferring points to station point.

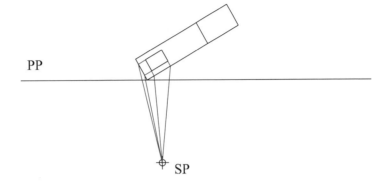

FIGURE 10.117 Grid on perspective.

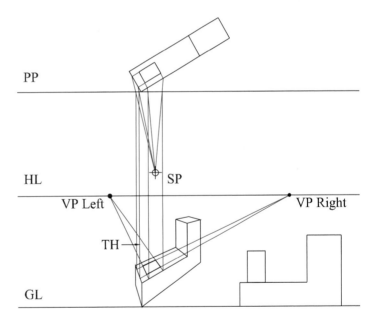

Note: In the beginning, some students have a problem knowing which vanishing points to use. It is helpful to look at the line in the plan view. If it is angling to the right side, then it goes to the right vanishing point; if it angles to the left, then it will vanish to the left point (see Figure 10.118).

Step 7. Now that the base of the minitower is complete, it is time to find the top grid. Go to the elevation and transfer the height of the minitower to the true-height line. Once you have done this, vanish this intersection to the left and right vanishing points, crossing the vertical lines to locate the grid placement (see Figure 10.119). Vanish the four points where vertical lines intersect at the top level to form your grid. Connect the bottom corners to the top corners of the grid with vertical lines. Your minitower as well as your two-point perspective is complete (see Figure 10.120).

FIGURE 10.118 Comparing plan with perspective.

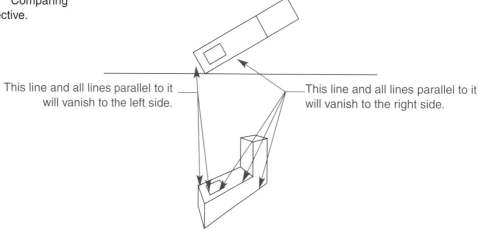

This line and all lines parallel to it will vanish to the left side.

This line and all lines parallel to it will vanish to the right side.

FIGURE 10.119 Grid top of tower.

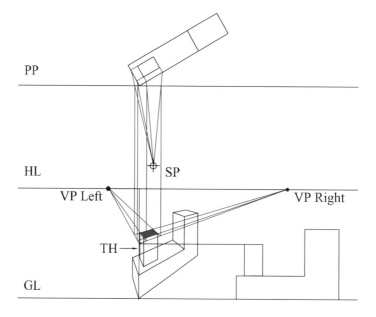

PP

HL   SP

VP Left   VP Right

TH →

GL

FIGURE 10.120 Complete two-point perspective.

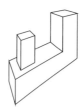

Three-Point Perspective Example

The steps used to draw a three-point perspective are the same as in the two-point example except once the object is drawn, a third vanishing point is added so some shade and shadow lines can be drawn to give the perspective drawing a little more life.

Figure 10.121 is a typical completed two-point perspective drawing with the standard setup. Making the third vanishing point is a matter of positioning where you want the sun (or a light source) to cast shadows on your drawing. In this example, we will place it in the left-hand sky (see Figure 10.122). Now, using the sun's location draw a vertical line straight down, intersecting the horizon line. This will be the third vanishing point (see Figure 10.123).

Remember that all the vanishing points will fall on the horizon line. The third vanishing point will be used in combination with the sun location to generate the shadow outline, using the following steps.

FIGURE 10.121 Three-point-perspective setup.

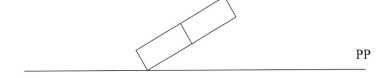

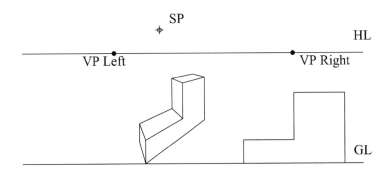

FIGURE 10.122 Three-point perspective showing sun.

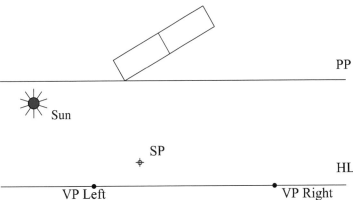

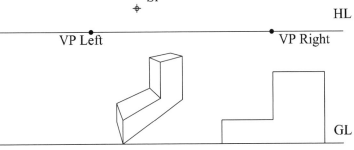

FIGURE 10.123 Finding the
third vanishing point.

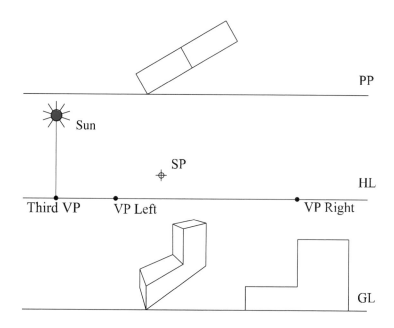

Step 1. The backside corners have been labeled to help you follow this example (see Figure 10.124). First, draw a line from the third vanishing point through point A (see Figure 10.125).

Step 2. Draw a straight line from the sun through point B, intersecting the last line you drew (see Figure 10.126).

Step 3. Draw a line from this intersection (point 1) to the right vanishing point (see Figure 10.127).

Step 4. Go back to the sun and draw a line from it through point C, extended until the line intersects with the line between point 1 and the right vanishing point. At this intersection go to the third vanishing point and project the line forward (see Figure 10.128).

Step 5. Draw a line from the sun through point D, intersecting the previous line (see Figure 10.129).

Step 6. Draw a line from this intersection to the right vanishing point (see Figure 10.130).

Step 7. Draw a straight line from the third vanishing point through point F, intersecting the last line drawn (see Figure 10.131).

This completes the shadow's outline for the object. Most drafters hatch the inside with lines that are drawn from the third vanishing point (see Figure 10.132). The shadow is the shape caused by the object when the light source shines on it. The shadow is cast on the ground or some other object. The shade falls on the object itself, so light is blocked out on that side. Simply draw lines parallel to the vertical ones shown on the object to hatch the shade.

FIGURE 10.124 Adding letters
to corners.

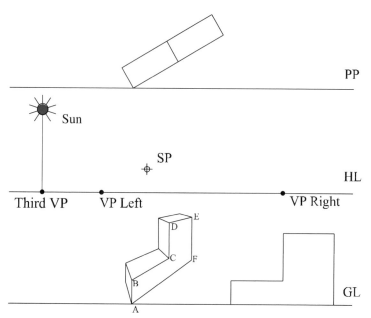

FIGURE 10.125 Drawing a line from the third point to point A.

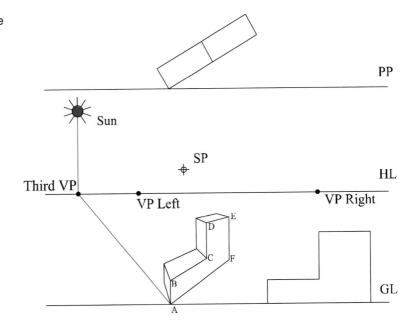

FIGURE 10.126 Drawing a line from the sun to point B.

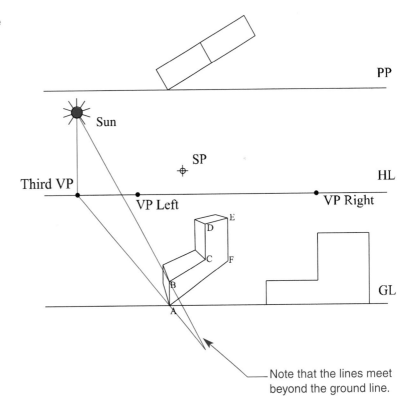

Note that the lines meet beyond the ground line.

FIGURE 10.127 Taking the intersection to the right vanishing point.

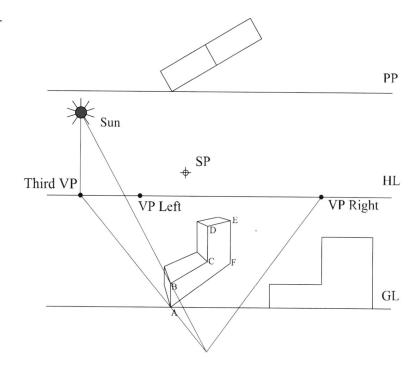

FIGURE 10.128 Drawing a line to the sun through point C and third point through C.

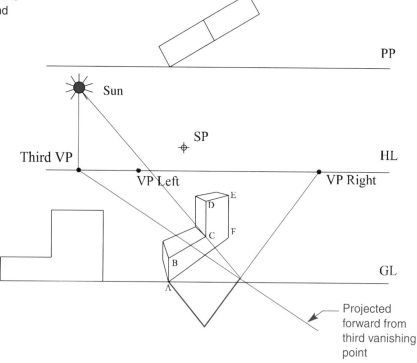

FIGURE 10.129 Drawing a line to the sun through point D.

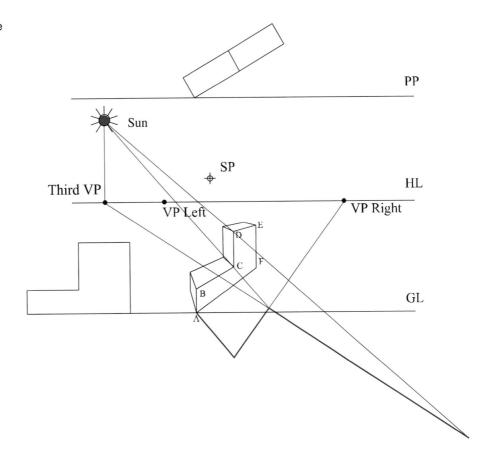

FIGURE 10.130 Taking the intersection point to the third vanishing point.

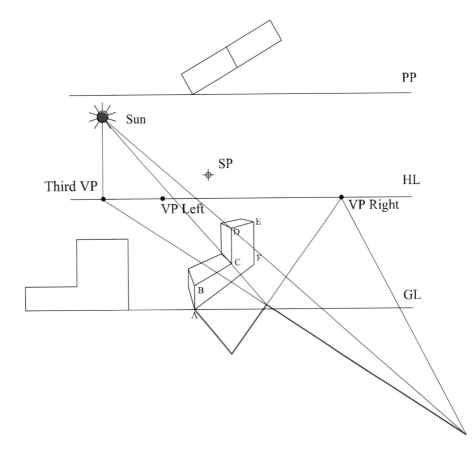

FIGURE 10.131 Completed three-point perspective.

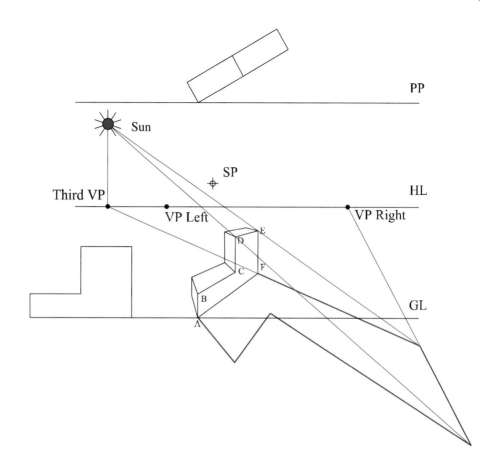

FIGURE 10.132 Drawing shade and shadow.

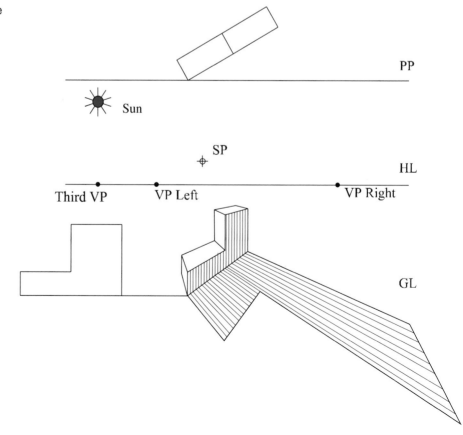

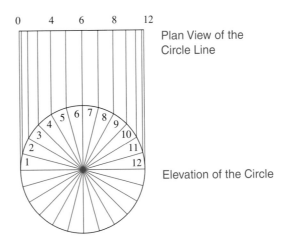

FIGURE 10.133 Circle divided into 15° segments.

Plan View of the Circle Line

Elevation of the Circle

Circles in Perspectives

There is no magical template for drawing circles or ellipses for perspectives. Positioning perspectives can vary so much that there is no easy out when drawing circles in perspective form. In perspective drawing, circles take the form of ellipses just like in axonometrics. In this case, two methods are very similar for constructing the elliptical shapes.

The first method involves drawing the circles in the elevation view and the plan view. Once the circles are drawn, divide the circle into 15° segments in the elevation view, then transfer the intersection points onto the plan view (see Figure 10.133).

At this point insert the views into the standard perspective setup at the location required in the plan view and elevation. The procedure at this point is the same for any perspective. Plot the points needed from the plan view and elevation, forming the outline in perspective form (see Figure 10.134). When you have plotted out enough points, use a French curve to connect the points to form the ellipse.

The other method is the grid method. It is done in the exact same order as the previous method and uses a similar technique. The difference is that the grid spacing determines the points to be plotted (see Figure 10.135).

FIGURE 10.134 Perspective plotting of circle.

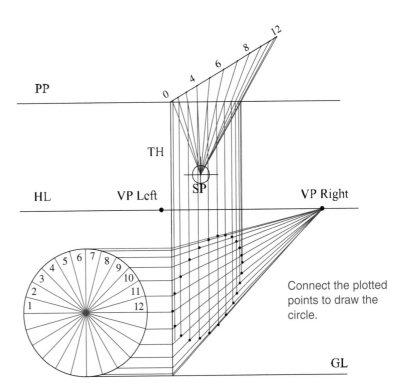

Connect the plotted points to draw the circle.

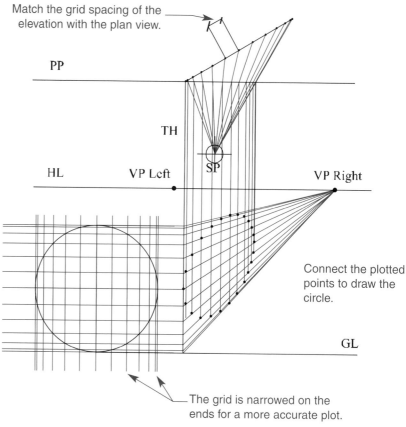

FIGURE 10.135 Perspective of gridded circle.

Match the grid spacing of the elevation with the plan view.

Connect the plotted points to draw the circle.

The grid is narrowed on the ends for a more accurate plot.

Sketching Pictorials

The techniques for sketching pictorials follow the same general guidelines used in technical drawing as discussed in Chapter 2.

For a drafter, the temptation to sketch like an artist becomes greater when it comes to pictorials. The pictorials are artistic, but do not allow yourself to get trapped into sketching like an artist unless you are one. A pictorial can be treated exactly like other sketches as a way to communicate and explain ideas.

Here is a review of sketching guidelines:

1. Draw visible lines with continuous strokes.
2. Do not use templates.
3. Use blue lead for plotting points, construction layout, and boxing out shapes.
4. Use grided vellum pads if needed.

Special isometric grid paper is available for sketching. The blue guidelines are set to 30°, 150°, and 90° angles. The iso boxes that are on the gird are not proportional vertically to the other directions. You cannot count boxes when trying to stay in scale vertically because of this discrepancy, so avoid this pitfall. Recall that one advantage of sketching is that no scale is required. (NTS means not to scale.) Just be proportional.

Grids are also used when plotting out ellipses. First, choose the correct isometric surface in which to place the ellipse (see Figure 10.136). Remember to turn or place the narrow or smaller ends of the ellipse into the small or acute angles (see Figure 10.137). Lay out the box for the surface and also the axis lines lightly or in blue lead (see Figure 10.138). Place points at the intersection of the axis and construction box (see Figure 10.139). Next, layout some small iso boxes inside the big box (see Figure 10.140). Once the grid is in place put some points at the far ends of the ellipse (see Figure 10.141).

At this stage there are eight points in place to help you sketch out the ellipse. Add a few more points if desired to lay out the ellipse, then keeping as steady as possible, sketch in the ellipse a quarter piece at a time.

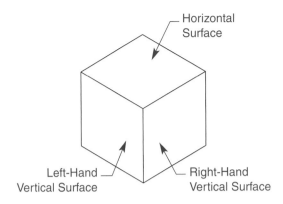

FIGURE 10.136 Identify the iso surface.

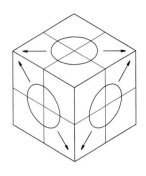

FIGURE 10.137 Ellipses on an iso cube.

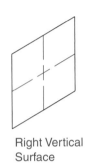

Horizontal Surface   Left Vertical Surface   Right Vertical Surface

FIGURE 10.138 Axis on iso ellipse.

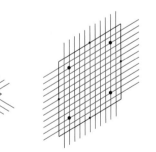

Four points on the ellipse and the two iso axes.

FIGURE 10.139 Finding points on the iso axes.

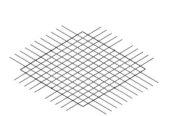

FIGURE 10.140 Grid of the iso surface.

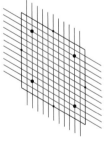

FIGURE 10.141 Using the grid to lay out points.

If a really smooth curve is desired, add more points to develop a better quality sketch (see Figure 10.142). Using this approach will give you smoother, nicer looking ellipses.

You can sketch an oblique on normal grid paper for the flat views, then use 45° for the angled depth. The iso grid paper works well when you are using a 30° angle for your depth.

Trying to sketch perspectives is a bit more challenging than other pictorials, but it is occasionally done. Set up a perspective sketch just like a drawing. Buy or make a perspective grid if you prefer using it. Handle the sketch just like a drawing. A sketch requires few tools; however, this does not mean the drawing should be sloppy or messy. As a drafter gets better, grids and pencils become a thing of the past; experienced professionals use transparent sketch paper rolls and felt markers. Look at sketching as a fast way to communicate ideas to others and not as something to be hung in an art gallery.

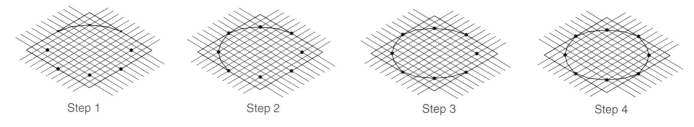

| Step 1 | Step 2 | Step 3 | Step 4 |

Sketch a quarter section at a time.

FIGURE 10.142   Sketching the ellipse.

REVIEW QUESTIONS

1. Sketch an example of a cube in isometric, dimetric, and trimetric form. Label the interior angles and the characteristics.
2. Why are depth scales adjusted on dimetric and trimetric drawings?
3. Explain the difference between ellipses drawn in isometric projection form versus isometric drawing.
4. List the different methods used to draw an ellipse in isometric form.
5. Draw an ellipse with a 1½″ radius using the four-center method. Put it on a right-hand vertical surface.
6. List the three different types of obliques and explain how they differ from one another.
7. Is it possible to have a circle and an ellipse in oblique forms on the same drawing?
8. Sketch an isometric and an oblique cube looking at the bottom horizontal surface.
9. Make a list of the major components used in a perspective setup.
10. How would a perspective be set (where would the horizon line be placed) to draw the following perspective views:
    a. Worm's-eye view
    b. Bird's-eye view
    c. Person's-eye view
11. From where is a true-height line generated on a perspective drawing?
12. In a perspective, what does the station point represent?
13. Explain how to find the vanishing points on a two-point perspective.

EXERCISES

EXERCISE 10.1

Using the isometric drawings in Figure 10.143, sketch the front view, side view, and the top view on 8 × 8 grided vellum.

EXERCISE 10.2

Sketch the figures in exercise 10.1 in oblique form using a 30° angle for the depth.

EXERCISE 10.3

Using the given views, sketch the isometric figures in Figure 10.144.

FIGURE 10.143 Exercise 10.1.

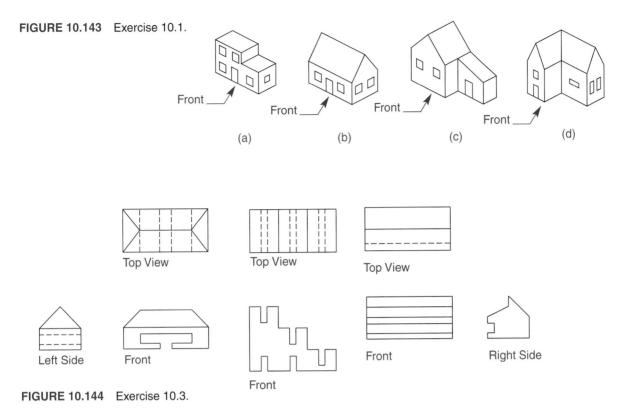

FIGURE 10.144 Exercise 10.3.

EXERCISE 10.4

Lay out the given one-point perspective setup in Figure 10.145 on an 11″ × 17″ sheet at a ¼″ = 1′-0″ scale. Construct a one-point perspective using the given setup showing all construction lines.

EXERCISE 10.5

Lay out the one-point perspective setup in Figure 10.146 on an 11″ × 17″ sheet at a ¼″ = 1′-0″ scale. Construct a one-point perspective using the given setup showing all construction lines. After completing the ceiling tile, add a 2′ × 2′ floor tile grid to your one-point perspective.

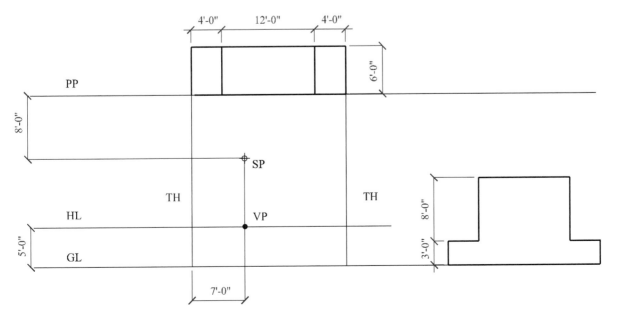

FIGURE 10.145 Exercise 10.4.

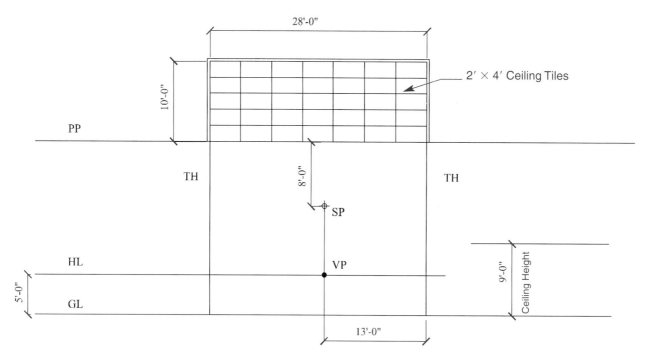

FIGURE 10.146 Exercise 10.5.

EXERCISE 10.6

Redraw the two-point perspective layouts in Figure 10.147 on an 11″ × 17″ sheet of vellum. Construct the two-point perspective showing all construction lines.

EXERCISE 10.7

Using Figure 10.148, add the shadows using a light source and a third vanishing point.

FIGURE 10.147 Exercise 10.6.
continued on next page

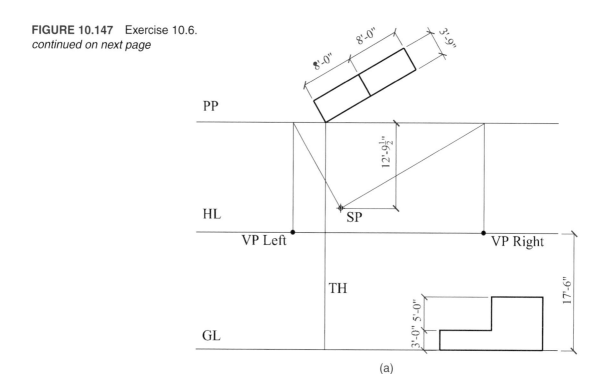

(a)

FIGURE 10.147 *continued*

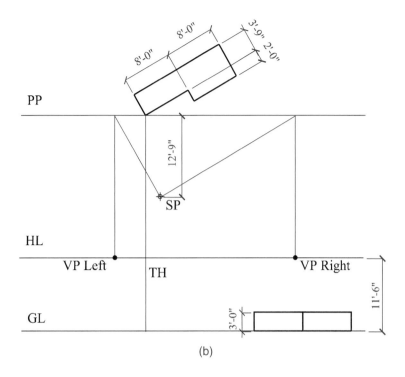

(b)

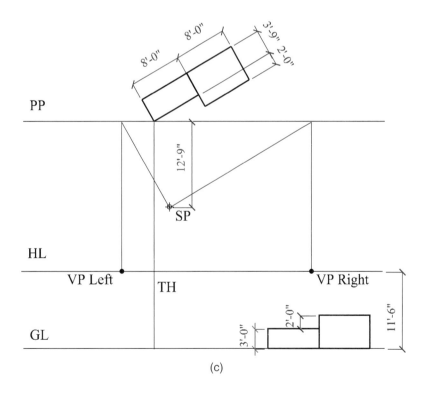

(c)

FIGURE 10.148   Exercise 10.7.

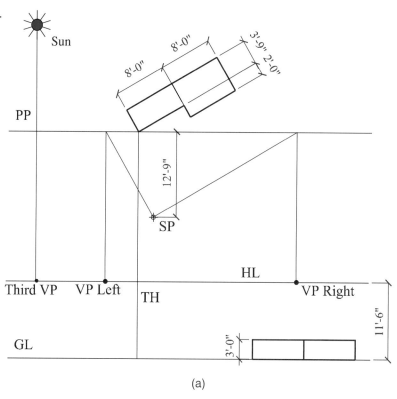

(a)

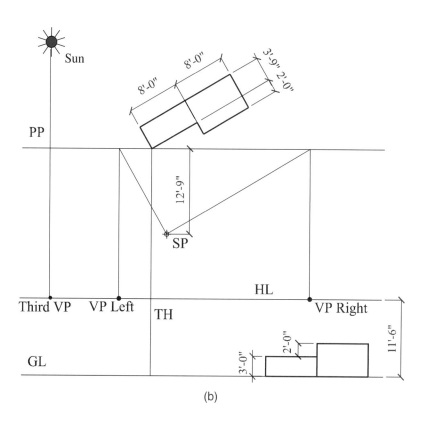

(b)

DRAWING ASSIGNMENTS

Use the plans and elevations given in Figure 10.149 to construct various pictorial drawings specified below.

1. Using architectural scales of your choice (⅜″ = 1′-0″ or ½″ = 1′-0″), construct isometric drawings of Figures a–h. Place the drawings on an 8½″ × 11″ sheet of vellum.

2. Using architectural scales of your choice (⅜″ = 1′-0″ or ½″ = 1′-0″), construct the following types of oblique drawings. Place the drawings on an 8½″ × 11″ sheet of vellum.

   a. Cabinet drawings for Figures a, b, c, d, g, and h.

   b. Cavalier drawing for Figures e and f.

3. Using an architectural scale and layout of your choice, construct a one-point perspective of Figures 10.149 a, b, c, d, e, and h. Put each drawing on a separate 17″ × 22″ or 18″ × 24″ vellum sheet.

4. Using an architectural scale and layout of your choice, construct a two-point perspective of Figures a, b, c, e, f, g, and h. Put each drawing on a separate vellum sheet of 17″ × 22″ or 18″ × 24″.

5. Take your two-point perspective drawings of Figures 10.149 a, e, and g and add a light source and third vanishing point to the drawings, and lay out the shadow of the figures.

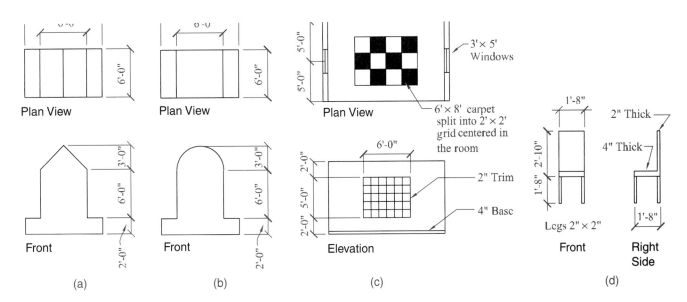

FIGURE 10.149   Drawing Assignment 1.
continued on next page

FIGURE 10.149   *continued*

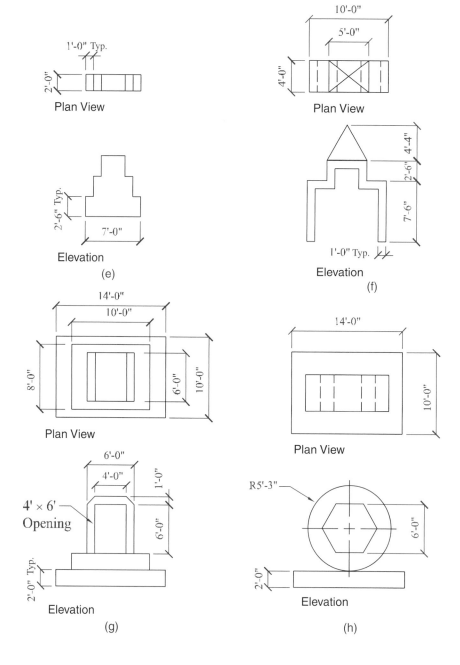

AutoCAD for Beginners

CHAPTER 11

Introduction to Computer Basics

The computer age arrived and took many people by surprise. Even today there are individuals in the drafting fields who have never touched a computer, and some brag that they never intend to do so. This is not something in which to take pride or live in ignorance of. Too many people lost their jobs in the 1990s because of insufficient computer and CAD skills. Today, people must learn new skills and update old ones to stay current with industry.

At some point those who are willing to learn about computers and CAD need a comfortable entry point, one that assumes no previous knowledge and, to use a common term, is user friendly. The following chapters are designed to ease a beginner into the computer and AutoCAD world.

11.1 The Computer/CAD Station

In this section the three elements that make drawing on a computer successful will be discussed and analyzed. These three elements are the CAD operator/drafter, the hardware (computer equipment), and the software (programs). Each of these elements is equally important, but starting with the human side will help you understand that people can draw some amazing things using this technology. Remember that hardware and software are tools for the drafter, they are controlled and managed by a human and not the other way around. Of course, sometimes it may not feel that way.

CAD Operator/Drafter

There are some people who believe that drawing on a computer eliminates the need to learn basic drafting skills. They believe they can simply jump right in and learn the software and become productive drafters instantly. A high percentage of these people are greatly disappointed. Can you imagine teaching someone to type who cannot read, spell, or punctuate yet can copy what he or she sees in front of him or her? Drafters in any discipline must understand what they are drawing in order to get promoted and better themselves. Make sure to learn the fundamentals of drafting first. It does not matter if they are taught to you on a drawing board or a computer. One good thing about drafting basics is that they do not change as rapidly as do computer software and hardware.

Interacting with Computers.

Making sure you are in a comfortable environment may help alleviate any anxiety you may be feeling about learning to use a computer. Check your equipment; the chair should be set to the right height for you and should support your back correctly. The keyboard and mouse also should be set to comfortable positions. If you have never seen a mouse or keyboard see Figure 11.1. Keyboard pads can be used for wrist support.

The room lighting and monitor angle are also important to your viewing comfort. Most monitors have adjustable settings that allow the viewer to tilt the screen parallel to eye level. Having a lot of light may be desirable around a drawing board but not around a monitor screen. The glare becomes a problem for the eyes, so generally a dull or soft light setting works better.

These measures are designed to prevent physical problems that have been known to develop over a period of time. Carpal tunnel syndrome is a repetitive wrist motion problem that affects some individuals, and

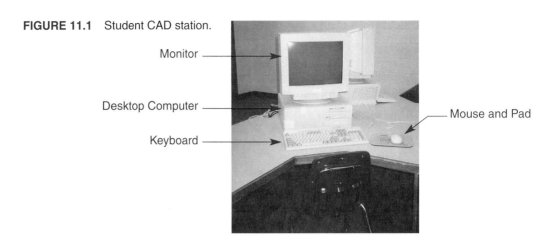

FIGURE 11.1   Student CAD station.

Monitor

Desktop Computer

Keyboard

Mouse and Pad

back problems can occur when chairs are not aligned properly. Studies in the United States and Sweden have been inconclusive in trying to link health problems to daily exposure to electromagnetic radiation from the computer's monitor. Proper lighting is essential for alleviating eyestrain. Remember to periodically look away from the screen. A basic student station looks similar to Figure 11.1.

Once you have established a good environment, it is time to become familiar with your computer equipment. Turning a computer station on and off is generally a matter of finding the correct switches. In a standard setup the computer, monitor, and printer must be turned on separately. Newer computers have a standby mode that is activated when the operator stops using it for a period of time. Pushing the on switch, moving the mouse, or pressing a key on the keyboard returns the computer to normal mode. There are normally two switches at the front of the computer: one turns the computer on and off, and the other resets or reboots the computer when it locks up or freezes during normal usage.

The monitor has its own on/off switch along with other switches for fine-tuning the brightness and adjusting the screen. If the screen needs changing, read the monitor's users guide or ask your instructor for help. These adjustments are easy to make to get the best quality viewing.

Another piece of equipment that commonly needs turning on and off is the printer. Printers will have any number of buttons depending on the complexity of the system. The buttons found most universally are the on/off, jam/form feed, and the test page. On some printers now the on/off switch has been phased out, and the printers programmed to come on automatically when the computer starts communicating with them.

The sooner you learn the basic setup, the more confident, comfortable, and relaxed an operator you can be. Look for small green indicator lights to come on when your equipment is turned on and running properly.

Computer Hardware

Hardware is the physical equipment or parts that make up the computer station. The following items are considered computer hardware:

- **Input Devices:** keyboard, mouse, trackball, microphone, and digitizer tablet/puck.
- **CPU (central processing unit) Components:** computer case/tower/desktop, processor, hard drive, motherboard, cache, RAM, power supply, floppy drive, video/graphics card, sound card, network card, CD-ROM/DVD, tape backup drive, zip drive, modem card.
- **Output Devices, External Hardware, and Peripheral Equipment:** monitor/printer/plotter/scanner, speakers, network server, fax machine, camera.

As you can see, many components work together to run a computer smoothly.

Input Devices

An *input device* is the means by which the operator transmits instructions to the computer. Some people say this is how the operator interacts with the computer. The operator gives an instruction or command, and the computer performs the request. That is the way it is supposed to work, but problems do occur. A malfunction in the hardware or glitch in the software occasionally happens, but the primary cause of problems is that the operator forgets to look at the screen for the feedback that the computer gives after receiving a command. Sometimes the operator is two commands ahead of the software before realizing that the software is hung up in a command that never got finished. The lesson here is always to read your monitor's screen for feedback. You must interact with your computer to avoid frustrating miscommunication. One-way conversations are rarely successful.

Keyboard. This input device is the most easily recognized of the computer components (see Figure 11.2). It has some keys that resemble a typewriter's alignment, and if the CAD operator knows how to type, it is a definite plus. Fear not, though, the keyboard and most software have built-in shortcuts that require using only one or two keys to generate a lot of commands. Computer and software manufacturers have realized that most people do not type at high rates of speed and have learned to cater to them.

Mouse. The mouse is a fast-working input device that allows the user to move all over the screen and select menu options (see Figure 11.3). To a CAD operator, the mouse is a tremendous aid in speeding up drawing. A two-button mouse is standard on most computer systems. The left-hand button is used to pick or select items from the screen menus. Some options require the user to press the left button two times quickly (double-click) to select an option. It takes a little time to get the feel or learn the touch, so practice.

In AutoCAD the right-hand button performs a return function like the Enter key on the keyboard. and can also exit a command or bring back the last command if used two times in a row. It will even access other commands in some cases. If you are left-handed, it may be more comfortable to make the right-hand button the pick option and the left one the return button. It is easy enough to do this, so ask your instructor to make the adjustment. Curved and contoured mice are available to give users as comfortable a feel as possible.

A three-button mouse became popular among AutoCAD users in the mid 1990s. The middle button allows a few more shortcuts or functions. Microsoft's IntelliMouse incorporates a wheel as the middle button. It can be pressed to function as a button and may be turned to perform other options. AutoDesk recommends using the IntelliMouse.

A digitizer with a puck is not an uncommon sight at a CAD station (see Figure 11.4). A digitizer tablet can incorporate a variety of menus to help speed up selection of commands. The puck has buttons like a mouse, but they are much smaller. This allows more buttons to be placed on the puck so that more options can be provided in the setup of the device. At one time this was a very popular input device, but as the Windows programs developed using on-screen icons/buttons the mouse became more effective.

A trackball is another input device that works similarly to a mouse. A mouse needs to be rolled around to move an arrow or a cursor to different locations on the screen. The trackball has a ball mounted on top that spins and moves the arrow around the screen. It also has buttons that can be used just like those on a mouse. People with limited hand mobility often favor a trackball.

A microphone is one of the newer input devices. It can be used to activate commands by voice signals. Improvements in technology have made the voice-activated system better with time, but bugs tend to be more prominent with a microphone. This device must also be trained to an individual's normal voice and requires special software to work with computer programs. Individuals who have limited use of their hands may find a microphone to be the key to being a successful CAD operator.

FIGURE 11.2 The parts of a keyboard.

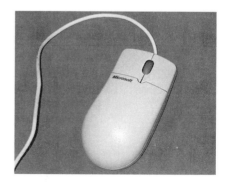

FIGURE 11.3 A mouse.

FIGURE 11.4 Digitizer and puck.

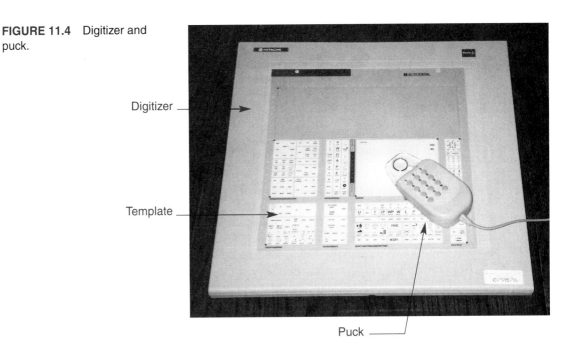

Digitizer

Template

Puck

Computer or Central Processing Unit and Components

The heart and soul of your computer is contained within the computer case, which can be either a tower or desktop style. The case protects the motherboard as well as other components such as the various disk drives. The motherboard can be thought of as the spinal cord for your computer because everything eventually connects into it. In addition to containing the memory and the microprocessor, the motherboard has slots for accessories such as video, network, modem, and sound cards.

Note: The term *random access* distinguishes RAM from other memory devices that are accessed sequentially. The hard disk, CD, and floppy disk are all sequential devices.

The CPU (central processing unit) is the brains of the computer. It has several vital parts. Let's start with the microprocessor. This is the "chip" that is so important when selecting a computer. It performs millions of computations per second. This value is sometimes quoted in MIPS—millions of instructions per second. The clock rate of the CPU chip is expressed in MHz or megahertz (millions of clock cycles per second). The microprocessor is fed a steady stream of instructions and data that come from memory devices. The primary source of the data stream is the main memory or RAM (Random Access Memory).

RAM is composed of chips as well and comes in several varieties: DRAM, SRAM, SDRAM. All RAM chips have one serious shortcoming; they are volatile, that is, they lose all their data when the power is turned off. (You may have experienced this situation!) The hard disk is used to store data on a "nonvolatile" medium—a magnetic disk. This is referred to as ROM or Read-Only Memory. Why can't the microprocessor just get its information from the disk? RAM is much faster (about 10 times faster), but it is also more expensive per unit of storage capacity (the megabyte), so most computers have 10 to 50 times more hard disk storage available than RAM.

Even though RAM chips are faster than the hard disk, the microprocessor could perform more operations (MIPS) if it could get the data faster still. Most current computers have a smaller amount of very fast RAM (which is also more expensive) called *cache*. Normally the entire program that you are running will be loaded from the hard drive into RAM along with all your data, which can occupy a lot of RAM. But at any given instant, the microprocessor is concerned with only a small subset of this information. The cache controller tries to anticipate what the microprocessor is going to need next and moves it from the main RAM into the cache RAM. Software is written so that in most cases the next instruction is nearby; thus, a small amount of cache can make the computer run much faster. Wouldn't it be great if the cache were on the microprocessor chip itself? In fact, the most powerful microprocessors do have some amount of built-in cache, which is faster still. There can also be cache on the motherboard.

Computer Memory

Memory is measured in *bytes*. For instance, a 3½″ floppy disk can hold approximately 1.44 megabytes (MB) of information. The byte unit can be broken down even further into smaller units called *bits*.

1 byte = 8 bits

Note: When you are buying a computer, "128 MB of memory" refers to the amount of main RAM, and "9.0 GB disk" refers to the amount of hard drive storage (GB is a gigabyte, or about a billion bytes, or about a thousand MB).

A bit is a single digit of binary information (number system base 2). It has two possible values: 1 or 0. A single bit can represent one of two choices, on or off, high or low, left or right, and so on. Because a byte is a collection of 8 bits, a byte can represent up to 256 choices. A byte can represent all the possible colors to be displayed, for example. Think of your area code and phone number. It is just a collection of 10 decimal digits. Your phone number has been assigned to represent your phone's address. With 10 decimal digits there are 10,000,000,000 (10 billion) possible choices.

8 bits = 1 byte
1 megabyte (MB) = approximately 1 million bytes (1,048,576 bytes)
1 gigabyte (GB) = approximately 1 billion bytes (1,073,741,824 bytes)

- 1 floppy disk holds 1.44 megabytes
- RAM is commonly measured in megabytes
- Hard drives are commonly measured in gigabytes
- AutoCAD 2000 fully loaded takes up approximately 169 megabytes.

The memory system of a computer is a multilevel conglomeration of different devices. On one end of the spectrum is very fast, very expensive, very limited capacity. On the other end is slower, cheaper, huge capacity, and, very importantly, nonvolatility.

Another component that is plugged into the motherboard is a video card, which enhances the graphic images on the monitor. The cards with the most video RAM will produce sharper images at a faster rate of speed. Network cards can also be found plugged into the motherboard. These cards support linked computers so they can communicate with one another and exchange data or information. A modem card is another common accessory, which can give a computer Internet access throughout the world by plugging into a telephone line. Documents can also be transferred by fax with this card. Sound cards are used in CPUs for any audio interaction, whether receiving or sending sounds.

Some of the more familiar devices are seen on the front of the computer. A floppy disk drive is used to save drawings and other computer work on a 3½″ inch disk, a common storage device. Another standard device that is well known is the CD-ROM (Compact Disk Read-Only Memory) drive. Most of today's software programs come on CDs and are installed onto the hard drive through the CD-ROM drive. Some software, however, must have the CD in the CD-ROM drive to operate. Software can also be installed through the floppy disk drive.

A DVD-ROM (Digital Video Disk Read-Only Memory) is becoming increasingly popular. The DVD drive is more versatile in that it will run a DVD or a CD. A CD-ROM drive will not run a DVD, so check the disks and drives to become familiar with your CAD station and the disks it will access.

Tape backup drives and zip disk drives are additional devices on a computer but are not necessarily standard yet. These hardware components are used to back up or save large chunks of information or files. A hard drive can be backed up using a tape drive. Remember that if information is irreplaceable, it needs to be backed up. Floppy disks and Zip disks look similar, but a 3½″ floppy will hold about 1.44 MB of data, whereas a Zip disk will hold up to 250 MB. A floppy disk can be write-protected by moving a plastic tab on it to prevent accidental overwriting.

Output Devices, External Hardware, and Peripheral Equipment (see Figure 11.5)

Basically, an *output device* transmits images or sounds. For example, a monitor is used to display images on a screen for the operator to see and interact with the software. A printer is used to print images on paper. There are a wide variety of options when it comes to selecting a printer for CAD. Many firms have two types of printers: a small laser printer and a large ink-jet printer.

A laser printer gives superior image quality and is a fairly inexpensive device for printing 8½″ × 11″ size sheets. Large drawings can be scaled down to an 8½″ × 11″ size on a laser printer and have great readability for checking in-house drawings. Ink-jet printers are commonly used to print out a variety of large sheets (24″ × 36″) that are big enough to read clearly and can be given to contractors for construction. Large electrostatic plotters are also available but cost a good deal more than the ink-jet. These printers are replacing ink-pen plotters that were used in CAD's earlier days. Pen plotters draw with single lines and are too slow to compete with the other plotters on complex drawings with many lines.

Fax machines and scanners can be used with a computer to transfer images. Scanners capture images that can then be attached to a variety of files, E-mails, and Web sites. Faxes are generally used to transmit black-line images to other machines at different locations. The quality of faxes is fair at best, and sheet sizes are limited to 8½″ × 11″ and legal-size (8½″ × 14″) sheets.

A network server has become a very valuable tool in the office environment (see Figure 11.6). Think of a server as a big storage bank or a detached hard drive that can be linked to other individual computers. The server can share information, software, or data with the other computers simultaneously. It also helps reduce the size of the storage memory on the smaller computer hard drives.

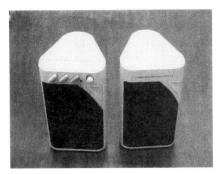
(a) Computer Speakers

(b) Network Server

(c) Small Printer (Desktop)

(d) Large Printer (Upright)

(e) Scanner and Fax

(f) Digital Camera

(g) Monitor

FIGURE 11.5   Computer peripherals.

FIGURE 11.6 A network setup.

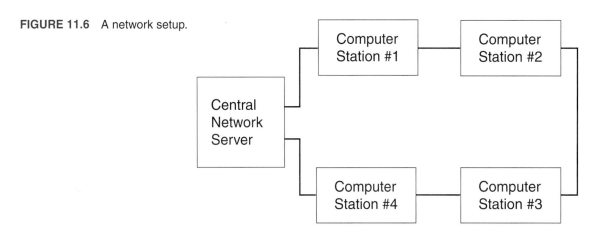

The downside to having a server is that when it goes down, it can suddenly bring work to a halt or to a snail's pace. Work can be done offline, but having limited access to outside information can be frustrating.

Digital cameras that interface with computers are one of the latest hardware additions to the world of technology. A picture taken with a digital camera can easily be put into a memory chip for sending with E-mail or displaying on Web pages.

Software and Basic Terminology

By definition, software programs are routines that perform some function or operation. Software provides the instructions that make the hardware work. A program normally comes on a CD or a 3½″ floppy disk, but some can be obtained electronically over the Internet using a process called *downloading* (see Figure 11.7). Software programs are written to do literally almost anything the human mind can conceive. It seems that if there is a need, some programmer will write a program to make it happen. That is how CAD has evolved.

The AutoCAD software is installed onto the hard drive for permanent storage. To be used, the software must be loaded from the hard drive to the RAM or working memory. The RAM does not transfer the whole program at once but instead processes what it needs as the CAD operator chooses various commands. This can take some time when using graphics software, which is why a fast CAD station needs a powerful micro-processor and up-to-date cache. Also, having a lot of RAM gives the computer more working memory, so it does not constantly have to tap into the hard drive to retrieve more information.

It is time to stop reading about computers and jump in and learn some fundamentals about operating them. Locate the on/off switches on the computer and monitor (*Hint*: Look in the lower right-hand corners. They are normally the largest buttons to be found.) and push them in and wait for the system to boot up. While you are waiting, look at the other buttons on the front face of the computer. One will open the CD-ROM drive, and another will eject a floppy disk if one has been previously loaded. A reset or reboot button can also be found on the front CPU face. It is used in case the software locks up the system. The monitor also has some buttons, but read the manual first before trying to adjust the screen. Several things can cause errors during the booting process: having a floppy disk inserted into the A: drive, pressing keys on the keyboard, or not having all the components (mouse/keyboard/monitor) plugged in correctly.

FIGURE 11.7 Floppy disks and a CD.

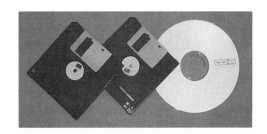

11.2   Using Windows with AutoCAD

A computer must have an operating system software to run programs. For years most computers used an operating system called DOS (Disk Operating System). It required a person to have a good memory and a lot of good typing skills to use it effectively. Fortunately, a more user-friendly operating system was developed called *Windows* (see Figure 11.8). This system uses pictures/icons for the user to select options to move through software operations rapidly. A lot of power was placed in the mouse to pick desired programs, commands, and subcommands on the screen. This made operating a computer system much easier for the average person, so Windows is a very popular operating system.

Learning how to handle the mouse will take a short period of time if you have never used one before. The terms *picking* and *clicking* are used interchangeably. They both mean the same thing: pressing the buttons on the mouse (see Figure 11.9).

The left pick button can be used when the mouse arrow is on an icon. Picking once highlights the icon/program. Watch the My Computer icon image change when you try this. If you choose the icon again, the font caption below it will be highlighted and will blink (see Figure 11.10). When the caption is highlighted, it can be edited, but if you are just learning, it is better to stay away from editing things you did not create or do not understand.

To start or launch a program place the mouse arrow over the icon and double-click the left pick button (press it twice very quickly). This should bring the program up into the RAM and allow you to use the opened software program.

Closing down a program or software package is quite easy. Look in the upper right-hand corner of the screen, and notice the three boxes side by side (see Figure 11.11). Simply place the mouse arrow on top of the box with the X and pick once with the left mouse button (left-click). As soon as you click on the X, the software program closes down and brings the desktop screen back so a new selection can be made.

FIGURE 11.8   Windows Desktop.

FIGURE 11.9 Mouse styles.

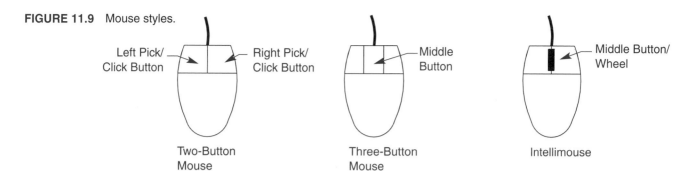

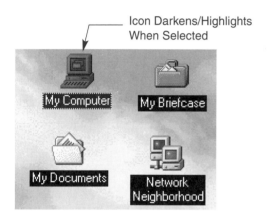

FIGURE 11.10 Icon with highlighted caption.

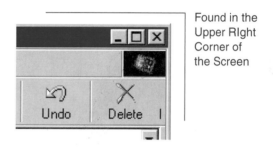

FIGURE 11.11 Minimize, Restore, Close buttons.

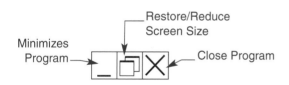

FIGURE 11.12 Minimize, Restore, Close buttons.

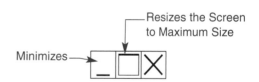

FIGURE 11.13 Minimize/maximize buttons.

The middle box is used to adjust the program's screen area (see Figure 11.12). It is used to fill up the screen completely or to reduce the size depending on your needs. It performs a restore or a maximize (see Figures 11.12 and 11.13 for the variations).

The left box with the dash is the minimize button. Clicking the left mouse button here minimizes the program or file to a small box at the base of the screen. The program remains loaded in RAM. The Windows operating system does not shut the program down; it just reduces it to the small rectangle box or button. To bring it back, place the mouse arrow on the reduced rectangle at the base of the screen (see Figure 11.14) and click with the left mouse button.

The right pick button can be used when the arrow is over an icon or off by itself. If the mouse arrow is over an icon when the right-hand pick (a right click) is selected, a menu of options pops up that allows you to view and edit program information (see Figure 11.15). One of the selections is Open, and if you move the mouse arrow on top of it and pick once with the left mouse button (left-click) it will open the software linked to that icon.

FIGURE 11.14   Minimized icons
on the task bar.

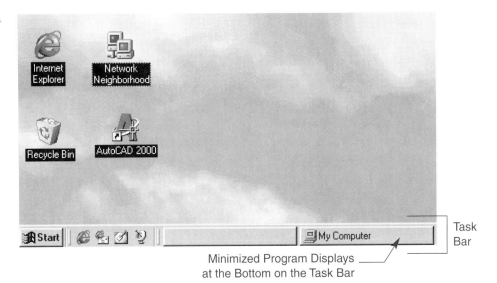

FIGURE 11.15   Pop-up menu.

FIGURE 11.16   Arrange Icons
suboptions menu.

If the mouse arrow is off to the side of an icon when you select (right-click) the right-hand mouse button, it opens a list of options for editing the desktop screen (see Figure 11.16). (The desktop is the screen that appears after the boot sequence is complete.) One of the options with which you can experiment without doing any harm is the Arrange Icons choice. Pick any of these suboptions and watch the icons get rearranged.

In the lower left corner of the Window's Desktop is the Start button. If you move the mouse arrow on top of it and left-click, a long list of options appears (see Figure 11.17).

The Shut Down option will become very familiar to you. It is used to shut the computer down safely when you are done using it. Make sure to shut down Windows before turning off the computer. If you choose the Shut Down option, three additional selections appear in the Shut Down Windows dialog box (see Figure 11.18): Restart, which will reboot the computer; Restart in MS-DOS mode; and Stand by, which will leave the operating system on. To display the Windows screen again, just push the CPU's ON button, and the Window's Desktop will return quickly.

Another suboption to the Start button is the Run option, which you use when you want to install new software on the hard drive. Many software programs today will go into an autorun mode when you insert the software's CD into the CD-ROM drive. If you need instructions, most software packages are set up to walk you through the installation process.

The Help option guides you through solving problems in Windows. On-line help is available over the Internet, and CDs can be purchased that are excellent for training someone new to the Windows environment. If you require hands-on, personal assistance, take a Windows Basics class.

A Programs option is also found in the Start button menu. This option lists all the programs loaded on the computer. Go to any program with the mouse arrow and pick the desired software, and it will open up. You will notice that cascading menus will pop up to the right (see Figure 11.19). Just be persistent and you will find the program you want.

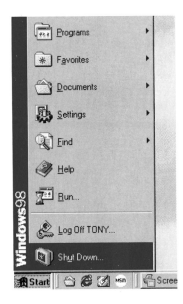

FIGURE 11.17 Shut Down… option of the Start pop-up menu.

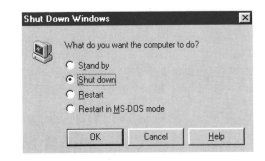

FIGURE 11.18 Shut Down Windows dialog box.

FIGURE 11.19 Cascade menu for Programs option of the Start pop-up menu.

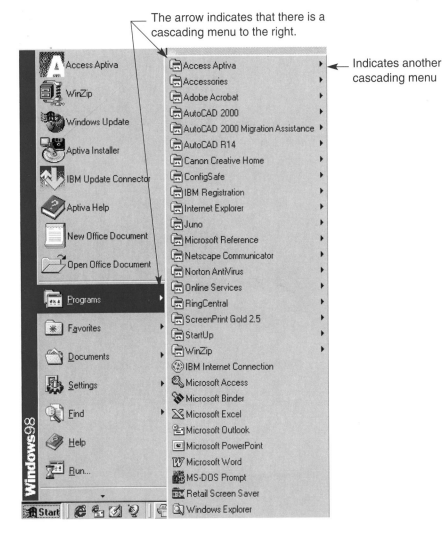

My Computer Icon

Becoming familiar with the power of the My Computer Windows Desktop icon is very important. Much can be gained by learning a few basic functions in this icon. The Explore option can be found by placing the mouse arrow on the My Computer icon and right-clicking (see Figure 11.20). Move down to the Explore option with the mouse arrow and left-click. Instantly you will see options that are critical to your success in operating the computer (see Figure 11.21).

The 3½ Floppy (A:) can be selected by double-clicking this option with the left-hand button. If a floppy disk is in the A: floppy drive, then it is possible to access information from A: using this route. Other options include the hard drive's root directory (C:), the CD-ROM drive, printer options, and control panel settings.

When you make a selection such as picking the 3½ floppy (A:), then it is possible to use the pull-down menus that are located across the top of the screen (see Figure 11.22). Left-clicking on the File pull-down menu displays many options below it (see Figure 11.23). The Open option displays all the files on the floppy disk. If you select a file with the mouse arrow and perform a left-double-click, the file will open if the soft-

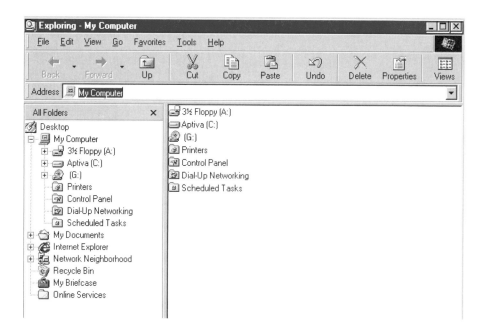

FIGURE 11.20   Windows explorer.

FIGURE 11.21   Explore option of the My Computer icon.

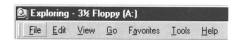

FIGURE 11.22   Pull-down file options for the A: floppy drive.

FIGURE 11.23   The File pull-down menu.

FIGURE 11.24 Menu options under 3½ Floppy (A:).

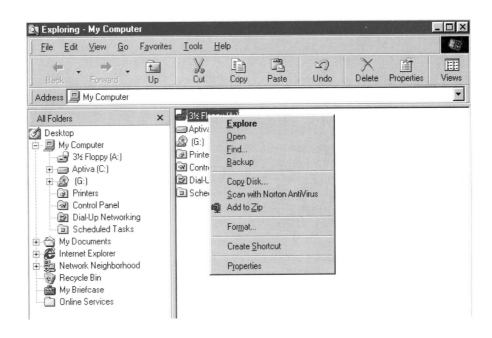

ware with which it was created can be found and accessed. A right-pick on 3½ Floppy (A:) will open some very useful commands (see Figure 11.24). Explore and Find are commonly used to do searches to locate files and other information.

The Backup option lets you make backup copies of large chunks of information such as the entire hard drive (C:) or separate programs. Backup hardware such as a tape is needed to do this.

The Copy Disk option lets you copy from one floppy disk to another. Just pick the copy from A: with the original floppy in the A: drive and the computer will temporarily store the information in RAM. When you are prompted to insert a new floppy, put it in and select the OK button. The information is copied from RAM to the new floppy disk.

The Format option wipes out all information on the disk and then prepares the disk for use in regular saving and retrieving functions.

Warning: Never format a disk unless you are prepared to lose all the information—programs, files, and everything. People have been known to wipe clean the entire hard drive, so be careful here.

Opening My Computer

Double-clicking with the left mouse button with the arrow on top of the icon opens the My Computer function. It has a somewhat different look than that under the Explorer option. Notice that folders are displayed in a larger icon or picture form, which is much easier on the eyes. The downside to this screen is that the All Folders sublist is not displayed, so navigating takes a little longer because in order to return to the previous screens the Back screen button must be clicked until the desired screen is reached. In the Explorer option, changing drives or directories is as easy as going to the All Folders display and picking where you want to go directly (see Figure 11.25).

Creating New Folders and Transferring Files (Check with your instructor before adding folders to the hard drive.)

There are two more topics to cover on our tour of Windows' survival skills. Making folders in which to store AutoCAD drawing files is a necessity. Folders help you stay organized with your drawing management.

Start by double-clicking on the My Computer icon to open it, then double-click on (C:). All the current folders are displayed. To add a folder for drawing files, left-click on the File pull-down menu (see Figure 11.26). Drop down to the New option and left-click on it, then go to the Folder option to the right and left-click on it. A new folder appears that must be named. Type in your name and hit the Return key. The folder has been created. Double-click on its icon to create folders inside the folder with your name (see Figure 11.27). Set up new folders in here for each drawing class for this semester or quarter. See the example in Figure 11.27, where two folders were created named Basic Design1 and Basic Drawing1. If you look at the address, you will see these folders are located in C:\Your Name.

If you want to delete these folders after the semester is over, just click on the folder and highlight it. Then press the Delete key on the keyboard, and the folder is sent to the Recycle Bin on the desktop (see Fig-

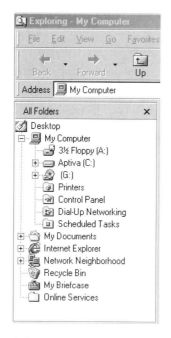

FIGURE 11.25 All Folders display in Explore.

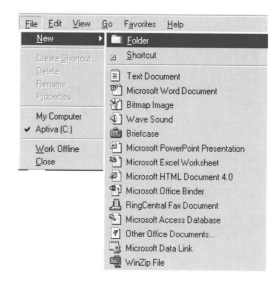

FIGURE 11.26 New, Folder selected on the File pull-down menu.

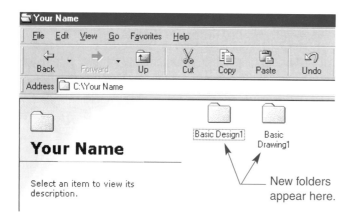

FIGURE 11.27 Two new folders created.

FIGURE 11.28 Recycle Bin icon.

ure 11.28). To permanently remove the files and folders from the computer, go back to the desktop and double-click on the Recycle Bin icon, then go to the File pull-down menu and select the Empty Recycle Bin. Do not do this unless you are sure you are not going to need these files any more.

Drawings can be transferred using the My Computer Explore option. Right-click on the My Computer icon and then drop down and left-click on Explore. Repeat the same sequence again so that two sessions of Explore are open. They will overlap each other somewhat and will need to be moved a little so you can see into both of them. Go to the top of the explorer display with your mouse arrow where you see Exploring – My Computer in blue or gray and pick with the left mouse button and hold it down. While holding down the button, drag or roll your mouse and watch the current Exploring session move across the screen (see Figure 11.29). Do the same thing to the other Exploring session, separating them just enough to see into the My Computer area of each one (see Figure 11.30).

Now, go to one of the sessions and double-click on 3½ Floppy (A:) to list the files on A:. Move to the other session and double-click on (C:) to list all the folders in that session. With this setup it is easy to move files around. Go to the session showing the files in A: and pick a file and hold the left mouse button down. Now, drag or roll the mouse arrow toward the screen of the other session. Notice as you cross over to the other session that the mouse arrow reappears there. At this point, pick the folder into which to drop the file from the other session. When the arrow is over the folder icon just let go of the left mouse button. The file you grabbed in the A: drive

Note: Saving drawings in a folder on the hard drive (C:) will give you one copy of the work. It is good practice to save to the hard drive first, then copy to a floppy later. If you save directly to floppy drive A:, AutoCAD starts using that drive to work on and will destroy the floppy disks over time.

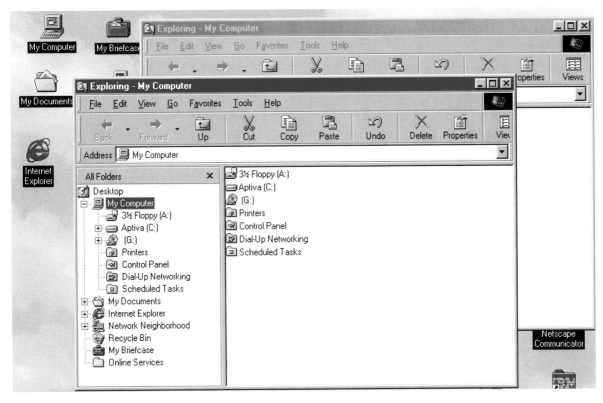

FIGURE 11.29 Opening double Explore sessions.

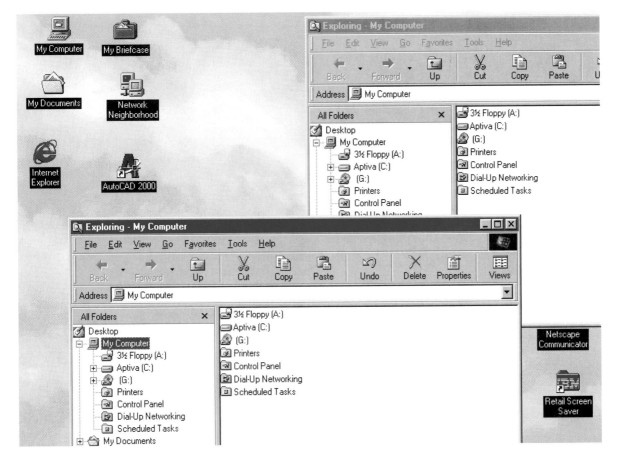

FIGURE 11.30 Moving double Explore sessions.

is instantly transferred into the folder on the C: drive. This operation can also be performed between directories and folders in C:. If you wish to keep a copy of a file in its original location, hold down the Ctrl key while dragging and dropping. Opening multiple sessions in Windows to copy or transfer data is a snap.

Tips for Copying Multiple Files

If you need to copy more than one file, here are two ways to do it.

1. While selecting files to be moved hold down the Ctrl key on the keyboard when picking the files you want to move with the left mouse button. When you have selected all the files to be moved, hold the left mouse button down on the last file chosen and drag over to the next session. All the selected files will move at the same time (see Figure 11.31).

2. If all the files you want to transfer are in sequence, go to the top or bottom and pick the first file you want. Next, hold down the Shift key on the keyboard and pick the last file desired. Notice that the whole string is highlighted. Keep holding down the left mouse button and drag the files over to the other open session. When the arrow is over the folder icon into which you wish to drop the files, simply let go of the left button (see Figure 11.32).

FIGURE 11.31 Using the Ctrl key to select files one at a time.

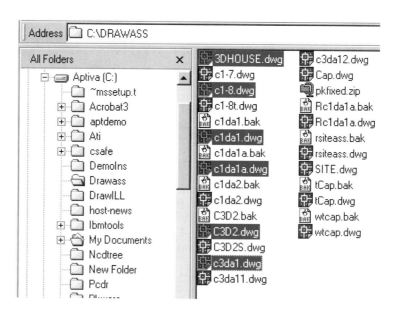

FIGURE 11.32 Using the Shift key to select whole columns of files.

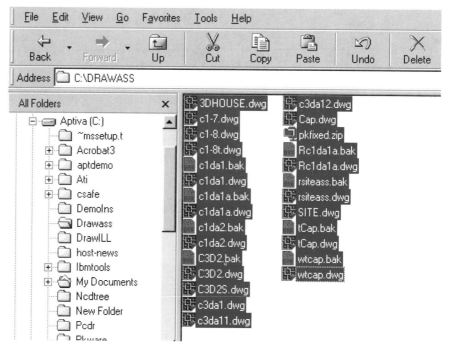

FIGURE 11.33 Closing a program.

Close Program

Tip for Tiling Multiple Sessions

Note: If a right click does not work in the toolbar area, move the cursor to a new location on the toolbar. Keep off the minimized icons.

After opening two sessions of Explore in Windows, move the cursor arrow down to the task bar at the bottom of the desktop, shown back in Figure 11.14. Right-click and select either Tile Windows Horizontal or Tile Windows Vertical. The screen will split up and make it easy to see each session clearly on the same screen.

If this is your first exposure to using the Windows operating system, it may take some time to get used to it along with the mouse picking and clicking operations. As long as you do not delete items that exist on the computer you are fairly safe in exploring and moving around in Windows. Remember to shut down programs when you are done using them (see Figure 11.33).

If you are shutting down the computer, go to the Start button in the bottom left corner and left-click on the icon. Then select the Shut down option and pick OK. The computer will then tell you when it is safe to turn it Off.

REVIEW QUESTIONS

1. List some of the physical problems that CAD operators have been known to develop over time.
2. Explain the difference between hardware and software.
3. What is the purpose of an input device?
4. How many buttons can a mouse have?
5. Make a list of all possible input devices to be found on a CAD station.
6. On what devices can information be stored?
7. What do the following abbreviations stand for?
   a. CPU
   b. RAM
   c. ROM
8. Explain some of the differences between RAM and ROM.
9. Make a list of external hardware and peripheral equipment.
10. List some of the advantages and disadvantages of being on a network server.
11. Define *software*.
12. How much memory can a floppy disk hold?
13. In what units is RAM commonly measured?
14. How do you start a program in Windows?
15. How do you minimize a program in Windows?
16. What are some of the important options found under the My Computer icon?
17. Why should you use caution when formatting disks?
18. How can the Explore option of My Computer be opened?
19. What is the purpose of the Recycle Bin?
20. What option is used to install software on a computer's hard drive?
21. How are files copied within the Windows environment?
22. Research DVDs, CDs, and their drives. Compare their quality, performance, and cost.

ASSIGNMENTS TO RESEARCH

1. Put together a checklist of computer requirements for a CAD station to run AutoCAD 2000.

2. Research AutoCAD LT and AutoCAD 2000 and compare them.

3. Call five architectural or interior design firms and ask them the following questions.

    a. How many different CAD software packages does your firm use?

    b. What operating systems are you using and why?

    c. How much CAD drawing versus board drawing is done in your office?

    d. What are some of the positive and negatives in CAD work?

4. Research the following software products made by AutoDesk.

    a. Architectural DeskTop

    b. 3D Studio

    c. Compare a and b with AutoCAD 2000.

CHAPTER 12

Introduction to AutoCAD

12.1 Starting Up the AutoCAD 2000 Program

Once AutoCAD has been loaded onto your computer, you can access it much like any other program by double-clicking on the AutoCAD 2000 icon (see Figure 12.1). You can also begin by clicking on the Start button at the bottom of your screen and then choosing Programs, AutoCAD 2000, AutoCAD 2000 in sequence (see Figure 12.2).

FIGURE 12.1 AutoCAD 2000 icon.

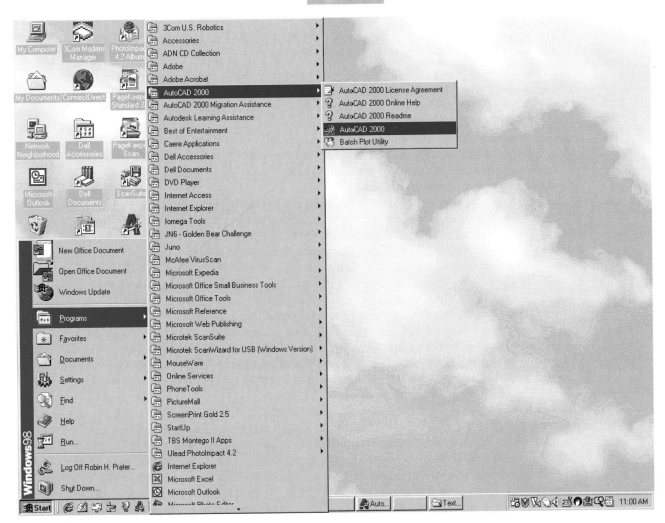

FIGURE 12.2 AutoCAD 2000 options in the Programs menu.

FIGURE 12.3   Startup dialog box.

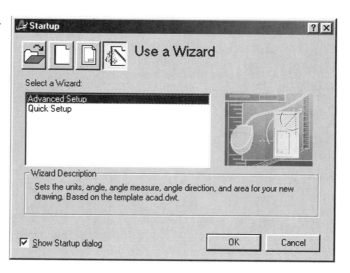

On startup, AutoCAD displays its standard screen with a Startup dialog box at its center (see Figure 12.3). **Dialog boxes** are one of the many ways that AutoCAD has to communicate with users. Basically, a dialog box walks you through a series of questions. We will go into more detail about dialog boxes later in the chapter, but for now, close the Startup dialog box by left-clicking on the X button at the top right of the dialog box (see Figure 12.3). This will allow you to experiment with the program as we introduce some basic concepts.

12.2   Becoming Familiar with the AutoCAD Graphics and Text Screens

Take a moment to look over the AutoCAD screen (see Figure 12.4). If you have used other programs in the Windows environment, the screen may look somewhat familiar. The bar along the top tells you that you are working in AutoCAD 2000. Notice what happens if you move your mouse around. A crosshair moves around the screen. The area in which the crosshairs move around is called the **graphics screen**. This is where your drawings will be displayed. Notice that a pair of numbers is displayed at the bottom of the screen. This area is called the **status bar**. The numbers are a coordinate display of the location of your cursor and will change as you move your cursor around the screen.

If you move your mouse outside the graphics screen, an arrow appears that allows you to pick from the buttons and pull-down menus. The pull-down menus are at the top of your screen. They include the Eile, Edit, View, Insert, Format, Draw, Dimension, Modify, Express, Window, and Help menus. Left-clicking on these buttons pulls down a menu of options. Try this now with the Draw pull-down menu.

Note: If you accidentally click on a command that you do not wish to execute, press the ESC button on your keyboard. This will take you out of the command.

Notice that some of the words in the menu have an arrowhead beside them. If you highlight one of these with your mouse, an additional menu will cascade out to the side. Try this now with the Circle command, found under the Draw menu (see Figure 12.5).

If there are three dots next to a word on the pull-down menu, that means a dialog box will appear if you click on that option. Try clicking on the Hatch command found under the Draw pull-down menu. If you open a dialog box that you do not want to use, simply click on the Cancel button in the dialog box. You can also click on the close or X button at the top right corner of the dialog box.

The command line at the bottom of your screen is one of the key ways in which the AutoCAD 2000 program communicates with you. If you get in the habit of checking the command line, you will always know what the computer thinks you are trying to do. If the line says Command, the computer is waiting for you to begin a new set of instructions. Otherwise, it displays the command that is currently being executed. In addition, this is where questions that the program needs you to answer will be displayed.

For example, click on the Draw pull-down menu, then click on Line. The command line should now display Command: _line Specify first point:. It is waiting for you to tell it the first point of a line. There are many ways to do this, but if you wish to play a little, try left-clicking a few points on the graphics screen. When you have drawn enough lines, press Enter on your keyboard. This will take you out of the Line command. Notice that the command line now displays only Command:.

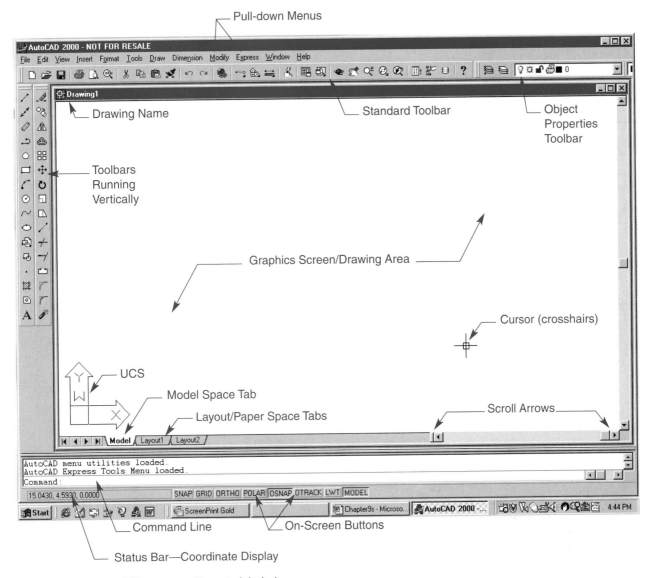

FIGURE 12.4 AutoCAD screen with parts labeled.

FIGURE 12.5 Cascade menu of the Circle command.

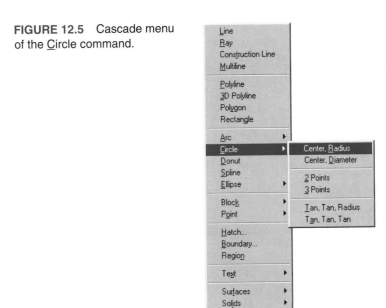

The two typewritten lines above the command line list the previous two commands issued. AutoCAD keeps a running history of the current session. The scroll bars on the side of these lines allow you to move up or down the list of commands that you have previously entered. If you press F2 on your keyboard, a list of all the commands you have given AutoCAD since you began the current session will be displayed in a larger window. If all the commands do not fit on the screen, you can scroll up or down to display them. When you have seen enough, press F2 again to close the window.

But what about all the other buttons around the graphics screen? If you move your cursor so that the arrow rests over one of the buttons, AutoCAD will display a tooltip or label that tells you what that button does. Notice that in addition to the tooltip, a description of the tool appears below the command line on the status bar. If a button has an arrow in the lower right hand corner of the image, clicking and holding down your left mouse button will cause a flyout menu to be displayed (see Figure 12.6). Keep the mouse button pushed down while you move the cursor down to the command you wish to execute. Releasing the mouse button will activate that command. It will also move that command to the top of the flyout menu so that this icon will now be displayed on the toolbar. Try this with the Zoom command by finding the icon that matches the one shown in Figure 12.6. Remember to check your command line to see what the program thinks is happening. Press Esc when you want to exit the command.

The buttons are grouped together on toolbars. The toolbars that are shown by default when you first load the program are the Standard Toolbar, the Draw toolbar, the Modify toolbar, and the Object Properties toolbar. You can find a list of additional toolbars by right-clicking on the toolbox (see Figure 12.7). The checks displayed next to each toolbar title tell you which toolbars are currently being displayed. To turn a new toolbar on, highlight the title with your cursor and left-click. To turn a toolbar off, repeat the process with a title that has a check mark beside it. Highlighting and clicking on the Customize feature at the bottom of the menu will allow you to customize the properties and icons displayed on your toolbars.

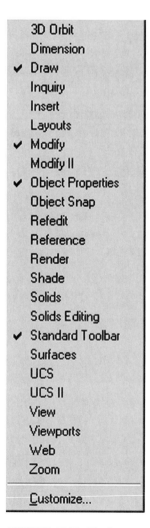

FIGURE 12.6   Zoom flyout menu.   **FIGURE 12.7**   Toolbar menu.

Left-clicking along the border around the toolbars or on the raised bars at the end of the toolbars will allow you to move your toolbar to another part of the screen. You can even place a toolbar in the middle of the graphics screen for quick access. Take a minute to experiment with moving one of your toolbars to a new location. Don't worry if the toolbar does not go exactly where you want it to the first time; you can always move it again. AutoCAD considers the toolbar to be "docked" when it is back along the borders of the graphics screen.

12.3 Communicating with AutoCAD

If you have read through the previous section, you have already seen several ways in which AutoCAD communicates with the program user. One of the great things about AutoCAD is that there are usually several different ways to input any given command. You have the flexibility of finding which way suits you best.

Using your keyboard to simply type in the name of the command will access all commands in AutoCAD. Most commands also have a keyboard shortcut that is often, but not always, the first letter of the word. Sometimes the letter must be combined with the Alt or Ctrl key. The shortcut letter is underlined whenever the word appears on the screen. The function keys across the top of the keyboard also access certain basic commands (see Figure 12.8). Each pull-down menu also contains a list of commands, grouped according to function. Another way to access commands is to left-click on the appropriate icon displayed on the toolbars. The icons are designed to provide visual clues to their purpose. In addition, a tooltip or label pops up when you place the cursor over a button, and a description of the function of the button appears at the bottom of the screen in the status window.

If you become a frequent user of AutoCAD, you will probably find yourself memorizing some of the shortcuts. If you use the program only occasionally, just try to find the method that is easiest for you to remember. Everyone has his/her own learning/working styles, and even frequent users will differ on which method holds the most appeal. Remember always to check the command line to ensure that AutoCAD is executing the correct command.

Example

Let's use the Line command as an example once again. To access the command, you have several options, all of which allow you to draw a line. The most obvious is to use your keyboard to type in the name of the command, **Line** or **(line)**. In the case of the Line Command, the letter **L** (or **l**) provides a shortcut. If you become a frequent user of the program, you will probably find yourself memorizing these shortcuts. Otherwise, it takes very little time to type in the full word.

Left-clicking on the Draw pull-down menu and then choosing Line will also access the Line command (See Figure 12.9).

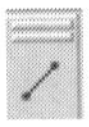

Look at the Draw toolbar. The default position is to the left of the graphics screen, but it may be located elsewhere on your display. The icon you are looking for looks like a diagonal line with red endpoints on each end. A left click on this icon accesses the Line command.

Try accessing the Line command using each of these methods. Which one did you find the easiest to use? Do not decide right away always to use only this technique. Experiment with the different methods of entry; your favorite may change after a few weeks of practice.

Line Icon

FIGURE 12.8 AutoCAD function keys.

F1	Help
F2	Text Window
F3	Osnap On/Off
F4	Tablet On/Off
F5	Isoplane
F6	Coordinates On/Off
F7	Grid On/Off
F8	Ortho On/Off
F9	Snap On/Off
F10	Polar On/Off
F11	Object Snap Tracking On/Off

FIGURE 12.9 Selecting the Line command in the Draw pull-down menu.

12.4   Crisis Control

One of the most comforting things to know about a computer program is what to do when things do not go exactly the way you expect them to go. The purpose of this section is to provide you with some valuable tools for just such a situation and to give you a feeling of being in control.

Canceling Commands in Progress

What happens when you realize that you have picked the wrong command, or maybe you just changed your mind? Are you stuck? No! AutoCAD allows you the flexibility of pressing the **Esc** key to cancel a command while it is running. Always check your command line to make sure it has returned to Command:. You may have to press the Esc key more than once.

   In addition, most dialog boxes have Cancel buttons as well as the X or close button in the upper right-hand corner. Picking the Cancel or Close button will close the current dialog box with no action taken, even if you have started picking options.

Help Command

AutoCAD provides you with lots of on-line help. Find Help at the top of your screen. The associated pull-down menu (see Figure 12.10) provides options including AutoCAD Help, Fast Track to Plotting, What's New, and Learning Assistance. AutoCAD Help allows you three ways of searching for information. Clicking on the Contents tab will show you a list of "chapters" dealing with various aspects of the program such as a Command Reference and a User's Guide. The Index tab functions much like a dictionary, allowing you to look up a word alphabetically. The Find tab gives you a search vehicle for locating the topic or command for which you need information. AutoCAD Help can also be located by typing **Help**, Alt + H, or pressing the F1 function key. Additionally, the question mark button on the Standard Toolbar will bring up the AutoCAD Help menu.

   If you click on the question mark button located in the upper right-hand corner of a dialog box, you receive a slightly different kind of help. A shadowed question mark appears next to your cursor. Click on the area of the dialog box about which you have a question, and a short description will appear. This should provide enough information to get you going again.

FIGURE 12.10 Help menu.

U and REDO

Undo Redo
Icon   Icon

If you have used a word processing program in the Windows environment, many of the buttons on the Standard Toolbar will be familiar to you. The two buttons showing curved lines with arrows access the **U** (Undo) and **Redo** commands. You can also access these commands by typing in **U** or **UNDO** and **REDO**. The Undo command allows you to take back the previous command. It can be used repeatedly so you can back up step-by-step canceling previously issued instructions. The Redo command allows you to reinstate a command that was undone by mistake. Redo can be used only once and must immediately follow an Undo. It works only for one command. So, for example, if you have used Undo to cancel five commands and then use Redo, only the last of the five commands will be reinstated. If you enter Redo again, you will get a message saying "REDO must immediately follow the U or Undo command," so choose your Undo and Redo commands carefully.

In addition to the curved arrow icon on the toolbar, Undo can also be accessed through the Edit pull-down menu, by pressing Ctrl + Z, by typing **U** at the command line, or by right-clicking to display the cursor menu, which contains Undo. Redo can be accessed by using the Edit pull-down menu, by pressing Ctrl + Y, by typing **REDO** at the command line, or by right-clicking to display the cursor menu.

The Save Time Command

Type **SAVE TIME** at the command prompt and then press Enter⏎. The function of Save Time is to perform an automatic save while AutoCAD is running. Once Save Time has been activated, type in the time in minutes to set the automatic save interval. About 20 minutes is what most professionals recommend. Another option is to set the time according to what you are willing to redraw. If you are drawing something really complicated, do not wait for a Save Time to kick in. Perform a save yourself.

The Save Time command saves the drawing to the Windows/Temp subdirectory. The file extension will not be .dwg but instead will be .SV$. If an automatic save is performed before the drawing is given a name, the file name will look similar to the following:

Drawing 1_1_1_6500.SV$

Giving the drawing a name such as Project prior to the automatic save would generate a save time file that looks similar to this:

Project_1_1_5724.SV$

The numbers shown are randomly assigned by AutoCAD, so when you are hunting down this file, look for the drawing name and the SV$ extension. The file must be renamed with a .dwg extension before it can be opened in AutoCAD.

12.5   File Management

Beginning a New Drawing: Drawing Setup

When you begin a new session of AutoCAD, the program automatically provides a Startup dialog box to walk you through opening up a new drawing. If you have already done some work in AutoCAD before you decide to start a new drawing, there are several ways to access the Create New Drawing dialog box. You may select File from the pull-down menu and then click on New. You may also simply type in the word **NEW**. The keyboard shortcut for opening a new file is to press Ctrl + N. Whether you open a new drawing with the Startup dialog box (see Figure 12.3) or the Create New Drawing dialog box (see Figure 12.11), the procedure is virtually the same; only the title in the blue band across the top differs.

FIGURE 12.11   Create New
Drawing dialog box.

Four large buttons are located just below the blue bar. Each button provides you with a different option for starting an AutoCAD drawing. The far left button opens an existing drawing. You are allowed to choose this button only in the Startup dialog box. Once you are working in the program, you most open an *existing* file using a different set of instructions, which are covered in the next section of this text.

The next three buttons help you start a new drawing. You have the option of starting completely from scratch, using a template, or using what AutoCAD calls a **Wizard**.

Using a Wizard

The far right button, the Wizard button, is picked by default. This is why the button looks like it has been pressed down, and the words "Use a Wizard" appear next to the buttons. If this is not the case, use your left mouse button to pick the Wizard button.

Once you decide to utilize a Wizard, your next choice is to use the **Advanced Setup** or the **Quick Setup.** The difference in these options is in the number of choices you are given. The Quick Setup asks you to make two choices, whereas the Advanced Setup asks you to make the same two choices plus three others. The common choices are units and area. Now you're probably hoping for a little more explanation than that, so here goes.

Units

The **Units** option refers to the type of units with which you would prefer to draw. The options include decimal, engineering, architectural, fractional, and scientific. You should make this choice based on the type of drawing that you wish to produce. Unless you work in several disciplines, most of your drawings will end up being in one particular system of units.

The default option is to use decimal units (see Figure 12.12). Decimal units can be used with either inches (English) or millimeters (Metric). This system of units is most often used for mechanical drawings, but it should work fine for initially exploring AutoCAD.

Engineering units contain feet and inches (see Figure 12.13). This type of unit is most often found on maps and civil engineering drawings. Civil drafting covers a wide range of projects ranging from plot plans and topography maps to bridge and dam design. Many landscape drawings will utilize engineering units.

You will no doubt have guessed that architects typically use architectural units. They contain feet, inches, and fractions of inches (see Figure 12.14). This system of units is typically found on drawings such as floor plans, elevation views, section views, and detail drawings. Most interior design drawings use architectural units.

The fractional system of units is helpful for drawings that consist of fractional parts rather than feet or meters (see Figure 12.15).

Scientific units are useful when the measurements in the drawing are either extremely large or extremely small. The letter *E* in the unit indicates that the first part of the number (such as 1.5500 in the example in Figure 12.16) is to be multiplied by an exponent of 10 given in the last part of the number (+01, or 10 to the first power, in the example shown in Figure 12.16). Another way to look at exponents of 10 is to think of the expo-

FIGURE 12.12   Units options with <u>D</u>ecimal units displayed.

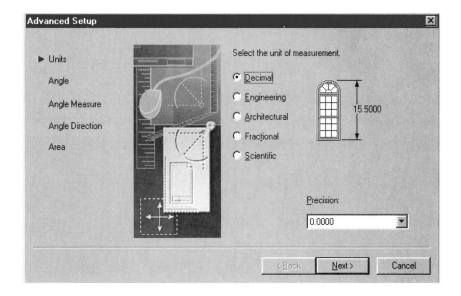

FIGURE 12.13   Units options with <u>E</u>ngineering units displayed.

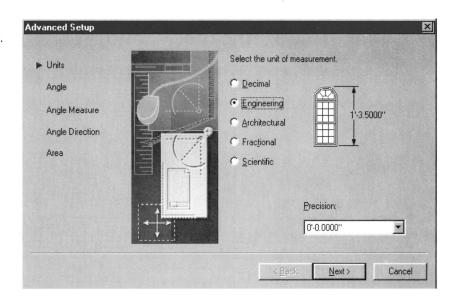

FIGURE 12.14   Units options with <u>A</u>rchitectural units displayed.

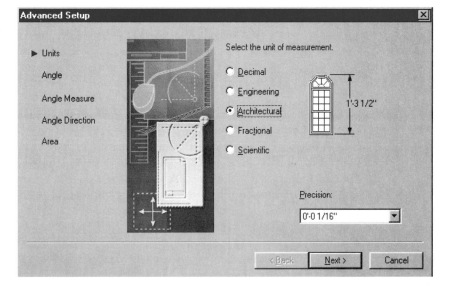

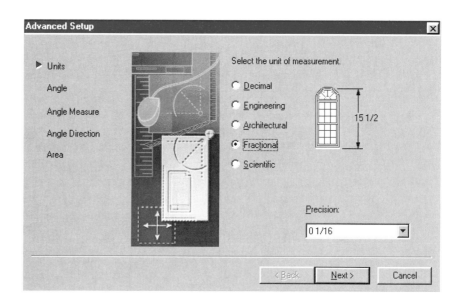

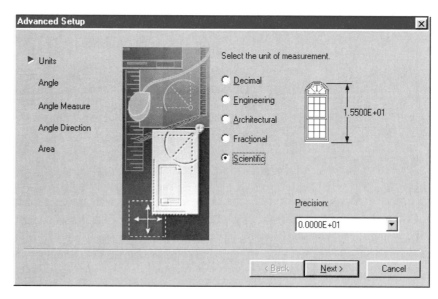

Note: If you are
doing the Advanced
Setup, you can
choose the amount of
precision you need
for your project. For
example, in decimal
units you can round
to the nearest whole
number, or take your
calculations out to the
eighth decimal place.
Architectural units
may be rounded to
the nearest inch or
carried out to the
nearest $\frac{1}{64}''$.

nent as indicating how many zeros will follow the 1, so 10^1 equals 10 and 10^2 equals 100. A negative exponent indicates the number of places the decimal point moves to the left. So 10^{-1} equals 0.1 and 10^{-2} equals 0.01. The number written as 1.5500E+01 equals $1.5500 \times 101 = 1.5500 \times 10 = 15.5$. That seems like a lot of work for such a small number, but imagine if the number you were dealing with involved 10 or 20 zeros.

Decide which system of units suits you the best, then use your left mouse button to choose that option. The circles next to the list of units are called **radio buttons**. If a black dot appears in the center of the circle, that choice is activated. If the circle is blank, that choice has not been selected.

Area. Once you have sorted out the type of units you will be using, the next step in the Quick Setup is to select the **Area** option for your drawing (see Figure 12.17). Select the size area that you will need to draw the object at full scale. For example, if your drawing would fit in an area 50′ by 75′ these are the numbers you input for the size of your drawing. You input dimensions at full scale. If a wall is 10′ long in "real life," you input the value into AutoCAD as 10′. You do not have to scale your input; AutoCAD will take care of that when it comes time to print. Now, obviously, your computer screen does not expand and contract depending on the size of your drawing. Nor would you want a 50′ by 75′ computer screen on your desk! The monitor works just like a television screen to display full-size elements in a small screen space. We will discuss scale and plotting in a later chapter.

Once you have chosen the units and area for your drawing, you are ready to click on the dialog box of the menu to complete the Quick Setup.

FIGURE 12.17 Area options.

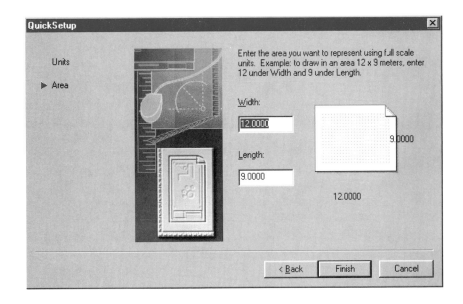

Angle. The Advanced Setup allows you to choose the way you want angles to be displayed on your drawing. You can choose among decimal degrees, degrees/minutes/seconds, grads, radians, or surveyor units. In addition, you can select the amount of precision necessary for your project.

- Decimal Degrees (see Figure 12.18) is the default option and is often used in mechanical drafting.

Reminder: There are 360° (degrees) in a complete circle, 60′ (minutes) in a degree, and 60″ (seconds) in a minute.

- Deg/Min/Sec (see Figure 12.19) displays the angle values in degrees, minutes, and seconds depending on the amount of precision desired. This option is used in some mechanical drawings as well as in some architectural and civil work.

- Grads (see Figure 12.20) is an abbreviation for gradients. Notice that the angle measure is followed by a lowercase *g*. In the gradient system, a complete circle is made up of 400 grads, so a 90° angle is equal to 100 g.

- Radians (Figure 12.21) is a way to measure an angle based on rotation using π, the ratio between the circumference of a circle and its diameter. A radian is the angle between two radii of a circle such that the length of the arc between them is equal to the radii. Using radian notation, π radians equal 180°. One radian is equal to approximately 57.2958°. Try choosing the radian option on the angle dialog box. Notice how the display changes as you increase the precision of the angle. With a precision of 0g, a 90° angle reads as 2r, but if the precision is increased to 0.00g, the same angle reads as 1.57r.

FIGURE 12.18 Area options with Decimal Degrees displayed.

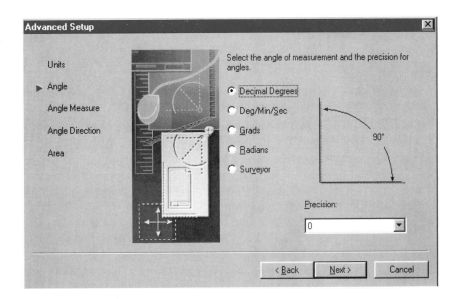

FIGURE 12.19   Area options with Deg/Min/Sec displayed.

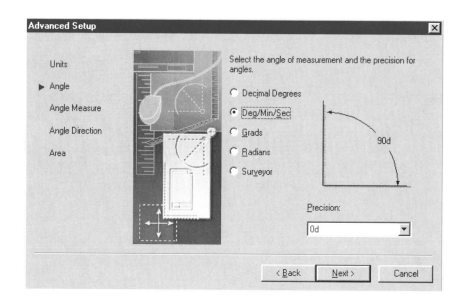

FIGURE 12.20   Area options with Grads displayed.

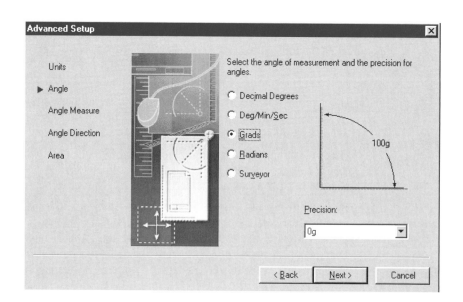

FIGURE 12.21   Area options with Radians displayed.

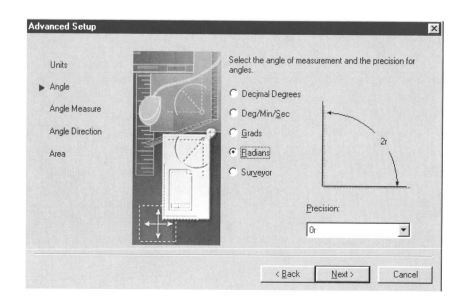

FIGURE 12.22 Area options
with Sur_veyor units displayed.

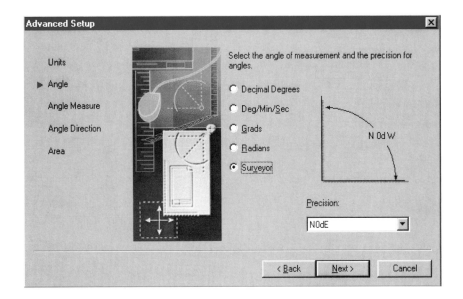

FIGURE 12.22 Area options
with Sur_veyor units displayed.

■ Sur_veyor (see Figure 12.22). Surveyors measure angles using bearings. Bearings are expressed in degrees, minutes, and seconds but differ from other angle expressions by having compass directions associated with them. The first part of the bearing gives the starting compass direction. The last part of the bearing gives the direction toward which the angle goes. So a compass bearing of N 45d E starts at north on the compass and measures 45° toward the east. Bearings are found on land surveys and plot plans.

Angle Measure. The **Angle Measure** option allows you to select the orientation for measuring angles. Normally, AutoCAD places 0° at due east on a compass. You can use this feature to begin measuring your angles at _East, No_rth, _West, _South, or any _Other compass reading (see Figure 12.23).

Angle Direction. The default in AutoCAD is to measure angles in a counterclockwise direction (see Figure 12.24). You can use this feature to choose between counterclockwise and clockwise rotation.

Once you have worked your way through the five choices provided in the Advanced Setup, you are ready to click on the Finish button. At any time during the setup you can click on the Back button to repeat a previous step. You can also use the Cancel button to jump out of the setup menu.

FIGURE 12.23 Angle measurement options.

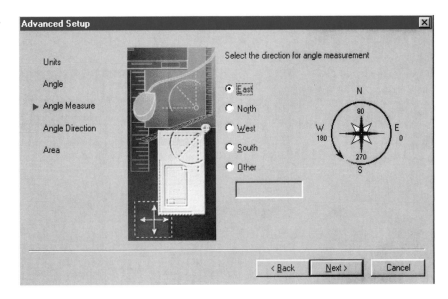

FIGURE 12.24 Angle Direction options.

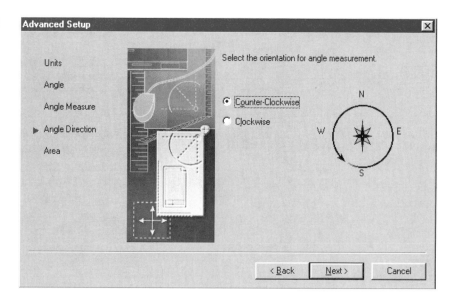

Starting from Scratch

The Start From Scratch button begins a new drawing with very minimal layout guidelines. You are asked only to choose between English and Metric units. This option is probably better suited for experienced users.

Using a Template

A template in AutoCAD is a drawing file with a predetermined set of standards and settings. Templates are available based on ANSI, ISO, DIN, JIS, and architectural standards. Once you click on the Template button in the Setup dialog box, a screen appears with a listing of all the existing templates. An area to the right of the box allows you to preview the templates. The most obvious differences will be in the way the borders and title blocks are set up. Other values such as grid and snap settings, units and angle values, and text and dimensioning conventions will be less apparent to the eye. Notice that the template files are saved as .dwt files. You can create your own template files or modify existing ones using the Save As command.

Opening an Existing Drawing

The Windows environment makes opening an existing AutoCAD drawing a very familiar process. As always, you have several options. You can go to the File pull-down menu and click on Open, you can also simply type in the word **open** at the command line, or you can click on the icon for opening a file on the Standard Toolbar. The icon looks like an open file folder. The keyboard shortcut for opening an existing file is to press Ctrl + O.

Any of the methods just listed will put you directly into the Select File dialog box (see Figure 12.25). This allows you to search the existing files for the drawing you require. AutoCAD drawings should be saved as .dwg files and will display a red icon next to the file name. A single left-click with the mouse will provide you with a preview of the drawing in a window on the right side of the dialog box. Double-click to open the drawing. If you have trouble locating a file, you can utilize the Find File . . . or Locate buttons found toward the bottom right of the screen.

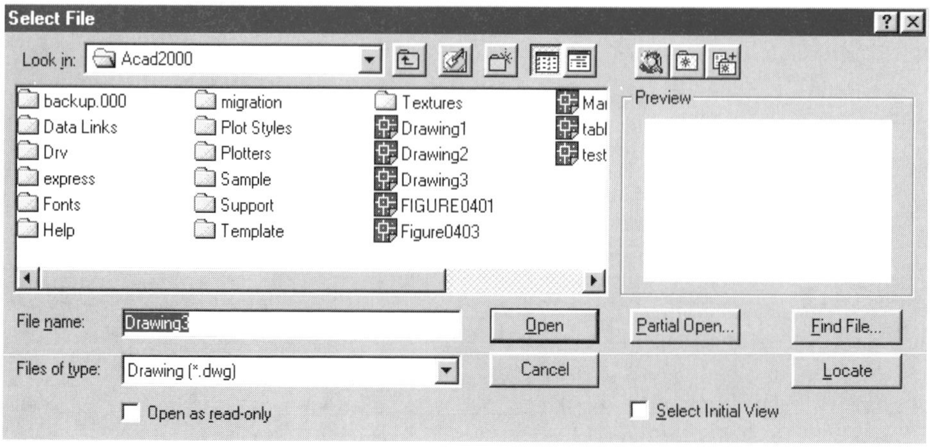

FIGURE 12.25 Select File dialog box.

FIGURE 12.26 Save Drawing
As dialog box.

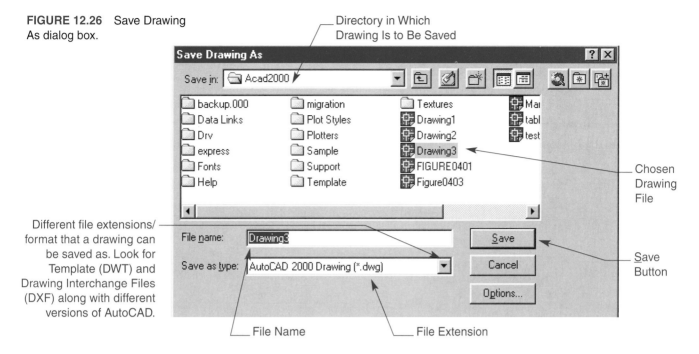

Directory in Which
Drawing Is to Be Saved

Chosen
Drawing
File

Save
Button

Different file extensions/
format that a drawing can
be saved as. Look for
Template (DWT) and
Drawing Interchange Files
(DXF) along with different
versions of AutoCAD.

File Name

File Extension

Saving a Drawing

Because AutoCAD 2000 functions in the Windows environment, saving a drawing is a very straightforward process. A cardinal rule is to remember to save early and save often. There are basically two save commands, **Save** and **Save As**. Both appear under the File pull-down menu. The first time a drawing is saved, the Save As dialog box (see Figure 12.26) automatically appears on the screen no matter which command you choose. At this point you must select the drive and folder where you wish to save your drawing. Be sure to check with your instructor before saving any drawing to the hard drive, usually the C: drive. The Save command can also be accessed by left-clicking on the icon on the Standard Toolbar that looks like a floppy disk. Typing in the word at the command line will also work. The keyboard shortcut for saving a drawing is Ctrl + S. Once a drawing has initially been saved with the Save As screen, the dialog box does not reappear when the basic save is used. This is referred to as a qsave and assumes that everything will be saved according to the status quo.

AutoCAD drawings are typically saved as .dwg files. However, you are also given the option of saving your drawing as a Drawing Interchange File (.dxf) or template file (.dwt). AutoCAD 2000 allows you to save a drawing in a format compatible with several of the previous AutoCAD releases. So, for example, if your office has updated to the 2000 release but several of your clients are still using the R14 release, you can save a drawing in R14 to allow the clients to access the file on their own systems. A list of the formats in which an AutoCAD drawing may be saved and exported follows. These options are found in the File pull-down menu. Just select the Export suboption to get the following list:

- WMF—Windows Metafile (see WMFOUT)
- SAT—ACIS solid object file (see ACISOUT)
- STL—Solid object stereolithography file (see STLOUT)
- EPS—Encapsulated PostScript file (see PSOUT)
- DXX—Attribute extract DXF® file (see ATTEXT)
- BMP—Device-independent bitmap file (see BMPOUT)
- 3DS—3D Studio® file (see 3DSOUT)
- DWG—AutoCAD drawing file (see WBLOCK)

If you want to create a new version of a drawing without affecting the existing version, call up the original and then do a Save As under a different name. This will provide you with two files of the original. You can now edit one while leaving the other intact.

The AutoCAD Design Center is another useful tool. The Design Center is accessed with the Tools pull-down menu or by pressing Ctrl + 2. The Design Center allows you to drag and drop existing drawings or portions of drawings into the file with which you are working.

12.6   Ending Your AutoCAD Session

Just as with the other commands, AutoCAD provides you with several options for ending your drawing session. Since AutoCAD 2000 runs in a Windows environment, you may close the program by clicking on the X button on the upper right of the screen. You may also type in **QUIT** or **EXIT** or select E_x_it from the _F_ile pull-down menu. If you have made no changes to the drawing, the program will immediately close down. If you have made changes, a dialog box will come up asking you whether you wish to save your changes. At this time, you may also choose to cancel the close command.

REVIEW QUESTIONS

1. What does it mean when three dots appear next to a command on a pull-down menu?
2. Where should you look on the computer screen to determine which command AutoCAD is currently trying to execute?
3. What key should you press to access a listing of previously entered commands?
4. Describe a flyout menu.
5. List four ways you can communicate with the AutoCAD program.
6. What key will cancel a command while it is running?
7. Where should you go if you need a quick review of how a command works?
8. What function does the Undo command perform?
9. How many times in a row can you use the Redo command? What command must it follow?
10. Convert each of the following numbers to decimal, engineering, architectural, fractional, and scientific units.
    a. 21.5″
    b. 1′-7.25″
    c. 2′-1½″
    d. 16.75″
    e. 2.5E+01
11. What angle option is used on some mechanical as well as on some civil and architectural work?

EXERCISES

Exercises Using the Wizard
EXERCISE 12.1

Double-left-click on the AutoCAD icon on the Windows Desktop (default Windows screen). When the Startup dialog box opens, use the Wizard icon, which will offer two selections.

- Select Quick Setup and then select the OK button.
- Select the _A_rchitectural unit of measurement and then select the _N_ext> button.
- In the _W_idth: box, type 34′ . (This is the ¼″ = 1′-0″ equivalent of an 8.5″ real-size plotting sheet.)
- Left-click in the _L_ength: box and highlight the existing number, then type in 44′. (This is the ¼″ = 1′-0″ equivalent of 11″ real-size plotting sheet.) This setup is good for ¼″ = 1′-0″ scale.
- The setup is complete. Check with your instructor to see if it is all right to perform a Save As to save your drawing to a student directory on the hard drive. Use the name 12EX-1. To close the drawing, select _C_lose from the _F_ile pull-down menu.

EXERCISE 12.2

With the AutoCAD main screen still showing from exercise 12.1, select the File pull-down menu and then select New with a left click to begin a new drawing. Use a Wizard displays again. This time use the Advanced Setup option and select the OK button.

- At the Advanced Setup dialog box select Decimal units if it is not already highlighted, then select the Next>button.
- Select Decimal Degrees option if not already highlighted, and select the Next>button.
- At the next display, leave the East default selected and select the Next>button.
- Leave the next dialog box at the Counter-Clockwise selection.
- In the Area dialog display type in 36 at the Width: box, then highlight the Length: box and type 24. Now select the Finish button.
- The setup is now complete to draw at 1″= 1″(full scale) and 36″ × 24″ limits.
- Perform a Save As and name the exercise 12EX-2. Close the drawing using Close in the File pull-down menu.

EXERCISE 12.3

From the File pull-down menu, select the New option. When the Startup dialog box opens, use the Wizard icon, which will offer two selections.

- Select the Quick Setup and then select the OK button.
- Select the Architectural unit of measurement and then select the Next> button
- In the Width: box, type in 8.5′. (This is the 1″ = 1′-0″ equivalent of an 8.5″ real-size plotting sheet.)
- Left-click in the Length: box and highlight the existing number, then type in 11′. (This is the 1″ = 1′-0″ equivalent of 11″ real-size plotting sheet.)
- Perform a Save As to save your drawing to a student directory on the hard drive. Use the name 12EX-3. To close the drawing, select Close from the File pull-down menu.

Exercises Using a Template
EXERCISE 12.4

From the File pull-down menu select New. Select the Use Template icon to the left of the Wizard icon. When the selection is made, a list of existing templates is shown in the text display area. Use the arrow buttons to the right and scan through the existing templates. Select **Architectural, English units – named plot styles dwt** with a double left click.

- When this selection is made, an Architectural title block is loaded into the Paper Space/Layout1 environment. This is a 3′ × 2′ or 36″ × 24″ sheet size with a preloaded setup for your use.
- Notice in the left bottom corner a triangle with the W and the X inside it (see Figure 12.27). This symbol indicates the drawing is in a full-scale paper space environment. It is fine to put text in the title block at this stage but not to draw on the objects.
- To draw in the model space environment, move the cursor into the middle of the drawing and perform a double left click. Notice that the triangle disappears and the UCS (User Coordinate System) symbol is shown in the bottom left corner (see Figure 12.28). It is the normal symbol you get when you begin a new drawing from scratch.

FIGURE 12.27 Paper space icon.

FIGURE 12.28 UCS symbol.

Once you have activated model space, you can feel free to start drawing. In Appendix A on plotting, zooming in floating model space will be explained. When you need to get back to paper space, simply double-click with the cursor pulled over in the gray area off the layout sheet.

- You can save the drawing in paper space or model space. The process is the same. The trick is to watch the icons so you can click back and forth to the environment you want.

- Repeat exercise 12.4 using a different template. If you want to try something interesting, select a German Template (DIN) or a Japanese Template (JIS).

Exercises Starting from Scratch
EXERCISE 12.5

In the AutoCAD main menu, select the New command in the File pull-down menu. When the Create New Drawing dialog box opens, select the Start from Scratch icon. Use the default English (Feet and Inches) setting and left-click on the OK button. The environment comes up with the following setup:

- $12'' \times 9''$ drawing limits and the units set to inches.

Remember to do a Save As to give your drawing a name, and perform a Close to shut down the drawing.

Exercises Opening Existing Drawing
EXERCISE 12.6

In the AutoCAD main menu select the open folder icon in the lower bottom left corner of the graphics area. The Select File dialog box appears and shows the current directory in the Look in: box. If the Acad 2000 directory is not listed, use the arrow button to the right and select it. In the listings below select the Sample subdirectory with a double left click (see Figure 12.29). At this point some sample drawings found in AutoCAD are listed.

- Select the Campus Dwg with a double left click.

This is one of the preloaded drawings in the AutoCAD sample directory. Scan through this directory and take a look at the different types of drawings. Open a few others to get some practice. Use the Close option in the File pull-down menu to shut down the drawings one at a time.

FIGURE 12.29   The Sample AutoCAD directory.

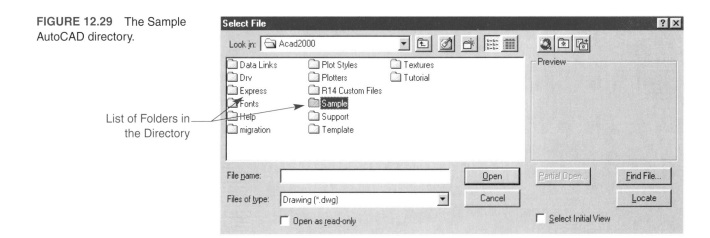

Exercise Creating Your Own Template
EXERCISE 12.7

Begin a new drawing by typing **NEW** at the command line.

- Select the Use a Wizard icon from the Create New Drawing dialog box, choose the Advanced Setup, and left-click on the OK button.
- Select Engineering units, then left-click on the Next> button.
- Choose the Surveyor angle settings, leave the Precision on N0dE, and left-click on the Next> button.
- Leave the direction for angle measurement set to East, and left-click on the Next> button.
- Select the Clockwise setting for the Angle Direction, then left-click on the Next> button again.
- Under the Area setting choose a Width: of 340′ and a Length: of 220′ and click the Finish button.

To save the drawing as a template file, type in **Save As**. At the File name: prompt, type Site1=20 to give the drawing a name. At the Save as type: prompt, select AutoCAD Drawing Template File [*.dwt] (see Figure 12.30). When prompted to Save in: the Template directory, type in Civil 11x17 to name the template (see Figure 12.31).

When prompted with a Template Description dialog box, keep the English Measurement, and click on the OK button (see Figure 12.32). The drawing setup you have just created is now a template and can be accessed when you begin a new drawing by using the Use a Template icon. Try starting a new drawing and see if you can find this template.

FIGURE 12.30 AutCAD template file

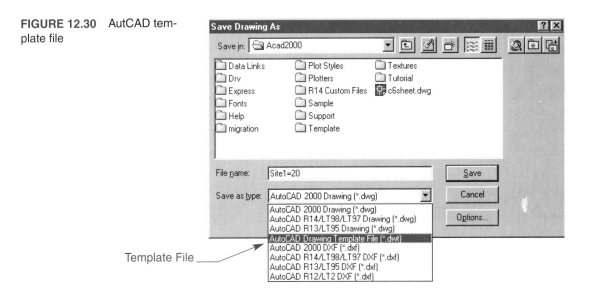

Template File

FIGURE 12.31   Civil template.

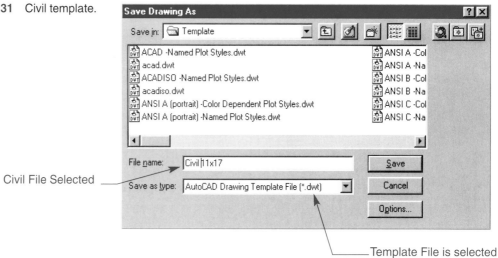

Civil File Selected

Template File is selected

FIGURE 12.32   Template Description dialog box.

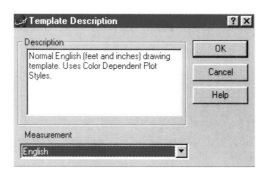

CHAPTER 13

○ ○

Beginning to Draw

13.1   The Point Command

- Type **PO** or **POINT** at the command prompt and then press Enter (↵).
- Left-click on Point in the Draw pull-down menu. This will cause another menu to cascade down containing the options Single Point, Multiple Point, Divide, and Measure.
- Pick the Point icon on the Draw toolbar. It looks like a single dot.

Point
Icon

The Point command creates points within your drawing. These points are useful not only for marking a particular location but for editing purposes. Once you have accessed the Point command, AutoCAD will ask you to Specify a point:. If you want to experiment with the command now, try left-clicking on a point anywhere on your graphics screen. Before this chapter is over, we will show you a more precise way to enter points. Pick Point and then Multiple Point on the Draw pull-down menu to draw several points without having to re-select the command. Multiple Point will remain active until you press the Esc button to exit the command. The Point icon will also allow you to draw multiple points. Typing in the command or selecting the Single Point option under the Draw pull-down menu will allow you to pick only one point.

You are also able to choose how you want your points to look. Go to the Format pull-down menu and select Point Style. Notice that Point Style is followed by three dots, so expect a dialog box to appear when you highlight it.

The Point Style dialog box (see Figure 13.1) offers 20 different looks or styles for your point. You can also size your points relative to the screen or in absolute units. Changing the point style changes *all* the points on your drawing, including the points you have already drawn, so you cannot have several different point styles within one drawing. You may have noticed that one of the point style boxes is blank. This option allows you to pick a point but not actually display the point on your drawing. This is useful for precise drawing and editing. You will hear more about this later in Chapter 16. In AutoCAD, a point is considered a node. This becomes important when you learn to use object snaps.

Note: The Point Style dialog box may also be accessed by typing in **DDPTYPE** at the command: line.)

Tip: The apparent size of the points on your screen may change as you use the Zoom command (see Section 14.2). You also need to use Regen for the style changes to appear on the screen (see Section 14.5).

Note: For an explanation of the Divide and Measure options of the Point command, see Section 16.7.

Tip: To continue placing points on a drawing without repeating the Point command, choose the Multiple Point option on the Point cascade menu.

FIGURE 13.1   Point Style dialog box.

Point Style

Point Size: 5.0000   %
⦿ Set Size Relative to Screen
○ Set Size in Absolute Units

OK   Cancel   Help

13.2   The Line Commands

Line
Icon

Note: If a letter is capitalized on the command line, you can use that letter as a shortcut to selecting that command rather than having to type out the complete word.

- Type **Line** or **L** at the command prompt and press Enter ↵.
- Select Line from the Draw pull-down menu.
- Pick the Line icon on the Draw toolbar. It looks like a single line with a red endpoint on each end.

Once you have selected the **Line** command by using one of the preceding methods, you are ready to begin drawing lines. Remember to check the command window to find out what AutoCAD expects of you. Once you enter the Line command, you will be asked to specify a first point. For now, you can do this by picking a point on the graphics screen with your left mouse button. From this point on you are given three options at each step. The default option is to specify the next point. Notice the words **Close** and **Undo** in the square brackets; these are your other two options. If you type in **Close** or **C** and press Enter↵ instead of selecting a next point, AutoCAD will draw a line connecting the last point you entered to the first point selected. Take a minute and try out this option. If you accidentally choose a wrong point or if you change your mind, the Undo option will help you out. Type in **Undo** or **U** and press Enter↵, and AutoCAD will erase the last line segment drawn. You can repeat this process for as many times as you have line segments to erase. But remember, you must stay in the Line command to exercise the Close and Undo options. Typing in **Undo** and pressing Enter↵ directly after you have exited Line will erase all the lines drawn (see Section 12.4).

13.3   The Erase and Redraw Commands

Erase
Icon

Note: Sometimes you wish to use a command on more than one item at a time. When you choose these items to be acted on as a group, this is called a *selection set.*

- Type **ERASE** or **E** at the Command: prompt and then press Enter↵.
- Select Erase from the Modify pull-down menu.
- Choose the Erase icon from the Modify toolbar. The icon looks like a pencil with an eraser on the end.

The **Erase** command may be one of the best tools in AutoCAD. It allows you to draw freely without worrying if you make a mistake or change your design. The first question AutoCAD will ask you after you have entered the Erase command is to select the objects you wish to erase. The program gives you several methods for doing this. You can select the object with a pick box, a window, a crossing, or a fence. We'll walk you through using each of the methods of selection. They will come in handy later when you begin to edit your drawings (Chapter 17). You can select multiple items within the same erase command. As you select the objects you wish to erase, they will be shown with a dashed line. Press Enter↵ when you have finished selecting, and the objects will then be erased. If you find that was not what you wanted to do after all, you can use the Undo command to put the objects back.

Selecting Objects One at a Time with a Pick Box (See Figure 13.2)

As soon as the Erase command begins, your on-screen cursor will change from a crosshair to a pick box (□). Use your mouse to position the pick box over any object you wish to erase. A single left click on the mouse pad causes the object to be shown with dashed lines (see Figure 13.2). You can pick as many objects as you want before pressing Enter↵ and exiting the command. If you accidentally select the wrong object, type **U** at

FIGURE 13.2   Selecting an object using a pick box.

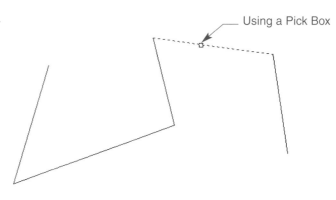

Using a Pick Box

the Select Objects: prompt. The last object chosen will be taken out of the selection set. You can continue to use **U** to back you through all the objects you have chosen. As an object is taken out of the selection set, it will go back to its original configuration. If you use the Undo command after the Erase command has been executed, *all* the objects that were erased will be restored on the drawing.

Undo, Redo, and Oops Commands

AutoCAD offers several options for undoing a previously issued command. The **Undo** command works after any command (see Chapter 12, Section 12.3). It also works within the **Erase** command sequence (as just described). In both cases, the command may be used repeatedly to step you back through the work you have just done. If you go back too far, you can use the **Redo** command to take away the *last* **Undo**. But be very careful, **Redo** works only once, so if you have undone five commands, **Redo** will restore only the last of the five. Be careful not to accidentally reissue the **Undo** command by pressing the space bar or Enter ↵.

Some people prefer to use the **Oops** command with the **Erase** command sequence. The **Oops** command works after the **Erase** command has been executed to take away only the last **Erase**. The **Oops** command works only with **Erase**, **BLOCK**, and **WBLOCK** (see Chapter 22) commands. **Oops** cannot be used over and over again. Take a minute to experiment with using the **Undo** and **Oops** commands in conjunction with the **Erase** command.

Choosing a Window (see Figure 13.3)

When you are talking about selection sets, a **window** is a rectangular area outlined on the screen with a solid line. Everything that is completely contained within the window will be selected. You generate the window by using your cursor to pick (single click with the left mouse button) a point that is not on an existing object on the screen. The command line will then prompt you to Specify opposite corner:. *You must pick from left to right.* As you move your cursor you will see the rectangle being formed. Once you have selected your window, the command line will tell you how many objects were found within the rectangle you specified. Sometimes, no objects are found, and it will appear that nothing has happened unless you check the command bar. You may continue to add objects to your selection set by using another window or by using another method of selection.

Utilizing a Crossing (see Figure 13.4)

A **crossing** is similar to a window. You use your cursor to pick a rectangular box. The difference is that you select a crossing by *picking from right to left*. Everything that is either contained within the box or crosses the box will be selected. A crossing shows up on your screen as a dashed line. Notice the difference between the lines selected in Figures 13.3 and 13.4.

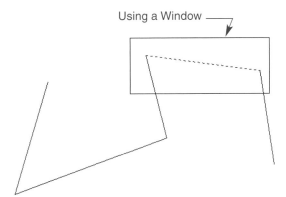

FIGURE 13.3 Selecting an object using a window selection.

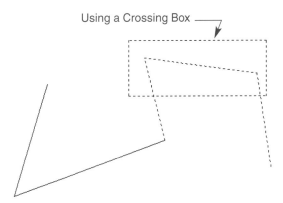

FIGURE 13.4 Selecting an object using a crossing box.

Employing an Irregular Window or Crossing (WP or CP) (see Figure 13.5)

Sometimes it is difficult to place everything within or on the boundaries of a rectangle. AutoCAD provides for this contingency by giving you the option of specifying an irregular window or crossing. Typing in **wp** at the Select Object: prompt and then pressing Enter↵ will place you in the **Window Polygon** command. The command line will prompt you to Specify first polygon point:. Then you will be asked to Specify endpoint of line or [Undo]. As you move your cursor to pick points, you will see a closed figure being formed. If you select a wrong point, simply type in **U** or **Undo** and press Enter↵, then return to selecting endpoints. When you are finished, press Enter↵. The objects chosen to be erased will be shown as dashed lines. You may continue to add to the selection set at this time or you may finish the command by pressing Enter↵.

The **Crossing Polygon** command works in the same manner as the Window Polygon command. Type **cp** at the Select Object: prompt and then press Enter↵. You will then be asked to select the endpoints of the lines making up your polygon crossing. These lines will show up as dashed lines to remind you that anything contained within or crossing the polygon will be selected.

Building a Fence (see Figure 13.6)

A **fence** is a little like a crossing box with the middle taken out of it. Only objects that cross the fence are selected. A fence does not necessarily form a closed figure. To get to the fence method of selection, type **f** at the command prompt asking you to specify or select an object. You will then be asked to pick the endpoints of the lines making up your fence. Just as with the other selection methods, you may use Undo to back out of any segment drawn. Just like a crossing, a fence shows up as a dashed line on your graphics screen.

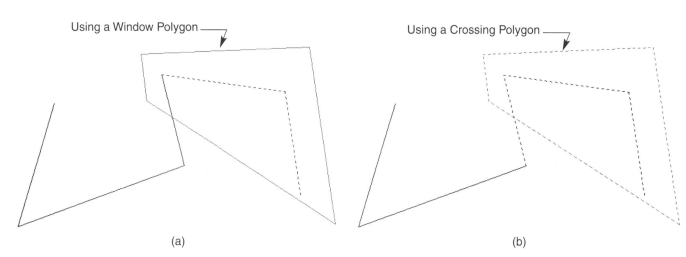

(a)   (b)

FIGURE 13.5   Selecting an object using (a) a window polygon; (b) a crossing polygon.

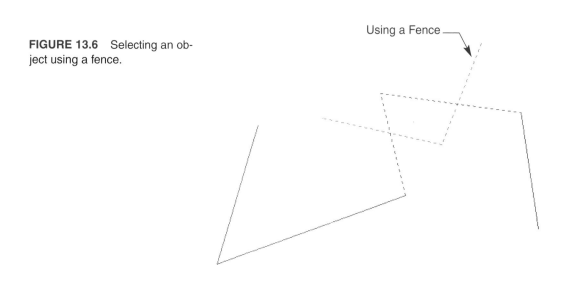

FIGURE 13.6   Selecting an object using a fence.

Selecting Objects That Are Too Close Together

Sometimes objects on the screen are so close together that it is difficult to pick the object you wish to select without also choosing an object you want to leave alone. If this happens, press the **Ctrl** button and then pick the location you are trying to select. AutoCAD will cycle through the objects in the vicinity. When you reach the one you want to choose, press Enter ↵.

13.4 AutoCAD Coordinate Systems

Picking points on a screen works just fine for some applications, but after a while you will need to draw with a little more precision. AutoCAD provides you with several methods of locating a point.

The Cartesian Coordinate System

Move your cursor around and notice that two of the three numbers on the status bar at the bottom of your screen change. If you move the cursor toward the left edge of the screen, the first number gets smaller. If you move the cursor toward the right edge of the screen, the first number gets larger. In the same way, moving the cursor toward the bottom of the screen makes the second number smaller. Moving toward the top of the screen makes the second number larger. The first number is the X-coordinate in the Cartesian coordinate system. The second number is the Y-coordinate. The third number is the Z-coordinate. It stays at zero because you are working in two dimensions. By default, you have been using Cartesian coordinates.

The **Cartesian coordinate system** (see Figure 13.7) provides you with a frame of reference for locating points. In this text we will be dealing only with two-dimensional drawing, so we will be discussing only X- and Y-coordinates. (The Z-coordinate remains zero until you switch to three-dimensional drawing.) All points are located based on their distance from a point called the **origin,** which is the intersection of two lines known as the X- and Y-axes. All points are given an X- and a Y-coordinate. The X-coordinate is the horizontal distance from the origin. The Y-coordinate is the vertical distance from the origin. The origin has (X,Y,) coordinates of (0,0). Any point to the right of the origin has a positive X-value, and any point to the left of the origin has a negative X-value. Any point above the origin has a positive Y-value, and any point below the origin has a negative Y-value. Looking at Figure 13.7, you can see that the X- and Y-axes divide the coordinate system into four sections called **quadrants**. Unless you specifically change the setup, AutoCAD automatically begins a drawing with the origin in the lower left-hand corner of your graphics screen. This setup provides for all the points shown on the screen to have positive X- and Y-values. You can input negative X- and Y-values, but you will have to change the screen view in order to see them.

When a command in AutoCAD asks you to specify a point, you now know how to use the Cartesian coordinate system to provide the absolute coordinates of that point. Always enter the X-coordinate first, followed by a comma, then the Y-coordinate. Press Enter↵ to proceed to the next step.

FIGURE 13.7 The Cartesian coordinate system.

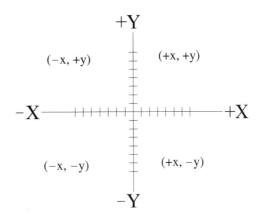

FIGURE 13.8   Drawing a line using coordinates.

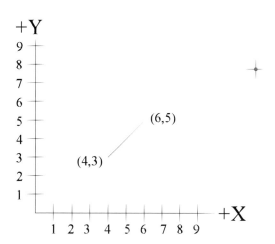

Example: Cartesian Coordinates (see Figure 13.8)

Draw a line from point (4,3) to point (6,5)

Command: **L or LINE**↵
Specify first point: **4,3**↵
Specify next point or [Undo]: **6,5**↵
Specify next point or [Undo]: ↵
Command:

The Polar Coordinate System

The **polar coordinate system** (see Figure 13.9) specifies the location of a point with a distance and an angle. If you use **absolute polar coordinates**, the distance and the angle will be measured from the origin. Unless you specify otherwise, the angle will be measured in a counterclockwise direction from the X-axis. If you want to specify a point using polar coordinates, enter the distance first followed by an angle symbol (<) and the value of the angle.

Example: Polar Coordinates (see Figure 13.10)

Pick points using polar coordinates.

Command: **POINT**↵
Specify a point: **2<225**↵
Command: **POINT**↵
Specify a point: **2<30**↵
Command: **POINT**↵
Specify a point: **4<0**↵
Command: **POINT**↵
Specify a point: **4<45**↵

The Relative Coordinate System

The two systems we just discussed use absolute coordinates to specify points, but sometimes you don't know the absolute coordinate of a desired point. Sometimes all you know is where a point is located in reference to another point. It is just like giving directions to the local grocery store. You don't need to know the global lo-

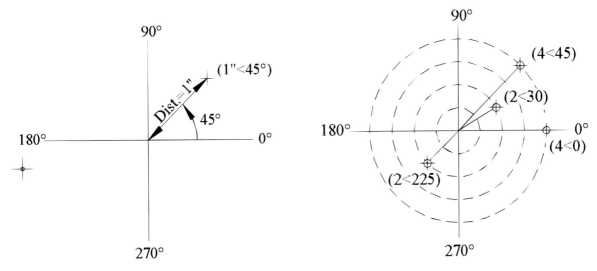

FIGURE 13.9   The polar coordinate system.

FIGURE 13.10   Specifying points using polar coordinates.

cation of the market in order to give someone directions. All you need to describe are the appropriate left or right turns to take starting from your house. That's the way relative coordinates work: you give AutoCAD directions based on the last point entered in the command. One of the nice things about relative coordinates is that they work with either Cartesian or polar coordinates. You indicate that you are using relative coordinates by placing the "@" symbol in front of your coordinates. Let's walk through a couple of examples using relative Cartesian and relative polar coordinates.

Example: Relative Cartesian Coordinates

Command: **LINE**↵
Specify first point: **2,3**↵   [You cannot use relative coordinates on the first point because AutoCAD would have no starting reference point.]

Specify next point or [Undo]: **@1,0**↵   [Go 1 unit in the positive X-direction and 0 units in the Y-direction from the last point (2,3); the new endpoint is (3,3).]

Specify next point or [Undo]: **@0,1**↵   [Go 0 units in the X-direction and 1 unit in the positive Y-direction from the last point (3,3); the new endpoint is (3,4).]

Specify next point or [Undo]: **@-1,0**↵   [Go 1 unit in the negative X-direction, 0 units in the Y-direction from the last point (3,4); the new endpoint is (2,4).]

Specify next point or [Undo]: **@0,-1**↵   [Go 0 units in the X-direction, 1 unit in the negative Y-direction from the last point (2,4); the new endpoint is (2,3)—back at the beginning.]

Specify next point or [Undo]: **@1,1**↵   [Go 1 unit in the positive X-direction, 1 unit in the positive Y-direction from the last point (2,3); the new endpoint is (3,4).]

Specify next point or [Undo]: ↵

See Figure 13.11 for the results of this input.

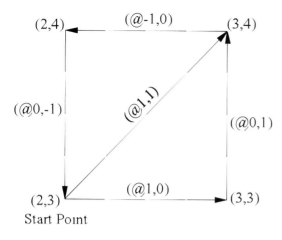

FIGURE 13.11   Relative Cartesian coordinates.

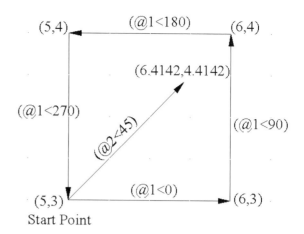

FIGURE 13.12   Relative polar coordinates.

Note: You can mix the methods of coordinate entry within one command. For example, you could input one endpoint in the line command using absolute Cartesian coordinates, the next endpoint with relative Cartesian, and the next with relative polar coordinates.

Example: Relative Polar Coordinates

Command: **LINE⏎**
Specify first point: **5,3⏎**   [Enter the first point with absolute
                                                        coordinates or pick the point.]

Specify next point or [Undo]: **@1<0⏎**   [Place the new endpoint at a distance of 1
                                                        unit at an angle of 0° from point (5,3); the
                                                        new endpoint will be (6,3).]

Specify next point or [Undo]: **@1<90⏎**   [Place the next endpoint at a distance of 1
                                                        unit at an angle of 90° from point (6,3);
                                                        the new endpoint will be (6,4).]

Specify next point or [Undo]: **@1<180⏎** [Place the next endpoint at a distance of 1
                                                        unit at an angle of 180° from the last
                                                        endpoint of (6,4); the new endpoint will be
                                                        (5,4).]

Specify next point or [Undo]: **@1<270⏎** [Place the new endpoint at a distance of 1
                                                        unit at an angle of 270° from the last
                                                        endpoint of (5,4); the new endpoint will be
                                                        (5,3).]

Specify next point or [Undo]: **@2<45⏎**   [Place the new endpoint at a distance of 2
                                                        units at an angle of 45° from the last
                                                        endpoint of (5,3); the new endpoint will be
                                                        (6.4142,4.4142).]

Specify next point or [Undo]: ⏎

See Figure 13.12 for the results of this input.

13.5   The Units Command

- Type **units** at the command prompt
- Select Units … from the Format pull-down menu.

AutoCAD will accept coordinates in whatever Units format you are currently working with. You usually select the type of units during the setup phase of the drawing. If you wish to change the type of units that you are using, use the **Units** command. Once the command has been entered, the Drawing Units dialog box will appear on the screen (see Figure 13.13).

FIGURE 13.13 Drawing Units dialog box.

Note: Typing –UNITS at the command prompt will walk you through the Units command with a text window instead of a dialog box.

Just as during the initial drawing setup (Chapter 12), you can choose from architectural, decimal, engineering, fractional, or scientific units for displaying length. Angles can be displayed using grads, radians, surveyor's units, or degree/minutes/seconds. The precision of both length and angle measurements can be set using this command. Just as in the setup menu, you can change the direction and rotation used to measure angles.

REVIEW QUESTIONS

1. List three ways to access the **Point** command.
2. What procedure would you follow to change the way the points in your drawing look?
3. How many point styles can you have within one drawing?
4. Describe the difference between using the **Undo** command within the **Line** command and using the **Undo** command after the **Line** command has been completed.
5. What is a selection set?
6. What are the differences between using a window, a crossing, or a fence to specify a selection set?
7. Compare the Cartesian coordinate system with the polar coordinate system.
8. How do relative coordinates compare with absolute coordinates?
9. Can you use relative and absolute coordinates within the same command?
10. What command would you use to change from architectural to engineering units?

EXERCISES

EXERCISE 13.1

Draw Figure 13.14 three times using the following methods. Use full scale.
1. Absolute
2. Relative
3. Polar and relative

EXERCISE 13.2

Draw Figure 13.15 using the following methods.
1. Absolute
2. Relative

EXERCISE 13.3

Draw the shapes in Figure 13.16 using the pick point method.

EXERCISE 13.4

Draw the shapes in Figure 13.17 using the polar method.

FIGURE 13.14 Exercise 13.1.

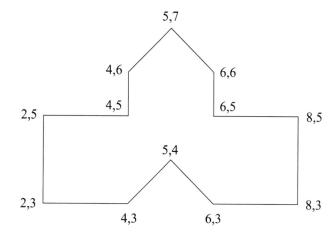

FIGURE 13.15 Exercise 13.2.

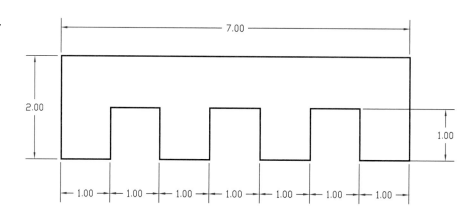

FIGURE 13.16 Exercise 13.3.

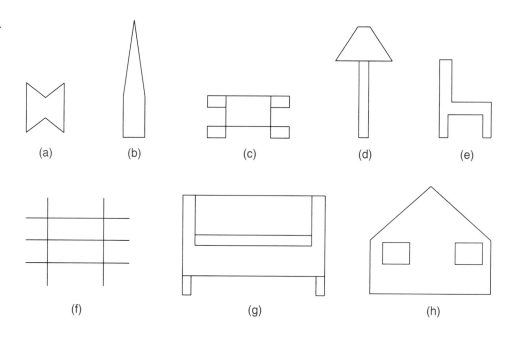

FIGURE 13.17 Exercise 13.4.

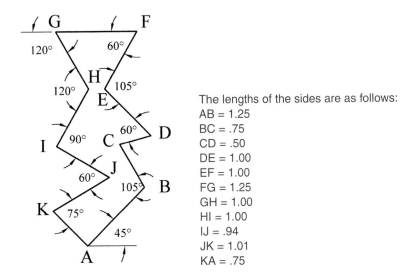

The lengths of the sides are as follows:
AB = 1.25
BC = .75
CD = .50
DE = 1.00
EF = 1.00
FG = 1.25
GH = 1.00
HI = 1.00
IJ = .94
JK = 1.01
KA = .75

DRAWING ASSIGNMENTS

1. Draw the shapes in Figure 13.18 using full scale. Use the relative method. Save the drawing as 13EX-1.

2. Draw the shapes using full scale. This time use the polar method.

3. Draw shapes A, E, and F using full scale. This time use the absolute method. Each time you begin a new drawing, use 4,4 as the bottom left corner of the object.

4. Using the Multiple Point command, place nodes where the corners are formed on shapes B and D.

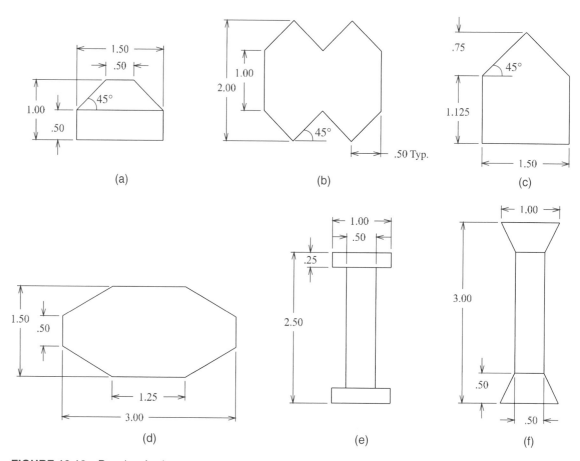

FIGURE 13.18   Drawing Assignment 1.

○ ○

CHAPTER 14

View Modification

14.1 The Limits Command

- Type **Limits** at the command prompt and then press Enter ↵.
- Select Drawing Limits from the Format pull-down menu.

AutoCAD allows you to place limits on a drawing. These limits can be used as a frame of reference as you construct your drawing. Left-click on the Grid button at the bottom of the screen. The dots appear only on the area defined by the limits. When you use a Drawing Setup Wizard, you define the limits of your drawing by specifying the area that will be represented on your drawing. AutoCAD then effectively sets aside an area of the screen for you to draw in. The program assumes that the bottom left corner of the drawing will be at the coordinate (0,0), which by default is located at the bottom left corner of the graphics screen. The upper right corner will be at the coordinates defined by the numbers you choose at the area input in the dialog box. So if you input an area with a width of 12 and a length of 9 (see Chapter 12), the limits of your drawing will be defined by a rectangle with opposite corners of (0,0) and (12,9).

Note: Limits checking only checks on points that are entered as part of a command. This may still allow portions of objects such as circles to overlap the limits. See Section 16.2 for more information on the Grid command.

The Limits command allows you to change the limits of your drawing. Once you have accessed the command, the prompt will ask you to Specify lower left corner or [ON/OFF] <0.0000, 0,00000>: The default value is given in the brackets < >. This tells you the current setting of the lower left corner of your limit. At this point, you can type in a new set of coordinates or accept the current set by simply pressing the Enter ↵ key. Typing in ON or OFF will turn the limits checking either on or off. If limits checking is on, AutoCAD will not allow you to input points outside the limits. Typing ON or OFF will also finish the Limits command. If you still wish to change the boundaries of the limits, you must go back into the command. Once you have input the requirements for the lower left-hand corner of your limits, the command will ask you to Specify upper right corner <12.0000,9.0000>:. Again, the numbers within the brackets < > will give the current limits setting. Once you have entered coordinates (or accepted the established limit) for the upper right corner, AutoCAD will automatically change the Grid display if that command is activated.

Example: The Limits Command

Use the Quick Setup Wizard to create a new drawing with decimal units. Set the width at 15 and the length at 10.

Turn the Grid setting on with a spacing of 0.5 in both the X- and Y-directions.

Access the Limits command either with the pull-down menu or by typing Limits at the command prompt. Accept the default value or (0.0000,0.0000) for the lower left corner. Input a new value of (20,15) for the upper right corner. Notice how the display changes.

Go into the Limits command and type in **ON** to activate the limit check. Now try to draw a line from (18,12) to (22,14). You should get a message telling you that the point is outside the limits. Go back into the Limits command and turn limit checking off. Now try to draw the line from (18,12) to (22,14). AutoCAD should now allow you to draw this line even though it is outside the limits shown by the grid. Notice that the grid remains at the limits even though limit checking has been turned off.

Save this drawing as "Limits" to use in experimenting with the **Zoom** command.

14.2   The Zoom Command

- Type **ZOOM** or **Z** at the command prompt and then press **Enter** ↵.
- Select Zoom from the View pull-down menu by left-clicking. This will cause another menu to cascade down containing a list of zoom options (Realtime, Previous, Window, Dynamic, Scale, Center, In, Out, All, Extents).

Zoom Icons

- Pick one of the Zoom icons from either the Standard toolbar or the Zoom toolbar. The Zoom icon looks like a handheld magnifying glass. Different symbols within the "glass" identify which type of Zoom command will be performed (see Figure 14.1). The Standard toolbar contains three Zoom icon buttons. One of the buttons has an arrowhead at the end of the handle of the magnifying glass. If you left-click on this icon and hold the mouse button down, a flyout menu will appear (see Figure 14.2). Still holding the mouse button down, move the cursor down until you reach the zoom option you wish to use. Releasing the mouse button will activate the Zoom command chosen.
- Without selecting an object, right-click in the graphics screen and choose Zoom from the menu that will appear. This will activate the Realtime Zoom command.

The **Zoom** command works like a microscope or a pair of binoculars to allow you to change your perspective on your drawing. You can zoom in to look at a closer view of your drawing or zoom out to "see" it from farther away. Just as looking through a pair of binoculars does not change the actual size of the players at a baseball game, using the Zoom command does not change any of the actual sizes of objects within your drawing; it just makes the objects look larger or smaller to you, so you can zoom in to see a small object on your drawing. You can draw lines or execute any of the AutoCAD commands on the screen shown after Zoom has been executed. If you Zoom back to the original screen, the new objects will be transferred at the correct size and proportions for the new screen.

AutoCAD provides you with several options for zooming. Let's take a moment to look at all the available options before experimenting with using the command.

FIGURE 14.1   The Zoom toolbar.

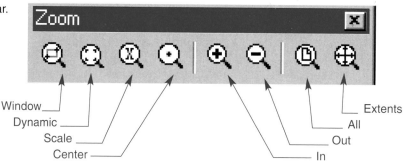

Window
Dynamic
Scale
Center
In
Out
All
Extents

FIGURE 14.2   The Zoom flyout menu.

Zoom All

At a minimum, the Zoom All command will display everything within the limits of your drawing. Even if you have drawn only a small object in the corner of your drawing area, the Zoom All command will zoom to the entire area covered by the limits. In addition, Zoom All will display any objects that have been drawn outside the limit area.

To continue with the ballpark analogy, if you set your limits to the size of the playing field, then the closest you could zoom in with Zoom All would be to a view that covered the entire playing field. If any home runs were hit out of the park, they could also be displayed using Zoom All.

Zoom Window

The **Zoom Window** command asks you to specify a rectangle by choosing the location of two opposite corners. The corners can be either picked with the left mouse button or keyed in with coordinates at the line. Once the rectangle is defined, AutoCAD zooms in as tightly as possible on that area of your drawing. Everything within the rectangle will be displayed as large as it can be displayed and still fit on the screen. One thing AutoCAD does not do is change the shape of the graphics screen display, so if you choose a rectangle that is not proportional to the screen, the program will display the contents of the screen plus whatever else fits within the graphics window to fill it up.

Returning once more to the ballpark analogy, Zoom Window allows you to define an area of the park such as first base and then zoom in tightly on that particular spot. You can see if the runner is really out or if the first base player missed the tag.

Zoom Extents

Zoom All and **Zoom Extents** are similar commands. Both display all the entities within the drawing. However, the area shown by Zoom All always includes the entire limits of the drawing. Zoom Extents shows only the area where objects have been drawn, so if you have used only a small section of your limits to draw in, Zoom Extents will fill the graphics screen with that section. If part of the limits area is blank, it will not be included in the display. Figure 14.3 provides a comparison between the two commands.

Zoom Previous

If you wish to go back to the way the screen looked before you used the Zoom command, **Zoom Previous** is the way to do so. The Zoom Previous command restores your screen to the previous view. It can be used up to 10 times to back out of several Zoom iterations.

Zoom Scale

The **Zoom Scale** command allows you to zoom relative to a value that you enter (see Figure 14.4). Entering a number greater than 1 will cause the display to zoom in tighter. In other words, the objects on the screen will look bigger. A number less than 1 will create a zoom out, and the objects will look smaller. There are three ways to enter a Zoom Scale. Entering a number as a scale factor will scale relative to the limits of your drawing. Entering a scale factor as a number followed by the letter X will scale the display relative to the view currently on your graphics screen. A scale factor made up of a number followed by the letters XP relates to paper space units (see Appendix A).

FIGURE 14.3 Comparison of (a) Zoom All and (b) Zoom Extents commands.

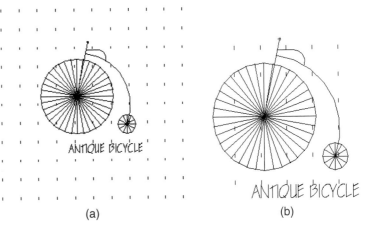

(a)

(b)

FIGURE 14.4 Zoom Scale.

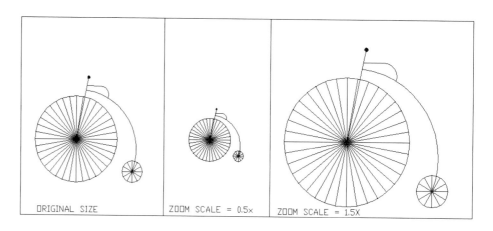

ORIGINAL SIZE   ZOOM SCALE = 0.5×   ZOOM SCALE = 1.5X

Zoom Realtime

Note: Once the Zoom command is entered at the command prompt a right click with the mouse will automatically give you a realtime zoom option. An additional right click will give you the Zoom shortcut menu (see Figure 14.5).

Choosing the Zoom icon that looks like a magnifying glass with a plus (+) and minus (−) sign next to it places you in the **Zoom Realtime** command. The first thing you will notice is that your cursor now looks like the Realtime icon button. This is to remind you that Realtime Zoom is an interactive command. Press down and hold the left mouse button. As you guide the magnifying glass cursor up and down the screen the image will expand and contract. Unlike the other types of zooms, there is no abrupt change on the screen; the image changes smoothly as you move your mouse. If you reach the edge of your screen and still need to zoom more, release the mouse button and reposition the cursor on the other side of the screen, left-click, hold, and move the cursor again to zoom.

Zoom Center

The **Zoom Center** option asks you to Specify a centerpoint: and Enter magnification or height <current>:. The display then changes to a window defined by the chosen center point with a zoom value based on the magnification or height specified. The zoom magnification will decrease as the magnification number gets larger.

Zoom In

The **Zoom In** command has the same effect as using a Zoom Scale with a factor of 2X. The objects shown in the current view will appear to be twice as large. The effect takes place as soon as you select the icon or choose the command from the pull-down menu.

Zoom Out

The **Zoom Out** command is the opposite of the Zoom In command. The objects shown on the screen will appear at half the size of the previous display. Zoom Out has the same effect as a Zoom Scale with a factor of 0.5X.

Zoom Dynamic

Zoom Dynamic is an interesting command. When you first select the command, the display changes to show all the parts of the drawing that you have generated. A blue dashed line is placed around the extents of the drawing, and a green dashed line indicates the area that was displayed when you entered the Zoom Dynamic command. A view box appears with a cross in the middle. You can move this box around with your mouse and left-click at the desired location. Now you can size the box by moving your mouse and left-clicking. This procedure can be repeated until you have framed in the exact area that you wish to choose for a zoom. Pressing **Enter.⌐** will execute the command.

Using an IntelliMouse

An **IntelliMouse** is a two-button mouse with a small wheel between the buttons. The buttons perform the same functions as a regular two-button mouse. In AutoCAD, the wheel can be used to **pan** or **zoom** without having to access the commands through the keyboard or the pull-down menu. The wheel rotates in discrete intervals that you feel as a click as you move the wheel. The default value for each movement or click is a zoom of 10%. (To change this value use the **Zoomfactor** system variable. The higher the number, the smaller the change will be.) Rotate the wheel forward or backward to Zoom In or Out. Press the wheel and then drag the mouse to pan across the screen.

FIGURE 14.5 The Zoom short-cut menu.

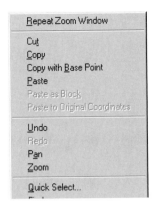

| Repeat Zoom Window |
| Cut |
| Copy |
| Copy with Base Point |
| Paste |
| Paste as Block |
| Paste to Original Coordinates |
| Undo |
| Redo |
| Pan |
| Zoom |
| Quick Select... |

14.3   The Pan Command

- Type **PAN** or **–pan** at the command prompt.
- Select Pan from the View pull-down menu. A menu will cascade out offering options for Real Time, Point, Left, Right, Up, and Down pans.
- Choose the Pan icon from the Standard Toolbar. The icon looks like a hand placed on top of a piece of paper.

Pan Icon

The Pan icon provides a good visual image for the way the commands functions. Imagine that your entire drawing is like a piece of paper, and the graphics screen is like a window. The **Pan** command functions like a hand to move the "drawing" around in the "window." It does not change the size of the objects displayed, merely where they are located on the screen. So if you are zoomed in on a small portion of your drawing, you can use the Pan command to "move" the drawing around and see the parts that are not currently visible.

There are several ways to pan. Choosing the Real Time option will cause a hand to appear on the screen in place of the cursor. You can then use your mouse to move or pan the drawing around. Hold down the left button and move the mouse around until the drawing is in the position you desire. Typing in **PAN** or choosing the Pan icon from the toolbar places you in **Real Time Pan**. If you reach the edge of the screen and still need to pan some more, release the mouse button, reposition the mouse, and continue.

Typing in **–pan** or choosing the Point option from the pull-down menu will allow you to pan by choosing a displacement. You will be provided with two command prompts. The first command prompt will ask you to Specify base point or displacement:. At this time you can enter either a specific point or the distance you want to pan the drawing. If you decide to specify a distance, use the same format as you would for a point entry. The pan will proceed just as though you had entered relative coordinates. Since the point and the displacement use the same format, AutoCAD will not know which you are entering until you answer the next command prompt. The second command prompt will read Specify second point:. If you wish to use the displacement option, press Enter↵, and the command will use the coordinates from the first command prompt as a displacement. If you want to use the point option, enter another point location. It will be as though you picked up the drawing at the first point and moved it to the second point. So if on the first entry you typed 2,3 and then pressed Enter↵ at the second prompt, AutoCAD would move the entire drawing 2 units in the X-direction and 3 units in the Y-direction. If you typed another set of coordinates such as 4,6, then AutoCAD would move the drawing from point (2,3) to point (4,6) or 2 units in the X-direction and 3 units in the Y-direction (see Figure 14.6).

The Left, Right, Up, and Down options provided in the Pan pull-down menu can be used to incrementally pan in the direction chosen.

Note: If your mouse has a wheel between the two mouse buttons, you can use this wheel to zoom and pan. The default value for each click of the wheel is 10%. You can change this variable with the Zoomfactor command.

FIGURE 14.6 Pan displacement.

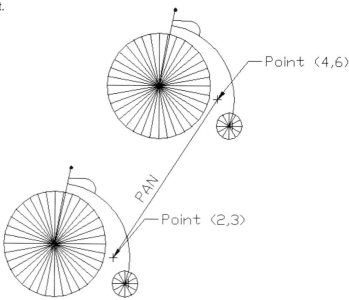

14.4 Drawing Scale

Architectural drawings use a wide variety of scales. There are two factors that determine how a drawing will be scaled:

- Paper or sheet sizes to fit the drawing for printing and plotting
- Readability for understanding the design

Paper can be manufactured in large sizes, but prints and plots need to be at a size that is convenient to carry. Most small printers have a standard size of 8½″ × 11″, which makes it easy to put in book form for a portfolio. The larger size sheets are given to contractors for carrying around to construction sites. A 24″ × 36″ sheet size is fairly convenient for a contractor's needs. The following is a range of standard sizes for architectural drawings, but keep in mind that printers and plotters have some control on the sheet sizes. Rolls of paper come in preset widths that lend themselves to certain sizes to avoid wasting paper.

	Architectural Sheet Sizes (Full Size)		Mechanical Sheet Sizes	
	Length	**Width**	**Length**	**Width**
A-Size Sheet	12″ × 9″		11″ × 8½″	
B-Size Sheet	18″ × 12″		17″ × 11″	
C-Size Sheet	24″ × 18″		22″ × 17″	
D-Size Sheet	36″ × 24″		34″ × 22″	
E-Size Sheet	48″ × 36″		44″ × 34″	

These sizes can be used in a wide range of fields. A 30″ × 42″ size is not uncommon to find in the architectural fields. The AutoCAD software will let you customize your sheet sizes according to your plotter's or printer's limitations.

Drawing Readability

Students tend to find full or real scale (1″ = 1″) the easiest to understand. This is the scale at which AutoCAD draws. (Of course, AutoCAD can plot a drawing to any scale that may be needed.) This scale is used in several disciplines, particularly mechanical drafting. Most of the parts drawn are fairly small and can be drawn at the real size and fit easily on typical sheet sizes.

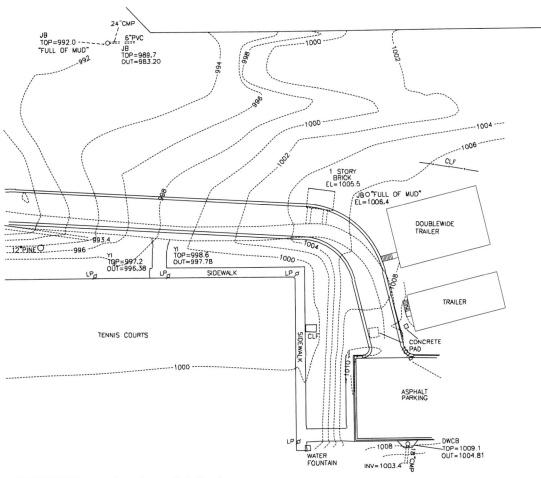

FIGURE 14.7 Drawing of a partial site plan.

Now think about the types of drawings used in architecture.

- Site plans
- Landscape plans
- Foundation plans
- Framing plans
- Floor plans
- Elevations
- Roof plans
- Wall sections
- Building sections
- Interior elevation and details
- Door, window, and finish schedules

A site is one of the largest things anyone will ever draw (see Figure 14.7). Let's say you want to draw a site plan that is 200′ long by 100′ wide. Immediately you should understand that there is no way to view this drawing at full scale/real size on a monitor. Printing this drawing at full scale is also not feasible, so it is your job to manage the drawing so that it can be viewed on the monitor as well as plotted on a standard sheet size. One thing to remember is that the drawing must print out in a size large enough to be easily read and understood. Some typical scales for site plans and landscape plans are shown here.

$$1'' = 10'$$

$$1'' = 16'$$

$$1'' = 20'$$

$$1'' = 30'$$

$$1'' = 40'$$

$$1'' = 50'$$

$$1'' = 60'$$

$$1'' = 100'$$

Note: Information on reading these scales was covered in Chapter 2.

Now let's look at the drawings that go with a building or structure (see Figure 14.8).

A set of architectural drawings comprises an assortment of plan views as well as elevations. If a building measures 80′ long by 35′ wide, it has to be scaled down to fit on a standard size drawing sheet while still at a scale that can easily be read. Floor plans and exterior elevations generally use scales in the following ranges:

$\frac{1}{4}'' = 1'\text{-}0''$ (most common for residential)

$\frac{3}{16}'' = 1'\text{-}0''$

$\frac{1}{8}'' = 1'\text{-}0''$ (most common for large commercial projects)

If a small area of a plan needs blown up even further, a $\frac{3}{8}'' = 1'\text{-}0''$ and $\frac{1}{2}'' = 1'\text{-}0''$ are not uncommon.

The larger architectural scales are used for wall sections and other detailed drawings (see Figure 14.9). These drawings show a lot of assembly and materials that need to be as clear as possible to be read correctly.

Large architectural scales are the following:

$\frac{3}{4}'' = 1'\text{-}0''$

$1'' = 1'\text{-}0''$

$1\frac{1}{2}'' = 1'\text{-}0''$

$3'' = 1'\text{-}0''$

As shown in the various figures, a wide variety of scales are used in architectural drawings. Understanding scale usage will help ease you into scaling a drawing in AutoCAD.

Scaled Drawings in AutoCAD

An AutoCAD drawing must be scaled for the same reasons mentioned earlier in this section, largely so that the end product or drawing can be printed out at a readable scale on a standard sheet size.

The actual drawing is drawn and stored in the computer's memory. Today's computers have enough memory capability to draw almost any drawing at full scale. AutoCAD drawings are drawn to full scale but are adjusted for viewing on a monitor and printing on standard sheets of paper.

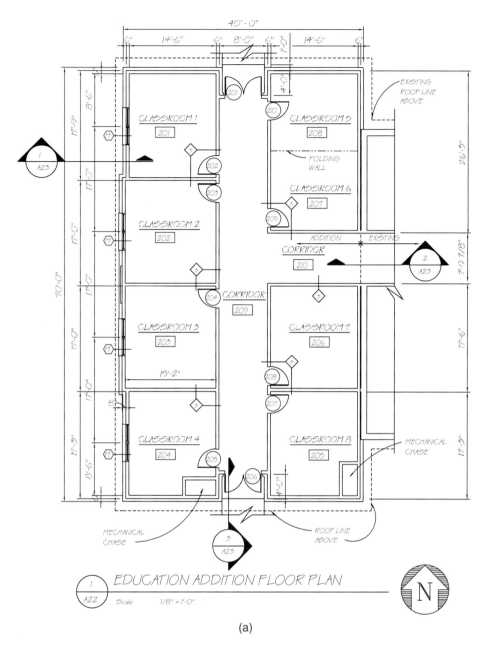

(a)

FIGURE 14.8 (a) Floor plan. (b) Elevation. Courtesy of Barker Cunningham Barrington Architects.
continued on next page

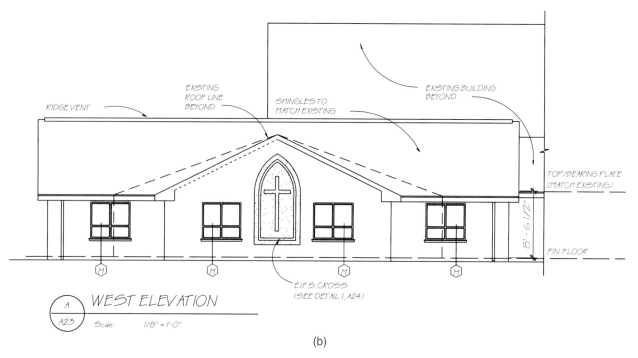

RIDGE VENT

EXISTING
ROOF LINE
BEYOND

SHINGLES TO
MATCH EXISTING

EXISTING BUILDING
BEYOND

TOP/BEARING PLATE
(MATCH EXISTING)

8'- 6 1/2"

FIN. FLOOR

E.I.F.S. CROSS
(SEE DETAIL 1, A24)

A
A23
WEST ELEVATION
Scale: 1/8" = 1'-0"

(b)

FIGURE 14.8 *continued*

Controlling the Scale in Model Space (See Appendix A on Plotting)

The Limits command setting is a useful tool for viewing a drawing to see if a certain scale will fit a standard sheet size. It is important to remember that the Scale command is not used to set scales in AutoCAD. It acts independently of the Limits command and will get you into a lot of trouble very quickly if you start using it to try and adjust scales in drawings.

The monitor is where a CAD operator views a drawing. Monitor sizes vary somewhat but setting up the limits of a drawing will allow you to see the whole drawing on the screen, even on a small one. Some examples for setting scales using limits follow.

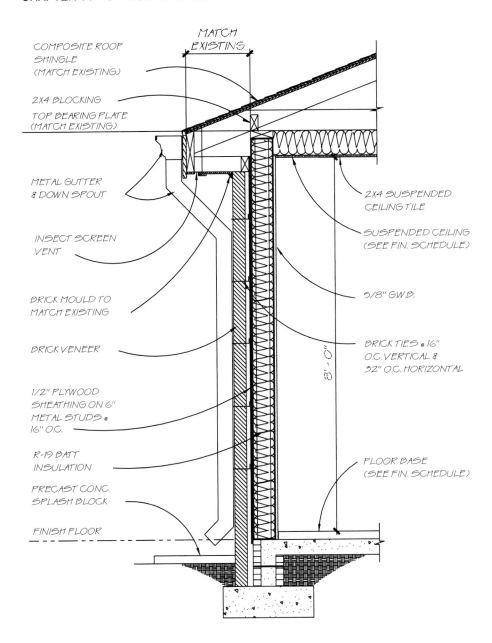

COMPOSITE ROOF
SHINGLE
(MATCH EXISTING)

MATCH
EXISTING

2X4 BLOCKING

TOP BEARING PLATE
(MATCH EXISTING)

METAL GUTTER
& DOWN SPOUT

INSECT SCREEN
VENT

BRICK MOULD TO
MATCH EXISTING

BRICK VENEER

1/2" PLYWOOD
SHEATHING ON 6"
METAL STUDS ●
16" O.C.

R-19 BATT
INSULATION

PRECAST CONC.
SPLASH BLOCK

FINISH FLOOR

2X4 SUSPENDED
CEILING TILE

SUSPENDED CEILING
(SEE FIN. SCHEDULE)

5/8" G.W.B.

BRICK TIES ● 16"
O.C. VERTICAL &
32" O.C. HORIZONTAL

8'-0"

FLOOR BASE
(SEE FIN. SCHEDULE)

1 / A23   WALL SECTION   Scale: 3/4" = 1'-0"

FIGURE 14.9

Example 1

A floor plan is to be drawn at ¼"= 1'-0" scale. The largest standard sheet size that your office plotter can handle is 24" × 36".

- Begin a new drawing and then select the Start from Scratch option when the Create New Drawing dialog box opens up. Left-click on OK.
- At the command line type in **Limits**.

Then when AutoCAD requests you to:

> Specify lower left corner or [ON/OFF] <0'-0", 0'-0">

Type **0,0** then AutoCAD command prompts you to:

> Specify upper right corner <1'-0", 0'-9">:

At this point type in **144', 96'.**

Now, where did the 144', 96' come from? Here is how those numbers were found. We start with the scale needed: ¼" = 1'-0". This means that a ¼" real size now represents 1'. There are a total of four (¼") in one real inch.

¼" + ¼" + ¼" + ¼" = 1" (therefore, 4' are represented in one inch)

Now, we use that knowledge to adjust the sheet size, which is a standard 36" × 24" real size.

Because each ¼" represents one foot, and there are four quarter-inches in an inch, we simply multiply the sheet size by 4:

(4' / 1") × 36" = 144'
(4' /1") × 24" = 96'

Another method for calculating these numbers is to find the scale factor. To do this, divide the 1' by ¼".

(1' / ¼") = (12" / ¼") = 48

48 is the scale factor.

Then, take the desired sheet size of 36" × 24" and multiply 36" by 48:

36" × 48 = 1728"

Next, multiply 24" by 48:

24" × 48 = 1152"

The sheet size is now 1728" × 1152", but architectural scales are based on one foot, so convert the inches to feet by dividing them by 12":

$$1728'' \times \frac{1\,\text{ft}}{12''} = 144'$$

$$1152'' \times \frac{1\,\text{ft}}{12''} = 96'$$

Thus, the limit of the upper right corner needs to be set to 144', 96' for this scale.

- Once the limits are set, do the following. At the command line use the **Grid** command and set the spacing at 2' apart.

    > Command: **Grid**
    > Specify grid spacing (X) or [ON/OFF/Snap/Aspect] < >: **2'**

- Next, use the **Zoom** command and choose the **All** option by typing **Z↵**, then type **A↵** at the command line.

    Now you are looking at a grid that is set to your limits and desired sheet size. If your drawing starts getting close to the edges of the grid, you may need to go to a smaller scale.

    If you do not want to use a grid but want to have a guide to see the sheet limits, then draw a rectangle with a lower left corner of 0,0 and an upper right-hand corner of 144', 96'.

Example 2

A simpler way to set the scale follows. This time we will use a scale of ⅛″ = 1′-0″ with the same sheet size of 36″ × 24″.

- Begin a new drawing. Select the Start from Scratch option in the Create New Drawing dialog box and left-click on the OK screen button.

- Type in **MVSETUP** at the command line, then answer **No** to Enable paper space?

> Command: **MVSETUP**↵
> Enable paper space? [No/Yes] <Y>: **No** or **N**

At the command line, AutoCAD prompts you to pick your drawing units. Pick A for architectural.

> Enter Units type [Scientific/Decimal/Engineering/Architectural/Metric]:
> A↵

Now the screen displays a list of scale factors in the left column and the scales in the right column (see Figure 14.10). At the bottom left of this window, type in the scale factor you need. In this case, 96 for ⅛″ = 1′-0″.

> Enter the scale factor: **96**

Now you are prompted for the paper width. Enter the real size in inches. (AutoCAD converts to feet automatically for you.)

> Enter paper width: **36.**↵

At the next prompt, it asks for the paper height, so type in **24.**

> Enter paper height: **24.**↵

As soon as the last number is entered, a rectangle appears showing you the limits or sheet outline automatically set at 288′,192′.

FIGURE 14.10 MVSETUP screen.

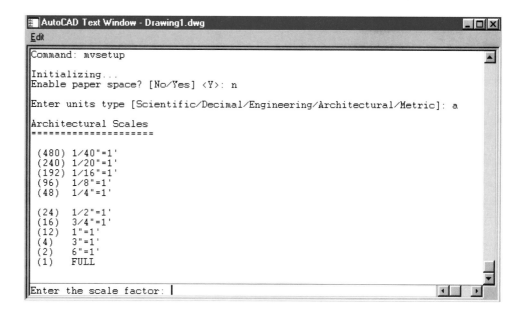

You are done. If you want a grid to display, pick 4 feet. This will work well at this scale. When typing in distances in architectural units, you can enter them as follows:

60″	inches
5′-0″	feet and inches with dash
5′0″	feet and inches without dash
5.5′	feet

These are the real sizes you are entering when drawing. The computer is drawing using real sizes at full scale. What you see on the monitor is the scale adjusted for your viewing.

When you zoom in and out on a drawing, you are constantly adjusting the viewing scale. To zoom to the limits of a drawing, use the Extents or All option.

MVSETUP

Using **MVSETUP** is a quick way to set up drawing specifications (see Figure 14.10). It does not show you all the scales that exist. You may have to calculate the scale factor yourself, using the following method.

If you want a scale factor for ⅜″ = 1′-0″, divide 1′ by ⅜″ to get the scale factor.

$$\left(\frac{1'}{\frac{3}{8}''} \right) = \left(\frac{12''}{\frac{3}{8}''} \right) = 32 \text{ scale factor}$$

When you use the MVSETUP command, you do not have to calculate the limits to a drawing. MVSETUP is not found in the Use a Wizard option in the Create New Drawing dialog box.

The two choices in the wizard setup are Advanced Setup and Quick Setup. If you choose to start a new drawing with either one of these options, at some point along the way you will need to calculate the limits. Both methods will ask you to enter your drawing area. You must enter a width and a length with the limits numbers converted to the desired scale, calculated as in Example 1. Learn to calculate limits to desired scales to make your life easier.

One thing to be aware of when using MVSETUP is that at the prompt

Enable paper space? [No/Yes] <Y>

answering No lets you customize your model space environment. Answering Yes will put you in the Paper Space Layout1 environment and give a list of options at the command line. Avoid going into paper space when you are just learning AutoCAD. Paper space is for the plotting environment and will be discussed later in Appendix A. The model space environment is for drawing and designing, so stay in model for now.

14.5   Additional Tools Useful for Modifying Views

Transparent Commands

Note: Using the **Undo** command will undo not only the command just executed but also any transparent commands used during the process.

Some commands in AutoCAD can be entered transparently, which means that you can execute a second command while working in the first command. For example, say you need to draw a line from a particular point. If you need to look more closely at your drawing to choose the location, you can transparently zoom in to that area, pick the point, and then zoom back out to select the next location. A command is entered transparently by putting an apostrophe (') in front of the command name. AutoCAD indicates that a transparent command is being executed by placing double angle brackets (>>) in front of the action shown in the command prompt.

Zoom and **Pan** are two commands that are well suited to transparent usage. **GRID**, **SNAP**, and **Object SNAP** also work well transparently. Many other commands can also be used transparently. The rule of thumb for transparency is that the command cannot select objects, cannot create new objects, cannot cause regenerations, and cannot end a drawing session.

Regen, Redraw, and Blipmode

Some people feel more comfortable when a mark is placed at any location picked by the cursor. The command that activates this feature is called **Blipmode**. It places a temporary mark in the shape of a small cross wherever the cursor picks. If an object such as a line is erased, the blips will remain on the screen. To activate the blips, type in **BLIPMODE** and choose **ON**. If you get tired of having blips appear on your screen, type in **BLIPMODE** and then choose **OFF**.

The only way to remove the existing blips from your screen is to use a command that regenerates or redraws. Either Zoom or Pan will accomplish this. You can also activate the **Redraw** command. Redraw is like taking an eraser brush and cleaning up your drawing. It refreshes the display currently on the graphics screen. Redraw can be accessed from the View pull-down menu by typing in **REDRAW** at the command prompt, or by choosing the **Redraw** icon, which looks like the writing end of a pencil. **Regen** is another command that will clean up your drawing. Regen cleans up the current display as well as updating the database. Select Regen from the View pull-down menu or type in **Regen** at the command prompt.

The View Command

Sometimes you will find that you are repeatedly zooming and panning back and forth between the same views. In this case, it might be easier to give each of these views a name and identity so that you can call up that view whenever you need it. Typing in **VIEW** at the command prompt will bring up the View dialog box, where you can store each view with a name, location, coordinate system, and properties. You can also store orthographic and isometric views. Picking the New button will bring up the New View dialog box. This allows you to define the new view as what is currently displayed on the graphics screen or by picking a window for the view. If you choose the window option, the pick button will be activated. Click on this button to return to your drawing and choose a window. Once the window is selected you will be returned to the dialog box. View names may have up to 255 characters and may include any letters, numbers, or characters that are not already being used by Microsoft Word or AutoCAD. Blank spaces may also be inserted. Once a view is defined, all you have to do to select it is highlight the name in the View dialog box, click on the Set Current button and pick **OK**.

REVIEW QUESTIONS

1. By default, where is the coordinate (0,0) located on the graphics screen?
2. Will AutoCAD allow you to draw outside the limits set in the initial drawing setup? Is so, when and how?
3. What command would you choose to increase the apparent size of an object on the graphics screen?
4. Would a Zoom scale factor of 0.5X make an object appear larger or smaller on the graphics screen?
5. Does the Zoom command change the actual size of an object within a drawing?
6. Explain the difference between the Zoom Extents and the Zoom All commands.
7. Which command allows you to zoom interactively?
8. What is the purpose of the Pan command? Compare the Pan and Zoom commands.
9. What does a transparent command do? How do you make a command transparent?
10. List five commands that can be performed transparently.
11. Suppose you have activated the Blipmode so that marks are left on the screen everywhere that a point is picked. How can you get rid of the blips left on your screen?
12. Explain the purpose of the View command.

EXERCISES

EXERCISE 14.1

Locate the AutoCAD 2000 directory found in the Program files. Double-click on the Sample subdirectory to get a listing of drawings. Double-click on the Wilhome.Dwg to open it.

a. Zoom in on Fireplace Detail 1-A1. Use the View command, and under Named Views, select the New button and name the view Fireplace, then select OK. Now perform a Zoom All.

b. Type **VIEW** at the command prompt and select the Fireplace view you just named. Pick the Set Current button, then select OK to bring the view back to the original position when you named it.

c. Zoom in on the floor plan and locate the kitchen sinks. Use Pan Real Time and pan to the right until you locate the other sink with the disposal.

d. Zoom to the stairs and find out how many risers are in the stairs.

e. Zoom in on the kitchen elevations and find the height of the countertop and ceiling in detail number 3.

EXERCISE 14.2

Open the Sample drawing named db_sample.dwg. Locate the following employees' cubicle numbers.

Keith Jackson

Roxie Smith

Yolanda Torbati

John Feaster

Cintra Haque

Lars Sachsen

EXERCISE 14.3

Open the drawing named City map.dwg in the Sample directory. Look for the following:

a. The street closest to the Metrodome.
b. The river splitting the University of Minnesota.
c. Find the names of all the lakes on the map.

EXERCISE 14.4

Using the given scale factor of 96 for a scale of ⅛″ = 1′-0″ set the limits in feet for the following sheet sizes.

        Y-value *X-value*
a. 8½″ × 11″ sheet
b. 11″ × 17″ sheet
c. 18″ × 24″ sheet
d. 24″ × 36″ sheet
e. 36″ × 48″ sheet

EXERCISE 14.5

Using the given scale factor of 240 for a scale of 1″ = 20′, set the limits in feet for the following sheet sizes.

        Y-value *X-value*
a. 8½″ × 11″ sheet
b. 11″ × 17″ sheet
c. 18″ × 24″ sheet
d. 24″ × 36″ sheet
e. 36″ × 48″ sheet

EXERCISE 14.6

Using the given scale factor of 2 for a scale of ½″ = 1″, set the limits in feet for the following sheet sizes.

        Y-value   *X-value*
a. 8½″ × 11″ sheet
b. 11″ × 17″ sheet
c. 18″ × 24″ sheet
d. 24″ × 36″ sheet
e. 36″ × 48″ sheet

EXERCISE 14.7

Using the given scale factor of 4 for a scale of 3″ = 1′-0″, set the limits in feet for the following sheet sizes.

        Y-value   *X-value*
a. 8½″ × 11″ sheet
b. 11″ × 17″ sheet
c. 18″ × 24″ sheet
d. 24″ × 36″ sheet
e. 36″ × 48″ sheet

EXERCISE 14.8

Using the given scale factor of 32 for a scale of ⅜″ = 1′-0″, set the limits in feet for the following sheet sizes.

        Y-value   *X-value*
a. 8½″ × 11″ sheet
b. 11″ × 17″ sheet
c. 18″ × 24″ sheet
d. 24″ × 36″ sheet
e. 36″ × 48″ sheet

EXERCISE 14.9

Using the given scale factor of 4 for a scale of ¼″ = 1″, set the limits in feet for the following sheet sizes.

        Y-value   *X-value*
a. 8½″ × 11″ sheet
b. 11″ × 17″ sheet
c. 18″ × 24″ sheet
d. 24″ × 36″ sheet
e. 36″ × 48″ sheet

EXERCISE 14.10

Using the given scale factor of 600 for a scale of 1″ = 50′, set the limits in feet for the following sheet sizes.

        Y-value   *X-value*
a. 8½″ × 11″ sheet
b. 11″ × 17″ sheet
c. 18″ × 24″ sheet
d. 24″ × 36″ sheet
e. 36″ × 48″ sheet

CHAPTER 15

○ ○

Creating Simple Geometric Entities

Note: For a review of the geometric terminology used in this chapter, see Chapter 4, Section 4.1.

15.1 The Circle Command

- Type **CIRCLE** or **C** at the command prompt.
- Select Circle from the Draw pull-down menu. This will cause a menu of options to cascade out (see Figure 15.1).
- Click on the Circle icon on the Draw toolbar. The icon looks like a circle with a red radius.

Circle Icon

AutoCAD provides you with six options for drawing circles. The default option is that you specify a center point and a radius. Both of these inputs may be picked with the mouse or entered as coordinates. Notice that this is the first option listed on the Circle cascade menu (Figure 15.1). When you activate the Circle command, the prompt will read Specify center point for circle or [3P/2P/Ttr (tan tan radius)]:. This tells you that AutoCAD will assume that you are inputting a center point unless you type in the abbreviation for one of the other choices.

The other options are fairly straightforward. The decision on which one is best for your application will depend on the information you know about the circle and where you wish to place it. The **Center, Diameter** option is similar to the **Center, Radius** option except that you are asked to input the diameter of your circle instead of the radius. The **2 Point** option asks you to specify two points that will define the diameter of the circle, which determines its location. The **3 Point** option defines a circle that passes through three given points. Recall the manual construction process for this same process covered in Section 4.1. Makes you ap-

FIGURE 15.1 Circle cascade menu.

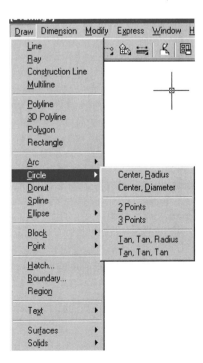

369

FIGURE 15.2 Circle selection options.

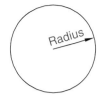

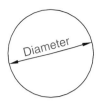

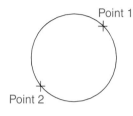

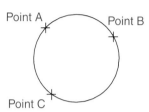

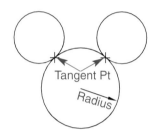

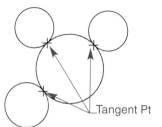

Note: Immediately after drawing a circle, you can return to the **Circle** command by pressing either the space bar or the Enter⏎ key. This procedure will work for most of the commands found in AutoCAD. Just remember not to use any other keystrokes or commands in between or you will have to access the command in the traditional manner.

preciate AutoCAD, doesn't it? For the **Tan, Tan, Radius** option you are required to input two tangent points that will be contained in the circle as well as the radius of the new circle. The **Tan, Tan, Tan** option is similar to the 3 Point option except that the three points are defined by three points of tangency (see Figure 15.2).

15.2 The Polygon Command

- Type **Polygon** or **pol** at the command prompt.
- Select Polygon from the <u>D</u>raw pull-down menu.
- Click on the Polygon icon on the Draw toolbar. The icon shows the shape of a pentagon (five sides).

Polygon
Icon

The first prompt that appears once you activate the **Polygon** command is Enter the number of sides < >:. The **Polygon** command allows you to draw regular polygons that have anywhere from 3 to 1024 sides. (The value shown within the angle brackets < > will be the default value based on the last time the command was used.) Once you have determined the shape of your polygon by picking the number of sides, you have the option of sizing and locating the figure either by specifying the center and the radius or by determining an edge.

The default option is to first choose the center point of the polygon. You may do this by picking a point with your mouse or by entering coordinates. Once you do this, you will be asked to Enter an option [Inscribed in circle/Circumscribed about circle]< I >:. This means you must decide whether you want your polygon constructed within the confines of the circle you will specify or around the circle (see Figure 15.3). The default value will initially be <u>I</u> for inscribed but will change to whatever was selected the last time the command was used. After you have entered either **I** for inscribed or **C** for circumscribed, you will be asked to Specify radius of circle:. Once the radius is entered, the polygon will appear on the drawing.

FIGURE 15.3 The difference between an inscribed polygon and a circumscribed polygon.

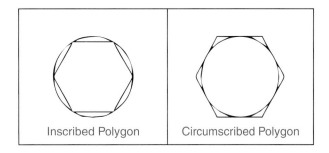

Inscribed Polygon | Circumscribed Polygon

15.3 The Arc Command

- Type **ARC or A** at the command prompt.
- Select Arc from the Draw pull-down menu. A cascading menu will appear with various input options (see Figure 15.4).
- Pick the Arc icon on the Draw toolbar. The icon looks like an arc with three red points shown on the endpoints and the center of the arc.

Arc
Icon

The **Arc** command is so versatile that it takes a little bit of experimenting to get used to it. The first step is to acquaint yourself with the various components of an arc (see Figure 15.5). You will find that once you begin needing the command, the choice of option will become obvious. Rarely do you have all the information about an arc. Your job is to find at least three pieces of data that can be used to input the arc.

Figure 15.6 illustrates each of the options available in the command. The **3 Point** option is the default if you access the command through the Arc icon or by typing the command name. Unless you change the setup, arcs are usually created in a counterclockwise direction, so put some thought into choosing your Start and End points in options that require that input.

Note: You can use the space bar or the Enter↵ key to make the endpoint of a previously drawn arc or line the starting point for a new arc.

The **Continue** option can be used to attach a new arc to the last arc or line drawn. The new arc will be tangent to the arc or line to which it is attached. If you wish to draw a series of continuing arcs, you can press the Enter↵ button twice to reactivate the command and then indicate the Continue option. Figure 15.7 shows several ways this command can be utilized.

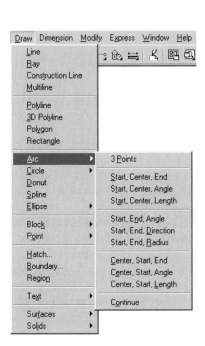

FIGURE 15.4 Arc command cascade menu.

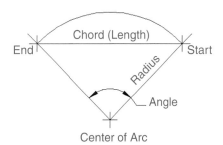

FIGURE 15.5 Components of an arc.

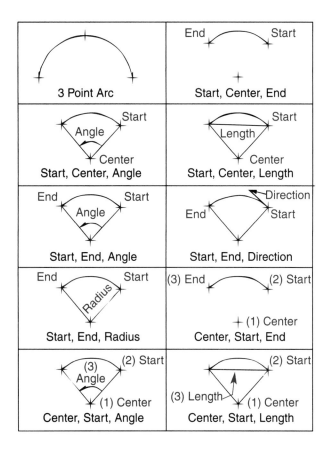

FIGURE 15.6 Examples of Arc input options.

FIGURE 15.7 Example of the Arc and Line Continue commands.

15.4 The Ellipse Command

- Type **ELLIPSE** or **EL** at the command prompt.
- Select Ellipse from the Draw pull-down menu. A cascading menu will appear, offering three options: (1) Center, (2) Axis, End, and (3) Arc.

Ellipse Icon

- Pick the Ellipse icon from the Draw toolbar. The icon image is an ellipse with two red dots at quadrants of the ellipse.

Axis, Endpoint Option

An ellipse possesses a major and a minor axis (see Figure 15.8). The **Axis, Endpoint** option asks you to specify the endpoints of one axis of the ellipse. These endpoints may define either the major or the minor axis. AutoCAD then requests the distance from the center point of the first axis to the endpoint of the second axis. These three points will define your ellipse. As you experiment with the command notice that a preliminary ellipse appears as soon as you pick the first two endpoints. If you move the cursor, you will see a line stretching from the center of the ellipse like a rubber band. As you move the cursor, and stretch this rubber band, the preliminary ellipse will expand and contract depending on the location of your cursor. This feature lets you preview the ellipse you are defining. The ellipse does not actually exist in the drawing until you choose the final distance to the other axis (see Figure 15.9).

AutoCAD gives you the option of defining a rotation instead of a distance in the last step. To take advantage of this option, you must type an **R** at the command prompt "Specify distance to other axis or [Rotation]:". To understand how this command works, visualize a circle. As you turn the circle away from you the circle begins to take on the appearance of an ellipse to your eye. The shape is determined by the way you view the object. In the first two steps of the **Ellipse** command, enough information is provided to pick one axis. If you choose the **Rotation** option, AutoCAD assumes that the information given is for the major axis,

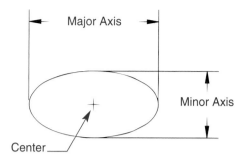

FIGURE 15.8 Components of an ellipse.

FIGURE 15.9 Axis, Endpoint option.

FIGURE 15.10 Ellipse rotation angles.

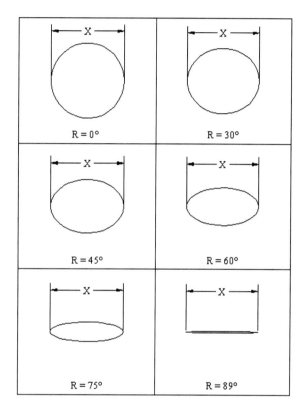

so at this point you have provided enough information to define a circle. Inputting a rotation angle will complete the information needed to define an ellipse. You tell AutoCAD how much to rotate the circle in order to construct the ellipse. A circle rotated 30° will create a 60° ellipse (see Figure 15.10).

Center Option

Another way to construct an ellipse with AutoCAD is to use the **Center** option. You can select this option from the menu that cascades next to Ellipse on the Draw pull-down menu. Otherwise, you will have to access this option by typing **C** at the command prompt "Specify axis endpoint of ellipse or [Arc/Center]:". AutoCAD will then ask you to Specify center of ellipse:. Once you have selected the center of your ellipse, you must specify the endpoint of one of the axes (see Figure 15.11). AutoCAD then asks for the distance to the other axis. You can input this value as a number or as a point location. As with the Axis, Endpoint option, you have the choice of choosing a rotation instead of a distance.

FIGURE 15.11 Center option for an ellipse.

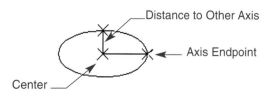

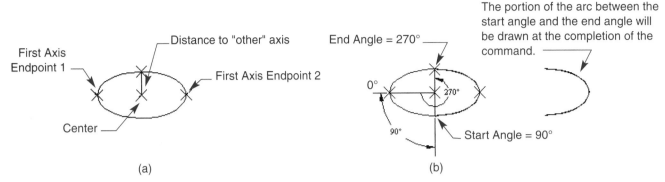

FIGURE 15.12   Selection point for elliptical arcs.

Elliptical Arcs

Just as a normal arc is a portion of a circle, an elliptical arc is a portion of an ellipse. You can access this command by choosing the **Arc** option once you enter the Ellipse command. The following is the command sequence:

Command: **ELLIPSE**
Specify axis endpoint of ellipse or [Arc/Center]: **A**
Specify axis endpoint of elliptical arc or [Center]: (Input the first axis endpoint.)
Specify other endpoint of axis: (Input the second axis endpoint.)
Specify distance to other axis or [Rotation]: (Input the distance for the second axis.)
Specify start angle or [Parameter]: (Input the start angle.)
Specify end angle or [Parameter/included angle]: (Input the end angle.)

If you access the command through the <u>D</u>raw pull-down menu, the sequence starts with the input of the first axis endpoint. Notice that this command as well as the next two follow a sequence almost identical with the Axis, Endpoint option for drawing an ellipse. This makes sense because at this point you are defining the ellipse which the arc will be part of. In fact, you will see the ellipse appear on the graphics screen, but do not worry because it is there only temporarily. Next, you will be asked for a start and an end angle. The part of the ellipse that is between these two angles is the part that will remain on the screen. Remember that these angles are not necessarily oriented like other angles in the program, with 0° being at due east. The start angle for an elliptical arc is oriented off the first endpoint of the first axis. A line between the center of the ellipse and the first endpoint of the first axis is considered to be at 0°. Angles are defined in a counterclockwise direction from there. Figure 15.12 shows an example of the selection points for an elliptical arc.

15.5 The Polyline Command

Pline
Icon

- Type **PLINE** or **PL** at the command prompt.
- Select <u>P</u>olyline from the <u>D</u>raw pull-down menu.
- Choose the Polyline icon from the Draw toolbar. The icon looks like a curved line with three dots placed along the line.

A polyline is basically a line with personality. A polyline can have width. In fact, the width can change over the course of a polyline. A polyline can even change direction. All segments of a polyline do not even have to be straight; arcs may be included. When you draw a line using the Line command, each segment of the line picks as a separate entity. When you select a polyline, all segments react as one unit. This comes in very handy when you begin editing your drawings.

When you first enter the **Pline** command, you will see a message at the command prompt that is very similar to the way the Line command begins. The message asks you to Specify start point:. You can specify this start point either by entering coordinates (relative or absolute) or by picking a point with your cursor. From then on the command prompt begins to look a little different. The first difference you will notice is a message telling you the Current line-width. The default value will be whatever value was used the last time the command was accessed, so the first time you invoke the Pline command, the default line width will be zero. The next line to appear at the command prompt should read Specify next point or [Arc/Close/Halfwidth/Length/Undo/Width]:. If you are happy with all the settings, you can just keep choosing point locations until your polyline is complete, then press Enter↵ to exit the command. If the linewidth is set at zero, the polyline will not look different from a series of lines drawn with the Line command. The difference will appear in editing the polyline.

If you want to draw something that does not look like a typical line, AutoCAD provides several options:

Specify next point or [Arc/Close/Halfwidth/Length/Undo/Width]:

Any of the options displayed within the square brackets can be selected by typing in either the complete word or the capitalized letter(s) of the option and then pressing Enter⤶. Two of the options should look familiar—**Close** and **Undo**. These two choices work just like they do for the Line command. If you draw a segment that you are unhappy with, choose Undo (while you are still in the Pline command), and the last segment you drew will be removed. You can repeat this option as many times as you want to until you reach the beginning of the polyline. If you have drawn two or more segments and wish to close the object to the first chosen point, you may select the Close option by typing either **Close** or **C.**

The **Width** and **Halfwidth** options allow you to specify the width you wish the next segment of your polyline to have. Once you select the Width option (type **Width** or **W** at the command prompt), you will be prompted to input a starting and an end width. The segment can start at one width and taper down or up to another. The default width will be shown in angle brackets. The default for the starting width will be whatever was used the last time the Pline command was accessed. If you change the starting width, the default for the ending width becomes the same number. Once you have input the desired widths, you are free to choose another option or select the next endpoint for the line segment. Be very aware of the information displayed at the command prompt; this will keep you from having to use the Undo command as often. The Halfwidth option works just like the Width option. The only difference is that instead of inputting the full width of the polyline, you input the width from the centerline of the polyline to one outside edge. Thus, choosing the Width option and specifying a width of 0.5 will give you the same result as selecting a Halfwidth of 0.25. It just depends of which input is easier to provide.

Choosing the **Arc** option provides for a departure from the straight-line segments you typically associate with a line. After you type in **Arc** or **A** and press Enter⤶, the command prompt will display the following message:

Specify endpoint of arc or
   [Angle/Center/CLose/Direction/Halfwidth/Line/Radius/Second pt./Undo/Width]:

The Close, Halfwidth, Undo, and Width are the same options you encountered in the straight-line part of the command. If you wish to go back to drawing straight lines, choose the Line option. The remaining options have to do with constructing the arc segment. (See Section 15.3 for a review of the components of an arc.) The **Angle** option (see Figure 15.13a) will prompt you to specify an included angle and then an endpoint. The command prompt for the **Center** option (see Figure 15.13b) will request the center and the endpoint of your arc. Inputting an arc segment with the **Radius** option (see Figure 15.13c) requires the radius of the arc and the endpoint of the arc. The **Second pt.** option (see Figure 15.13d) prompts you to enter a second point of your arc and then the endpoint. Remember that the AutoCAD default is to construct arcs in a counterclockwise direction. Thus, for example, a positive included angle will be oriented from the start point to the endpoint in a counterclockwise direction. A negative included angle will be oriented clockwise from the start point of the arc segment.

FIGURE 15.13 Drawing arc segments with the Pline command. (a) Angle option. (b) Center option. (c) Radius option. (d) Second pt. option.

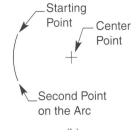
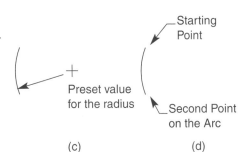

(a)
Angle option: This option in the pline arc sequence lets the user specify the included angle that forms the arc.

(b)
Center option: This option in the pline arc sequence lets the user specify the center point of the arc after supplying a starting point. A second point is needed to complete the arc sequence.

(c)
Radius option: This option presets the value of the arc's radius automatically.

(d)
Second pt. option: This option allows the user to simply pick the point where the arc will end.

Use the **Length** option to input a distance rather than a set of coordinates for the next point on the polyline. The next segment of the polyline will be drawn at the specified length at the same angle as the previous polyline segment. If the previous segment was an arc, the new segment will be drawn as a straight-line tangent to the arc.

Example.   Using the Polyline command (Figure 15.14)

Command: **pline**
Specify start point: (Pick a point.)
Current line-width is **0'-0"**
Specify next point or [Arc/Close/Halfwidth/Length/Undo/Width]: **@1"<270**↵
Specify next point or [Arc/Close/Halfwidth/Length/Undo/Width]: **W.**↵
Specify starting width <0'-0">: **0.125"** ↵
Specify ending width <0'-0 1/8">: **0.**↵
Specify next point or [Arc/Close/Halfwidth/Length/Undo/Width]: **@0.5"<270** ↵
Specify next point or [Arc/Close/Halfwidth/Length/Undo/Width]: **W.**↵
Specify starting width <0'-0">: **0.**↵
Specify ending width <0'-0">: **0.**↵
Specify next point or [Arc/Close/Halfwidth/Length/Undo/Width]: **@0.5"<270.**↵
Specify next point or [Arc/Close/Halfwidth/Length/Undo/Width]: **A.**↵
Angle/CEnter/CLose/Direction/Halfwidth/Line/Radius/Second pt/Undo/Width: **A.**↵
Specify included angle: **90.**↵
Specify endpoint of arc or [Center/Radius]: (Pick a point.)
Specify endpoint of arc or
   [Angle/CEnter/CLose/Direction/Halfwidth/Line/Radius/Second pt/Undo/Width]: **L.**↵
Specify next point or [Arc/Close/Halfwidth/Length/Undo/Width]: **W.**↵
Specify starting width <0'-0">: **0.**↵
Specify ending width <0'-0 ">: **0.25"** ↵
Specify next point or [Arc/Close/Halfwidth/Length/Undo/Width]: **@.25"<0.**↵
Specify next point or [Arc/Close/Halfwidth/Length/Undo/Width]: **@0.5"<0.**↵
Specify next point or [Arc/Close/Halfwidth/Length/Undo/Width]: **W.**↵
Specify starting width <0'-0 ¼">: **.**↵
Specify ending width <0'-0">: **0.**↵
Specify next point or [Arc/Close/Halfwidth/Length/Undo/Width]: **@0.25"<0.**↵
Specify next point or [Arc/Close/Halfwidth/Length/Undo/Width]: **@0.5"<0.**↵
Specify next point or [Arc/Close/Halfwidth/Length/Undo/Width]: **A.**↵
Angle/Center/Close/Direction/Halfwidth/Line/Radius/Second pt/Undo/Width: (Pick
   endpoint.)
Angle/Center/Close/Direction/Halfwidth/Line/Radius/Second pt/Undo/Width: **L.**↵
Specify next point or [Arc/Close/Halfwidth/Length/Undo/Width]: **@0.25"<90.**↵
Specify next point or [Arc/Close/Halfwidth/Length/Undo/Width]: **W.**↵
Specify starting width <0'-0">: **0.125"** ↵
Specify ending width <0'-0 ⅛">: **.**↵
Specify next point or [Arc/Close/Halfwidth/Length/Undo/Width]: **@0.5"<90.**↵
Specify next point or [Arc/Close/Halfwidth/Length/Undo/Width]: **W.**↵
Specify starting width <0'-0 ⅛">: **0.0.**↵
Specify ending width <0'-0">: **.**↵
Specify next point or [Arc/Close/Halfwidth/Length/Undo/Width]: **CL.**↵

FIGURE 15.14

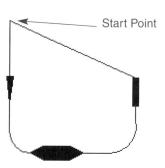

Start Point

Editing Polylines

PEDIT is a special command used to edit polylines only. It also has the power to change lines into polylines, which allows the **PEDIT** command to be used on those converted lines.

Use the following command sequence to edit a pline:

- Type **PEDIT** or **PE** at the command prompt.
- Select Polyline from the <u>M</u>odify pull-down menu.
- Choose the PEDIT icon from the Modify II toolbar.

PEDIT
Icon

When you enter the command, you will be prompted to select a polyline:

Command: PE↵
PEDIT Select polyline:

You may choose only one polyline at a time with the pick box during this process. Once you have selected a polyline, the command line displays the suboptions of the PEDIT command:

Enter an option [Close/Join/Width/Edit vertex/Fit/Spline/Decurve/Ltype gen/Undo]:

The different suboptions perform the following tasks:

- **Close**: If an object made of polylines is open, then this suboption will draw a polyline from the first point drawn with the **PLINE** command to the last point drawn, closing the shape and forming a polygon (see Figure 15.15).
- **Join:** This suboption is used to join polylines together so they act as one object. This means that after a group of polylines is joined together they must be treated as one object. If you try to erase one polyline, they will all disappear because the first polyline has been joined to the others (see Figure 15.18a).
- **Width:** This option is used to edit a polyline's width. Type in the desired thickness (see Figure 15.16).
- **Edit Vertex**: This suboption allows the relocation of the polyline endpoint as well as some other vertex-related functions (see Figure 15.17).

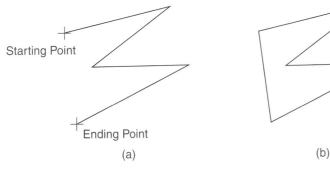

Starting Point

Ending Point

(a)   (b)

FIGURE 15.15 (a) A group of polylines. (b) The same group of polylines edited with the Close suboption of PEDIT.

FIGURE 15.16 A polyline whose width has been increased with the Width suboption of the PEDIT command.

FIGURE 15.17 (a) A group of joined polylines. (b) The same group of joined polylines with the right outside corners moved in with the Vertex suboption of PEDIT.

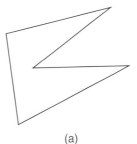

(a)   (b)

FIGURE 15.18 (a) A group of joined polylines. (b) The same group of polylines with the Fit suboption of PEDIT applied. (c) The same group of polylines as in (a) with the Spline suboption of PEDIT applied.

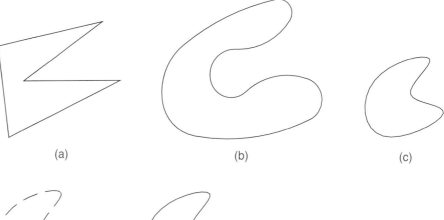

(a) (b) (c)

FIGURE 15.19 (a) A Spline curve with Ltype gen turned on. (b) The same curve with Ltype gen turned off.

(a) (b)

- **Fit**: This suboption is used to change a polyline from a straight line into a curved line passing through the original endpoints (see Figure 15.18b).
- **Spline**: The spline suboption provides a smoother curve than the Fit option. The curve does not pass through the original endpoints of the polyline, so its shape is not restricted (see Figure 15.18c).
- **Decurve**: The Decurve option removes the curves on polylines that were constructed with the Fit or the Spline suboption.
- **Ltype gen**: Ellipses and hidden-line curves constructed with polyline suboptions such as Fit or Spline sometimes have a problem displaying the hidden linetypes around the curves. Ltype gen is a switch that when turned on helps display the gaps better when linetypes with spaces in between such as hidden, phantom, and centerlines are used (see Figure 15.19).
- **Undo**: This option takes back the previous PEDIT suboptions used while inside that command sequence.

Converting a Line into a Polyline

To change a line into a polyline, you must use the PEDIT command. Follow the same command sequence.

Command: **PE↵**
PEDIT Select Polyline: (Touch the line with the pick box.)

When you select the line, AutoCAD recognizes that it is not a polyline, and the following is shown at the command prompt.

Object selected is not a polyline
Do you want to turn it into one? <Y>

Ener Y at the command prompt for yes, and the line is converted into a polyline. You can then use the PEDIT command to edit the former line.

15.6 The Donut Command

- Type **DONUT** (or **DOUGHNUT**) or **DO** at the command prompt.
- Select Donut from the Draw pull-down menu.

The **Donut** command creates objects shaped like a doughnut. A Donut is actually constructed of two polyline arcs of a given width. Once you enter the command, you will be asked to Specify inside diameter of donut <current >:. Then you need to Specify outside diameter of donut <current >: (see Figure 15.20). Once

FIGURE 15.20 Components of a Donut.

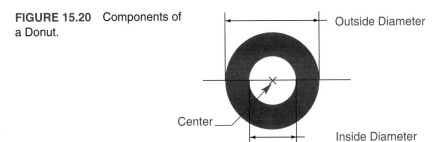

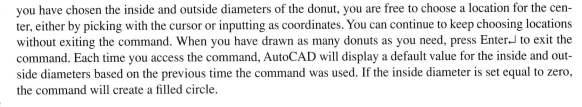

Note: The **Fill** command determines the way AutoCAD fills the body of the donut. In a large job, a solid fill may cause the regeneration of a drawing to slow. In addition, solid fill uses more ink. You may want to temporarily change the **Fill** setting during the preliminary stages of the drawing and have it solid only for the final output.

you have chosen the inside and outside diameters of the donut, you are free to choose a location for the center, either by picking with the cursor or inputting as coordinates. You can continue to keep choosing locations without exiting the command. When you have drawn as many donuts as you need, press Enter↵ to exit the command. Each time you access the command, AutoCAD will display a default value for the inside and outside diameters based on the previous time the command was used. If the inside diameter is set equal to zero, the command will create a filled circle.

15.7 The Rectangle Command

- Type **RECTANGLE** or **rec** at the command prompt.
- Select Rectangle from the Draw pull-down menu.
- Choose the Rectangle icon from the Draw toolbar. The icon looks like a rectangle with a dot shown on opposite corners.

Rectangle Icon

Drawing with the rectangle command is extremely simple. All you have to do is specify two points on opposite corners of the rectangle from each other, either by picking with the cursor or specifying by coordinates.

A figure constructed with the Rectangle command is considered to be a polygon made from polylines. As such it can be edited with PEDIT. You can also construct a rectangle with chamfers, fillets, width, and several 3-D options.

REVIEW QUESTIONS

1. What are two ways to indicate the location of the center of a circle in AutoCAD? Must you know the location of the center in order to construct a circle?

2. If you have just finished drawing a circle, either of two keys will provide a quick shortcut back to the Circle command. Name these two keys.

3. What command should you use to draw a triangle?

4. Which would be larger—a polygon circumscribed or inscribed around a circle of the same diameter?

5. What information does AutoCAD require in order to construct a polygon?

6. Other than by selecting the Continue option, how could you continue an arc from the endpoint of a previously drawn line or arc?

7. Would you use the Arc, Ellipse, or Polygon command to draw an elliptical arc?

8. Discuss the differences between an object drawn with the Line command and an object drawn with the Polyline command.

9. What happens if you set the inside diameter of a Donut to zero?

10. List two commands that can be used to draw a square.

11. Other than the Polyline command, list three commands that draw objects using polylines.

12. Can an object drawn with the Line command be edited with the PEDIT command?

13. What command should be used to fillet a polyline?

14. Which of the PEDIT options allows you to change the width of various segments within a polyline?

15. What command would be used to create smooth curves that pass through the vertices of a polyline?

EXERCISES

EXERCISE 15.1
Draw the shapes in Figure 15.21 at full scale.

EXERCISE 15.2
Create two rugs using patterns consisting of two geometric shapes, one rectangular and the other elliptical.

EXERCISE 15.3
Create an elevation of a fireplace with a mantle. Use two geometric shapes in the design.

EXERCISE 15.4
Using the Line and Arc commands, draw the wood stud shading pattern in Figure 15.22 in plan view.

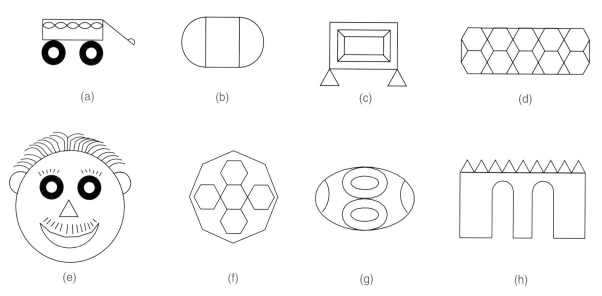

FIGURE 15.21   Exercise 15.1.

FIGURE 15.22   Exercise 15.4.
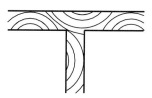

DRAWING ASSIGNMENTS

1. Draw the figures in 15.23 using full scale.
2. Draw the figures in 15.24 at a scale of $2'' = 1''$. Set your limits so you can plot on an $11'' \times 17''$ sheet size.

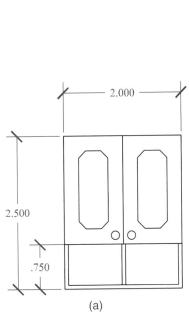

(a)
Choose any dimensions that are
not given and custom-design the
rest of the cabinet

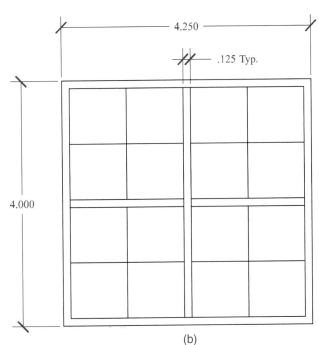

(b)
Divide the window into four equal sections and
then divide the glass into four equal sections.

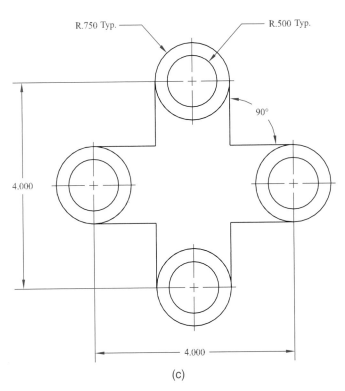

(c)

FIGURE 15.23 Drawing Assignment 1.
continued on next page

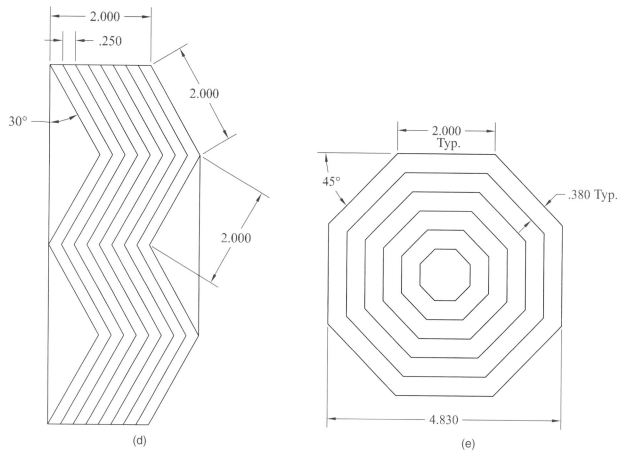

(d)

(e)

FIGURE 15.23   *continued*

FIGURE 15.24 Drawing Assignment 2.

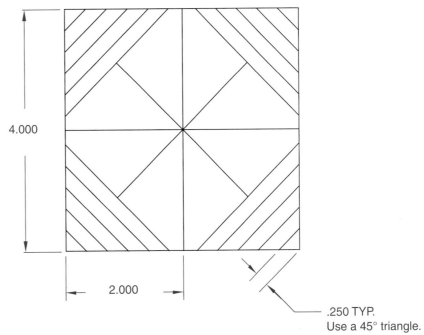

4.000

2.000

.250 TYP.
Use a 45° triangle.

CHAPTER 16

Drawing Aids

Drawing quickly and accurately are skills a CAD operator must develop. AutoCAD provides many tools to speed up drawing time and make a drawing as precise as a calculator. Drafting on a drawing board quickly and accurately was a developed skill. All the manual equipment had human limitations built into them. Drawing with small scales and laying out construction lines with parallel bars and triangles to find intersections and corners always included some amount of error. This was accepted on the drawing board but now has been corrected using CAD software such as AutoCAD.

The terms *drawing aids* and *tools* have been used in AutoCAD for a long time. Mastering these commands and settings will increase your drawing speed and accuracy almost automatically.

The following commands will be covered in this chapter:

ORTHO

GRID

SNAP

POLAR Tracking

OSNAP (Object Snap)

- Orthogonal or **ORTHO** controls vertical and horizontal alignment or 90° features. When this command is turned on, lines or objects can be drawn in a vertical or horizontal arrangement (see Figure 16.1). The ORTHO command restricts drawing and editing commands to function only in 90°or 270° (vertical) and 0° or 180° (horizontal) directions.

- The **GRID** command places small dots on the drawing screen as a guide to layout and drawing.

- The **SNAP** command gives the CAD operator the ability to move along and in between grids to precise increments.

- **POLAR Tracking** allows the user to see preset angles along with a distance in an on-screen text display. It is like an angle guidance system; however, it does not restrict you to drawing only with the preset angle.

- **OSNAP,** or **Object Snap,** gives the AutoCAD operator the ability to lock onto or grab parts of a drawing based on its geometry, such as endpoints and the midpoint of shapes.

FIGURE 16.1 The Ortho option will allow commands to work only in the directions shown.

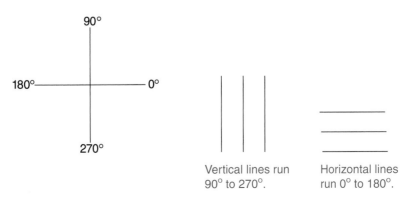

Vertical lines run 90° to 270°.

Horizontal lines run 0° to 180°.

16.1   The ORTHO Command

A great many lines in architectural drawing are drawn vertically or horizontally. The ORTHO command forces the software to draw in this mode. The only angles that are allowed to be used when ORTHO is turned on are 0°, 90°, 180°, and 270°. The **ORTHO** command is simple to set since it is an on or off setting found on the status bar at the base of the AutoCAD screen (see Figure 16.2).

Locating the ORTHO Command

There are several quick routes for turning ORTHO on and off.

- The F8 function key in the top row of the keyboard will toggle or switch ORTHO on and off. Just press it and watch the command line display whether it is on or off.
- The ORTHO on-screen button is at the bottom middle of the AutoCAD graphics window (see Figure 16.3).
- When the ORTHO command is turned on, the ORTHO button displays a line on the left side and top of the button giving the impression that the button is pushed in (see Figure 16.4). The Off position does not show these lines highlighted (see Figure 16.5).
- Type **ORTHO** at the command prompt.

Command: **ORTHO** ⏎
Enter mode [ON/OFF]: *(Type in **On** or **Off**, then press the Enter ⏎ key.)*

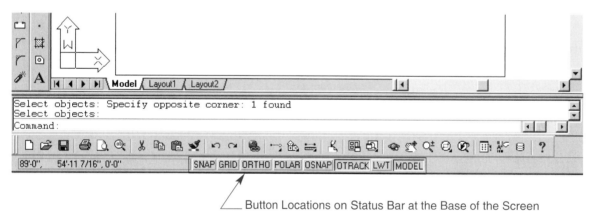

Button Locations on Status Bar at the Base of the Screen

FIGURE 16.2   Location of the ORTHO button on the AutoCAD status bar.

Lines indicate that the button in turned on.

The button is turned off.

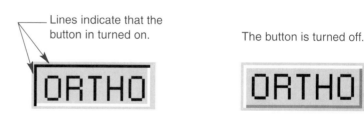

FIGURE 16.3   The status bar buttons.

FIGURE 16.4   ORTHO button on

FIGURE 16.5   ORTHO button off.

Note: Figure 16.6 is a good example of the rubber band effect on lines. It gives you a visual look at the path of the line before the final endpoint is selected.

FIGURE 16.6 Moving the cursor with ORTHO off.

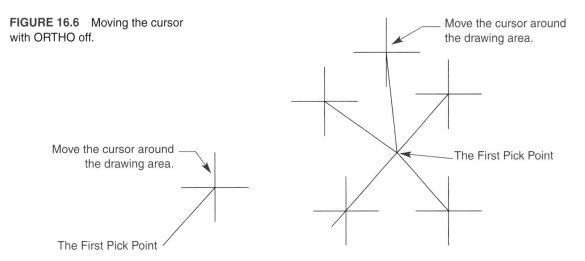

Move the cursor around the drawing area.

The First Pick Point

Move the cursor around the drawing area.

The First Pick Point

Example: Using the ORTHO Command

To see the direct effect of drawing with the ORTHO command, let's take a look at using the Line command with ORTHO turned off and then on.

Command: **LINE** ↵
LINE Specify first point: *(Left-click anywhere in the middle of the screen.)*

Now move the cursor around in a circular pattern. Notice that the line follows the cursor around wherever it goes (see Figure 16.6). Left-click to draw the line at any angle. The Off option allows lines to be drawn with the pick point method at any angle to which the cursor is moved.

Now let's set the ORTHO command to the On position and try the same thing using the Line command. Take a look at the screen while dragging the cursor around. Only vertical and horizontal lines appear, and when the second point is selected for the end of a line, what is drawn is vertical or horizontal (see Figure 16.7).

Obviously there are times when the ORTHO setting needs to be alternated between the On and Off options. If you need to draw lines at different angles other than vertical or horizontal turn it off. Note that you can turn it on or off in the middle of the Line command or other commands. If you are drawing only horizontal and vertical lines then leave ORTHO on (see Figure 16.8). The Grid and Snap Commands do have some control over Ortho. Their settings will determine how far the cursor needs to be moved before a line will change from the vertical direction to the horizontal.

Note: Watch the line follow the cursor movement when in the Ortho mode. Snap and Grid settings may be too restrictive for your needs so do not hesitate to turn them off.

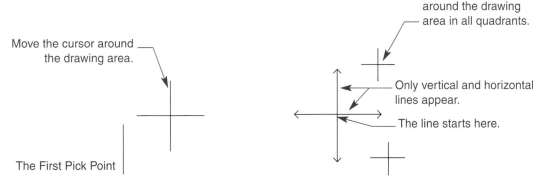

Move the cursor around the drawing area.

The First Pick Point

Move the cursor around the drawing area in all quadrants.

Only vertical and horizontal lines appear.

The line starts here.

FIGURE 16.7 Moving the cursor with ORTHO on.

FIGURE 16.8 Drawing with ORTHO on and off.

Turn ORTHO off to draw angles that are not vertical or horizontal.

Turn ORTHO on to draw vertical and horizontal lines.

Direct Distance

The ORTHO command must be turned on when using the **direct distance** method for drawing horizontal and vertical lines. Simply turn ORTHO on, then select the Line command. Pick the first or starting point, then pull the cursor in the direction the line should go. Then, instead of picking with the mouse or using another entry method, type in the distance needed at the command line and press Enter↵.

Some of the other commands that you will learn later such as Move and Copy can be used with OR-THO and direct distance as well.

16.2   The GRID Command

Setting up a grid as a drawing guide can be helpful when you are first learning how to use AutoCAD to draw lines. The grid will appear as a pattern of dots and will be located within the drawing limits. The grid dots can be switched on and off just like the ORTHO command. The grid dots will not print out. The grid dots are for laying out drawings and are not supposed to show up on the printout.

Locating the GRID Command

The **GRID** command is used to display a pattern of dots on the drawing screen.

- Type **GRID** at the command prompt.
- Under the Tools pull-down menu is a Drafting Settings option (see Figure 16.9). Just left-click on it, and the Drafting Settings dialog box will appear (see Figure 16.10).

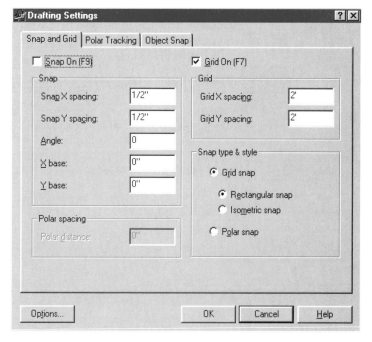

FIGURE 16.9 Drafting Settings option selected on the Tools pull-down menu.

FIGURE 16.10 Drafting Settings dialog box.

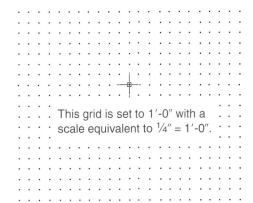

This grid is set to 1'-0" with a scale equivalent to ¼" = 1'-0".

FIGURE 16.11 GRID pop-up menu.

FIGURE 16.12 Grid spacing.

- The GRID button is found to the left of the ORTHO button on the status bar at the base of the Auto-CAD graphics area (see Figure 16.2).

To open the dialog box, right-click with the mouse cursor arrow on top of the GRID button. Left-click on Settings in the pop-up menu and the Drafting Settings box will appear (see Figure 16.11). Left-click on the Snap and Grid tab in the upper left corner of the dialog box. The Grid settings will appear on the upper right side. Left-click in the Grid X spacing and Y spacing boxes and type in the desired grid spacing (see Figure 16.12). The grid spacing will vary depending on the limits and drawing scale. One problem that occurs occasionally is that the grid spacing is too close together. When this occurs, a message, *Grid too dense to display,* will come up on the command line, and the grid will not show. When this happens, increase the spacing distance until the grid displays.

Turning the GRID On and Off

The GRID screen button can be turned on and off by left-clicking on it. The F7 function key on the top row of the keyboard will also toggle the GRID on and off. There are other ways to perform this function, but these two are the fastest methods.

16.3 The SNAP Command

The SNAP command works well with the GRID command. SNAP gives you the ability to move the cursor inside the grid pattern in precise increments. For instance, if a grid pattern is set to a 1' spacing, then the snap can be set to a 6" increment. This will cause the cursor to snap on the nearest 6" increment as it moves across the grid, falling on the grid dots and halfway points (6") between them (see Figure 16.13). This can be helpful if most of the lines being drawn are in 6" divisions. If there were a lot of lines ending in 3" increments, for example, then the snap could be set to 3". The SNAP and GRID can be reset to different spacing in a drawing at any time.

Locating the SNAP Command

- Type **SNAP** at the command prompt.
- Select the Drafting Settings option under the Tools pull-down menu.

FIGURE 16.13 Using Snap with Grid.

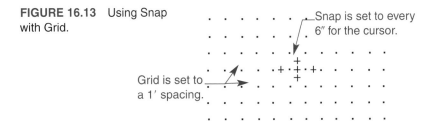

Snap is set to every 6" for the cursor.

Grid is set to a 1' spacing.

FIGURE 16.14 SNAP pop-up menu.

- Select the on-screen SNAP button on the status bar at the base of the drawing area. A right-click on the SNAP button will pop up a small menu (see Figure 16.14). A left-click on Settings will open the Drafting Setting dialog box (see Figure 16.10). Once the dialog box is open, the Snap setting can be adjusted to the drawing needs.

Adjusting the Snap Settings

There are quite a few Snap settings in the Drafting Setting dialog box. Left-click on the Snap and Grid tab to find the Snap adjustments. Two areas are used to create Snap settings, Snap X spacing: and Snap Y spacing (see Figure 16.15), and Snap type and style (see Figure 16.16).

The Snap X and Snap Y settings control the movement of the snap increments in the X-direction (left to right) and the Y-direction (top to bottom). Just left-click in the box and type in the snap increments desired. When you select OK at the bottom of the Drafting Settings dialog box, the snap setting will take effect.

The Angle: snap setting will rotate the grid and the snap to the angle typed in at the box. Angle can be useful for drawing shapes turned or rotated at different angles (see Figure 16.17 with a 45° angle setting). Note that the X and Y grid and snap now work along this angle or rotation setting along with the ORTHO command. To change back to a 0 angle, replace the 45° angle with a 0. The grid returns to a rectangular alignment.

The X base and Y base settings control the origin of the grid and snap. Changing these settings repositions the grid and snap or shifts them to a new origin.

Settings in the Snap type and style area control the directional movement of the snap. For example, when the Grid snap radio button is selected along with the Rectangular snap, the snap moves along the rectangular shape of the grid (see Figure 16.18). If the Isometric radio button is selected, the snap changes from the X and Y rectangular pattern to the Iso snap mode. The grip and snap now are aligned to draw in an isometric drawing format. ORTHO will also work with this iso snap setting when turned on. After activating the Isometric snap and ORTHO modes, try drawing a line. Watch how the line moves as you move the cursor to pick a second point to complete the line. The cursor is limited to drawing only lines that fall along the isometric drawing format. Lines can be drawn only along iso axes set at 30°, 90°, 150°, 210°, 270°, and 330°

FIGURE 16.15 Snap and Grid tab options from Drafting Settings dialog box.

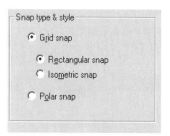

FIGURE 16.16 Snap type and style options from Drafting Settings dialog box.

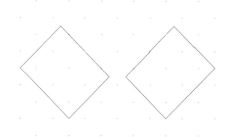

FIGURE 16.17 Using Angle snap.

FIGURE 16.18 Using Rectangular snap.

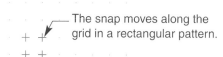

The snap moves along the grid in a rectangular pattern.

FIGURE 16.19 Using Isometric snap with ORTHO on.

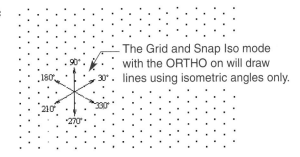

The Grid and Snap Iso mode with the ORTHO on will draw lines using isometric angles only.

(see Figure 16.19). To change directions along the iso axes with the SNAP on, use the F5 function key or hold down the Ctrl key and the E key on the keyboard. Doing this will let you draw to all the iso axes. These settings can speed up isometric drawing tremendously. When it is time to draw a nonisometric line, just turn SNAP off.

Another valuable feature of the Isometric Snap is that when it is turned on the Ellipse command will display an Isocircle option. It is located in the Draw pull-down menu as an option in the cascade menu under Ellipse (see Figure 16.20). The Isocircle option is in the Axis, End selection. After left-clicking on the Axis, End option, look down at the command line. The command line will list the options in brackets [Arc/Center/Isocircle]. Type **I** and press the Enter↵ key to select the Isocircle option. Then you will be requested to pick a center. Use a left click or type in X and Y coordinates. Now, roll the mouse to drag out the ellipse. A defaulted radius size is set at the command line. Just type in the radius size or type a **D** for diameter, then specify a diameter value. Another choice is to use the cursor to drag and left-click to draw the isocircle. Note the direction in which the isocircle is heading. It can be drawn in a horizontal position, left vertical, or a right vertical. Press **F5** to change the ellipse alignment before you select the diameter of the isocircle. Keep pressing **F5** until it falls on the correct isosurface, then type in the diameter value (see Figure 16.21).

The final option in the Snap type and style box is the Polar snap. Instead of using X and Y rectangular values as snaps, polar snap measures the snap distance along an angle. The Polar distance can be set in the box to the immediate left of Polar snap. The values will be displayed in the form Distance < Angle (Example: $2' < 30°$).

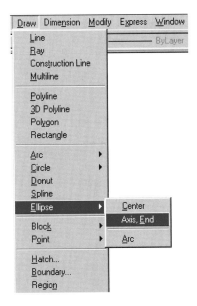

FIGURE 16.20 Ellipse, Axis End selected on the Draw pull-down menu.

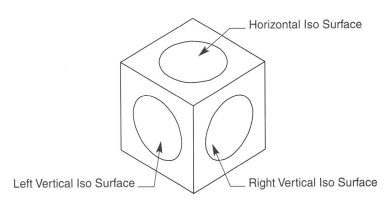

FIGURE 16.21 Iso surfaces.

FIGURE 16.22   Using polar snap.

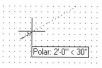

Example: Using Polar Snap

To see the effect of this setting, turn the Polar snap on and set a polar distance (see Figure 16.22). In our example, we used a 2′ distance at a ¼″ = 1′-0″ scale. The increment angle is set to 30°. Once these are set use the Line command.

> Command: **LINE** ⏎
> LINE Specify first point: *(Pick any point.)*

Now, drag the cursor around the screen and click the **F10** function key (Polar Tracking On/Off switch), turning it to the On position. Look at the command line for the ON/OFF prompt to see when it comes on. While dragging the cursor around watch the polar snap values pop up on the screen when the increments are reached (see Figure 16.22). Every time a coordinate is found while dragging the cursor around, the display pops up to let you know the polar value.

The SNAP command works hand in hand with the GRID command and is turned on and off just as easily as the grid. A left-click on the SNAP screen button on the status bar at the bottom center of the AutoCAD graphics screen turns the snap option on and off. The F9 function key also turns SNAP on and off.

In the beginning most students learn to use grids and snaps with most of their drawings. As a student progresses through AutoCAD and becomes more confident grids and snaps play a less prominent role in drawing.

16.4   Polar Tracking

■ The Polar Tracking settings are found in the Drafting Settings dialog box, which, as shown previously, can be accessed through the Tools pull-down menu.

■ A POLAR on-screen button is also located in the bottom center of the AutoCAD graphics screen to the right of the ORTHO button. Right-click on the POLAR button, then left-click on the Settings option. Left-clicking on the Polar Tracking tab in the Drafting Settings dialog box displays the screen shown in Figure 16.23. In the upper left corner is an On/Off switch for Polar Tracking. A left-click in the check box will turn it on and off from this dialog display.

In AutoCAD, polar is a designation for a distance value at a given angle. In the Line command when you used the Polar method, points were entered in the format (@Distance < Angle). Polar tracking works similarly to the Ortho option, but any angle increment can be set as a guide, not just 90° increments.

The Polar Angle Settings area is used to set up the tracking angle needed. The Increment angle: box lists some of the more commonly used angles. Left-click on the down arrow and scan through the selections. Angles are in degrees and can be set to the following selections: 5, 10, 15, 18, 22.5, 30, 45, and 90. Left-click on the angle needed to select it, and it appears in the Increment angle: box.

If the Additional angles box is checked, then more angles can be added to the Increment angles. First, left-click on the New button and then type in the extra angle to be displayed. Use the New button to set more angles if needed. When the settings are in place, left-click on the OK button, and the angles will be seen in the polar display box (see Figure 16.24, where an additional angle of 33° was added).

There are two selections in the Object Snap Tracking Settings area. Object Snaps will be covered in more depth later on in this chapter, but we mention these two choices here. Basically, Object Snaps lock on to a wide variety of preset points such as endpoints of lines and tangents of circles. The tracking can be set to display the orthogonal only (90° angles) object snap tracking or the polar tracking, which tracks along preset polar angles.

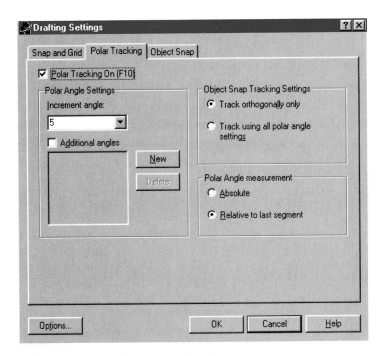

FIGURE 16.23 Polar Tracking tab options.

FIGURE 16.24 Polar with additional angle of 33°.

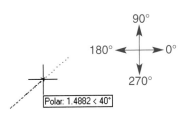

FIGURE 16.25 Measuring with Absolute polar. Absolute always references 0° to the right.

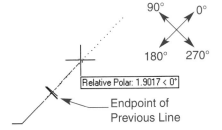

FIGURE 16.26 Measuring with Relative polar. It refers to the last drawn line for its new 0° reference.

FIGURE 16.27 Setting angle increment value.

Tip: If you want the angle to measure every degree, left-click on the Polar Tracking tab. Highlight the angle in the Increment angle box, and then type **1** to make the tracking read every single degree increment (see Figure 16.27). Many CAD operators prefer this setting.

Finally, the Polar Angle measurement area controls the reference for the polar angle. The Absolute setting will use the current 0,0 location as a base for measuring angles (see Figure 16.25). A Relative to last segment setting will use the last segment drawn as the base 0,0 point (see Figure 16.26). This means that every time a new line is drawn, the 0 angle will move to the endpoint of the last segment drawn. Polar tracking is essentially a visual guidance system that gives the distance and angle readout before the line is drawn. It can be used very effectively on a drawing with a wide range of angled lines.

16.5 OSNAP (Object Snap)

One of the most valuable drawing tools is the Object Snap. Using the Object Snap is an exact method of grabbing and locking in on points that would be difficult to find using any other method in AutoCAD. You no longer have to rely on the precision of your hand to pick endpoints of a line. Always use OSNAP whenever possible. Being a beginner does not excuse anyone from not using them. The Object Snaps can lock in on the following:

- Endpoints of lines and objects
- Midpoints of lines
- Centers of circles
- Nodes, which are points placed on a drawing with some of these options: Point, Measure, or Divide commands

- Quadrants of circles and ellipses (points at 0, 90, 180, and 270°)
- Intersections of lines and objects
- Extension will lock on the end of a line and float an extension with the cursor
- Insertion snaps to a predetermined insert point on any number of objects
- Perpendicular snaps 90° to a selected object or line
- Tangents of circles and arcs
- Nearest will snap to the first part of the object identified
- Apparent Intersection will lock in on where two lines that almost touch would intersect if they were extended to touch
- Parallel snap will draw a line parallel to an existing line

These are the basic explanations of what the Object Snaps can do. They will be easier to understand when examples are shown a little later on.

Object Snaps can be used in one of two ways. They can be activated manually each time they are needed, but it can be time consuming to have to activate an Osnap in the middle of a command. If an automatic setting is desired, then a Running Osnap can be set. When this is turned on, every time the cursor moves and encounters an Osnap condition, it automatically highlights it with a symbol. A left click will choose the highlighted Osnap. To override a current Running Osnap setting one time, simply manually pick the Osnap you desire to use, and it will supercede the running Osnap.

Turning on all the object snaps may seem like a good idea, but sometimes it provides too many options for a condition, and it will take a little time to separate out the correct one. As a general rule, look over your drawing and turn on the Running Osnaps that will be used frequently. The Running Osnaps are great to use. It takes just a little while to get used to them and how they work.

Setting OSNAPS

- Hold down the Shift key and right-click to display a list of OSNAPS (see Figure 16.28). Left-click on the desired selection and complete the command you are in.
- In the View pull-down menu left-click on the Toolbars... option to turn on an Osnap toolbar (see Figure 16.29). Scroll through the Toolbars options using the arrows on the right. Left-click on the box to the left of the Object Snap option (see Figure 16.30). The Object Snap toolbar will be displayed on the drawing screen (see Figure 16.31). When you lay the cursor arrow on top of an icon, a caption will appear identifying the symbol (see Figure 16.32). Left-click on the symbol to select the option.

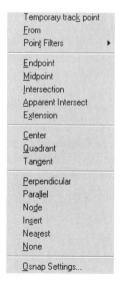

FIGURE 16.28 List of Osnaps.

FIGURE 16.29 Toolbars selected on the View pull-down menu.

FIGURE 16.30 Toolbars dialog box.

FIGURE 16.31 Object Snap toolbar.

FIGURE 16.32 Intersection icon with caption.

■ Type **OSNAP** at the command prompt (OSNAP can also be set with a transparent command). Remember that Osnaps work while in a command. For instance, if a line had to be drawn from the endpoint of an object to the endpoint of a different object, the following sequence would be used:

Command: **LINE** ↵
LINE Specify first point: *(Select the Osnap Endpoint.)*

Touch near the object's endpoint and watch the yellow endpoint box light up when it is located, then left-click. The command line will now read:

Specify next point or [Undo]: *(Select the Osnap Endpoint again.)*

Touch near the endpoint of the second object, and when the yellow box is highlighted, left-click to select it.

A less preferred method of entering Osnaps is at the command line. The following abbreviations for each Osnap can be entered at the keyboard to activate it. The first three letters are used.

Osnap's Abbreviations

FRO—From a referenced base point

END—Endpoints of lines

MID—Midpoints of lines

INT—Intersections of lines

EXT—Extensions of lines

APP—Apparent intersections of lines

CEN—Centers of circles

NOD—Nodes generated by Point, Divide, and Measure

QUA—Quadrants of circles

INS—Insertion points from Block or other objects

PER—Perpendicular to a line or object

TAN—Tangent to circle, arc, or ellipse

NEA—Nearest grabs first point it sees

PAR—Parallel snaps to a line and then creates a parallel path for the line currently being drawn

Even when using the on-screen methods for activating Osnaps, look at the command line to make sure the correct selection was made.

Turning On the Running Osnaps

Running Osnaps are quickly accessed through the Drafting Settings dialog box. As shown earlier in this chapter, the Drafting Settings dialog box can be opened up using the Tools pull-down menu and left-clicking on Drafting Settings. Another quick way to get to the Drafting Settings dialog box is to go to the bottom center of the graphics area and right-click on the OSNAP button, then left-click on the Setting option that pops up (see Figure 16.33). Notice the alignment of the screen. The symbol that will appear in the drawing area when selected is on the left. The small check box in the middle is where you left-click to turn the Osnaps on and off. Study the symbols carefully. They are your on-screen aids for verifying that you are selecting correctly.

Also in this dialog box is a Select All button, which will turn on all the Osnaps. The Clear All button will turn all the Osnaps off. Try these buttons and watch for the checks to appear in the small squares.

FIGURE 16.33   Object Snap
tab options.

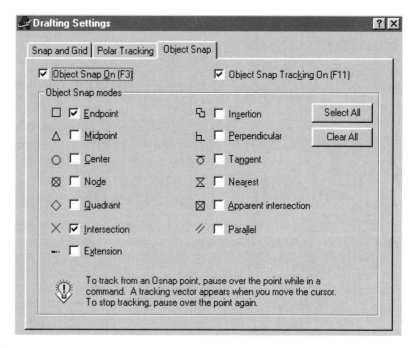

Turning Osnaps On and Off as a Group

Osnaps are needed the most when you are drawing lines with the pick point method. The other methods such as Polar, Relation, Absolute, and Direct Distance already have values inserted to complete the line. Conflicts will occur with these methods, so AutoCAD has some quick and easy switches for turning the Running Osnap mode on and off.

- F3 function key
- Left-click on the OSNAP button at the bottom of the graphics area
- Right-click on the OSNAP button, then left-click on the On or Off display

These are quick ways to toggle back and forth between different methods of drawing. Try each to see which one is easiest for you.

Using Osnaps on a Drawing

Osnaps start to work when a command has been requested such as Line or Circle. Here are some examples of each Osnap.

Example: From

In this example a 4″ rectangle has already been drawn (see Figure 16.34). Another rectangle needs to be drawn inside the existing one precisely .25 in all directions. The From Osnap works well in this case. Before starting, turn on the Intersection Running Osnap.

> Command: **REC**↵
> Specify first corner point or [Chamfer/Elevation/Fillet/Thickened Width]:
>   **FRO**
> Base point: *(Move the cursor to the lower left corner and click when the*
>   *intersection symbol appears (see Figure 16.35)).*
> Base point: <Offset>: **@.25, .25**
> Specify other corner point: **FRO**
> Specify other corner point: from Base point: *(Click on the intersection of*
>   *the upper right corner (see Figure 16.36)).*
> Specify other corner point: from Base point: <Offset>: **@-.25,-.25** *(See*
>   *Figure 16.37.)*

The end result should show a perfectly centered rectangle inside the 4″ rectangle.

FIGURE 16.34

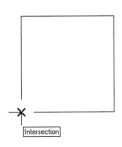

FIGURE 16.35

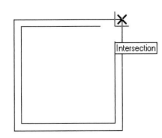

FIGURE 16.36

FIGURE 16.37 Completed rectangle.

Example: Endpoint Osnap

In this example two lines have already been drawn, and we have started the Line command to draw another line across two of the endpoints of the existing lines (see Figure 16.38). We have turned on the Endpoint Running Osnap, and we have turned off Snap (F9), Grid (F7), and Ortho (F8) for all these examples.

    Command: **LINE.**↵
    LINE Specify first point:

Touch the top half of the line on the left. When the endpoint box displays, left-click, and that endpoint is grabbed (see Figure 16.39).

    Specify next point or [Undo]:

Move over to the line on the right and touch its top half until the endpoint symbol displays and then left-click (see Figure 16.40). The line has now been drawn from endpoint to endpoint (see Figure 16.41).

Two Existing Lines

FIGURE 16.38

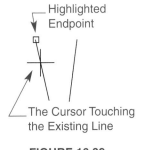

Highlighted Endpoint

The Cursor Touching the Existing Line

FIGURE 16.39

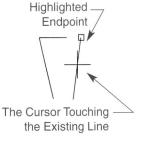

Highlighted Endpoint

The Cursor Touching the Existing Line

FIGURE 16.40

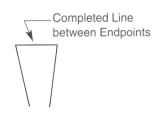

Completed Line between Endpoints

FIGURE 16.41

You Try It

Try this example for yourself: Draw two lines similar to Figure 16.38. Connect the endpoints on top with the line command using the endpoint Osnaps. Now connect the endpoints on the bottom without using the Osnaps; rely on your eyesight. After you're done, zoom in and see the difference in accuracy.

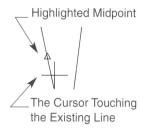

Highlighted Midpoint

The Cursor Touching
the Existing Line

FIGURE 16.42

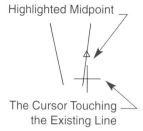

Highlighted Midpoint

The Cursor Touching
the Existing Line

FIGURE 16.43

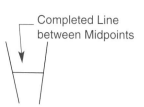

Completed Line
between Midpoints

FIGURE 16.44   Example complete.

Example: Midpoint Osnap

In this example, a line will be drawn from the midpoint of an existing line to the midpoint of another existing line. Midpoint Running Osnap is turned on.

> Command: **LINE**↵
> LINE Specify first point:

Touch the line on the left-hand side. When the midpoint symbol appears, left-click, and the midpoint is grabbed (see Figure 16.42).

> Specify next point or [Undo]:

Move to the line on the right side and wait for the midpoint symbol to appear and perform another left click (see Figure 16.43). The line has now been drawn from midpoint to midpoint (see Figure 16.44).

Several other Osnaps work in a similar manner to the preceding ones. It is a matter of understanding the definitions and symbols (see Figure 16.45).

The following examples show perpendicular and parallel Osnaps in operation. They work a little differently.

FIGURE 16.45

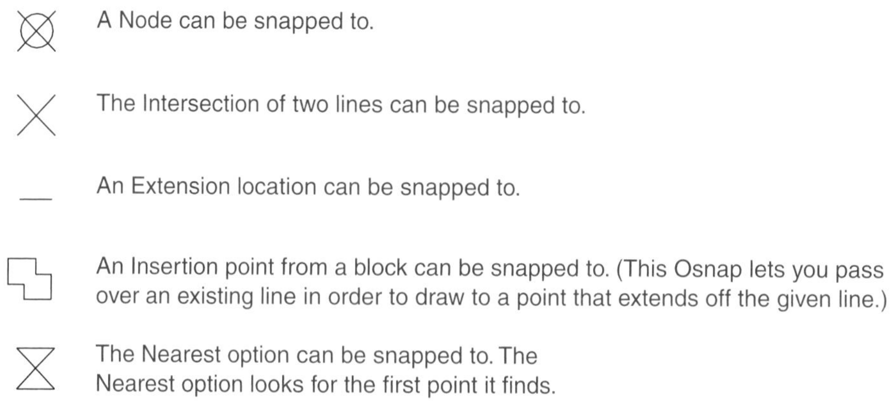

⊗   A Node can be snapped to.

✕   The Intersection of two lines can be snapped to.

—   An Extension location can be snapped to.

⌐   An Insertion point from a block can be snapped to. (This Osnap lets you pass over an existing line in order to draw to a point that extends off the given line.)

⋈   The Nearest option can be snapped to. The Nearest option looks for the first point it finds.

FIGURE 16.46   **FIGURE 16.47**

Example: Perpendicular Osnap

In this example, there is an existing line and node. A new line will be drawn perpendicular to the existing one. Remember that the Node and Perpendicular Osnaps are turned on in this example.

Use the Line command, select the Node Osnap, and touch the point until the node symbol displays (see Figure 16.46).

Next, touch the existing line, and when the perpendicular symbol appears, left click to draw the line (see Figure 16.47). In this example the Osnap Tracking was turned on, so the word *perpendicular* is displayed.

Example: Parallel Osnap

In this example, there is an existing line along with a node. Start drawing a line from the node, and then touch the line with the cursor until the parallel symbol is highlighted (see Figure 16.48). When this happens move the cursor out below the point until the parallel tracking caption comes on, then left-click (see Figure 16.49). A parallel line will be drawn from the node. The node and parallel Osnaps need to be turned on in this example.

The final example will show some circle characteristics. The following Osnaps are used for circles: Tangent, Center, and Quadrant. In this example, the Tangent, Center, and Quadrant Osnaps are turned on along with Osnap Tracking. A total of three circles are drawn.

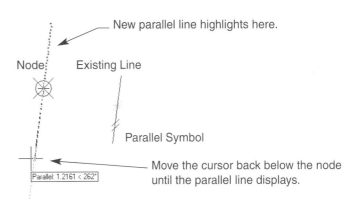

FIGURE 16.48   **FIGURE 16.49**   Parallel example complete.

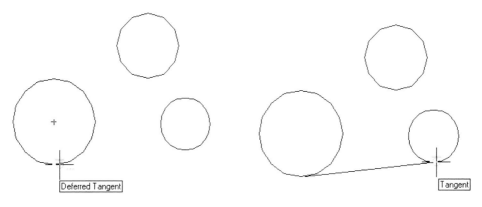

FIGURE 16.50   **FIGURE 16.51**

Example: Tangent Osnap

Using the Line command, draw a tangent line at the bottom of two circles.

    Command: **LINE**↵
    Specify first point:

   With only the Tangent Osnap On, touch the bottom of the big circle until the Deferred Tangent caption appears, then left-click (see Figure 16.50).

    Specify next point or [Undo]:

   Go to the bottom of the circle on the right, and when the Tangent caption appears, left-click (see Figure 16.51). Press the space bar to exit the Line command.

Example: Center Osnap

Use the same example, but this time turn on only the Center Osnap option.
   Use the Line command as before by touching each circle on its perimeter.
   As you watch the Center caption appear, left-click, then move the cursor to the perimeter of the second circle (see Figure 16.52). When the Center caption appears again, left-click (see Figure 16.53). Press the space bar to cancel the Line command.
   A line now appears between the exact centers of the circles (see Figure 16.54).

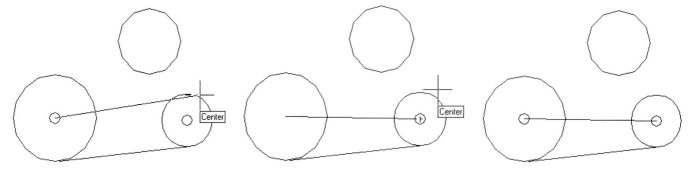

FIGURE 16.52   **FIGURE 16.53**   **FIGURE 16.54**

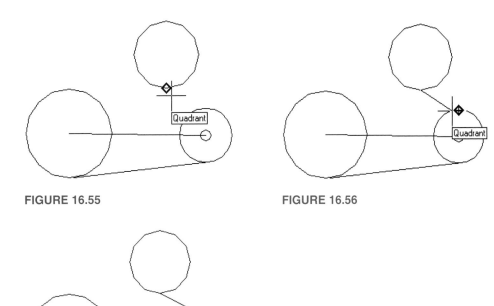

FIGURE 16.55   FIGURE 16.56

FIGURE 16.57

Example: Quadrant Osnap

Use the same example, but this time turn on only Quadrant Osnap.

Use the Line command and when it asks for the first point, touch the bottom of the top circle. When the Quadrant caption is displayed, left-click (see Figure 16.55).

Move the cursor to the circle on the right. Touch the top portion of the circle until the Quadrant caption appears, then left-click (see Figures 16.56 and 16.57).

Osnaps are an AutoCAD operator's best friend when it comes to drawing freely and quickly to exact points. They can be challenging in the beginning, but do not give up on them. Our examples utilized the Line command, but Osnaps work with modifying commands as well. Copying and Moving objects, just to name a few, are made much easier with Osnaps. Go back and draw out the examples and work them yourself, turning the running snaps on. Then do them again with the running snaps off. Pick the Osnap manually using the right mouse button while holding down the Shift key.

16.6   The List, ID, Dist, and Area Commands

Occasionally you will realize that you don't know the exact location of an object in your drawing, or you may be unsure of the layer (Chapter 19) on which something was placed. You may find that you need to know the distance between two points in a drawing or the area and perimeter of a portion of a drawing. AutoCAD provides several tools for answering these types of questions. Most of these tools are placed on the Inquiry toolbar (see Figure 16.58).

FIGURE 16.58   The Inquiry toolbar.

The List Command

List
Icon

- Type **LIST** or **LI** at the command prompt.
- Select Inquiry from the Tools pull-down menu. A flyout menu including List will appear.
- Pick the List icon from the Inquiry toolbar. The icon looks like a white sheet of paper covered with lines (or a list).

The **List** command provides a wealth of information about objects in a drawing. Once you enter the command you will be asked to select the objects about which you wish to inquire. You can use the List command on more than one object at a time. A list will be provided of each object's type and layer. In addition, the X-, Y-, and Z-coordinates will be provided based on the current User Coordinate System (UCS). If the object has a thickness other than zero, that information will be provided. Color, linetype, and lineweight are indicated as being set Bylayer or specific for that particular object.

The ID Command

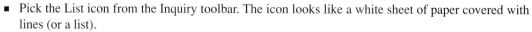

(ID) Identification
Icon

- Type **ID** at the command prompt
- Select Inquiry from the Tools pull-down menu. A flyout menu including ID Point will appear.
- Pick the ID icon from the Inquiry toolbar. The icon looks like a thin yellow bar or ruler with the letters x,y,z above it.

The **ID** command provides the coordinate value of a location within the drawing. The coordinates are provided relative to the current User Coordinate System (UCS). Once you enter the command, select the point you wish to identify. Look at the command line to see the coordinates for that point. This new ID point has been set as a relative 0,0 coordinate.

The Dist Command

Distance
Icon

- Type **DIST** or **DI** at the command prompt.
- Select Inquiry from the Tools pull-down menu. A flyout menu including Distance will appear.
- Pick the Distance icon from the Inquiry toolbar. The icon looks like a thin yellow bar or ruler topped by a line with arrowheads on each end.

The **Dist** command enables you to determine the distance and angle between two given points in the drawing. Once you enter the command you will be prompted to pick your first point, then your second. Look at the command line for distance information. Make sure to read the first distance not the ΔX or ΔY that follows.

The Area Command

Area
Icon

- Type **AREA** at the command prompt.
- Select Inquiry from the Tools pull-down menu. A flyout menu including Area will appear.
- Pick the Area icon from the Inquiry toolbar. The icon looks like a thin yellow bar or ruler topped by a figure shaped like a trapezoid.

The **Area** command calculates the area and perimeter of objects within your drawing. You can also use the command to calculate the area and perimeter of sections you choose to define. After you enter the Area command, you will need to select the Object suboption, then touch a polygon or circle. The area and perimeter information is displayed at the command line. You may also just pick the endpoints along the outside of the object instead of using the object suboption. The Area command has a lot in it to learn but we are only describing its very basic use.

16.7   The Divide and Measure Commands

The Divide Command

- Type **DIVIDE** or **DIV** at the command prompt.
- Select Point from the Draw pull-down menu by left-clicking. A cascading menu will appear containing the options Single Point, Multiple Point, Divide, and Measure. Pick Divide.

The **Divide** command allows you to partition an object with a number of equally spaced points or blocks. These nodes do not actually break the object; they only distinguish locations on the object. Thus, for

FIGURE 16.59

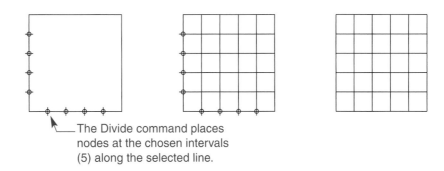

└─ The Divide command places
nodes at the chosen intervals
(5) along the selected line.

Note: Nodes will print out on the drawing. To remove them, type PD mode at the command line and set the value to 1. To see different node options go to the Format pull-down menu and select Point Styles for the displays.

example, if you pick the divided object as part of a selection set, the entire object will be chosen, not individual segments, but you can set Osnap to snap to any of the nodes defined by the Divide command.

Think back to the process for using manual drafting techniques to divide a line into equal sections (Chapter 4). This command accomplishes the same thing simply by your entering the command, selecting the object to divide, and specifying the number of divisions required. Imagine that you need to draw a checkerboard pattern (see Figure 16.59). Draw the lines defining the perimeter of the checkerboard area, then use the Divide command to define nodes (or points) along the perimeter lines dividing the lines into the number of spaces needed for the pattern. Then by turning on Node Osnap, you can easily draw the dividing lines by snapping to each node along the line. The Divide command can be used on arcs, circles, ellipses, elliptical arcs, polylines, and splines.

The Measure Command

Note: The nodes defined in the Divide and Measure commands may come in handy later in helping you define displacement for commands such as Copy (see Chapter 18).

The Measure command is similar to the Divide command. In the Divide command objects are divided with nodes whose spacing is determined by the overall length of the object. In the Measure command the spacing of the nodes is input within the command. For example, you could specify that nodes be placed every 2″ along the length of the object. AutoCAD will begin measuring from the end of the object closest to the pick point, so if your pick point for the object is closest to the left end of the object, the program will begin measuring from the left end. If you pick from the right, the measuring will begin from the right.

REVIEW QUESTIONS

1. Name three ways to turn Ortho on and off.
2. What are some of the drawbacks to drawing with the Ortho command on?
3. How does Ortho work with the Direct Distance point entry method?
4. How can the Ortho mode be changed to an Iso mode?
5. Name two ways to turn the Grid on and off?
6. What determines the overall area in which the grid dots are displayed?
7. How can the grid X spacing be set differently from the Y spacing?
8. If a grid is too dense to display, what can be done to fix this problem?
9. In how many different ways can the Snap command be activated?
10. Explain how the Snap command works with the Grid.
11. Right-clicking on the Snap button at the bottom of the drawing area will activate what?
12. Does the Snap turn off when the Grid is turned off?
13. How many different ways can the Polar Tracking be turned on and off?
14. How can the Polar Tracking be set to display at every 10 increments?
15. Make a list of all the Object Snaps and sketch the corresponding AutoSnap symbol.
16. Define a Running Object Snap.

17. How can the Drafting Settings dialog box be opened?

18. What kind of problems can occur when all the object snaps are turned on?

19. Can the Running Object Snaps be overridden?

20. What information does the List command supply? Make a complete list.

21. What function does the ID command serve?

22. What information does the Distance command provide?

23. List the command aliases for Distance and List.

24. Identify the function keys for the following:

    a. Grid

    b. Snap

    c. Ortho

    d. Isometric cursor switch

EXERCISES

EXERCISE 16.1

Set up a drawing environment with the following:

- Use ¼" = 1" scale with limits of 0,0 and 34",44".
- Set up an X and a Y Grid of 2".
- Set a Snap of .5" with Rectangular snap on.
- Turn on the Endpoint and Perpendicular running Osnaps.
- Draw a rectangle 1" inside the limits to form a border line.
- Using the Endpoint object snap, draw diagonal lines from corner to opposite corner to form an X.
- Save the drawing as 16EX-1.

EXERCISE 16.2

Using the setup in 16EX-1, do the following:

- Change the Rectangular Snap to the Isometric setting.
- Draw three iso circles in different corners with the Ellipse command: one in the horizontal plane direction, one in the left vertical plane direction, and one in the right vertical plane direction.
- Turn on the Center Osnap and draw a line from center to center on all the ellipses.
- Turn off the Center Osnap and turn on the Tangent Osnap. Try to draw tangent lines on the outsides of the ellipses. (Expect a little challenge. Tangents work well on circles but not so well on ellipses.)

EXERCISES 16.3

Open the 16EX-1 original drawing. Make the following changes.

- Turn on the Polar snap.
- Set Polar distance to 3".
- Turn on Polar Tracking.
- Set the Increment angle to 45°.
- Set the Polar Angle measurement to Relative to last segment.
- Click on Track using all polar angle settings.

- With these settings watch the readouts on the screen and draw the following diamond-shaped boxes.
- Draw two diamonds with 6″ sides.
- Draw one diamond with 12″ sides.
- Save the drawing as 16EX-3.

EXERCISE 16.4

Using drawing 16EX-3, do the following:

- Turn on Midpoint Osnap and draw lines in the big diamond from the midpoint of a side to the midpoint of the opposite side.
- Turn on Perpendicular Osnap and draw lines from the midpoint of the sides perpendicular to the opposite sides in the small diamonds.

EXERCISE 16.5

Using different combinations of Osnaps redraw the drawings in Figure 16.60.

EXERCISE 16.6

Create a floor pattern that would fit in a 6″ × 6″ square at 1″ = 1″. Use a minimum of two different geometric shapes.

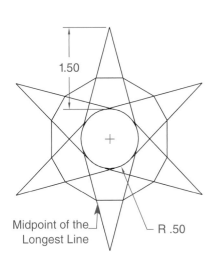
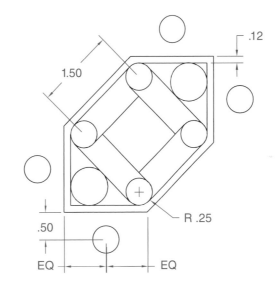

FIGURE 16.60 Exercise 16.5.

DRAWING ASSIGNMENTS

1. Use Polar Tracking to construct the drawing in Figure 16.61.

2. Draw the objects in Figure 16.62a–e using the full scale. Set up the limits so that the drawings will fit on standard sheet sizes. Some dimensions are left off so that you may customize some of the drawings.

3. Set up AutoCAD to draw the objects in Figure 16.62a–e in isometric form.

4. Draw the parts in Figure 16.63 in oblique cabinet form, using a 30° angle for depth.

FIGURE 16.61   Drawing Assignment 1.

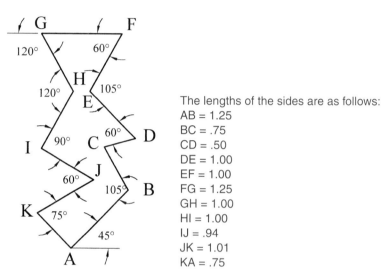

The lengths of the sides are as follows:
AB = 1.25
BC = .75
CD = .50
DE = 1.00
EF = 1.00
FG = 1.25
GH = 1.00
HI = 1.00
IJ = .94
JK = 1.01
KA = .75

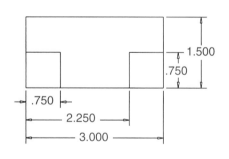

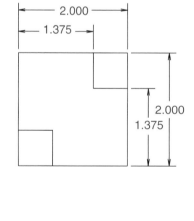

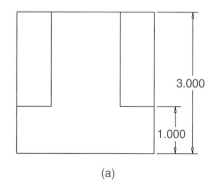

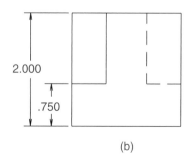

(a)   (b)

FIGURE 16.62   Drawing Assignment 2

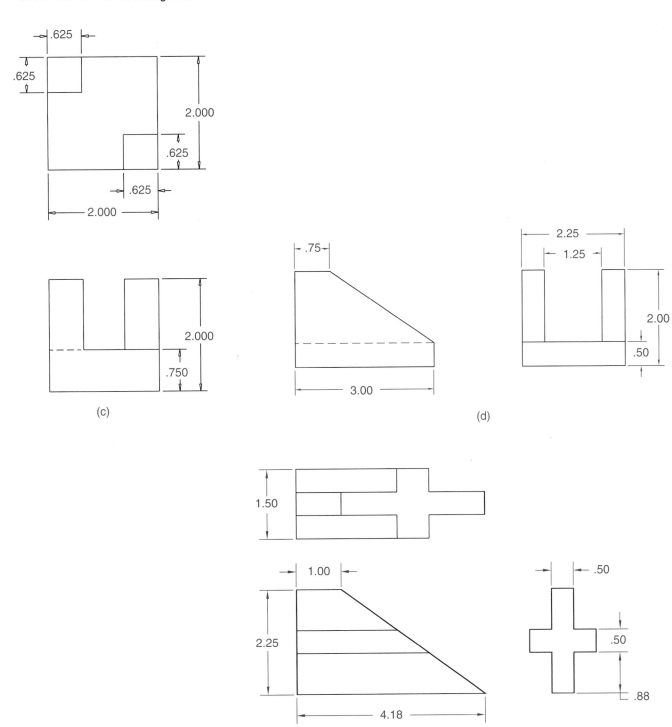

FIGURE 16.62 *continued*

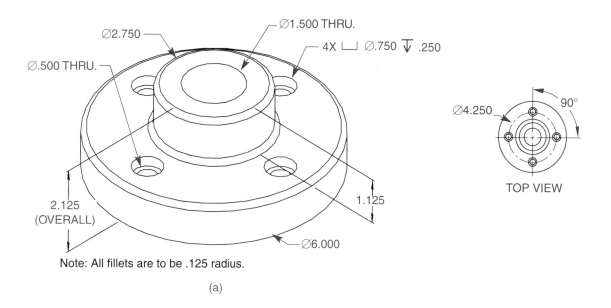

Note: All fillets are to be .125 radius.

(a)

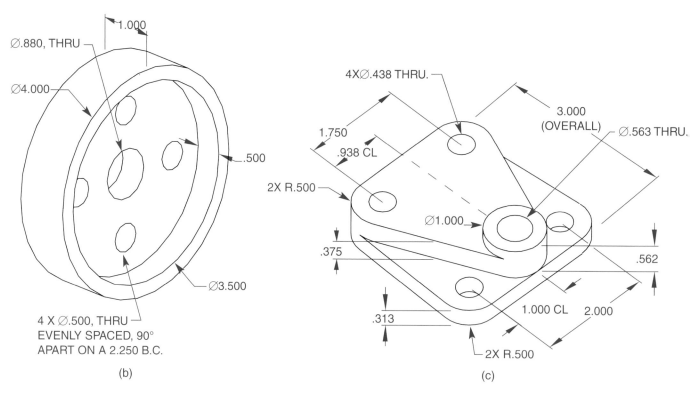

(b)

(c)

FIGURE 16.63

CHAPTER 17

Editing and Altering Entities

AutoCAD has many commands for editing or modifying existing entities or objects in a drawing. Learning to use such commands will make you faster and more efficient. The following editing commands will be demonstrated in this chapter (see Figures 17.1–17.3).

Commands

Trim

Extend

Break

Chamfer

Fillet

Stretch

Scale

Lengthen

Grips

Properties

Match Properties

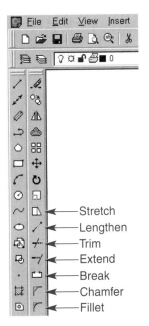

FIGURE 17.1 The Modify toolbar.

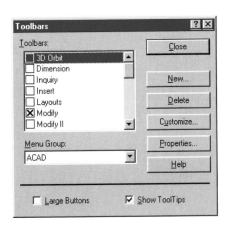

FIGURE 17.2 Turning on the Modify toolbar.

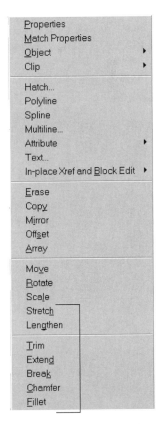

FIGURE 17.3 The Modify pulldown menu.

409

17.1   Using the Trim Command

- Type **TRIM** or **TR** at the command prompt.
- Select <u>T</u>rim from the <u>M</u>odify pull-down menu.
- Pick the Trim icon from the Modify toolbar.

Trim
Icon

The **Trim** command is used to clip off ends or overhangs of lines or objects. Figure 17.4 shows some situations where you could use the Trim command. The Trim command can remove only lines that touch or lap. Look at Figure 17.4 and think about what parts could be altered with the Trim command. Then look at Figure 17.5 to see if you came up with all these possibilities.

The Trim command is very easy to learn. The Trim command sequence would read as follows:

Command: **TR**⏎
Select Objects: *(Select an edge.)*⏎

*At this point you have two options to choose from when picking an edge.

Option 1

You can select a specific cutting edge by touching any line or lines with the cursor's pick box. (Do not touch the line you want to clip off first.) By touching the edge line you define where the trim will be made. To use a scissors analogy, the trim edge defines where the scissors will cut. After left-clicking on the cutting edge or edges, right-click to let AutoCAD know you are done picking cutting edges. Now, pick the lines to be removed with a left-click. As you pick these lines, they disappear (see Figure 17.6). Press Enter ⏎ to exit the command.

Option 2

When the Trim command asks you to Select Objects: right-click to select all the lines as cutting edges (known as the *smart mode*). Now, select any lines that intersect with a left click, and they will be trimmed off.

- Try the example in Figure 17.6. Draw your own lines at any scale you want. Try both options.

Tips for Working with Trim

Sometimes lines look like they touch or intersect, but in reality they do not. If the lines are not trimming for you, try erasing them. This problem occurs every so often, so watch for it. Later you will learn about the Extend command (Section 17.2), which can also solve some trimming problems by making lines touch.

Certain entities will not work with the Trim command. A Block Entity (see Chapter 22), for instance, will not allow trimming. One solution is to use the Explode command to break the block into individual lines and trim them.

To Explode a Block, type in **X**⏎ at the command line, then left-click on the object that is a block.

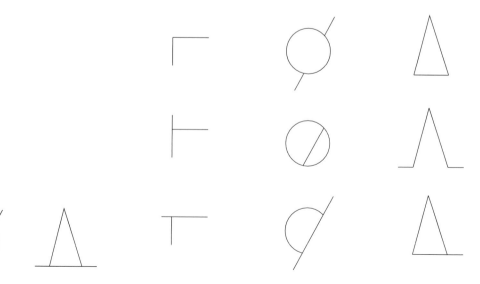

FIGURE 17.4 Shapes needing trimming.   **FIGURE 17.5**   Shapes showing how Trim can be applied in different ways.

FIGURE 17.6 Application of the Trim command.

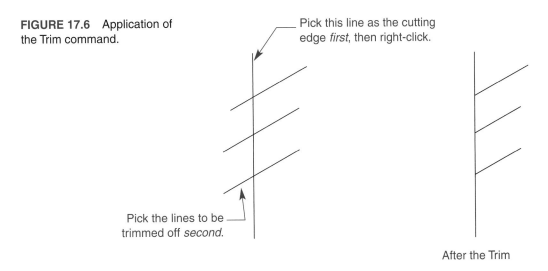

Pick this line as the cutting edge *first*, then right-click.

Pick the lines to be trimmed off *second*.

After the Trim

17.2 Using the Extend Command

- Type **Extend** or **EX** at the command prompt.
- Select Extend from the Modify pull-down menu.
- Pick the Extend icon from the Modify toolbar.

External
Icon

The **Extend** command can be used to make lines intersect other lines. For example, in Figure 17.7 several lines stop short of another line. If you wanted the lines to touch the other line as shown in Figure 17.8, you would use the Extend command to do this.

Using the Extend command is very similar to using the Trim command. The order in which you select lines is very important. Just as with the Trim command, you must select an edge or edges first in the Extend command, then you select the lines that must be extended. Use the following sequence for the Extend command:

At the command line type in **EX** or **EXTEND**.

Command line: **EX**↵
Current settings: Projection = UCS Edge None
Select Boundary edges: *(Choose a boundary edge.)* ↵
Select Objects:

*At this point you have the same two options you had in the Trim command.

FIGURE 17.7 Lines to be extended.

FIGURE 17.8 Extend example complete.

Option 1

Pick the edge to which you want other lines to extend and left-click on them, then right click. Now, touch the lines that need extending and left-click on them. They will extend as you select them.

Option 2

Right-click (smart mode) with the mouse. This automatically makes all lines on the drawing edges. After the right click the command line reads:

> Select object to extend or [Project /Edge /Undo]:

Start left-clicking on the lines that need extending. When the extending is complete, press Enter ↵.

Example: Using Extend

Draw a hexagon of any size you want, then draw two lines below the hexagon and one line inside the hexagon (see Figure 17.9). Use the Extend command. When it asks **Select Object:**, right-click.

   Left-click on the two vertical lines below the hexagon one at a time (see Figure 17.10). They should extend to the hexagon as you touch them.

   The horizontal line inside the hexagon can extend to two different edges, so it will require two separate picks. Left-click on the line on its left-hand side, and it extends to the left (see Figure 17.11). Now, click on the line's right side, and it extends to the right, touching the hexagon.

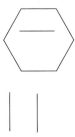

FIGURE 17.9   Lines to be extended.

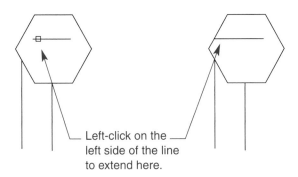

Left-click on the left side of the line to extend here.

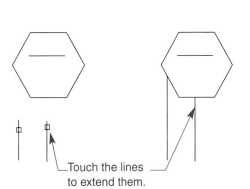

Touch the lines to extend them.

FIGURE 17.10   Application of the Extend command.

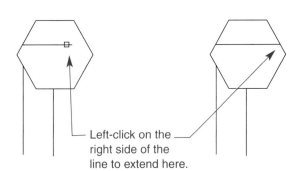

Left-click on the right side of the line to extend here.

FIGURE 17.11   Extend example complete.

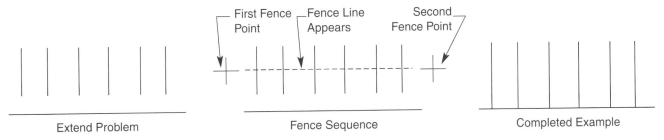

First Fence Point
Fence Line Appears
Second Fence Point

Extend Problem

Fence Sequence

Completed Example

FIGURE 17.12 Using the Extend command with a fence.

Tips for Working with the Extend Command

1. If a line does not Extend, it may not have an edge directly in front of it. This will require you to either place an edge line in front of the line or use the Edge option found inside the Extend command.

2. As with the Trim command, some entities do not work with the Extend command. A Block will not read as an edge and will not let lines extend to it. Either Explode the Block or draw a line on top of the Block, then use the Extend command.

3. The crossing and window options will not work when selecting several lines to extend. You may use the Fence option to pick more than one line at a time. To use the Fence option, activate the Extend command, and select your edges as shown in the earlier examples. At the command line type F,

   Select Object to Extend or [Project/ Edge / Undo]: **F**↵
   First Fence point:

   Pick a point on the far left side of the lines that need extending (see Figure 17.12). Now, drag the cursor to the right across your lines, and when you reach the other side, left-click to select a second fence point. Press Enter↵, and the lines should extend all at once. (The Fence option also works with the Trim command.)

4. If you pick lines to Extend one at a time, you may type in **U** (for Undo) to take back the last line you extended. To undo as many lines as you need, just keep typing U. If you exit out of the command and then perform an Undo at the command line, the whole Extend command will be Undone.

17.3 Using the Break Command

- Type **Break** or **BR** at the command prompt.
- Select Brea<u>k</u> from the <u>M</u>odify pull-down menu.
- Pick the Break icon from the Modify toolbar.

Break
Icon

The two previous commands, Extend and Trim, required an edge for the commands to work. The **Break** command does not need an edge to function. It has a great deal more freedom and flexibility (see Figure 17.13).

Let's look at the command line sequence when the Break command is used:

Command: **BR**↵
BREAK Select Object:

When the Select Object: line appears, the software is requesting you to pick a line or object to break. When you touch a line to be broken, the command line will then read:

Specify second break point or [First Point]:

FIGURE 17.13   Applications of
the Break command.

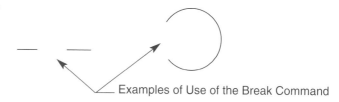

Examples of Use of the Break Command

Option 1

At this point AutoCAD has selected the object to be broken and marked the first point on the line to be broken.

You can then pick the second point on the line and have a piece of it erased (see Figure 17.14), or you can move completely off the line and left-click. The part of the line to the left of the first pick point will be removed (see Figure 17.15).

Option 2

If you wish to select a different first break point from the one AutoCAD selected, type in **F⏎** after [First Point] and the command line will read

Select first break point:

Now, select your first break point location by left-clicking on it. Next, you will be requested to pick the second break point on the object.

You can break only one object at a time with this command. Osnaps will work when selecting break points, so you can be very exact with the break locations. If you select a break point with the cursor off the object, then AutoCAD will find the nearest point along the object closest to the pick point.

Breaking an Object into Two Pieces without Erasing a Line

The examples so far have removed chunks or pieces from the objects. At certain times you will need to split an object in two and keep both sides. You can do this in one of two ways.

1. Make your first break point at the location where you want the split to occur. When AutoCAD asks for the second break point, type in the @ symbol. This will put the second break point in the same location as the first, thereby leaving no gap in the line.

2. You can use Osnaps to select your first and second break points at the exact same location. There will then be no gap, and the line will be split into two different lines, but leaving both sides intact (see Figure 17.16).

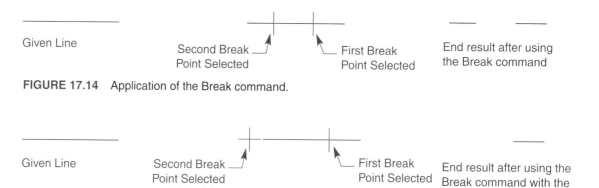

Given Line   Second Break ___   First Break   End result after using
                  Point Selected   Point Selected   the Break command

FIGURE 17.14   Application of the Break command.

Given Line   Second Break ___   First Break   End result after using the
                  Point Selected   Point Selected   Break command with the
                  off the Line   second pick point off the line

FIGURE 17.15   Application of the Break command.

Given Line   First and Second Break ___   End result after using the Break command at
                  Point Selected at the   the same break points. No gap is shown, but
                  Same Location   the line is now in two pieces. (Try to erase one
                                                           side to prove it.)

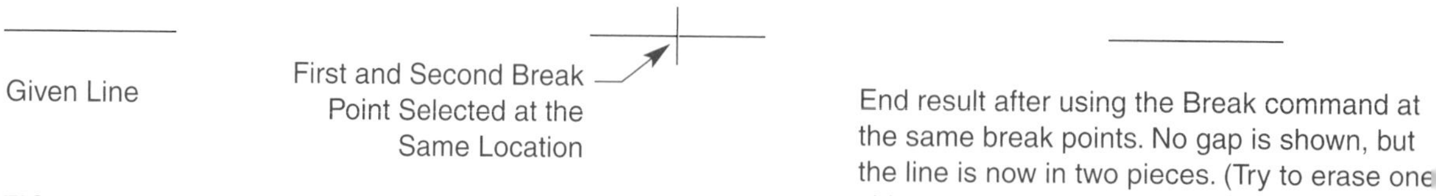

FIGURE 17.16   Application of the Break command.

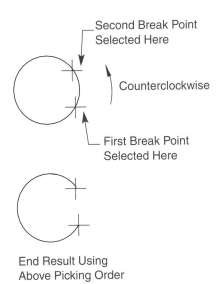

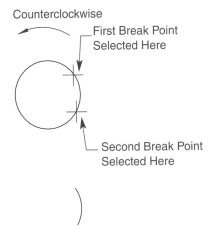

FIGURE 17.17 Breaking a circle.

Tips for Working with the Break Command

1. As with some of the previous editing commands, certain objects cannot be broken. A Blocked object must be exploded into individual lines before a Break command will work.

2. Many of the objects with which you are familiar can easily be broken; however, on certain round objects such as circles and ellipses the break points must be selected in a certain order because AutoCAD breaks in counterclockwise order by default (see Figure 17.17).

The command takes some getting used to at first. A little practice goes a long way.

Practice Example: Using the Break Command

Draw four circles of any size as shown in Figure 17.18. Follow the picking order given. Try to predict what shape will be left, then look at your end result after the command is finished. Did you anticipate it correctly? If not, try again.

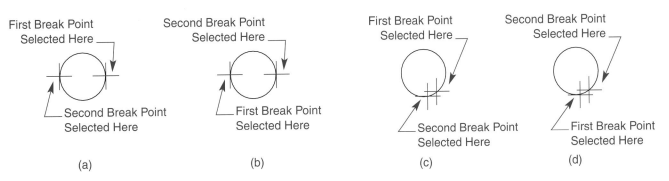

FIGURE 17.18 Practice example.

17.4   Using the Lengthen Command

- Type **LENGTHEN** or **LEN** at the command prompt.
- Select Lengthen from the <u>M</u>odify pull-down menu.
- Pick the Lengthen icon from the Modify toolbar.

Lengthen
Icon

The **Lengthen** command can alter the length of a line or arc in a variety of ways, depending on the need. Let's look at the command line sequence when the Lengthen command is used.

Command: **LEN** ↵
Select an object or [Delta / Percent / Total / Dynamic]:

If you select a line, the current length is displayed at the command line and returns you to the same prompt. The four options within the brackets give some flexibility in adjusting the length of a line or arc.

The Delta Option

The **Delta** option of selection works in the following way. Type **DE** and the command line shows:

Select an object or [Delta / Percent / Total / Dynamic]: **DE**↵
Enter Delta length or [Angle] < 0.000 >:

At this point typing a positive unit distance will increase the length of a line or arc, and a negative distance will shorten the objects. Right-click after entering a distance.

Select an object to change or [Undo]:

Just touch the object, and the line will change by the specified distance (see Figure 17.19).

Enter delta length or [Angle] < 0.000 >: **A** ↵
Enter delta angle <0>: *(Choose the desired angle.)*

Type in the angle desired, right-click, then select the arc to change.

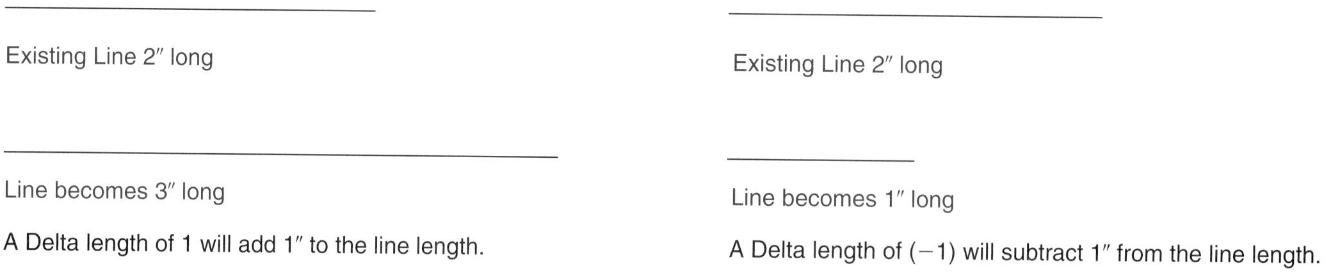

Note: The Angle selection in the Delta option works on an arc by using an angle to add or subtract a length (see Figure 17.20):

Existing Line 2″ long

Existing Line 2″ long

Line becomes 3″ long

Line becomes 1″ long

A Delta length of 1 will add 1″ to the line length.

A Delta length of (−1) will subtract 1″ from the line length.

FIGURE 17.19   Application of the Delta option of the Lengthen command.

FIGURE 17.20   Lengthening an arc with the Angle suboption.

Original Arc

30°

A 30° segment is added.

The Percent Option

The **Percent** selection is used with a line's original length. The original length is used as a unit, and a percentage of that unit is applied to alter its size. For example, a line is drawn 4″ long. If the Percent option is set to 50, the line will be reduced by 50% or half its size:

$$4'' \times \frac{50}{100} = 2''$$

$$4'' \times \frac{1}{2} = 2''$$

If the same 4″ line was lengthened by 200%, its size would double:

$$4'' \times \frac{200}{100} = 8''$$

$$4'' \times \frac{2}{1} = 8''$$

Example: Using Percent

Draw a line 1″ long.
    Follow this selection sequence:

    Command: **LEN**↵
    Select an object or [Delta / Percent / Total / Dynamic]: **P**↵
    Enter percentage length < 0.000>: *(Enter desired percentage here. 200 is okay.)*
    Select an object to change or [Undo]: *(Pick the line or arc to be changed.)*
    The length of the line should double in size.

Total Option

The **Total** option changes the object to the distance that is set. For instance, if a line is originally drawn 2.5′ long, and the Total option is used in the Lengthen command, the command line will read:

    Command: **LEN**↵
    Select object or [Delta / Percent / Total / Dynamic]: **T**↵
    Specify Total length or [Angle]: *(Enter Value.)*↵

If a value of 6′ is used, then when a line or arc is selected, its total length will be set to 6′.

Example: Total Option Using Angles

Instead of typing a value, type **A** for Angle, which will work on arcs. The command line will read:

Specify total angle <0>: *(Enter the angle value.)*↵
Select object to change or [Undo]: *(Pick the arc.)*

If a value of 90° is used, the arc will be drawn as a quarter of a circle. Input 180° to draw a half circle (see Figure 17.21).

FIGURE 17.21 Lengthening an arc with the Total suboption.

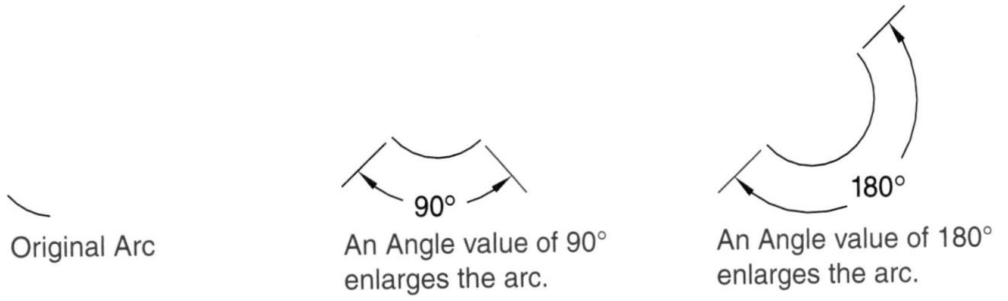

Original Arc

An Angle value of 90° enlarges the arc.

An Angle value of 180° enlarges the arc.

Dynamic Option

The **Dynamic** option is used with the cursor. When this option is selected, the command line reads:

Select an object to change or [Undo]: *(Pick a line or arc.)*
Specify new end point:

Move the cursor around and watch the line float along with the cursor. The next point selected with a left click will lengthen the line to that location. You can just pick points, but the following two tips will help give you some control.

Tips for Working with the Lengthen Command

1. Osnaps can be used to snap to exact locations.
2. Direct Distance can be used. (Pull the cursor in the direction you want to draw, then type in the distance by which to lengthen, and press Enter↵.) The command works with Ortho turned off.
3. As in previous editing commands some entities cannot be lengthened, such as closed objects and Blocked objects.
4. Some of the angle options will have some restrictions on size. Choosing angles between 0° and 360° will solve most of those problems.

17.5   Using the Stretch Command

Stretch
Icon

- Type **Stretch** or **S** at the command prompt.
- Select Stretc<u>h</u> from the <u>M</u>odify pull-down menu.
- Pick the Stretch icon from the Modify toolbar.

The **Stretch** command can be used on polygons and shapes with two or more connected lines. It basically performs some of the same functions as the Lengthen command, but Stretch works on more than a single line. Figure 17.22 shows some of the shapes that can be stretched.

With the Stretch command, there are only two methods of selecting objects: with a crossing box (**C**↵) or a crossing polygon (CP↵).

Crossing Boxes

By now you should have a good understanding of crossing boxes. Left-clicking and moving the cursor to the left gives you a crossing box. Make sure the box crosses or touches all the sides involved with the Stretch being performed (see Figure 17.23).

Pick the object to stretch, and right-click.

Select Object: *(Pick objects with a crossing box.)*↵
Specify a base point or displacement:

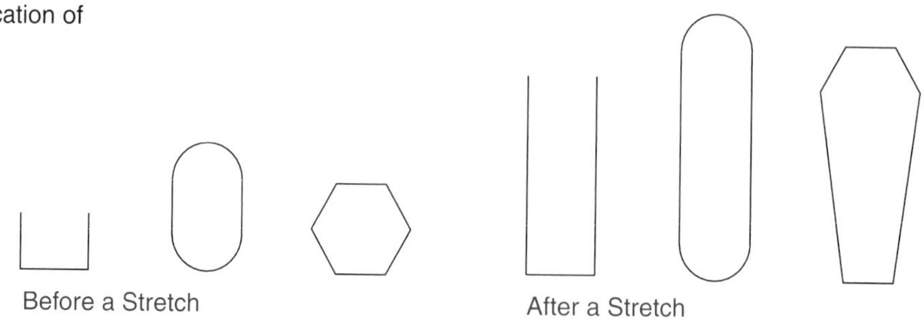

FIGURE 17.22   Application of the Stretch command.

Before a Stretch

After a Stretch

FIGURE 17.23 Application of the Stretch command.

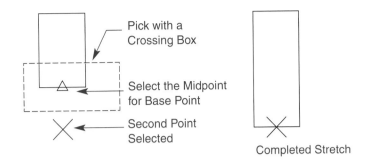

Pick with a Crossing Box

Select the Midpoint for Base Point

Second Point Selected

Completed Stretch

When a base point is requested, you must choose a point from which to reference the stretch. A midpoint or endpoint on the object will work fine for a base point even though picking anywhere will work.

Specify second point of displacement:

After picking a base point, select a second point to which to stretch the object. The distance between the base point and the second point determines how much the object will be stretched.

Crossing Polygon

Objects can also be selected with a crossing polygon (shown in Chapter 13). This option allows you to construct a shape by picking points and closing the polygon. Just make sure to cross or touch all lines involved with the stretch.

Tips for Working with the Stretch Command

1. Turn on ORTHO if you need the object to stretch vertically or horizontally.
2. The Direct Distance method works well for selecting the second point to which to stretch. Turn ORTHO on, pull the cursor in the direction the stretch should go, type in the distance needed for the stretch, and press Enter↵.
3. The majority of problems with the Stretch command involve trying to pick objects with some method other than a crossing box or polygon or selecting objects that cannot be stretched, like a circle or a Block.

17.6 Using the Scale Command

- Type **SCALE** or **SC** at the command prompt.
- Select Scal̲e from the M̲odify pull-down menu.
- Pick the Scale Icon from the Modify toolbar.

Scale Icon

The **Scale** command is used to change the size of objects (see Figure 17.24). It is *not* used to change the scale of a drawing or its limits. For example, the Scale command is used to resize a hole's diameter that has been drawn too large.

The Scale command sequence is as follows:

Command: **SC**↵
Select Object: *(Pick objects.) (Use any selection method.)*
Specify base point: *(Pick a point from which the Scale can be referenced.)*
Specify scale factor or [Reference]:

FIGURE 17.24 Application of the Scale command.

Scale Factor of 1

Scale Factor of 2

Scale Factor of 2.5

For the scale factor, type in a numerical value and press Enter⏎. Typing in 2⏎ will double the size of a selected object. Drag the cursor to any point and click. The object will enlarge or shrink as the cursor is moved, much like the Dynamic option works in the Lengthen command.

Type **R**⏎ to choose the Reference option. It lets you select a size or pick two points as a distance reference, then it scales proportionally based on the determined reference distance.

Example 1

Command: **SC.**⏎
Select objects: *Pick circle* ⏎
Specify base point: *(Use Center Osnap.)*
Specify scale factor or [Reference]: **3.**⏎

The circle will triple in size (see Figure 17.25).

Example 2

Command: **SC.**⏎
Select objects: *Pick circle* ⏎
Specify base point: *(Use Center Osnap.)*
Specify scale factor or [Reference]: *(Drag the cursor a distance outside the circle.)*

Watch the circle as the cursor drags, and left-click when the circle reaches the desired size (see Figure 17.26).

Example 3

Command: **SC.**⏎
Select objects: *(Select the circle.)*
Specify base point: *(Pick the center of the circle.)*
Specify scale factor or [Reference]: **R.**⏎
Specify reference length <1>: **.5** *(diameter of circle)*
Specify new length: **1.5** (see Figure 17.27)

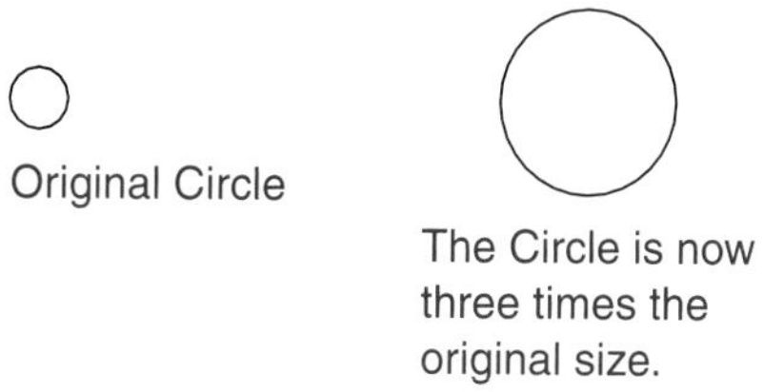

Original Circle

The Circle is now three times the original size.

The circle will scale out to the cursor placement.

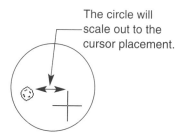

Original Circle with a .5″ diameter

Circle after using the Reference option with a new diameter of 1.5″.

FIGURE 17.25   Scaling a circle.

FIGURE 17.26   Scaling a circle with the cursor.

FIGURE 17.27   Scaling a circle with the Reference option.

FIGURE 17.28 Scaling a circle with the Reference option and quadrants.

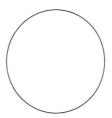

Use the 0° quadrant for your first reference point.

Use the 180° quadrant for your second reference point.

Before
Original Circle with a .5″ diameter

After
Circle after using the Reference option with a new diameter of 1.5″

Example 4

Command: **SC**↵
Select objects: *(Select the circle.)*
Specify base point: *(Pick the center of the circle.)*
Specify scale factor or [Reference]: **R**↵
Specify reference length <1>: *(Pick the 0° quadrant on the given circle.)*
Specify second point: *(Pick the 180° quadrant.)*
Specify new length: **1.5**↵ *(See Figure 17.28.)*

Tips for Working with the Scale Command

There are very few problems with the Scale command. Most entities can be scaled without any problem, including Blocks.

The biggest problem occurs when the Scale option is misused by individuals trying to adjust the drawing scale or limits with it. The Scale command will not change the limits environment; it is used to change an object's size, *not* its environment. The Limits command must be used to change limits.

17.7 Using the Chamfer Command

- Type **CHAMFER** or **CHA** at the command prompt.
- Select <u>C</u>hamfer from the <u>M</u>odify pull-down menu.
- Pick the Chamfer icon from the Modify toolbar.

Chamfer Icon

A *chamfer* is an angled corner found between two lines or objects, such as at the corner of a table to eliminate a sharp point (see Figure 17.29). The **Chamfer** command has a **Trim** mode that can be used to leave the intersection in place or to remove the intersection and show only the chamfer (see Figure 17.30).

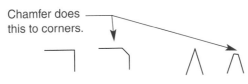

Chamfer does this to corners.

FIGURE 17.29 Application of the Chamfer command.

No Trim Option   Trim Option

FIGURE 17.30 Chamfering with and without the Trim option.

To use the Chamfer command, walk through the following steps. Type **CHA** at the command line.

Command: **CHA** ↵
(TRIM Mode) = Current Chamfer Dist1 = 0.500, Dist2 = 0.500
Select first line or [Polyline / Distance / Angle / Trim / Method]:

Take a look at the information in the command line. The second line gives you a list of current settings.

- (TRIM Mode) means the Trim is on, and the intersection will be removed. This is the default setting.
- The current chamfer distances are shown. Distance 1 (Dist1) is applied to the first line touched in the chamfer picking order. Dist2 is applied to the second line selected.

The last line in the command prompt lists the options from which to choose.

Select first line:

If the distances are OK, then simply click the two lines one at a time and the chamfer is performed (see Figure 17.31).

Polyline:

If the object being edited was constructed with polylines, then they must be chamfered with this option. Type **P**↵, then click the polylines one at a time. This option can chamfer more than one corner at a time when performed on a closed polyline figure (see Figure 17.32).

Distance:

Note: Distance 1 and Distance 2 do not have to be the same number.

Type **D**↵ to change the values of the distance settings. The command sequence will look like this:

Select first line or [Polyline/Distance/angle/Trim/Method]: **D**↵
Specify first chamfer distance <0.5000>: *(Select new distance for 1.)* ↵
Specify second chamfer distance <0.5000>: *(Select new distance for 2.)* ↵
Command: ↵
Select first line or [Polyline/Distance/Angle/Trim/Method]:

Notice that after the second distance is set, you are returned to a blank command line. You must press **Enter**↵ or right-click to return to the Chamfer command so that you can start selecting the lines to chamfer.

Angle

Type **A**↵ to use an angle to determine the second chamfer point. The sequence looks like this:

Select first line or [Polyline/Distance/Angle/Trim/Method]: **A**↵
Specify chamfer length on the first line <1.000>: *(Pick first distance.)* ↵
Specify chamfer angle from the first line <0>: *(Type angle needed.)* ↵
Command: ↵

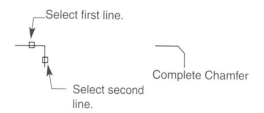

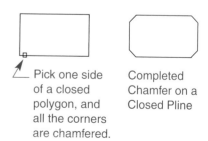

FIGURE 17.31   The Select first line option.

FIGURE 17.32   The Polyline option of Chamfer.

Notice again that after setting the angle, you must press **Enter.⏎** to return to the chamfer picking sequence. Just touch the first line and second line when the command line asks, and the chamfer will be drawn using the angle value instead of a distance for the second point.

Trim:

The Trim mode is set with this option by typing **T⏎**.

> Select first line or [Polyline/Distance/Angle/Trim/Method]: **T⏎**
> Enter Trim mode option [Trim/No trim] <Current Setting>:

Typing **N⏎** will leave the intersection untrimmed.

- **Method:** This option allows you to jump back and forth between the Distance choice with its current setting and the Angle choice with its current settings. The command line sequence is as follows.

> Select first line or [Polyline/Distance/Angle/Trim/Method]: **M⏎**
> Enter trim method [Distance/Angle] <Current setting>:

Select **D** to use the Distance method, or choose **A** to make an angle selection.

Tips for Working with the CHAMFER Command

Obviously, some shapes, such as circles and Blocks, will not chamfer. A common problem is that the distance and angle setting may be too large to work on small corners. If this happens you must change the chamfer settings or the size of the object.

17.8 Using the Fillet Command

- Type **FILLET** or **F** at the command prompt.
- Select Fillet from the <u>M</u>odify pull-down menu.
- Pick the Fillet icon from the Modify toolbar.

Fillet
Icon

A **fillet** is a radius tangenting into two objects (see Figure 17.33). **Fillet** is a very frequently used command in AutoCAD because of its ability to automatically trim out edges. The picking sequence is very similar to that used with the Chamfer command. You must return to the command after selecting the radius of the fillet. Fillet also has a [Trim/No Trim] option, just like the Chamfer command.

Let's walk through the command line when the Fillet command is activated.

> Command: **F⏎**
> Select first object or [Polyline/Radius/Trim]:

The **Polyline** and **Trim** options should be familiar to you; they are used in the same fashion as in the Chamfer command.

Polyline:

If lines or arcs are polylines, you must use this option to attach a fillet to them.

> Select first object or [Polyline/Radius/Trim]: **P⏎**
> Select 2D polyline: *(Pick a Pline on a closed object.)*

FIGURE 17.33 Application of the Fillet command.

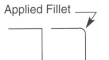  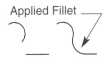

Applied Fillet
Applied Fillet
Applied Fillet

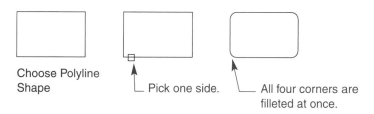

Choose Polyline
Shape

└─ Pick one side.   └─ All four corners are
                        filleted at once.

FIGURE 17.34   The Polyline option of Fillet.

Trim Option   No Trim Option

FIGURE 17.35   Fillet with and without Trim.

Make sure the polyline/Plines are touching, then select one Pline and the fillet is drawn. As in the Chamfer command, if the Polyline object is closed, then all the corners will get Fillets in a single selection (see Figure 17.34).

Trim:

This selection is the same as in the Chamfer command. Selecting **T** for Trim will remove the intersection, and the No Trim option will leave the intersecting lines untrimmed (see Figure 17.35).

Radius:

The **Radius** option allows you to change the fillet size. The following sequence shows how to select a new fillet radius.

    Command: **F**↵
    Select first object or [Polyline/Radius/Trim]: **R**↵
    Specify fillet radius <Current value>: *(Type new value.)* ↵
    Command: *(Press Enter↵)*
    Select first object or [Polyline/Radius/Trim]: *(Select first side.)*
    Select second object: *(Select second side.)*

Notice that you need to return to the Fillet command after choosing a new radius. Simply press Enter↵ or right-click to return to the Fillet command to start selecting the objects.

One very useful function of the Fillet and Chamfer commands is the ability to square off corners that stop short or overlap (see Figure 17.36). With the Fillet command just use a 0 radius and then follow through the normal sequence. Instead of a curve, a corner is formed.

Tips for Working with the FILLET Command

1. The most common problem with the Fillet command is using a radius that is too large. If this happens, the command line will let you know. Choosing a smaller radius is a solution.

2. Another problem is having the fillet go in the wrong direction at an intersection (see Figure 17.37). The Fillet will follow the counterclockwise selecting order; however, if there is not a clearly defined corner, you may need to break a line to dictate the path for the Fillet to follow (see Figure 17.38). Once the line is broken, it is easy to have the fillet go in the direction you need.

3. As in most of the editing commands, some things cannot be changed. Filleting a Block will not work without exploding the Block. As you try editing different entities you will develop an understanding of what will work well. (See Chapter 22 for more information about Blocks.)

FIGURE 17.36   Fillet with radius of 0.

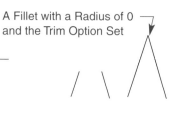

A Fillet with a Radius of 0
and the Trim Option Set

Note: If the fillet is placed on the wrong side, try selecting the lines in a different order.

FIGURE 17.37 Fillet @90° angle.

FIGURE 17.38 Fillet @90° intersection.

17.9 The Basics of Using the Grips Command

Usually, an AutoCAD user is first exposed to grips when he or she accidentally turns them on by selecting an object without choosing a command. **Grips** are the small blue rectangles that appear on the drawing as a result (see Figure 17.39). The first reaction most people have is, How do I get rid of them? Pressing the Escape key twice will remove them.

Grips are an important editing tool. They are like little identification or definition points that are found at critical areas that make up the geometric shape of the object. If you draw a variety of shapes and activate the grips, you will find some of these characteristics.

Grips are found on endpoints and midpoints, and on tangents, centers, and quadrants. Grips can be in three different states: cold, warm, or hot.

1. A grip is considered *cold* when the hollow grip boxes remain on an object while the object is a continuous line. This object is not affected by what you do to entities with warm grips.

2. An object is in a *warm* grip mode when the objects selected are shown as a broken line. The grip boxes are still and remain hollow on the object. The objects selected will be affected if a grip is made hot (see Figure 17.40).

3. A *hot* grip is an active grip. A left click with the cursor over a warm or cold grip box will make it hot and active. The rectangle boxes, which are hollow and blue in the warm and cold states, now become solid red boxes. When a grip is hot, cursor movement will alter the object when shifted around. To make more than one grip hot, hold down the Shift key and left-click on as many grip boxes as needed. The more grips that are lit up, the more the grip option will affect the whole object (see Figure 17.41). Press the Esc key to change the state of the grips.

The next question most people ask is, What does an active grip do? Look at the command line when the grip is hot to see which function is active. The **Grips** command will default to the Stretch option.

    STRETCH
    Specify stretch point or [Base point/ Copy / Undo /Exit]:

Just move the cursor to any location and watch the line stretch there when you left-click. Osnaps can be used when moving a hot grip being stretched to an exact location (see Figure 17.42). This Stretch will work with single lines, unlike the other Stretch command introduced earlier in this chapter.

Grips can perform the following functions:

Stretch

Move

Rotate

Scale

Mirror

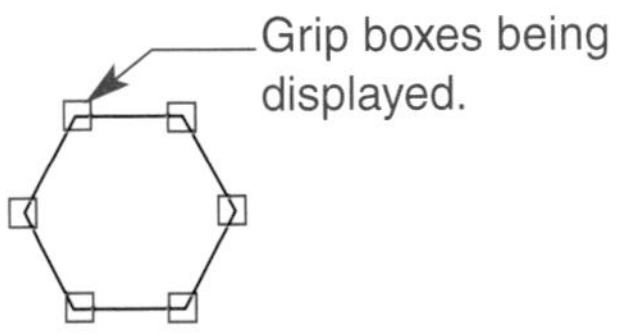

Grip boxes being displayed.

FIGURE 17.39 Grips.

FIGURE 17.40 Grips on multiple objects.

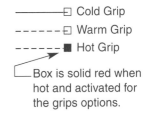

Cold Grip

Warm Grip

Hot Grip

Box is solid red when hot and activated for the grips options.

FIGURE 17.41 Hot grip.

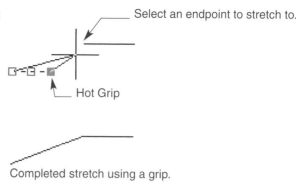

FIGURE 17.42   Stretching using a grip.

Select an endpoint to stretch to.

Hot Grip

Completed stretch using a grip.

To access these selections, go through the following sequence to use the grips.

1. Left-click on an object.
2. Make a grip hot by left-clicking on top of the blue rectangular box.
3. Look at the command line, which is defaulted to Stretch. Press Enter↵ repeatedly to cycle through the other options. Look at the command line each time you press Enter↵. Keep pressing until you reach the option you need.

The following are common options inside brackets. You have used most of these previously. Each of these will work with the Grip functions (Stretch, Move, Rotate, Scale, and Mirror).

Base point: Gives you a choice to locate a starting point for a base reference.

Copy: Will make a duplicate copy of the highlighted object.

Undo: Will take back the last grip placement used.

eXit: Exits the Grip command.

Reference: This option is found in Scale and Rotate. In Scale, it references a distance, then changes the scale base on a new assigned length. (See the Scale command found earlier in this chapter.) In Rotate, it references an angle you assign, then uses a second angle in combination to shift the rotation of a line.

The grips are like shortcuts to Stretch, Move, Rotate, Scale, and Mirror. They work very similarly to these commands accessed in the Modify menu. It is better to learn the basics of these commands, then come back and experiment with the grips options.

Some users do not like grips at all and turn them off. To do this, use the following sequence:

Command: **Grips**↵
Enter new value for Grips <1>: **0**↵

The ability to stretch and move objects quickly makes the grips a very useful tool. Be patient with the grips; they are a great tool to use.

17.10   The Properties Command

One of the most powerful editing tools in AutoCAD is the **Properties** command. It can change many features or characteristics of an object, such as the following:

Layers

Colors

Linetypes

Lineweights

Text

Geometry of shapes

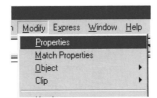

FIGURE 17.43 Properties pull-down menu.

- Type **PROPERTIES** or **MO** at the command prompt.
- Select Properties from the Modify pull-down menu (see Figure 17.43).
- Pick the Properties icon from the Standard toolbar.

Properties Icon

When the Properties command is activated, a dialog box appears and displays the characteristics that can be changed (see Figure 17.44). You can select the objects to be modified before activating the Properties command or immediately following. Left-click on the object to be altered, or use a window or a crossing box to activate the warm grips on an object. Depending on what is selected or highlighted, the options shown in the Properties dialog box will vary somewhat.

Two tabs that always appear at the top of the dialog box are Alphabetic and Categorized.

If the Alphabetic tab is chosen, then all the properties are put in alphabetical order (see Figure 17.45). The Categorized tab organizes the different property characteristics by groups or categories. As shown in Figure 17.44, the categories break down into areas such as General and Geometry. Notice the little boxes to the left with a minus sign in them. If you left-click on one, then that category is minimized and a plus symbol appears in the box (see Figure 17.46). Left-click on the plus symbol to restore the category.

The categories will change as the properties vary with different types of entities. Figure 17.47 shows an example of a new category when a string of text or lettering is selected for modification.

Notice that Text has its own category with its own unique properties. Each new entity you learn can have a different makeup and therefore may have its own individual category created. In the beginning, look for new categories to pop up.

FIGURE 17.44 Properties dialog box.

FIGURE 17.45 Properties displayed in alphabetic order.

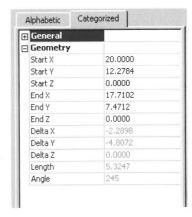

FIGURE 17.46 The General options of the Categorized tab.

FIGURE 17.47   Text options of the Categorized tab.

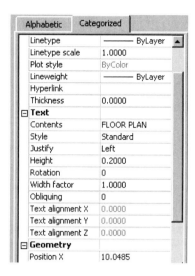

How to Use the Properties Command

To move through the Properties dialog box, left-click on the scroll arrows on the right. Once you find the property to change, left-click on the description to the left. After the description is highlighted, move the cursor to the right and pick on the current property setting. In the following example we will change the color from ByLayer to Cyan.

Example 1

1. Left-click on a line and activate the grips.
2. Activate the Properties command: **MO.**⏎
3. Left-click on the word Color in the dialog box (see Figure 17.48).
4. Left-click on the down arrow, then left-click on Cyan (see Figure 17.49).
5. The Cyan color now displays in the right column.
6. Close the Properties dialog box by left-clicking on the X in the upper right corner (see Figure 17.50).
7. Press the Esc key twice to turn off the grips. The line that was selected now has a cyan color.

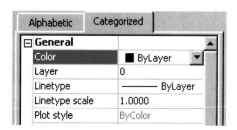

FIGURE 17.48   Properties Color option.

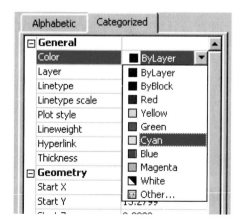

FIGURE 17.49   Changing color.

FIGURE 17.50 The Close button.

FIGURE 17.51 Geometry options.

FIGURE 17.52 Quick Select icon.

FIGURE 17.53 Quick Select dialog box.

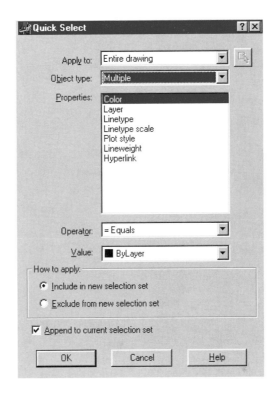

The sequence just used in Example 1 is typical when changing properties of objects. Sometimes you may need to type in the change at the setting location on the right. Just highlight the entire box, then type in the new value (see Figure 17.51).

Making changes with the Geometry tab is best left to experienced CAD users who know the coordinate systems fairly well. As you gain some confidence you may want to start making modifications here.

The Quick Select button is found in the upper right corner of the dialog box (see Figure 17.52). It opens up the dialog box shown in Figure 17.53. It gives you a method of filtering through the selections quickly. It performs the same functions as the Properties box but focuses more on user-specified areas.

The Properties command is one of the more frequently used options in AutoCAD. You can use other editing commands to do some of the functions of Properties, but learning to use this command will give you a greater control over editing.

17.11 The Match Properties Command

- Type **MA** at the command prompt.
- Select <u>M</u>atch Properties from the <u>M</u>odify pull-down menu (see Figure 17.54).
- Pick the Match Properties icon from the Standard toolbar.

Match
Properties
Icon

The **Match Properties** command is used to quickly pick out the properties of an existing object, then to change the properties of other existing objects to match the properties of the first. It sounds complicated, but it is not. Here is an example of how it works.

FIGURE 17.54   Match Properties selected in the Modify pull-
down menu.

FIGURE 17.55   Three circles,
one black, two blue.

FIGURE 17.56   Using the
Match Properties command.

FIGURE 17.57   Example complete.

Example: Match Properties Command

In this example, three circles will be drawn. The first one will be black, and the other two will be blue (see Figure 17.55).

Select Match Properties from the Modify pull-down menu.

Select source object:

Left-click on the black circle. A pick box and a paintbrush appear.

Select destination objects or [Setting]:

Touch each blue circle with the pick box and left-click each time. As you pick the circle its color changes to match the first one. Press **Enter** ↵ when you are done picking (see Figures 17.56 and 17.57).

Match Properties is quick and easy to use on all kinds of entities. When you get into Chapters 19 and 21 on Layers and Text, you will learn to like it a lot.

REVIEW QUESTIONS

1. How can the Modify toolbar be placed on the screen if it is turned off?
2. If a line does not Trim, what could be the problem?
3. List all the options inside the Grips command.
4. Explain the Trim/No Trim option in the Fillet and Chamfer commands.
5. How is the Lengthen command different from the Extend command?
6. How many options are found in the Scale command?
7. How do you activate grips?
8. When using the Stretch command, objects can be selected using only two methods. What are they?
9. What factors determine whether to use the Trim or Break command?
10. Why is Properties one of the more powerful editing commands in AutoCAD?
11. How does Match Properties work?
12. List the options inside the Chamfer command.
13. How can the Break command be used to break a line into two pieces without removing a portion?
14. Explain how the Break command selects the break points.

15. How do you remove the grip boxes from the AutoCAD screen?

16. List the command aliases for:
    a. Trim
    b. Extend
    c. Break
    d. Chamfer
    e. Fillet
    f. Stretch
    g. Lengthen

17. What are some problems that occur with the Extend command?

18. Explain the options inside the Lengthen command.

19. Draw a circle using any radius. Select the circle, then activate the Properties command. How many different changes can be made to the circle?

EXERCISES

EXERCISE 17.1

Draw a 2″ × 4″ rectangle. Place a chamfer on each corner using .25 on both distances.

EXERCISE 17.2

Draw a hexagon circumscribed around a circle with a 1.5″ radius using the Fillet command with a radius of .18. Fillet each corner.

EXERCISE 17.3

Draw a tick-tack-toe setup. Trim off all the lines that overhang so that all you are left with is one square block.

EXERCISE 17.4

Using the Properties command, change the color of the lines in exercise 17.1 to magenta.

EXERCISE 17.5

Draw the given example on the left in Figure 17.58 using .25″ spacing in between the horizontal lines. Use the Extend command to form 90° corners with the vertical line as shown on the right.

EXERCISE 17.6

Use the example in exercise 17.5 as the basic setup. Try the Lengthen command to force the horizontal lines to touch the vertical line. Use the Dynamic option along with Perpendicular Osnap.

EXERCISE 17.7

Draw a 3″ × 3″ square. Using the Stretch command change the shape to 3″ × 6″. Do it using the Direct Distance method with ORTHO turned on.

FIGURE 17.58 Exercise 17.5.

FIGURE 17.59   Exercise 17.8.

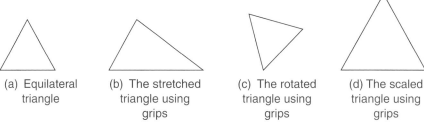

(a) Equilateral triangle   (b) The stretched triangle using grips   (c) The rotated triangle using grips   (d) The scaled triangle using grips

EXERCISE 17.8

Draw an equilateral triangle with the sides measuring 1.5″ (see Figure 17.59a).

 a. Use grips to make the right corner of the triangle the hot grip. Use the Stretch option and move the corner 1″ in the X-direction. Use Direct Distance with ORTHO on (see Figure 17.59b).

 b. Repeat the same sequence with the original triangle as in part (a), except use the Rotate option with a 30° rotation angle (see Figure 17.59c).

 c. Using the same basic triangle and gripping sequence, use the Scale option this time with a scale factor of 1.5 (see Figure 17.59d).

EXERCISE 17.9

Draw the shape shown in Figure 17.60a using a radius of .75″. Draw lines across the quadrants. Using the Break command, break the circle from 90° to 180° as well as from 270° to 0°.

EXERCISE 17.10

Draw the shape shown in Figure 17.61a. Break the lines in the middle of the circle.

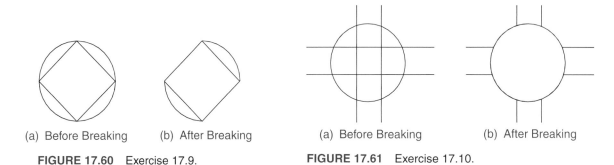

(a) Before Breaking   (b) After Breaking

FIGURE 17.60   Exercise 17.9.

(a) Before Breaking   (b) After Breaking

FIGURE 17.61   Exercise 17.10.

DRAWING ASSIGNMENT

1. Draw all the parts of Figure 17.62 with the assigned scales.

FIGURE 17.62 Drawing Assignment 1.

continued on next page

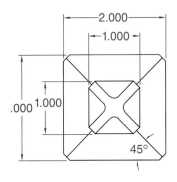

(a)
Scale: 1″ = 1″
Note: All chamfer distances
and fillet radii = .125″

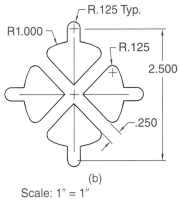

(b)
Scale: 1″ = 1″

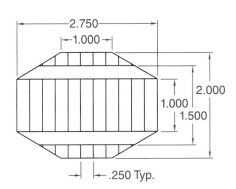

(c)
Scale: 1″ = 1″

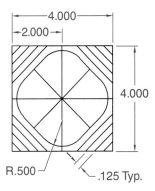

(d)
Scale: 1″ = 1″

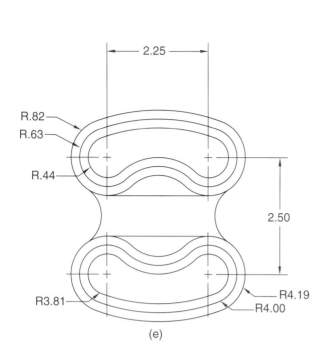

(e)

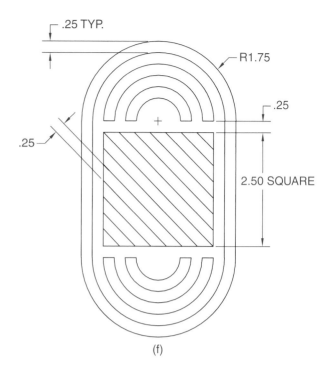

(f)

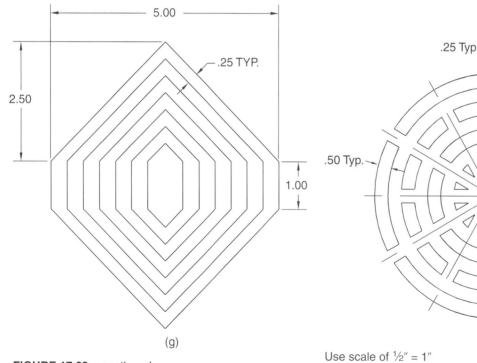

(g)

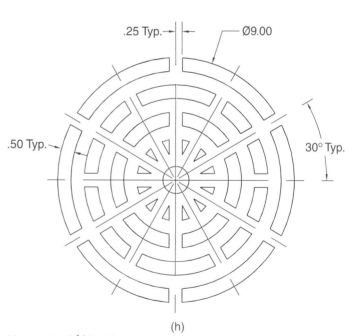

(h)

Use scale of ½″ = 1″

FIGURE 17.62   *continued*

CHAPTER 18

○ ○

Moving and Duplicating Objects

18.1 The Move Command

Move
Icon

- Type **MOVE** or **M** at the command prompt.
- Select Mo<u>v</u>e from the <u>M</u>odify pull-down menu.
- Pick the Move icon from the Modify toolbar. The icon looks like two lines at right angles to each other with arrows on the ends of both lines.

The **Move** command relocates an object in your drawing. Unlike with the Pan command, once you move the object it goes to a different place on the drawing relative to the other objects drawn. The first step once you initiate the Move command is to Select objects:. You can move more than one object at a time. Select the objects with any of the selection methods you learned for the Erase command (Section 13.3). You can pick with the cursor, define a window or a crossing, or type **f** to use a fence. Once you have chosen all the objects you wish to move, press Enter↵.

You should then see a command prompt asking you to Specify base point or displacement:. This is the part of the command where you begin to specify exactly how you want to move the object(s). Several methods are available. Think of trying to give directions to friends helping you move a couch. You might tell them to put the left corner of the couch in the northwest corner of the living room. In an AutoCAD drawing, you could do this by using OSNAP to pick the corner of the couch. (This would specify the base point.) Then when prompted for the second point of displacement, you would use OSNAP to pick the northwest corner of the room. Every object you selected initially would then be moved, with the objects staying in the same relative positions to one another. To continue the couch example—if you selected the couch as well as the pillows on the couch, they would all be moved together. Figure 18.1 shows the sequence for executing this command.

You may also enter coordinates for the base point and second point of displacement, using either absolute or relative coordinates, or you may use the Direct Distance method of entry. The base point does not have to be located on any of the objects being moved (see Figure 18.2). The two points you select simply provide the program with a relative displacement for your object(s).

Now suppose you know that you want your couch moved 2′ toward one wall and 3′ toward the other wall. You can input this information in AutoCAD by using the displacement option. When the command prompt asks you to Specify base point or displacement:, type in the displacement you need. In this case, you would type in @**2,3**. Press Enter↵ at the next prompt, Specify second point of displacement or <use first point as displacement>:. This tells AutoCAD to use the values input in the previous step (2,3) as relative X- and Y-coordinates for displacement. The objects selected will be moved 2 units in the positive X-direction and 3 units in the positive Y-direction (see Figure 18.3).

435

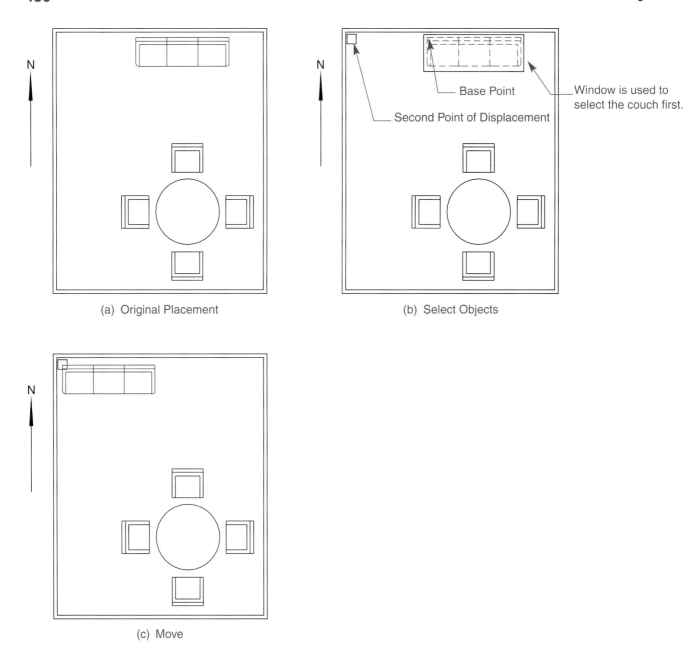

(a) Original Placement

(b) Select Objects

Base Point

Second Point of Displacement

Window is used to
select the couch first.

N

N

N

(c) Move

FIGURE 18.1   Application of the Move command.

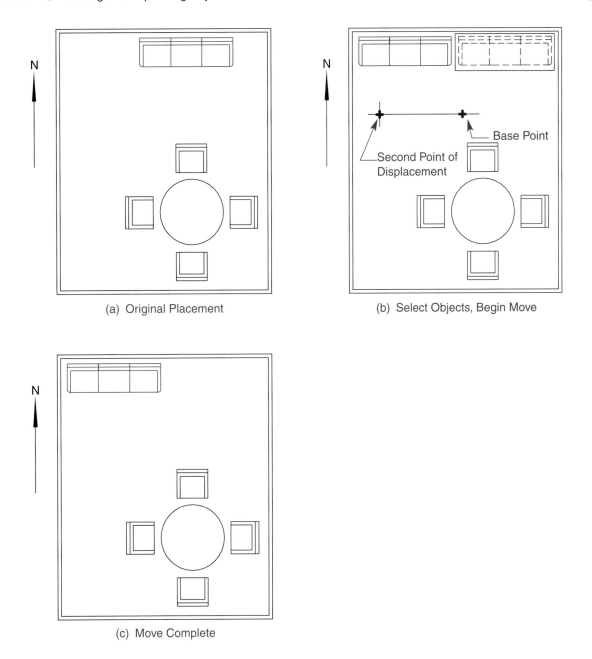

(a) Original Placement

(b) Select Objects, Begin Move

Base Point

Second Point of
Displacement

(c) Move Complete

FIGURE 18.2 Moving an object with a base point not located on the object.

FIGURE 18.3 Moving an object with relative displacement.

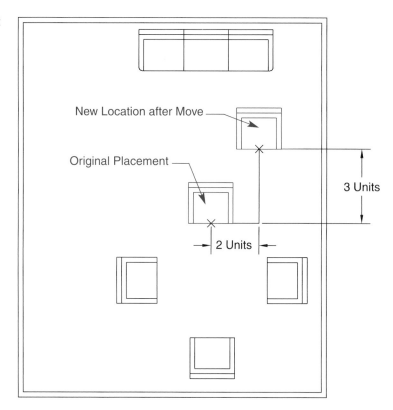

18.2   The Copy Command

Copy
Icon

- Type **Copy** or **CO** or **CP** at the command prompt.
- Select Cop<u>y</u> from the <u>M</u>odify pull-down menu.
- Pick the Copy icon from the Modify toolbar. The icon displays a circle at the top left with an arrow pointing to two overlapping circles at the bottom right.

The **Copy** command works very much like the Move command, so it is important to understand the differences before you begin using the commands. When you Move an object, the object disappears from its original location and becomes established at the new location. The Copy command leaves the original object in the same location and makes one or more copies in a new location. You can copy more than one object at a time using any of the selection options provided by AutoCAD. You specify where to place the copied item using the same procedures for specifying base points or displacement as you do for the Move command.

Take a moment to look over the Copy command sequence:

Select objects:
Specify base point or displacement, or [Multiple]:
Specify second point of displacement or <use first point as displacement>:

The sequence is almost identical with the Move command sequence with the exception of the Multiple option. If you wish to make more than one copy of an object, type **M** then press Enter↵ at that point in the command sequence. The command prompt will then again ask you to Specify base point:. When you start specifying second points, you can make multiple copies without having to reenter the command. When you have made all the copies you want, press Enter↵ to exit the command (see Figure 18.4).

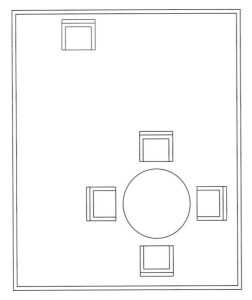

(a) Original

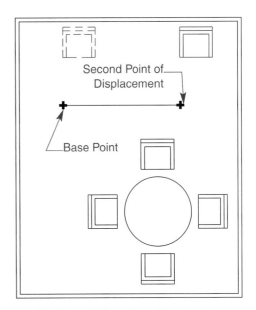

(b) Select Object, Base Point, and
Second Point of Displacement

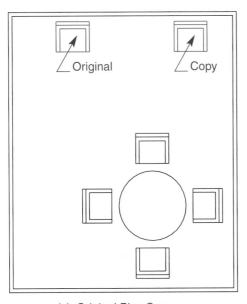

(c) Original Plus Copy

FIGURE 18.4 Application of the Copy command.

18.3 The Mirror Command

- Type **MIRROR** or **MI** at the command prompt.
- Select Mirror from the Modify pull-down menu.
- Pick the Mirror icon from the Modify toolbar. The icon has two triangles mirrored around a thin red line.

Mirror
Icon

When Alice walked through the mirror into Looking Glass Land, everything was exactly the same as the "real" world, only opposite. Sometimes you need to create that same effect in a drawing. The Mirror command allows you to create a mirror image of any object(s) in your drawing. This is a great tool. For example, if you have a section of your drawing that is perfectly symmetrical, you can draw half of the item and then use Mirror (see Figure 18.5).

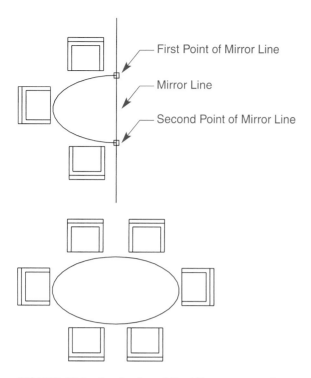

FIGURE 18.5   Application of the Mirror command.

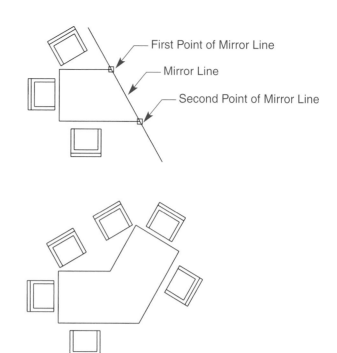

FIGURE 18.6   Example of an angled mirror line.

Once you enter the Mirror command, the first step is to select the objects you wish to mirror. The command prompt displays the message Specify first point of mirror line, then you are asked to Specify second point of mirror line:. You are defining where the mirror is to be situated. If you select two points that define a line 4′ from the original object, the mirrored object will be constructed at a distance 4′ from the mirror line or 8′ from the original object. If the mirror line is at an angle relative to the original object, the mirrored object will be constructed at an angle to the original (see Figure 18.6).

The final question before the Mirror command is executed is Delete source objects? [Yes/No]<N>:. If you do not delete the source objects, the original objects selected at the beginning of the command will be left in place, just as they were before you entered the Mirror command. If you answer yes to this question, the original objects will be deleted from your drawing and only the mirrored objects will appear. Notice that the default answer, shown in the angled brackets, is N for no. Simply pressing Enter↵ and accepting the default will leave your original object in place along with the new mirrored object.

Note: Try turning the ORTHO on when mirroring objects in a vertical or horizontal alignment.

18.4   The Offset Command

- Type **OFFSET** or **O** at the command prompt.
- Select Offset from the Modify pull-down menu.
- Pick the Offset icon from the Modify toolbar. The icon shows two irregularly shaped objects, one inside the other. The inside shape is red.

Offset
Icon

The **Offset** command is useful for creating parallel lines or concentric circles, arcs, and ellipses. When used with an existing line, the Offset command generates a copy of the line at a specified distance away (see Figure 18.7a). When used with an arc, a circle, ellipse, or polygon, the Offset command generates a new entity of the same basic shape as the original at the specified distance away (see Figure 18.7b). For example, if you use the command to create concentric circles, choosing an offset toward the inside of the circle will create a smaller circle centered inside the original circle. Choosing an offset toward the outside of the circle will create a larger circle around the original circle.

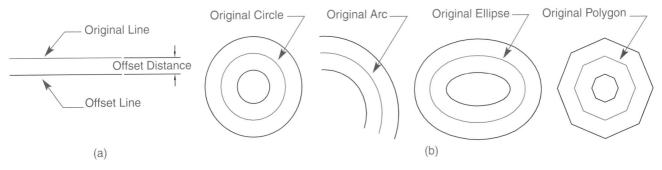

FIGURE 18.7 Using the Offset command on a line, arc, circle, and ellipse. Offsets may be placed on either side of a line or object.

Take a moment to look over the offset command sequence.

Specify offset distance or [Through]<Through>:
Specify second point:
Select object to offset or <exit>:
Specify point on side to offset:

The first steps in the command deal with setting the offset distance. Two options are available for setting this distance. You can simply input a number indicating the distance that you want placed between the objects being offset. If you do this, the request for a second point does not appear. The other option is to utilize the **Through** option, which asks you to specify two points that will define the offset distance.

Once the offset distance is set, you are ready to begin selecting objects to offset. At this point your cursor changes from a crosshair to a small square. Offsets are performed on one entity at a time, so the only method of selection allowed is to choose the object with the pick box. As soon as the object is selected Auto-CAD displays it as a dashed line. If you are paying attention, this should prevent you from offsetting the wrong object. If you are having trouble picking an object, you may need to use a transparent Zoom (see Chapter 14, Section 14.5) to get "close" enough to select the desired entity.

AutoCAD will repeat the last two steps of the command until you press Enter↵ (or Esc or the space bar) to exit the command sequence. You can continue to offset as many times as you need. You can even offset from an object that has just been created. Of course, the offset distance will remain the same. To change the distance you must exit and reenter the command.

Note: The Offset command cannot be used with 3D objects or faces.

Offset works with 2D polylines as well. A polyline offsets as a single entity, so if you select a rectangle that has been created with the Pline or Rectangle command, the entire rectangle will offset. If the rectangle was constructed with four separate line segments, you will have to offset each line separately. In addition, the offset will be exactly the same length as the original lines, so you will need to trim or extend them to obtain a perfect rectangle. Figure 18.8 illustrates these differences.

FIGURE 18.8 Using the Offset command on a Pline rectangle versus a rectangle made of separate lines.

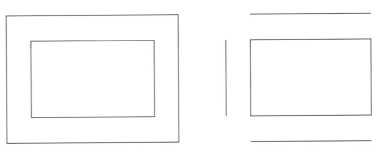

(a) Figure Drawn with Rectangle Command (Polyline) then Offset

(b) Figure Drawn with Line Command then Offset

18.5   The Rotate Command

Rotate
Icon

- Type **ROTATE** or **RO** at the command prompt.
- Select Rotate from the Modify pull-down menu.
- Pick the Rotate icon from the Modify toolbar. The icon contains a circular line with an arrow showing a clockwise direction.

The **Rotate** command allows you to rotate items within your drawing. You can select several items at once using any of the selection methods including the pick box, a window, a crossing, or a fence. The objects will be rotated around a base point that you select. This base point can be on one of the objects, or it can be totally removed from the objects. Object snaps (OSNAP) can be very useful in selecting this base point. Figures 18.9 and 18.10 show examples of using the Rotate command with different base points.

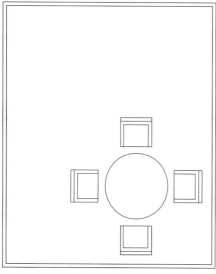

(a) Original Location

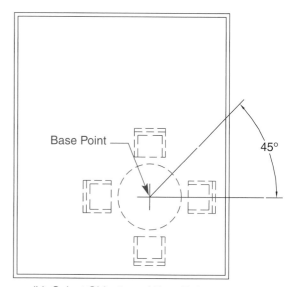

(b) Select Objects and Base Point

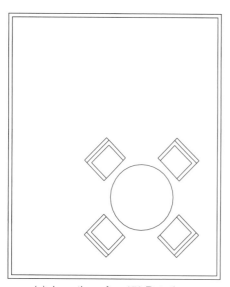

(c) Location after 45° Rotation

FIGURE 18.9   Using the Rotate command with the base point on an object.

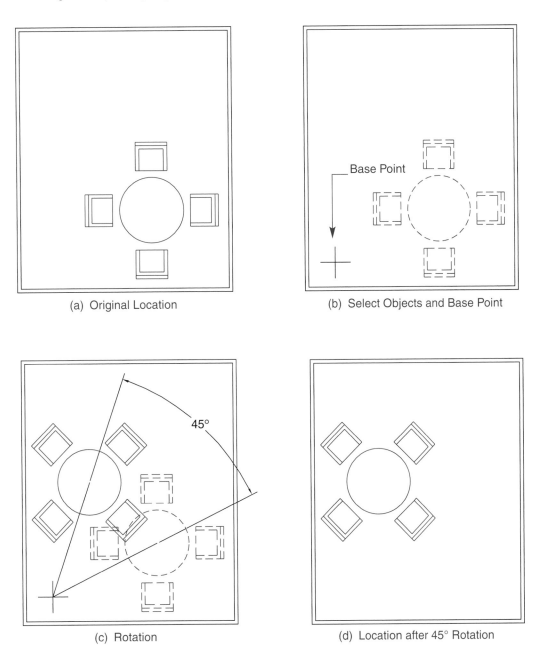

(a) Original Location

(b) Select Objects and Base Point

Base Point

(c) Rotation

45°

(d) Location after 45° Rotation

FIGURE 18.10 Using the Rotate command with the base point away from an object.

Take a moment to look over the Rotate command sequence.

Command: **ROTATE**
Current positive angle in UCS: ANGDIR=counterclockwise ANGBASE=0
Select objects:
Specify base point:
Specify rotation angle or [Reference]:

As soon as you enter the command AutoCAD displays the current settings for constructing angles. In this example, the angle direction (ANGDIR) is set at counterclockwise while the base angle (ANGBAS) is set at zero. These are the default values. They can be changed either when you set up the drawing or separately during the course of the session. When the command line prompts you to select the objects to be rotated, the cursor changes to a pick box. As you pick items to be rotated they will appear on the screen as dashed lines. When you have chosen all the objects you wish to rotate, press Enter↵ to indicate that you wish

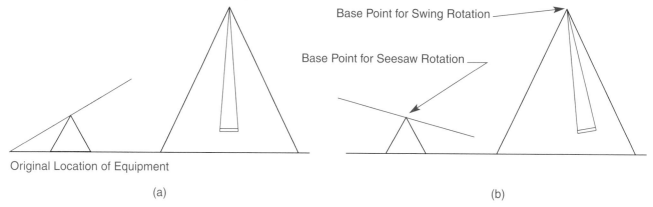

Base Point for Swing Rotation

Base Point for Seesaw Rotation

Original Location of Equipment

(a)

(b)

FIGURE 18.11   Application of the Rotate command.

to proceed to the next step. Now you are ready to specify a base point. This is the point about which all the objects selected will be rotated. The objects rotate about this point as a group; their positions relative to each other do not change. The last step of the process is to specify a rotation angle (or reference angles). The direction and basis for the angles will be based on the information displayed at the beginning of the command. The following example walks you through using the command. You will want to experiment with using the command on your own. Make sure you understand the difference between the Move command and the Rotate command.

Example: The Rotate Command

Step 1.   Use a Wizard to Start a New Drawing. Use the Quick Setup with Decimal Units and an area of 8.5 × 11. Use the Zoom Extents commands to zoom to the limits of your drawing. (If you want to "see" the Limits on your screen, turn the GRID on.)

Step 2.   Use the Line command to draw figures similar to the playground equipment shown in Figure 18.11a. Feel free to utilize any other commands that make drawing the figure easier for you.

Step 3.   Use the Rotate command to tilt the seesaw −45° and swing +10°. Rotate the seesaw about the top point of the triangle (the fulcrum). Rotate the swing around the pivot point at the top where the two supports come together (see Figure 18.11b).

18.6   The Array Command

- Type **ARRAY** or **AR** at the command prompt.
- Select <u>A</u>rray from the <u>M</u>odify pull-down menu.
- Pick the Array icon from the Modify toolbar. The icon displays four square boxes in a rectangular array.

Array
Icon

Like most of the other commands in this chapter, the **Array** command has the potential to save a lot of drawing time. The command takes an object (or several objects) and makes copies that are placed in an ordered pattern. The pattern may be either rectangular or polar.

Rectangular Array

Choosing the **rectangular array** option will copy your objects into a regularly spaced arrangement of rows and columns. The following command sequence is used for a rectangular array.

Command: **ARRAY**
Select objects:
Enter the type of array [Rectangular/Polar]<R>:
Enter the number of rows (---)<1>:
Enter the number of columns (| | |):
Enter the distance between rows or specify unit cell (---):
Specify the distance between columns (| | |):

Both the rectangular and the polar arrays start out by prompting you to select objects. These objects can be chosen using any of the normal selection methods such as windows, crossings, or fences. You can select one object or several to array. When you have included all the entities required, press Enter↵ to indicate that you are ready to proceed to the next step, which is selecting the type of array. If you want to construct a rectangular array, type in **R** and press Enter↵. The letter in the angle brackets indicates the default setting from the previous time the command was used. If the angle brackets already contain an *R*, you can simply press Enter↵ to accept the default option.

Now you must indicate the number of rows and columns you wish to have in your array. You can have an array with one row *or* one column, but you cannot have an array with one row *and* one column. In other words, either the number of rows or the number of columns must be greater than 1. This makes sense because a 1 × 1 array would leave you with the original object and no copies, so the command would accomplish absolutely nothing. In case you have trouble remembering the directions in which rows and columns run, AutoCAD provides you with a handy reminder in the command line. Rows run horizontally, so the program puts three horizontal dashes inside parentheses as a reminder. Likewise, columns run vertically, so three vertical dashes are shown.

Note: If you have only one row, the prompt will ask you to specify only the distance between columns.

Once you have selected the number of rows and columns, the next prompt to appear is to determine the distance between the rows. You can do this in one of two ways. One way is to directly enter a number, which will be the distance between each row plus the length of the object being arrayed. So, for example, if you were arraying a rectangle, the distance between rows would be from the top of one row to the top of the next row (see Figure 18.12). The command assumes that the objects selected will be in the lower left corner of the array. If this configuration is not what you have in mind, you can place a negative sign in front of the distance between rows to indicate that the array should be constructed downward instead of upward. The distance between columns works in much the same way (see Figure 18.12). If you input a negative number for the column distance, the array will be constructed to the left of the original object(s) instead of in the default direction to the right.

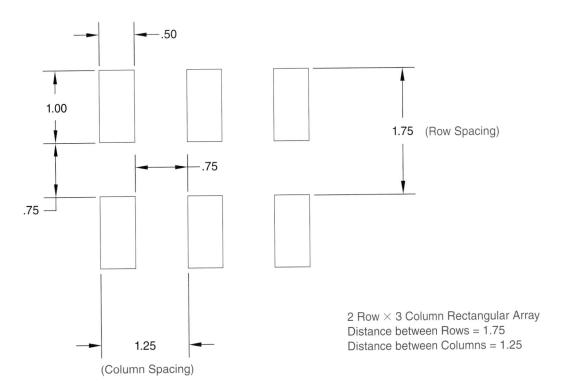

FIGURE 18.12 Determining the distance between rows and columns in an array.

The other way to indicate the distance between rows in an array is to specify a unit cell. A **unit cell** is a rectangle that you define by specifying two points at opposite corners. You can identify the unit cell either by picking the corners with the cursor or by entering a set of absolute or relative coordinates. If you use the cursor, a window will appear after the first point is picked. This window serves to show you the tentative size of the window at the present cursor location. The cell is not actually defined until you pick a second point. It is important to realize that the unit cell defines only *distance*. It does not define *location*. Because the unit cell has length as well as width, the program uses the cell to define the distance between the columns as well as between the rows. Thus, if you utilize this option, the command line will not prompt you to specify the distance between columns.

Example: Rectangular Array—Table and Chairs

Arrays are very useful in architectural drawings. Drawing multiple seat layouts in movie theaters, churches, and school classrooms becomes a snap. Look at Figure 18.13, which shows a rectangular array of a table and chair. Draw your own table and chair using your own dimensions and make a similar array. Use a ¼"=1'-0" scale with 5 columns and 4 rows.

Polar Array

Instead of arraying an object (or objects) into a configuration of rows and columns, the **polar array** command constructs a circular pattern of objects around a central point (see Figure 18.14). The command sequence starts off just like the rectangular array by prompting you to select objects. You have to indicate that you wish to construct a polar array by typing in **P** and then pressing Enter.⏎. Take a moment to look over the command sequence.

```
Command: ARRAY
Select objects:
Enter the type of array [Rectangular/Polar]<R>:
Specify center point of array:
Enter the number of items in the array:
Specify the angle to fill (+=ccw,- =cw)<360>:
Rotate arrayed objects?[Yes/No]<Y>:
```

FIGURE 18.13 A rectangular array.

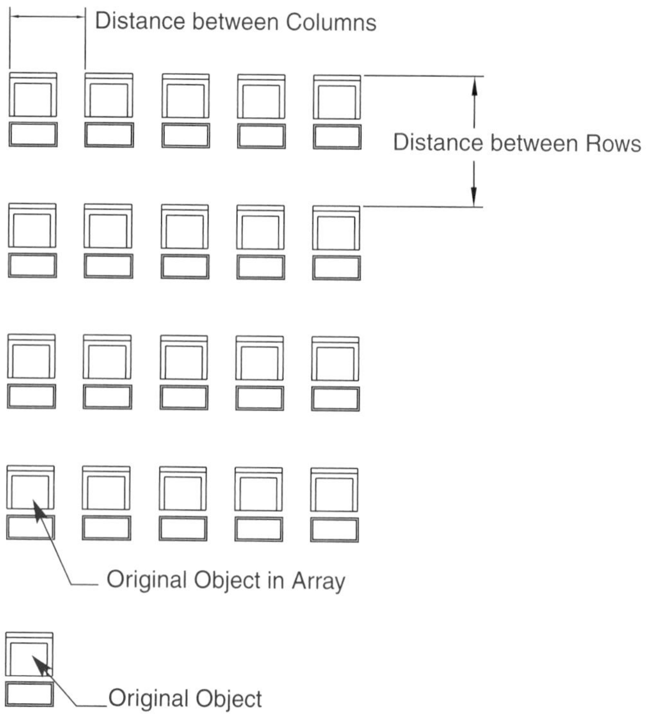

FIGURE 18.14 A polar array.

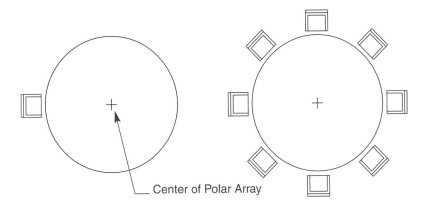

Center of Polar Array

Think of the center point of a polar array as the center of a clock face. All the objects in the array will be constructed in positions relative to this point. The center point can be chosen using coordinates or by picking with the cursor. The number of objects in the array is the final number once the array is complete, so the original object should be included in this count. If, for example, you enter **4** as the number of objects in the array, your final polar array will include four objects—the original plus three copies. The next step in the process allows you to choose the angle that you want your array to include. A polar array does not have to go around a complete circle (or 360°). The prompt reminds you that positive numbers will indicate a counterclockwise (ccw) angle, whereas negative numbers indicate a clockwise angle (cw). The last decision you must make is whether to rotate the objects being arrayed. If you accept the default value, which is Yes, the items will be rotated around the center point (see Figure 18.15a). If you type **NO**↵ at the prompt, the items will be displayed in the exact same position as the original (see Figure 18.15b).

FIGURE 18.15 Effect of rotating on a polar array.

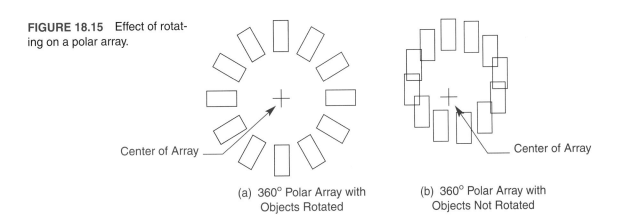

Center of Array

Center of Array

(a) 360° Polar Array with Objects Rotated

(b) 360° Polar Array with Objects Not Rotated

REVIEW QUESTIONS

1. Can you move more than one object at a time?

2. Is it possible to use relative coordinates to specify the displacement for an object?

3. What is the difference between the Move command and the Copy command?

4. What option would you utilize to copy an object several times without exiting and reentering the Copy command?

5. When you Mirror an object in your drawing are you always left with both the original and the mirrored image? Explain your answer.

6. Give a short explanation of the Offset command.

7. How do the Move and Rotate commands differ? How are they similar?

8. Explain how OSNAPs can be helpful when moving and duplicating objects.

9. Think of two examples in which the Array command could be used on a drawing. Give an example for both polar and rectangular arrays.

10. If you are drawing a rectangular array in which the objects are 3″ tall and need a 1″ space between each object, what value should you use for the distance between the rows?

EXERCISES

EXERCISE 18.1

Draw the table and chairs shown in Figure 18.16. Use an overall size of 3′ × 6′ for the table and a 10″ radius for the outside circle of the chairs. Use the figure as a typical layout and size for a restaurant's dining room. Take a 30′ × 60′ room and put as many tables in it as possible using a spacing of 5′ between chair backs and walls. Use a scale of ¼″ = 1′-0″. Use a Limits setup of 0,0 and 68′,44′.

EXERCISE 18.2

Draw a circle with a 2″ diameter. Using the Array command array the line 10 times using a polar array. Choose the midpoint of the line as a base point and use a 180° angle to make three copies of the tree (see Figure 18.17).

EXERCISE 18.3

a. Draw a rectangle to enclose the four trees of exercise 18.2 (see Figure 18.18a).

b. Move each tree and place the centers at the corners of the rectangle (see Figure 18.18b).

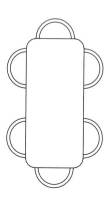

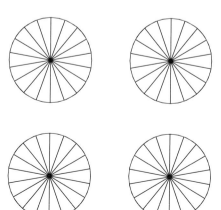

FIGURE 18.16   Exercise 18.1.   **FIGURE 18.17**   Exercise 18.2.

c. Rotate the entire drawing at a 45° angle using the center of the bottom left circle (see Figure 18.18c).

d. Draw a vertical line to the right of the shape. Use the endpoints of the line as a reference for a Mirror command. Mirror the entire shape to the right side leaving the original objects in place (see Figure 18.18d).

e. Using the Offset command, Offset the circle .50 inside and outside the originals (see Figure 18.18e).

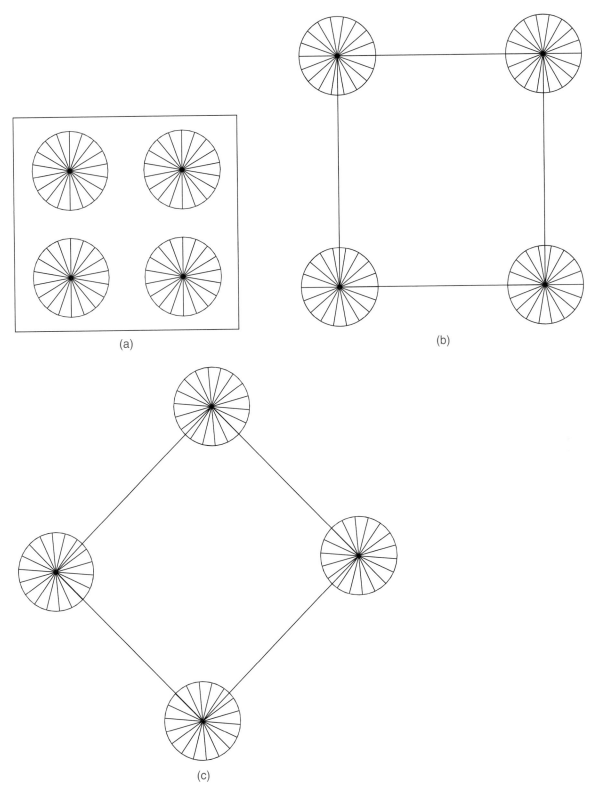

(a)

(b)

(c)

FIGURE 18.18 Exercise 18.3.
continued on next page

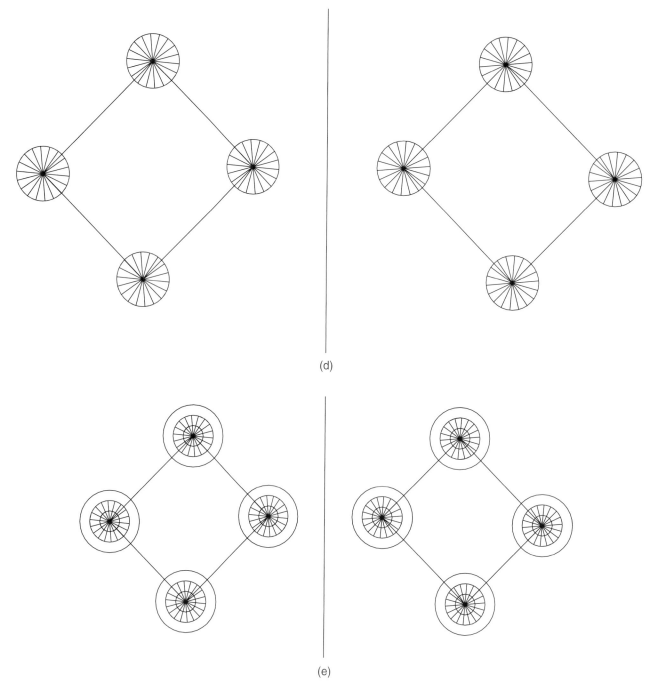

(d)

(e)

FIGURE 18.18 *continued*

EXERCISE 18.4

Using the Polygon command, draw a hexagon circumscribed around a circle with .75″ radius. Create the shape seen in Figure 18.19.

FIGURE 18.19 Exercise 18.4.

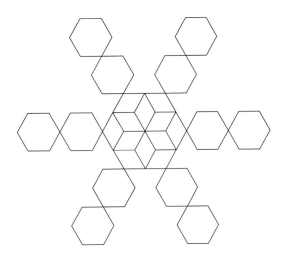

DRAWING ASSIGNMENTS

1. Draw the door elevation in Figure 18.20 using a scale of ⅜″ = 1′-0″. Use an offset of 2″ for the panels.

2. Draw the window elevation in Figure 18.21 using a scale of ⅜″ = 1′-0″. Divide the window into four equal sections, then divide the glass into four equal sections. Use an offset of 2″ for the panels.

3. Draw the deck in Figure 18.22 at a ¼″ = 1′-0″ scale. The deck has 6″-wide deck boards. Create some plants around the perimeter.

4. Draw the elevation in Figure 18.23 at a scale of ¼″ = 1′-0″.

5. Draw the two-bedroom apartment shown in Figure 18.24 at a ¼″ = 1′-0″ scale. Set limits at 0,0 and 68′,88′ (17″ × 22″ plotted sheet). Mirror the plan to create a duplex. Use 4½″-thick interior walls with 6″ exterior walls.

6. Draw the front side and rear elevations to the duplex in assignment 5. Use a ¼″ = 1′-0″ scale.

7. Draw the orthographic views for the objects in Figure 18.25.

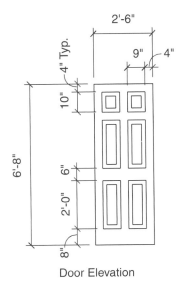

Door Elevation

FIGURE 18.20 Drawing Assignment 1.

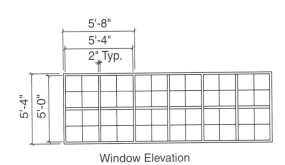

Window Elevation

FIGURE 18.21 Drawing Assignment 2.

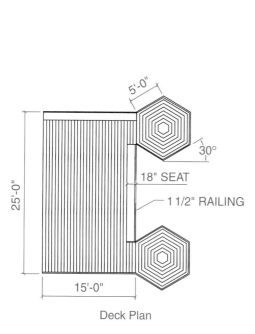

Deck Plan

FIGURE 18.22   Drawing Assignment 3.

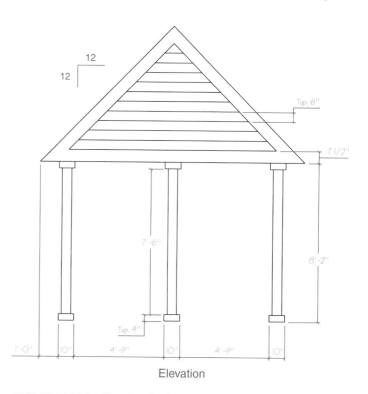

Elevation

FIGURE 18.23   Drawing Assignment 4.

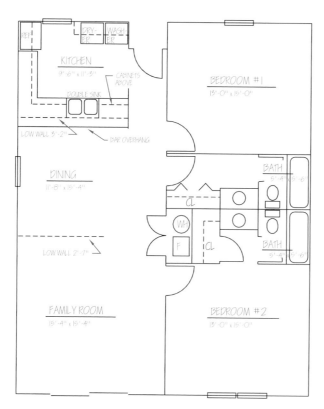

Two-Bedroom Apartment

FIGURE 18.24   Drawing Assignment 5.

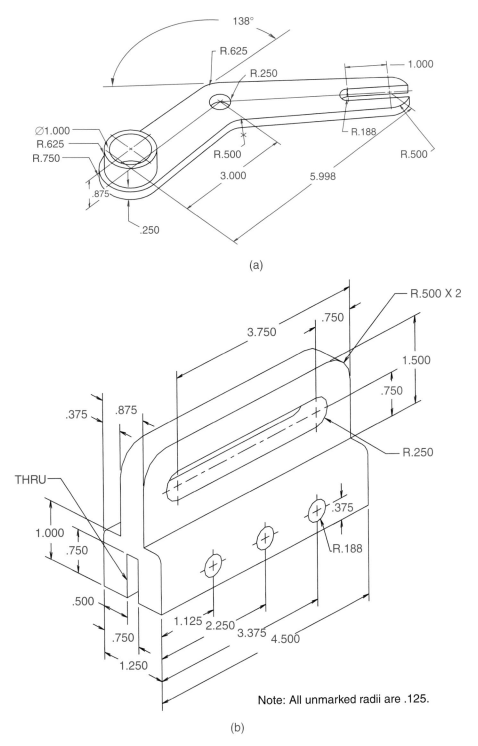

(a)

(b)

Note: All unmarked radii are .125.

FIGURE 18.25
continued on next page

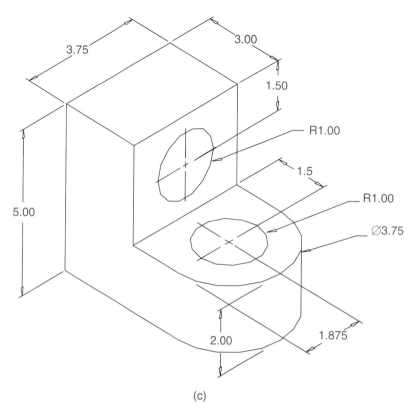

(c)

FIGURE 18.25
continued

CHAPTER **19**

○ ○

Layers

19.1 Why Use Layers?

First, let's talk about what layers are, then we'll move on to why you might use them. Layers are a way to group together parts of a drawing that have some logical connection with one another. Each layer can be assigned a different color, linetype, and lineweight. Each layer can be viewed by itself or with a group of other layers. When you initially set up a drawing, AutoCAD provides you with a single layer. This is the only layer that is absolutely required. As long as the drawings remain simple, one layer may be all that you will need, but as you become more proficient with the program, you may find yourself looking for tools to organize your information.

Think of layers as a series of transparent overlays used for presentation on an overhead projector. Each overlay relates to the others but can also be shown alone. Science teachers in elementary school use a set of overlays to teach children about the human body. Placed one on top of another, the overlays show systems of a human body. Overlays are a good way to show the relationships among the various parts of the body, but it is also helpful to peel off layers and study each system separately. Layers work the same way in AutoCAD. You can group objects in your drawing based on common characteristics. For example, on a house plan you could put the walls on one layer, the dimensions on another, and the text on another. The electrical, plumbing, and HVAC could also be placed on separate layers. The interior designer could create a furniture layout on a separate layer. Since you can choose which layers to display, the designer might choose not to show the electrical and mechanical layers while working on the drawings. In addition, several different furniture layouts could be produced and then placed on separate layers. Because AutoCAD allows you to choose which layers are plotted, several layouts could be printed without erasing and starting over each time.

In the same way, a landscape designer could use layers to create several landscape designs. The initial drawing might contain all the information provided for the site plan. The designer could then create a layer for an initial landscape plan. Another layer could be created for plantings to be added over a 5-year period. Another alternative would be to place all trees on one layer, shrubs on another, and base plantings on another. AutoCAD allows each layer to be displayed and printed in separate colors, linetypes, and lineweights. These options can help bring clarity to your drawings.

19.2 Accessing the Layer Properties Manager

- Type **LAYER** or **LA** at the command prompt.
- Select <u>L</u>ayer from the <u>F</u>ormat pull-down menu.
- Click on the Layer icon on the Object Properties toolbar. The icon shows a stack of papers.

Layer
Icon

Once you have accessed the Layer Properties Manager (see Figure 19.1), you have a variety of options from which to choose. The next few sections of the text describe how to take advantage of the choices available.

FIGURE 19.1 Layer Properties Manager showing default layer.

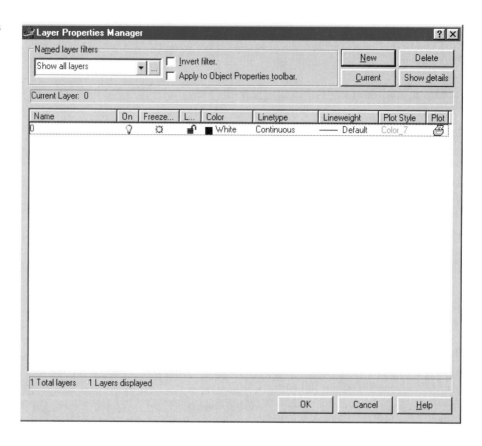

19.3 Naming and Creating New Layers

The first time you enter the Layer Properties Manager, only one layer, named 0, will be shown (see Figure 19.1). This is the default layer that is automatically created when you start a new drawing. This is the only layer required by AutoCAD, and it cannot be purged or renamed.

You can create additional layers in your drawing by picking the New button in the Layer Properties Manager dialog box. A new layer listing will appear highlighted on the screen with the name of the layer outlined with a box (see Figure 19.2). AutoCAD defaults to numbering the layers; however, you can use up to 255 characters to create your own names. Letters, numbers, and certain special characters such as spaces can be used. If you use an invalid character (such as ,.Λ':?=`) the program will let you know immediately with a polite message.

Layers can be based on a number of different systems. For simple drawings, it may be easiest to group layers by color and linetype. For more complex drawings, layers may be determined by the function of the objects in the layer. Notice as you create new layers that the layers are listed using alphanumeric sorting. Numbered layers are listed first, followed by an alphabetical listing of the additional layers.

Once you have entered a new layer, you can make it current by highlighting the layer and picking the Current button. Once a layer is current, any new objects drawn will be placed on that layer until another layer is selected as current. The exception to this rule is objects being edited using some of the modify commands such as Match Properties or Properties. If the program uses an existing object to construct a new entity, the new entity will be placed on the same layer as the existing one. Different colors are often assigned to different layers as a visual clue of an object's affiliation.

Several layer names can be entered at one time without having to choose the New button between each layer. Simply type in the new layer name followed by a comma each time. When you are finished entering new layer names press Enter↵ or pick OK if you are finished with the Layer Properties Manager.

19.4 Layer Properties

Color

The default color for AutoCAD is white. Objects will be shown as white on a screen with a black background. This does not mean that the lines will be invisible if you are using a white background for your screen. With a white background, the lines are shown as black. In the same way, any layers plotted on white paper will be drawn in black.

Note: To highlight a layer, left-click in the name area for that particular layer.

Note: In the releases prior to Auto-CAD 2000, names could not be longer than 31 characters and could not contain spaces. If you save a drawing from AutoCAD 2000 in the format of an earlier release, the program will automatically shorten the layer names and replace any spaces with underscores (_).

Note: AutoCAD will create a layer called Defpoints when certain commands are used. Leave this layer alone. This is *not* a layer for you to use.

FIGURE 19.2 Layer Properties
Manager with New layer being
created.

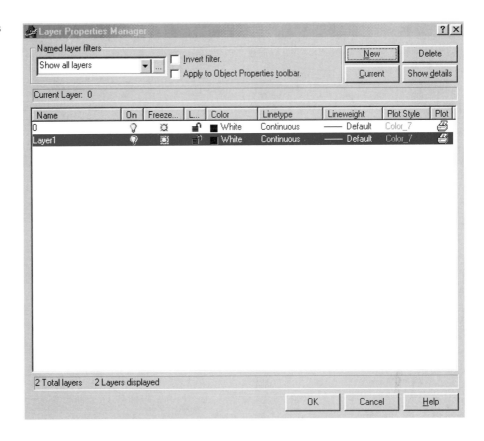

FIGURE 19.3 Select Color dialog box.

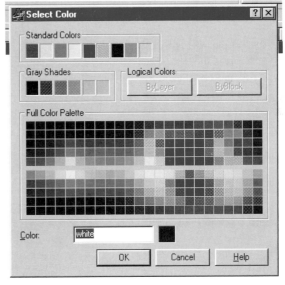

Note: The ACI
number will appear
in the Color: text box
once the color has
been chosen. Once
you have selected a
color, pick OK to exit
the Select Color dia-
log box. The new
color for the layer
should now be dis-
played in the Layer
Properties Manager.

To select the color for a layer, highlight the layer and left-click on the color displayed. The Select Color dialog box will appear on your screen (see Figure 19.3). Layer colors are coded by name and by number. You can
select a color by picking it directly from the display or by entering the name or number in the Color: text box.

The number of colors available will depend on the graphics card and the monitor of your system. Seven
standard colors as well as several gray shades are displayed at the top of the Select Color dialog box. The
numbers assigned to each color are as follows:

1   Red

2   Yellow

3   Green

Color is most often assigned BYLAYER or BYBLOCK, which means that all the objects in a particular layer or block are the same color. You can use the Properties command to modify the color of single objects within a layer; however, we do not recommend this.

Note: The gaps and spaces found on different linetypes (hidden, center, and phantom) may appear as continuous lines if the **Ltscale** (Linetype scale) is set incorrectly for the current drawing scale. The default Ltscale is set at 1 when a new drawing is started from scratch. A good practice is to set the Ltscale as you choose what drawing setup is needed for the drawing scale to be used. See Appendix B for typical Ltscale settings.
To change a Ltscale setting is easy. At the command line type in the following:
Command: **LTS** ⏎
LTSCALE Enter new linetype scale factor <1.0000>:
At this point just type in the desired value for your drawing scale. This value is good for all the lines on the drawing. To change a single line's Ltscale, you must use the Properties command, which is described in Chapter 17.

4   Cyan

5   Blue

6   Magenta

7   White

Linetype

Unless you decide otherwise, all lines drawn by AutoCAD will be of the continuous type. Notice that the linetype for your default layer 0 is Continuous. If you wish to change the linetype for a layer, you need to highlight the layer and left-click on the Linetype column to display the Select Linetype dialog box (see Figure 19.4).

The first time you open this dialog box only one linetype will be displayed. The standard linetypes are stored in an external file named acad.lin. Storing the files externally allows you to load only those linetypes required for your specific application. If the linetype you wish to use is not displayed in the Select Linetype box, pick the Load… button to activate the Load or Reload Linetypes dialog box (see Figure 19.5). The linetypes available are listed along with their appearance and a brief description. Highlight the linetype desired and pick OK. Back in the Select Linetype dialog box, highlight the linetype desired and pick OK again. The correct linetype should now appear in the Layer Properties Manager. Pick OK once again to return to your drawing.

FIGURE 19.4   Select Linetype dialog box.

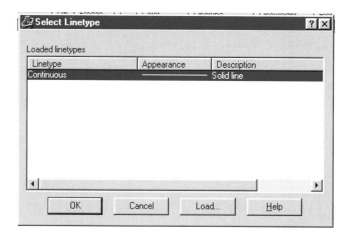

FIGURE 19.5   Load or Reload Linetypes dialog box.

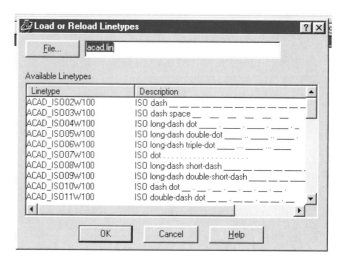

Note: An ISO library of linetypes is available by picking the File . . . button in the Load or Reload Linetypes dialog box and selecting acadiso.lin (see Figure 19.6). The ISO linetypes are identical in the acad.lin and acadiso.lin files. The difference lies in the non-ISO linetypes. These are scaled up by a factor of 25.4 to convert them from inches into millimeters.

ACAD_ISOO2W100	ISO dash
ACAD_ISOO3W100	ISO dash space
ACAD_ISOO4W100	ISO long-dash dot
ACAD_ISOO5W100	ISO long-dash double dot
ACAD_ISOO6W100	ISO long-dash triple dot
ACAD_ISOO7W100	ISO dot
ACAD_ISOO8W100	ISO long-dash short-dash
ACAD_ISOO9W100	ISO long-dash double-short-dash
ACAD_ISOO10W100	ISO dash dot
ACAD_ISOO11W100	ISO double-dash dot
ACAD_ISOO12W100	ISO dash double-dash
ACAD_ISOO13W100	ISO double-dash double-dot
ACAD_ISOO14W100	ISO dash triple-dot
ACAD_ISOO15W100	ISO double-dash triple-dot
BATTING	Batting
BORDER	Border
BORDER2	Border (.5x)
BORDERX2	Border (2x)
CENTER	Center
CENTER2	Center (.5x)
CENTERX2	Center (2x)
DASHDOT	Dash dot
DASHDOT2	Dash dot (.5x)
DASHDOTX2	Dash dot (2x)
DASHED	Dashed
DASHED2	Dashed (.5x)
DASHEDX2	Dashed (2x)
DIVIDE	Divide
DIVIDE2	Divide (.5x)
DIVIDEX2	Divide (2x)
DOT	Dot
DOT2	Dot (.5x)
DOTX2	Dot (2x)
FENCELINE1	Fenceline circle
FENCELINE2	Fenceline square
GAS_LINE	Gas line
HIDDEN	Hidden
HIDDEN2	Hidden (.5x)
HIDDENX2	Hidden (2x)
HOT_WATER_SUPPLY	Hot Water Supply
PHANTOM	Phantom
PHANTOM2	Phantom (.5x)
PHANTOMX2	Phantom (2x)
TRACKS	Tracks
ZIGZAG	Zigzag

FIGURE 19.6 AutoCAD linetype library of standard, ISO, and complex linetypes.

Lineweight

AutoCAD 2000 is the first release to allow weight or thickness to be assigned to objects that were not polylines. The default Lineweight is set at 0.01″ or 0.25 mm. To change the lineweight, highlight the layer and pick the lineweight column. The Lineweight dialog box should appear (see Figure 19.7). The available lineweights are based on those most commonly used in drawing (see Figure 19.8). The width varies from 0.00 mm to 2.11 mm. The original as well as the new lineweight will be shown in the area near the bottom of the dialog box.

FIGURE 19.7   Lineweight dialog box.

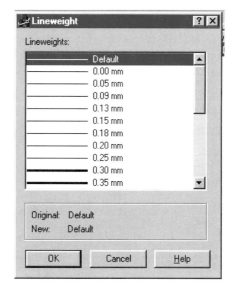

Alphabet of Lines for Mechanical Drawing

Thicker/Wide lines
Line width around 1/32″ or about the same width as a 0.7-mm drawing pencil

Thin lines
Line width around 1/64″ or a little wider than a 0.3-mm pencil lead

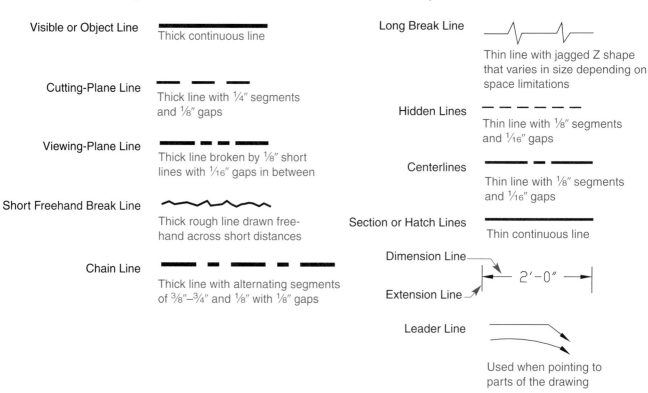

Visible or Object Line
Thick continuous line

Cutting-Plane Line
Thick line with 1/4″ segments and 1/8″ gaps

Viewing-Plane Line
Thick line broken by 1/8″ short lines with 1/16″ gaps in between

Short Freehand Break Line
Thick rough line drawn freehand across short distances

Chain Line
Thick line with alternating segments of 3/8″–3/4″ and 1/8″ with 1/8″ gaps

Long Break Line
Thin line with jagged Z shape that varies in size depending on space limitations

Hidden Lines
Thin line with 1/8″ segments and 1/16″ gaps

Centerlines
Thin line with 1/8″ segments and 1/16″ gaps

Section or Hatch Lines
Thin continuous line

Dimension Line
Extension Line
2′-0″

Leader Line
Used when pointing to parts of the drawing

Phantom Line
Thin line broken every 3/4″–1.5″ by two 1/8″ lines with 1/16″ gaps in between

FIGURE 19.8   Alphabet of lineweights.

19.5 On/Off, Freeze/Thaw, and Locking Layers

Turning Layers On and Off

Note: To regenerate a drawing type Regen at the command line. At times AutoCAD will automatically perform a regeneration after a command. A Regen command will recalculate the screen, refreshing and sharpening the lines and shapes.

Looking at the Layer Properties Manager dialog box (see Figure 19.9) you will notice that the first column after the Name is designated On and contains a column of light bulbs. If the bulb shows yellow, the layer is turned on. If the bulb is gray, the layer is off. The light bulb toggles between off and on as you pick it with the cursor.

If the layer is turned off, the objects within that layer will not be displayed on the screen and will not show up on a plot. However, the objects can still be affected by certain editing techniques. For example, if you enter the Erase command and select the All option, the objects in the layers that are turned off will still be erased. If you Regen your drawing, the layers that are turned off will still be regenerated.

Layers are often turned off to avoid confusion on a crowded screen. Sometimes you wish to plot only certain features of a drawing. For example, a floor plan drawing will not always have the electrical information plotted.

Freezing and Thawing Layers

The third column in the Layer Properties Manager dialog box is entitled Freeze…. The layers displaying a yellow sun under this column are considered *thawed*. The layers displaying a white snowflake are *frozen*. Frozen layers are not displayed on the screen, nor are they plotted. In addition, frozen layers cannot be edited or regenerated. Freezing a layer may speed up system performance in a very complex drawing. The Freeze/Thaw icons can be toggled just like the On/Off icons by picking on the icon.

Locking and Unlocking Layers

The fourth column in the Layer Properties Manager dialog box in entitled L… for Lock. The icons displayed in this column are either closed or open padlocks. The locks can be toggled open and shut by picking the icon. If a layer is locked (padlock closed), the objects on the layer will be visible on the screen but AutoCAD will not allow you to edit or change them. New objects can be added to the layer.

This option is particularly useful in situations where several people will be using the same drawing file. Layers can be locked to ensure that they are not inadvertently changed.

FIGURE 19.9 Layer Properties Manager showing layers.

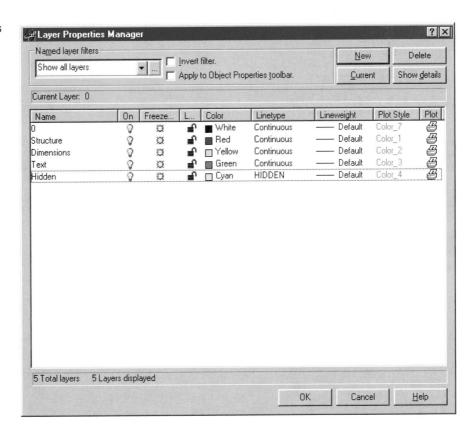

19.6   Managing Layers

Deleting a Layer

The remaining two buttons displayed in the Layer Properties Manager dialog box are the Delete and the Show details buttons. Highlighting a layer and then selecting the Delete button will remove that layer from the drawing. AutoCAD will not allow you to delete Layer 0, the current layer, or any layer containing objects.

The Show details Option

The Show details button toggles with the Hide details button. The Show details button works only when a layer is highlighted. It displays basically the same details about color, linetype, and lineweight displayed in the upper level but with pull-down menus to allow you to make any necessary changes to the layer (see Figure 19.10). You can also access the On/Off, Freeze/Thaw, and Lock/Unlock options with this button.

Changing the Name of a Layer

To change the name of a layer, highlight the layer and pick the Name column. A box will then appear around the current name. Type in the new name and press Enter↵. Pick OK to accept the change and exit the dialog box. The only layer you cannot rename is the default Layer 0.

Shortcuts for Modifying Layers

You can select several layers at one time by holding down the Shift key as you pick the layers. If you continue to hold the Shift key down while you highlight two layers that are not adjacent to each other, the layers in between the two picked will also be selected.

Pressing the Ctrl key also lets you pick several layers at once. The Ctrl key allows you to pick layers that are not adjacent to one another without also selecting the layers in between.

Right-clicking while you are in the Layer Properties Manager will bring up a shortcut menu. Figure 19.11 shows the options available for managing your layers with this menu.

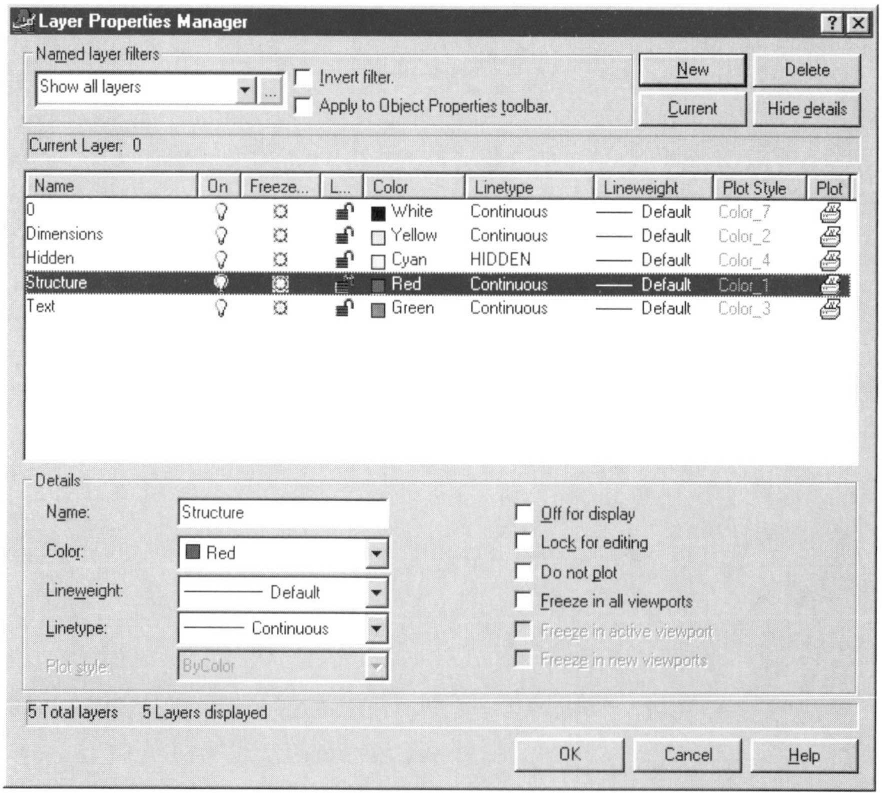

FIGURE 19.10   Layer Properties Manager showing details.

FIGURE 19.11 Layers shortcut menu.

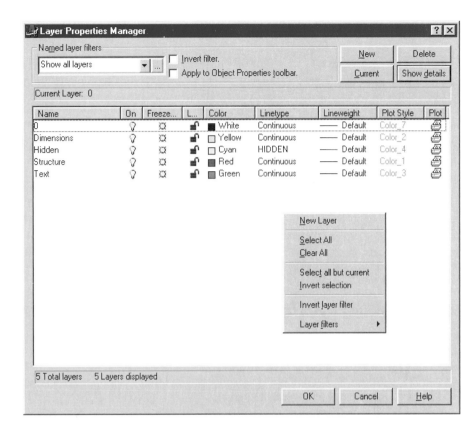

Select here to view your layers.

FIGURE 19.12 Object Properties toolbar.

The Object Properties Toolbar

The Object Properties Toolbar (see Figure 19.12) makes it easier for you to manage your layers. The first icon on the toolbar looks like a stack of papers, with the bottom paper in the pile being yellow. This is the Make Object's Layer Current icon. Select a particular object in your drawing. Click on the icon. The current layer will now be set to the layer of the selected object.

The next icon on the toolbar is the Layers icon. It looks like a stack of white papers. Picking this icon will bring up the Layer Properties Manager. The first window in the toolbar provides a pull-down menu of all the layers in the drawing. The layer being displayed will be the current layer in the drawing. You can pull down the list and highlight a different layer to make it current.

19.7 Using AutoCAD DesignCenter to Import Layers

- Select AutoCAD DesignCenter from the Tools pull-down menu.
- Pick the AutoCAD DesignCenter icon from the Standard Toolbar. The icon looks like a calculator with multicolored buttons.

DesignCenter Icon

The AutoCAD DesignCenter allows you to import features of previous drawings into the current drawing. One of the features you can import is the layers defined in a previous drawing. Not only does this save time, since you do not have to create all those new layers, but it leads to consistency between drawings. Once you have activated the command, the DesignCenter will appear on the left side of the graphics screen. A list of blocks, layers, and other features of the drawing such as dimension and text styles will be displayed. To import one of these features into the current drawing, simply drag and drop the information with your cursor.

REVIEW QUESTIONS

1. What is a layer? What purpose do layers serve in a drawing?

2. Where would you go to create a new layer in your drawing?

3. How many layers are required by AutoCAD?

4. What is the default linetype and the default color in AutoCAD?

5. Do all objects within a layer have to be the same color and linetype?

6. What does it mean to freeze a layer? How does this differ from turning a layer off?

7. Can you erase a line in a locked layer?

8. What procedure would you follow to change from working in one layer to working in another layer?

9. If you realize that you have drawn a line while working in the wrong layer, what can you do to put the line on the correct layer? (You may need to refer to Chapter 17.)

EXERCISES

EXERCISE 19.1

A floor plan of a house is to be drawn and layers need to be set up. Your task is to set up a drawing with the following layers and characteristics.

- Create a layer named Text. Set the color to Red and use Continuous linetype.
- Create a layer named Wall. Set the color to White and the linetype to Continuous along with a lineweight setting of .35 mm.
- Create a layer named Overhead Cabinets. Set the color to Cyan and the linetype to Hidden.
- Create a layer named Ceiling Line. Set the color to Blue and the linetype to Hidden (2X).
- Create a layer named Cabinet. Set the color to White and the linetype to Continuous.
- Create a layer named Appliances/Fixture. Set the color to Magenta and the linetype to Continuous.

Save the drawing and name it 19EX-1.

EXERCISE 19.2

In this exercise lay out a kitchen plan using the exercise 19.1 layer setup. Here are some minimum guidelines for the plan:

- Use a ³⁄₈″ = 1′-0″ scale.
- Use a rectangular plan with approximately 225 square foot layout.
- The total perimeter distance between the refrigerator, stove/oven, and the sink should be between 18′ and 22′.
- Recess part of the ceiling.
- Overhead cabinets need to be 12″ deep.
- Counters need to be 25″ deep.
- Use a 4½″ wall thickness
- If you need some ideas on kitchen layouts, refer to the *AIA Graphic Standards* or the *Interior Graphic Standards*.

Match the layers with the correct objects when you draw them. Save the drawing as 19EX-2.

EXERCISE 19.3

Construct some interior elevations of the kitchen plan in exercise 19.2. Use the following guidelines.

- Use 19EX-1 layers.
- Use ⅜″ = 1′-0″ scale.
- The counter height should be 36″ above the floor line.
- The bottom of the overhead cabinets should be 54″ above the floor line.
- Use a 4″ recessed base and a 4″ countertop base.
- Create a new layer and name it Shelves. Make the color Cyan and the linetype Hidden.

Draw the shelves in the Cabinet elevations with the new layer.

DRAWING ASSIGNMENTS

1. Redraw the plan view in Figure 19.13 at a ¼″ = 1′-0″ scale. Use the following settings for the drawing. Layers to create:

Layer Name	Color	Linetype	Lineweight
WALLS	White	Continuous	.7 mm
TEXT	Red	Continuous	Default
DIMENSION	Blue	Continuous	Default
Rod	Cyan	Hidden	Default
Fixtures	Blue	Continuous	Default
Appliances	Green	Continuous	Default
Cabinet and Shelves	Blue	Continuous	Default

Set Ltscale to 35.

2. Draw two interior elevations for the Master Bath plan found in Figure 19.13. Create a layer for walls, dimensions, and fixtures. Research bathroom information in the AIA Graphic Standards to get accurate sizes.

3. Redraw the given views in Figures 19.14–19.18, showing all the visible, hidden, and centerlines. Modify each linetype on its own layer and color.

4. Draw the given pictorials in Figures 19.19–19.21 in orthographic form choosing the best views.

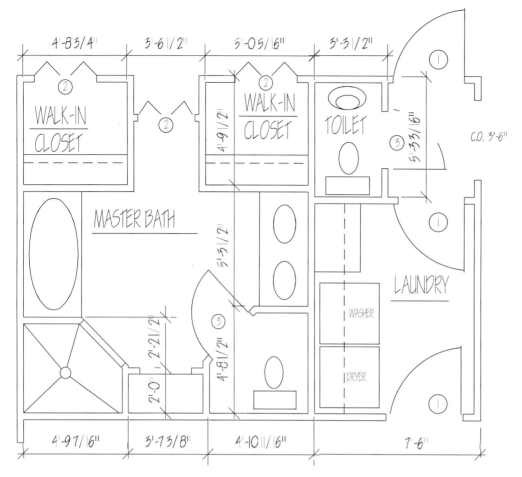

FIGURE 19.13 Drawing Assignment 1

FIGURE 19.14

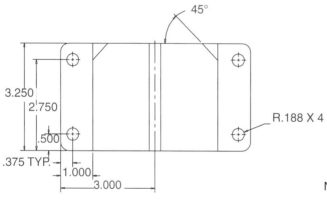

45°

3.250

2.750

.500

.375 TYP.

1.000

3.000

R.188 X 4

Note: All unmarked radii are R.250.

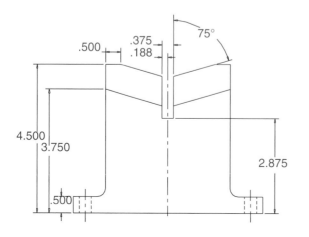

.500

.375

.188

75°

4.500

3.750

2.875

.500

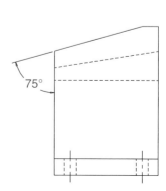

75°

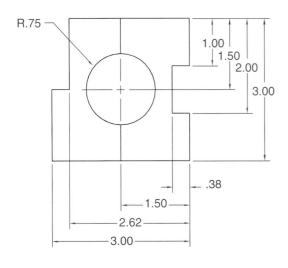

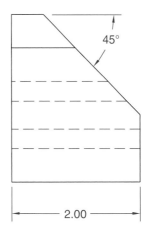

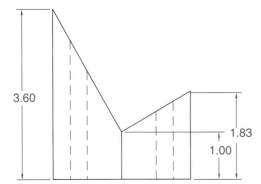

FIGURE 19.15

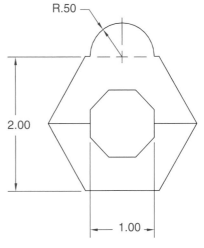

FIGURE 19.16

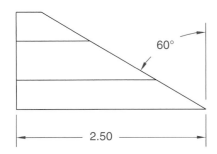

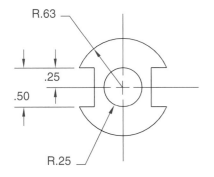

FIGURE 19.17

FIGURE 19.18

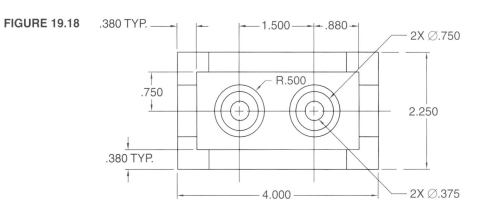

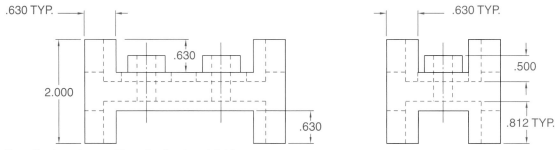

Draw the top view and turn the front and right
side orthographic views into sections.

FIGURE 19.19

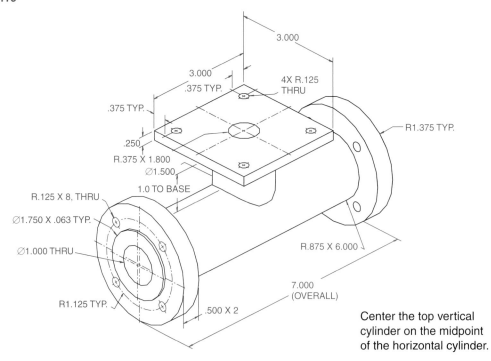

Center the top vertical
cylinder on the midpoint
of the horizontal cylinder.

FIGURE 19.20

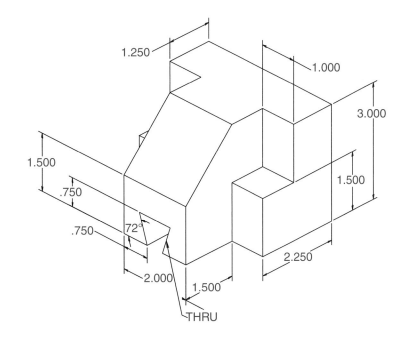

FIGURE 19.21

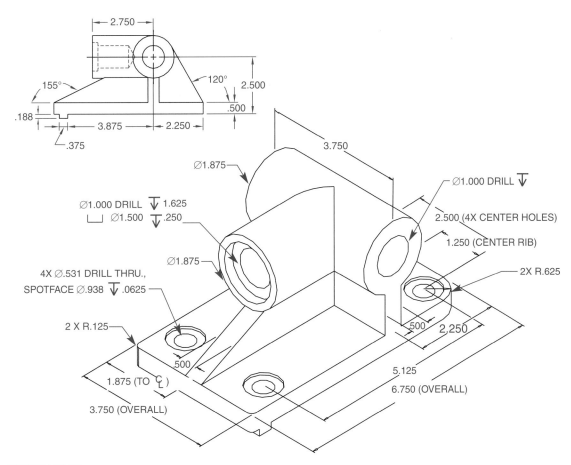

CHAPTER 20

Dimensioning

Dimensioning on the drawing board seemed to take as much time to do as the drawing itself. Planning the layouts, constructing the guidelines, and finally placing the correct dimensions in their desired locations was very time consuming. There is no comparison when it comes to dimensioning with AutoCAD.

One thing AutoCAD does not automatically do is dimension to standards or practices. Learning to dimension using the same standard as everyone else in an office or classroom takes a little practice, time, and guidance. Check with your instructor or office manager for dimensioning guidelines such as ASME Y14.5M. Knowing the system will help cut down on early errors. The speed of placing and editing dimensions in AutoCAD will enhance the learning process. A little bit of patience when planning dimensions and learning the ropes goes a long way toward making an excellent looking drawing.

It does take time initially to set up a dimensioning style that works for each type of drawing required as well as meeting standards. The advantage to all this dimension planning and setup is that once you create a style you can use it again on different drawings, either by putting it into a saved template or dragging and dropping it from the DesignCenter.

Another advantage to dimensioning with AutoCAD is that it is much easier to control office dimensioning standards. A copy of the office's standard dimensioning styles can be saved for each computer, so there is no excuse for anyone not to use them. All offices strive for consistency on drawings; it makes the drawings look better and eliminates confusion when reading them.

In this chapter learning about dimensioning with AutoCAD is broken into three parts:

1. Creating dimension styles and settings
2. Placing dimensions on a drawing
3. Editing dimensions on a drawing

The AutoCAD software has gone through quite an evolution when it comes to dimensioning. In the early stages of AutoCAD, all the settings (variables) had to be input by typing on the keyboard. Remembering what all the different settings did without any visual aids was a major task, but now most of the dimension variables show an example of how the dimensions will look when a setting is adjusted.

20.1 Creating Dimension Styles

This section will show how to create dimension styles.

Figure 20.1 shows the Dimension Style Manager dialog box, which is where the AutoCAD 2000 dimension styles are created.

The Dimstyle command

Dimension Style
Icon

- Type **Dimstyle** or **D** at the command prompt.
- Select Dimension Style from the Format pull-down menu (see Figure 20.2).
- Click on the Dimension Style icon on the Dimension toolbar (see Figure 20.3).
- Select Style from the Dimension pull-down menu (see Figure 20.4). To turn on the Dimension toolbar select Toolbars . . . from the View pull-down menu (see Figure 20.5).

FIGURE 20.1 Dimension Style Manager dialog box.

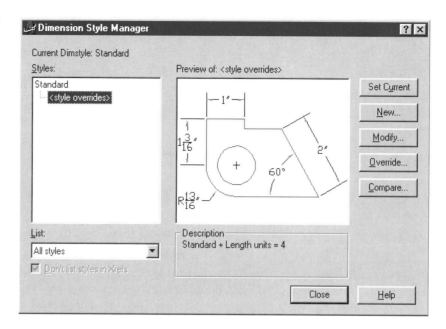

FIGURE 20.2 Dimension Style selected on the Format pull-down menu.

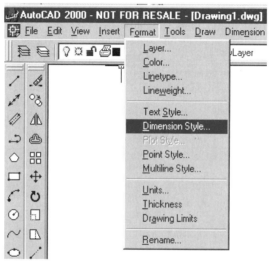

FIGURE 20.3 Dimension toolbar.

The Toolbars dialog box appears (see Figure 20.6). To turn on the Dimension toolbar simply left-click in the box to the left of Dimension. Left-click on the Close button on the Toolbars dialog box to close the toolbar selection. (Do not close the Dimension toolbar, only the Toolbar dialog box.) The Dimension toolbar will remain as seen in Figure 20.3.

Planning what the dimensions should look like will help in the long run, and creating a standard style to use will save time.

Helpful Hints

1. Create a separate layer for dimensions.

2. Adjust dimensioning settings to make the text height and arrowhead sizes appear and plot at the correct size. See Solutions 1 and 2 in the Mechanical Example section on page 474 (also see Figure 20.34).

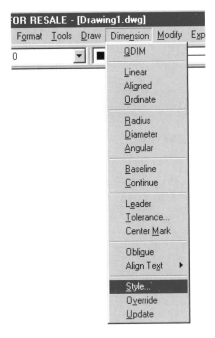

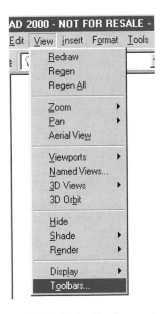

FIGURE 20.4 Style selected on the Dimension pull-down menu.

FIGURE 20.5 Toolbars selected on the View pull-down menu.

FIGURE 20.6 Toolbars dialog box.

Select here to turn on the Dimension Toolbar.

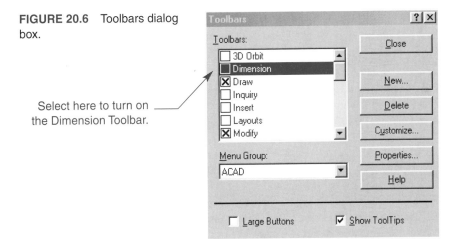

Desired ASME Y14.5 Dimension Settings

- Use a text height of ⅛″ (.12) if the drawing is at full scale.
- Use ⅛″ (.12) of arrows at full scale.
- Place text between the ends of the dimension line.
- Use a ¹⁄₁₆″ (.06) origin gap. (Gap off the object before the extension line begins.)
- Use a baseline spacing of ⅜″ (.38).

Architectural Example

For instance, let's say a 50′ line needs to be dimensioned. When this line is dimensioned, the ⅛″ text and ticks will be too small and will not display well because the limits are set for a ¼″ = 1′-0″ scale. There are two approaches to selecting scales and sizes.

Solution 1

Leave the sizes in the full-size or real height or size setting and change the Scale for Dimension Features to fit a ¼″ = 1′-0″ scale by dividing ¼ inch into 1 foot, or 12 inches:

$$\frac{12''}{.25''} = 48$$

This calculation can be performed the same way for any scale. The 48 would be the number used in the Scale for Dimension Features box. (Where to do this will be shown a little later.)

Solution 2

Leave the Scale for Dimension Features at 1 and change the sizes to what they should be in the scale you wish to use. Thus, a ⅛″ dimension text height in a ¼″ = 1′-0″ scale would need to be set to 6″ high. The height is calculated by using the scale factor and multiplying it by the ⅛″ desired height:

$$\text{Scale Factor} \quad \frac{1'}{\frac{1}{4}''} = \frac{12''}{.25''} = 48$$

Scale Factor	Real Size	Text Height Setting
48	× ⅛″	= 6″

For further information on this topic, refer to Appendix A.

Mechanical Example

Mechanical drawings tend to deal with smaller scales than drawings in other fields. Full scale is used whenever possible, but a few other scales are used frequently. A scale of ½″ = 1″ is illustrated in this example.

A metal plate is 20″ long by 10″ wide. It needs to fit on an 11″ × 17″ full size sheet. The limits will be set for 34″ × 22″. The dimension text height and arrowheads must plot out to the ASME minimum sizes of .12 tall (text) and .12 long (arrowheads).

Solution 1

Leave the arrowheads in the full-size or real-size setting. Change the Scale for Dimension Features to fit a ½″ = 1″ scale by dividing ½″ into 1″.

$$1''/.5'' = 2$$

The 2 would be the number used in the Scale for Dimension Features box.

Solution 2

Leave the Scale for Dimension Features at 1, and change the text and arrowhead sizes to adjust for the ½″ = 1″ environment. Since everything will be cut in half, just multiply the real sizes by the scale factor for the new sizes.

Scale Factor $1''/.5'' = 2$

Scale Factor	Real Size	New Text Height Setting
2	× ⅛″	= ¼″

Opening the Dimension Style Manager

At the command line type in **DIMSTYLE** or **D** and press Enter↵. The Dimension Style Manager dialog box appears. Left-click on the <u>N</u>ew . . . button on the right side of the dialog box. The Create New Dimension

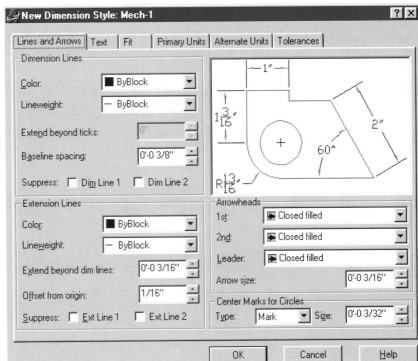

FIGURE 20.8 New Dimension Style dialog box.

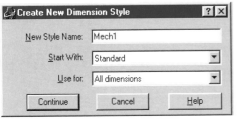

FIGURE 20.7 Create New Dimension Style dialog box.

Style dialog box opens up (see Figure 20.7). At the New Style Name: text box type in a name for a style to be created. We will use Mech 1 for our example. Once the name is typed, select the Continue button in the lower left corner of this display box. Another dialog box, which is the heart and soul of the dimension settings, opens up with the heading New Dimension Style: Mech 1 (see Figure 20.8). There are six major tabs across the top of the box for the following settings:

- Lines and Arrows
- Text
- Fit
- Primary Units
- Alternate Units
- Tolerances

Lines and Arrows Tab

When the Lines and Arrows option is selected with a left click, the following five areas appear (see Figure 20.9): a graphic illustration in the upper right-hand corner, Dimension Lines, Extension Lines, Arrowheads, and Center Marks for Circles.

1. The **graphic illustration** shows a drawing and dimensions. As changes are made to the settings the dimensions change to show the effects of the new settings.

2. **Dimension Lines** can be changed in the following ways:

- **Colors** for dimensions can be changed ByLayer, ByBlock, or by individual colors found in AutoCAD.

- **Lineweights** can also be altered by using the arrow to the right of the text box to access the desired setting. (The Display Lineweight setting must be turned on in the Lineweight Setting dialog box under the Format pull-down menu in order to generate lineweight changes.)

- **Extend beyond ticks** allows the extension lines to be set above the arrowheads with a positive value. A value of ⅛″ (.12) is acceptable (see Figure 20.10).

FIGURE 20.9 Lines and Arrows
tab menu.

Tab for Lines and Arrows

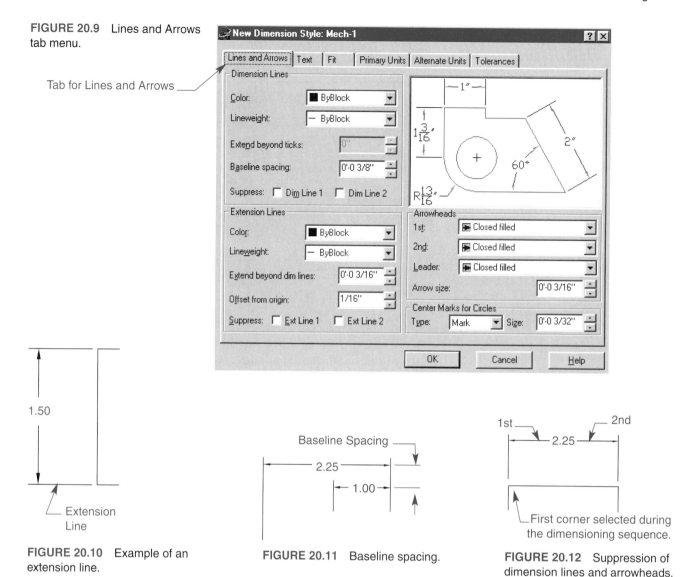

FIGURE 20.10 Example of an
extension line.

FIGURE 20.11 Baseline spacing.

FIGURE 20.12 Suppression of
dimension lines and arrowheads.

- **Baseline spacing** sets a standard space between dimensions when they are stacked on top of one another (see Figure 20.11).

- **Suppress** will cut off the first or second dimension lines and arrowheads when they are not desired. For example, you would use Suppress when you dimension from an existing dimension and you do not want to duplicate the line and arrowhead that already exists (see Figure 20.12).

3. **Extension Lines** are the lines that extend from the object being dimensioned (see Figure 20.10). They can be changed in some of the same ways that dimension lines get altered. Color, lineweight, extension beyond arrowheads, and suppression of lines are changed in exactly the same way as for the dimension lines; however, baseline spacing is replaced with an Offset from origin setting (see Figures 20.13 and 20.14). This controls the gap between the object being dimensioned and the start of the extension line (see Figure 20.15).

4. **Arrowheads** can be changed by selecting options in the text boxes (see Figure 20.16).

The 1st and 2nd options control how the dimensioning symbol will be displayed. A wide assortment of arrowheads, tick marks, dots, and just about anything found in the various drafting fields is provided. Left-click on the arrows to the right to check them out. Select the closed filled arrowheads.

The Leader option will also be a closed filled arrowhead. Leaders are used for notes and dimension circles (see Figure 20.17). The size of the dimensioning ticks and arrowheads is specified in the Arrow size: box. The minimum size used should be ⅛″ (.12).

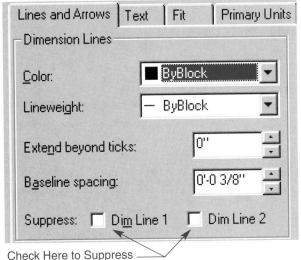

Check Here to Suppress

FIGURE 20.13 Dimension Lines options.

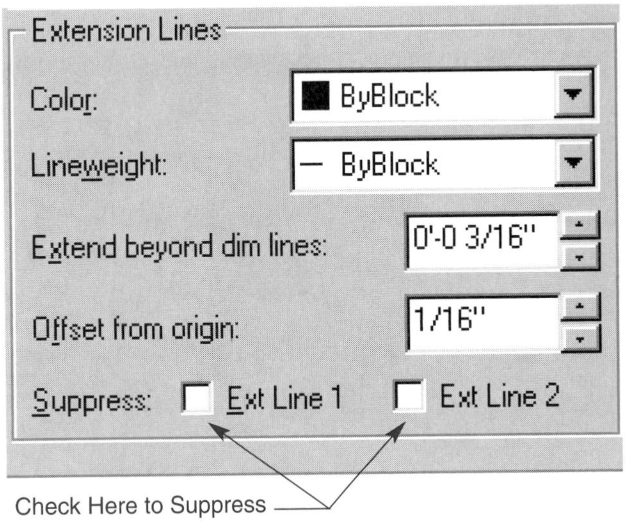

Check Here to Suppress

FIGURE 20.14 Extension Lines options.

5. **Center Marks for Circles**—This box has two controls in it to mark the center of circles: Type: and Size:. See Figure 20.18 for the Type options. The size control to the right adjusts the size of the mark or line setting. Type may be set to none, mark, or line (see Figure 20.19).

Text Tab

The Text Tab consists of four areas (see Figure 20.20): the graphics display, Text Appearance, Text Placement, and Text Alignment.

1. The **graphics display** shows how the changes affect the dimension settings and is located in the upper right corner. As you make changes look at the graphics display and make sure this is the way your dimensions should look.

2. **Text Appearance**—This box has five settings that control the text aspects (see Figure 20.21).

■ **Text style** lets you change font styles for the dimension text. Left-clicking on the down arrow will display font styles that have been loaded. Left-clicking on the box with three periods in it will bring up the Text Style dialog box and let you pick a style name and font style. (This is discussed in Chapter 22.)

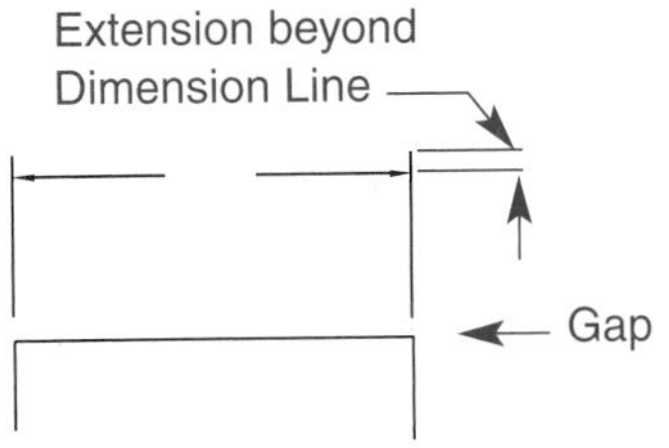

Extension beyond
Dimension Line

Gap

FIGURE 20.15 Shows the gap for the Origin option on the extension beyond the dimension lines.

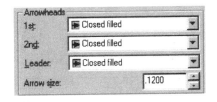

FIGURE 20.16 Arrowheads options.

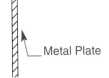

Metal Plate

FIGURE 20.17 Example of a leader.

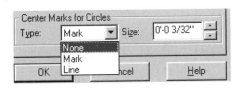

FIGURE 20.18 Center mark options for circles.

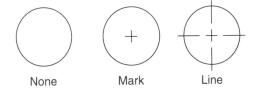

None   Mark   Line

FIGURE 20.19 Types of center marks.

Text Tab

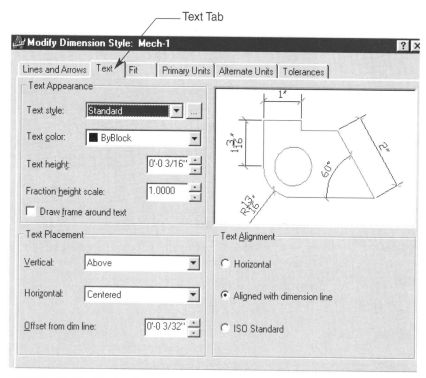

FIGURE 20.20   Text options.

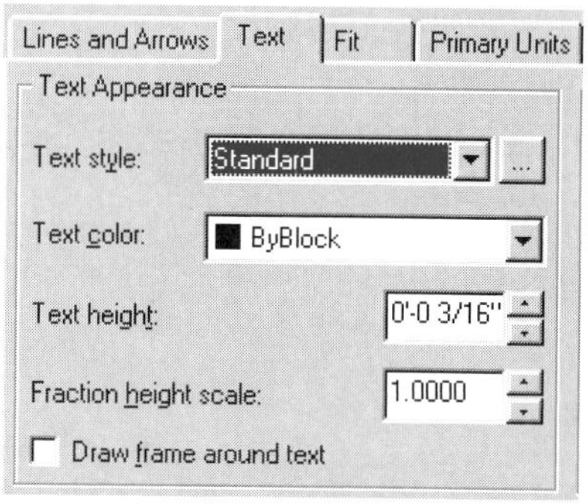

FIGURE 20.21   Text appearance options.

- The **Text color** box allows you to set the color of the text or coordinate it with a ByBlock or ByLayer selection. We recommend selecting the ByLayer option, placing the color in the layer controls.

- **Text height** needs to be set in this box. The minimum plotting height needs to be ⅛″ for full-scale drawings. If you want to dimension a drawing at a scale other than full, then leave the height at ⅛″ and change the scale factor in the Scale for Dimension Features located under the Fit tab to match the Limit settings.

- The **Fraction height scale** is based on a proportion of the text height. Use 1 for mechanical drawings.

- The final option is the **Draw frame around text** box. A left click in the box will turn it on. It is used to draw a basic dimension.

3. **Text Placement** – Three options are located in this display (see Figure 20.22).

- The **vertical** setting offers four choices, as seen in Figure 20.23. The Above selection is commonly used in architectural work; however, the Centered option is used in mechanical drawings (see Figure 20.24).

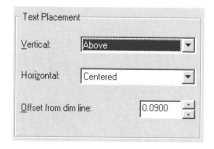

FIGURE 20.22   Text placement options.

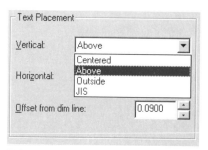

FIGURE 20.23   Vertical text placement.

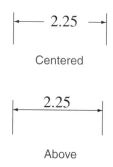

FIGURE 20.24   The Above and Center options.

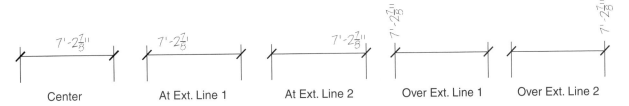

FIGURE 20.25 Horizontal options.

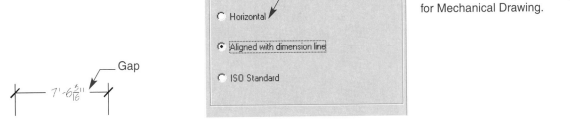

FIGURE 20.26 Offset from dimension line.

FIGURE 20.27 Text alignment options.

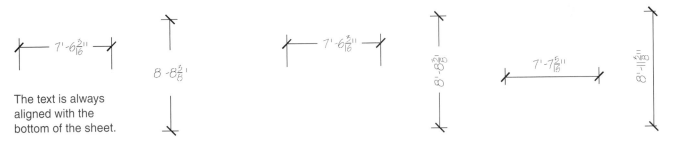

FIGURE 20.28 Unidirectional alignment (horizontal). Use this in mechanical drawing.

FIGURE 20.29 Aligned with dimension line setting. Text above lines is used mostly for architectural drawings.

- The **Horizontal** option can be left on centered for most mechanical drawing styles and can be adjusted later if needed. The function of this variable is to shift the text along the dimension line (see Figure 20.25). There is a lot of flexibility here, but stick with Centered and use the grips to move the text around if editing is needed later.

- The **Offset from dim line** is used to set the gap between the text and the dimension line (see Figure 20.26).

4. **Text Alignment**—There are three selections from which to choose in this box (see Figure 20.27).

- The **Horizontal** setting will keep the text in a position known as *unidirectional*. Figure 20.28 shows this type of alignment, which is used primarily in mechanical drafting.

- The **Aligned with dimension line** setting is more typically used in architectural drawing. The text will shift with the dimension lines, as shown in Figure 20.29.

- The final option is the international **ISO Standard**, which is used in most countries outside the United States and Canada.

Fit Tab

As text is placed on a drawing, everything can get crowded. The Fit menu gives you some choices when tight conditions arise (see Figure 20.30).

As in the previous menus, a graphics screen is situated in the upper right corner. Four other areas are displayed in this menu.

FIGURE 20.30   Fit options.

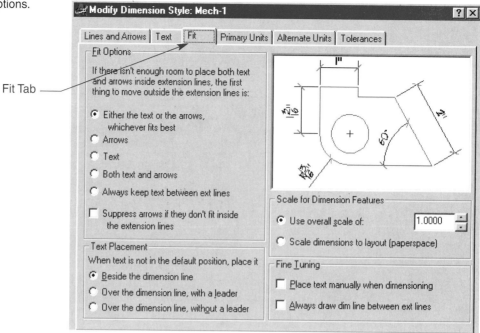

Fit Tab

FIGURE 20.31   Fit Options menu.

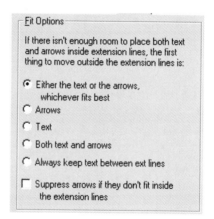

1. **Fit Options** is the largest display area. This box lets you pick how to handle the condition stated at the top of the display (see Figure 20.31). When there is not enough space between extension lines to fit the arrows and text inside them, then what should AutoCAD do with text and arrows?

   The choices are as follows:

   - Either the text or the arrows, whichever fits best
   - Arrows
   - Text
   - Both text and arrows
   - Always keep text between ext lines
   - Suppress arrows if they don't fit inside the extension lines

   Whichever option is chosen, it is easily edited later. Placing the text outside and using a leader to point back between the extension lines is common in architectural, not in mechanical, drawings (see Figure 20.32). Selecting the *Text* setting will generate this option.

2. The **Text Placement** display area has three options from which to choose (see Figure 20.33). It goes into effect when the text is not in the default position. AutoCAD will place the text in one of three ways:

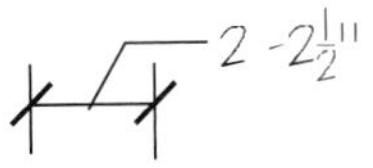

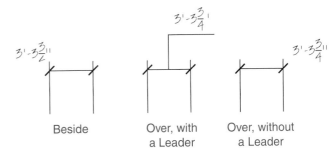

FIGURE 20.33 Text placement options.

Beside   Over, with   Over, without
a Leader   a Leader

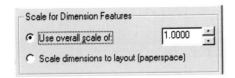

FIGURE 20.32 Using a leader
with dimension text.

FIGURE 20.34 Scale for Dimension
Features options.

- Beside the dimension line
- Over the dimension line, with a leader
- Over the dimension line, without a leader

3. A **Scale for Dimension Features** area is found directly below the graphics or drawing example (see Figure 20.34).

As shown in the figure, there are two choices. The option **Scale dimensions to layout (paper space)** is used if the drawing is to be placed into the paper space environment later. (See Appendix A, Plotting: Dimensioning in Floating Model Space.)

The option **Use overall scale of** is used when dimensioning is done in the model space environment. For example, if model space scale or limits are set to a scale of ½″ = 1″ and you want to leave the text setting at the real scale, such as ⅛″ for text height and ticks, then you must insert a scale factor here to match the drawing scale. For ½″ = 1″ it would be 2.

To find the scale factor for a given scale see Figure 20.35. This method will work for any desired scale.

4. The **Fine Tuning** display area has two options (see Figure 20.36).

- **Place text manually when dimensioning**—Checking this box on will allow you to move the cursor around and drag the floating text to various positions (see Figure 20.37). Once you find the right location a left click will apply the dimension.
- **Always draw dim line between ext lines**—This setting when checked on will always generate a dimension line between the two extension lines. Having both these boxes turned on works very well with architectural drawings.

Scale ½″ = 1″   Scale Factor = $\dfrac{1″}{.5″}$ = 2

Scale 2″ = 1″   Scale Factor = $\dfrac{1″}{2″}$ = .5

FIGURE 20.35 Calculating scale factors.

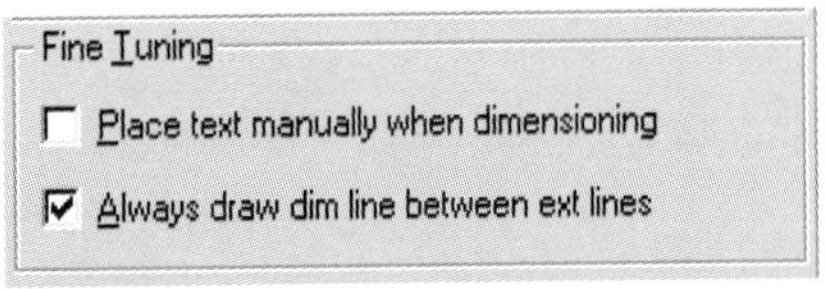

FIGURE 20.36 Fine Tuning options.

FIGURE 20.37 Placing text with the cursor.

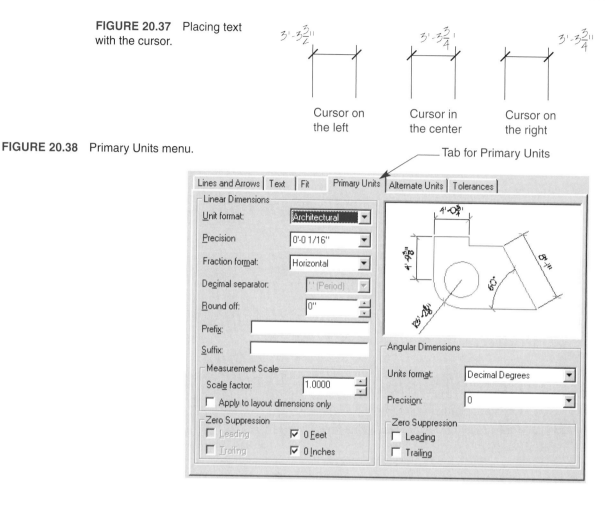

Cursor on the left

Cursor in the center

Cursor on the right

FIGURE 20.38 Primary Units menu.

Primary Units Tab

This group of settings pertains to unit displays and controls (see Figure 20.38).

1. **Linear Dimensions** is the largest display area with seven settings.

- Unit format—There is a list of formats for each drafting profession (see Figure 20.39).

Scientific—uses exponential forms

Decimal—uses inches or milimeters for mechanical drafting

Engineering—uses feet for civil drafting

Architectural—uses feet and inches for architectural drafting

Fractional—uses whole numbers and fractions only

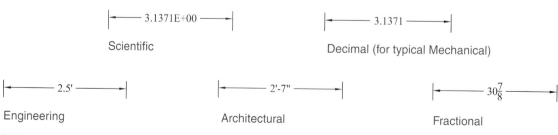

FIGURE 20.39 Unit Format options.

FIGURE 20.40 Precision menu.

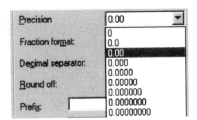

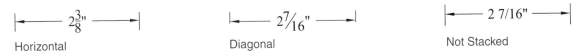

Horizontal   Diagonal   Not Stacked

FIGURE 20.41 Fraction format options.

- **Precision**—You may select the accuracy with which the text should be displayed. The decimal choices range from 0 to 0.00000000 (see Figure 20.40).
- **Fraction format**—The style of fractions can be set to one of three ways (see Figure 20.41). The horizontal is standard for mechanical drawing.
- **Decimal separator**—When decimal units are selected, the decimal (.) in a number (2.75) can be altered to a comma (2,75) or an empty space (2 75).
- **Round Off**—This setting allows you to determine how the dimension text will round off. Leave it at zero to get an exact value.
- **Prefix**—If a text display in front of the dimension is desired, it can be typed in at the prefix box, for example, 2X ∅1.500.
- **Suffix**—This setting applies text after the dimension, for example, ∅1.500 TYP.

2. **Measurement Scale**—This area is dedicated to adjusting dimension readings based on scale changes (see Figure 20.42). Let's say a full-scale drawing is too big to fit on a standard sheet size, so you draw the objects in the drawing at half scale to get a good fit on the sheet. Just because the objects are drawn at half size does not mean the dimensions should read half; they must read and show the real size on the drawing. In this case the Measurement Scale can be set to 2 to show the correct dimension. It measures the half scale then doubles the size. The **Apply to layout dimensions only** box can be checked on when you're going to dimension in the layout/paper space environment.

3. **Zero Suppression** for linear dimensions is found in the bottom left corner. When checked on with a left click this setting will remove zeros from dimension text as follows:

Zero Suppression for Architectural Units

- Leading off shows 0.875
- Leading on shows .875
- Trailing off shows 20.0
- Trailing on shows 20

Notice that the zero disappears when the suppression is activated.

FIGURE 20.42 Measurement Scale options.

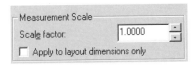

FIGURE 20.43 Angular Dimensions menu.

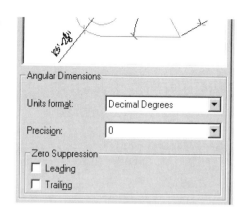

4. **Angular Dimensions**—Angle dimension settings are input in this area, which is located in the bottom right corner below the graphics area (see Figure 20.43).

The *Units format* sets the units for the angles. Angles can be displayed in the following units:

- Decimals   30.75°
- Degrees, Minutes, Seconds   30° 45′ 30″
- Gradians   100g
- Radians   3r

Most individuals are familiar with degrees. See Chapter 4 for a review of angle units. The *Precision* box allows you to select the accuracy with which the dimension should display.

Setting	Angle Reading
0	30
.0	30.0
.00	30.00

Zero Suppression for angles is in the bottom right corner. This setting affects angle values only.

Zero Supression	Angle Reads
Leading on	.5
Leading off	0.5
Trailing on	30
Trailing off	30.00

Alternate Units Tab

This tab is used when more than one system of units needs to be displayed. A good example is a drawing that needs to show decimal inches as well as metric millimeters. This situation can be handled very easily using the setting in this tab.

Look at Figure 20.44 as we walk through the example. Notice that all the settings are grayed out or are inactive. The first step is to place a check in the **Display alternate units** box. Doing this will activate the options for your use. Look in the Alternate Units area as shown in Figure 20.45. The first choice is the Unit format selection, which is very similar to what was shown earlier. The following choices are available:

Scientific

Decimal

Engineering

Tab for Alternate Units

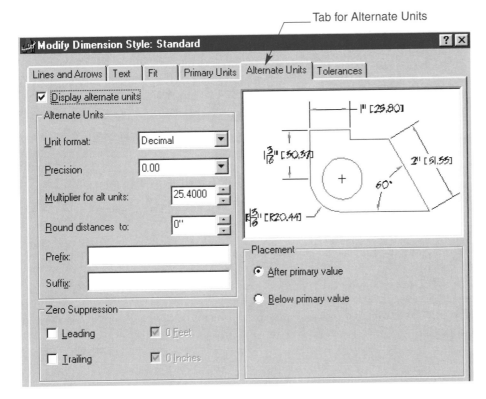

FIGURE 20.44 Alternate Units menu.

FIGURE 20.45 Tolerances menu.

Architectural Stacked

Fractional Stacked

Architectural

Fractional

Windows Desktop

Unit format

Just select the unit format you would like to be displayed along with the Primary Units you should have set up in the previous tab. If you are planning to display metric units such as millimeters with your decimal dimensions, just leave the unit format set to Decimal.

Precision. In the Precision box select the 0.0 setting if you want the correct decimal places for millimeters. This setting allows you to set the exactness of the alternate units. The precision will vary depending on the units selected in the Unit format box. It works just like the Primary Units setting.

Multiplier for alt. units. In this box you can set the units multiplication factor, as in the following examples:

Primary Units Decimals	*Alternate Unit (Millimeter)*
1″ or 1.00	25.4 mm = 1″
	25.4 is the multiplier value to be used when millimeters are desired.
1 ft	3 ft = 1 yd
	⅓ or .3333 is the multiplier value to be used to show alternate units in yards.

Round distances to:. This setting controls the exactness of the rounded-off value.

FIGURE 20.46

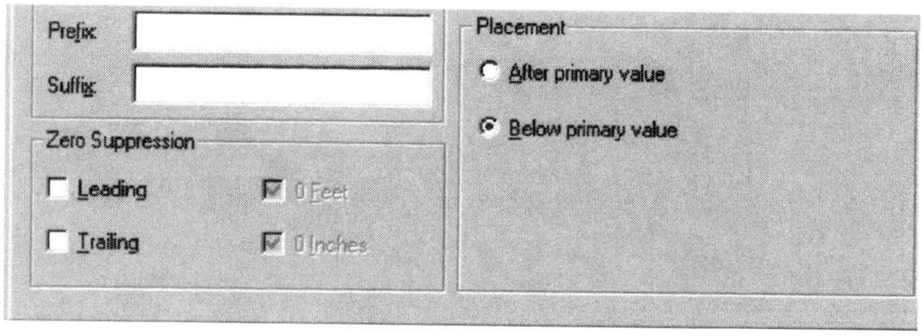

Prefix and Suffix.   You probably learned the difference between the two terms in an English class. This example should refresh your memory.

A prefix will place text before the alternate units. In the example a dollar sign is the prefix.
$20

A suffix will place text after the alternate units. In the example MM stands for millimeters.
20.0 MM

Zero Suppression

The Zero Suppression option for the alternate units allows you to suppress the leading zero in the alternate units. Simply left-click a check mark in the box to the left of Leading (see Figure 20.46).

Leader suppression on: .500
Leader suppression off: 0.500

Trailing zeros also may be suppressed by checking the box to the left of Trailing.

Trailing zero suppression turned on: 25
Trailing zero suppression turned off: 25.0

Placement

The Placement area contains the last set of choices in the Alternate Units tab. You have only two choices here:

- Selecting the After primary value places the alternate units after the primary units:

1.00 [25.4]
inches [millimeters]

- The Below primary value places the alternate units below the primary units:

1.00
[25.4]

Tolerances Tab

The tolerances tab is used to place tolerances on a drawing automatically with the dimensions (see Figure 20.47).

Tolerance Format

This area controls the tolerance that is applied to the primary units.

Method.   As you learned in Chapter 9, tolerance can appear in various forms. AutoCAD has the following options.

- **None**— no tolerance is applied.
- **Symmetrical**—This option is selected when a tolerance value such as $\pm.02$ is the same both in the positive and negative directions (see Figure 20.48).
- **Deviation**—This option is selected when a nonsymmetrical tolerance is applied, such as +.03 and −.01 (see Figure 20.49).

FIGURE 20.47 Tolerances tab open

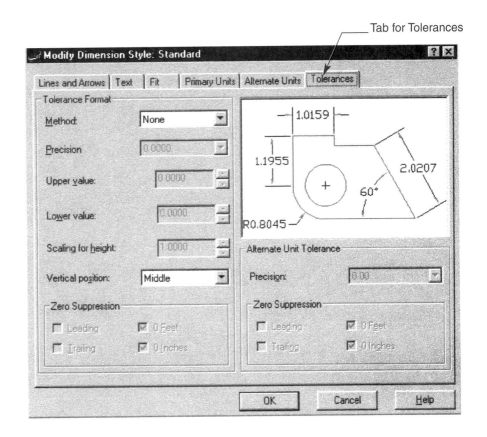

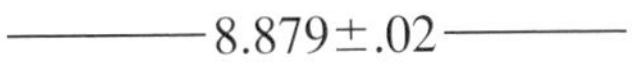

Tab for Tolerances

———— 8.879±.02 ————

FIGURE 20.48 Symmetrical tolerance

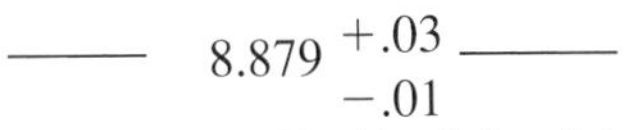

———— 8.879 $^{+.03}_{-.01}$ ————

FIGURE 20.49 Deviation tolerance

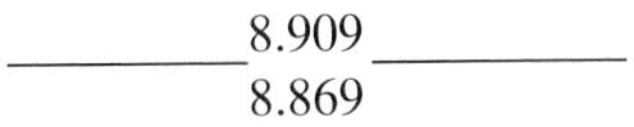

$$\frac{8.909}{8.869}$$

FIGURE 20.50 Limits example

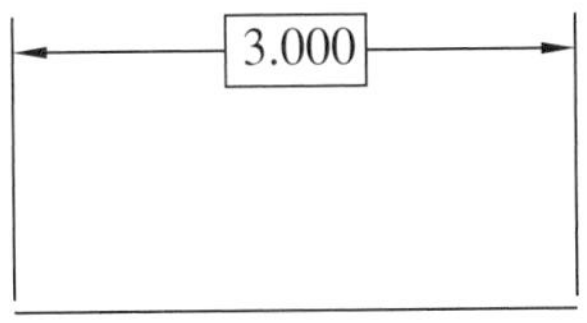

3.000

FIGURE 20.51 Basic dimension

- **Limits**—This option applies the tolerance to the dimension and gives both a maximum and a minimum dimension value when the dimension is placed on the drawing (see Figure 20.50).
- **Basic**—This option is used when a basic dimension is needed rather than a tolerance (see Figure 20.51).

Precision. The Precision setting establishes the number of decimal places to which the tolerance should be carried. In mechanical drawing some of the more common settings are two, three, and four decimal places to the right of the decimal.

Upper value. This setting establishes the positive tolerance value, such as +.02.

Lower value. This setting establishes the negative tolerance value, such as −.03.

Both the upper and lower value settings work with the method option that is chosen. You need to practice different combinations to get a feel for the possibilities. Always check out the graphics area to verify your selection.

Scaling for height.   The tolerance sizes are controlled with this setting. Sizes are based on a percentage of the text height of the dimension text. For example, a setting of .75 will reduce the individual tolerance text height to 75% of the size of the dimension height. Thus, a dimension height set to .25 would generate a tolerance height of .18. A setting of 1 will set the tolerance text height equal to that of the dimension. Remember that the smallest text on a drawing must be a minimum of ⅛″ (.12) high.

Vertical position.   The tolerances may be aligned in various positions around the dimension:

Top	$2.00 + .02$
	$-.03$
Middle	$2.00\,{}^{+\,.02}_{-\,.03}$
Bottom	$2.00\,{}^{+\,.02}_{-\,.03}$

Zero Suppression

The options in this area are used to supress zeros for the tolerance values. Checking Leading suppresses the zero to the left of the decimal:

Zero suppression off: ± 0.020
Zero suppression on: ± .020

Checking Trailing suppresses trailing zeros:

Zero suppression off: ± .020
Zero suppression on: ± .02

Alternate Unit Tolerances

The final options in the Tolerances Format area the alternate units. The Alternate control Units settings in the previous tab must be turned on before this area can be used.

Precision.   The tolerance of the alternate units can be expressed with a chosen number of decimal places. In the example in Figure 20.52 the millimeters are given to one decimal place.

Zero Suppression

As in some of the earlier examples, zero suppression may be applied to the alternate unit tolerance:

Leading zero suppression off: 25.5 ± 0.20
Leading zero suppression on: 25.5 ± .20
Trailing zero suppression off: 25.5 ± .20
Trailing zero suppression on: 25.5 ± .2

Dimension Style Manager

Let's take another look at the Dimension Style Manager dialog display (see Figure 20.53). A list of dimension styles is displayed in the Styles: box. The styles you create through the New. . . button are found here along with AutoCAD's default Standard styles. Once a style is listed here you can use it by highlighting it with a left mouse click, then moving the cursor to the Set Current screen button and left-clicking there. If you need to change a style, highlight the style you want to change with Set Current, then left-click on Modify. The Modify Dimension Style dialog box will appear, which looks exactly the same as when you create a new style. The same optional settings are available in the six menus: Lines and Arrows, Text, Fit, Primary Units, Alternate Units, and Tolerances.

FIGURE 20.52   Alternate Unit Tolerance

$$\longleftarrow 3.000\,{}^{+0.030}_{-0.010}\ \left[76.2\,{}^{+0.8}_{-0.3}\right]\longrightarrow$$

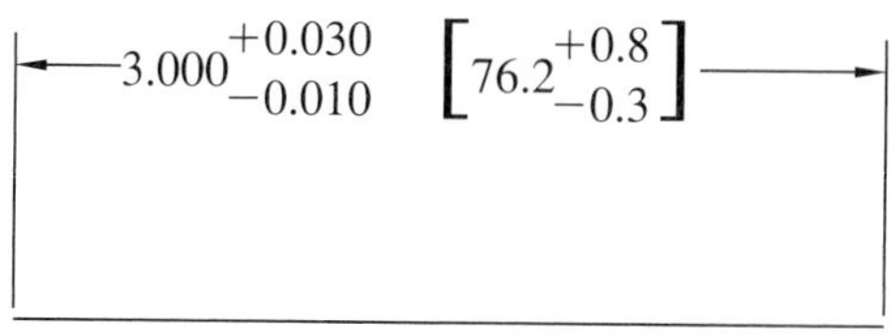

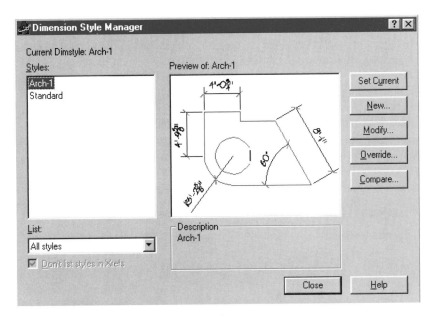

FIGURE 20.53 Dimension Style Manager dialog box.

FIGURE 20.54 Override display.

Editing or making changes to an existing style instead of making a new style is exactly the same as in the New setup. Make any necessary changes in the settings, then click on the OK button to activate the new settings.

The Override... button gives you the ability to make a temporary change to the current style setting. To use the override command make the desired style current, then left-click on the Override... button. The override dialog display appears with the six standard menus for dimension variable settings that you have seen before. Make your changes and pick OK when you are finished. Notice in the Styles: listing that the override is listed as a branch off the original style (see Figure 20.54).

Close the Dimension Style Manager display, and the override changes will take effect when dimensions are applied to a drawing. When it is time to return to the original style, open the Dimension Style Manager dialog box, left-click on that style and then left-click on the Set Current button. An AutoCAD Alert box appears and lets you know that the override settings will be discarded if the OK button is selected (see Figure 20.55).

If you wish to keep the overrides and the original style, then create a New style using the override changes. That way it will be possible to switch back and forth between the two styles without deleting any settings.

The Compare... button will display dimension variable settings. At the top of the Compare Dimension Styles dialog box are two text boxes where you can select styles and compare them with other existing styles (see Figure 20.56). The screen lists the Description and the Variable in the DIM mode and the setting of this variable in both styles. Only two styles can be compared at a time.

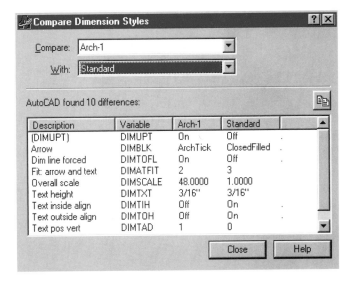

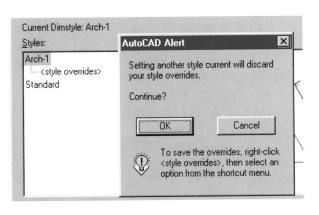

FIGURE 20.55 AutoCAD alert.

FIGURE 20.56 Compare Dimension Styles dialog box.

Dimension Variables (DIM)

In early AutoCAD releases, dimension variable settings were typed in at the command line. There were no icons or displays to help the user set up dimension styles. It took a lot of time and a great memory to set the DIM variables in those days. These variables still exist, and we are going to show them to you with the current dimension boxes. Select the Help pull-down menu on the standard AutoCAD screen and left-click on the first option (AutoCAD Help F1). Under the Contents pull-down double-left-click on the Command Reference option. Next, double-left-click on the suboption, Dimension Variables Quick Reference. This is the best place to look when checking out the DIM variables.

If you want a taste of the pre-Windows AutoCAD era left-click on the Dimension Styles button. Notice that there is a written description along with the variable abbreviation (see Figure 20.57). It is easy to see that setting dimension variables was a real memory game. This screen also included standard DIM variable settings for:

ANSI—American National Standards Institute

ISO-25—International Standards Organization

DIN—Deutsche Industrie Norm

JIS—Japanese Industrial Standard

Use the scroll bars to the right and scan through all the variables. Sixty-four (64) DIM variables are listed here, and it is a real challenge to remember what each one does. Today's AutoCAD gives you a choice of using dialog boxes and icons instead of typing these DIM variables.

We need to look at one more option in this Help screen menu. Use the Back button at the top of the screen to return to the Dimension Variables Quick Reference (see Figure 20.58). Now, left-click on the Dimension System Variable button and check out the screen that appears (see Figure 20.59).

Use the Maximize button in the top right corner of the screen to display the entire visual. What a great index or reference! The screen displays the pictures and dialog boxes along with the DIM variables. Use the scroll bars and scan through completely. Use this help screen whenever dealing with DIM variable settings for quick answers.

Now that we have shown you how to set up the appearance of dimensions, it is time to learn how to place them on a drawing. This is the fast, fun part of dimensioning.

FIGURE 20.57 Dimension Style Variables.

Dimension Style Variables

Variable	Description	ANSI	ISO-25	DIN	JIS
DIMADEC	Decimal places for angular dimensions	0	0	0	0
DIMALT	Alternate units selected	Off	Off	Off	Off
DIMALTD	Alternate unit decimal places	2	4	2	2
DIMALTF	Alternate unit scale factor	25.4000	0.0394	0.0394	0.0394
DIMALTRND	Alternate unit rounding value	0.0000	0.0000	0.0000	0.0000
DIMALTTD	Alternate tolerance decimal places	2	4	2	2

FIGURE 20.58 Location of the Back button.

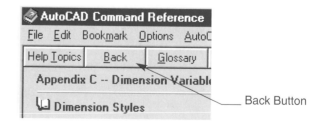

Back Button

The following illustration shows how the dimension system variables are organized on tabs in the New Dimension Style dialog box. Although not shown, these system variables are organized the same way on the Modify Dimension Style and Override Dimension Style dialog boxes.

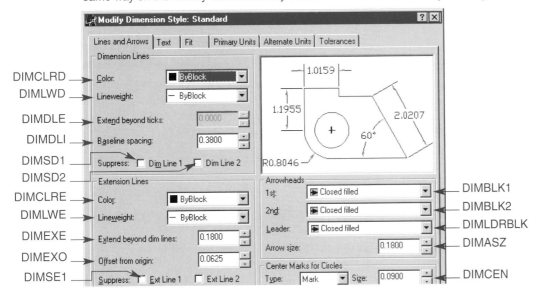

FIGURE 20.59 Dimension System variables.

20.2 Placing Dimensions on a Drawing

You can put dimensions on a drawing in a variety of forms. The two ways most preferred are through the Dimension pull-down menu and the Dimension toolbar.

The Dimension pull-down menu can be opened with a left click to show all the following options (see Figure 20.60).

- **QDIM**—Quick dimensioning applies dimensions fast to individual selections or a group selection. Dimensions are applied on a straight alignment (see Figure 20.61).

- **Linear**—Linear dimensioning is used when a dimension is needed between two points or between two given lines or objects. Dimensions are applied on vertical or horizontal lines (see Figure 20.62).

- **Aligned**—The Aligned option is used to place a straight-line dimension on an angled line (see Figure 20.63).

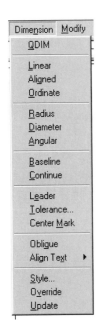

FIGURE 20.60 Dimension pull-down menu.

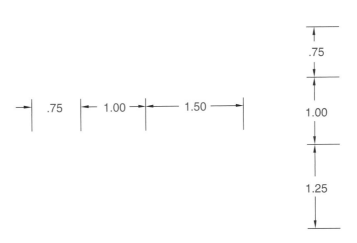

FIGURE 20.61 QDIM using the chain option.

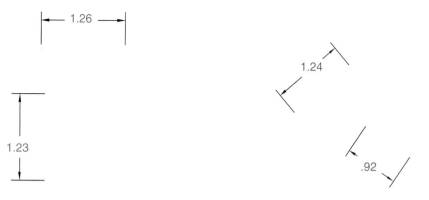

FIGURE 20.62   Linear dimensioning.   **FIGURE 20.63**   Aligned dimensioning.

- **Ordinate**—Ordinate dimensioning does not use arrows but instead references from a (0,0) coordinate and uses an extension line (see Figure 20.64).
- **Radius**—Radius dimensioning is applied to circles or arcs, measuring from the center to the outside (see Figure 20.65).
- **Diameter**—Diameter dimensioning is applied to circles or arcs, measuring across the circle or twice the radius (see Figure 20.66).
- **Angular**—The Angular option is used to dimension angles. Pick the two lines that make up the angle, and you can place the dimension on the drawing in a variety of ways (see Figure 20.67).
- **Baseline**—The Baseline option is used to datum dimensions. Establish a datum line with a linear dimension first, then you can use the baseline option with multiple picks (see Figure 20.68).
- **Continue**—The Continue option strings dimensions in a straight line, also known as a *chain*. The first dimension must be placed with the Linear option (see Figure 20.69).

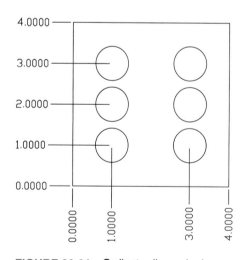

FIGURE 20.64   Ordinate dimensioning.

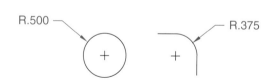

FIGURE 20.65   Radius dimensioning.

FIGURE 20.66   Diameter dimensioning.   **FIGURE 20.67**   Angular dimensioning.

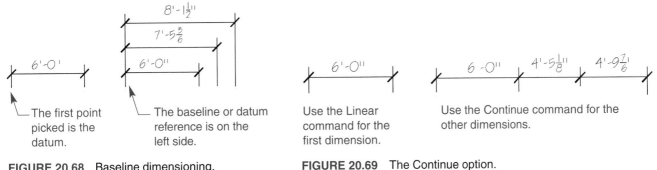

FIGURE 20.68 Baseline dimensioning.

FIGURE 20.69 The Continue option.

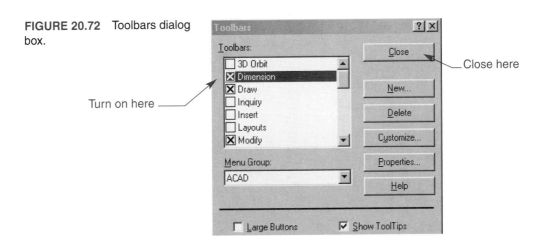

FIGURE 20.70 The Leader option.

FIGURE 20.71 Center mark options.

- **Leader**—The Leader option generates an arrowhead with a leader line plus an MTEXT option for notes (see Figure 20.70).

- **Tolerance**—The Tolerance option is for geometric tolerancing which is used for advanced mechanical drawings.

- **Center Mark**—This selection places center ticks and lines on circles and arcs depending on the setting in the Dimension Style Manager (see Figure 20.71).

Some remaining options (Oblique, Align Text, Override, and Update) are used for editing dimensions after they have been placed on the drawing. The Style option was demonstrated earlier to show how to create styles and set variables. Any of these dimension options can be activated with a left-click on the Dimension pull-down menu.

The Dimension Toolbar

Using the on-screen Dimension toolbar is another popular way of placing dimension options on the screen. The toolbar will stay on the screen until it is closed, which is a shorter, quicker way to access commands. The Dimension toolbar can be turned on by left-clicking on the View pull-down menu and then left-clicking again on Toolbars at the bottom (shown earlier in this chapter). Check the Dimension box selection and close the Toolbars dialog box (see Figures 20.72 and 20.73).

FIGURE 20.72 Toolbars dialog box.

FIGURE 20.73   Dimension toolbar.

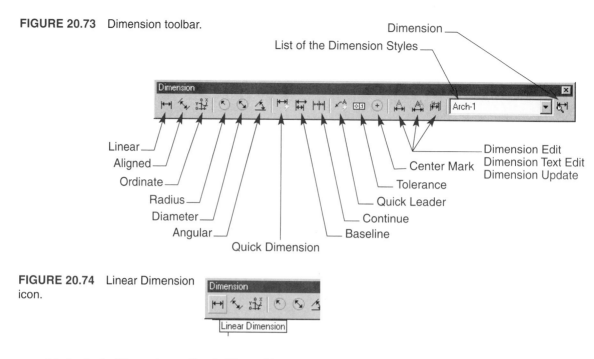

FIGURE 20.74   Linear Dimension icon.

Notice in the Dimension toolbar in Figure 20.73 that the options are the same as in the pull-down menu version. If you forget what a button does, just put the mouse arrow on top of the icon for a few seconds, and the description will appear just below the icon (see Figure 20.74).

The lone drawback to using the toolbar is that it takes up some room on the drawing screen. It is a floating toolbar and can easily be moved around if you hold down the left-click button while in the dark blue shaded area of the toolbar with the cursor and drag it across the screen. If dragged far enough to the left or right the toolbar will align vertically (see Figure 20.75). Aligning a toolbar is a matter of preference. If too much of the screen is being covered up, turn it off and use the pull-down menu instead.

FIGURE 20.75   Aligning the toolbar vertically.

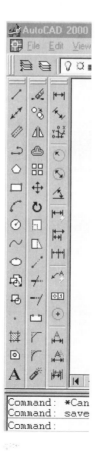

Using the Linear Option

Dimensioning with the Linear option can be done in two ways. Once you have selected the command, look at the command line. It reads:

> Command: **dimlinear**
> Specify first extension line origin or <select object>:

Option 1: *<select object>*

Note: The Direct Distance method can be used for placing dimension.

The option in the brackets <select object> is the default. Just press Enter↵ or right-click to accept the default option. Notice that the cursor changes into a small rectangular box (pick box). When this box appears, just touch the line to be dimensioned (see Figure 20.76). Next, roll the mouse above or below the object. The dimension text, dimension line, ticks, and extension line will follow the cursor around. Place the dimension by left-clicking when the desired location is reached. Alternately, pull the cursor in the direction the dimension should go and type in the distance you want the dimension line to be placed away from the object (see Figures 20.77 and 20.78).

Option 2: *Specify first extension line origin*

Using the other option at this command line, pick the ends of the line or object to be dimensioned. Using object snaps, grab the endpoint of the line on one side, then the endpoint of the other side (see Figure 20.79). Once you have chosen the second point the dimension appears and can be placed in the same manner as in the previous example in option 1 (see Figure 20.80).

Both of these methods show the following text options at the command line that can be used by typing them in at the command line.

> [Mtext/Text/Angle/Horizontal/Vertical/Rotated]:

Typing **Mtext** will bring up the Multiline Text Editor, where the text can be altered or changed. The angle brackets (<>) found in the text area represent the current dimension value. You can type notes in front of it or behind it, and they will show up with the dimension after you select the OK button and place the dimension on the drawing. Typing Text will allow you to replace the current dimension text at the command line.

The other four choices (Angle, Horizontal, Vertical, and Rotated) deal with different alignments and positions. Go ahead and try a few of these options. Once in a while you might need one of these.

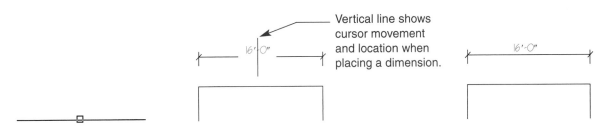

FIGURE 20.76 Selecting line to be dimensioned.

FIGURE 20.77 Dimension placement by moving the cursor.

FIGURE 20.78 Completed dimension.

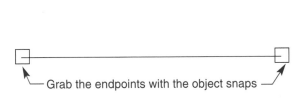

FIGURE 20.79 Picking line endpoints.

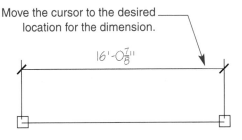

FIGURE 20.80 Completed dimension.

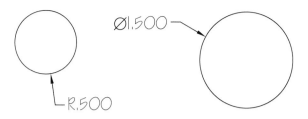

FIGURE 20.81   Aligned dimension.   **FIGURE 20.82**   Circle dimensioning with the Radius and Diameter options.

Using the Aligned Option

The Aligned option is for dimensioning along an angled line or surface (see Figure 20.81). The Aligned option works in the same way as the Linear feature. Both option 1, selecting the object, and option 2, picking the endpoints of the object, will work in the same way. The following three options become available in the command line after the object is selected.

[Mtext/Text/Angle]:

These choices also work identically with those of the linear command.

The Ordinate option is not used in architectural drawing. It is normally found in some electronic fields. It is easy to use—just pick a point and the dimension text and extension line are placed on the drawing.

Using the Radius and Diameter Options

Dimensioning with the Radius or Diameter option is similar to using the Aligned option. Select Radius, and the command line will read:

Command: **dimradius**
Select arc or circle:

Touch the circle that needs dimensioning with the pick box, and the dimension will appear, ready to be positioned. Place the dimension in the desired location with the mouse, and left-click to apply it to the drawing (see Figure 20.82). The command line will also allow you to change the dimension with the standard options [Mtext/Text/Angle]. To use these choices make sure to select them between selecting the circle and applying the text to its final position.

Hint for Radius and Diameters

Set up a separate dimensioning style to be used when dealing with circles. It is desirable to use arrowheads along with horizontal text. It may be desirable to use the Leader command to dimension circles and arcs.

Using the Angular Option
Dimensioning angles gives you three choices for picking objects (see Figure 20.83).

1. You can select two lines that form an angle.
2. You can select an arc.
3. You can select a vertex of an angle along with the endpoints of the angle.

The [Mtext/Text/Angle] option will appear again in the command line for additional modifications of the text if desired.

FIGURE 20.83 Dimensioning with the Angular option.

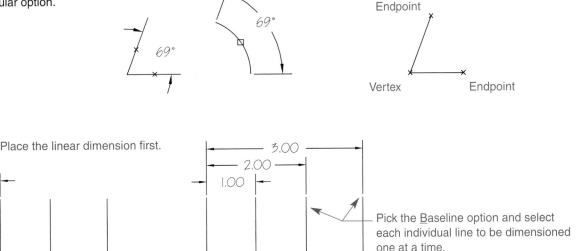

FIGURE 20.84 Baseline dimensioning.

Using the Baseline Option

The Baseline will work once a base or datum is established. This means that another dimension such as a linear dimension must be placed first. Pick the lines in sequence so they stack properly (see Figure 20.84). Baseline dimensioning is seldom used in architectural drawings, but occasionally a variation of it may be used.

Using the Continue Option

Dimensioning along a straight line is a common practice on architectural drawings. The process is much like using the Baseline command: a reference such as a linear dimension is needed before the Continue command will work. Then it becomes a matter of picking each individual line (see Figure 20.85). Watch the dimension appear as you pick.

Using the Leader Option/Quick Leader

Leaders are used to call out dimensions or notes and point to their location. Select the Leader option, also known as Q leader, in the Dimension pull-down menu, and the command line will show:

Specify first leader point or [Settings] <Setting>:

Press Enter↵ to open the Leader Settings dialog box, which contains three pull-down menu tabs (see Figure 20.86).

FIGURE 20.85 Using the Continue option.

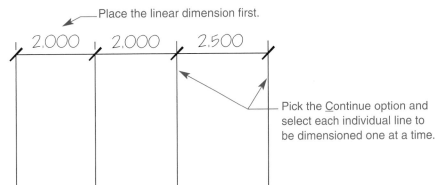

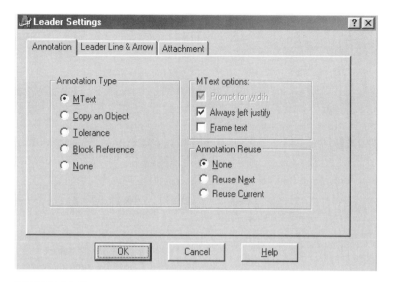

FIGURE 20.86	Leader annotation menu.

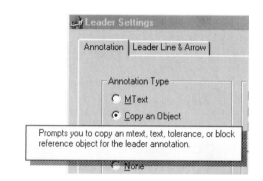

FIGURE 20.87	Leader help.

Annotation

The settings in the Annotation menu will allow Mtext to work with the Leader option to generate notes at the same time. The Always left justify option will align the text on the left-hand side. One useful help feature is the question mark in the upper right corner. Left-click on it, then pick the option you have a question about. A description or definition will appear, to aid you (see Figure 20.87).

Leader Line & Arrow

This menu tab does quite a bit. The Leader Line can be set to draw a straight line or a curved spline (see Figure 20.88). The Number of Points box will let you set how many points can be used to draw the leader line (see Figure 20.89).

You can set different types of arrowheads here along with choosing typical angles on the leader lines. Leaving them at Any angle will give you more flexibility when laying out dimensions.

Attachment

The Attachment pull-down tab lets you decide how the leader will intersect with the text (see Figures 20.90 and 20.91).

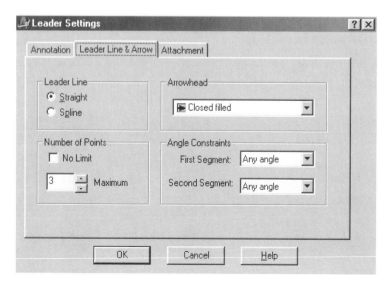

FIGURE 20.88	Leader Line & Arrow menu.

The line can change direction four times.

The line can change direction twice.

Leader Set to 4-Point Option

Leader Set to 2-Point Option

FIGURE 20.89	Using the Number of Points option.

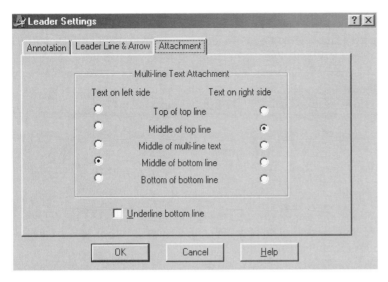

FIGURE 20.90 Attachment menu.

Top Settings   Middle Settings   Bottom Settings

FIGURE 20.91 Leader Mtext.

The Leader Settings are fairly easy to use. One setting that CAD operators change often is the None option at the bottom of the menu under the Annotation tab (see Figure 20.86). This option is used when no text is wanted with the leader. The text may already have been created and the leader is needed.

When the None option is set you can just left-click to draw the leader, and the Mtext option will not appear while the leader line is placed on the screen. The None option can be used when a large number of notes and leaders are needed. It can be faster to place the notes on the drawing continuously with the AutoCAD Text commands and add the leaders to the notes later.

Using Mtext with the leader is fairly simple. Click on the MText option in the Annotation pull-down tab, and click on None under Annotation Reuse selections. These choices will activate the Mtext option each time the leader command is used. After the leader is drawn, the command line will read:

Enter first line of annotation text <Mtext>:

At this point you can type in the note or press Enter↵ to bring up the Multiline Text Editor (see Figure 20.92). Just type in the note and left-click on the OK button, and the note will appear with the leader. If the same note and leader needs to be repeated, click on Reuse Next, and each time the leader command is used the previous note or text will be repeated automatically (see Figure 20.93).

FIGURE 20.92 Multiline Text Editor dialog box.

FIGURE 20.93 Reuse Leader option.

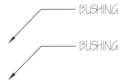

Using the Center Mark Option.

The Center Mark command is fairly simple to use. The Center Mark command is found in the Dimension pull-down menu. Left-click on the Center Mark option and then left-click, touching the circle or arc. If it does not work, check the center mark settings in the Dimension Style's Lines and Arrows menu to make sure the Line or Mark choice is set. If the None option is set, then the center mark will not be shown. Set the Mark option, select the OK button, close the dialog display, and retry the Leader command again.

Using Quick Dimensions (QDIM)

The Quick Dimension command can apply dimensions to a drawing with tremendous speed. It can work in two different ways when selected:

1. You can pick individual lines one at a time and generate a group of dimensions in the defaulted Continuous mode (see Figure 20.94). Right-click after selecting the last line, then drag the dimension line into position and left-click to place the string of dimensions.
2. When selecting lines to be dimensioned, use a crossing box and touch every line that needs a dimension (see Figure 20.95). After selecting the lines with the crossing box, drag the dimension line into position and left-click when ready. This is a great new feature in AutoCAD that makes dimensioning faster than ever.

QDIM Options

After you have selected the lines or objects and it is time to place the dimension line, take a look at the command line in the lower left corner:

Specify dimension line position, or
[Continuous/Stagger/Baseline/Ordinate/Radius/Diameter/datum Point/Edit]
   <Continuous>:

You can select these choices by typing them in at the command line. Figure 20.96 gives examples of each.

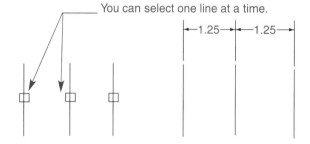

FIGURE 20.94   Quick Dimensioning picking one line at a time.

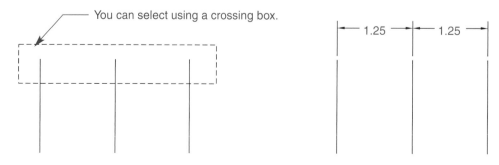

FIGURE 20.95   Using a crossing box to Quick Dimension.

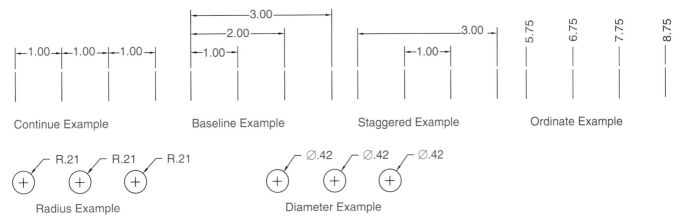

FIGURE 20.96 Quick Dimension options.

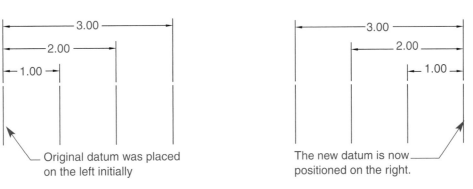

FIGURE 20.97 Using a datum point.

The datum Point option can be used right after the Baseline option has been selected. The datum Point for the Baseline is established by the order in which lines are selected. However, the datum point can be changed by using the datum Point and picking a new location for the datum (see Figure 20.97).

The Edit option is the final selection in this list of options. When chosen it displays Xs on all the lines that were selected to be dimensioned (see Figure 20.98). The purpose here is to change the dimension locations that were originally selected. A Remove option is the default setting. A left-click with the cursor placed on top of an X causes the X to disappear and to be removed from the original selection. The Add option is activated by typing **A** and pressing Enter↵. A left-click can place a new X, which will be included in the dimension selection (see Figure 20.99). Once you are finished making the selections, exit with a right-click, then left-click where the dimensions are to be placed (see Figure 20.100). The dimensions will show up where the Xs were left on the drawing.

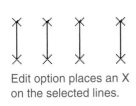

Edit option places an X
on the selected lines.

FIGURE 20.98 Using the Edit option.

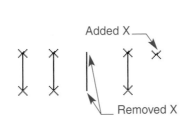

Added X

Removed X

FIGURE 20.99 Editing options.

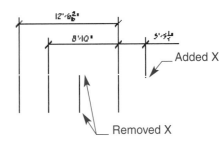

Added X

Removed X

FIGURE 20.100 Dimensions edited.

20.3 Editing Existing Dimensions

You have many choices when it comes to changing dimensions after they are placed on a drawing. When a dimension is put on a drawing, it is a Block and is treated as one object. It is edited differently than a string of text or a line. A dimension can be edited by two methods:

1. The dimension can be left as a Block and altered with some of the following choices.

   - Grips
   - MO—Properties
   - DIMTEDIT—Dimension Text Edit
   - DIMEDIT

2. A dimension can be Exploded or have its DIMASO (Associative Dimensioning) cut off (prior to dimensioning).

Both the options in number 2 have consequences and should be used only in rare cases. When these options are used the dimension is no longer a block, and the individual pieces must be dealt with as single entities.

Editing Dimensions with Grips

Grips are a great dimension editing tool. The following grips options are available: Stretch, Move, Rotate, Scale, Mirror, and Copy.

To activate the grips, left-click on the dimension block (the command line should be clear). Little boxes should show up all along the dimension. These are the warm grip boxes. Next, put the cursor on the middle box near the dimension text, and left-click when the box changes color. The box becomes solid and is considered a hot grip (see Figure 20.101). That means it is ready to perform a Grip option.

The default option is the Stretch. Watch what happens when you move the mouse in all directions (see Figure 20.102).

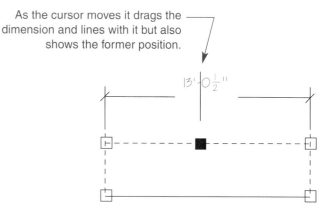

As the cursor moves it drags the dimension and lines with it but also shows the former position.

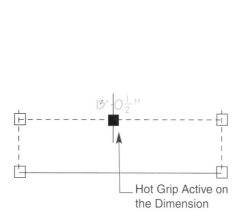

Hot Grip Active on the Dimension

FIGURE 20.101 Hot grip on dimension.

FIGURE 20.102 Stretching lines and dimensions with grips.

FIGURE 20.103 Moving lines and dimensions with grips.

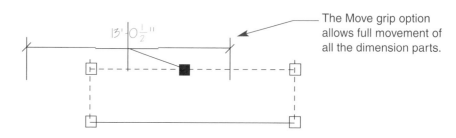

The Move grip option allows full movement of all the dimension parts.

The Grips Stretch option helps shift text around in crowded areas. To change to the Move option hold the Shift key down and press Enter↵ once (see Figure 20.103). The Stretch and Move options are used frequently to edit dimensions. To cycle through the Grip options continue holding down the Shift key and pressing Enter↵.

> ### Example
>
> Draw a dimension anywhere with any variable settings. Using the grips, experiment with the Stretch and Move options.
>
> The Stretch option works very well for moving dimensions around for better fits. When you are done, hit the Esc key twice to turn the grips off. Once will take you from warm grips to cold and twice will turn off the grips completely.

Editing Dimensions with Properties Command

The most powerful editing tool in AutoCAD is the **Properties** command because it gives you access to a great many choices. Normally it is the first option used because it can do so much at one time. For instance, turn on the grip boxes on an existing dimension (do not make the grip hot), then activate the **Properties** command.

Properties Icon

- Type **MO** at the command prompt.
- Select **Properties** from the Modify pull-down menu (see Figure 20.104).
- Pick the **Properties** icon from the Standard Toolbar.

Figure 20.105 shows all the settings that can be changed under the Alphabetic pull-down menu tab. All the Dimension Variables are listed there for editing dimensions. Left-click on the Categorized pull-down menu tab, and the dimension settings are grouped in their six main categories (see Figure 20.106). Click on the + signs to open them. Also, notice the other options under General.

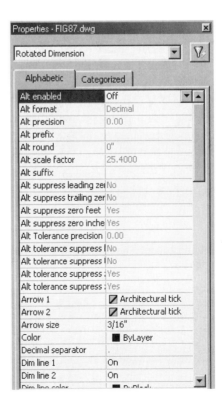

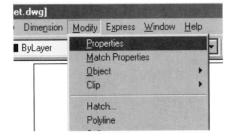

FIGURE 20.104 Modify pull-down menu.

FIGURE 20.105 Alphabetic tab menu.

FIGURE 20.106 General menu under the Categorized tab.

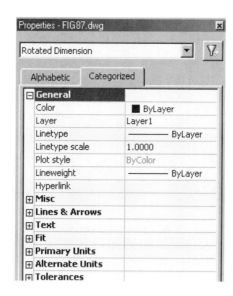

To make changes left-click on the written description, and when it is highlighted left-click on the value to be changed to the right. Type in the new values, and when the change is made close the Properties dialog box and click the Esc key twice.

Editing Dimensions with Dimension Edit (DIMEDIT) and Dimension Text Edit (DIMTEDIT)

The **DIMEDIT** and **DIMTEDIT** commands are used for changing dimensions. Each has a different function. **DIMEDIT** changes the text in the dimension Block.

DIMEDIT Icon

- Type **DIMEDIT** at the command prompt.
- Select the **DIMEDIT** icon from the Dimension toolbar.

The following choices in **DIMEDIT** are shown at the command line:

[Home/New/Rotate/Oblique] <Home>:

Type in the suboptions. Press Enter↵ for the Home suboption, which will place the text in its default position in the middle of the dimension line (see Figure 20.107).

The New suboption will allow you to change the text value using the Mtext Editor (see Figure 20.108).

The Rotate suboption will ask you to specify an angle for the dimension text. The example in Figure 20.109 used a 30° angle.

The Oblique suboption will change the angle of the extension lines (see Figure 20.110).

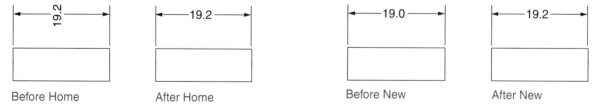

Before Home   After Home

FIGURE 20.107 Home suboption of DIMEDIT to change the text position.

Before New   After New

FIGURE 20.108 New suboption of DIMEDIT to change the text.

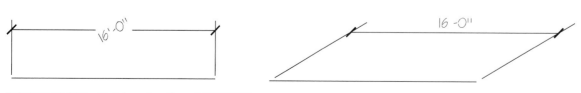

FIGURE 20.109 Rotate suboption of DIMEDIT.

FIGURE 20.110 Oblique suboption of DIMEDIT.

DIMTEDIT has some similarities to the Grip option and DIMEDIT. It can adjust the location of the text and dimension line like a stretch grip, but it also will reposition the text along the dimension line.

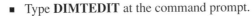

- Type **DIMTEDIT** at the command prompt.
- Select the **DIMTEDIT** icon from the Dimension toolbar.

DIMTEDIT
Icon

At the command line the following suboptions are shown.

[Home/New/Rotate/Oblique] <Home>:

There are no new options in this command, just a different set of combinations.

Edit DIM Text Value DDEDIT

- Type **DDEDIT** at the command prompt.

Using this command brings up the Multiline Text Editor for changing text values. Just type in **DDEDIT** at the command line, press Enter↵, and select the dimension text with a left click.

There are other offshoots to these commands, but the following are some of the most beneficial in the beginning. The Update command is an important one. When modifications to dimension settings or variables are made, sometimes they will not take effect until the Update command is used. The Update option is at the very bottom of the Dimension pull-down menu. Select it and then touch the dimension to be updated. Do not expect the Update to work on all the commands. It has limitations just like the other editing commands, and it may take several combinations to get the desired layout.

Editing Dimensioning Command with DIMASO

- Type **DIM** at the command line and press Enter↵, then type DIMASO and press Enter↵ again.

Associative Dimensioning, also known as the DIMASO variable, controls the dimension block or unit. The dimension is defaulted to the DIMASO On setting, which makes the dimension one unit or block. This means that if you tried to erase a tick mark by itself, the whole dimension, being one unit, would be erased totally. Turning the DIMASO off before applying the dimension to the drawing will insert it in individual pieces. Each part of the dimension can then be edited separately as lines and text (see Figure 20.111).

The **DIMASO** variable can be changed at the command line:

Command: **DIM**↵
Dim: **DIMASO**↵
Enter new value for dimension variable <ON> OFF↵:

At this point type the setting desired and press Enter↵, then press the Esc key.

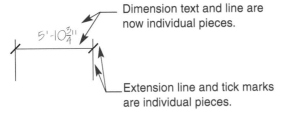

Dimension text and line are now individual pieces.

Extension line and tick marks are individual pieces.

FIGURE 20.111   Associative dimensioning turned off.

Tips for Using DIMASO Turned Off

When DIMASO is turned off, the normal dimension editing commands will not work on the split-up dimension. For example, the following will not work:

- Dimension Edit
- Dimension Text Edit
- Gripping as a unit
- Updating, Overriding, Modifying as a Unit

You must then manually edit every piece. This is a major drawback, but sometimes this is the only option to get what is needed. Use this as a last option.

Another drastic option is Exploding a dimension unit. This will also split up the dimension into pieces. The same problems will exist after an Explode; a lot of the most powerful dimension editing tools will be wasted.

Tips for Efficient Dimensioning

1. Create an architectural style that works well for horizontal and vertical dimensions.
2. Create a style to switch to when placing dimensions on circles and pointing with leaders. (Use arrows instead of ticks, and set the text to the horizontal position.) Save Dimension Styles on a template drawing.
3. Always use Osnaps when dimensioning.
4. Turn on DIMUPT. (Place text manually when dimensioning.)
5. Create a layer just for dimensions.
6. Use **DIMASO** off and Explode only after all other editing features have failed.

REVIEW QUESTIONS

1. List the different methods used to open the Dimension Style Manager dialog box.
2. What does the Scale for Dimension Features control?
3. List the six major Tabs found in the New Dimension Style dialog display.
4. Where is the setting that changes the arrowheads to tick marks located?
5. What setting will help when dimensions are too crowded together?
6. How should the Zero Suppression be set for mechanical drawings? Refer to Chapter 9 if needed.
7. What does the Override command do?
8. What do the following abbreviations stand for?
   a. ANSI
   b. ISO-25
   c. DIN
   d. JIS
9. Sketch an example of an aligned dimension, baseline dimension, and continue dimensioning.
10. How does the Quick dimensioning work?
11. Which dimension setting has a Spline option in it?

12. What are four ways to edit existing dimensions?

13. What options are found in the DIMEDIT command and what do they do?

14. DIMASO controls what function?

15. DIMUPT can be used to control what?

16. At what point should a dimension be exploded and why?

EXERCISES

EXERCISE 20.1

Begin a new drawing from scratch and create a Dimensioning Style for a ¼″ = 1′-0″ scale drawing with the following settings.

In the Lines and Arrows tab:

- Name the New Style Mech Full.
- Set the Extend beyond dim lines to .12.
- Set the Arrowheads 1st and 2nd to closed fill.
- Set Arrow size to .125.

In the Text tab:

- Set Text style to Technic Bold.
- Set Text height to .125.
- Set Fraction height scale to 1.
- Set Text Placement Vertical to Center and Horizontal to Centered.
- Set Text Alignment to Horizontal with dimension line.

In the Fit tab:

- Under Scale for Dimension Features set Use an Overall scale of: to 1.
- Under Fine Tuning turn on Place text manually when dimensioning.

In the Primary Units tab:

- Under Linear Dimensions set Unit format to Decimal.
- In the Zero Suppression box to the left, place a check in the Leading box.

Perform a Save As and name the drawing 20EX-1.

EXERCISE 20.2

Begin a new drawing from scratch and create a Dimensioning Style for a ½″ = 1″ scale drawing with the following settings.

In the Lines and Arrows tab:

- Name the New Style Mech half.
- Set the Extend beyond dim lines to .125.
- Set the Arrowheads 1st and 2nd to Open 30.
- Set Arrow size to .18.

In the Text tab:

- Set Text style to Times New Roman.
- Set Text height to .18.
- Set Fraction height scale to .8.
- Set Text Placement Vertical to Above and Horizontal to Centered.
- Set Text Alignment to Aligned with dimension line.

In the Fit tab:

- Under Scale for Dimension Features set Use an Overall scale of: to 2.
- Under Fine Tuning turn on both Place text manually when dimensioning and Always draw dimline between ext lines.

In the Primary Units tab:

- Under Linear Dimensions set Unit format to Architectural.
- In the Zero Suppression box to the left place a check in the Trailing 0 Inches.

Perform a Save As and name the drawing 20EX-2.

EXERCISE 20.3

Begin a new drawing from scratch and create a Dimensioning Style for a 1″ = 1′-0″ scale drawing with the following settings.

In the Lines and Arrows tab:

- Name the New Style 1 Arch.
- Set the Extend beyond dim lines to 1/16″.
- Set the Arrowheads 1st and 2nd to Closed Arrows.
- Set Arrow size to .18.

In the Text tab:

- Set Text style to Country Blueprint.
- Set Text height to .18.
- Set Fraction height scale to .75.
- Set Text Placement Vertical to Above and Horizontal to Centered.
- Set Text Alignment to Aligned with dimension line.

In the Fit tab:

- Under Scale for Dimensions Features set Use an Overall scale of: to 12.
- Under Fine Tuning turn on both Place text manually when dimensioning and Always draw dimline between ext lines.

In the Primary Units tab:

- Under Linear Dimensions set Unit format to Architectural.
- In the Zero Suppression box to the left remove the check from the Trailing 0 Inches.

Perform a Save As and name the drawing 20EX-3.

EXERCISE 20.4

Begin a new drawing from scratch and create a Dimensioning Style for a metric full scale drawing with the following settings.

In the Lines and Arrows tab:

- Name the New Style Met 1.
- Set the Extend beyond dim lines to 3.5.
- Set the Arrowheads 1st and 2nd to closed filled.
- Set Arrow size to 3.5.

In the Text tab:

- Set Text style to Times New Roman.
- Set Text height to 3.5.
- Set Fraction height scale to 1.
- Set Text Placement Vertical to Centered and Horizontal to Centered.
- Set Text Alignment to Horizontal with dimension line.
- Set Offset from dim line to 2.5.

In the Fit Tab:

- Under Scale for Dimension Features set Use an Overall scale of: to 1.
- Under Fine Tuning turn on Place text manually when dimensioning.

In Primary Units Tab:

- Under Linear Dimensions set Unit format to Decimal.
- In the Zero Suppression box to the left place the check by the Trailing 0 Inches.
- In Precision box set to 0.0.

Perform a Save As and name the drawing 20EX-4.

DRAWING ASSIGNMENTS

1. Using the Mechanical Dimensioning setup of exercise 20.1, draw and dimension the drawings shown in Figure 20.112. Make copies of the drawings and redimension them with two other methods.
2. Draw the pictorials or given views in Figure 20.113 in technical drawing form (auxiliarys, sections, and orthographics) and dimension them with an ASME Y14.5 style of your own.

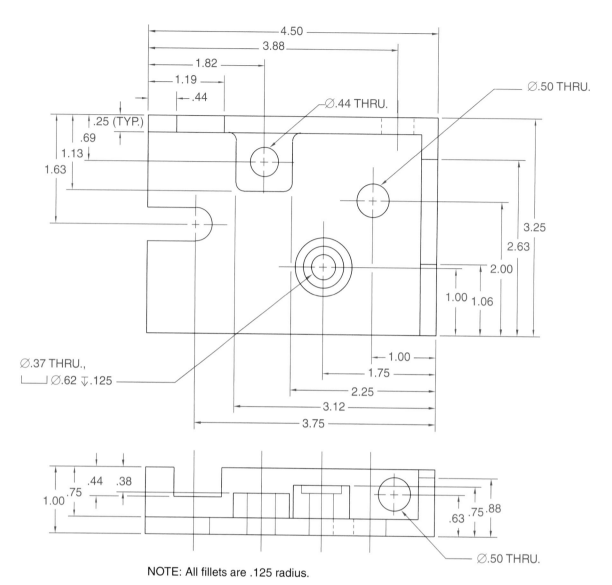

NOTE: All fillets are .125 radius.

FIGURE 20.112   Drawing Assignment 1.

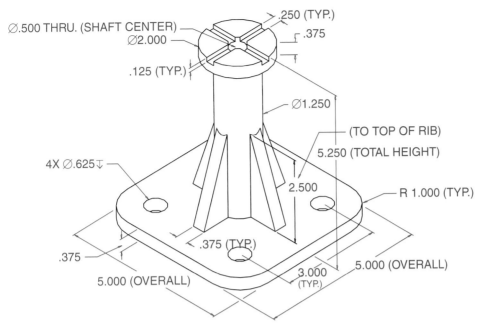

Ø.500 THRU. (SHAFT CENTER)
Ø2.000
.250 (TYP.)
.375
.125 (TYP.)
Ø1.250
(TO TOP OF RIB)
5.250 (TOTAL HEIGHT)
4X Ø.625⤓
2.500
R 1.000 (TYP.)
.375
.375 (TYP.)
5.000 (OVERALL)
3.000 (TYP.)
5.000 (OVERALL)
5.000 (OVERALL)

NOTE: Center all ribs on base plate.

(a)

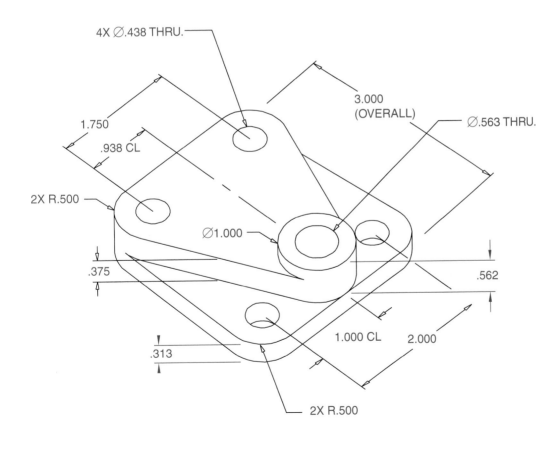

4X Ø.438 THRU.
3.000 (OVERALL)
1.750
Ø.563 THRU.
.938 CL
2X R.500
Ø1.000
.375
.562
.313
1.000 CL
2.000
2X R.500

(b)

FIGURE 20.113 Drawing Assignment 2.
continued on next page

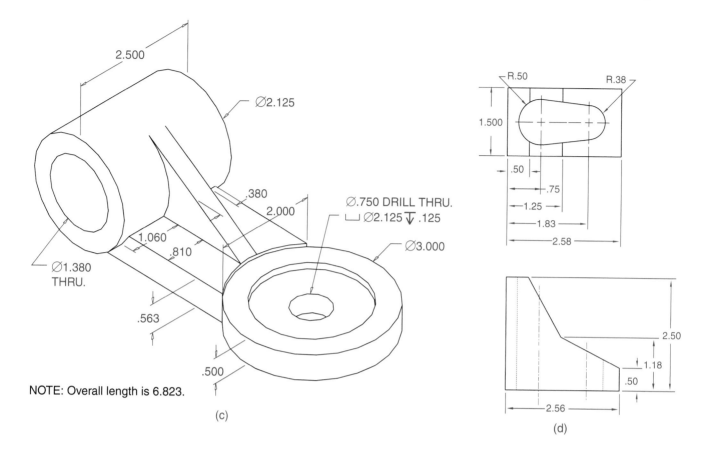

2.500

Ø2.125

.380

2.000

Ø.750 DRILL THRU.
⌴ Ø2.125 ▽ .125

1.060

.810

Ø3.000

Ø1.380
THRU.

.563

.500

NOTE: Overall length is 6.823.

(c)

R.50   R.38

1.500

.50

.75

1.25

1.83

2.58

2.50

1.18

.50

2.56

(d)

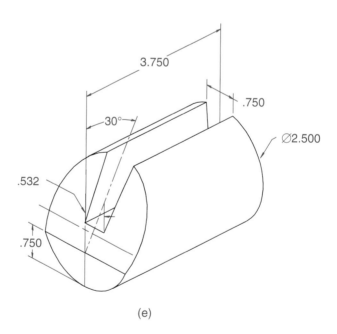

3.750

.750

30°

Ø2.500

.532

.750

FIGURE 20.113   *continued*

(e)

CHAPTER 21

Using AutoCAD Text Commands

Mechanical drawings have notes along with other text placed on them. The more technical a drawing is the more notes are needed for explaining details. In the days of board drawing, hand lettering was extremely time consuming even for the fastest drafters.

In computer-aided drawing the art of lettering has been turned into more of an exact science. Each CAD drawing can have the exact same lettering style no matter how many different people work on the same drawing. Being consistent is a must in drafting, and with CAD it is very achievable.

Typing and editing text are big advantages on a CAD project. Even someone who is a fairly slow typist can place and revise text faster than a drafter who is hand lettering a drawing.

The term *text* in CAD has replaced what was once called *lettering*. This chapter is broken into three sections:

1. Creating Text Settings and Formats
2. Placing Text on a Drawing
3. Editing and Modifying Existing Text on a Drawing

21.1 Creating Text Settings and Formats

Here are some guidelines to use when setting up text formats. A minimum ⅛″ (.125″) text height should be set for dimensions and notes. Some companies will even bump up this height to ³⁄₁₆″ (.18″) if there is a possibility that the drawings will be reduced in size at some point. Titles on drawings should be set to a minimum of ¼″ (.25″) (see Figure 21.1). When text appears in paragraph form the spacing between the sentences should be half the text height (see Figure 21.2).

The drawing scale can affect the text height and needs to be carefully planned. To set the text height, take the scale factor and multiply it by the text height as if it were at the full plotting size. See the examples in Figure 21.3. Understanding how this works will help set the right text height correctly each time a drawing is done at a different scale.

FIGURE 21.1 Text height.

USE HIGH STRESS STEEL FOR THE PULLEY.
Notes ⅛″ Height

PULLEY DETAIL
Titles ¼″ Height

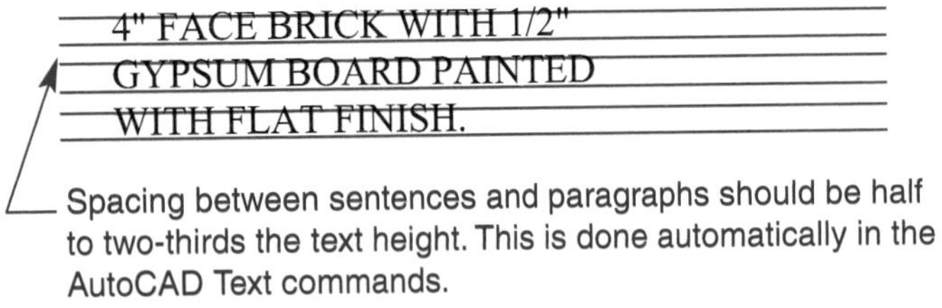

FIGURE 21.2 Text spacing.

4″ FACE BRICK WITH 1/2″
GYPSUM BOARD PAINTED
WITH FLAT FINISH.

Spacing between sentences and paragraphs should be half to two-thirds the text height. This is done automatically in the AutoCAD Text commands.

FIGURE 21.3   Setting text heights.

Setting Text for ¼″ = 1′-0″ Scale
If the drawing is to be drawn at a scale of ¼″ = 1′-0″, calculate the text height as follows:

    1. Divide the 1′ by the ¼″ of the scale to find the scale factor:

$$\frac{1'}{\frac{1}{4}''} = \frac{12''}{.25''} = 48 \qquad \text{48 is the scale factor needed.}$$

    2. Multiply the desired text height of ⅛″ for notes by the scale factor of 48:

      ⅛″ × 48 = 6″   This will be the text height for your notes.

Use the same format to find the text height for ¼″ titles:

      ¼″ × 48 = 12″   This will be the text height for your titles.

Setting Text for 1″ = 1′-0″ Scale
If a wall section is to be drawn at a scale of 1″ = 1′-0″, calculate the text height as follows:

    1. Divide the 1′ by the 1″ of the scale to find the scale factor:

$$\frac{12''}{1''} = 12 \qquad \text{12 is the scale factor needed.}$$

    2. Multiply the desired text height of ⅛″ for notes by the scale factor of 12:

      ⅛″ × 12 = 1.5″   This will be the text height for your notes.

Use the same format to find the text height for ¼″ titles:

      ¼″ × 12 = 3″   This will be the text height for your titles.

Setting Text for ¼″ = 1″ Scale
If the drawing is to be drawn at a scale of ¼″ = 1″, calculate the text height as follows:

    1. Divide the 1″ by the ¼″ of the scale to find the scale factor:

$$\frac{1''}{\frac{1}{4}''} = 4 \qquad \text{4 is the scale factor needed.}$$

    2. Multiply the desired text height of ⅛″ for notes by the scale factor of 4:

      ⅛″ × 4 = ½″   This will be the text height for your notes.

Use the same format to find the text height for ¼″ titles:

      ¼″ × 4 = 1″   This will be the text height for your titles.

The Text Style Command.

- Type **DDSTYLE** or **ST** at the command prompt.
- Select Text <u>S</u>tyle from the F<u>o</u>rmat pull-down menu (see Figure 21.4).
- Pick <u>S</u>tyle from the Dimension pull-down menu.

The Text Style dialog box appears, where you can make some selections concerning text appearance (see Figure 21.5).

The **Effects** section has five options that alter the appearance of basic text.

- **Upsi<u>d</u>e down**—Left-click on the little boxes to the left of the words to activate the settings. If this option is activated, the text will appear upside down when placed on the screen (see Figure 21.6).

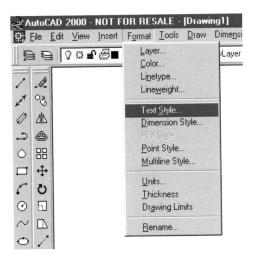

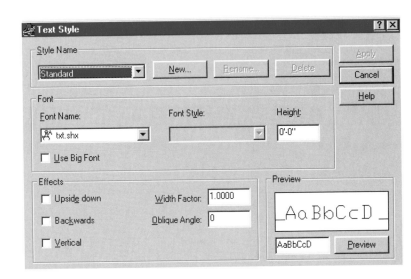

FIGURE 21.4 Text Style selected on the Format pull-down menu.

FIGURE 21.5 Text Style dialog box.

IHE ᖷLᑐᑐᖴ ᖷLᗄᑎ

FIGURE 21.6 Upside-Down text.

ИA⅃ꟼ ᖴOO⅃ᖷ ƎHT

FIGURE 21.7 Backwards text.

T
H
E

F
L
O
O
R

P
L
A
N

FIGURE 21.8 Vertical text.

F L O O R

Width Factor
Set at 2

FLOOR

Width Factor
Set at .5

FIGURE 21.9 Setting text width.

THE BEST OF THE BEST

Oblique Angle Set to 23°

THE BEST OF THE BEST

Oblique Angle Set to −23°

FIGURE 21.10 Oblique text.

- **Backwards**—This setting will cause the text to appear from right to left (see Figure 21.7).
- **Vertical**—This setting will cause the text to run vertically on the drawing instead of the standard horizontally (see Figure 21.8).
- **Width Factor**—Left-click in the box to the right of the words, and type in the width factor desired. The normal or default setting for text is 1. Increasing this number will widen the text, and reducing it will compress it (see Figure 21.9).
- **Oblique Angle**—Left-click in the box to the right of the words and change the default setting of zero by typing in a new angle setting. Changing this setting will give the letters a slant or slope (see Figure 21.10). A positive angle slopes the text to the right. (A slope between 0 and 23 is acceptable in some fields of drafting.) A negative angle is not acceptable for any drafting field.

Creating Style Names and Fonts

As an AutoCAD user, you can create a name for any style that you customize. Do so by left-clicking on the New... option in the Style Name section. The New Text Style dialog box pops up (see Figure 21.11). Type in

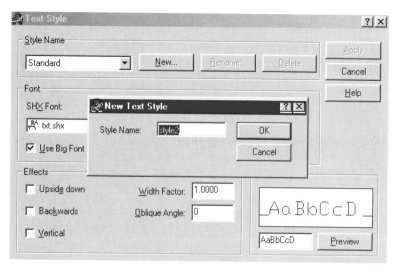

FIGURE 21.11   New Text Style dialog box.

FIGURE 21.12   Choosing a font.

the Style Name desired and left-click on the OK screen button. The new name is placed in the style name list. Left-click on the arrow to the left of the New... button and check the list for the new style name just created. Select the new style name to make it the current one.

With the new name current, it is easy to pick out a font or lettering style for it. Left-click on the arrow found under the Font Name option (see Figure 21.12).

AutoCAD has a wide range of fonts. Scroll down with the arrows in the Font Name: text box to see all the styles loaded that can be selected. Find the City Blueprint and left-click on the words to select it.

In the lower right corner of the dialog display the Preview box shows you what this font style looks like. Other font controls are found to the right of the font name. Some fonts may have additional choices in the Font Style box. For instance, the Times New Roman font has four choices in this box: Bold, Bold Italic, Italic, or Regular.

The height setting box is found just to the right of the Font Style text box. This is where the height can be set if desired. Notice that the default height is set to 0. If this setting is used, then every time the text commands are requested, the program will automatically ask/prompt you for a height to be used. This works well if you are changing text height frequently on the drawing. Another benefit to using a 0 setting is that font height will not override the text height setting for dimensions when those are in place.

It is also possible to Rename and Delete style names in the Text Style dialog display. Left-click on the style name to highlight it and then Rename or Delete it.

The best order to set up your lettering is as follows:

Note:
Remember to calculate the text height based on the drawing scale.

1. Select a new style name.
2. Select a font to be used.
3. Choose a font height.
4. Select any other setting desired for this style.
5. Make sure to left-click on the Apply... box or the font settings will not hold.
6. Left-click on the Close button to close the Text Style dialog box.

Deciding on a Font to Use

AutoCAD has an extensive number of fonts with an extreme range of styles. Choosing a style for the right job is a matter of purpose. When you are looking for a font, clarity and legibility must play a major factor in selection. Fonts in AutoCAD that fit mechanical drawings are plentiful. Stay away from fonts that are difficult to read on working drawings. Simplex, Romans, and Romand work well.

Fonts for special usage such as logos and title blocks may shift to the more extreme fonts. A logo is a company symbol or trademark with a design that is intended to get attention or make a statement about a company. Businesses want something their clients will recognize and remember.

21.2 Placing Text on a Drawing

Lettering can be placed on a drawing using a variety of methods, which are split into two categories: single line text and multiline text.

The DTEXT Command

- Type **DTEXT** or **DT** at the command prompt.
- Select Te**x**t from the **D**raw pull-down menu, then select **S**ingle Line Text from the cascade menu to the right (see Figure 21.13).

The command prompt line then reads:

Specify start point of text or [Justify/Style]:

At this point you have three choices.

1. You can pick a text starting point by left-clicking once, and the single line of text will begin there running from left to right, after you supply it with two more bits of information.

   Check out the command line. If the text height was set to 0 in the initial text style settings as discussed in the previous section, then you are being asked to pick a height for that line of text. Next, the command line will prompt you for an angle to incline the text. The 0° angle is the default, but it can easily be changed here by typing in a new value (see Figure 21.14, which shows a 45° example).

2. Look at the original command line after typing in **DT**. You may choose what is inside the brackets [Justify/Style].

   Typing **JUSTIFY** or **J** will give you the following options in the command line: [Align/Fit/Center/Middle/Right/TL/TC/TR/ML/MC/MR/BL/BC/BR].

   The Align option can be selected by typing **A** ↵. Then you will be asked to pick a first text point and a second text point using the mouse's left-click button and the cursor. Once you do this and start typing, the software will do whatever it needs to do to place the text between the two points. This includes expanding and shrinking text sizes in all directions.

   The Fit option will do the same thing as Align; however, you can set the height to remain the same, so at least it will be consistent (see Figure 21.15).

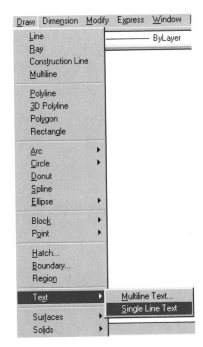

FIGURE 21.13 Text, **S**ingle Line Text selected on the **D**raw pull-down menu.

FIGURE 21.14 Angled text.

Note: Avoid using the Align and Fit settings on technical drawings. They are too inconsistent.

It is more acceptable to use the following options, as they do not distort the letter sizes.

Options	Shortcut Keystrokes
Center	C (press Enter ↵)
Middle	M (press Enter ↵)
Right	R (press Enter ↵)

The Center option will start where you left-click and place the text center bottom of the text (see Figure 21.16). Other choices inside the Center option are Height and Rotation angle. The command sequence appears as follows:

Align/Fit/Center/Middle/Right/TL/TC/TR/ML/MC/MR/BL/BC/BR:
Specify center point of text: *(Pick a point with left click.)*
Specify height <current setting>: *(Type new setting.)*
Specify rotation angle <0>: *(Type your angle.)*
Enter text:

The Middle option is almost identical with the Center option except that the starting point is in the middle of the letters, not at the bottom. See Figure 21.17 for a comparison of the letter locations around the starting point.

The Right option is a right-side justify. This causes the text to align on the right-hand side where the initial starting point was selected (see Figure 21.18).

The rest of the options are abbreviated. The abbreviations represent the starting point and general text alignments (see Figure 21.19).

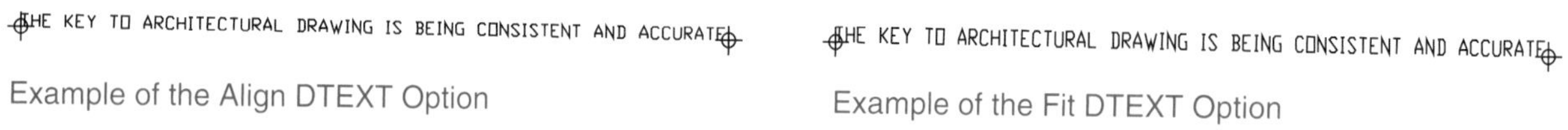
THE KEY TO ARCHITECTURAL DRAWING IS BEING CONSISTENT AND ACCURATE
Example of the Align DTEXT Option
THE KEY TO ARCHITECTURAL DRAWING IS BEING CONSISTENT AND ACCURATE
Example of the Fit DTEXT Option

FIGURE 21.15 Align and Fit options.

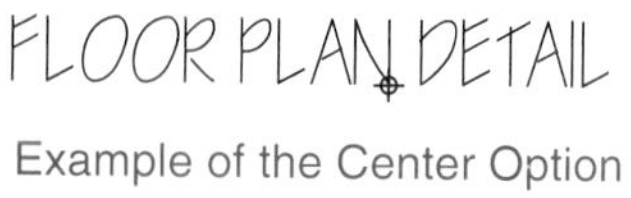
FLOOR PLAN DETAIL
Example of the Center Option

FIGURE 21.16 Center option.

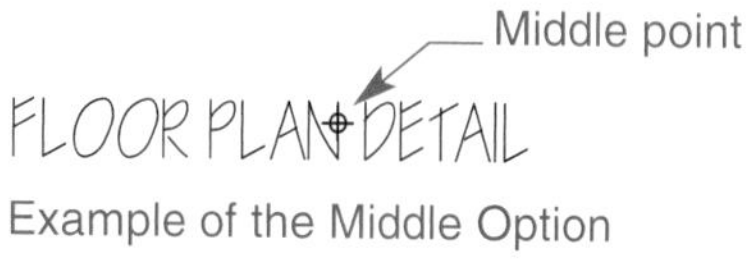
Middle point
FLOOR PLAN DETAIL
Example of the Middle Option

FIGURE 21.17 Middle option.

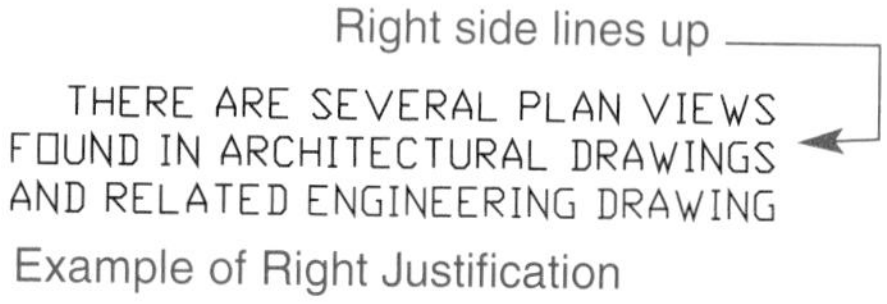
Right side lines up
THERE ARE SEVERAL PLAN VIEWS
FOUND IN ARCHITECTURAL DRAWINGS
AND RELATED ENGINEERING DRAWING
Example of Right Justification

FIGURE 21.18 Right justification.

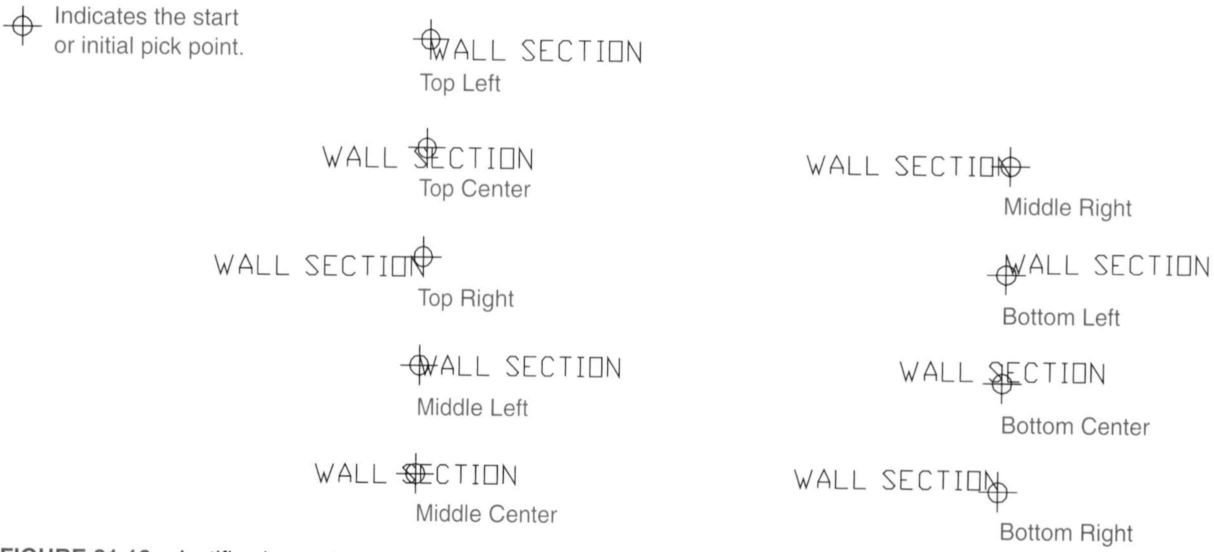
Indicates the start or initial pick point.
WALL SECTION
Top Left
WALL SECTION
Top Center
WALL SECTION
Top Right
WALL SECTION
Middle Left
WALL SECTION
Middle Center
WALL SECTION
Middle Right
WALL SECTION
Bottom Left
WALL SECTION
Bottom Center
WALL SECTION
Bottom Right

FIGURE 21.19 Justification options.

(TL) TOP LEFT

(TC) TOP CENTER

(TR) TOP RIGHT

(ML) MIDDLE LEFT

(MC) MIDDLE CENTER

(MR) MIDDLE RIGHT

(BL) BOTTOM LEFT

(BC) BOTTOM CENTER

(BR) BOTTOM RIGHT

The choices are many, so check with your instructor for the classroom standards.

3. The last choice at the DTEXT command line is style.

> Specify start point of text or [Justify/Style]:

> If you type **S**↵, then you can change the font style name to a different selection if it has been previously created in the Text Style setting. If you type **?**↵ at the prompt, then you can access a list of the created styles by pressing Enter↵ again at the <*> prompt. An advantage to using **DTEXT** is that you see the text on the screen as it is being typed.

The MTEXT Command

The multiline text option is used to generate a lot of text in paragraphs or sentences. It is not seen as it is typed on the drawing. The multiline command has its own dialog display box for the text (see Figure 21.20).

- Type **MTEXT**, **MT,** or **T** at the command prompt.
- Select Te**x**t from the **D**raw pull-down menu, then select **M**ultiline Text... from the cascade menu to the right (see Figure 21.21).
- Select the Multiline Text icon from the Draw toolbar.

MTEXT
Icon

The command line then prompts you to pick a first corner with the left mouse button. Once you have done this the command shows a variety of choices:

Specify first corner: *(Pick any point.)*
Specify opposite corner or [Height/Justify/Line Spacing/Rotation/Style/Width]:

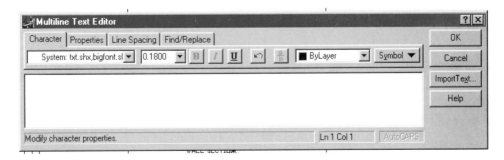

FIGURE 21.20 Multiline Text Editor dialog box.

FIGURE 21.21 Text, Multiline Text... selected on the Draw pull-down menu.

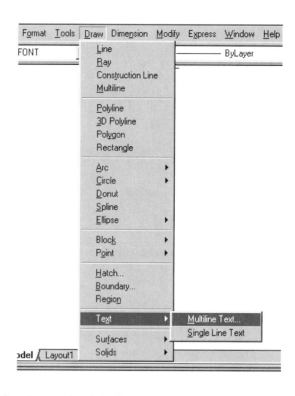

Dragging the cursor and performing another left click will pop up the Multiline Text Editor dialog box. (see Figure 21.20).

The Character tab is open, which shows the following options:

- Selecting font styles
- Selecting a height for text
- Underscoring or underlining (U)
- Selecting colors for the text
- Picking a symbol

Note: For mechanical symbols choose the GDT.shx font style.

The Symbol choices include Degrees, Plus/Minus, and Diameter (see Figure 21.22). The Other... option brings up a Character Map of symbols unique to the font style that is selected (see Figure 21.23).

To use a symbol from the chart, left-click on one, then move the mouse arrow to the Select button and left-click. Next, move to the Copy button and left-click on it, then left-click on the Close button. Finally, insert the symbol by right-clicking and then choosing Paste with a left click.

If the Properties tab is selected, the following set of options pops up (see Figure 21.24).

- Style
- Justification
- Width
- Rotation

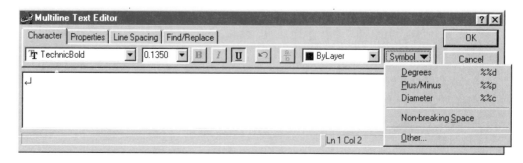

FIGURE 21.22 Symbol options.

FIGURE 21.23 Character map.

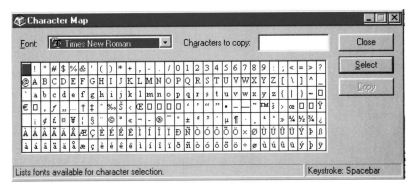

FIGURE 21.24 Multiline Text Editor.

The Line Spacing tab will open two line spacing settings to control the distance between text lines stacked on top of one another. The Final/Replace tab can be used to scan the text for editing.

There are four screen buttons on the right-hand side of the dialog display.

- The **OK** button puts the text on the drawing and exits the Text Editor.
- The **Cancel** button terminates the text in the mline text area and exits the Text Editor.
- The **Import Text...** button allows you to search and bring in text from another program or file and use it in this drawing.
- The **Help** button displays the help screen for MTEXT.

The multiline text editor is preferred by most CAD operators; however, keyboard options are available. Look at the command sequence again after typing **MTEXT** and selecting the starting corner. You can type in the options shown at the command line prompt:

[Height/Justify/Line Spacing/Rotation/Style/Width]:

All these options have just previously been shown. They are found in the dialog boxes, but sometimes a fast CAD operator can use a single keystroke for making changes instead of going into the dialog box. Once you have selected the command by typing the first letter and pressing Enter↵, the Multiline Text Editor pops up ready for you to type.

21.3 Editing and Modifying Existing Text

Once you have placed text on a drawing and exited the DTEXT or MTEXT options, you must use special editing commands to make changes. **Properties** and **DDEDIT** are two excellent text editing commands used in AutoCAD (see Figures 21.25, 21.26, and 21.27).

The Properties Command

Properties Icon

- Type **PROPERTIES** or **MO** at the command prompt.
- Select **Properties** from the Modify pull-down menu (see Figure 21.28).
- Pick the **Properties** icon from the Modify toolbar.

The DDEDIT Command

Edit Text Icon

- Type **DDEDIT** or **ED** at the command prompt.
- Select Text from the Modify pull-down menu (see Figure 21.29).
- Pick the **Edit Text** icon from the Modify II toolbar.

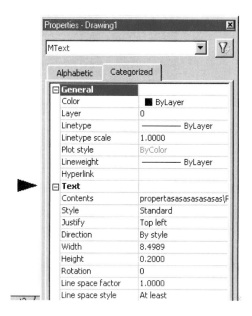

FIGURE 21.25   Properties tab options.

FIGURE 21.26   Edit Text dialog box for single-line text.

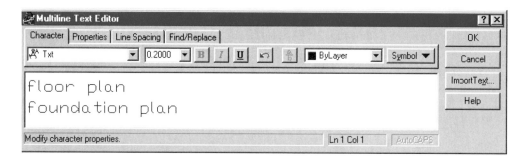

FIGURE 21.27   Multiline Text Editor dialog box.

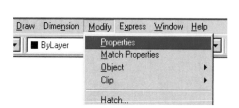

FIGURE 21.28   Properties selected on the Modify pull-down menu.

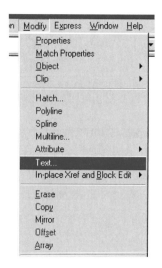

FIGURE 21.29   Text... selected on the Modify pull-down menu.

When selecting text to edit, you have a choice of either picking and highlighting the DT text string or MTEXT paragraph first and selecting DDEDIT (ED) or DDMODIFY (MO) second, or picking the editing commands first and selecting the text second. It is purely a matter of preference. In both cases the Text Editor dialog box will open ready for changes.

Text Tips

The DDEDIT command shows a blinking vertical bar so you can locate where the changes are being made. Use the keyboard's four arrow keys to maneuver around the text, or just place the mouse arrow at the desired location and left-click to get the blinking bar. Once you have changed the text, make sure to select the OK button to keep the changes.

Modifying with Properties has a lot more options than just editing text, but it is the most powerful and commonly used editing AutoCAD command. When dealing with text, make sure that you have selected the text with a window or by left-clicking on part of it in order for the Text options to open in the Properties dialog box. When it opens, go to the right of the vertical line down the middle and select what is to be edited. In the Contents group of text to the right, you may need to select a box with three little dashes to open the full text editor window. After making the changes, make sure to close the Properties dialog display by left-clicking on the X in the little box in the upper right-hand corner. To turn off the grips (the little blue boxes that show up when clicking on objects and entities) press the Esc key on the keyboard twice.

The MTEXT command will have many symbols to pick from in its setup. In contrast, only a few symbols can be generated in DTEXT, such as:

%%% will show a % symbol

%%U will underline text if used before the text

%%D will add an angle degree symbol

%%O will draw a line above the letters if used before the text

%%C will generate a diameter symbol

Note: The symbols will not appear until you press Enter⏎ twice or once followed by pressing the Esc key.

The command called **QTEXT** is used to display a rectangular box where the text will be located. Just type in **QTEXT** at the command line and then type **ON**.

Command: **QTEXT**⏎
Enter node [ON/OFF] <OFF>: **ON**

This setting is used to reduce the amount of memory that text uses for a drawing; therefore, if there is a lot of text on a drawing, then turning **QTEXT** on will speed up the computer. To get the letters back, just turn **QTEXT** off and follow it with the **Regen** command. The Regen performs a recalculation of the screen and will bring the text back.

Another feature in AutoCAD is the spelling check, which is located under the Tools pull-down menu. Select Spelling and left-click on top of the text and it will scan the text for misspelled words. This spell checker works similarly to ones that are found in word processing software packages. If a spell check of the whole drawing is desired, just type **ALL**⏎, then press Enter⏎ when the Select objects prompt appears at the command line, and every piece of text will be checked.

Example: DTEXT

In this example we will create a new style name called Arch1 and pick a font style called CountryBlueprint from the Font Name selection. The text height will be set to 1/4″ (.25″) with a Width Factor set to .75. The text to be typed:

AutoCAD® 2000 HAS A WIDE
RANGE OF FONT STYLES.

Right after the text is placed on the drawing with the **DTEXT** command, then it will be changed using **Properties (MO)** to the following:

- Text height of 1/8″ (.125″)
- Width Factor of (.9)
- Obliquing angle of 15°

Begin by selecting Text Style from the Format pull-down menu (see Figure 21.30), which will open up the Text Style dialog box (see Figure 21.31).

Left-click on the New box to activate the New Text Style dialog box and type in Arch1. Left-click on the OK box to return to the Text Style display, and left-click on the arrow in the Font Name text box. Two new arrows appear, and when you left-click on either one it will start moving through the different fonts (see Figure 21.32). When you come to CountryBlueprint left-click on it to select it (see Figure 21.33). Make sure the setting in the Height box is at 0, which will force the **DTEXT** command to ask you for a text height when it is used later. Left-click in the Width Factor text box and set the Width Factor to .75. The settings are complete, so left-click on the Apply button, then on the Close button (see Figure 21.34).

To start the **DTEXT** command type in **DT** at the command line and press Enter↵.

Command: **DT** ↵

Next, left-click near the middle of the graphics screen when the command line reads as shown in Figure 21.35. The command line will then show a current text height. Type in the .25 height desired after the colon.

Specify height <Current Height Shown Here>: **.25**↵

Press Enter↵ when the next command prompt comes up displaying a default rotation angle of 0.

Specify rotation angle of text <0>: ↵

The command line now prompts you to enter the text desired. At this point type in your text.

Enter text: **AutoCAD® 2000 HAS A WIDE** ↵
Enter text: **RANGE OF FONT STYLES** ↵
Enter text: ↵↵ (press Enter↵ twice)

The DT command is complete, and the text appears on the screen as shown in Figure 21.36.

To edit the existing text, let's use the **PROPERTIES** command to make the changes. Pick both lines of text with a crossing window until the blue grip boxes appear, then type in **MO** at the command line.

Command: **MO**

The Properties box will appear displaying the Text options (see Figure 21.37).

Left-click on the height setting on the right side of the box, and change it from .25 to .125. Next, left-click on the width factor, highlighting the .75 setting, and change it to .9. Finally, change the Obliquing setting from a 0 slope to a 15° slope (see Figure 21.38).

When you are finished, close the Properties display by left-clicking on the small X in the upper right corner. The text is now displayed with the new changes (see Figure 21.39). Press the Esc key twice to turn off the grip boxes.

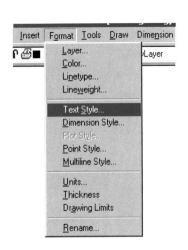

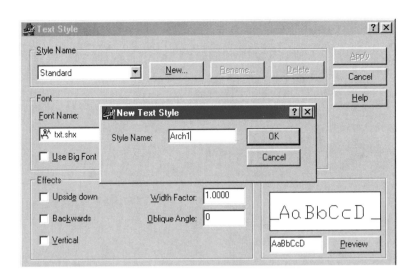

FIGURE 21.30 Text Style selected on the Format pull-down menu.

FIGURE 21.31 New Text Style dialog box.

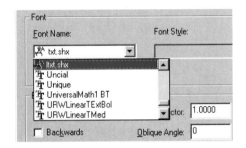

FIGURE 21.32 Font style options.

FIGURE 21.33 Font style highlighted.

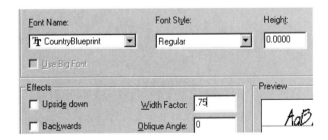

FIGURE 21.34 CountryBlueprint font style selected.

```
DTEXT
Current text style:  "ARCH1"  Text height:  0.2500
Specify start point of text or [Justify/Style]:
```

FIGURE 21.35 Command line text.

AutoCAD 2000 HAS A WIDE
RANGE OF FONT STYLES

FIGURE 21.36 Text display.

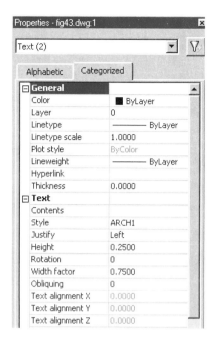

FIGURE 21.37   Text options.

Thickness	0.0000
Text	
Contents	
Style	ARCH1
Justify	Left
Height	0.1250
Rotation	0
Width factor	0.9000
Obliquing	15
Text alignment X	0.0000
Text alignment Y	0.0000
Text alignment Z	0.0000

FIGURE 21.38   Obliquing option in the Properties dialog box.

AutoCAD 2000 HAS A WIDE RANGE OF FONT STYLES

FIGURE 21.39   Text with grips.

Example: MTEXT

In this example we will create a new style name called Interior and pick a font style called City-Blueprint. The text height will be ½″ (.5″) with a Width Factor of 1.25. Using the MTEXT (MT or T) command we will type the following:

The lobby will have a brick tile floor with a 4″ base. A semi-gloss paint for all gypsum board walls. The counter will have a glass bock exterior face.

Once we exit the **MTEXT** command, we will use a DDEDIT to change the wording in the text. Begin by typing in **STYLE** or **ST** at the command line.

Command: **ST** ↵

The Text Style dialog display immediately pops up. Use the New... button to create a Style Name called Interior by typing it in when the style1 is highlighted. Left-click on the OK button, and the new style name will appear. In the Font Name box use the arrow to scroll through the list of the AutoCAD font styles. When you find the CityBlueprint font, select it by left-clicking on it. Left-click in the Height box and type in a text height of ½″ (.5″). Left-click in the Width Factor box and change the setting to 1.25. When you are done click the Apply button, then Close. The settings should look like Figure 21.40 before closing.

To start using **MTEXT**, type **MT** at the command line.

Command: **MT**

Left-click in the lower left corner for the Specify first corner, then move the mouse to the upper right corner and click again. The Multiline Text Editor dialog box opens, and you can begin typing. The screen should look like Figure 21.41 when the text is complete.

Left-click on the OK button, and the text is placed on the drawing.

To start editing the paragraph (words only) type DDEDIT or ED at the command line:

Command: **ED**

The command prompt requests a selection, so the text on the drawing must be highlighted/selected for editing. Once you have done this the Text Editor dialog box opens. Now, place the cursor inside the text area and make changes from the keyboard after a left click (see Figure 21.42 for the new text).

FIGURE 21.40   Text Style dialog box.

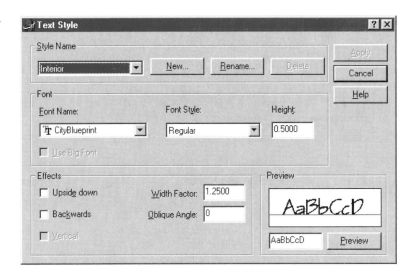

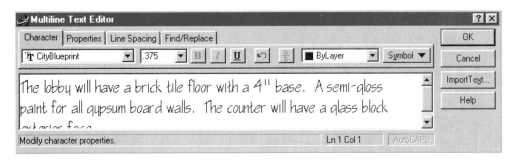

FIGURE 21.41   Multiline Text Editor.

FIGURE 21.42   Multiline Text Editor with changes.

These two examples combined some basic skills to place text on a drawing. The problems at the end of the chapter will give you some more practice getting used to the commands.

REVIEW QUESTIONS

1. How are lettering styles set up in AutoCAD?
2. What happens when the text height is set to 0?
3. Explain the difference between DTEXT and MTEXT.
4. List the options found in the Justify selection in the DTEXT command.
5. How can symbols be used inside the MTEXT command?

6. Qtext displays letters in what format?

7. Name three ways to edit existing text.

8. What are the aliases for the following commands?

    a. Properties

    b. DDEdit

    c. MTEXT

    d. DTEXT

9. How are the following symbols generated with DTEXT?

    a. Percent symbol

    b. Underlined text

    c. Diameter symbol

    d. Degree symbol

10. What effect will an Obliquing angle cause on the text?

11. A Width Factor of .5 will do what to a letter?

12. What are some of the factors considered in selecting a font style for technical drawings?

EXERCISES

EXERCISE 21.1

Start a **New** drawing **Starting from Scratch** and create a Text Style with the following settings:

- Set <u>S</u>tyle Name as Mech.
- Set Font St<u>y</u>le to Simplex.
- Use a .75 <u>W</u>idth Factor.
- Set Heig<u>h</u>t to .5″.

Type the following using MTEXT:

DRAWING INDEX

M-1 TITLE SHEET

M-2 PICTORIAL DWG.

M-3 TECHNICAL DWG.

M-4 BILL OF MATERIAL.

M-5 SPECIFICATIONS.

Save the drawing as 21EX1.

EXERCISE 21.2

Edit the drawing 21EX1 with the following changes:

- Change the letter height to .25 for every line except DRAWING INDEX.
- Change the <u>W</u>idth Factor on all letters to .5.
- **Save** changes as 21EX2.

EXERCISE 21.3

Start a **New** drawing with the **Use a Wizard's** Quick Setup. Use **Architectural Unit**, then set a 34′ width and 44′ length. Create a Text Style with the following settings:

- Set <u>S</u>tyle Name as INT2.
- Set Font St<u>y</u>le to City Blueprint.
- Use a 5° <u>O</u>blique Angle.
- Set text Heigh<u>t</u> to 6″.

Type the following paragraph using the MTEXT command:

Before deciding on an office chair, it is important to understand the CAD operator's habits. If the operator will be in the chair eight to ten hours a day, then the desired comfort level may be high.

Save the drawing as 21EX3.

EXERCISE 21.4

Use the title block shown in Figure 21.43 from Chapter 3.

- Create a New Style and use the Times New Roman font.
- Draw the title block for an 8.5″ × 11″ sheet at full scale.
- Place the text in the title block area using the sizes specified on the sheet.

Save the drawing as 21EX4.

EXERCISE 21.5

Create a title block of your own for a sheet set to limits of 0,0 lower left corner and 144′, 96′ upper right corner. Make sure to use an 8′ left-hand margin (equivalent to 2″) and 4′ margins (equivalent to 1″) on the three remaining sides.

FIGURE 21.43 Title block.

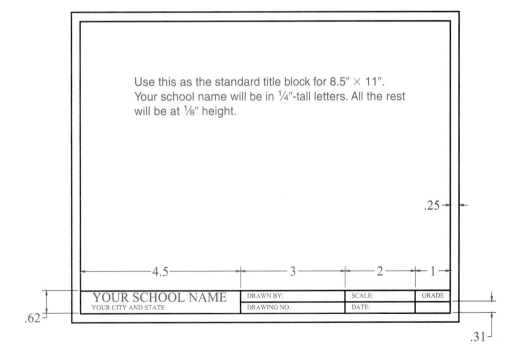

DRAWING ASSIGNMENTS

1. Using the Door Schedule in Figure 21.44 as a guide, make a version of your own. Put it on an 8.5″ × 11″ sheet at full scale.

   - Use three text heights:

     .25 large letters

     .18 medium letters

     .125 small letters

   - Make sure the text fits comfortably between the lines both vertically and horizontally. Use guidelines to place the text on the schedule. Turn the guidelines' layer off when the schedule is complete.

2. Using the Window Schedule in Figure 21.45 as a guide, make a version of your own. Put it on an 8.5″ × 11″ sheet at full scale.

   - Use three text heights:

     .25 large letters

     .18 medium letters

     .125 small letters

   - Make sure the text fits comfortably between the lines both vertically and horizontally. Use guidelines to place the text on the schedule. Turn the guidelines' layer off when the schedule is complete.

3. Using the Finish Schedule in Figure 21.46 as a guide, make a version of your own. Put it on an 8.5″ × 11″ sheet at full scale.

   - Use three text heights:

     .25 large letters

     .18 medium letters

     .125 small letters

   - Make sure the text fits comfortably between the lines both vertically and horizontally. Use guidelines to place the text on the schedule. Turn the guidelines' layer off when the schedule is complete.

4. Design three different logos for the following businesses.

   a. Architectural firm
   b. Mechanical engineering company
   c. Pocket Knife company

5. Use the logos in assignment 4 to design business cards for each one. Include a company name, address, phone number, fax number, and E-mail address. The cards should be 3.5″ × 2″.

6. Create your own style and sizes for the Bill of Materials in Figure 21.47.

FIGURE 21.44 Drawing Assignment 1.

DOOR SCHEDULE			
MARK	SIZE	TYPE	REMARKS
1	$3^0 \times 7^0 \times 1\frac{3}{4}$"	PANEL WOOD	SOLID CORE
2	$2^8 \times 6^8 \times 1\frac{3}{4}$"	FRENCH	S.C. W/ FIXED GLASS
3	$3^0 \times 6^8 \times 1\frac{3}{4}$"	FLUSH	SOLID CORE
4	$2^8 \times 6^8 \times 1\frac{3}{4}$"	DUTCH	SOLID CORE
5	$2^8 \times 6^8 \times 1\frac{3}{8}$"	PANEL	HOLLOW CORE
6	$2^8 \times 6^8 \times 1\frac{3}{8}$"	PANEL	HOLLOW CORE
7	$2^2 \times 6^8 \times 1\frac{3}{8}$"	LOUVERS	H.C. PANTRY DOORS
8	$2^8 \times 6^8 \times 1\frac{3}{8}$"	PANEL	HIDDEN-POCKET
9	$4^0 \times 6^8$	LOUVERS	FOLDING CL UNIT
10	$9^0 \times 7^0$	PANEL WOOD	GARAGE DOOR
11	$3^8 \times 6^8$	PANEL	H.C. HIDDEN-POCKET CL DOORS

FIGURE 21.45 Drawing Assignment 2.

WINDOW SCHEDULE			
MARK	SIZE	TYPE	REMARKS
A	10" x 6'-10"	SIDE LITE	WD. & BRICK JAMB
B	1'-10" x 4'-9"	FIXED	WD. & BRICK JAMB
C	2'-6" x 6'-6"	D.H.	WD. & BRICK JAMB
D	3'-6" x 4'-9"	D.H.	PICTURE WINDOW IN BREAK. RM.
E	5'-1" x 5'-6"	PICTURE	WD. & BRICK JAMB
F	2'-6" x 2'-0"	HORIZON	WD. & BRICK JAMB
G	5'-1" x 2'-6"	HORIZON	WD. & BRICK JAMB
H	1'-10" x 2'-6"	D.H.	WD. & BRICK JAMB
I	3'-6" x 2'-6"	HORIZON	WD. & BRICK JAMB
J	3'-6" x 1'-6"	DECOR	W/ 3'-6" x 3'-0" FIXED GLASS BELOW

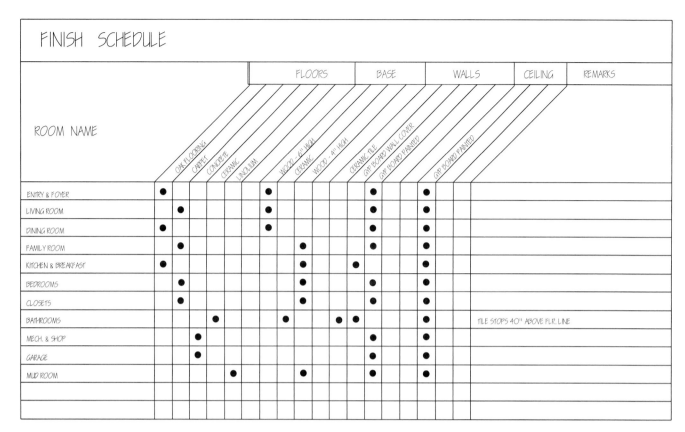

ROOM NAME	FLOORS					BASE			WALLS			CEILING	REMARKS
	OAK FLOORING	CARPET	CONCRETE	CERAMIC	LINOLEUM	WOOD - 6" HIGH	CERAMIC	WOOD - 4" HIGH	CERAMIC TILE	GYP BOARD WALL COVER	GYP BOARD PAINTED	GYP BOARD PAINTED	
ENTRY & FOYER	●					●			●		●		
LIVING ROOM		●				●			●		●		
DINING ROOM	●					●			●		●		
FAMILY ROOM		●					●		●		●		
KITCHEN & BREAKFAST	●						●			●	●		
BEDROOMS		●					●		●		●		
CLOSETS		●					●		●		●		
BATHROOMS				●				●	●	●		●	TILE STOPS 40" ABOVE FLR. LINE
MECH. & SHOP			●						●		●		
GARAGE			●						●		●		
MUD ROOM				●			●		●		●		

FIGURE 21.46   Drawing Assignment 3.

BILL OF MATERIALS

PART NO.	DESCRIPTION	QUANTITY
100	SHAFT - CAST STEEL	1
101	BODY- CAST IRON	1
102	PULLEY- CAST IRON	1
103	MOUNT - STEEL	2
104	BUSHING - BRONZE	2
105	SEALS- RUBBER	4
106	TAPER PIN - STEEL	1

FIGURE 21.47

CHAPTER 22

○ ○

Learning to Create Blocks and WBlocks

One of the real pleasures of using AutoCAD is the ability to reuse existing information. AutoCAD commands can transfer images within a single drawing or from one drawing to another. The smallest of elements or an entire drawing can be put together as a unit called a block or a Wblock by using various methods.

The goals of this chapter are to show you how to use the Block and Wblock commands. These commands will be broken down into the following parts:

1. Creating Blocks and Wblocks.
2. Inserting Blocks and WBlocks into drawings.
3. Editing Blocks.

22.1 Creating Blocks and WBlocks

The Block Definition dialog box can be accessed in the following ways.

- Type **BLOCK** or **B** at the command prompt.
- Select the Make flyout option of Block in the Draw pull-down menu (see Figure 22.1).
- Pick the Block icon from the Draw toolbar.

Block
Icon

Once you are in the Block Definition dialog box, use the following sequence when making a Block (see Figure 22.2).

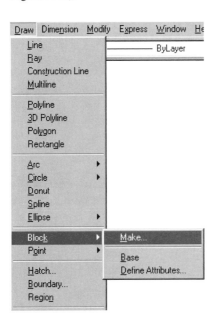

FIGURE 22.1 Block, Make... selected on the Draw pull-down menu.

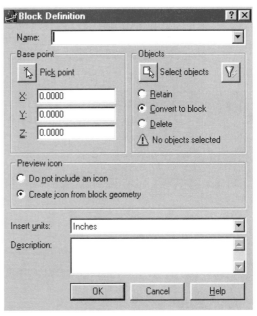

FIGURE 22.2 Block Definition dialog box.

533

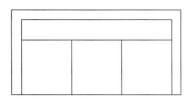

FIGURE 22.3   Object selected.

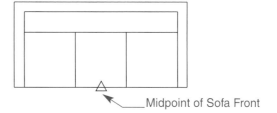

Midpoint of Sofa Front

FIGURE 22.4   Midpoint of sofa.

1. Name the Block. (This example will be called Sofa.) Type the name in the Name text box.

2. Left-click on the Select Objects screen button.

3. The Block definition box will close. Select the objects or items on the drawing that need to be included in the Block (see Figure 22.3).

4. Once you have selected all the lines on the Sofa, right-click to return to the Block definition screen. Left-click on the Pick point screen button.

5. The original drawing screen reappears and waits for you to pick a reference or insertion point. Choose a point. Osnaps are recommended when doing this. We will choose the midpoint on the front of the sofa (see Figure 22.4).

6. As soon as the Midpoint is selected, the Block Definition dialog box reappears. Left-click on the OK screen button and the Block creation is finished.

Several options exist in the Objects area of the dialog box:

- The **Retain** option will leave the block object in its original position and form.
- **Convert to Block** will leave the original object, but it will be a block and will act as one unit if selected.
- **Delete** will remove the original object from the drawing.
- The **Quick Select** selection will give you some additional options to filter in or remove components from the blocks (more for the advanced user) (see Figure 22.5).

In the Base point area of the dialog box the Pick point screen button is used for identifying where the block is to be inserted. Another method is to pick the insertion point by typing in the X, Y, and Z coordinates (see Figure 22.6). Either method will get the job done. It just depends on what information is available at the time.

The bottom half of the Block Definition dialog box has four choices. The Preview icon area lets you create an icon or picture to be included in a preview. This is the default setting that can be turned off by left-clicking on the Do not include an icon radio button. A text description can be associated with the block definition and will display in the area where it is typed. The final option is Insert units (see Figure 22.7). It will assign a unit value to which the block is scaled when it is dragged from the AutoCAD DesignCenter.

Insert unit contains the following options: Unitless, Inches, Feet, Miles, Millimeters, Centimeters, Meters, and Kilometers.

Depending on the environment any of these could be needed. In the mechanical environment, drawings are normally done in inches or millimeters, but Unitless will adjust sizes to fit the different scaled environments.

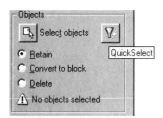

FIGURE 22.5   Objects options.

FIGURE 22.6   Base point options.

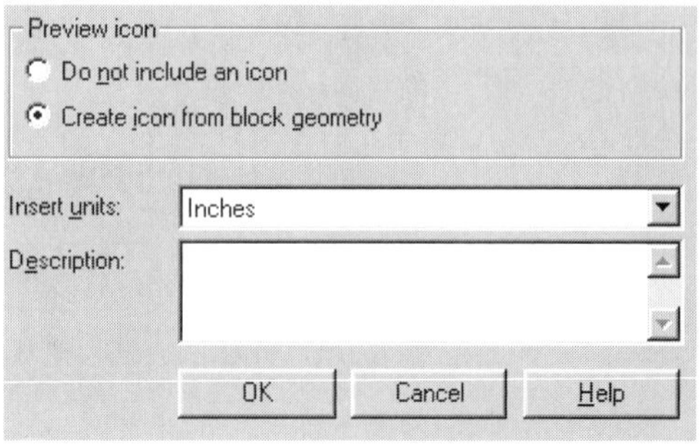

Preview icon
Do not include an icon
Create icon from block geometry

Insert units: Inches

Description:

OK   Cancel   Help

FIGURE 22.7   Preview icon options.

The WBLOCK Command.

■ Type **WBLOCK** at the command prompt.

A Wblock is different from a Block in the following way. The W in the command stands for Write. By definition, a Wblock writes a file name or creates a drawing file. In the previous releases of AutoCAD, a Wblock was the best method for inserting Blocks from one drawing environment into another. When a Wblock is created, it gets a .dwg file extension, for example, Sofa.dwg. A Block, on the other hand, does not get a file extension and therefore is part of the original drawing in which it was created. The only way to transfer a Blocked unit from its original drawing to a brand new drawing is through the AutoCAD Design-Center.

Take a look at the Write Block dialog box and note some of the differences between it and the Block Definition display (see Figure 22.8).

The Source area has radio button options for Block, Entire drawing, and Objects.

These are the choices you make when creating a Wblock.

1. A block can be made into a Wblock and is given a file extension.

2. An entire drawing can be a Wblock. (Any drawing with a .dwg file extension can be inserted whether or not it was created with the Write Block command or was saved as a normal drawing.) With the **Wblock** comand you can select what item you want to reuse instead of taking the whole drawing as a unit.

3. You can select individual objects to make up the Wblock.

The Destination area in this dialog box contains the File name text box where the Wblock is named. Use the same rules as when naming a new drawing or saving a drawing. The Location text box lets you save the Wblock to a particular directory or to a floppy disk. The Insert units box serves the same purpose as in the Block Definition dialog display.

As you can see, making Blocks and Wblocks will take a little bit of practice to learn the sequence. Read through the steps as you learn to make your own Blocks.

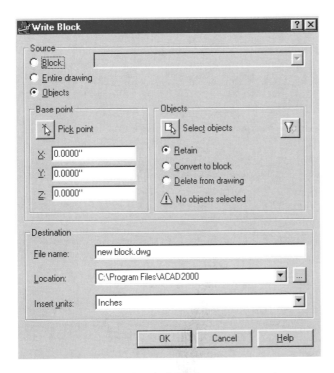

FIGURE 22.8 Write Block dialog box.

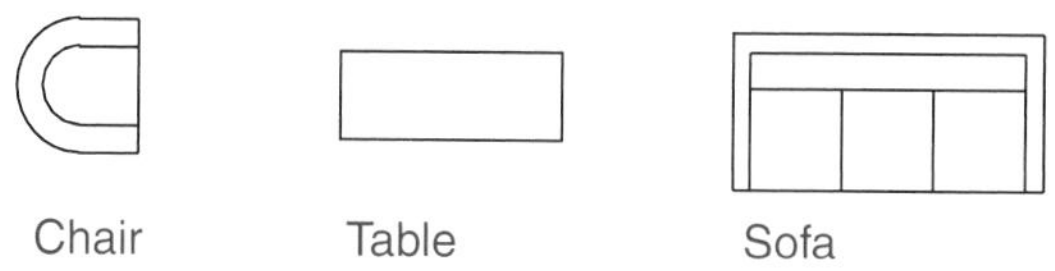

FIGURE 22.9   Three blocks.

Chair   Table   Sofa

22.2   Inserting Blocks and WBlocks into Drawings

This first example will demonstrate how to insert Blocks from an existing drawing into a new drawing using AutoCAD 2000's DesignCenter. The following example will have three blocks that have previously been created using the same steps explained in the first part of this chapter. The three Blocks are of a chair, a table, and a sofa (see Figure 22.9). After blocking each object separately, we will save the drawing and give it the name **oblocks**.

Example

Close the drawing named oblocks and start a new drawing by left-clicking on the File pull-down menu and then left-clicking on the New option. Using the Wizard in the Create New Drawing dialog box, select the Quick Setup option and click OK (see Figure 22.10).

The Quick Setup dialog box opens. Choose the Architectural option and left-click on the Next button. Set the width to 34′ and the length to 44′ and then left-click on the Finish button at the base of the dialog box. This drawing is the one we will drag the blocks into.

Now left-click on the DesignCenter icon (see Figure 22.11). It is on the Standard Toolbar between the Zoom Previous icon and the Properties icon.

The DesignCenter dialog box opens up split into two screens (see Figure 22.12). The left screen is basically the Exploring option showing all the directories and folders. The right side shows a detailed listing of what has been selected in the left screen. In this example we scanned through the files to find the oblocks.dwg stored in the user/Blockchapter folder. A double left click on the Blockchapter folder, followed by a double left click on the oblocks.dwg generated Figure 22.13.

The right-hand screen displays the components of this drawing (see Figure 22.14). A double left click on the Blocks icon produces the three Blocks that exist in this drawing (see Figure 22.15).

To move a copy of the Blocks into the new drawing, left-click on the sofa block icon seen in Figure 22.15 and hold down the left mouse button (see Figure 22.16). While holding the button down roll the mouse out of the DesignCenter area and drag it into the new drawing area. Once in this area simply let go of the mouse button, and the Block appears (see Figure 22.17).

Repeat the left-click, hold, and drag method on the chair and the table to place them into the new drawing (see Figure 22.18).

FIGURE 22.10   Create New Drawing dialog box.

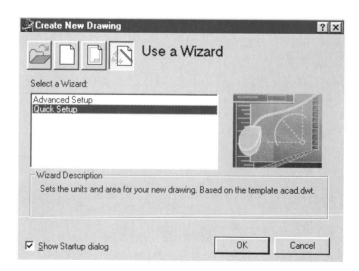

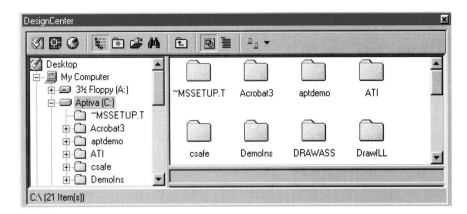

FIGURE 22.11 DesignCenter icon. **FIGURE 22.12** DesignCenter dialog box.

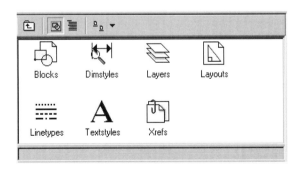

FIGURE 22.13 DesignCenter showing oblocks open.

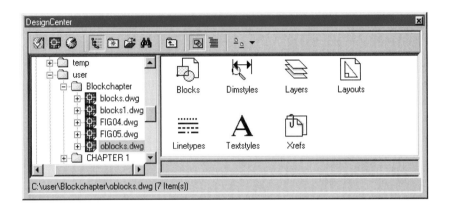

FIGURE 22.14 Blocks folder.

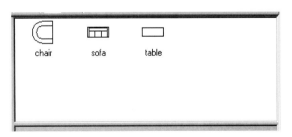

FIGURE 22.15 Chair, sofa, and table in DesignCenter.

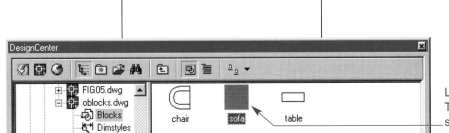

Left-click holding down the button. Then roll the mouse up, dragging the sofa into the other drawing above.

FIGURE 22.16 Sofa highlighted in DesignCenter.

Dragged in from
the DesignCenter

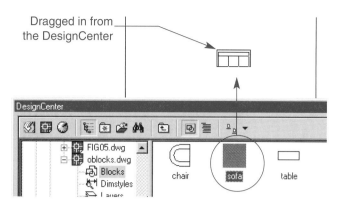

FIGURE 22.17   Dragged sofa in DesignCenter.

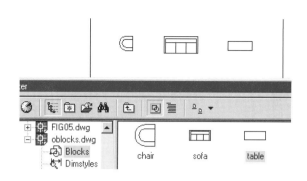

FIGURE 22.18   Dragged sofa, chair, and table in DesignCenter.

At this point, a copy of the Blocks has been placed on this drawing, and the blocks are now part of this drawing and can be used again without going through the DesignCenter. The Insert command (discussed in the following section) can now be used on the Block in a new drawing.

Using the Insert Block Command

This command will let you place Blocks or Wblocks on a drawing.

Insert
Block

- Type **DDINSERT** at the command prompt.
- Select <u>B</u>lock from the <u>I</u>nsert pull-down menu (see Figure 22.19).
- Pick the Insert Block icon from the Draw toolbar.

The Insert dialog box appears (see Figure 22.20). The <u>N</u>ame box lists all the Blocks that are part of the current drawing (see Figure 22.21). Currently the chair, the sofa, and the table are the Blocks that were copied from oblocks.dwg. Pick the Block you want to use and left-click on the OK screen button. That Block appears on the drawing and can be dragged by rolling the mouse around. (Notice that the cursor is pointing to the base point that was chosen in the original Make Block option.)

This point is locked in, and the only way to change the base point is to make another Block and choose a different base point at a new location. To place the Block on the drawing, just left-click, and the block will be placed. For a precise placement, use the Osnaps to lock in on an endpoint, intersection, or wherever the Block is desired. Another way to place the Block is to check the Sp<u>e</u>cify On-screen button and type in the co-ordinates at the <u>X</u>, <u>Y</u>, and <u>Z</u> text boxes (see Figure 22.22). Keep in mind the units of the drawing and also that

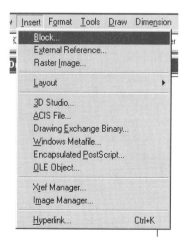

FIGURE 22.19   <u>B</u>lock selected on the <u>I</u>nsert pull-down menu.

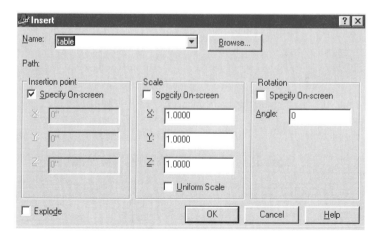

FIGURE 22.20   Insert dialog box.

FIGURE 22.21   Insert text box.   **FIGURE 22.22**   Insertion point options.

the X- and Y-coordinates are for two-dimensional drawings. The Scale display area has a few choices for the CAD operator.

Specify On-screen will default the Block scale to the command line if this option is checked. At the command line the display shows:

Specify insertion point or [Scale/X/Y/Z/Rotate/PScale/PX/PY/PZ/PRotate]:

These options will do the following:

- **Scale** will set a uniform scale for X, Y, and Z.
- **X** will change the X-coordinate scale.
- **Y** will change the Y-coordinate scale.
- **Z** will change the Z-coordinate scale.
- **Rotate** will set a rotation angle to turn the Block.

The rest of the options preceded by a **P** are a repeat of the previous options with the following exception: The **P** stands for preview. It allows you to preview the scale before it gets inserted in the drawing. The sequence at the command line goes like this.

1. Type in **PX** to preview and select an X scale.
2. Specify a preview X scale factor.
3. Pick an insertion point on the drawing while looking at the Block's preview scale.
4. After the pick enter the scale again or change it to something else. A Y scale factor will also be available.

There is also a **Rotation** option in the dialog box. Checking the box marked Specify On-screen will initiate a sequence at the command line that will ask you for a rotation angle. Specifying an Angle setting will automatically rotate the block to a predetermined angle. A setting of 45° would turn the sofa as shown in Figure 22.23.

Left-clicking on the Explode box in the lower left corner will break up the Block cell into individual lines and pieces.

The Insert command also inserts Wblocks. Because Wblocks are basically drawing files with extensions, they will not be listed where the Blocks are shown in the Name text box. You must left-click on the Browse... screen button located to the right of the Name box. Browsing is like using the exploring option. The Select Drawing File dialog box opens, and you can scan through all the directories and folders and find where the Wblock was saved (see Figure 22.24). In this example a drawing named CIRCLES.dwg is highlighted.

FIGURE 22.23   Sofa rotated.

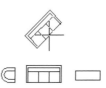

FIGURE 22.24 Select Drawing
File dialog box.

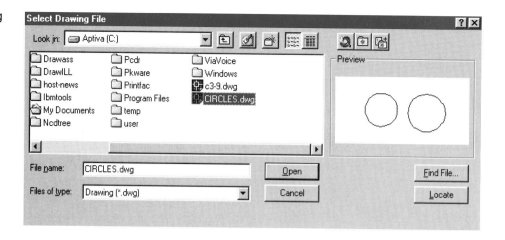

The Preview area on the right-hand side gives you a peak at the highlighted drawing file. When you find Wblock, left-click on the Open button, and you return to the Insert box. Left-click on the OK button and then left-click in the drawing area when it opens to place the Wblock on the drawing. All the options work the same for the Blocks as for the Wblocks.

Note: Block and Wblock existed before the Windows Copy and Paste commands. A new student to AutoCAD might try to use these because they are more familiar to them. This method of copying and pasting between different drawings will work, but it does not have the scale control or other options of the Block command. You may find the scale change a drawback to using copy and paste options.

The Minsert Command

- Type in **MINSERT** at the command prompt.

A Minsert may be desired when a rectangular array is needed to insert many blocks in a rows-and-columns pattern. The Minsert command is very similar to the Insert command, with a couple of exceptions. It has an Array option, and MINSERT cannot be exploded into separate parts. Minsert is not used very much, so you will not find it in a toolbar or a pull-down menu; it must be typed in at the command line.

Command: **MINSERT**
Enter block name or [?] <Table>:

Type in the block name or a question mark to get a list of the existing blocks and make a selection. If you want to Minsert a Wblock, type the exact location of the file in the computer. For example, if a Minsert is required for a drawing named Door1.dwg that is in a directory labeled DoorElevation, then type in DoorElevation/Door1.dwg at the command line, and the computer will search the path and find the Wblock.

Command: MINSERT
Enter Block name or [?]: DoorElevation/Door1.dwg

Layering Tips for Blocks and Wblocks

Even though a Block or a Wblock acts as one unit or a cell, they can have different characteristics within that cell. A wide variety of lineweights, colors, and linetypes may be found in a Block. Good layer management can help keep the Block properties intact after the Insert or Minsert command is completed. Plan out the layers and properties that will make up the Block before it is created.

- Do not use Layer 0 (zero) as part of your Block. It will not hold the properties you establish when inserted if another layer is current during the insertion process. The Block takes on the properties of the current layer.

- When a Block is inserted into an existing drawing and the Block's layer names match some in the existing drawing but have different properties, the existing drawing will dominate and change the properties of the Block layers to match its own.

- You may use Layer 0 for a block if you want the block to assume the properties of the current layer when inserted.

Example of Insertion Problems with Layer

A Block with a layer named Chair that has a red color and a Hidden linetype is inserted into another drawing. This drawing already has a layer named Chair, but the color and linetype assigned are Blue and Continuous. What is going to happen? The Block will insert, but the Block properties will change to a blue color and a continuous line type.

Set up your Blocks with special layer names that do not repeat in any other drawings or Blocks. This should keep your Blocks from becoming chameleons.

Redefining a Block

If a Block has been inserted into a drawing many times and it needs to be revised, redefining it is a good time-saver. The process is easy. Make the necessary changes to one of the existing blocks on the drawing. When the changes are complete, go through the Block command again. Name the edited Block the same name as the old Block. AutoCAD will ask if the Block should be redefined. Click on the Yes button. Watch the other existing Blocks update themselves. If the original block disappears, use the Oops command to get it back. Do not use the Undo command because it will not keep the created Block.

22.3 Editing Blocks

A Block cell acts as one unit or element, so it is easy to change a Block as a whole. Blocks can be edited to a certain extent. Some of the Block properties are easy to change. Layers, colors, and linetypes can be modified using the Properties command, as demonstrated in Chapter 17.

Note: The Explode command does not work on the Minsert command.

Trying to change an individual part of a Block separately from the rest of the unit is a problem. To do this, you must disassemble the Block cell with the Explode command. The pieces can then be altered individually. Remember that all the parts act separately now and must be edited one at a time.

An exploded cell can be put back together by going through the steps of making a Block again. Early planning to get your Block in the correct format so that little or no editing will be required later is the best way to go. Another way to handle changes ahead of time is to make several Blocks with the changes in the different Blocks. Create a library of Blocks with all the possible changes already made before using the Make Block command. Add new Blocks to your master drawing library as needed.

REVIEW QUESTIONS

1. Explain the difference between the Block and Wblock commands.
2. How do you start the Wblock command?
3. How do you make a Block?
4. What are the four choices in the Block Definition dialog box?
5. How can the AutoCAD DesignCenter be of benefit when dealing with Blocks?
6. In what toolbar will you find the Insert Block icon?
7. How does Exploding affect Blocks and Wblocks?
8. What options are available in Minserting a Block?
9. How can inserted Blocks and Wblocks be edited in AutoCAD?
10. Why should you avoid using layer 0 on components of a Block?
11. Explain some of the problems that occur with layers when a Block or Wblock is inserted into another drawing.

EXERCISES

EXERCISE 22.1

Draw the bathroom fixtures shown in Figure 22.25a and make them into Blocks. Name the Blocks shower, toilet, sink, and tub. Save the drawing and name it Bath. Next, start a New drawing using architectural drawing units and set the drawing limits to (0,0) lower left corner and (34′,44′) in the upper right corner. Draw the given master bath plan in Figure 22.25b.

Use the AutoCAD DesignCenter on this first exercise. Open it and find the drawing named Bath in the left-side area. Once you find it, keep opening it until the Block drawings appear. Use the drag-and-drop method to complete the drawing shown in Figure 22.25c. Save this drawing as Bath1.dwg.

EXERCISE 22.2

Begin a new drawing. Set up architectural units with limits at (0,0) in the lower left corner and (34′,44′) in the upper right corner. Use the Browse option of the Insert Block command to find the drawing name Bath1.dwg created in exercise 22.1. Insert it into your new drawing. Mirror the Wblock so the drawing looks like Figure 22.26. Save this drawing as Bath2.dwg.

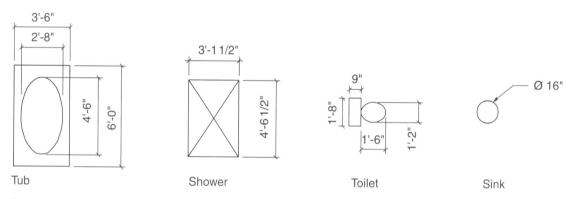

Draw the fixtures, not the titles or dimensions.

(a)

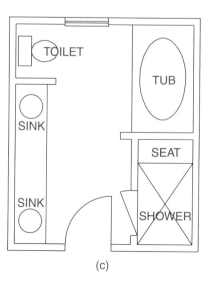

Note:
1. Use a 4″-thick wall.
2. Use a 30″-wide window with a 6″-thick frame.
3. Use a 30″-wide shower door and a 32″-wide entry door.

(b)   (c)

FIGURE 22.25   Exercise 22.1.

FIGURE 22.26 Exercise 22.2

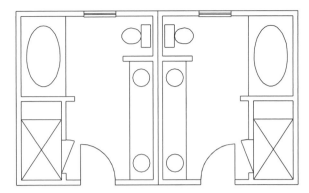

FIGURE 22.27 Exercise 22.3

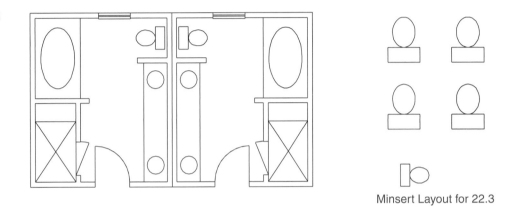

Minsert Layout for 22.3

EXERCISE 22.3

Open drawing Bath2.dwg. Explode the Wblock, make a copy of the toilet, and drag it to the bottom of the sheet. Make a new Block of the toilet at the bottom. Minsert the new toilet block. Set the scale to 1.5 and change the rotation angle to 90°. Enter 2 rows and 2 columns with a distance between the rows and columns of 5′ as shown in Figure 22.27.

DRAWING ASSIGNMENTS

Use the following figures as a guide for creating some of the furniture blocks for the assignments. Add new furniture as needed. Research sizes in the *Architectural Graphic Standards*.

1. The furniture in Figure 22.28 is in 3-D form. Make a plan view of each piece of furniture from its 3-D drawing. After each piece is drawn make a Block for each individual one. If you desire more choices, research the sizes and create your own. Once the Blocks are complete, label them with text and print them on individual title block sheets at a ¼″ = 1′-0″ scale.

2. Draw the problems in Figure 22.29. Make Blocks and insert them. Repeat the assignment, this time using the MINSERT command when possible.

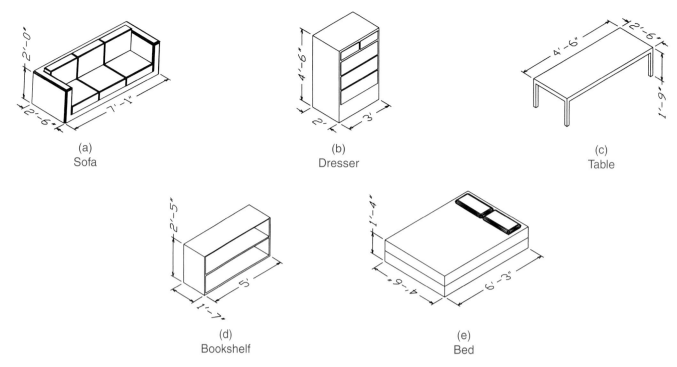

FIGURE 22.28   Drawing Assignment 1.

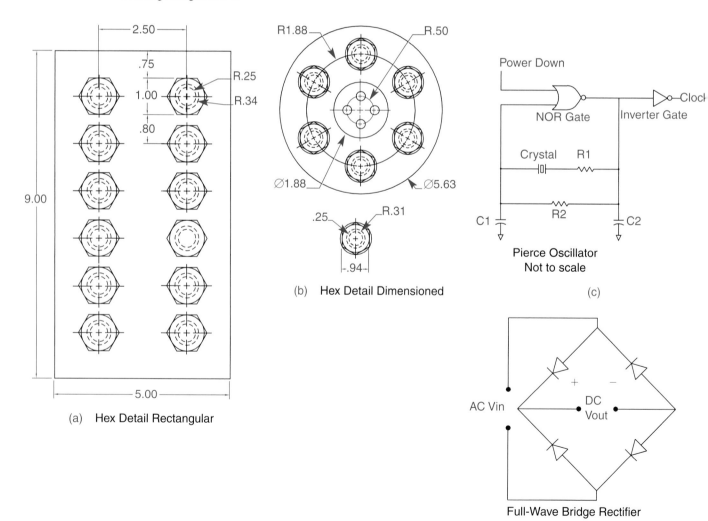

FIGURE 22.29   Drawing Assignment 2.

Insight into Plotting and Paper Space

Most individuals who have used a computer have printed a copy of something. Once the basic printing settings are established the process is quite easy. Plotting a drawing in AutoCAD tends to be more challenging. Some of the principles are the same as when printing in other software packages, but in AutoCAD 2000 the options seem endless.

AutoCAD 2000 plotting is very powerful and loaded with options. Many training centers and schools offer classes in plotting alone. As with the rest of this book our aim is to introduce you to the basics of Auto-CAD plotting and printing. We will explain concepts and walk through a basic plot in this appendix.

Model Space, Layout/Paper Space, and Floating Model Space

It is possible to plot in model space as well as in the Layout format. Some AutoCAD users do not use the Layout plotting environment (known as the Paper Space environment in earlier releases of AutoCAD). The Layout format is a bit of a different world with its own set of guidelines but is not always necessary for plotting. We will start by defining the different environments, then we will explain how to choose a plotting environment.

Model Space

Model space is the drawing and designing environment. When you see the UCS icon on the drawing screen, as shown in Figure A.1, your drawing is in model space or floating model space, which is explained a little later. There are very few limitations on drawing in this environment, but model space is a single environment where everything is handled the same way. Placing text, dimensions, and a title block in this world means tying them to the limits or scale set up in this environment.

Layout/Paper Space

The Layout/Paper Space environment enhances your ability to plot using multiple options. The icon in Figure A.2 is showing that Paper Space is being used. This format allows two different environments to coexist (see Figure A.3). For instance, a title block can be placed in the layout at a full scale of $1'' = 1''$ in paper space. Inside that title block a window or, in AutoCAD terms, a viewport can be opened to display a drawing from model space at any desired scale. This is called *floating model space,* as shown n Figure A.4. In this world you can jump back and forth between paper space and model space by double-left-clicking outside the viewport to switch to paper space. Likewise, double-left-clicking inside the viewport will place you in floating model space.

A viewport is analogous to a TV screen that can be used as one large screen or has the ability to be split into smaller ones. Viewports can be created in the Model Space or in the Layout/Paper Space option.

FIGURE A.1   UCS icon.

FIGURE A.2   Paper space icon.

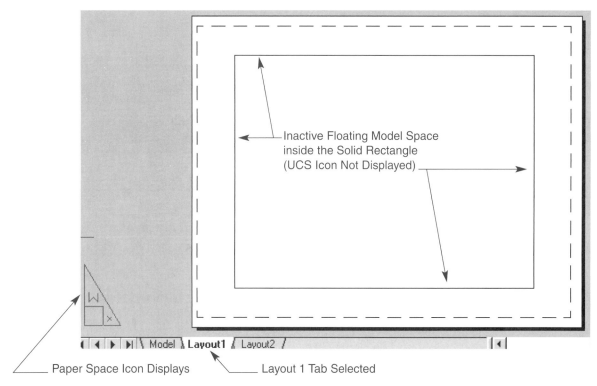

Inactive Floating Model Space inside the Solid Rectangle (UCS Icon Not Displayed)

Paper Space Icon Displays   Layout 1 Tab Selected

FIGURE A.3 Layout1 tab selected.

Thick Viewport Line in Floating Model Space

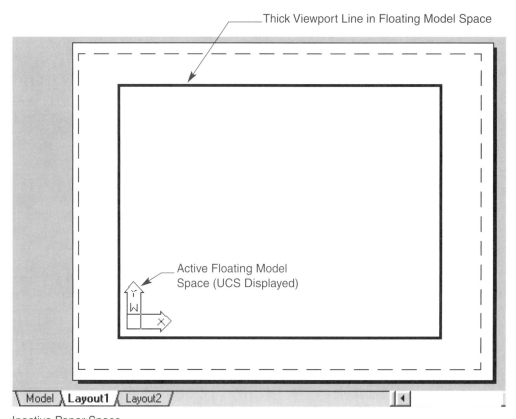

Active Floating Model Space (UCS Displayed)

Inactive Paper Space
No (PS) Icon Displayed

FIGURE A.4 UCS in floating model space.

■ To create viewports type **VPORTS** at the command prompt. The Viewports dialog box appears (see Figure A.5).

Any number of viewport alignments are found under the Standard viewports heading. Figure A.6 shows the result of choosing the *Four: Equal* option. The screen is split into four equal spaces.

FIGURE A.5 Viewport dialog box.

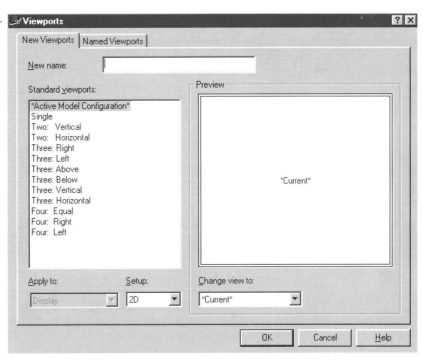

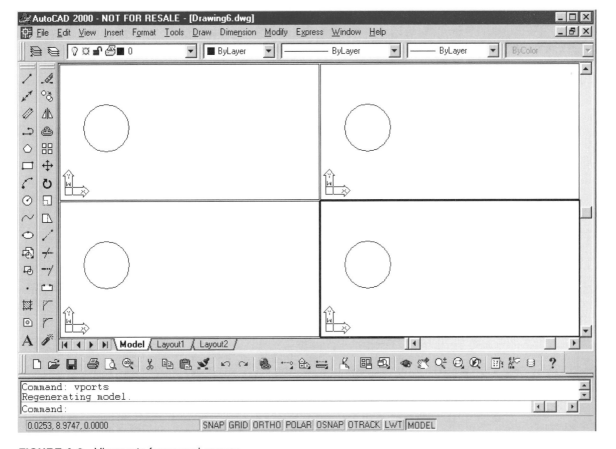

FIGURE A.6 Viewports four equal spaces.

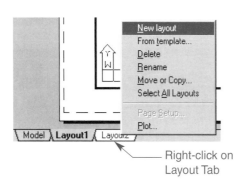

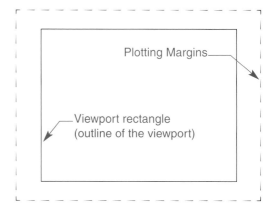

FIGURE A.7 Layout2 selected.   **FIGURE A.8** Components of Layout screen.

Viewports in model space are generated immediately after you select the alignment and press the OK button in the dialog box. Creating viewports in the Layout environment takes an extra step.

If you select a Layout tab at the bottom of the drawing screen, a single viewport window is automatically cut into the paper space environment. Two Layout tabs (Layout1 and Layout2) are the default in paper space. Each can represent a different viewport to the same drawing. If you need a customized viewport or layout, right-click on either Layout tab (see Figure A.7). Left click on the New layout selection, and a new layout is created.

Sometimes you might need multiple viewports in a single layout. A quick and easy way to do this is to left-pick on the viewport rectangle (while in paper space) located on the inside of the broken rectangle that represents the margins (see Figure A.8). Once you have selected the viewport rectangle, press the Delete key on the keyboard to eliminate the single viewport. Now you can use the Viewports command to create multiple ports in a layout. There are fewer alignments to choose from in paper space and the defaulted fit window option will require you to cut the floating model space viewport opening in paper space. After you select the alignment the command line prompts you to Specify the first corner: of the viewport window. Left-pick inside the plotting margins in the lower left corner. Move the cursor to the upper right corner, staying inside the dashed margin, left-pick again, and the viewport will be placed in the Layout/Paper Space environment. Paper space is active or current at this time. Simply double-left-click inside the viewport in which you wish to draw, and the viewport becomes active in floating model space. This may be more than you want to know at this time, but viewports play a major part in deciding whether to plot in model space versus layout/paper space. The advanced AutoCAD user will use the Viewports command while in paper space. It will enable the user to use paper space scaling and to hide lines in the different viewports, which is discussed later.

Should the Drawing Be Plotted Using a Layout or in Model Space?

Model space has the following plotting limitations:

1. The title block must be drawn to the same limits or scale as the rest of the drawing.
2. Only the current viewport can be printed in model space.

The Layout/Paper Space environment has the following plotting features.

1. A title block can be placed in paper space at full scale. A floating viewport can be placed inside the title block. The floating viewport can be set to different scales using the Zoom XP option.

   For instance, make the floating model space viewport active by double-left-clicking in the middle of the viewport rectangle. At the command line use the following sequence:

Command: **ZOOM**↵
Specify corner of window, enter a scale factor (nX or nXP), or
    [All/Center/Dynamic/Extents/Previous/Scale/Window] <real time>: **1/48 XP**

For a ¼″ = 1′-0″ scale type **1/48 xp**. This is how scales are set in floating model space. It does not matter what the limits settings were in the original model space. The Zoom XP command must be used to set up

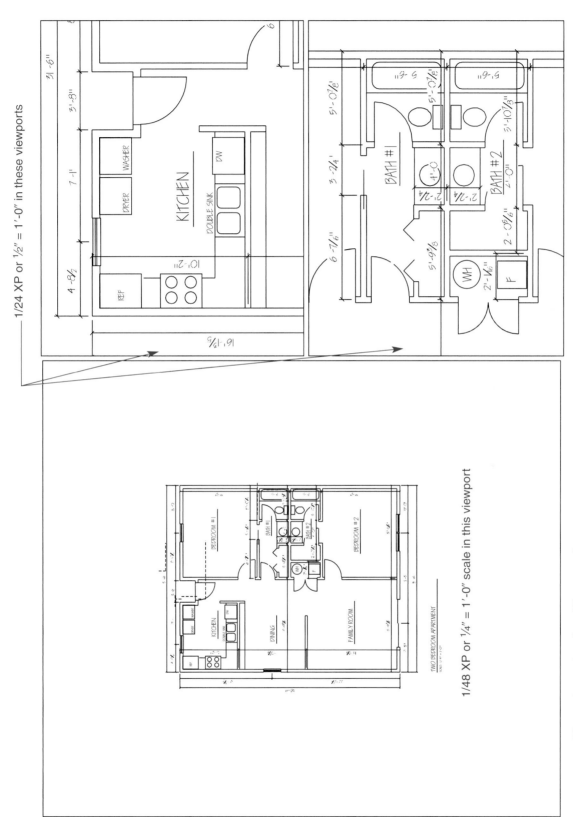

1/24 XP or ½" = 1'-0" in these viewports

1/48 XP or ¼" = 1'-0" scale in this viewport

FIGURE A.9 Three viewports using different scales.

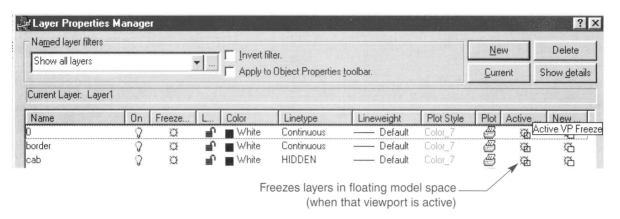

Freezes layers in floating model space ———
(when that viewport is active)

FIGURE A.10   Layer Properties Manager dialog box.

a scale to plot everything inside that viewport to that scale. The title block should be outside the viewport rectangle. This is a full-scale paper space area. Double-left-click outside the viewport rectangle to set the paper space active, and plot the drawing and title block together using full scale.

Tip for Dimensioning in Floating Model Space
Create a dimension layer for each individual viewport. Use that layer when dimensioning in that viewport.

Note: When a dimension is placed in its desired viewport, it also shows up in the other viewports. When a dimension shows up in a viewport in which it was not created, a scaling problem can occur when that viewport is zoomed to a different scale. The dimension size is not proportional to that viewport, so it will need to be removed from the viewport in which it was not created. To do this you must hide that layer with that viewport active. You can do this using the Layer Properties Manager (see Figure A.12).

2. Multiple viewports can be plotted at the same time with different scales in the same layout. This means that a single layout can contain one viewport showing the whole floor plan at ¼″ = 1′-0″ (1/48 XP) scale along with two other viewports of the same drawing blowing up a plan view of the kitchen and bathroom at a larger scale (see Figure A.9).

3. Lines may be removed or hidden in one viewport but remain visible or displayed in another viewport. Remember that whatever is drawn in the active floating viewport will be drawn in the inactive ones also.

For example, dimensions could be added to a drawing in one viewport but would not be needed in other viewports. To remove the dimensions from a particular viewport make it active or current, then open the Layer Properties Manager dialog box. On the far right-hand side is an Active heading where each layer can be frozen in that selected viewport if desired (see Figure A.10).

Dimensioning in Floating Model Space via Paper Space

A powerful feature to use in paper space is the paper space scaling of dimensions. This is an automatic adjustment that can be turned on while you are dimensioning in floating model space. DIMSCALE can be set to work in real model space as well. A DIMSCALE of 48 would be used in model space to plot ¼″ = 1′-0″. DIMSCALE is calculated in the same way as the scale factor (see Appendix B for different scale factors, and "Drawing Scale" in Chapter 14).

As discussed earlier in this appendix, a single drawing floating in model space can have different viewports or layouts with independent scales in each. A viewport is scaled with the Zoom XP option, as shown earlier.

In the Dimension Style dialog box, the Fit tab has the **Scale dimensions to layout (paper space)** selection (see Figure A.11). This must be selected for paper space scaling of dimensions floating in model space.

Turning this option on will force the DIMSCALE to adjust with the Zoom XP each time it is used. Make sure that the Zoom XP is set correctly before dimensioning. If the Zoom function is changed, the dimension sizes will adjust to the new zoom factor.

Example: Paper Space Dimension

A house floor plan is split into two separate viewports. One is scaled with the **Zoom** command at 1/48 XP for a ¼″ = 1′-0″ scale to view the whole drawing while the other viewport is scaled at 1/24 XP for a ½″ = 1′-0″ scale to blow up the kitchen area.

Dimensions placed in the 1/48 XP scaled viewport will have the DIMSCALE automatically set when that viewport is active. When the other viewport is active, dimensions can be placed in that viewport and the 1/24 XP scale will force the DIMSCALE to automatically fit that scale. See Note.

FIGURE A.11 Scale dimensions to layout (paperspace) button.

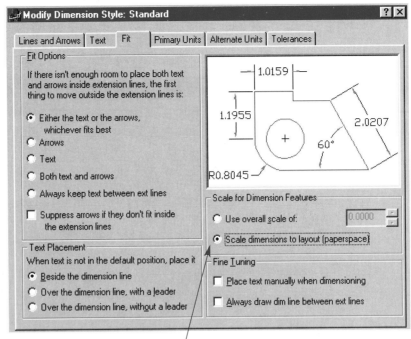

To be turned on in paper space when dimensioning in the floating model space mode.

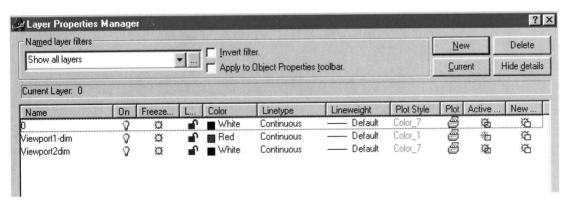

FIGURE A.12 Layer Properties Manager dialog box.

The AutoCAD Training Centers introduce viewports and paper space usage in a student's Level II training. The training is more advanced and takes some time to learn. Do not get overwhelmed by this information in the beginning. There are still a few professionals who shy away from using it.

The reasons for choosing a plotting environment are fairly straightforward: If you do not need to

- plot at different scales in a viewport,
- plot multiple viewports on the same sheet, or
- hide lines in one viewport but not in another,

then plotting a drawing in model space may be the best choice if you have a title block for every sheet size and scale used.

Plotting in AutoCAD 2000

In previous AutoCAD releases, there were minimal upgrades and features to learn about plotting. Release 2000 plotting has much more power and many more settings for the user to learn. It can seem overwhelming even to those who have experience in early releases, but AutoCAD provides support in learning to plot.

FIGURE A.13   Fast Track to Plotting option of the Help dialog box.

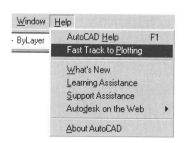

Fast Track to Plotting is loaded with all kinds of help. Instructions with audiovideo support can be accessed through the AutoCAD Help pull-down menu (see Figure A.13). Go through the Fast Tracking to Plotting before attempting your first plot. It is not important that you understand everything about plotting. The best teacher when it comes to plotting is experience, but the Fast Track crash course will give you some preparation and background before attempting to plot.

Getting Ready to Plot a Drawing

Check the following with your instructor before trying to plot.

1. Find out what plotter is configured in your lab.
2. Find out what page or sheet sizes are available in that plotter.
3. Figure out the scale in which your drawing should be plotted.

- Layout/Paper Space scaling is controlled by the Zoom command while in floating model space. The individual viewport must be activated before the Zoom command can be used for XP scaling. The following sequence is used to input a scale of ¼″ = 1′-0″, which has a scale factor of 48.

  Command: **ZOOM**↵
  Specify corner of window, enter scale factor (nX or NXP), or
     [All/Center/Dynamic/Extents/Previous/Scale/Window] <real time>: **1/48 XP**

- The model space scale for plotting the drawing can be set in the Layout Settings tab in the plotting sequence. As a guide, use the same scale that you created with the limits or wizard setup.

4. Determine which environment (Model Space or Layout/Paper Space) will be best for your drawing to be plotted in. Practice plotting in both environments for the experience.
5. Check with your instructor to verify your printable area. Each printer/plotter has a dead zone around the perimeter that is determined by the plotting device. Make sure your border and title block will be inside the printable area.

Plotting a Drawing in Model Space

To plot the entire drawing, start by zooming to the limits of your drawing while in model space.

1. To choose the Plot command, do one of the following:

- Left-click on the Plot icon on the Standard Toolbar.
- Select Plot from the File pull-down menu.
- Type **Plot**↵ at the command line.

Note: If the Fast Track to Plotting dialog box appears, close it by choosing the No option.

The Plot dialog box appears (see Figure A.14).

2. Left-click on the Plot Device tab first to bring up the options found in this tab (see Figure A.15).

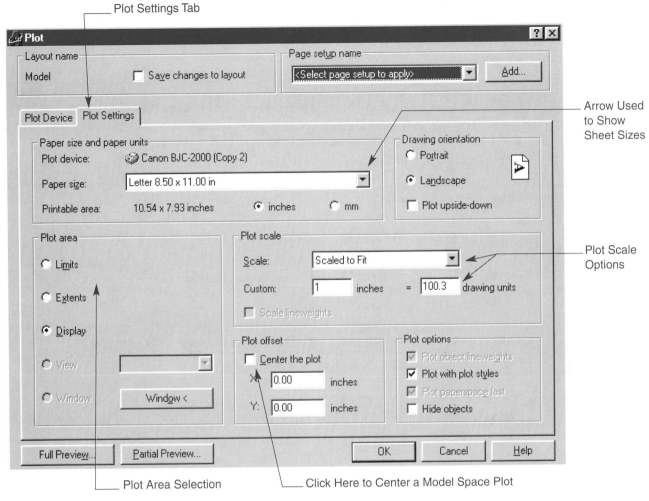

FIGURE A.14 Plot dialog box.

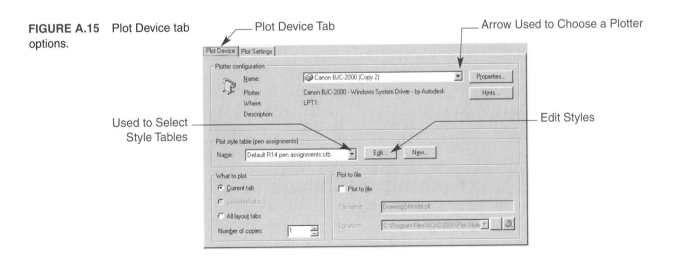

FIGURE A.15 Plot Device tab options.

- In the **Plotter configuration** area select the plotter to be used by using the down arrow on the right.
- In the **Plot style table (pen assignments)** area, choose a plot style name. It is OK to choose the **Default R14 pen assignments.ctb** or **acad.ctb** when just starting out and learning the plotting sequence.

3. Left-click on the Plot Settings tab and make the following selections (see Figure A.14):

Note: The paper size must be supported by the plotter/printer chosen or a warning will display on the screen.

- In the Paper size and paper units area, choose a paper size for printing and then pick inches or mm (millimeters) for the units of the drawing to be plotted in.
- In the **Drawing Orientation** area choose from the following alignments:

Portrait

Landscape

Plot upside-down

Watch the small graphic window to the right to check the alignment visually.

- The **Plot area** options include the following choices:

Note: Use the **Limits** choice to plot the whole defined area of your drawing setup.

Limits—This will plot the limits that have been established on the drawing.

Extents—This will plot only all the objects in the drawing with no respect to the limits.

Display—This will plot only what is seen or displayed on the screen.

View—Views created with the **View** command previously can be selected to be plotted.

Window—This button allows you to pick an area/window with the cursor and mouse or by typing in coordinates forming a rectangular shape.

- The **Plot scale** area is where you set the desired plotting scale to plot a model space drawing to a scale (see Figure A.16). Two choices are available:

Scale – There are 31 scale choices, ranging from mechanical to civil engineering to architectural. **Scaled to Fit** and **Custom choices** are also available (see Figure A.15).

Scaled to Fit will adjust the drawing to fit in the plotting area. This creates some very unorthodox scales and should be used only when the scale is not a factor.

Custom – This choice allows you to set any desired scale in the Custom text boxes (see Figure A.17).

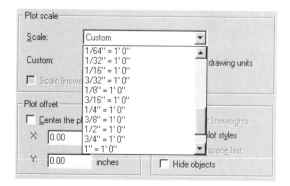

FIGURE A.16   Plot scale choices.

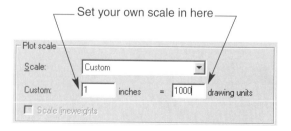

FIGURE A.17   Plot scale for customizing.

    ■ Set the **Plot offset** area to <u>Center the plot</u> for model space plotting (left-click in the box).

4. After picking the settings, it is time to preview what the plot will look like. At the bottom left corner of the Plot dialog box are two Preview buttons:

<u>Partial Preview</u>—This selection shows the plotting area in relation to the selected paper size. It also will display warnings when a plotting problem exists. A partial preview will not display objects in the drawing.

<u>Full Preview</u>—This option shows all the objects that will be printed as well as the outline of the paper size. Any part of the drawing not shown in the preview will not print.

5. If the full preview looks acceptable, right-click and choose Plot. If you select Exit instead, then the screen returns to the Plot dialog box. Choose the OK button at the bottom right of the Plot dialog screen to execute the plot. If you click Cancel, then the standard AutoCAD screen returns.

Plotting from a Layout or Paper Space

Layout plotting works a little differently, but it really is just a matter of understanding paper space and how to scale floating model space inside paper space.

If you chose a template from the Startup dialog box when you began your drawing, then a Layout/Paper Space environment was automatically created for you. If the drawing was done in model space, then you must select the Layout1 tab at the bottom of the graphics screen. When you click on the Layout1 tab, the Page Setup dialog box appears, and you will need to make some choices similar to those in model space plotting.

1. Left-click on the Plot Device tab (see Figure A.18).

    ■ Choose the plotter.
    ■ Choose a Plot style (pen assignments).

FIGURE A.18 Plot Style Table R14 pen assignments.

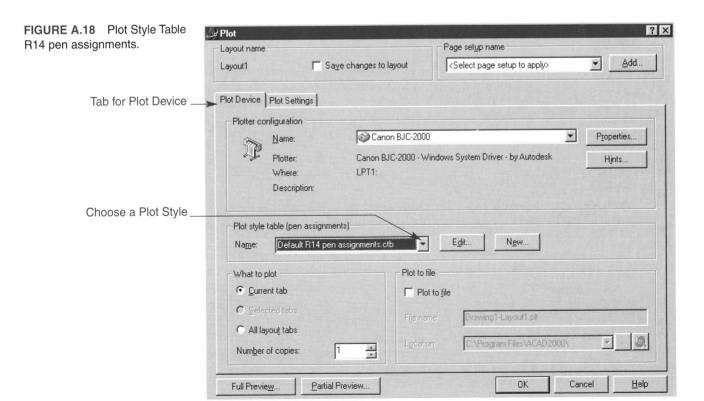

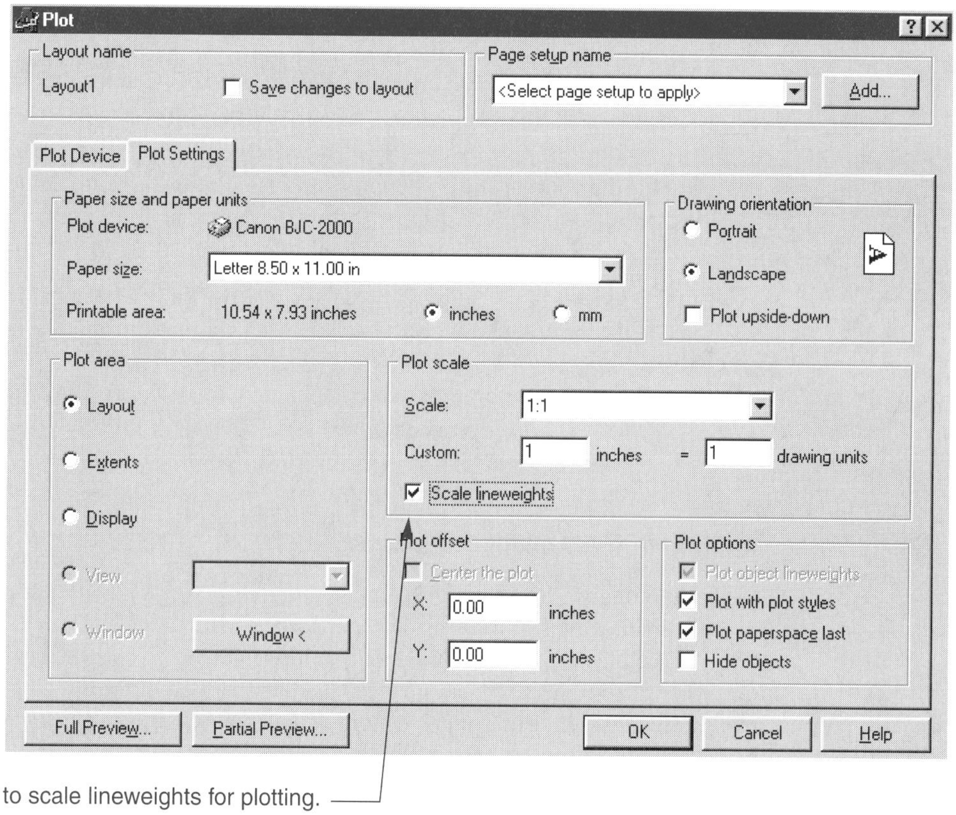

FIGURE A.19   Scale to lineweight for plotting.

Check to scale lineweights for plotting.

2. Left-click on the Plot Settings tab and make a few more choices (see Figure A.19).

- Choose a paper size that works well with your drawing.
- Notice your printable area. It can be displayed in inches or millimeters.
- Check the drawing orientation area just as in the previous model space example.
- Notice that the Plot area is set to Layout. This is because you are intending to plot from the Layout/Paper Space option, so leave this setting alone.
- In the Plot scale area you have choices similar to the ones found in model space. Use 1:1 scale typically for your paper space plot scale. Left-click in the Scale lineweights box to turn it on so that lineweights will be scaled in proportion to the plot scale (see Figure A.19).
- Click the OK button at the bottom of the Plot dialog box to exit the layout/page setup.

Tips   The paper space portion of your drawing, which typically contains a title block and border, is drawn at 1″ = 1″. This is the reason for setting the plot scale to 1:1 for Layout/Paper Space plotting.

Inside the Viewport Window

Remember that viewport lines exist within the Layout mode. A viewport separates paper space from floating model space. Inside the viewport's rectangular lines is floating model space, a window to a different world, analogous to a glass bottom boat looking into the sea. You draw and design in model space. It is active when you double-click inside the viewport rectangle and the UCS icon appears (see Figure A.20).

The final step before exiting floating mode space is to scale it. The Zoom command is one way to do this, using the scale factor for your desired scale. Suppose you wanted floating model space to plot at ¼″ = 1′-0″ scale (scale factor of 48). Type the following at the command line to set this environment:

```
Command: ZOOM↵
Specify corner of window, enter scale factor (nX or NXP), or
    [All/Center/Dynamic/Extents/Previous/Scale/Window] <real time>: 1/48 XP
```

Exit floating model space by double-clicking outside the viewport rectangle.

FIGURE A.20 Floating model space identification.

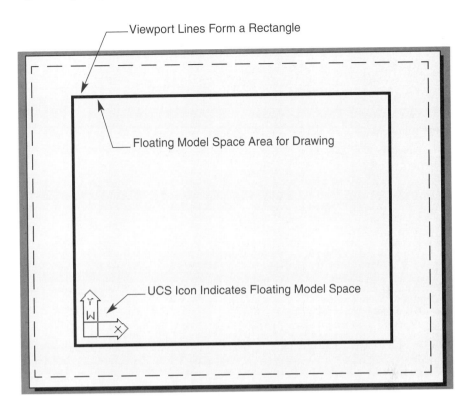

Viewport Lines Form a Rectangle

Floating Model Space Area for Drawing

UCS Icon Indicates Floating Model Space

Outside the Viewport Window

Outside the viewport rectangle and inside the dashed rectangle is where you need to use a full-scale environment. The drawing's border lines and title block should be placed in here. If you selected a template with a title block and border from the Create a New Drawing dialog box when you first began a drawing, notice that its position is outside the viewport lines. This is where the full-scale world exists. If you want to bring in your own full-scale title block and border, use the Insert command to import a drawing file (.dwg) or import it from another drawing as a Block using the AutoCAD DesignCenter. Recall that you can draw and place text there at their real sizes. Make sure the paper space icon is displayed when you are working with the full-scale environment (title block and border) (see Figure A.21).

Previewing a Plot

Once the floating model space and the Layout/Paper space environments are set, it is time to preview the plot. Make sure the paper space icon is present on your screen to plot the whole layout. Select the Plot command to begin. Settings reappear in the Plot dialog box that were made when the Layout button was first used. This time, however, there are two buttons at the bottom left corner of the screen for plot previews.

- Partial Preview—Lines representing the plotting area (dashed line) and paper size (continuous line) will appear on the screen. None of the drawing appears for you to see. Partial preview will also display warnings of possible problems with the plot being previewed.
- Full Preview—This option shows the drawing that will be plotted. Look at the screen picture very carefully to make sure everything on the drawing will be printed. Right-click to access the following choices:

- **Exit**—This choice takes you back to the Plot dialog box.
- **Plot**—This choice executes the plot.
- **Pan**—This selection lets you hold the left mouse button down and pan around the drawing.
- **Zoom** (default)—Holding the left mouse button down and moving the magnifying glass up and down will adjust the zoom.

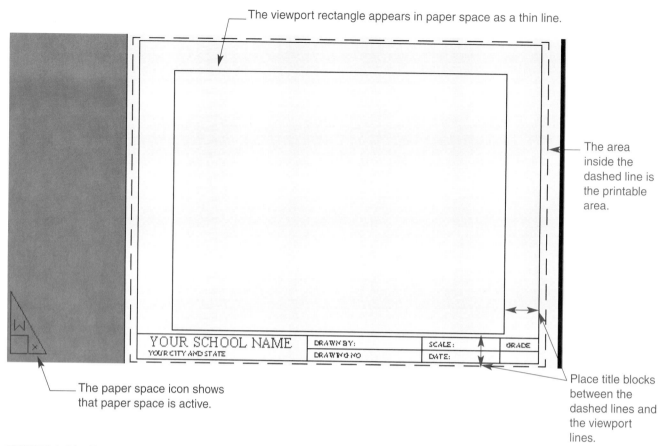

FIGURE A.21 Paper space identification

- **Zoom Window**—This choice lets you define a zoom window by holding down the left mouse button to start the window and releasing it to complete the zoom window.
- **Zoom Original**—Returns the screen to the original size when the preview button was selected initially.

Choose the Plot option to execute the plot.

APPENDIX B

Settings for Sheet Sizes and Limits (Architectural, Civil, and Mechanical Engineering Drawings)

Architectural Settings

Scale	**Scale Factor**	**Paper Space Zoom Factor**	**Text Height** 1/8″ 3/16″ 1/4″	**LTSCALE**
1/16″ = 1′-0″	192	1/192 XP	24″ 36″ 48″	96
1/32″ = 1′-0″	128	1/128 XP	16″ 24″ 32″	64
1/8″ = 1′-0″	96	1/96 XP	12″ 18″ 24″	48
3/16″ = 1′-0″	64	1/64 XP	8″ 12″ 16″	32
1/4″ = 1′-0″	48	1/48 XP	6″ 9″ 12″	24
3/8″ = 1′-0″	32	1/32 XP	4″ 6″ 8″	16
1/2″ = 1′-0″	24	1/24 XP	3″ 4.5″ 6″	12
3/4″ = 1′-0″	16	1/16 XP	2″ 3″ 4″	8
1″ = 1′-0″	12	1/12 XP	1.5″ 2.25″ 3″	6
1½″ = 1′-0″	8	1/8 XP	1″ 1.5″ 2″	4
3″ = 1′-0″	4	1/4 XP	.5″ .75″ 1″	2
1″ = 1″	1	1/1 XP	.125″ .188″ .25″	.5

** LTSCALEs are approximate and should be used as an initial starting value and adjusted as needed.*

Architectural Limits for Different Sheet Sizes

	Sheet Size 11″ × 8.5″	**Sheet Size 12″ × 9″**	**Sheet Size 17″ × 11″**	**Sheet Size 18″ × 12″**	**Sheet Size 24″ × 18″**	**Sheet Size 36″ × 24″**
Scale	**(X,Y)**	**(X,Y)**	**(X,Y)**	**(X,Y)**	**(X,Y)**	**(X,Y)**
1/16″ = 1′-0″	(176′,136′)	(192′,144′)	(272′,176′)	(288′,192′)	(384′,288′)	(576′,384′)
3/32″ = 1′-0″	(117′-4″,90′-8″)	(128′,96′)	(181′-4″,117′-4″)	(192′,128′)	(256′,192′)	(384′,256′)
1/8″ = 1′-0″	(88′,68′)	(96′,72′)	(136′,88′)	(144′,96′)	(192′,144′)	(288′,192′)
3/16″ = 1′-0″	(58′-8″, 45′-4″)	(64′,48′)	(90′-8″, 58′-8″)	(96′,64′)	(128′,96′)	(192′,128′)
1/4″ = 1′-0″	(44′,34′)	(48′,36′)	(68′,44′)	(72′,48′)	(96′,72′)	(144′,96′)
3/8″ = 1′-0″	(29′-4″, 22′-8″)	(32′,24′)	(45′-4″, 29′-4″)	(48′,32′)	(64′,48′)	(96′,64′)
1/2″ = 1′-0″	(22′,17′)	(24′,18′)	(34′,22′)	(36′,24′)	(48′,36′)	(72′,48′)
3/4″ = 1′-0″	(14′-8″, 11′-4″)	(16′,12′)	(22′-8″, 14′-8″)	(24′,16′)	(32′,24′)	(48′,32′)
1″ = 1′-0″	(11′,8′-6″)	(12′,9′)	(17′,11′)	(18′,12′)	(24′,18′)	(36′,24′)
1½″ = 1′-0″	(7′-4″, 5′-8″)	(8′,6′)	(11′-4″, 7′-4″)	(12′,8′)	(16′,12′)	(24′,16′)
3″ = 1′-0″	(3′-8″, 2′-10″)	(4′,3′)	(5′-8″, 3′-8″)	(6′,4′)	(8′,6′)	(12′,8′)
1″ = 1″	(11″,8.5″)	(12″,9″)	(17″,11″)	(18″,12″)	(24″,18″)	(36″,24″)

Civil Engineering Settings

Scale	Scale Factor	Paper Space Zoom Factor	Text Height ⅛″ ³⁄₁₆″ ¼″	LTSCALE
1″ = 10′	120	¹⁄₁₂₀ XP	15″ 22.5″ 30″	60
1″ = 20′	240	¹⁄₂₄₀ XP	30″ 45″ 60″	120
1″ = 30′	360	¹⁄₃₆₀ XP	45″ 67.5″ 90″	180
1″ = 40′	480	¹⁄₄₈₀ XP	60″ 90″ 120″	240
1″ = 50′	600	¹⁄₆₀₀ XP	75″ 112.5″ 150″	300
1″ = 60′	720	¹⁄₇₂₀ XP	90″ 135″ 180″	360
1″ = 100′	1200	¹⁄₁₂₀₀ XP	150″ 225″ 300″	600

Civil Engineering Limits for Different Sheet Sizes

Scale	Sheet Size 11″ × 8.5″ (X,Y)	Sheet Size 12″ × 9″ (X,Y)	Sheet Size 17″ × 11″ (X,Y)	Sheet Size 18″ × 12″ (X,Y)	Sheet Size 24″ × 18″ (X,Y)	Sheet Size 36″ × 24″ (X,Y)
1″ = 10′	(110′,85′)	(120′,90′)	(170′,110′)	(180′,120′)	(240′,180′)	(360′,240′)
1″ = 20′	(220′,170′)	(240′,180′)	(340′,220′)	(360′,240′)	(480′,360′)	(720′,480′)
1″ = 30′	(330′,225′)	(360′,270′)	(510′,330′)	(540′,360′)	(720′,540′)	(1080′,720′)
1″ = 40′	(440′,340′)	(480′,360′)	(680′,440′)	(720′,480′)	(960′,720′)	(1440′,960′)
1″ = 50′	(550′,425′)	(600′,450′)	(850′,550′)	(900′,600′)	(1200′,900′)	(1800′,1200′)
1″ = 60′	(660′,510′)	(720′,540′)	(1020′,660′)	(1080′,720′)	(1440′,1080′)	(2160′,1440′)
1″ = 100′	(1100′,850′)	(1200′,900′)	(1700′,1100′)	(1800′,1200′)	(2400′,1800′)	(3600′,2400′)

Mechanical Engineering Settings

Scale	Scale Factor	Paper Space Zoom Factor	Text Height ⅛″ ³⁄₁₆″ ¼″	LTSCALE
1″ = 1″	1	1/1 x P	.125″ .187″ .250″	.5
2″ = 1″	.5	2/1 x P	.062″ .093″ .125″	.25
½″ = 1″	2	½ x P	.250″ .375″ .500″	1
¼″ = 1″	4	¼ x P	.500″ .750″ 1.00″	2
⅛″ = 1″	8	⅛ x P	1.00″ 1.5″ 2″	4

* LTSCALEs are approximate and should be used as
an initial starting value and adjusted as needed.

Mechanical Engineering Limits for Different Sheet Sizes

Scale	Sheet Size 11″ × 8.5″ (X,Y)	Sheet Size 17″ × 11″ (X,Y)	Sheet Size 22″ × 17″ (X,Y)	Sheet Size 34″ × 22″ (X,Y)	Sheet Size 44″ × 34″ (X,Y)
1″ = 1″	(11″,8.5″)	(17″,11″)	(22″,17″)	(34″,22″)	(44″,34″)
2″ = 1″	(5.5″,4.25″)	(8.5″,5.5″)	(11″,8.5″)	(17″,11″)	(22″,17″)
½″ = 1″	(22″,17″)	(34″,22″)	(44″,34″)	(68″,44″)	(88″,68″)
¼″ = 1″	(44″,34″)	(68″,44″)	(88″,68″)	(136″,88″)	(176″,136″)
⅛″ = 1″	(88″,68″)	(136″,88″)	(176″,136″)	(272″,176″)	(352″,272″)

Thread Symbols

In mechanical drawings threads are used for various functions such as holding, adjusting, and transferring power between different parts. Threads are common to pipes, screws, nuts, and bolts. In a drawing threads are symbolic. Thus, threads may be drawn in different forms on a technical drawing and they may not look at all like the threads on the finished product. The *Machinery's Handbook* is a source for exact data and information on threads. The tables and charts in this handbook are used by machinists to manufacture threads. Threads can be unique depending on their form or profile. For exact information always use the handbook.

A drawing is used to give enough thread information to the machinists so they can build the part, not hold it up and compare it with the drawing. Look at the three different thread representations in Figure C.1. Threads may be drawn using simplified, schematic, or detailed representation. Any of these representations is acceptable for use on a technical drawing. After looking at the drawings in Figure C.1 you should realize that the appearance of threads on a drawing has little to do with how the machined part will look. You may be asking yourself what controls the way a threaded part will turn out.The answer is the thread note that accompanies the part's representation. We shall walk through some typical thread notes then show you some basic methods for drawing thread representation. Figure C.2 gives examples of thread notes in the inch system and in the metric system. We shall now examine the information in the notes.

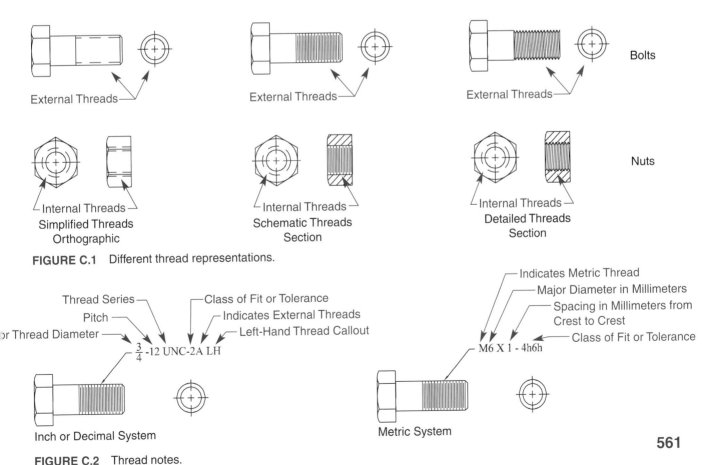

FIGURE C.1   Different thread representations.

FIGURE C.2   Thread notes.

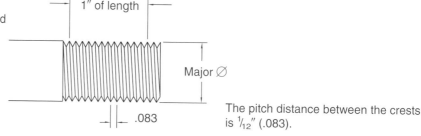

Measure 1″ along the crests centers, then count the number of threads to find the pitch. Here the pitch is 12 threads per inch.

The pitch distance between the crests is $\frac{1}{12}$″ (.083).

FIGURE C.3   Example showing Major ⌀ and Pitch.

Inch System

1. The major diameter of the threads is given. It may be shown in fraction or in decimal form. This measurement is taken from the tip of the crest on one side of the thread to the corresponding crest on the other side. In simple terms it is the largest diameter on the threads (see Figure C.3).

2. The pitch is listed after the major diameter. The value designates the number of threads per 1″ along the shaft. To determine the exact distance between the crests divide the number of threads into 1″. For example, a thread with a pitch of 16 has a distance between crests of 1/16″.

3. Each thread has a series or profile shape. There is a wide range of profiles, and each has an abbreviation. For a complete list check the handbook or the ASME Y14.6 standards on screw threads.

4. The class of fit is indicated with a value of 1, 2, or 3. A loose thread fit or one with a lot of play is a 1. A medium or average fit is indicated with a 2, and a really tight fitting thread is indicated with a 3.

5. External threads such as those on a shaft are called out with the letter A. Internal threads like those inside a nut are called out with a B.

6. Threads are assumed to be right-handed unless the LH callout is used. When threads appear in simplified or schematic form it is impossible to determine if they are right- or left-handed by visual examination of the drawing; therefore, it is critical to have a left-handed callout in the thread note.

7. An additional note may be added to the end of the callout giving the length of the shaft. For instance, a 5 x LG at the end of a thread note indicates the shaft is 5″ long.

Metric Threads

1. The first letter of the thread note, M, is the callout for a metric profile thread.

2. Following the M is the value of the major diameter of the thread in millimeters.

3. An X is used to separate the major diameter from the next number, which gives the pitch spacing from crest to crest. The value is in millimeters.

4. The class of fit or tolerance in the metric thread is a little more detailed than in the inch system. Lowercase letters (g) indicate the tolerance on the external threads, whereas uppercase letters (H) relate to the internal threads. Refer to the handbook when applying metric tolerances. They are somewhat more detailed than in the inch system. In the metric system the lower numbers such as 4 or 5 indicate a tight tolerance. A 6 is considered a medium fit, and numbers 7 and higher indicate loose fits.

As you can see, the note is critical to producing the correct threads. The graphic representation is more show than function. The real job of the thread graphic is to make the threads easy to identify and to stand out on the drawing.

Now, it is time to learn how to draw some basic threads.

Drawing Simplified Threads

1. Start by drawing the rectangular outline of the overall size of the threads. Use the major diameter and the length of the shaft or hole the threads go on (see Figure C.4a).

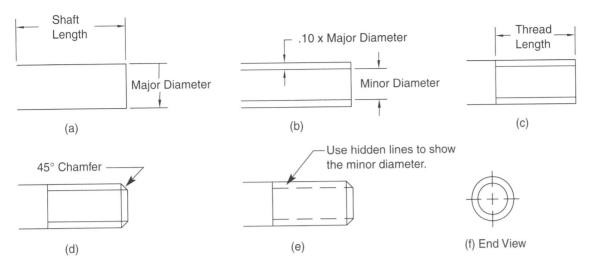

FIGURE C.4 Drawing simplified threads.

2. Next, lightly draw some lines parallel to the shaft's length inside the rectangular area approximately .10 times the major diameter of the thread. These lines represent the minor diameter on the threads and will be hidden when darkened. For an exact measurement look up the minor diameter in the handbook (see Figure C.4b).

3. If the threads do not run the full length of the shaft, you may also approximate the length by taking the major diameter and multiplying it by 1.5. If the shaft is 6″ or less, add an additional .25″. For lengths over 6″ add .5″ (see Figure C.4c).

4. Add a 45° chamfer starting on the end of the thread where it intersects the beginning of the minor diameter (see Figure C.4d).

5. Darken the lines. The lines representing the minor diameter will be hidden (see Figure C.4e). An end view shows two visible-line circles representing the major and minor diameters (see Figure C.4f).

Drawing Schematic Threads

1. Follow the first four steps shown in the simplified example to get to the layout shown in Figure C.5a.

2. Starting on the chamfered end draw parallel lines inside using a spacing of half the pitch distance (see Figure C.5b).

3. Use the line on the chamfer peak as a guide to start the major diameter. Trim every other line at half the pitch distance when they cross the line representing the minor diameter (see Figure C.5c).

4. Erase the guide line used to trim out the minor diameter, and darken the threads. You may use a little thicker line on the smaller lines that now represent the root of the minor diameter (see Figure C.5d).

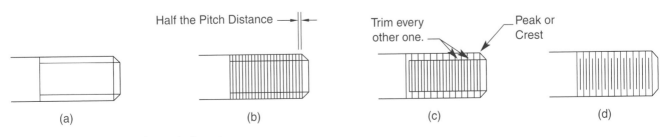

FIGURE C.5 Drawing schematic threads.

FIGURE C.6 Sample thread forms.

Detailed Threads

Drawing the threads in detailed form makes the thread look more like the real part versus the simplified or the schematic. Such drawings also take the most time to draw. One thing to remember is that the simplified and schematic are universally used on all thread forms. The detailed thread drawing will vary depending on the thread form. A few of the forms are shown in Figure C.6.

We shall use the Sharp V thread form in our example. The steps can vary a little depending on the thread form, but they will follow the same basic approach for visualizing a detailed thread form.

Steps to Draw a Sharp V in Detailed Form

1. Draw the rectangular outline as previously shown in the simplified example (see Figure C.7a).
2. Starting from the end, use the pitch distance and measure full pitch distances along the bottom line (see Figure C.7b).
3. Move to the top line and measure half the pitch distance for the first point only. After marking the first point, measure along the line using full pitch distances. This small offset will allow you to put a slope on the threads (see Figure C.7c).
4. Research the shape and measurements that are unique to the thread form. For a Sharp V draw an overall 60°angle at each point with the peaks on the outer edge of the shaft. Use different combinations of 60° increments (see Figure C.7d). The intersection of the angles on the inside of the shaft will determine the minor diameter.

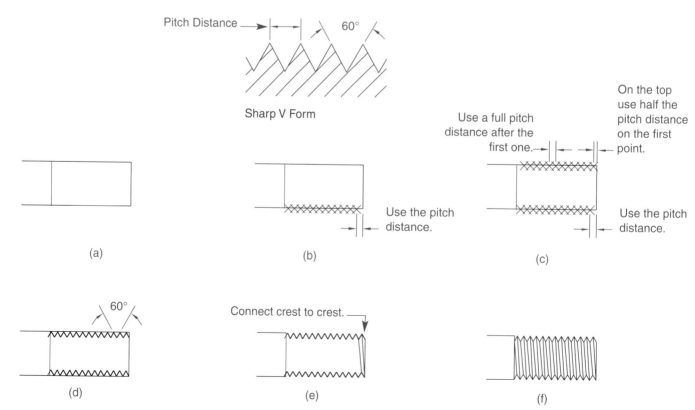

FIGURE C.7 Drawing Sharp V detailed threads.

5. When the thread outline is complete on the top and bottom it is time to connect the lines that run from one side to the other. Start on the bottom half crest on the far right side and draw a line to the first full crest on the top right side. Move over to the root intersection and connect the two roots with a line on the immediate left of the previously drawn line (see Figure C.7e). Continue until all the lines connecting the peaks and the roots are drawn (see Figure C.7f). Left-handed threads would slope in the opposite direction (see Figure C.8).

This method does take more time and effort but it represents the uniqueness of the individual thread forms. The good news is that the threads may be saved and reused in CAD. AutoCAD and other manufacturers have packages of symbols that may be used to insert different threads items such as nuts and bolts into a drawing. Figure C.9 shows the nomenclature for thread. It will help you when drawing and researching different threads.

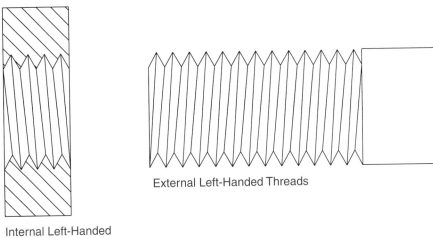

External Left-Handed Threads

Internal Left-Handed Threads

FIGURE C.8 Left-Handed thread example.

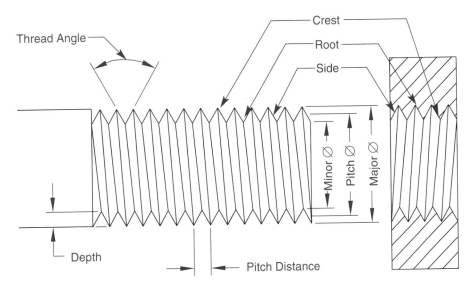

FIGURE C.9 Thread nomenclature.

Fraction and Decimal Conversions

Divisions of an inch by Fractions

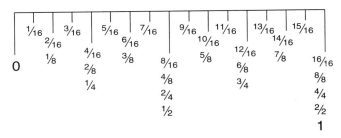

Divisions of an inch by 1/16″ only

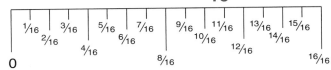

Divisions of an inch by 1/8″

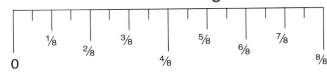

Divisions of an inch by 1/4″ and 1/2″

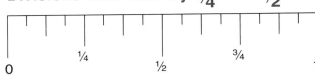

Decimal Equivalents

4ths	8ths	16ths	32nds	64ths	To 4 Places	To 3 Places	To 2 Places	4ths	8ths	16ths	32nds	64ths	To 4 Places	To 3 Places	To 2 Places
				1/64	.0156	.016	.02					33/64	.5156	.516	.52
			1/32		.0312	.031	.03				17/32		.5312	.531	.53
				3/64	.0469	.047	.04					35/64	.5469	.547	.55
		1/16			.0625	.062	.06			9/16			.5625	.562	.56
				5/64	.0781	.078	.08					37/64	.5781	.578	.58
			3/32		.0938	.094	.09				19/32		.5938	.594	.59
				7/64	.1094	.109	.11					39/64	.6094	.609	.61
	1/8				.1250	.125	.12		5/8				.6250	.625	.62
				9/64	.1406	.141	.14					41/64	.6406	.641	.64
			5/32		.1562	.156	.16				21/32		.6562	.656	.66
				11/64	.1719	.172	.17					43/64	.6719	.672	.67
		3/16			.1875	.188	.19			11/16			.6875	.688	.69
				13/64	.2031	.203	.20					45/64	.7031	.703	.70
			7/32		.2188	.219	.22				23/32		.7188	.719	.72
				15/64	.2344	.234	.23					47/64	.7344	.734	.73
1/4					.2500	.250	.25	3/4					.7500	.750	.75
				17/64	.2656	.266	.27					49/64	.7656	.766	.77
			9/32		.2812	.281	.28				25/32		.7812	.781	.78
				19/64	.2969	.297	.30					51/64	.7969	.797	.80
		5/16			.3125	.312	.31			13/16			.8125	.812	.81
				21/64	.3281	.328	.33					53/64	.8281	.828	.83
			11/32		.3438	.344	.34				27/32		.8438	.844	.84
				23/64	.3594	.359	.36					55/64	.8594	.859	.86
	3/8				.3750	.375	.38		7/8				.8750	.875	.88
				25/64	.3906	.391	.39					57/64	.8906	.891	.89
			13/32		.4062	.406	.41				29/32		.9062	.906	.91
				27/64	.4219	.422	.42					59/64	.9219	.922	.92
		7/16			.4375	.438	.44			15/16			.9375	.938	.94
				29/64	.4531	.453	.45					61/64	.9531	.953	.95
			15/32		.4688	.469	.47				31/32		.9688	.969	.97
				31/64	.4844	.484	.48					63/64	.9844	.984	.98
1/2					.5000	.500	.50						1.000	1.000	1.00

Additional Drawings

The drawings in Figures E.1 through E.11 are to be assigned by the instructor using requirements and specifications for the individual students. A mix of detailed drawings, assemblies, and pictorials can be applied at the instructor's discretion.

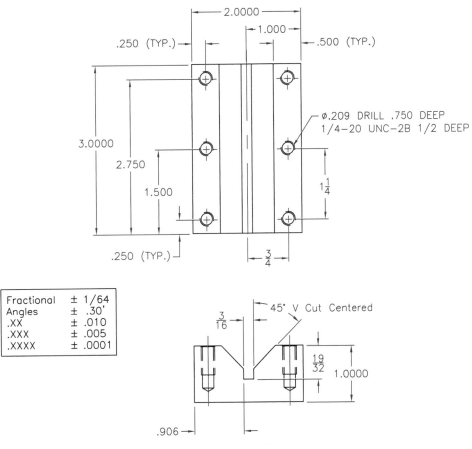

FIGURE E.1 One two three block.

FIGURE E.2 RH tool post.

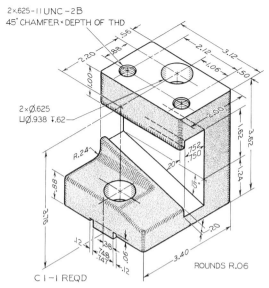

Make detail drawing using size B or A3 sheet. If assigned, convert dimensions to metric system.

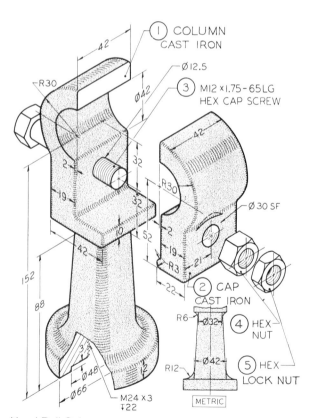

Hand Rail Column
(1) Draw details. If assigned, complete with dimensions.
(2) Draw assembly.

FIGURE E.3 Hand rail column.

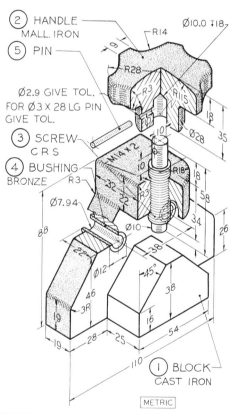

Drill Jig
(1) Draw details. If assigned, complete with dimensions.
(2) Draw assembly.

FIGURE E.4 Drill jig.

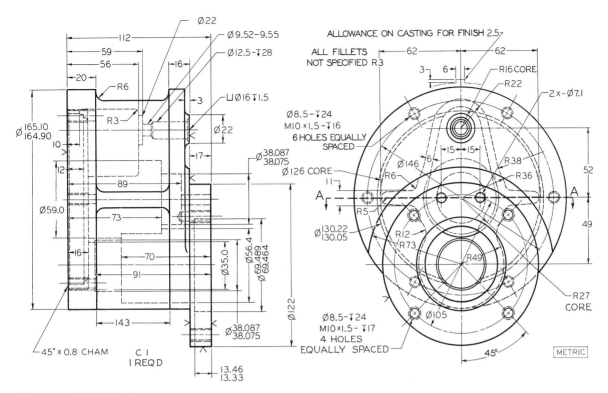

Generator Drive Housing
Given: Front and left-side views.
Required: Front view, right-side view in full section, and top view in full section on A-A.
Draw full size on size C or A2 sheet. If assigned, complete with dimensions.

FIGURE E.5 Generator drive housing.

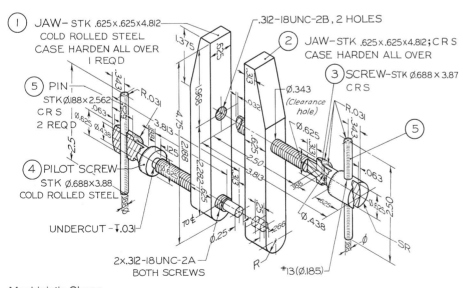

Machinist's Clamp
Draw details and assembly. If assigned, use unidirectional two-place
decimal-inch dimensions, or redesign for metric dimensions.

FIGURE E.6 Machinist's clamp.

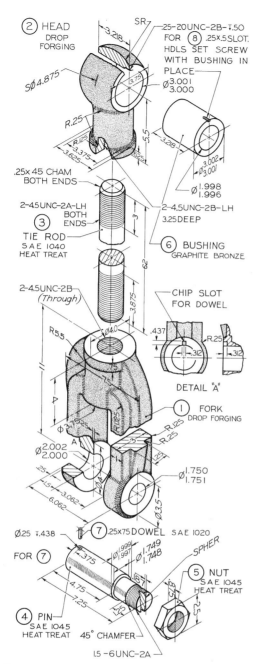

Connecting Bar
(1) Draw details.
(2) Draw assembly. If assigned, convert dimensions to metric or decimal-inch system.

FIGURE E.7 Connecting bar.

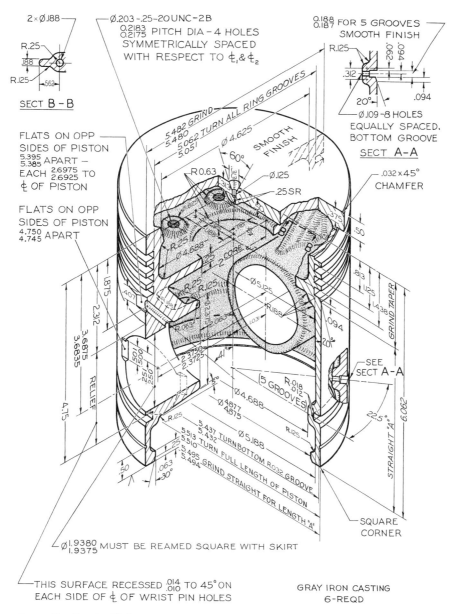

Caterpillar Tractor Piston
Make detail drawing full size on size C or A2 sheet. If assigned,
use unidirectional decimal-inch system, converting all fractions to
two-place decimal dimensions, or convert all dimensions to metric.

FIGURE E.8 Caterpillar tractor piston.

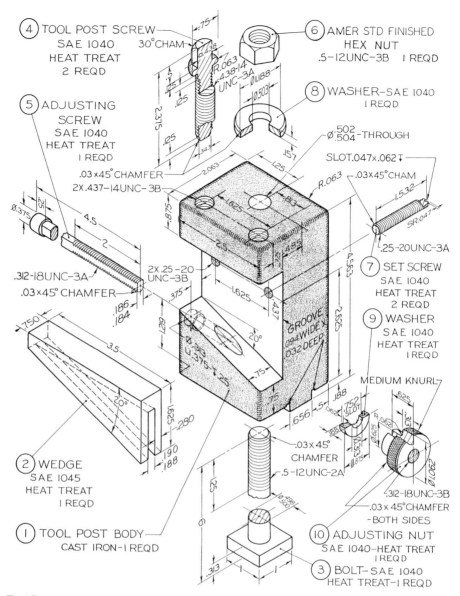

FIGURE E.9   Tool post.

Tool Post
(1) Draw details.
(2) Draw assembly. If assigned, use unidirectional two-place decimals for all fractional dimensions, or redesign for all metric dimensions.

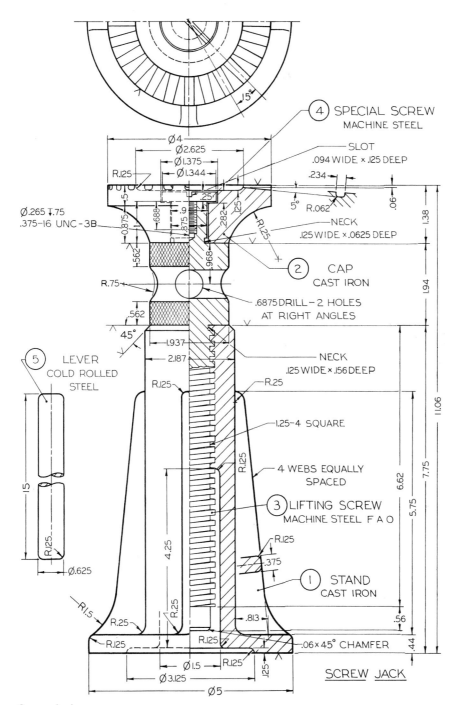

Screw Jack
Draw details using orthographic views and sections where
needed to complete a fully detailed drawing for the parts.

FIGURE E.10 Screw jack.

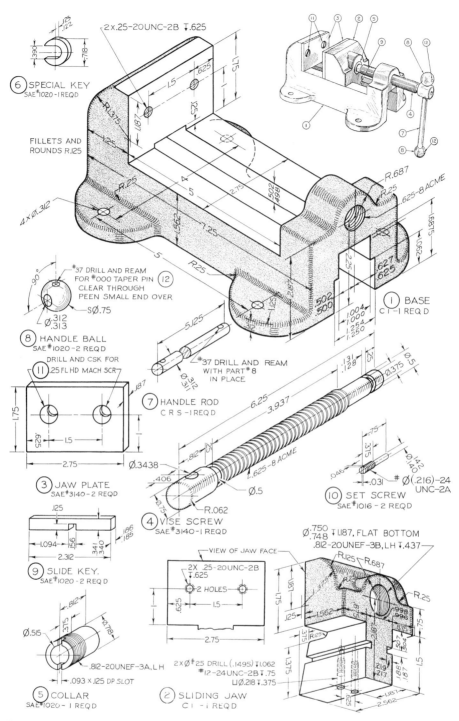

Machine Vise
(1) Draw details.
(2) Draw assembly. If assigned, convert dimensions to the
decimal-inch system, or redesign with metric dimensions.

FIGURE E.11   Machine vise.

Index